The Paradox of Ukrainian Lviv

The Paradox of Ukrainian Lviv

A Borderland City between Stalinists, Nazis, and Nationalists

Tarik Cyril Amar

Cornell University Press

Ithaca and London

First published 2015 by Cornell University Press
First paperback printing 2019

Library of Congress Cataloging-in-Publication Data

Amar, Tarik Cyril, 1969– author.
The paradox of Ukrainian Lviv : a borderland city between Stalinists, Nazis, and nationalists / Tarik Cyril Amar.

pages cm
Includes bibliographical references and index. ISBN 978-0-8014-5391-5 (cloth) ISBN 978-1-5017-3580-6 (pbk.)

1. L'viv (Ukraine)—History—20th century. 2. Ukraine—History—German occupation, 1941–1944. 3. World War, 1939–1945—Ukraine—L'viv. I. Title.
DK508.95.L86A46 2015
947.7'9—dc23 2015010558

Contents

Acknowledgments

It is, unfortunately, unlikely that I will remember and properly acknowledge all the many individuals and institutions that have helped me write this book, and I offer my apologies to those I inadvertently omit. Special thanks are due to my adviser, Stephen Kotkin, and to Jan T. Gross, Harold James, and Amir Weiner, who oversaw the early stages of this project. None of this work would have been possible without the Department of History at Princeton University. Before I came to Princeton, I benefited from the support and insights of my teachers at the London School of Economics and Political Science and at Balliol College, Oxford University, especially my tutor Martin Conway.

In Ukraine, especially Lviv and Kyiv, as well as in Poland, Russia, Germany, and the United States, I have been fortunate to encounter many committed and helpful archivists and librarians, sometimes working under difficult conditions. Over the years, many historians and scholars from other humanities and social-science disciplines have also helped, supported, and challenged me, including Felix Ackermann, Omer Bartov, Jan Behrends, Volker Berghahn, Michael David-Fox, Gloria and István Deák, Sofia Dyak, David Engel, Laura Engelstein, Gennady Estraikh, Franziska Exeler, Mayhill Fowler, Yoram Gorlizki, Victoria de Grazia, Ruth Ellen Gruber, Mark von Hagen, John-Paul Himka, Jochen Hellbeck, Susan Heuman, Peter Holquist, Cynthia Hooper, Liudmyla and Vladyslav Hrynevych (who also housed me during the Orange Revolution), the late Yaroslav Isaievych, Yanni Kotsonis, Maike Lehmann, Ola Linkiewicz, Eric Lohr, Mark Mazower, Ekaterina Melnikova, Stefan Plaggenborg, Susan Pedersen, Olena Petrenko, Ekaterina Pravilova, Vasyl Rasevych, Andreas Renner, Malte Rolf, Per Anders Rudling, Seth Schwartz, Max Schweer, Helene Sinnreich, Timothy Snyder, Michael Stanislawski, Keely Stauter-Halsted, Theodore Weeks, Richard Wortman, Serhy Yekelchyk, and Rakefet Zalashik.

I have had the opportunity to present my research and ideas at various venues, including the Russian and Soviet History Kruzhok at Columbia University, the history department at Bochum University, the German Historical Institute in Warsaw, the Russian History Seminar of the Department of History at Georgetown University, the *Ab imperio* Annual Seminar (then in Kazan), the Kandersteig Seminar of the Remarque Institute at New York University, the "Borderlands of Empire: Imperialism, Colonialism, Environment, and Culture" workshop organized by Omer Bartov, Wendy Lower, and Eric Weitz in Vilnius, the Munk School of Global Affairs at the University of Toronto, the Skirball Department of Hebrew and Judaic Studies at New York University, the Council of European Studies and history department at Yale University, and the workshop "Sovietizing the Periphery, a Comparative Approach," organized by the Graduate School for East and South East European Studies at Ludwig Maximilians University, Munich.

In Kyiv, Lviv, Moscow, Warsaw, and Berlin I have been fortunate to receive much hospitality and help from Teofil Dyak, Kornelia Holiyat, Ola Linkiewicz, Ira and Mykhailo Tsimmerman, and Rakefet Zalashik.

I gratefully acknowledge that work on this book has been facilitated by a number of grants and fellowships received from Princeton and Columbia Universities, the United States Holocaust Memorial Museum, the Harvard Ukrainian Research Institute, and the Ukrainian Studies Program and the Harriman Institute at Columbia University. Last but not least, special thanks are due to my editors at Cornell University Press, John G. Ackerman and Roger Malcolm Haydon, to Kirsten Painter and Carolyn Pouncy, who have made this book much more readable than I could have done on my own, as well as to the anonymous reviewers of my manuscript.

Note on Terminology

The city at the center of this study has had a long history, most of it multiethnic. Variations of Lviv's name have included Lwów, Lemberik, Lwi Gród, Lemburg, Lemberg, Loewensburg, Leopolis, Civitas Leona, Leontopolis, and Lvov. This book strives to simplify usage by mostly using the modern Ukrainian "Lviv" for the post-1944 period and as a default when no other name clearly applies. However, to avoid an anachronism that could be misread as endorsing one national narrative over others and to realistically signal Lviv's historical diversity to the reader, when the historic context is not Ukrainian, this text will also use Lwów, Lvov, and Lemberg, all names for the city in local—though not continuous or uncontentious—use during the twentieth century.

This book also addresses regions whose belonging or character has been contested. As a result, their names can express claims and the reifying simplifications they require. Thus, the terms Eastern Galicia, Western Ukraine, and Eastern Ukraine differ from eastern Galicia, western Ukraine, and eastern Ukraine. This fact poses a special challenge to the historian: the claims and reifications need to be rendered but not reproduced uncritically. I have adopted the rule that capitalization is used only in quotes or to indicate the perspective of historical actors. As with Lviv's multiple names, this approach makes for less surface consistency but more historical accuracy. I have also occasionally referred to (eastern) Galicia after the end of the Habsburg Empire, which is, strictly speaking, an anachronism but sometimes useful as a shorthand to refer to (largely) the territory of what used to be (eastern) Galicia.

The Soviet Union was ruled through a parallel structure of state and party, in which, on the whole and with few, if important, exceptions, the party was dominant. At the same time, members of the Soviet state elite usually were also party members. Formally, the Soviet Union was not a unitary state but a federation of republics, which were defined by ethno-territorial or national criteria. Among these republics, the Russian Soviet Federative Socialist Republic (RSFSR) was by far the most important and powerful. The second most important republic was Soviet Ukraine, with its capital (since 1934) in the city of Kyiv (in Ukrainian) or Kiev (in Russian). In reality, the Soviet Union was highly centralized, which is why a book about a major city in Soviet Ukraine has to address rule from both Moscow and Kyiv.

For this study, a limited number of institutions and offices are especially important and occur frequently in the text. Their full official names have been replaced by short forms: the Central Committee of the Communist Party of the Soviet Union, TsK VKP(b) and after 1952 TsK KPSS(b), is referred to as the Moscow Central Committee. At its top was the Politburo, called the Presidium between 1952 and 1966. The Central Committee of the Communist Party of Ukraine, TsK KP(b)U and after 1952 TsK KPU, is referred to as the Kyiv Central Committee or as the Central Committee of Ukraine; it also had a politburo at the top. Both central committees had their own bureaucracies, which paralleled and overshadowed the state administration.

In Lviv, generally the most powerful institution, effectively ruling the city and its region (the oblast), was the oblast party committee; the most powerful man in the oblast and the city was its first secretary or head. The oblast party committee was almost always referred to by its abbreviated name, the obkom, which is the term also used in this book. The Lviv obkom had its own equivalent of a politburo, the obkom buro and a bureaucracy or apparat, structured, in essence, along the same lines as the central committees, which has left rich (and unlike in some other oblasts) nearly undamaged archival holdings for the postwar period. Lviv also had a city party committee, which was subordinate to the obkom but still important. It was referred to by two abbreviated names: one Ukrainian, miskom; and one Russian, gorkom. The lowest level of the party's spatially structured hierarchy (excluding party structures based on individual institutions, such as factories, academic institutions, and collective farms) were the raion committees or raikoms.

The Soviet secret police played a major role and underwent several reorganizations and official names. It was of special significance in Lviv and Western Ukraine because it was fighting Ukrainian nationalism, generally associated with this area. To make this text more readable, it is usually referred to simply as the secret police.

During the Second World War, the German administration of the Generalgouvernement (in essence, those parts of Poland not annexed to Nazi Germany in addition to, from 1941, parts of western Ukraine) licensed one institution to represent some Ukrainian interests. This body was called the Hauptausschuss (the Main Commission) in German and the Ukrainskyi tsentralnyi komitet (literally, the Ukrainian Central Committee) in Ukrainian. To avoid confusion with the

Central Committee of the Communist Party, the Hauptausschuss is referred to by that name or its Ukrainian abbreviation, UTsK.

Polish, Ukrainian, and Russian terms are transcribed in a simplified manner that prioritizes ease of reading and, in particular, usually leaves out soft signs (in Ukrainian and Russian), since experts will easily refer to the original spellings (in quotations or titles I follow the source spelling). When quoted from a Russian or Ukrainian source, proper names, including place names, are transcribed according to the source language: for example, Kiev from Russian, Kyiv from Ukrainian; Odessa from Russian, Odesa from Ukrainian.

Many archives used in this study are organized by *fond*, a large holding usually organized by provenance; *opys* (*opis*), a *fond* subsection, often chronologically defined; and *sprava* (Ukrainian) or *delo* (Russian), usually a set of individual files. Files from such archives are referred to by the archive's name (abbreviated), followed by the *fond*, *opys*, and *sprava/delo* numbers, separated by commas and followed by a colon and the relevant pagination numbers. Documents from archives with different structures (such as the Ukrainian SBU secret police archives which use *tomy*, volumes) are referenced in more detail as needed.

Archival Abbreviations

AAN	Archiwum akt nowych, Warsaw
AUJ	Archiwum Uniwersytetu Jagiellońskiego, Cracow
BA	Bundesarchiv, Berlin
DALO	Derzhavnyi arkhiv Lvivskoi oblasti, Lviv
GDA SBU	Haluznyi derzhavnyi arkhiv Sluzhba bezpeky Ukrainy, Kyiv
GARF	Gosudarstvennyi arkhiv Rossiiskoi Federatsii, Moscow
IUA	Institute of Ukrainian Studies Archive, Ukrainian Academy of Sciences, Lviv Branch
NARA	National Archives and Records Administration, College Park
RGAE	Rossiiskii gosudarstvennyi arkhiv ekonomiki, Moscow
RGANI	Rossiiskii gosudarstvennyi arkhiv noveishei istorii, Moscow
RGASPI	Rossiiskii gosudarstvennyi arkhiv sotsialno-politicheskoi istorii, Moscow
TsDAHOU	Tsentralnyi derzhavnyi arkhiv hromadskykh obiednan Ukrainy, Kyiv
TsDAMLM	Tsentralnyi derzhavnyi arkhiv-muzei literatury i mystetstva, Kyiv
TsDAVOU	Tsentralnyi derzhavnyi arkhiv vyshchykh orhaniv vlady Ukrainy, Kyiv
TsDIA	Tsentralnyi istorychnyi arkhiv, Lviv Branch
TsDKFFA	Tsentralnyi derzhavnyi kinofotofonoarkhiv Ukrainy, Kyiv
USHMM	United States Holocaust Memorial Museum
YIVO	YIVO Institute for Jewish Research
ŻIH	Jewish Historical Institute, Warsaw

Introduction

This book is a local and transnational study of the twentieth-century experience of a European borderland city with four key forces of European and global twentieth-century history: Soviet Communism, Soviet nation shaping (here, Ukrainization), nationalism, and Nazism. It examines a fundamental stage in the making of modern Lviv by focusing on its Second World War and postwar transformation from an important multiethnic city (formerly known mostly as Lwów and Lemberg) into a Soviet and Ukrainian urban center.

Now in the west of an independent Ukrainian nation-state, during the last century Lviv also belonged to the Habsburg Empire, interwar Poland, and the Soviet Union. During the First World War, the city was under Russian imperial occupation; during the Second World War, it endured over three years of German occupation. Moreover, Lviv was caught not only between empires—Habsburg and Romanov, Nazi German and Soviet—but also between competing nationalisms, successful at local mass mobilization and increasingly militant. Yet empire and nationalism, while often at odds, were not mutually exclusive: Lviv was made Ukrainian not only very recently, during and after the Second World War, but also by a Soviet Union committed to overcoming the nation, if in general and in the long run, and waging an unforgiving war against Ukrainian nationalism. It was not merely the persistence of pre-Soviet traditions, as asserted in traditional explanations and national narratives, but the effects of Soviet rule, intentional as well as not, that made and shaped Lviv's Ukrainian and specifically Western Ukrainian identity.

In addition, German occupation left a deep and terrible imprint on the making of Ukrainian Lviv by killing the city's Jews, demoting its Poles, and offering conditional and relative preference to Ukrainians. Thus, the modern foundations of today's Lviv, geographically on the margins but central to Ukraine's identity, politics, and culture of memory, encapsulate a double—and recent—paradox: the city was molded into a modern national center by two highly authoritarian and massively violent regimes—Nazi Germany and the Stalinist Soviet Union—which usually defined each other as abhorred opposites. Most of this transformation, moreover, occurred under Soviet rule, when the Soviet Union was fighting Ukrainian nationalism as an absolute evil.[1]

Historical context is indispensable to understanding the rupture of the mid-twentieth century and its results. Until 1939, Lviv was Lwów, a city of mostly Poles, Jews, and Ukrainians.[2] At first, during a long nineteenth century, it existed within the Habsburg Empire as the capital of the Crownland province of Galicia. It then became a provincial center in the ethnically diverse eastern borderlands of an increasingly authoritarian interwar Poland. Making up a sixth of its population before the Second World War, Ukrainians were the smallest as well as the least powerful among the city's major ethnic groups. By the end of Soviet rule in 1991, Lviv was—in ethnic, linguistic, and cultural terms—the most Ukrainian of all major Ukrainian cities, and it has continued to play a special role as a center of national identity as well as of nationalism. In fact, Lviv is the only major city in Ukraine whose public space is preponderantly Ukrainophone.[3]

Yet historically Lviv had been a site of real coexistence, both tense and productive. Only after the beginning of the Second World War did international and local factors combine to unleash a perfect storm of political, military, and ethnic mass violence, which lasted for years, changed the city forever, and was facilitated on an unprecedented scale by states as well as organizations fighting for state status, by outside invaders as well as locals.

A Borderland City

Regardless of the state to which Lviv belonged at any given time after the establishment of local Habsburg rule in 1772, the city always displayed a combination

1. Lviv, like the multiethnic and borderland metropole of Thessaloniki (Salonica), cannot be understood without confronting the paradoxical nature of its history. For Salonica, see Mark Mazower, *Salonica, City of Ghosts: Christians, Muslims, and Jews, 1430–1950* (New York: Vintage, 2006), 6. My work, however, focuses on Lviv's recent history and the paradoxes of its twentieth-century transformation.

2. There were other, smaller groups, too, such as Lviv's Armenians. See for instance, Dorota Ziętek, *Tożsamość i religia: Ormianie w krakowskiej i lwowskiej diasporze* (Cracow: Nomos, 2008). Their history was complex, important, and often tragic. Yet for reasons of space and consistency, this work focuses on the larger ethnic groups that were at the center of Lviv's modern national politics.

3. There are smaller cities and towns where Ukrainian clearly predominates, such as Ivano-Frankivsk. Lviv, however, is the only generally acknowledged regional metropole that has this feature.

of typical as well as paradoxical borderland features, as summarized by Omer Bartov and Eric Weitz: it was "geographically or culturally distant from the seat of power," be it Vienna, Warsaw, or Moscow and Kyiv. But these state centers always made special efforts "to subsume or integrate" the city into their respective political systems, social orders, and imperial or national imaginaries.[4]

However, states and their strategies were not everything. Lviv was also shaped by its special diversity: a site of exchange and encounter, embedded in local and translocal networks, traditionally the city had been home to several kinds of Christianity as well as Judaism and, to a much smaller extent, Islam. To search for modern national identities in premodern Lviv would be to reproduce the anachronisms of modern nationalism. The city was, however, always ethnically diverse, inhabited by groups that by the late nineteenth century mostly identified themselves and each other as Poles, Jews, or Ukrainians.[5] Thus, it became a site of modern national projects, increasingly mobilizing—and mobilized by—its inhabitants. For about a century, between the "Springtime of Nations" of 1848 and the violent ethnic "unmixing" of the Second World War, much of the city's history became a story of ethnic communities, growing distinct and national enough to know their differences and deny their similarities and treated as different by their rulers. In this period, Lviv turned into both a center and a prize of Polish nationalism, as well as a symbol for the ambitions of a Ukrainian nationalism which envied Polish ascendancy and emulated Polish mobilization. Surrounded by a countryside mostly inhabited by peasants learning to see themselves as Ukrainians, the city was usually known by its Polish name of Lwów, and its public space was dominated by Polish culture up to and into the Second World War.

The war, starting in Europe with a partition of Poland between Nazi Germany and the Soviet Union, brought Soviet occupation from the fall of 1939 to the summer of 1941, then German occupation until the Soviet reconquest in the summer of 1944. Lviv experienced Sovietization twice: first under the conditions of what Timothy Snyder has aptly called the Molotov-Ribbentrop Europe of a de facto German-Soviet alliance based on the pact of August 1939, then again after German occupation but within a new context of Soviet victory in the Soviet-German

4. Omer Bartov and Eric D. Weitz, "Introduction," in *Shatterzone of Empires: Coexistence and Violence in the German, Habsburg, Russian, and Ottoman Borderlands*, ed. Bartov and Weitz (Bloomington: Indiana University Press, 2013), 1.

5. On Lviv and Galicia as multiethnic sites, see also the contributions in Christopher Hann and Paul Robert Magocsi, eds., *Galicia: A Multicultured Land* (Toronto: University of Toronto Press, 2005).

war of 1941 to 1945.[6] This Soviet expansion, usually analyzed in terms of geopolitics and repression, also created new spaces, physical and imagined, of Soviet practices—political as well as everyday, noisy as well as silent—in which a meaning of being Soviet, an ethos, was articulated. After 1939 and again after 1944, Lviv was a key site for these processes.

At the same time, the city's ethnic composition was changed in an unprecedented and irrevocable manner. Between 1939 and 1946, while alliances and enemies changed radically, there was a de facto Soviet-German-Soviet continuity of demoting and finally expelling Lviv's Polish population. During the Holocaust, the Jewish population of the city was murdered. Starting in 1944, the Soviet Union brought in unprecedentedly large numbers of eastern Ukrainian as well as Russian and other Soviet cadres.

Violence was crucial to Lviv's transformation, but it was not everything. Three principal Soviet policies also shaped that transformation: Sovietization, Ukrainization, and, interacting with both of these, rapid catch-up industrialization and modernization in the Soviet mode. All three policies combined universal Soviet approaches to reshaping societies and specific responses to Lviv's borderland position.

One change that has sometimes been alleged and decried, however, did not happen: Lviv was not Russified. In fact, it was only under the Soviet regime that, for the first time in its history, Lviv was made overwhelmingly Ukrainian: it came to be inhabited mainly by people who would call it Lviv, spoke Ukrainian, saw themselves as Ukrainians, were recognized and defined as such by their rulers, and agreed with them on this categorization—if often, at least initially, on little else.[7]

6. Timothy Snyder, *Bloodlands: Europe between Hitler and Stalin* (New York: Basic Books, 2010), 119. As Gabriel Gorodetsky has shown, available evidence on Soviet thinking and the international context of the 1930s does not support an explanation of Soviet policy from 1939 to 1941 as a single, long-term blueprint of expansionism. He has warned against anachronism in interpreting Soviet actions, perceptions, and plans. See Gabriel Gorodetsky, "The Impact of the Molotov-Ribbentrop Pact on the Course of Soviet Foreign Policy," *Cahiers du monde russe et soviétique* 31 (1990): esp. 27, 36-37. At the same time, to read Stalin's mind in 1939 as bent on empire, as Vojtech Mastny has, seems plausible but not compelling. See Vojtech Mastny, *The Cold War and Soviet Insecurity: The Stalin Years* (Oxford: Oxford University Press, 1996), 16. Yet the issue of Soviet motivations is not identical with that of outcomes.

7. This late, postwar stage of the Ukrainization of urban space and urbanization of Ukrainian identity was not a special trait of any Ukrainian region. As Roman Szporluk has pointed out, it was equally true for western and eastern Ukraine that urbanization, in spite of changes in the 1930s, was still mostly a postwar phenomenon, so that by 1959 (the first postwar general census) "for the first time in their modern history, Ukrainians made up the majority of the population in their own cities." See Roman Szporluk, "Urbanization in Ukraine since the Second World War," in his *Russia, Ukraine, and the Breakup of the Soviet Union* (Stanford, CA: Hoover Institution Press, 2000), 141. Lviv was special but not unique. Generally, its fate most resembled that of the city of Vilnius (Wilno,

Sovietization: Contexts and Meanings

In Lviv, Soviet rule, based on a modern ideology of radical revolution, was new, but it should also be understood in the context of two broader issues: the development of Sovietization as a theory and practice of transferring superior Soviet modernity, especially to territories and societies perceived as frontiers of the Soviet building of socialism and, at the same time, the persistence of Lviv's borderland dynamics.[8]

Traditionally, the historiography of Sovietization has focused on the postwar period and an area stretching from the Soviet zone of occupation in Germany (later East Germany) to the western borders of the Soviet Union, and from the Baltic coast to the southern border of Bulgaria, a region where Soviet hegemony was established through formally sovereign client states.[9]

Vilna, Vilne), also a multiethnic provincial metropole in interwar Poland's eastern borderlands, shaped by Polish and Jewish culture and transformed by war, genocide, expulsion, nationalism, and Sovietization. In the case of Vilnius, the contrast between the prewar and the postwar periods was even starker: Before the war, Lithuanians were a smaller minority in Vilnius than Ukrainians in Lviv, but subsequently Vilnius was not only Lithuanianized but became the capital of a Lithuanian Soviet republic. In Vilnius, too, Sovietization did not aim at Russification. Instead it sought to foster a Lithuanian identity with a "new socialist and pro-Russian" content. See Theodore R. Weeks, "A Multi-Ethnic City in Transition: Vilnius's Stormy Decade, 1939–1949," *Eurasian Geography and Economics* 47 (2006): esp. 153–56, 169.

8. As Ronald Grigor Suny has concluded, ideology is a capacious as well as an indispensable concept, and the Soviet case of an "explicitly articulated political ideology" belonged to the "quintessentially modern" ("On Ideology, Subjectivity, and Modernity: Disparate Thoughts about Doing Soviet History," *Russian History/Histoire russe* 35 [2008], 253, 258).

9. The literature on Sovietization is extensive. Key works, representative of an approach focusing on the postwar period and the satellite states, include Zbigniew K. Brzezinski, *The Soviet Bloc: Unity and Conflict. Ideology and Power in the Relations among the USSR, Poland, Yugoslavia, China, and Other Communist States* (Cambridge, MA: Harvard University Press, 1960). More recent works with a similar approach include Balázs Apor, Péter Apor, and E. A. Rees, eds., *The Sovietization of Eastern Europe: New Perspectives on the Postwar Period* (Washington, DC: New Academia Publishing, 2008); Peter Kenez, *Hungary from the Nazis to the Soviets: The Establishment of the Communist Regime in Hungary, 1944–1948* (Cambridge: Cambridge University Press, 2006); John Connelly, *Captive University: The Sovietization of East German, Czech, and Polish Higher Education, 1945–1956* (Berkeley: University of California Press, 2000); Norman M. Naimark and Leonid Gibianskii, eds., *The Establishment of Communist Regimes in Eastern Europe, 1944–1949* (Boulder, CO: Westview, 1997); Naimark, *The Russians in Germany: A History of the Soviet Zone of Occupation, 1945–1949* (Cambridge, MA: Harvard University Press, 1995); Krystyna Kersten, *The Establishment of Communist Rule in Poland, 1943–1948* (Berkeley: University of California Press, 1991); and Richard Staar, *Poland, 1944–1962: The Sovietization of a Captive People* (Baton Rouge: Louisiana State University Press, 1962). In this literature, Yugoslavia and Albania are often regarded as special cases. Writers and memoirists have also made important, even seminal contributions on Sovietization: for instance, Czesław Milosz, *The Captive Mind* (New York: Knopf, 1953); Wolfgang Leonhard, *Die Revolution entläßt ihre Kinder* (Cologne: Kiepenheuer & Witsch, 1955); Hugo Steinhaus, *Wspomnienia i zapiski*, ed. Aleksandra Zgorzelska (London: Aneks, 1992); and Sándor Márai, *Memoir of Hungary, 1944–1948* (Budapest: Central European University Press, 1996).

But it was the German-Soviet pact of 1939, not the Soviet triumph of 1945, that marked the beginning of Sovietization in eastern Europe.[10] Lviv was typical of a broad stretch of territory from the Baltic to the Black Sea where Soviet conquest occurred twice, was interrupted by German occupation, and led to annexation.[11] Yet studies of Sovietization in Eastern Europe beyond the geographical and chronological framework of the postwar client states have become more numerous only since the early 2000s.[12]

Conceptually, debates about Sovietization have been organized around two related dichotomies: monotony versus diversity and outside imposition versus endogenous factors. Terms to describe the outcome of Sovietization have differed, including the "imposition of communist-controlled government" or a "Stalinist blueprint," "Stalinization," "Communist takeover," "Satellization," "the introduction

10. To be precise, what started in 1939 were the first attempts at Sovietization after the establishment of Bolshevik rule and the Soviet Union between 1917 and 1922/1923. Eastern and Central Ukraine were among the most important sites of Sovietization during that initial period of Soviet state building, as Jurij Borys has detailed (*The Sovietization of Ukraine, 1917–1923: The Communist Doctrine and Practice of National Self-Determination* [Edmonton: University of Ontario Press, 1980]). Yet because of the Soviet failure to defeat Poland in the war of 1919–1920, Sovietization as a process reaching beyond the former area of the Russian Empire in Eastern Europe began, in a sustained manner, only in 1939.

11. As Stephan Merl has pointed out, there is no reason to omit "territories occupied by the Soviet Union in 1939" from our understanding of Sovietization, since "the issues there were very much the same" as in territories Sovietized only after the war. See Stephan Merl, "Review of David Feest, *Zwangskollektivierung im Baltikum: Die Sowjetisierung des estnischen Dorfes 1944–1953* (Cologne: Böhlau, 2007)," *Kritika: Explorations in Russian and Eurasian History* 10 (2009): 377. In particular, as Jan Gross has stressed repeatedly, most of the Sovietized societies in Europe—whether annexed or dominated through client status—had in common the experience of German occupation, German influence, and war, which needs to be factored into any explanation of Sovietization and its results ("Themes for a Social History of War Experience and Collaboration," in *The Politics of Retribution in Europe: World War II and Its Aftermath*, ed. István Deák, Jan T. Gross, and Tony Judt [Princeton, NJ: Princeton University Press, 2000], 23). On territories and societies disrupted and transformed by both Nazi Germany and the Stalinist Soviet Union, see Snyder, *Bloodlands*. For a recent study integrating local primary and oral history sources of Sovietization following Japanese rule, see the contributions in Sören Urbansky, ed., *"Unsere Insel": Sowjetische Identitätspolitik auf Sachalin nach 1945* (Berlin: be.bra, 2013).

12. David Feest, *Zwangskollektivierung im Baltikum: Die Sowjetisierung des estnischen Dorfes 1944–1953* (Cologne: Böhlau, 2007); Olaf Mertelsmann, ed., *The Sovietization of the Baltic States, 1940–1956* (Tartu: Kleio, 2003); Martin Mevius, *Agents of Moscow: The Hungarian Communist Party and the Origins of Socialist Patriotism, 1941–1953* (Oxford: Oxford University Press, 2005). Sabine Dullin has emphasized the continuity of Soviet border regimes between Sovietization before 1941 and after 1944/45 (*La frontière épaisse. Aux origins des politiques soviétiques, 1920-1940* [Paris: Éditions de l'École des hautes études en sciences sociales, 2014], 307). Earlier examples of work more fully integrating prewar, war, and postwar developments include David R. Marples, *Stalinism in Ukraine in the 1940s* (New York: St. Martin's Press, 1992); and Sanford R. Lieberman, "The Re-Sovietization of Formerly Occupied Areas of the USSR during World War II," in *The Soviet Empire Reconsidered: Essays in Honor of Adam B. Ulam*, ed. Lieberman et al. (Boulder, CO: Westview, 1994).

of Soviet totalitarianism into Eastern Europe," and "Marxisation."[13] But there is a broad consensus that, in one way or another and notwithstanding variations over time and space, Sovietzation was a highly compulsory process. In Eastern Europe, it was not difficult for contemporaries and later observers to identify its core elements in action, including the making of institutions led by a party-state monopolizing power, property, truth, and careers; administrative-territorial changes; the abolition of private property in the means of production and the market, the expropriation of industry and trade, and, usually, the collectivization of agriculture; the suppression of public spheres and autonomous social structures and the making of centrally controlled ones; and, facilitating it all, a hypertrophic system of policing and state terror.

But what did Sovietization mean for the Sovietizers? By addressing this question, we can examine the phenomenon of Sovietization to learn more about the Soviet order as a whole. The first thing to note is that the term "Sovietization" did not originate as a Cold War denunciation but as an explicit and proud Bolshevik ambition, cutting across borders. As early as 1920, Lenin hoped for the "Sovietization" of Lithuania, Hungary, the Czech lands, Romania, and Poland.[14] By the Second World War, a major Soviet Russian dictionary registered Sovietization, with entries for noun and verb: applicable to something as well as somebody, to places, institutions, and subjects, it meant to "organize Soviet power" and "to inculcate Soviet ideology" and "worldview."[15]

While extending beyond Soviet borders, Sovietization's meaning was integrated with the Soviet project as a whole and at home: the attempt to create, through radical social and individual transformation, a utopian socialist, or Communist, society. The 1940 dictionary adduced post-Civil-War Siberia, a traditional part of the Russian Empire, as an example.[16] Despite trivializing usage during the Cold War, Sovietization cannot be reduced to Russian imperialism in a new guise. Embedded in Communist ideas and practices, it was an

13. For these terms, see Vladimir Tismaneanu, *Stalinism for All Seasons: A Political History of Romanian Communism* (Berkeley: University of California Press, 2003), 107; François Fejtö, *A History of the People's Democracies: Eastern Europe since Stalin* (London: Pall Mall Press, 1969), 12; Charles Gati, *The Bloc That Failed: Soviet-East European Relations in Transition* (Bloomington: Indiana University Press, 1990), 19; and Stefan Mękarski, *Sowietyzacja kulturalna Polski* (London: Reduta, 1949), 17.

14. Olaf Mertelsmann, "Introduction," in his *Sovietization of the Baltic States*, 9; Richard Pipes, ed., *The Unknown Lenin: From the Secret Archive* (New Haven: Yale University Press, 1998), 85, 90, 97–98.

15. B. M. Volin and D. N. Ushakov, eds., *Tolkovyi slovar russkogo iazyka* (Moscow, 1940), 4:342. Both the original and the Cold War "Sovietization" concepts should not be confused with a recent new meaning employed in some writings on post-Soviet Russia to describe tendencies of centralization and a return to "principles of . . . rule characteristic for the late Soviet period" (Olga V. Kryshtanovskaya, "Sovietization of Russia, 2000–2008," *Eurasian Review* 2 [2009]: 127).

16. Volin and Ushakov, *Tolkovyi slovar russkogo iazyka*, 342.

authoritarian socialist mission of modernity making, giving meaning to internal transformation as well as conquest and expansion.[17]

There is a broader literature that addresses, in effect, Sovietization before 1939: historians such as Jörg Baberowski, Francine Hirsch, Terry Martin, Douglas Northrop, and Yuri Slezkine have discussed what amounted to the Soviet variant of a "civilizing mission" among the eastern, Asian, Muslim, and/or small tribal people of the Soviet Union as it was constituted after the Civil War on the remaining territory of the former tsarist empire.[18] It was this continuing project that Lviv was supposed to join through Sovietization, which bridged traditional concepts of East and West because it was universalist and rested on its own categories of historical teleology: from a Soviet perspective, Soviet civilization was the way of the future for everyone; and the backward included both the premodern and a backward form of modernity itself—the superseded stage of bourgeois capitalism. Thus, Lviv was imagined not only as a frontier of Soviet nation building through Ukrainization, modernization, and postwar industrialization but also as a "forepost" (in Soviet terminology) of Soviet civilization overcoming legacies of both "feudalism" (premodern backwardness) and "capitalism" (backward modernity).

It is worth underlining that the historical stakes were high because Lviv's Soviet rulers chose to make them so, publicly construing Western Ukraine as a laboratory of competitive borderland modernization where Soviet socialism would prove its superiority. In a famed speech at a Western Ukrainian teachers' meeting in 1945, the high-ranking cadre Dmytro Manuilskyi compared the policies of Habsburg, Polish, and Soviet rulers: they had all had to deal with a periphery. Yet where Habsburgs and Poles were accused of intentionally increasing the region's backwardness to maintain a regime of internal colonialism, the Soviet party-state would make it catch up by developing it faster than the center.[19] Like some Cold War Western development theorists, the Soviets believed that there

17. There was also a long Russian imperial tradition of pitting a modernizing state against its own society in a struggle "to overtake and surpass the world leaders in modernization." See David Joravsky, "The Stalinist Mentality and Higher Learning," *Slavic Review* 42 (1983): 580. Yet the Bolsheviks had not only partly assimilated but radicalized this tradition: overcoming backwardness was indispensable and linked to the foundation myth of the Great October Revolution. See Yuri Slezkine, "Imperialism as the Highest Stage of Socialism," *Russian Review* 59 (2000): 228 (my emphasis).

18. Jörg Baberowski, *Der Feind ist überall: Stalinismus im Kaukasus* (Munich: Deutsche Verlags-Anstalt, 2003); Francine Hirsch, *Empire of Nations: Ethnographic Knowledge and the Making of the Soviet Union* (Ithaca, NY: Cornell University Press, 2005); Slezkine, "Imperialism as the Highest Stage," 227–34; Terry Martin, *The Affirmative Action Empire: Nations and Nationalism in the Soviet Union, 1923–1939* (Ithaca, NY: Cornell University Press, 2001); Douglas Northrop, *Veiled Empire: Gender and Power in Stalinist Central Asia* (Ithaca, NY: Cornell University Press, 2003).

19. RGASPI 17, 125, 351: 24–25.

was one best way toward a modernity defined as industrial and that the model could be exported.[20]

The central importance of Marxist-Leninist ideology for Soviet history is generally acknowledged.[21] Modernity, however, is still a contentious notion. As Michael David-Fox has shown, the split between scholars favoring the concept of modernity and those who have emphasized neotraditionalism has been a key feature of the post-Soviet historiography of the Soviet Union, although this debate may have reached an impasse.[22] Lviv's Soviet experience bears out the importance of modernity for understanding Soviet history and for the self-understanding of those who made it.[23] Against the long-standing background of a "mutual culture of evaluation," Lviv's Sovietization was an outstanding example of the self-defining desire to prove the superiority of Soviet modernity and, in the process, to invert the discursive construct of a "West-East cultural gradient."[24]

Certainly, there is a conceptual price tag not only to neglecting but also to universalizing modernity.[25] In general, modernity has not been a "single process of

20. On general patterns of development as modernization from afar, see Paul R. Josephson, *Resources under Regimes: Technology, Environment, and the State* (Cambridge, MA: Harvard University Press, 2005), 15.

21. Suny, "On Ideology, Subjectivity, and Modernity."

22. Michael David-Fox, "Multiple Modernities vs. Neo-Traditionalism: On Recent Debates in Russian and Soviet History," *Jahrbücher für Geschichte Osteuropas* 54 (2006): 535–36, 551. See also Daniel Beer, "Origins, Modernity, and Resistance in the Historiography of Stalinism," *Journal of Contemporary History* 40 (2005): 363–79. Important works within the paradigm of modernity include Stephen Kotkin's *Magnetic Mountain: Stalinism as a Civilization* (Berkeley: University of California Press, 1995); Amir Weiner, *Making Sense of War: The Second World War and the Fate of the Bolshevik Revolution* (Princeton, NJ: Princeton University Press, 2001); Steven A. Barnes, *Death and Redemption: The Gulag and the Shaping of Soviet Society* (Princeton, NJ: Princeton University Press, 2011); and David L. Hoffmann, *Cultivating the Masses: Modern State Practices and Soviet Socialism, 1914–1939* (Ithaca, NY: Cornell University Press, 2011).

23. Modernity is no less elusive and productive a concept than ideology, as Michael David-Fox has also stressed ("Multiple Modernities," 536). The two concepts have in common that we cannot do without them: their elusiveness is not a flaw but a challenge that cannot be met by avoiding or debunking them.

24. On the importance of the idea of the West-East gradient and its inversion, see David-Fox, "Multiple Modernities," 552; and Michael David-Fox, *Showcasing the Great Experiment: Cultural Diplomacy and Western Visitors to the Soviet Union, 1921–1941* (Oxford: Oxford University Press, 2012), 12–27, esp. 25. For the broad context, see the contributions in Catherine Evtuhov and Stephen Kotkin, eds., *The Cultural Gradient: The Transmission of Ideas in Europe, 1789–1991* (Lanham, MD: Rowman and Littlefield, 2003).

25. Weiner, Amir, and Aigi Rahi-Tamm, "Getting to Know You: The Soviet Surveillance System, 1939–57," *Kritika: Explorations in Russian and Eurasian History* 13 (2012): 6. There were also important differences between, roughly speaking, Western colonial and imperial discourse before the First World War, on one side, and Cold War Western modernization discourse, on the other, despite substantial continuities. See the contributions by Michael Adas and Michael Latham in *Staging Growth: Modernization, Development, and the Global Cold War*, ed. David C. Engerman et al. (Amherst: University of Massachusetts Press, 2003), 4–5, 35–39.

which Europe is the paradigm."[26] It has also not been perfect anywhere: like other forms, the Soviet variant was aspirational no less than realized. In the Soviet Union traditions, changing as well as recast, did not only persist or resist but substantially influenced politics and society; moreover, the Bolsheviks exaggerated their claims to modernity.[27] Clearly, no study of things Soviet—and many others—can disregard long continuities, informal practices, and the "(re-)invention of traditions" emphasized in neo-traditionalist approaches.[28] But understanding the Soviet order requires not dismissing or refuting but integrating its formative claims as well as real practices of modernity because if we fail to do so we can neither grasp why it was diffferent nor, which is arguably more important, the difference that it made.

Moreover, within a world of not only multiple but antagonistic and competitive modernities, the specific features of Soviet society were crucially important, and the historical moment also mattered. By 1939, a new Soviet civilization had been created.[29] It was illiberal and Stalinist. Soviet modernity thus went west at a particular point in its own history, when Stalinism had just reached its prewar peak. Against the backdrop of its first five-year plans, collectivization, purges, and "social cleansing," in 1936 the regime declared that the foundations of socialism had been built.[30] The terrors of 1936 to 1938 then demonstrated that they remained violently authoritarian, with party dictatorship narrowed down to individual and unprecedentedly powerful, if ordinarily imperfect, despotism.

As a result of these developments, 1939 carried west a continuing project of Soviet socialist modernity, a mature Stalinist regime, and a Stalinist way of life. The ensuing encounter was both highly charged and abrupt. Discourse on a threatening outside permeated prewar Stalinism's everyday life, while the regime also sought to create "something of a world closed in on itself."[31] A sealing of

26. Charles Taylor, *Modern Social Imaginaries* (Durham, NC: Duke University Press, 2004), 196.

27. J. Arch Getty, *Practicing Stalinism: Bolsheviks, Boyars, and the Persistence of Tradition* (New Haven: Yale University Press, 2013), esp. 2, 17.

28. Beer, "Origins, Modernity, and Resistance," 367.

29. Barnes, *Death and Redemption*, 110.

30. On the mass operations of the 1930s as a distinct attempt to cleanse the body politic of "socially harmful elements," see Paul Hagenloh, *Stalin's Police: Public Order and Mass Repression in the USSR, 1926–1941* (Baltimore: Johns Hopkins University Press, 2009), 1–12. On Stalin's boasts of fundamental transformation, see David L. Hoffmann, *Stalinist Values: The Cultural Norms of Soviet Modernity, 1917–1941* (Ithaca, NY: Cornell University Press, 2003), 150.

31. Kotkin, *Magnetic Mountain*, 206, 357. Katerina Clark has recently shown that even at the height of pre-1941 Stalinism, its self-isolation and self-aggrandizement did not exclude internationalist tendencies. Her study is a high-cultural history of the Moscow artistic and intellectual elite, deliberately not addressing "political or institutional history" or "the masses." See Katerina Clark, *Moscow, the Fourth Rome: Stalinism, Cosmopolitanism, and the Evolution of Soviet Culture, 1931–1941* (Cambridge, MA: Harvard University Press, 2011), 5–7. Thus, its findings do not principally contradict Stalinism's reclusive effects but add to our understanding of its capacity to accommodate contradictory developments in "simultaneity" and "imbrication," in Clark's apt terminology.

Soviet space and a "cult of the borderguard" marked official mass culture.[32] Feeling subject to "hostile encirclement" and "believing in the intrinsic civilizational conflict between socialism and capitalism," the Soviet leadership spread a sense of impending war.[33]

In the fall of 1939, the inhabitants of this often fatal utopia entered and met a real outside, one that was "utterly different," shaped by a combination of "new nation-states, national majorities and minorities, right-wing rule, and multiple competing political parties and movements."[34] To understand the individual and social effects of Sovietization on the Sovietized as well as the Sovietizers, this encounter is no less important than the state strategies of expansion and transformation, on which much of the traditional literature has focused.

Sovietization and Ukrainization

Traditional narratives of postwar Lviv's Ukrainian national perseverance miss much of the interaction between its pre-Soviet legacies and the Soviet transformation drive. In reality, Ukrainization and Sovietization were inseparable in Lviv. Some contemporaries and later observers, however, have preferred a simpler picture, distinguishing an abhorred Sovietization from a welcome Ukrainization. In the 1950s, for instance, Kost Pankivskyi—a Ukrainian national activist, politician, and collaborator with the Germans—would remember Lviv's first Soviet occupation between 1939 and 1941 as divided sharply into a "soft" period of Ukrainization followed by a "fierce" period of Sovietization.[35]

Yet in Lviv as elsewhere in the twentieth century, Communism and nationalism came to converge on violent ethnic reordering and simplification. The unprecedented Ukrainization of the towns and cities of western Ukraine occurred in the decades after 1939, under long Soviet—as well as short German—rule. The Soviet census of 1959 counted three-fifths of Lviv's population as Ukrainian, a share that had increased fivefold since 1931, the year of the last prewar census.

32. Emma Widdis, *Visions of a New Land: Soviet Film from the Revolution to the Second World War* (New Haven: Yale University Press, 2003), 143–44.

33. Olga Kucherenko, *Little Soldiers: How Soviet Children Went to War, 1941–1945* (Oxford: Oxford University Press, 2011), 23. War *was* impending, and to a substantial extent but not exclusively because of Soviet policies widespread international hostility to the Soviet Union was a reality. None of this diminishes the importance of Soviet ideological and propaganda choices. If anything, these realities reinforced their effect.

34. Barnes, *Death and Redemption*, 110. When the Soviet camp system absorbed many of the inhabitants of this new old world, they were collectively labeled "Westerners," "defined primarily in opposition to those who had long been Soviet citizens" (ibid., 111).

35. Kost Pankivskyi, *Vid derzhavy do komitetu* (New York: Kliuchi, 1957), 22.

While Ukrainians became a majority for the first time, there were about one-tenth as many Poles as on the eve of the war and about one-fourth as many Jews.[36] Although both groups had been more numerous and socially prominent than Ukrainians before the war, they were now, respectively, about 4 and 6 percent of the population.

At the same time, although Lviv was not Russified, by 1959 more than a quarter of the population was Russian, and Soviet Russian culture and language loomed large. Yet it is important to note that this peak of Lviv's demographic Russianness was historically brief. Over the remaining Soviet period, the percentage of Ukrainians continued to grow, while that of Russians decreased. By 1989, Ukrainians constituted four-fifths of Lviv's population. Meanwhile, the Russian population dropped to about 16 percent by the end of the Soviet period—as it happened, roughly the same as the Ukrainian minority's share in prewar Lwów.

In Soviet Lviv, it was dangerous to challenge the importance and general hegemony of Russian culture. In 1952, the director of one of Lviv's minor academic institutions lost his position for abolishing exams in Russian literature.[37] Yet such evidence needs contextualization. Clearly, on the whole, it is the *absence* of Russification in Soviet Lviv that stands out. In the wider Soviet Union, Russian facilitated careers and dominated the media and public space. Yet in Lviv, one of the first speeches at a 1951 conference for women academics, at the height of postwar Stalinism, was dedicated to the "Question of a Single Ukrainian National [*natsionalnu*] Language." In 1952, a head of a Marxism-Leninism subdepartment (*kafedra*) in Lviv lost his position for, among other offenses, deriding the "local Ukrainian language." In 1968, Lviv's History Museum offered signs only in Ukrainian although over half its visitors were "tourists" from other parts of the Soviet Union and abroad, as a Soviet report lamented.[38] By 1970, after the postwar decade with the steepest increase in the number of Lviv's Ukrainians, nearly 94 percent of them declared Ukrainian to be their native language. In 1987, nearly three-quarters of all pupils in the city were taking their lessons in Ukrainian. It was little wonder, then, and not due to sudden perestroika effects but to long-term

36. Roman Lozynskyi, *Etnichnyi sklad naselennia Lvova* (Lviv: Vydavnychnyi tsentr LNU imeni Ivana Franka, 2005), 211. The preponderant majority of Lviv's Jews in 1959 were not from the pre-1941 population, out of which only a few had survived the Holocaust; moreover, these survivors mostly left Soviet Ukraine after 1945.

37. DALO P-3, 4, 431: 56. In 1956, it was a high Soviet official who complained that, although most workers at Lviv factories were Ukrainian-speaking locals "from the villages," "all, even the least notable positions" of authority were occupied by "people who do not know Ukrainian at all." He deplored the "strange phenomenon" of management and slogans in Russian but workers, "of course," speaking Ukrainian (DALO P-3, 5, 330: 87).

38. DALO P-3, 4, 331: 66, P-3, 4, 431: 14; P-3, 10, 223: 69.

developments and Soviet policies, that by 1989, nearly 97 percent of Lviv's population declared Ukrainian to be their native language.[39] Clearly, the footprint of Russification would have looked very different. Soviet Lviv was not Russified but Ukrainianized, while the Soviet idea of Ukrainian identity presupposed a subordinate relationship to a Soviet version of Russian culture.

The Making of the Local and the Shaping of Western Ukraine

Turning Lwów into Lviv was the most important instance of the attempt to shape a Western Ukrainian identity fit for the Soviet Union. Yet this process was neither preordained nor straightforward.[40] Indeed, initially it was unclear what exactly Western Ukraine was.[41] There was a sense that it was different as well as already gone: in 1939, Lviv's new Soviet and Ukrainian-language newspaper *Vilna Ukraina* reported on a meeting between writers from "Soviet Ukraine" and "Western Ukraine"; in November, a Kyiv Central Committee decree spoke of the "former Western Ukraine."[42]

39. Lozynskyi, *Etnichnyi sklad naselennia Lvova*, 231–32. For school statistics, see Iaroslav Isaievych et al., eds., *Istoriia Lvova* (Lviv: Ivan Krypiakevych Institute of Ukrainian Studies, National Academy of Sciences of Ukraine, Tsentr Evropy, 2006–7), 3:317.

40. Paul Robert Magocsi, "A Subordinate or Submerged People: The Ukrainians of Galicia under Habsburg and Soviet Rule," in his *The Roots of Ukrainian Nationalism: Galicia as Ukraine's Piedmont* (Toronto: University of Toronto Press, 2002), 61.

41. In Soviet terminology there were—mostly—two names for the territories conquered and added to Soviet Ukraine as a result of the Second World War: Western Ukraine and the western oblasts. Frequently, the "western oblasts" were meant to be more comprehensive, including the oblasts of Zakarpattia, Chernivtsi, Lviv, Drohobych (incorporated into Lviv in 1958), Ivano-Frankivsk, Ternopil, Volyn, and Rivne. When the term "Western Ukraine" was used, it often excluded Zakarpattia and Izmail oblasts, which were also Second-World-War acquisitions but categorized differently. Even official documents, however, were not always precise about the relationship between "Zakarpattia" and "Western Ukraine," with the latter term employed to mean both of them together. Moreover, variants persisted, including the rare "Western Ukrainian Krai" or the unusual capitalization of the "Western Oblasts." See RGAE 4372, 47, 145: 76 and RGANI 5, 17, 484: 15. Even "Galicia," usually avoided, sometimes resurfaced in Soviet discourse, as in 1946, when Lviv's local newspaper called "Galician" the area usually referred to as "Western Ukraine," while also, interchangeably, writing about the "western oblasts" and "Western Ukraine" (*Vilna Ukraina*, 8 March 1946, 7, 8). Clearly, here was a site of concepts still under construction. By 1977, the second edition of the *Ukrainian Soviet Encyclopedia*, in its entry on the "unification" of the Ukrainian Soviet Republic in the Second World War, defined Western Ukraine as eastern Galicia and western Volyn. (Mykola Bazhan et al., eds. *Ukrainska radianska entsyklopediia* [Kyiv: URE, 1977-85], 2:358). Yet, this definition did not fit the usage of Soviet authorities in the postwar years. Rather, their documents indicated not only their looser and wider usage of the term for almost everything that had not been part of Ukraine before 1945 (except, of course, Crimea after 1954), but also that for the authorities Lviv was always the center of this wider Western Ukraine around which their strategies and problems of Sovietization clustered.

42. Volodymyr Serhiychuk, ed., *Ukrainskyi zdvyh* (Kyiv: Ukrainska vydavnycha spilka, 2005), 2:18; *Vilna Ukraina*, 14 October 1939, 6.

Soviet intentions, unclear to begin with, were also not the same as Soviet outcomes. Was the effect of Soviet policies to "profoundly transform" eastern Galicia so that it became like "any other part of Soviet Ukraine," as Paul Robert Magocsi has surmised?[43] Or was there a different, if also profound transformation, with a different result: a Soviet Western Ukraine unlike its past but also unlike the Soviet present further east?

This question can only be answered with respect to the Soviet category of the local, whose history in Western Ukraine has, however, mostly been overlooked. To Sovietize Western Ukraine, the Sovietizers made fundamental distinctions between those who shape and those who must be shaped, those who bring progress and those who must catch up, which were reminiscent of distinctions made in Western empires and colonies, the southern and eastern parts of the late Romanov empire, and Cold War hegemonic development projects.[44] Yet within a shared but diverse modernity, the Bolsheviks really were as special as they insisted: with Sovietization, distinctions of domination were fused with the fundamental Soviet ethos of class struggle, while the interwar Soviet Union developed a specific technique of combining that ethos with ethnic categorizations.[45]

In this context, the expulsion of Western Ukraine's Poles between late 1944 and early 1947 came at the end of a transition period in Soviet nationality policy when, in Terry Martin's terms, xenophobia and fear of irredentism won out over ethnophilia. Yet expelling local Poles did not mean expelling the local as a key category for making sense of borderland Sovietization. Once Poles were gone, the place of the local was left to those of Lviv's often new Ukrainian inhabitants who had belonged to the pre-Soviet population of remade Western Ukraine. This was the starting point of what would turn into the making of a Soviet Western Ukrainian identity.

This local identity, during a long and traumatically violent initial period, was shaped decisively by what was in effect a Bolshevik *civilizing mission*: to be Sovietized, the Western Ukrainian local had to be saved, elevated, and developed no less than, for instance, an Azeri inhabitant of interwar Baku. The Western Ukrainian local, too, was seen as backward, often exasperatingly unwilling to be improved but—given enough compulsion, selection, and conditional

43. Paul Robert Magocsi, *Galicia: A Historical Survey and Bibliographic Guide* (Toronto: University of Toronto Press, 1983), 218.

44. On development and modernization as key elements of US hegemony, see David Ekbladh, *The Great American Mission: Modernization and the Construction of an American World Order* (Princeton, NJ: Princeton University Press, 2010). On a self-consciously European-type practice of colonialism in the eastern borderlands of the late Romanov empire, see Adeeb Khalid, *The Politics of Muslim Cultural Reform: Jadidism in Central Asia* (Berkeley: University of California Press, 1998), 51-53; and Northrop, *Veiled Empire*, 7-9.

45. Baberowski, *Der Feind ist überall*, 109–83; Martin, *Affirmative Action Empire*, 311–43.

rewards—redeemable. Having entered the persona of the local, literally emptied by the Soviet authorities of its first postwar Polish co-occupant, Western Ukraine's and Lviv's pre-Soviet Ukrainians faced the Soviet demand to prove that they were improvable.

This compulsory option also implied the second fundamental, though not absolute, difference between Soviet and non-Soviet forms of imperialism. In the latter, racism was "an inherent product of the colonial encounter."[46] The making of decisive distinctions between one's superior own and an inferior Other was immersed in paradigms of an essentially unequal humanity. Although in practice Soviet socialism was not immune to racist ideas or ethnically targeted discrimination and violence, it fundamentally rejected racism.[47] At the same time, resisting the temptation of essentializing those deemed at once backward *and* equal remained a challenge.

In Soviet Western Ukraine, this fact of discourse shaped the fate and identity of the local no less than the practices of deportation, repression, and discrimination so liberally employed.[48] Certainly, both nonsocialist and socialist imperialism relied on a "culturally sanctioned habit of deploying large generalizations."[49] Yet even while their new western borderlands tempted Sovietizers to confound ethnicity and class, explicit racist essentialization remained unavailable and—almost literally—unthinkable to them.[50] Thus, in 1953, after Stalin's death, the Soviet

46. Ann Laura Stoler, *Carnal Knowledge and Imperial Power: Race and the Intimate in Colonial Rule* (Berkeley: University of California Press, 2010), 24–25.

47. On the distinction between the phenomenon of ethnically targeted or biased state violence, clearly occurring in the Soviet case, and systematized racism as a fundamental element of regime ideology or public discourse, see especially Amir Weiner's concise discussion, "Nothing but Certainty," *Slavic Review* 61 (2002): 44–53.

48. Whereas Edward Said focused on the strictly exclusive aspects of Western imperialism, offering its Other no options of promotion via change, assimilation, and alienation, David Ekbladh has pointed out North American and European beliefs in lifting the Other out of "backwardness" through modern tutelage and domination, with—at least before the First World War—the paradigm of tutelage more important in the American than in the British or French cases. See Edward W. Said, *Orientalism* (New York: Vintage Books: 1979); Ekbladh, *Great American Mission*, 19–20, 37. Although part of the difference between Said and Ekbladh is clearly due to their looking at different empires at different times, on the whole, the Soviet case seems closer to the American than to the British or French.

49. Said, *Orientalism*, 226.

50. On the challenged but not broken persistence, in the Soviet Union, of the primacy of nurture over nature, of "acculturation" over the option of a "biological-racial ethos," as exemplified by Nazi Germany, with special reference to Ukraine and the Second World War, see Weiner, *Making Sense of War*, 26–27, 201–7. On prerevolutionary Russian cultural and intellectual developments that may have contributed to the Soviet lack of modern racism, see Nathaniel Knight, "Ethnicity, Nationality, and the Masses: *Narodnost'* and Modernity in Imperial Russia," in *Russian Modernity: Politics, Knowledge, Practices*, ed. David L. Hoffmann and Yanni Kotsonis (New York: Macmillan, 2000), 58; and Hoffmann, *Cultivating the Masses*, 33.

approach to Western Ukraine became a battleground in the lethally fierce succession struggle among his chief accomplices and potential heirs. Lavrentii Beria's criticism of Soviet repression and violence there allowed some local as well as loyal critics in Lviv to join in with accusations that the Sovietizers had treated the locals as a "qualitatively lower sort of human existence," condemned by their own "dishonesty" and "banditism" to remain mired in "absolute backwardness."[51] Yet in the Soviet case, it was the rejection of such attitudes that prevailed. This rejection was not due merely to Beria's strategizing: it was not contingent but inherent to the Soviet phenomenon. A "utopia manqué," with all its hypocrisy and oppression, the Soviet Union could not permanently abandon the axiom of the perfectibility of categorically all.[52] In a Soviet context, the obstacles separating the locals from being fully Soviet had to be imagined as surmountable in the name of a kind of socialism unable to see itself as anything other than humanity's most advanced modern civilization.

This idea of Sovietization also implied capital-h History as a teaching of origins and pasts overcome and of the future as a claiming of ends. Like Soviet civilization as a whole, Sovietization was inconceivable without its *telos*, the belief that it was the one and only and inevitable escape from a history of humanity construed as a long ascent based on an initial fall into exploitation and inequality. In Soviet Lviv, in 1946, it was the director of the city's History Museum who stressed the long Ukrainian struggle against Polish, Austrian, and German colonizers and the backwardness they had imposed; now the city would have "a future."[53] In a mode fundamentally resembling the operating principle of Socialist Realism, in the *Gesamtkunstwerk* of Sovietization Western Ukraine's locals were expected to incarnate the present and the end—a present still reflecting an unredeemed past but about to be overcome by a socialist future.[54]

The opposites of the locals were the so-called "easterners," Soviet immigrants of various ethnic backgrounds who came to the city after its conquest. For at least seven years after 1946, until the death of Stalin and a subsequent turn in Soviet strategy in Western Ukraine, locals and easterners were the most pervasive

51. Iuriy Slyvka et al., *Kulturne zhyttia v Ukraini: Zakhidni zemli. Dokumenty i materialy*, (Kyiv and Lviv: Instytut ukrainoznavstva im. I. I. Krypiakevycha, Natsionalna akademia nauk Ukrainy, 1995, 1996, 2006), 2: 32, 45.

52. Clark, *Moscow, the Fourth Rome*, 128.

53. *Lvovskaia pravda*, 2 February 1946, 3.

54. As Michael David-Fox has pointed out, the doctrine of Socialist Realism was also a response to the Soviet need to compete with the West (*Showcasing the Great Experiment*, 147). From 1939, Lviv, and Western Ukraine in general, became an important site and symbol of that competition. The structural similarity between the local as a work in progress of Sovietization and the Soviet Union's art doctrine is striking.

categories deployed by the party-state. Thus, if the question of why and how Sovietization ended up shaping a Western Ukrainian identity has to be answered with reference to the local, understanding the meaning of the local requires understanding the meaning of the "easterner": the easterner—by no means only ethnic Russians, though these often, especially initially, played a key role—had to be advanced, avoid assimilating to the locals, and often be strict and demanding with them but also—in theory and self-image at least—self-sacrificing. The easterners' encounter with the locals shaped their own sense of how to be Soviet.[55] In particular, after 1939, Soviet Western Ukraine was a place where easterners learned to take Stalinist civilization west.

If Soviet Man was carrying a socialist burden to Western Ukraine, the locals responded in complex ways: they were silent and sullen; practiced foot-dragging, deception, and careerism; or sought ways to preserve dignity and autonomy in the face of humiliation, compulsion, and opportunity. Tens of thousands of locals fought a desperate and brutal guerilla-war-cum-terrorist campaign for Ukrainian nationalism's idea of independence. But the party-state won its dirty war of counterinsurgency, killing more than 150,000, deporting more than 200,000, and incarcerating nearly 110,000 locals.[56]

Before being formally declared to have caught up with fully developed Soviet socialism in 1958, all pre-Soviet inhabitants of Western Ukraine went through the stage of being local. In the initial phase, the party-state's policy toward locals varied extremely, combining continual calls to mobilize and promote them with recurring fits of distrust, discrimination, and punishment. After Stalin's death, Lavrentii Beria's strategizing in Moscow marked a lasting turn in the locals' favor, accompanied by some severe criticism of those who had mistreated them. First Secretary of Ukraine Leonid Melnikov lost his position for having been hard on Western Ukrainian locals as well as Jews everywhere in Ukraine, and a first secretary of Lviv's obkom, Vasyl Chuchukalo, lost his position for having been a Melnikov favorite.[57]

55. This, too, resembled earlier processes: as Douglas Northrop has pointed out, Central Asia, before and after 1917, was a place where Russian colonizers and Sovietizers learned roles of superiority and tutelage (*Veiled Empire*, 8).

56. For these figures, covering the period from the summer of 1944 to the spring of 1953, see Lavrentii Beria's report of 16 May 1953, RGASPI 82, 2, 897: 144.

57. TsDAHOU 1, 24, 3487 on Melnikov's and Chuchukalo's linked disgrace. Borys Lewytzkyj has claimed that the "official reasons" for Melnikov's dismissal were largely unimportant and that his career did not suffer substantially from his fall (*Politics and Society in Soviet Ukraine, 1953–1980* [Edmonton: Canadian Institute of Ukrainian Studies Press, 1984], 4). Lewytzkyj had to rely on published sources. However, Ukrainian Politburo documents, discussed in more detail below and including the minutes of the major Melnikov-bashing meeting of this body in the summer of 1953, show that the accusations against Melnikov were taken seriously.

It is important to note that the promotion and discrimination of locals between 1944 and 1953 did not form a predictable pattern. Discrimination was strong and pervasive, but promotion never ceased either. Its results usually did not satisfy Soviet authorities, but they were not negligible. At the beginning of 1951, locals made up 8.5 percent of Lviv's regional elite as registered and administered in the official nomenklatura system; by March 1953, before Beria's initiative, the same indicator stood at 21.3 percent.[58]

Locals, caught in and engaged with these confusing party-state strategies, had to learn to play without reliable rules or power. They could, however, learn one fundamental rule: being local, for better or for worse, was the new most important identity category. This process needs to be put in the context of what they had learned before about being Polish, Ukrainian, and Jewish—especially, but not only, starting in 1939. The cumulative effect of Soviet techniques of categorization, prewar national mobilization, and Second World War escalation, ethnic discrimination, segregation, and annihilation solidified the local as a category: similarity combined with difference to produce counterdistinction. The pervasive Soviet reliance on the category of the local and the effects of the war reinforced each other to create a lasting force field of identity politics reaching across the war and postwar periods.

The postwar local, however, was made not to be exterminated or expelled but for self-overcoming. Bohdan Dudykevych was one of the few elite locals who were also early key Sovietizers.[59] For him, speaking at a closed meeting in 1945, the division of the population into "locals" and "'Soviets'" had to be replaced not by immediate unity but by an equally strict division into "Soviet" and "non-Soviet."[60] Yet history showed itself to be cunning, and the way turned out to

58. TsDAHOU 1, 24, 2946: 8–9. The nomenklatura system, however, was hierarchical and distinguished an elite within the elite. The most important positions at the regional level, too, were part of the Kyiv Central Committee's nomenklatura, whereas less important ones belonged to that of the obkom. It was easier for locals to advance in this second tier of local power. According to the document cited at the beginning of this note, in 1951 they made up 9.8 percent of the local elite but 24.9 percent in March 1953, whereas their share of the positions under the nomenklatura of the Kyiv Central Committee was smaller and increased more slowly, from 5.03 to 7.4 percent.

59. DALO P-3, 5, 356: 6–7. A Ukrainian born in 1907, Dudykevych had been a Communist since 1929, had done trade union and pedagogical work during the first Soviet occupation, fled east when the Germans attacked, served for several months in the Soviet army, then spent the rest of the war in various positions in the Soviet Union. He was admitted to candidate Communist Party membership in 1946, followed by full membership in 1948. Apart from his long service as the director of Lviv's Lenin Museum, in 1953 and 1954 he would serve as the second secretary of the Lviv obkom.

60. DALO P-4, 1, 58: 207. In Dudykevych's original phrasing, the difference between what was and what ought to be was clearer. He used the non-Ukrainian word *sovety*—in quotation marks—when contrasting the latter with the "locals," implying a typically local, hostile use of the term. Calling for a new, categorically delocalized segregation into "Soviet" and "non-Soviet," he used the correct and official Ukrainian term for Soviet, *radianskyi*.

be the goal. The intentional Soviet making of the local—in the form of a distinct but transitory type of not-yet-Sovietized western borderland Ukrainian—had the unintended effect of shaping and solidifying a special and persistent Western Ukrainian identity, which was distinct from the eastern, pre-1939 variant of Soviet Ukrainian identity. Moreover, and equally important, the party-state never reversed this outcome but rather adapted to it. Unsurprisingly, post-Soviet Western Ukraine is a product of its history, as has often been pointed out. Equally unsurprisingly but much less often noted these days, much of this history was Soviet and authoritarian-socialist.

In Western Ukraine and Lviv, Sovietization also turned into a meeting between different ways of being Ukrainian. It was under Soviet rule that postwar Lviv emerged as a truly common as well as divisive all-Ukrainian project. Although the local functioned in some respects like a surrogate ethnic category, those to whom it was ascribed were often ethnically the same as those labeled easterners. Thus, if Lviv became the single most important site of local-easterner encounter, this also implied an intra-Ukrainian struggle. This, too, was a historic change: in some respects, the easterners took over the place and roles of the two groups who had dominated prewar Lwów. Yet Polish and Jewish elites had not pursued a project of making the city Ukrainian. After the war, with prewar Poles and Jews dead and gone and with the addition of Russians, Soviet socialism, and Soviet inter/nationalism, the majority of Lviv's new population became Ukrainian.

Chapter 1 sets the historical background of Lviv's transformation after 1939 by sketching its history between its founding in the thirteenth century and the beginning of the Second World War. Tracing the perhaps not inevitable but certainly real increase of national tension and nationalist mobilization from the middle of the nineteenth century on, the chapter also shows that outcomes were not preordained. In Lviv, nineteenth-century nationalism was powerful but neither omnipotent nor without rival ideologies. The First World War was crucial in boosting the politics and mentalities of nationalism. Against this backdrop, the chapter explains the effects of Polish interwar rule and the making and remaking of a Ukrainian nationalism, deeply frustrated by the outcome of the First World War and turning increasingly violent, conspiratorial, and authoritarian.

Chapter 2 addresses the first Soviet occupation of Lviv between the fall of 1939 and the summer of 1941. It details Soviet policies of political, cultural, and social transformation—often violent—and local responses. In particular, the chapter focuses on the encounter between the city's inhabitants and the Soviet conqueror-newcomers, highlighting how both drew on and articulated their sense of self and the Other. Moreover, the chapter traces the similarities and crucial differences in the effects of Soviet policies on Lviv's main national groups.

Chapter 3 describes the three years of German occupation from 1941 to 1944, when Lviv's Jewish population was murdered in the Holocaust and the conflict between its Polish and Ukrainian inhabitants escalated. Analyzing continuities and discontinuities between Soviet and German rule, the chapter reconstructs the specific ways in which Soviet and German initiatives affected the city of Lviv and its inhabitants. The chapter also shows the interlocking of German and local agency in the implementation of the Holocaust as well as how, for its German occupiers, Lviv became a site of symbolic delimitation against their Soviet opponents as well as fantasies of the "East."

Chapter 4 treats the years immediately after the Soviet reconquest between 1944 and 1946/1947 as a seminal transition period, when Lwów's Polish majority population was expelled and a rapid repopulation of the city laid the foundation for Lviv's postwar Ukrainization. After the initial Soviet-local encounter between 1939 and 1941, it was during this period that lasting patterns developed for the making of the mutually constitutive identities of locals and easterners. The chapter reconstructs the expulsion of the city's Poles as not the sudden event into which it has often been foreshortened in memory and history but a process protracted enough to fundamentally influence the making of the new postwar Lviv.

Chapter 5 addresses Lviv's postwar industrialization and the creation of a large population of workers from two kinds of immigrants: locals from the western Ukrainian countryside and easterners. These new workers were crucial to Lviv's Sovietization not only as labor power but also as an essential element of the city's Soviet identity or, as the Soviet authorities often put it, "face." With Lviv recast not only as a Soviet but as an industrial city, a large working class was indispensable. There was no urban experience of Sovietization as personal transformation more widespread than that of Lviv's new worker locals.

If the experience of workers was a mass phenomenon, Chapter 6 focuses on the most condensed display of the remaking of the local by discussing the so-called Old Intelligentsia of the city—a sample of postwar Ukrainian scholars, writers, and artists who had been trained before 1939—and their painful and public transformation into Soviet intelligentsia. The chapter also addresses Lviv's last specifically local and especially intelligentsia-focused mass repression campaign after the killing of a Soviet local writer and propagandist in the fall of 1949. Moreover, through this campaign, the chapter looks at the relationship between the party-state and the new generation of students in Lviv's academic institutions.

Chapter 7 is dedicated to the postwar history and closing of the only synagogue in Lviv that was reopened after the Holocaust. Marginalized and harassed yet intermittently important to Soviet concerns and policies, Lviv's postwar synagogue was the last institution that publicly represented a distinctly Jewish identity in a city that, before the Holocaust, had been one of the major centers of

Jewish life in east central Europe. The synagogue implied a complicated but extant link with a local prewar Jewish past. At the same time, it was subjected to the same pressures exerted on Jewish life in the postwar Soviet Union in general. The chapter reconstructs Lviv's postwar synagogue as a site of national and religious identity and a target of Soviet repressive policies and stereotypes.

Chapter 8 analyzes Lviv's official postwar culture of memory as a borderland of the past, a liminal space of the Soviet historical imagination, simultaneously connecting and dividing the city's pre-Soviet history and its Soviet present. Through this exploration of the Sovietization of Lviv's past, the chapter addresses what happened after the identity of the local had turned out to be persistent and the Soviet authorities no longer sought to overcome it but to work with it.

CHAPTER ONE

Lviv/Lwów/Lemberg before 1939

Today, Lviv is a city of about 750,000 inhabitants and 65 square miles in the West of an independent Ukrainian nation-state.[1] It is the center of one of Ukraine's twenty-seven main administrative units, Lviv oblast, and the urban center of Western Ukraine (a generally, if unofficially, recognized region), with about nine-and-a-half million inhabitants, roughly the equivalent of Hungary's and a fifth of Ukraine's total populations.[2]

This contemporary Lviv is a historically recent creation, decisively shaped by the Second World War and the postwar period; it is not the outcome of inexorable national fate. Yet these twentieth-century processes, while anything but preordained, cannot be understood in isolation from either earlier developments or the latter's echo in twentieth-century memory, ambitions, and conditions. This chapter puts Lviv's history, as it unfolded after the beginning of the Second World War, in its broader context.

Origins at Stake

There is general consensus that Lviv was founded as a fortress in the thirteenth century and named after its founder's son, Lev, the Lion. Medieval Lviv quickly became the capital of the Halyts-Volyn principality. Its rulers descended from but also defied the rulers of the ancient Rus' state centered on Kyiv.[3] Modern

1 Brenda Lafleur et al., *Lviv City Profile: Demographic, Economic, Fiscal* (The Conference Board of Canada, Canadian International Development Agency, 2012), 6, http://www.ebed.org.ua/sites/expertise.one2action.com/files/repo/ebed_lviv_city_profile_eng.pdf.

2 Sebastian Klüsener, "Die Regionen der Ukraine: Abgrenzung und Charakterisierung," *Ukraineanalysen*, no. 23 (8 May 2007): 3. The number of twenty-seven administrative units includes Crimea and the Crimean city of Sevastopol, which used to have a special status in Ukraine, were annexed by Russia in 2014, and (as of 2015) are under de facto rule from Moscow.

3 Natalya Yakowenko, *Narys istorii seredniovichnoi ta ranniomodernoi Ukrainy*, 2nd ed. (Kyiv: Krytyka, 2005), 98–99. There are different variations of the Halyts-Volyn state's designation in the pertinent literature. I have tried to adopt a transcription of Natalya Yakowenko's "Halytsko-Volynske kniazivstvo." My sketch of the history of the Halyts-Volyn state is derived from ibid., 96–109.

national narratives claim the latter as the origin of Russia or Ukraine. In reality, it was neither Ukrainian in any modern sense nor "one of the most reliable outposts in the West of the old Russian lands."[4] Its history does not fit myths of nationalism, imperialism, or hegemony.

By the mid-thirteenth century, the Halyts-Volyn ruler had received papal recognition as *Rex Russiae*. In the fourteenth century, the principality was divided, with its Halyts part and Lviv going to the Roman Catholic kings of medieval Poland. One of them declared a crusade against Orthodox schismatics.[5] Later, conflicting interpretations contested the memory of this Halyts-Volyn state. By the end of the nineteenth century, modern Ukrainian historiography in then Habsburg Galicia rejected Polish rule as a dark hiatus and claimed Lviv as originally and authentically eastern Slavonic, Orthodox, and (proto-)Ukrainian—not western Slavonic, Catholic, or (proto-)Polish.[6]

Moreover, the Kyiv and the Lviv myths were linked. Early dynastic affiliations with Kyiv were deployed to assert the national claim that the Halyts-Volyn state had continued an ancient Rus' tradition, preserving legitimacy for a Ukrainian nation. Assigning the Kyiv Rus' origins anywhere else than to the Grand Duchy of Moscow/Russian Empire, however, challenged Russian claims of having alone preserved the Rus' tradition. As a symbol, Lviv could turn, in Andreas Kappeler's succinct phrase, a "Ukrainian question" into a "key problem of the nation-building and national identity of the Russians."[7] By the end of the twentieth century, Lviv's

4 Roman Lubkivskyi, *Lviv: Misto ochyma pysmennyka* (Lviv: Kameniar, 1985), 76.

5 Yakowenko, *Narys istorii*, 105–9; Orest Subtelny, *Ukraina: Istoriia*, 3rd rev. ed. (Kyiv: Lybid, 1993), 100–101.

6 Serhii Plokhy, *Unmaking Imperial Russia: Mykhailo Hrushevsky and the Writing of Ukrainian History* (Toronto: University of Toronto Press, 2005), 165.

7 Andreas Kappeler, "Aspekte der ukrainischen Nationalbewegung im 19. Jahrhundert und frühen 20. Jahrhundert," in *Ukraine: Gegenwart und Geschichte eines neuen Staates*, ed. Guido Hausmann and Andreas Kappeler (Baden-Baden: Nomos, 1993), 77. For a concise overview of the history of the relationship between Ukrainian and Russian identity and nation and state building projects, see Andreas Kappeler, "'Great Russians' and 'Little Russians': Russian-Ukrainian Relations and Perceptions in Historical Perspective," *Donald W. Treadgold Papers in Russian, East European, and Central Asian Studies*, no. 39 (2003): 22–28. Alexei Miller has shown how, in the second half of the nineteenth century, the "Ukrainian nationalist challenge [became] an exceptionally important catalyst for the debate on . . . the making of the Russian nation itself" (*The Ukrainian Question: The Russian Empire and Nationalism in the Nineteenth Century* [Budapest: Central European University Press, 2003], 249). Conversely, Faith Hillis has explained how the Ukrainian borderlands of the nineteenth-century Russian empire played a crucial role in the search for Russian national identity (*Children of Rus': Right-Bank Ukraine and the Invention of a Russian Nation* [Ithaca, NY: Cornell University Press, 2013], esp. 3). Focusing on the period of modern nation building is not to deny that, as with Moscow's political imaginary, there were earlier, premodern constructions of alternative lines of succession and communities. Thus, in the sixteenth and seventeenth centuries, Kyiv thinkers set up genealogies leading from Kyiv via Halyts and Lithuania back to Kyiv (Yakowenko, *Narys istorii*, 109–10.). In the seventeenth century, Orthodox clergy and Cossack leaders imagined a confessional, not a modern national community (Hillis, *Children of Rus'*, 12).

definitive—and last—Soviet history, published in Kyiv, lauded early Lviv as an eastern Slavonic bulwark against Western Catholics.[8]

The Making of a Multiethnic Borderland City

After Lviv became part of medieval Poland—subsequently the Polish-Lithuanian Commonwealth—the old settlement became a suburb to a new walled city and the ethno-religious structure of the population changed, with Catholic Polish and German immigrants added to Orthodox inhabitants.[9] By the beginning of the sixteenth century, Roman Catholics made up the majority of the city's population and dominated its institutions.[10]

While Jewish settlement in the area began earlier, the first evidence of two Jewish communities in Lviv dates to the middle of the fourteenth century, when Ashkenazi Jews arrived and shaped the city's Jewish life.[11] For Lviv's Jews the period of Polish rule brought advances followed by a decline. Pogroms and "blood libel" persecutions grew more frequent starting in the seventeenth century.[12]

At the end of the eighteenth century, as a result of the partitions of the Polish-Lithuanian Commonwealth, Lviv and its region came under Habsburg rule as the eastern half of a new Crown Land province called, in a short version, "Galizien-Lodomerien" or simply "Galizien." Poles initially resisted the new name, but soon it was generally used.[13] What Larry Wolff has described as the invention of Galicia had begun.[14]

The Habsburgs called Galicia's chief city "Lemberg." During their rule, from the late eighteenth to the early twentieth centuries, its population increased

8 V. V. Sekretariuk et al., *Istoriia Lvova* (Kyiv: Naukova dumka, 1984), 12–28.

9 Anna Veronika Wendland, *Die Russophilen in Galizien: Ukrainische Konservative zwischen Österrreich und Rußland 1848–1915* (Vienna: Verlag der Österreichischen Akademie der Wissenschaften, 2001), 35; Dieter Pohl, *Nationalsozialistische Judenverfolgung in Ostgalizien 1941–1944: Organisation und Durchführung eines staatlichen Massenverbrechens* (Munich: Oldenbourg, 1996), 23; Sergey R. Kravtsov, *Di Gildene Royze: The Turei Zahav Synagogue in Lviv* (Petersberg: Michael Imhof, 2011), 9–10.

10 Isaievych et al., *Istoriia Lvova*, 1:78.

11 Eliyahu Jones [Yones], *Żydzi Lwowa w okresie okupacji 1939–1945* (Łodź: Oficyna Bibliofilów, 1999), 9; Kravtsov, *Di Gildene Royze*, 9. Yones described his own fate as a slave laborer and survivor in his *Die Straße nach Lemberg: Zwangsarbeit und Widerstand in Ostgalizien 1941–1944* (Frankfurt am Main: Fischer, 1999)

12 Israel Bartal and Antony Polonsky, "The Jews of Galicia under the Habsburgs," *Polin* 12 (1999): 4, 9.

13 Grzegorz Hryciuk, *Przemiany narodowościowe i ludnościowe w Galicji Wschodniej i na Wołyniu w latach 1931–1948* (Toruń: Wydawnictwo Adam Marszałek, 2005), 26.

14 Larry Wolff, *The Idea of Galicia: History and Fantasy in Habsburg Political Culture* (Stanford, CA: Stanford University Press: 2010).

sevenfold, surpassing 200,000 in 1910.[15] But no fundamental changes in its ethnic composition occurred. What was really new about Habsburg rule was its ethos. This was the first time in Lviv's history that its rulers embraced an enlightenment-driven ideology of superior and imperial modernity imposed on a periphery categorized as backward. As Larry Wolff has stressed, Galicia's status as an "invented entity" made it a "perfect target for systematic enlightened transformation."[16] Lviv and *Galizien* were now objects of a civilizing mission. While geographically on—imagined—margins, they now also constituted an important laboratory of the central project of Enlightenment Europe: modernity.

The dynastic Habsburg Empire promoted this modernity with a national accent. The Habsburgs replaced Lemberg's medieval privileges with a centralizing bureaucracy initially staffed by German and Germanophone officials and aimed at the cultural Germanization of elites.[17] But, hobbled by limited resources and coordination, Habsburg Germanization was not nationalist but remained imperial, oscillating with reactionary responses to revolutionary crises.[18]

Habsburg rule brought Lemberg economic growth and changed its look, with substantial urban renewal. Lemberg's architects, many of them imported from Vienna, introduced a neoclassicist style meant to imprint a new, rational order on the cityscape, and travelers duly praised Lemberg for looking not like itself but like a little "Vienna of the East."[19] Within less than a century, however, Habsburg Lemberg became a shell for Lwów, a city belonging to Vienna but shaped by Polish elites, a Polish majority, and Polish cultural predominance.[20] Gradualist Habsburg fantasies failed—or, perhaps, succeeded, if in unforeseen ways.

15 Christoph Mick, "Nationalismus und Modernisierung in Lemberg 1867–1914," in *Städte im östlichen Europa: Zur Problematik von Modernisierung und Raum vom Spätmittelalter bis zum 20. Jahrhundert*, ed. Carsten Goehrke and Bianka Pietrow-Ennker (Zürich: Chronos, 2006), 178.

16 Wolff, *Idea of Galicia*, 20.

17 Rudolf A. Mark, "'Polnische Bastion und ukrainisches Piedmont': Lemberg 1772–1921," in *Lemberg, Lwów, Lviv: Eine Stadt im Schnittpunkt europäischer Kulturen*, ed. Peter Fäßler, Thomas Held, und Dirk Sawitzki (Cologne: Böhlau, 1993), 52; Yaroslav Hrytsak, *Prorok u svoi vitchyzni: Franko ta ioho spilnota* (Kyiv: Krytyka, 2006), 38.

18 Isabel Röskau-Rydel, "Galizien," in *Galizien, Bukowina, Moldau: Deutsche Geschichte im Osten Europas*, ed. Röskau-Rydel (Berlin: Siedler, 1999), 46, 99; Roman Szporluk, "The Making of Modern Ukraine: The Western Dimension," in *A Laboratory of Transnational History: Ukraine and Recent Ukrainian Historiography*, ed. Georgiy Kasianov and Philipp Ther (Budapest: Central European University Press, 2009), 255.

19 Isabel Röskau-Rydel, "'Die Stadt der verwischten Grenzen': Die Geschichte Lembergs von der Gründung bis zur ersten Teilung Polens (1772)," in *Lemberg, Lwów, Lviv*, ed. Faßler, Held, and Sawitzki, 29-30; Röskau-Rydel, "Galizien," in *Galizien, Bukowina, Moldau*, ed. Röskau-Rydel, 57; Markian Prokopovych, *Habsburg Lemberg: Architecture, Public Space, and Politics in the Galician Capital, 1772–1914* (West Lafayette, IN: Purdue University Press, 2009), 22–31, 278.

20 Röskau-Rydel, "Galizien," 77–80.

Although the idea had been "not to make Poles into Germans all at once" but to construct a "genuine" if new Galician identity as a halfway house for the Polish elite, the provisional became permanent and Germanization withered away.[21] In Lviv, the Habsburgs would not be the last ones to experience the insidious solidification of the transitory.

Habsburg Lemberg never presided over a prosperous province. Galicia remained poor and mostly agricultural, but it was not stagnant, profiting from an early oil industry.[22] Around the turn of the century, Lemberg/Lwów boomed, and its architects—now increasingly from the city's new Polytechnic Institute—turned it into a jewel of *Secesja* or *Jugendstil* building.[23]

Fin-de-siècle Lemberg was a provincial hub of Europe's urban modernity. In 1894, it was the empire's first city and Europe's fourth to introduce electric streetcars, which by 1938 would employ a staff of thirteen hundred.[24] By the early twentieth century, it had one of the empire's largest electric power stations.[25] In 1896, almost all the children in the city attended school, and among the young, illiteracy had been nearly eradicated. Lemberg witnessed an "explosive development" of print media, and the first commercial cinema precursors started working before the turn of the century. By the end of the First World War, over twenty-four cinemas had opened, and local intellectuals had contributed to early Polish film criticism. Lwów's coffee houses and the unveiling of the city's monument to the Polish national poet Adam Mickiewicz were both shown on film to socially mixed audiences, witnessing Lemberg's own version of the "utterly untraditional artistic modernism," in Eric Hobsbawm's apt phrase, that cinema represented.[26]

Jewish Lemberg

The city's Jewish population suffered discrimination for most of the nineteenth century, but achieved legal emancipation and formal equality in 1868. Between

21 See Wolff, *Idea of Galicia*, 80, for Metternich's 1815 fantasies of making Poles first into Galicians with the end goal of producing Germans.

22 On the importance and limits of Galicia's oil boom, see Alison Fleig Frank, *Oil Empire: Visions of Prosperity in Austrian Galicia* (Cambridge, MA: Harvard University Press, 2005).

23 Röskau-Rydel, "Galizien,"117–18; Hrytsak, *Prorok u svoi vitchyzni*, 29–30.

24 Jan Gieryński, *Lwów nie znany* (Lwów: Nakładem Księgarni A. Krawczyńskiego, 1938), 54; Mick, "Nationalismus und Modernisierung," 180.

25 Christoph Mick, *Kriegserfahrungen in einer multiethnischen Stadt: Lemberg 1914–1947* (Wiesbaden: Harrassowitz, 2010), 35-37.

26 On print media, see Mick, "Nationalismus und Modernisierung," 191, 195. On cinemas, see Barbara Gierszewska, *Kino i film we Lwowie do 1939 roku* (Kielce: Wydawnictwo Akademii świętokrzyskiej, 2006), 425–27; Eric Hobsbawn, *The Age of Empire, 1875–1914* (London: Abacus, 1994), 238.

1772 and 1848, Habsburg rule combined traditional discrimination against Jews with modernizing policies seeking to turn Jews into draftable citizen-subjects. Galicia was the first province where Jews faced both emancipation and military conscription, putting a region new, poor, and peripheral at the center of a monarchy-wide "discourse on Jewish equality and the price of citizenship."[27]

After the establishment of legal equality, the "first purely political organization of Jews not only in Galicia but in Austria as a whole" was the assimilationist Shomer Yisrael, founded in Lwów in 1868.[28] On its own terms, assimilation or acculturation produced some results. In the 1890s, out of one hundred city councilors, five or six were Jewish. By 1914, their number had increased to fifteen.[29] Yet on the whole, Jewish elite assimilation, first to German culture, then to Polish, failed. By the 1870s, the local ascendancy of Polish elites diminished the relevance of German culture; then the growth of modern Polish antisemitism squashed Polish-Jewish visions. Their former main representative in Lemberg, Alfred Nossig, recognizing antisemitism as "characteristic of our situation," renounced assimilation in favor of Zionism.[30]

Under Habsburg rule, the city's Jewish population generally prospered economically and advanced socially. But these benefits were spread unevenly. By the turn of the century, a disproportionate share of Lemberg's wealthy as well as poor were Jewish.[31] By 1897, Jews accounted for one-fifth of Lwów University's students; by 1914, 60 percent of the city's doctors were Jewish, as well as 70 percent of its lawyers and members of the chamber of trade and commerce.[32] For many Galician Jews, however, life in one of the poorest parts of the Habsburg monarchy remained hard. Between 1880 and 1914, about 350,000 Jews emigrated from Galicia.[33]

27 Michael K. Silber, "From Tolerated Aliens to Citizen-Soldiers: Jewish Military Service in the Era of Joseph II," in *Constructing Nationalities in East Central Europe*, ed. Pieter M. Judson and Marsha L. Rozenblit (New York: Berghahn, 2005), 24; Röskau-Rydel, "Galizien," 70.

28 Harald Binder, *Galizien in Wien: Parteien, Wahlen, Fraktionen und Abgeordnete im übergang zur Massenpolitik* (Vienna: Verlag der österreichischen Akademie der Wissenschaften, 2005), 53. On Shomer Yisrael's assimilationist orientation toward German culture, see Ezra Mendelsohn, "From Assimilation to Zionism in Lvov: The Case of Alfred Nossig," *Slavonic and East European Review* 49 (1971): 521–23.

29 Mick, "Nationalismus und Modernisierung," 176; Mick, *Kriegserfahrungen in einer multiethnischen Stadt*, 59.

30 Mendelsohn, "From Assimilation to Zionism in Lvov," 524–30; Theodore R. Weeks, *From Assimilation to Antisemitism: The "Jewish Question" in Poland, 1850–1914* (DeKalb: Northern Illinois University Press, 2006), 120–21.

31 Mick, *Kriegserfahrungen in einer multiethnischen Stadt*, 53.

32 Jones, *Żydzi Lwowa*, 11; Bartal and Polonsky, "Jews of Galicia," 19; Mick, "Nationalismus und Modernisierung," 205.

33 Pohl, *Nationalsozialistische Judenverfolgung*, 23.

Between Empires and Nationalisms

In the later nineteenth century, Galicia, like much of the empire, turned into an arena for competing nationalisms. After 1867, it belonged to the half of the empire ruled from Vienna, where, according to Peter Judson, the state set an "example of modern state building *not* linked to nation building" but to a framework of dynastic patriotism.[34] These policies, while not seeking to create *one* nation, did promote the making of many, if indirectly. Reacting to local national activists and seeking local national settlements, they furthered national mobilizations.

In Lwów, too, a multiply nationalist polity was emerging from the city's traditional multiethnicity.[35] After considering dividing the province of Galicia between Poles and Ruthenian-Ukrainians to punish the former for an uprising in 1846, Vienna instead soon relied on Polish elites, disappointing Ruthenian-Ukrainian activists.[36] This Habsburg pro-Polish turn contrasted sharply with the brutal repression of the Polish 1863–64 uprising in Russian Poland.[37] In Habsburg Lemberg, Polish was added to German as the official language of administration.[38] The result was local Polish ascendancy in a city Poles called Lwów as well as a "unique

34 Pieter M. Judson, "Constructing Nationalities in East Central Europe: Introduction," in *Constructing Nationalities in East Central Europe*, ed. Judson and Rozenblit, 2–3 (my emphasis).

35 Ibid., 3.

36 In the Habsburg Empire, although distinctions between endonyms and exonyms as well as overlapping terminologies and political and polemical subtexts complicate the picture, the ethnic group or nation that is now called Ukrainian was often called Ruthenian. The concept of eastern Galicia referred to a reasonably clearly understood space as well as contentious national ambitions, even though it was never defined with the deceptive precision produced by state bureaucracies. As Grzegorz Hryciuk has put it—pointing out some further complications—"Eastern Galicia . . . is not an unambiguous term. In the case of the territories . . . under Austrian rule from 1772 to 1918, the concept . . . can refer to a geographical term, meaning the eastern districts [*powiaty*] of a . . . Crown Land of the Austrian empire or . . . to a political term, designating the project of the creation of a separate territorial entity within the . . . Habsburg monarchy, [or] as an independent state, or as an autonomous territory within the . . . Second [Polish] Republic" (Hryciuk, *Przemiany narodowościowe i ludnościowe*, 25). Projects of somehow and to some degree separating eastern Galicia from its surrounding state and from western Galicia were usually promoted by Ukrainian nationalism. Since, however, they did not succeed, an administrative definition of eastern Galicia never proceeded beyond what could have been its precedent and has remained the consensual default reference point: "In spite of the difficulties with a precise definition of the territory of eastern Galicia, the most frequent assumption is that it encompassed the districts, which from 1850 came under the jurisdiction of the . . . *Oberlandesgericht* appeals court in Lwów. These were territories, in which the Ukrainian (Rus') population made up the majority, although in the west [of the court's district] Eastern Galicia also included territories . . . where the Polish element was preponderant" (ibid.).

37 On the effect of the suppression of the uprising on Galicia's Polish society, see Magdalena Micińska, *Inteligencja na rozdrożach, 1864–1918* (Warsaw: Neriton, 2008), 81–86.

38 Mick, "Nationalismus und Modernisierung," 174–76.

special position" in the empire, often called "Galician autonomy."[39] Lwów regained substantial municipal self-government and prospered economically.[40] Poles, however, were a majority only in the eastern half of Galicia. Yet their elites, politically ascendant throughout Galicia, dominated both its major cities, West and East: Cracow and Lwów. Polish elites claimed the whole province as their Piedmont, a rallying point for Polish cultural and political renewal. Ukrainian-Ruthenian elites sought to divide Galicia and dominate its eastern half with its center in a city they called Lviv, but that remained beyond their power.

The contrast between Lwów and its surroundings was stark. By the end of the Habsburg Empire, almost all administrative divisions of eastern Galicia had non-Polish majority populations and "two-thirds of the population was Greek-Catholic."[41] The latter group were mostly peasants who were learning to see themselves as Ukrainians. The one administrative entity in eastern Galicia with a Polish population majority was Lwów.[42] Poles, however, were not alone there. By 1900, only slightly more than half of the city's population consisted of Polish Roman Catholics. Most other inhabitants were Jews, nearly a third of the population, and Ukrainians, a sixth to a fifth, and all increasingly saw themselves in modern national terms.[43]

For Lviv's small Ukrainian elite, it was a time of high goals and deep frustration. After the Second World War, the city's Ukrainian historian and national activist Ivan Krypiakevych would recall his early twentieth-century walks through Lviv in search of Ukrainians. Back then he had mused about how to take over a city, where Ukrainians made up "not more than 15 percent" of the population and showed, as he recalled, "little [national] consciousness or organization." In 1915, meeting a Lviv policeman speaking "beautiful Ukrainian," Krypiakevych felt certain that he was "from the village."[44]

39 Röskau-Rydel, "Galizien," 107; Harald Binder, "Die Polonisierung Lembergs im 19. Jahrhundert—Konzeption und Realität," in *Stadtleben und Nationalität: Ausgewählte Beiträge zur Stadtgeschichtsforschung in Ostmitteleuropa im 19. und 20. Jahrhundert*, ed. Markus Krzoska and Isabel Röskau-Rydel (Munich: Meidenbauer, 2006), 109–10; Mick, *Kriegserfahrungen in einer multiethnischen Stadt*, 141. The persistence of the formally incorrect term "autonomy" marked the success of the Polish project to nationalize Galicia and its capital city within the Habsburg Empire.

40 Heidi Hein-Kircher, "Die Entwicklung der Lemberger Selbstverwaltung im Rahmen der Habsburgischen Gemeindeordnung von der Revolution 1848 bis zur Verabschiedung des Statuts 1870," in *Stadtleben und Nationalität*, ed. Krzoska and Röskau-Rydel, 93–97, 104.

41 Timothy Snyder, *The Reconstruction of Nations: Poland, Ukraine, Lithuania, Belarus, 1569–1999* (New Haven: Yale University Press, 2003), 134. For another concise overview of nationality/confessional statistics for Galicia, see Röskau-Rydel, "Galizien," 48–49.

42 Snyder, *Reconstruction of Nations*, 134.

43 Jones, *Żydzi Lwowa*, 12.

44 Ivan Krypiakevych, "Spohady," in Iaroslav Isaievych, ed. *Ivan Krypiakevych u rodynnii tradytsii, nautsi, suspilstvi* (Lviv: Instytut ukrainoznavstva im. I. Krypiakevycha NAN Ukrainy, 2001), 96.

Alternatives?

Nationalist mobilization was one of the most important political forces in late Habsburg Lemberg, as it was in the empire as a whole. In 1908, a Ukrainian nationalist assassinated the Polish governor and viceroy of Galicia. Metropolitan Andrei Sheptytskyi, the widely respected and Ukrainian-patriotic head of the Greek-Catholic Church to which most Ukrainians belonged, condemned the murder as a sign of "politics without God."[45] But some Polish newspapers still accused him of sympathy for terrorism.[46] In hindsight, Sheptytskyi's insistence on ethics even for nationalists represented a fading past, as did the Habsburg Empire. Yet to consider inevitable the triumphant—if often self-defeating—nationalist outcomes of nationalist mobilization would mean to share nationalist assumptions. As Mark Mazower has pointed out, at the turn of the century, "belief in the empire as a multi-national space spanned the political spectrum from Catholic monarchists to Austrian Marxists."[47] Markian Prokopovych has emphasized that late Habsburg Lwów/Lemberg was not only a place of proliferating nationalism, but also remained one of the most dynastically loyal (*kaisertreu*) cities of the empire.[48] Careers, status, and identities could still be reconciled with loyalty to the empire.

World War

It was the First World War that brought catastrophic change, closing and opening historical paths while severely harming Lemberg/Lwów, destroying the Habsburg Empire, and triggering multiple conflicts over the imperial inheritance. By the end of the war, having been subjected to Russian occupation, Habsburg reconquest, national struggles, and a massive pogrom, Lwów was in not only a different but a new state. Physically, the city had suffered comparatively little. Yet war-related reconstruction absorbed public funds as late as 1929, when the Great Depression was beginning to deliver another devastating blow. For years, Lwów remained an impoverished municipality.[49]

45 John-Paul Himka, "Christianity and Radical Nationalism: Metropolitan Andrei Sheptytsky and the Bandera Movement," in *State Secularism and Lived Religion in Soviet Russia and Ukraine*, ed. Catherine Wanner (Washington, DC: Woodrow Wilson Center Press; New York: Oxford University Press, 2012), 95.

46 Ryszard Torzecki, "Sheptyts'kyi and Polish Society," in *Morality and Reality: The Life and Times of Andrei Sheptyts'kyi*, ed. Paul Robert Magocsi (Edmonton: Canadian Institute of Ukrainian Studies Press, 1989), 79; Andrzej A. Zięba, "Sheptyts'kyi in Polish Public Opinion," in *Morality and Reality*, ed. Magocsi, 30.

47 Mark Mazower, *Hitler's Empire: Nazi Rule in Occupied Europe* (London: Allen Lane, 2008), 18.

48 Prokopovych, *Habsburg Lemberg*, 9.

49 Mick, *Kriegserfahrungen in einer multiethnischen Stadt*, 290.

Eastern Galicia as a whole was "among the regions most devastated" by the war.[50] It was also, as Peter Gatrell has shown, "the first major site of civilian mass displacement."[51] Both source and destination for thousands of refugees, by 1917 Lwów saw food protests and strikes.[52] Just after the Great War's end, in January 1919, the Polish diarist Zofia Romanowiczówna lamented the "unheard-of" and terrible destruction of municipal infrastructure, with the trams out of commission, residences and streets dark, and water and food scarce.[53]

The worst result of the war, however, was the irreparable harm done to interethnic relationships. Even while compromise was still being discussed on the eve of the war, Polish-Ukrainian tension already dominated Galicia's politics.[54] Subsequent wartime Habsburg and Russian policies and mass repressions left the local population polarized over perceptions of unequal treatment and mutual betrayal.[55] But the First World War, unlike the second one, did not change the overall ethnic composition of Lwów's population.[56] Demographic growth, however, stalled: increasing to about 212,000 by 1914, by 1918 the population was less than 188,000, with prewar levels restored in 1920/21. Thousands of Lwówians—preponderantly but not exclusively men—fought, and an estimated 12,000 of the city's prewar inhabitants were killed in the war. Tens of thousands became refugees.[57]

According to the Jewish ethnographer and activist S. An-sky, antisemitism was the one thing non-Jews—friend and foe—shared during the First World War,

50 Ibid., 130; Philipp Ther, "Chancen und Untergang einer multinationalen Stadt: Die Beziehungen zwischen den Nationalitäten in Lemberg in der ersten Hälfte des 20. Jahrhunderts," in *Nationalitätenkonflikte im 20. Jahrhundert: Ursachen von inter-ethnischer Gewalt im Vergleich*, ed. Ther and Holm Sundhausen (Wiesbaden: Harrasowitz, 2001), 130; Alexander V. Prusin, *Nationalizing a Borderland: War, Ethnicity, and Anti-Jewish Violence in East Galicia, 1914–1920* (Tuscaloosa: University of Alabama Press, 2005), ix.

51 Peter Gatrell, *A Whole Empire Walking: Refugees in Russia during World War I* (Bloomington: Indiana University Press, 1999), 18.

52 Mick, *Kriegserfahrungen in einer multiethnischen Stadt*, 181–88.

53 Zofia Romanowiczówna, *Dziennik lwowski 1842–1930*, vol. 2: *1888–1930*, ed. Zbigniew Sudolski (Warsaw: Ancher, 2005), 310, 313.

54 Mick, *Kriegserfahrungen in einer multiethnischen Stadt*, 64–65.

55 Aleksandra Iu. Bakhturina, *Okrainy rossiiskoi imperii: gosudarstvennoe upravlenie i natsionalnaia politika v gody pervoi mirovoi voiny, 1914–1917 gg.* (Moscow: Rosspen, 2004), 140–41; Mick, *Kriegserfahrungen in einer multiethnischen Stadt*, 72–74; Alexander V. Prusin, *The Lands Between: Conflict in the East European Borderlands, 1870–1992* (Oxford: Oxford University Press, 2010), 44–59.

56 Isaievych et al., *Istoriia Lvova*, 3:10, 43.

57 Mick, *Kriegserfahrungen in einer multiethnischen Stadt*, 69–70; Andrzej Bonusiak, *Lwów w latach 1918–1939. Ludność-Przestrzeń-Samorząd* (Rzeszów: Wydawnictwo Wyższej Szkoły Pedagogicznej, 2000), 173–75; Isaievych et al., *Istoriia Lvova*, 3:10. Lviv was part of a larger catastrophe of displacement. Alone during the initial Habsburg 1914 retreat before the Russian invasion, 250,000 to 300,000 refugees fled from the provinces of Galicia and Bukovina, south of Galicia (Prusin, *Lands Between*, 54).

Figure 1.1 Habsburg troops reentering Lviv in the First World War, June 1915. Bundesarchiv, Bild 146-2006-0158. German Federal Archives.

and antisemitic assaults left deep scars on the Jews of Galicia.[58] They did not fully recover from the First World War before the second brought the Holocaust.[59] While not comparable to the latter, the antisemitism of 1914–1918 deposited

58 Szymon An-ski, *Tragedia Żydów galicyjskich w czasie I wojny światowej: Wrażenia i refleksje z podróży po kraju* (Przemyśl: Południowo-Wschodni Instytut Naukowy w Przemyślu, 2010), 197–99, 209–10; Mick, *Kriegserfahrungen in einer multiethnischen Stadt*, 189–95, Prusin, *Lands Between*, 47–49, 53–54.

59 Bartal and Polonsky, "Jews of Galicia," 19–21.

stockpiles of weaponized prejudice about Jewish war profiteering, collaboration with the enemy, and, in particular, the stereotype of a special Jewish-Communist affinity: "Judeo-Bolshevism."[60]

The Postwar War: From Clashing Empires to Street-Fighting Nationalisms

With the end of both the war and the Habsburgs, Ukrainians and Poles started fighting openly over Lwów/Lviv.[61] The idea of seizing the city was not new. Habsburg wartime policies oscillated between favoring Polish and Ukrainian hopes, increasing national tension. Moreover, there was no official local forum for debate between the groups after Galicia's provincial assembly in Lemberg closed for the duration of the war. Against a background of unpredictability, suspicion, and opportunity, Galician Ukrainian elites feared and Polish elites hoped that Vienna would win the First World War and reward Polish loyalty with an autonomous Polish kingdom, including all of Galicia. Alternatively, but no better from a Ukrainian perspective, the establishment of a Kingdom of Poland under German control in 1916 opened the prospect of Galicia in a postwar Poland dependent on Germany.[62] By early 1917, Lwów's Polish mayor, returning from Russian deportation, announced that the prize was no longer autonomy, but a Polish state.[63] With the tsar's empire destroyed, two kaisers in distress, and President Woodrow Wilson's Fourteen Points appearing to

60 Prusin, *Nationalizing a Borderland*, 117–18; Mick, *Kriegserfahrungen in einer multiethnischen Stadt*, 146–53. For a detailed study of the nineteenth-century roots and twentieth-century development of the Judeo-Bolshevism stereotype in the case of Poland, see Joanna Michlic, "The Soviet Occupation of Poland, 1939–1941, and the Stereotype of the Anti-Polish and Pro-Soviet Jew," *Jewish Social Studies* 13 (2007): 135–76.

61 Not to claim the city did not signal a lack of political mobilization. With the Jews of Lwów and eastern Galicia, too, the end of the Habsburg Empire led to a surge in activity. In October 1918, a Jewish National Council of Eastern Galicia was established in Lviv, and a Congress of Eastern Galicia Zionists debated emigration to Palestine, national autonomy within Europe, and how to respond to the Polish-Ukrainian conflict. A minority, impressed by the Ukrainian National Council's offer of autonomy, argued for taking the Ukrainian side. The majority, seeking neutrality, prevailed. Grzegorz Mazur, "Skic do dziejów stosumków polsko-żydowskich we Lwowie w okresie międzywojennym," in *Świat niepożegany: Żydzi na dawnych ziemiach wschodnich Rzeczypospolitej w XVIII—XX wieku*, ed. Krzysztof Jasiewicz (Warsaw: RYTM, 2004), 401–3.

62 Michał Klimecki, *Polski-ukraińska wojna o Lwów i Galicję Wschodnią 1918–1919* (Warsaw: Bellona, 2000), 25–26, 244–45; Torzecki, "Sheptyts'kyi and Polish Society," 80; Timothy Snyder, *The Red Prince: The Secret Lives of a Habsburg Archduke* (New York: Basic Books, 2008), 88; Mick, *Kriegserfahrungen in einer multiethnischen Stadt*, 156–59.

63 Mick, *Kriegserfahrungen in einer multiethnischen Stadt*, 85–96, 161.

promise a new and national world order, Polish elites aimed at independence. Official reports found that the Polish population had mostly lost belief in the Habsburg Empire.[64]

Galicia's Ukrainian leaders, however, stuck to that faith. At the war's hopeful beginning, Sheptytskyi pitched ambitious projects to the Habsburgs of how to occupy, unify, and alienate from Russia all of Ukraine, which was to be fitted with a single Catholic Church, quite possibly under himself. By 1917/1918, Russian revolutionary collapse and a joint German-Habsburg occupation of Ukraine seemed to make these dreams come true.[65] Apart from maximalist visions, the minimum aim of Galician Ukrainian elites was a Ukrainian province in a postwar Habsburg state or, perhaps, attached to Germany.[66] During the war, the Ukrainian national activist and intellectual Dmytro Dontsov combined perceptive if jaundiced predictions of a future Polish state's discriminatory minority policies with projects for a Ukrainian Crown Land or province of Germany.[67]

The 1917/1918 establishment of an independent Ukrainian National Republic based in Kyiv in the southwestern provinces of a Russian empire in revolutionary disintegration evoked an ambiguous response from Galicia's Ukrainian leaders.[68] Some called for unification, but a majority preferred making their Ukraine with the Habsburgs.[69] The alternative of joining eastern Ukraine could mean the loss of territories to postwar Poland, but this was not the only concern. There was also fear of eastern disorder and nationalism deficits. In February 1918, Lonhyn Tsehelskyi, a Galician Ukrainian national activist and politician, publicly celebrated the independent Ukrainian state.[70] Later, however, he wrote that to unite "orderly" Galicia with eastern Ukraine, "without national awareness, anarchized and bolshevized," was a "leap in the dark." It would expose Galician Ukrainian "national achievements" to the "crazy vortex of social revolution" and "the mercy of the Bolsheviks and their equally mad Ukrainian chieftains." Galician Ukrainian leaders should save Galicia from eastern "anarchy and ruin" with the

64 Klimecki, *Polski-ukraińska wojna*, 40–41; Mick, *Kriegserfahrungen in einer multiethnischen Stadt*, 196.

65 Bohdan Budurowycz, "Sheptyts'kyi and the Ukrainian National Movement after 1914," in *Morality and Reality*, ed. Magosci, 48–50; Snyder, *Red Prince*, 95–120.

66 Magocsi, *Galicia*, 171–72.

67 Dmytro Dontsov, *Groß-Polen und die Zentralmächte* (Berlin: Carl Kroll, 1915), 62.

68 The Ukrainian National Republic was established in 1917; it declared full independence from Russia in January 1918.

69 Mick, *Kriegserfahrungen in einer multiethnischen Stadt*, 166, 205–7; Klimecki, *Polski-ukraińska wojna*, 31–33.

70 Mick, *Kriegserfahrungen in einer multiethnischen Stadt*, 178.

assistance of "all of Austria." Perhaps, they could even "drag Austria into war against Bolshevism."[71]

Central Power secret diplomacy around the February/March 1918 treaties of Brest-Litovsk seemed to promise a Ukrainian Crown Land inside the Habsburg Empire.[72] Yet under Polish pressure, the Habsburgs then dashed these hopes.[73] This was a crucial moment, not merely because it closed one path to Ukrainian national aims, but also because it triggered a tectonic shift inside Ukrainian nationalism that reverberated into the interwar period and the Second World War. The historic hour of Galicia's Ukrainian traditional elites seemed to have struck, but it was over before it began. Its unfulfilled passing would undermine the older generation's authority and favor a young generation of terrorist nationalists.

By October 1918, Galician Ukrainians were carving out territory of their own in, mostly, eastern Galicia and neighboring Bukovina. Their state would be called the Western Ukrainian National Republic (ZUNR).[74] The attempt to take over eastern Galicia as Western Ukraine and Lwów as Lviv for its capital "this night, before the Poles do it tomorrow," as one Ukrainian leader urged, was at first underestimated and then fiercely resisted by the city's Poles and their reemerging state.[75] The ensuing struggle pitted both Ukrainians against Poles and the city against the countryside. Lviv's Ukrainian minority played only a small role in the fighting; most Ukrainian troops came from surrounding villages, with rural Ukrainian commanders' reluctance to send reinforcements contributing to defeat, while Lwów's Polish majority mobilized strongly inside the city before receiving help from central Poland.[76]

Sheptytskyi's initial joy at a bloodless national triumph proved premature.[77] Quickly escalating, the street fighting would leave Lviv's buildings pockmarked

71 Lonhyn Tsehelskyi, *Vid legendy do pravdy: Spomyny pro podii v Ukraini zviazani z Pershym Lystopadom 1918 r.* (New York: Bulava, 1960; repr. Lviv: Svichado, 2003), 31. In January 1919, when military setbacks made it necessary to unite anti-Bolshevik forces in western and central Ukraine, Tsehelskyi spoke in more all-Ukrainian patriotic tones. His retrospective or rediscovered skepticism, cited above, has been criticized. See Oleksandr Rubl'ov, *Zakhidnoukrainska intelihentsiia u zahalnonatsionalnykh politychnykh ta kulturnykh protsesakh, 1914–1939* (Kyiv: Instytut istorii Ukrainy, NAN Ukrainy, 2004), 72.

72 The Ukrainian National Republic, having declared full independence, signed the Brest-Litovsk Treaty in February, Bolshevik Russia in March.

73 Klimecki, *Polski-ukraińska wojna*, 34, 38–39; Snyder, *Red Prince*; and Vasyl Rasevych, "Wilhelm von Habsburg—Sproba staty ukrainskym korolem," in *Podorozh do Evropy: Halychyna, Bukovyna i Viden na tsentralnoevropeiskii kulturnii shakhivnytsi*, ed. Oksana Havryliv and Timofy Havryliv (Lviv: VNTL, 2005), 210–21; Röskau-Rydel, "Galizien," 164–65.

74 Klimecki, *Polski-ukraińska wojna*, 49; Isaievych et al., *Istoriia Lvova*, 3:10–11.

75 Isaievych et al., *Istoriia Lvova*, 3:12.

76 Mick, *Kriegserfahrungen in einer multiethnischen Stadt*, 228–29.

77 Budurowycz, "Sheptyts'kyi and the Ukrainian National Movement," 51.

by what its inhabitants called "Wilson's Points," made by grenades and machine-gun fire.[78] It also added another toxic layer of bitter memory and recrimination. Ordinarily lethal combat came with plundering, atrocities, and civilian casualties.[79] Although the Polish diarist Zofia Romanowiczówna initially deplored a fratricidal war, with extremists prevailing over moderates on both sides, the clash taught her to see Ukrainians as a "savage horde" of "bandits" and "monsters."[80] Ivan Krypiakevych, on the other side, recalled treacherous Polish neighbors, abusing Ukrainian trust to conspire "just behind our walls."[81] Osyp Nazaruk, a Ukrainian politician and writer, never forgave his fellow Ukrainians for ignoring his advice to take Polish hostages. His frenzied fear that the Poles sought to "destroy the whole Ukrainian cultural class" demanded relief. Even surviving defeat would make him feel right about his ruthlessness, not wrong about his wild anxieties.[82] Yevhen Nakonechnyi, born between the wars and a proud Ukrainian nationalist, would recall other Ukrainians remembering "every day" of the fighting "with clockwork precision."[83]

Driven from Lviv, Ukrainian troops besieged the city for several months. A failed Bolshevik attempt in 1920 to carry revolution west through Poland also temporarily threatened Lwów, but it was the local Polish-Ukrainian struggle that quickly filled books of disclosure and advocacy.[84]

For the German modernist author Alfred Döblin, it was the pogrom that followed the Polish-Ukrainian fighting in Lwów/Lviv—facilitated by the Polish military and carried out by Polish soldiers and inhabitants of the city—that made "these struggles [internationally] known." The pogrom lasted for three days, cost at least seventy-three lives, and left thousands injured, humiliated, and plundered. Incidents of violence and pillaging continued for weeks. The

78 Mark Mazower, "Minorities and the League of Nations in Interwar Europe," *Daedalus* 126 (1997): 50.

79 Prusin, *Nationalizing a Borderland*, 79–80; Mick, *Kriegserfahrungen in einer multiethnischen Stadt*, 223–26.

80 Romanowiczówna, *Dziennik lwowski*, 2:313, 321.

81 Krypiakevych, "Spohady," 116.

82 Osyp Nazaruk, *Rik na velykii Ukraini: Konspekt spomyniv z ukrainskoi revolutsii* (New York: Hoverlia, 1978), 6. For Nazaruk's interwar work for the Ukrainian Catholic Party, which demanded Ukrainian autonomy within Poland, see Isaievych et al., *Istoriia Lvova*, 3:58–59.

83 Yevhen Nakonechnyi, *"Shoa" u Lvovi: Spohady* (Lviv: Naukova biblioteka im. V. Stefanyka, 2004), 135. Nakonechnyi's memoirs were written with an explicit apologetic agenda to refute what the author considered unjustified allegations of Ukrainian participation in the Holocaust, as John-Paul Himka has discussed in "Debates in Ukraine over Nationalist Involvement in the Holocaust, 2004–2008," *Nationalities Papers* 39 (2011): 353–56. In this work, Nakonechnyi's writing is used where plausible.

84 Mick, *Kriegserfahrungen in einer multiethnischen Stadt*, 256–60, 278–82; Magocsi, *Galicia*, 182, 185.

perpetrators were usually Polish and came from various social backgrounds. The victims reported massive robbery and blackmail, with much approval and little help from bystanders. When Döblin visited Lwów in 1924, charred ruins of Jewish houses still scarred the city.[85] The writer, former Habsburg subject, and desperate Habsburg mythmaker Joseph Roth could have been thinking of Lwów when describing the Habsburg Empire's Jews as the "third" who lost when others clashed.[86] In interwar Polish memory, the relationship between Jewish pogrom victims and largely Polish perpetrators was inverted, with the latter resenting the former, while Jews who had taken part in the Polish defense of Lwów were marginalized.[87]

Despite unprecedented violence, the First World War left the city's ethnic composition largely intact, but memories of fierce conflict endured. In the end, after much diplomacy, confusion, delusion, deception, and realpolitik, Lwów became part of interwar Poland. This was confirmed by a Polish-Soviet peace agreement in 1921, then by the Council of Ambassadors in 1923, representing the Western victors of the First World War. Galician Ukrainians had reason to feel that they had not received a fair deal.[88] In Lwów, they held mass meetings, vowing never to recognize Polish rule.[89]

A Marginal Center

On the whole, Lwów's importance declined in interwar Poland. With Poland on the map of states again and its capital in Warsaw, there was no need for a Piedmont anymore. Yet Lwów's symbolical significance increased, reaching what Grzegorz Mazur has aptly called "magic" dimensions: keeping Lwów Polish was of special public importance.[90] Poland's reemergence was accompanied by six wars between 1918 and 1921. The first of these foundational struggles, the fight over eastern Galicia and Lwów, generated a powerful Polish myth of heroism,

85 Alfred Döblin, *Reise in Polen* (Munich: DTV, 2000), 201. On the pogrom, see Mick, *Kriegserfahrungen in einer multiethnischen Stadt*, 232–34, 245–47.

86 Joseph Roth, "Juden auf Wanderschaft," in his *Orte: Ausgewählte Texte* (Berlin: Reclam, 1990), 217.

87 David Engel, "Lwów, 1918: The Transmutation of a Symbol and Its Legacy in the Holocaust," in *Contested Memories: Poles and Jews during the Holocaust and Its Aftermath*, ed. Joshua D. Zimmerman (New Brunswick, NJ: Rutgers University Press, 2003), 32–44; Prusin, *Nationalizing a Borderland*, 75–91; Mick, *Kriegserfahrungen in einer multiethnischen Stadt*, 346–50, 356.

88 Frank, *Oil Empire*, 214–36.

89 Isaievych et al., *Istoriia Lvova*, 3:56; Grzegorz Mazur, *Życie polityczne polskiego Lwowa, 1918–1939* (Cracow: Księgarnia Akademicka, 2007), 97.

90 Mazur, *Życie polityczne polskiego Lwowa*, 429.

linking past national uprisings to present patriotic duties.[91] Poles also blamed German and Austrian intrigue for the Ukrainian attempt to seize Lviv.[92] Such Polish observers saw Ukrainians as dependent enough to need outside agitators yet autonomous enough to be traitors in cahoots with powers that had once partitioned Poland. Some Polish authors distinguished between good, loyal "Ruthenians" and bad, treacherous "Ukrainians." In general, in the Polish imagination the struggle over Lviv/Lwów shaped lasting images of both Polish heroes and Ukrainian villains.[93]

Interwar Lwów became a center of the Polish nationalist right, with the self-promoting leader of the defense of Lwów lending it his authority.[94] Yet interwar Polish Lwów triumphant was also Ukrainian Lviv defeated. The city's Ukrainians developed their own memorial cult of what they called the "November Deed," glorified in what Christoph Mick has identified as a "culture of defeat."[95]

Ukrainians mattered beyond Lviv, and no city in Poland mattered more to Ukrainians than Lviv. In terms of population structure, like other nation-states emerging out of Central Europe's shattered imperial order, interwar Poland was at least as much a multiethnic "mini empire."[96] Of the country's citizens about five million, or 16 percent, were Ukrainians, mostly living in those southeastern territories secured by fighting and diplomacy between 1918 and 1923.[97] Almost all

91 Norman Davies, *God's Playground: A History of Poland* (Oxford: Oxford University Press, 2005), 2:292; Mazur, *Życie polityczne polskiego Lwowa*, 431. For more detail on the mythology of the Polish defense of Lwów and its commemorative practices, see Mick, *Kriegserfahrungen in einer multiethnischen Stadt*, 322–37, 353–75.

92 Mick, *Kriegserfahrungen in einer multiethnischen Stadt*, 323.

93 Snyder, *Reconstruction of Nations*, 134; Marek Figura, *Konflikt polsko-ukraiński w prasie Polski Zachodniej w latach 1918–1923* (Poznań: Wydawnictwo Poznańskie, 2001), esp. 357; Cornelia Schenke, *Nationalstaat und nationale Frage: Polen und die Ukrainer 1921–1939* (Hamburg: Dölling und Glitz, 2004), 43. On the practice of distinguishing good Ruthenians and bad Ukrainians, see Mick, *Kriegserfahrungen in einer multiethnischen Stadt*, 324.

94 Mazur, *Życie polityczne polskiego Lwowa*, 432. As M. B. B. Biskupski has pointed out, the symbolism of Lwów was heightened for the nationalist right because the fighting over Lwów "served [the nationalist right] as a counter to the Piłsudskiite-dominated events in Warsaw" (*Independence Day: Myth, Symbol, and the Creation of Modern Poland* [Oxford: Oxford University Press, 2012], 41).

95 On the Ukrainian cult around the November fighting, see Mick, *Kriegserfahrungen in einer multiethnischen Stadt*, 337–43, 376–80.

96 David Reynolds, *The Long Shadow: The Legacies of the Great War in the Twentieth Century* (New York: W. W. Norton, 2014), 12.

97 Grzegorz Motyka, *Tak było w bieszczadach: Walki polsko-ukraińskie 1943–1948* (Warsaw: Oficyna Wydawnicza Volumen, 1999), 26–27. About "three million Ukrainian speakers" in the former Galicia and about two million in the neighboring region of Volhynia (Wołyń in Polish, Volyn in Ukrainian) were citizens of the interwar Polish state due to Poland's victories and diplomatic successes of 1918–1923 (Snyder, *Reconstruction of Nations*, 138, 144).

of Poland's Ukrainians lived in villages; a small percentage belonged to the urban intelligentsia, often nationally mobilized and mobilizing.[98] If one place epitomized the Ukrainians' experience of bitter defeat, painful yet incomplete repression, and persistent ambitions, that place was Lviv.

After their victory, the Polish authorities persecuted suspect Ukrainians and restricted Ukrainian public activity. They replaced Habsburg Galicia with four *województwa* districts, renaming the three of them—Lwów, Stanislawów, and Tarnopól—that essentially overlapped with eastern Galicia into Eastern Little Poland. In official use, Ukrainians lost their name, replaced by the now archaic term "Ruthenians," implying they were no nation but merely a subordinate ethnic group.[99] Yet Lviv remained "the greatest urban accumulation of Ukrainians in Poland, their intellectual and political center, the seat of many Ukrainian institutions and organizations."[100]

Many Ukrainians strove for different degrees of autonomy in or independence from Poland. This fueled intra-Ukrainian generational conflict. Shortly before the Polish national leader and hero Józef Piłsudski visited Lwów in 1921, Stepan Fedak, a Ukrainian lawyer and politician, welcomed him on behalf of the city's Ukrainian community. Yet when Piłsudski arrived in Lwów, Fedak's student son fired on his car.[101] This was also the Lviv of Dmytro Dontsov, then becoming the main ideologist of a Ukrainian ethnic nationalism moving toward racist fascism, editor of a leading Ukrainian literary journal, and author of works calling for violent struggle.[102]

98 Motyka, *Tak było w bieszczadach*, 26.

99 Magocsi, *Galicia*, 175–76.

100 Cited in Motyka, *Tak było w bieszczadach*, 26.

101 Mazur, *Życie polityczne polskiego Lwowa*, 114–15. Fedak Junior may have been aiming not at Piłsudski but at the local Polish *wojewoda* (ibid. 115–16).

102 Magocsi, *Galicia*, 192. For Dontsov's dour elitism and admiration for Nietzsche, see Dmytro Dontsov, *Dukh nashoi davnyny* (Prague: Vydavnytstvo Yuriia Tyshchenka, 1944), 241–43. Alexander Motyl has suggested that despite the existence—and proud self-designation—of Ukrainian fascists in the interwar nationalist movement, its real core was "right-wing" and homemade (*The Turn to the Right: The Ideological Origins and Development of Ukrainian Nationalism, 1919-1929* [New York: Columbia University Press, 1980], 166–73). The underlying dichotomies between domestic factors and foreign influences as well as "fascist" and extremely "right-wing" seem so rigid as to miss fascism's international diversity, idiosyncracies, and flexibility. Considering Dontsov, Motyl has insisted on his complexity and called for a full consideration of all his ideas at any given time "as a logical whole." The assumption that this whole followed an identifiable logic seems problematic. In any case, Motyl's restricting his study of Dontsov to the 1919–1929 period seems to militate against a genuinely comprehensive approach. Motyl insists that it is "incorrect to label Dontsov a fascist for the ideas he professed in the 1920s (but only in the 1920s!) if only because one could just as easily and logically brand him a Yankee or a Bolshevik" (*Turn to the Right*, 60). This conclusion does not seem compelling on its own terms and is a curious way of turning a caveat into an argument. At least, it seems to implicitly acknowledge that something important is being omitted by stopping in 1929.

Starting with a difficult, if partly self-imposed, legacy and great as well as unprecedented international expectations and obligations, Polish interwar minority policy was a failure.[103] Despite a broad Polish consensus on assimilation—except for Jews—of national minorities, electoral procedures were biased to underrepresent such groups in unquiet borderlands considered crucial for national security.[104] Moreover, the meaning of assimilation was a divisive issue, causing shifts in Polish policy and a sense of Polish unreliability among minorities.

The two main concepts of minority policy dominating Polish discourse were national-ethnic assimilation, *asymilacja narodowa*, and state-oriented assimilation, *asymilacja państwowa*. Whereas national-ethnic assimilation aimed at linguistic, cultural, and sometimes religious Polonization, state assimilation allowed limited space for other ethnic identities, combined with submission to the emphatically Polish state. The policy difference was relative: national assimilation dominated Polish minority policy in the first half of the 1920s and in the second half of the 1930s; in the intervening decade, state assimilation and ideas to deploy flexible minority policies against the multinational Soviet neighbor prevailed. In the 1930s, state assimilation was seen as a first step toward national-ethnic assimilation.[105]

Although national minorities constituted one-third of Poland's population, most ethnic Poles regarded it as "absolutely self-evident" that only Poles should govern and define the national interest.[106] Ethnically Polish society was not monolithic, but for those it relegated to inferior status that mattered little; those not ethnically Polish faced an unjust and mostly unyielding state. Among Ukrainians, dissatisfaction was growing, exacerbated in 1930 by a disastrous Polish pacification campaign of collective punishment in response to nationalist Ukrainian terrorism.[107] For the most part, Lwów did not directly experience this

103 On the Polish case as a model for the new regime of minority rights treaties after the First World War under the supervision of the League of Nations, see Mark Mazower, *Dark Continent: Europe's Twentieth Century* (New York: Vintage, 1998), 53–55; and Mazower, *Governing the World: The History of an Idea, 1815 to the Present* (New York: Penguin, 2012), 159–62.

104 Snyder, *Reconstruction of Nations*, 136; Snyder, "The Life and Death of Western Volhynian Jewry, 1921–1945," in *The Shoah in Ukraine: History, Testimony, Memorialization*, ed. Ray Brandon and Wendy Lower (Bloomington: Indiana University Press, in association with the United States Holocaust Memorial Museum, 2008), 79; Schenke, *Nationalstaat und nationale Frage*, 58.

105 On national-ethnic and state assimilation, see Schenke, *Nationalstaat und nationale Frage*, 17, 51.

106 Motyka, *Bieszczadach*, 36; Schenke, *Nationalstaat*, 16.

107 Schenke, *Nationalstaat*, 222.

campaign, but it brought to the city bad news, violent incidents, arrests, and a mobilization of nationalist Polish youth.[108]

Pacification also fed into the propaganda of Ukrainian nationalism. Although it was less lethal than critics claimed, estimated Ukrainian casualties ranged from four to thirty-five. In any case, the campaign had mass effects. Several hundred assaults brought arrests, public beatings, punitive house searches, forced contributions, and the leveling of Ukrainian institutions.[109] The literature of accusations and recriminations grew again.[110] Later, a potentially auspicious agreement between the moderate—and majority—Ukrainian center-right Ukrainian National Democratic Alliance (UNDO) and the Polish authorities was doomed when it coincided with increasing Polish intransigence after Piłsudski's death in 1935.

For the Ukrainian intelligentsia Polish rule meant diminished careers. As Ivan Krypiakevych understood, Polish discrimination against leading Ukrainians enhanced Ukrainian national mobilization.[111] Yet probably the single most powerful irritant of Polish borderland policy was the deployment of agricultural-military settlers in territories regarded by many minority inhabitants as their own.[112] Ironically, this settlement policy was both divisive—even within ethnically Polish society—and ineffective: it produced settler numbers far below expectations and did not secure the borderlands, but it rekindled hostility to Poles, in particular in periods of agricultural crisis.[113]

Poland paid a high price for a misconceived policy good never fully delivered.[114] Invading Poland in 1939, Soviet authorities exploited local frustration over the settlements.[115] Nikita Khrushchev, then head of the Kyiv Central

108 Mazur, *Życie polityczne polskiego Lwowa*, 129–30.

109 Motyka, *Tak było w bieszczadach*, 37–38. For detail especially on the contentious quantitative dimensions of pacification, see Robert Potocki, *Polityka państwa polskiego wobec zagadnienia ukraińskiego w latach 1930–1939* (Lublin: Instytut Europy Środkowo-Wschodniej, 2003), 76–85.

110 Magocsi, *Galicia*, 192–93.

111 Krypiakevych to Stepan Tomashivskyi, 2 January 1923, repr. in Isaievych, *Ivan Krypiakevych u rodynnii tradytsii*, 402–5 (here 403).

112 Motyka, *Tak było w bieszczadach*, 36–37. On taxes in Volhynia and their uses for mobilization against the Polish state especially, see Schenke, *Nationalstaat und nationale Frage*, 94.

113 Werner Benecke, *Die Ostgebiete der Zweiten Polnischen Republik: Staatsmacht und öffentliche Ordnung in einer Minderheitenregion 1918–1939* (Cologne: Böhlau, 1999), 123; Schenke, *Nationalstaat und nationale Frage*, 94, 366.

114 The government had aimed for forty thousand settler farms but got only eight thousand. In Volhynia, settlers occupied 3.9 percent of the land. Their share of the district's population did not quite reach 1 percent, or less than 18,165 settlers. Nearly half of them did come from central Poland, which was likely to increase resentment (Karol Grünberg and Bolesław Sprengel, *Trudne sąsiedztwo: Stosunki polsko-ukraińskie w X–XX wieku* [Warsaw: Książka i Wiedza, 2005], 363–64).

115 Katherine R. Jolluck, *Exile and Identity: Polish Women in the Soviet Union during World War II* (Pittsburgh: University of Pittsburgh Press, 2002), 14.

Committee and de facto ruler of Soviet Ukraine, would maintain that the "Polish lords" had planned to use settlements to create "a staging area for attacking the Soviet Union."[116]

Ukrainians were also hit by the Polonization of education.[117] In Lwów, the establishment of a Ukrainian university was not permitted, while its existing university was Polonized.[118] Ukrainian underground university activities united student activists with respected academics such as Ivan Krypiakevych.[119] In 1926, after the suppression of this initiative, two young Ukrainian nationalist terrorists murdered a Polish school inspector.[120] With the intellectual poverty typical of terrorism, shooting a bureaucrat on his way home from the cinema appeared to be self-assertion and protest. One of the murderers was Roman Shukhevych, the talented scion of a family of Ukrainian notables, who would go on to become a nationalist military leader and ethnic cleanser during the Second World War.

The prosecution of militant nationalism increased its popularity. In 1936, Lwów witnessed a major trial of the leadership of the Organization of Ukrainian Nationalists (OUN), the main underground group of angry young men (mostly men) who believed in ethnic nationalism, authoritarianism, and fascist models. For them, only armed struggle and terrorism could liberate Ukrainians from Poland.[121] The accused included not only Shukhevych but also another young nationalist leader, Stepan Bandera, who would become the political leader of the most important faction of the OUN, usually referred to as the OUN-B.[122]

Buttressed by his victimization at the hands of Russian occupiers during the First World War and postwar Polish authorities, Metropolitan Sheptytskyi enjoyed authoritative stature as the spiritual leader of Poland's Ukrainians.[123] Yet even his authority met its limits with a younger generation when he decried both Polish "pacification" and nationalist terrorism. When nationalists murdered a

116 TsDAHOU 1, 1, 604: 19. Konstantin Simonov, the writer and war correspondent embedded with what he saw as Soviet "liberators," would remember his "unrestricted joy." Believing in the campaign's necessity to protect vital Soviet security interests, he also condemned Polish settlement (*Glazami cheloveka moego pokoleniia: Razmyshleniia o I. V. Staline* [Moscow: Kniga, 1990], 68–69).

117 Snyder, *Reconstruction of Nations*, 144; Grünberg and Sprengel, *Trudne sąsiedztwo*, 365–66.

118 Grünberg and Sprengel, *Trudne sąsiedztwo*, 366; Mick, *Kriegserfahrungen in einer multiethnischen Stadt*, 62–63.

119 Krypiakevych, "Spohady," 118.

120 Petro Duzhii, *Roman Shukhevych—polityk, voin, hromadianyn* (Lviv: Halytska vydavnycha spilka, 1998), 76–78.

121 For a recent, comprehensive, and up-to-date account of the OUN's history, see Grzegorz Motyka, *Ukraińska partyzantka 1942–1960* (Warsaw: RYTM, 2006).

122 Mazur, *Życie polityczne polskiego Lwowa*, 134. The history of the OUN is marked by two main factions emerging after a split in 1940: Bandera's OUN-B and the OUN-M under Andriy Melnyk.

123 On Sheptytskyi's "ostracism" from large parts of Polish society, including the Roman-Catholic higher clergy, see Zięba, "Sheptyts'kyi in Polish Public Opinion," 381–87.

Ukrainian school director for putative collaboration with Poland, Sheptytskyi castigated them for "using our children to kill their parents."[124] But his admonition, carefully calibrated as it was, had little effect.

Even though national tension was increasing and state policies were deeply flawed, the outcomes were not predetermined. It was neither Ukrainian nationalism nor Polish minority policy that brought about the end of interwar Poland but the German-Soviet assault of September 1939. When it came, the response was complex and contradictory. There was no general uprising of the minorities, but there were many local clashes between members of minority groups, partly organized in groups and militias, on one side, and Polish forces, on the other, as well as killings of Poles and non-Poles who represented neither the state nor any militias. In the area of the former eastern Galicia, Ukrainian nationalists stepped up attacks on Poles; especially in Volhynia, Ukrainian Communists started attacks with the Soviet invasion on 17 September.[125] Yet Sheptytskyi and UNDO declared their loyalty to the Polish state. While several hundred Ukrainians were marching as German auxiliaries, more than a hundred thousand Ukrainians were mobilized into Polish forces, more than half of them from eastern Galicia.[126]

In September 1939, Lwów, while not multicultural in the contemporary, often normative sense of the term, was still multiethnic. By the end of the Second World War, however, its population had changed radically. The discontinuity was not complete but crushing. This historic break was produced during the Soviet and German conquests and occupations beginning in 1939. Although local antagonisms fed into the extremely violent history of this hinge period, its devastating dynamics unfolded only when these two outside conquerors intervened.

124 Budurowycz, "Sheptyts'kyi and the Ukrainian National Movement"; Torzecki, "Sheptyts"kyi and Polish Society," 86.

125 Ryszard Torzecki, *Polacy i Ukraińcy: Sprawa ukraińska w czasie II wojny światowej na terenie II Rzeczpospolitej* (Warsaw: Wydawnyctwo Naukowe PWN, 1993), 24–28; Motyka, *Ukraińska partyzantka 1942–1960*, 72; Rafał Wnuk, *"Za pierwszego Sowieta": Polska konspiracja na Kresach Wschodnich II Rzeczypospolitej, wrzesień 1939–czerwiec 1941*(Warsaw: PAN ISP, 2007), 19–20; Prusin, *Lands Between*, 129.

126 Mazur, *Życie polityczne polskiego Lwowa*, 423–24; Hryciuk, *Przemiany narodowościowe i ludnościowe*, 164. Motyka refers to 150,000–200,000 Ukrainian soldiers in the Polish army. Part of the divergence may be due to the difference between the total number of Ukrainian soldiers in the Polish army and those who were mobilized in September 1939. See Motyka, *Ukraińska partyzantka*, 69; and Motyka, *Tak było w bieszczadach*, 39. On Sheptytskyi, see Budurowycz, "Sheptyts'ky and the Ukrainian National Movement," 60. The OUN may, in fact, have wanted to start an uprising but was constrained by German desire not to antagonize their Soviet allies by mobilizing Ukrainian nationalists too openly (Motyka, *Tak było w bieszczadach*, 68). The OUN leadership is likely to have been split over this restraint and may have kept to it partly for show or to spare its forces for the time after a Polish defeat (John A. Armstrong, *Ukrainian Nationalism*, 3rd ed. [New York: Columbia University Press, 1963], 44). The OUN did instruct its members to prepare against possible Polish repression (Torzecki, *Polacy i ukraińcy*, 27–28).

CHAPTER TWO

The First Soviet Lviv, 1939–1941

The German-Soviet partition of Poland in the fall of 1939 opened a grim path to a Soviet and Ukrainian Lviv: in the end, Europe's nightmare would ironically realize both Stalinist and Ukrainian nationalist dreams. Lviv's path through the Second World War was crooked and tortuous—leading through occupation, exploitation and deterioration, growing interethnic tension and conflict, genocide, and expulsion. To understand the transformation of Lviv, its Sovietization and Ukrainization, it is necessary not only to take into account the geopolitical outcome of the war but to integrate our picture of the grand strategies pursued by conquering states bent on fulfilling violent, ideology-driven projects with an account of local experiences. This chapter traces this interaction during Lviv's Soviet occupation between 1939 and 1941.

Taking Lwów

One of the first effects of the German attack on Poland was to increase the population of Lwów. On the eve of the war, the city had about 330,000 inhabitants; by October 1939, it would have about half a million and at least seventy major facilities housing refugees.[1] Then Lwów was first besieged by Germans and subsequently occupied by Soviet forces who also invaded Poland. Resistance was futile, German propaganda reminded Lwów's defenders, with Germans and their Soviet allies encircling them.[2] On 22 September, Soviet troops entered Lwów after its defenders had capitulated.[3] Soviet propagandists depicted enthusiastic local

1 Hryciuk, *Polacy we Lwowie*, 50; Isaievych et al., *Istoriia Lvova*, 3:175.

2 Leo Leixner, *Von Lemberg bis Bordeaux: Fronterlebnisse eines Kriegsberichterstatters*, 4th ed. (Munich: Zentralverlag der NSDAP, 1942), 84.

3 For the most detailed description of Lwów's military role in the fall of 1939, see Wojciech Włodarkiewicz, *Lwów 1939* (Warsaw: Bellona, 2003).

Figure 2.1 German and Soviet soldiers meeting in Lviv, September 1939 (from a German soldier's album). Yad Vashem Photo Archive album, archival signature 5323.

crowds greeting their soldiers, but it is unclear who exactly was cheering: some Poles and Ukrainians accused Jews of welcoming the Soviets; some Poles accused Ukrainians, too.[4] Jews and Ukrainians were, in fact, more likely to welcome Soviet forces than Poles. For Jews, Soviets were not-Germans.[5] For Ukrainians and Jews, interwar Poland had left memories of national discrimination. But it bears emphasis that contemporaries could not actually *know* anything about who greeted the Soviets the most. Instead, in an ethnically fissiparous city in a state of emergency, fragmented impressions and rumors combined with prior stereotypes.[6] Jews were condemned for both obsequiousness and alleged assistance to

4 Hryciuk, *Polacy we Lwowie*, 17; Andriy Kosytskyi, *Entsyklopediia Lvova* (Lviv: Litopys, 2007–8), 2:158. Reports from smaller, more intimate places yield cases of some representatives of all four main ethnic groups of the conquered region—Poles, Jews, Ukrainians, and Belarusians—greeting Soviet troops. See Yehuda Bauer, *The Death of the Shtetl* (New Haven: Yale University Press, 2009), 35–36.

5 Jan T. Gross, *Revolution from Abroad: The Soviet Conquest of Poland's Western Ukraine and estern Belorussia*, exp. ed. (Princeton, NJ: Princeton University Press, 2002), 28–35; Bauer, *Death of the Shtetl*, 36.

6 On antisemitic stereotypes in Polish and Ukrainian underground reporting in particular, see Christoph Mick, "Incompatible Experiences: Poles, Ukrainians, and Jews in Lviv under Soviet and German Occupation, 1939–1944," *Journal of Contemporary History* 46 (2011): 343–45.

the invaders: denounced for kissing cavalry horses in the last world war, now they were accused of kissing Soviet tanks.[7]

Soviet forces took Lviv without major fighting.[8] They generally did not commit massacres there, as they did in some other locations in 1939 and would in Lviv when fleeing in 1941, but they did kill a large number of unarmed Polish police officers. About fifteen thousand of the city's defenders, including more than one thousand officers, were taken captive.[9] Many of the officers were later murdered while in detention.[10] Soviet propaganda omitted much that was war, chaos, panic, and plunder. Soviet photojournalism from the new western territories did not show warfare but only "liberation."[11] Ivan Serov, the freshly appointed people's commissar of the interior as well as deputy commissar of state security of Soviet Ukraine, marched in with the first columns and reported that Poles had observed the surrender conditions. In response to a few shots fired nevertheless, Soviet troops panicked and shot around wildly. The following day, a Soviet correspondent was killed at a window by, Serov was certain, a nervous Red Army soldier.[12]

Keeping Lviv

In the eastern Polish territories occupied by Soviet forces, more than 40 percent of the population was Polish and a third Ukrainian, while Belarusians and Jews each made up a tenth respectively.[13] Quickly annexing these lands, their new Soviet rulers chose to add all of them to Soviet Belarus and Soviet Ukraine. Given the plurality of the Polish population, this decision reflected the fact that Stalin, in Mark Mazower's terms, was at least as adamant as Hitler that "no independent Polish state should remain."[14]

7 Mick, *Kriegserfahrungen in einer multiethnischen Stadt*, 150; Gross, *Revolution from Abroad*, 29.

8 TsDAHOU 1, 1, 603: 11–13; Hryciuk, *Polacy we Lwowie*, 17–18.

9 Grünberg and Sprengel, *Trudne sąsiedztwo*, 547; Hryciuk, *Polacy we Lwowie*, 18; Mick, *Kriegserfahrungen in einer multiethnischen Stadt*, 421–22. On Soviet massacres in 1939, see Prusin, *Lands Between*, 129.

10 For an overview of the Soviet detention and mass murder of Polish officers, see Snyder, *Bloodlands*, 134–40.

11 David Shneer, *Through Soviet Jewish Eyes: Photography, War, and the Holocaust* (New Brunswick, NJ: Rutgers University Press, 2011), 87.

12 Vasyl Danylenko et al., eds., *Radianski orhany derzhavnoi bezpeky u 1939—chervni 1941 roku: Dokumenty HDA SB Ukrainy* (Kyiv: Kyevo-Mohylanska akademiia, 2009), 195 (doc. 106).

13 Snyder, *Bloodlands*, 128.

14 Mazower, *Hitler's Empire*, 96. As Alexander Prusin has emphasized, by purely ethnodemographic criteria, at least the Łomża district should have become Polish under Soviet rule, whereas Vilnius could not have been transferred to Lithuania (*Lands Between*, 122–23.).

Soviet officials boasted of conceptual as well as literal conquest, securing the new territory "under lock and key" as a "powerful forepost of our motherland."[15] Its annexation combined formal government acts and mock-plebiscite popular assemblies, exercises in hypervirtual democracy. Fusing deception and self-deception, the Bolsheviks interpreted what they imposed as evidence of autonomous progress. Khrushchev claimed the assemblies as an early success, which left him "stunned" and reassured that "no bourgeois borders" could "withstand the idea of our Bolshevik party."[16] In interwar Poland, boycotting elections had been a form of passive resistance.[17] Compelling participation while setting results, the Soviet authorities deployed advanced authoritarianism. Captive voters were humiliated by "a great feeling of bad taste," as Karolina Lanckorońska, a young Polish art history lecturer at Lwów University, recalled.[18] Less than two months after the Soviets took Lwów, annexation was complete and Soviet citizenship imposed.[19] Officially, Lwów was now Lviv, both a new Soviet and an "ancient Ukrainian city": Soviet terminology signaled that Soviet power would draw on traditional Ukrainian nationalist slogans.

An internal police border replaced the former Soviet-Polish border.[20] "Western Ukraine" or "the western oblasts" initially came to mean the 34,000 square miles of six new Soviet districts or oblasts.[21] One year after the conquest, Lviv was made a city of the first category of official residence restriction, making it particularly hard to obtain a residence permit.[22] Such zoning and control

15 TsDAHOU 1, 1, 603: 14–16. Between October 1939 and November 1940 alone, Soviet border guards captured almost seventy thousand persons at the new border (Prusin, *Lands Between*, 135).

16 TsDAHOU 1, 1, 604: 19–20. On the elections, see Grünberg and Sprengel, *Trudne sąsiedztwo*, 545. In 1940, Lwów's population was compelled to participate in three similar exercises, in effect acclaiming the Supreme Soviets of the Soviet Union and of the Ukrainian Republic and local authorities (ibid., 547).

17 Schenke, *Nationalstaat und nationale Frage*, 44; Jan T. Gross, *Polish Society under German Occupation: The Generalgouvernement, 1939–1944* (Princeton, NJ: Princeton University Press, 1979), 24.

18 Hryciuk, *Polacy we Lwowie*, 24. On elections in the conquered territories as subjugation by alienation through individual humiliation and shared shame, see Gross, *Revolution from Abroad*, 71–113.

19 Hryciuk, *Polacy we Lwowie*, 22–23; Grünberg and Sprengel, *Trudne sąsiedztwo*, 545.

20 Hryciuk, *Polacy we Lwowie*, 87; Dullin, *La frontière épaisse*, 237.

21 These six regions were Volyn, Drohobych, Lviv, Rivne, Stanislav, and Ternopil oblasts. This definition of Western Ukraine as everything newly annexed to the Ukrainian Soviet republic did not exactly match the areas of eastern Galicia or Eastern Little Poland. The latter had consisted of the territory turned into the Soviet oblasts of Lviv, Drohobych, Stanislav, and Ternopil and is estimated to have had slightly more than five million inhabitants. Nevertheless, as pointed out above, the Soviet authorities sometimes used the terms Galicia, the western oblasts, and Western Ukraine interchangeably. Lviv always had a special, dominating position, be it in Western Ukraine, eastern Galicia, or Galicia.

22 DALO P-3, 3, 460: 46.

practices, a domestic Soviet practice, indicated the full integration of the new territories.[23]

Staff for Soviet nomenklatura positions, for obkom regional party committees, the secret police, and newspapers was quickly imported.[24] Co-optation also started immediately; by May 1940, there were nearly twenty-nine thousand persons promoted from among the conquered population, including seven thousand in Lviv oblast, the greatest concentration in Western Ukraine.[25] Thousands of village soviets were established and soldiers recruited; suspected of religion and nationalism, however, they were scattered among units farther east and kept under special observation.[26]

Propaganda was ubiquitous. Polish symbols were purged, street names Ukrainianized and Sovietized. Posters and new monuments gave the city a new look, and it became a stage for celebrations on the First of May and the anniversaries of the October Revolution, the Stalin Constitution, or the "liberation" of 1939 itself.[27] Lviv was divided into four quarters, or raions, named after Stalin, the Red Army, the Railways, and the Ukrainian national poet Taras Shevchenko.[28] The supreme leader, Soviet militarism, modernization, and a Soviet canon of national-romantic Ukrainian culture now marked Lviv's territory. Its time was synchronized with Moscow, its calendar of annual festivals purged of religious holidays.[29]

23 On the development of zoning practices for purposes of security, control, and purging that applied to both border and core areas of the Soviet Union, see Dullin, *La frontière épaisse*, 209.

24 Mykola Holovko, *Suspilno-politychni orhanizatsii ta rukhy Ukrainy v period druhoi svitovoi viiny, 1939–1945 rr.* (Kyiv: Olan, 2004), 198–99.

25 TsDAHOU 1, 1, 601: 125.

26 Ivan Bilas, *Represivno-karalna systema v Ukraini 1917–1953: Suspilno-politychny ta istoryko-pravovy analiz* (Kyiv: Libid, 1994), 1:118-19; TsDAHOU 1, 1, 627: 74. According to Grzegorz Hryciuk, the Soviet draft targeted the years of 1919, 1918, and part of 1917 and can be extrapolated to have levied about fifty thousand young men of the hundred thousand available from these cohorts in a territory roughly congruent with eastern Galicia. In the whole Soviet zone of occupation, estimates vary between 100,000 and 150,000 levied. See Hryciuk, *Przemiany narodowościowe i ludnościowe*, 177; and Catherine Merridale, *Ivan's War: Life and Death in the Red Army, 1939–1945* (New York: Picador, 2006), 75.

27 Hryciuk, *Polacy we Lwowie*, 34. In standard Soviet fashion, mass participation in celebrating the new Soviet holidays was encouraged by compulsion and the creative use of scarcity. First of May, for instance, got a sugar boost: usually hard to get, sugar was offered in large quantities for the special occasion. See Anna Czekanowska, *Świat rzeczywisty—świat zapamiętany: Losy Polaków we Lwowie, 1939–1941* (Lublin: Norbertinum, 2010), 144.

28 Isaievych et al., *Istoriia Lvova*, 3:192.

29 Czekanowska, *Świat rzeczywisty*, 79–80, 141.

Exploitation, Repression, Immiseration, Corruption: Building Stalinist Socialism

"Building Socialism" in a Soviet key began quickly in the new territories: large estates, monasteries, and high-ranking civil servants were expropriated.[30] The replacement of private farming by collectivization was the final goal here as elsewhere; by May 1940, Lviv's Communist leader, Leonid Hryshchuk (first head of the oblast party committee, the obkom), claimed forty-three collective farms in his oblast.[31]

All major enterprises became state property.[32] Trade was effectively expropriated by a combination of the invaders' artificially inflated purchasing power and a sudden abolition of the Polish złoty.[33] Prewar Lwów had been a city of many small shops and workshops; Soviet Lviv destroyed them.[34] By November 1940, Hryshchuk, quizzed by an angry Khrushchev, conceded the presence of what he called distortions in "liquidating the private trader," with, at one point, almost all shops closed and the city left without any food supply. Hryshchuk also conceded that it had been a mistake to overtax peasants or fight "speculation" with roadblocks.[35] Long lines in front of empty shops and a spreading black market had provoked the Bolshevik panacea of blanket suppression.[36] In February 1940, the obkom head of a neighboring oblast complained about "speculators" taking goods to Lviv and recommended fighting them by opening Polish graves, suspected of housing contraband.[37] Eventually, Lviv's food crisis was alleviated, but

30 Under the usual conditions of compulsory volunteering, 2,589 kolkhozes were set up in all of Western Ukraine before June 1940, including 222 in Lviv oblast (Grünberg and Sprengel, *Trudne sąsiedztwo*, 546; RGASPI 17, 138, 9: 86). While according to Soviet data, on the eve of the German attack, 13.5 percent of all farms in Western Ukraine had been collectivized, the real number of collective farms was "significantly lower" because some existed "on paper only." See Mykhailo Senkiv, *Zakhidnoukrainske selo: nasylnytska kolektyvizatsiia—40—poch. 50-kh rr. XX st.* (Lviv: Instytut ukrainoznavstva im. I. Krypiakevycha, 2002), 91.

31 TsDAHOU 1, 1, 602: 43. In Soviet Ukraine, the official lexicon for peasant re-enserfment was bilingual, Ukrainian and Russian. Collective farms were kolhosps or kolkhozes; peasants who were in the way were kurkuls or kulaks. Hryshchuk, born in 1906, a member of the Komsomol from 1923 and the party from 1930, had spent the 1930s in "responsible political and command duties" in the Soviet Far East and in one of Kyiv's raions. He had also taken part in the Twenty-Five-Thousander campaign, serving in glorified shock troops of urban activists that drove peasants into collective farms (DALO P-1, 1, 319: 12).

32 Bonusiak, "Sowietyzacja kultury Lwowa," 563–64, 569.

33 Isaievych et al., *Istoriia Lvova*, 3:173.

34 Nakonechnyi, *"Shoa" u Lvovi*, 44–46, 48.

35 TsDAHOU 1, 1, 627: 21.

36 Tomasz Bereza, ed., *Lwowskie pod okupacją sowiecką 1939–1941* (Rzeszów: Instytut Pamięci Narodowej, 2006), 179.

37 TsDAHOU 1, 20, 7441: 10–12, 22.

its impoverishment deepened when it began to get food again from its surroundings, bartered for city dwellers' belongings.

Housing expropriation, in theory, followed rules, but the practice was corrupt. By November 1939, Lviv's authorities had officially seized 2,649 residences. Propaganda described this act as social redistribution: a 1940 documentary on "Soviet Lvov" reported that ten thousand workers' families had been resettled from the city's outskirts into the central apartments of the "fugitive Polish bourgeoisie"; in 1941, participants in a meeting heard how thousands had been "pulled from" squalid basements up into the places of "their former masters."[38] In reality, much seized *zhilploshchad*, or living space, went to newly arrived eastern cadres.[39] By June 1941, almost half of Lviv's approximately fifteen thousand buildings had been seized, especially in better quarters.[40]

As happened throughout the Soviet Union, clergy and religious believers were oppressed. The authorities' explicit if still disguised aim regarding the Greek Catholic Church was systematic "disintegration." While expropriating religious institutions, they also imposed punitive taxes, in effect massive tributes doubling as targeted disruption devices.[41]

In 1940, all inhabitants of Lviv oblast were forced to "voluntarily" yield a total of 45.5 million rubles for a de facto mandatory "state loan"—in effect, a tribute.[42] Soviet currency manipulations wiped out about two-thirds of the purchasing power of those holding złoty—that is, everyone—then almost all private savings.[43] For refugees currency manipulations were especially harmful, turning

38 Documentary *Sovetskii Lvov*, produced by Ukrkinokhronika, Tsentralnyi derzhavnyi kinofotofonoarkhiv Ukrainy, archive number 1699; Isaievych et al., *Istoriia Lvova*, 3:197.

39 Of the 2,649 residences expropriated by November 1939, 951 were for Soviet security personnel—the biggest single share—and another 1,167 for other regime functionaries, the vast majority of whom were incoming occupation staff. Officially, 379 places were assigned to workers and 152 to intelligentsia members (Bonusiak, "Sowietyzacja kultury Lwowa," 565).

40 Thomas Sandkühler, *"Endlösung" in Galizien: Der Judenmord in Ostpolen und die Rettungsinitiativen von Berthold Beitz 1941–1944* (Bonn: Dietz, 1996), 58.

41 Kurt I. Lewin, *Przeżylem: Saga świętego Jura spisana w roku 1946 przez syna rabina Lwowa*, ed. Barbara Toruńczyk, annotated by Andrzej Żbikowski (Warsaw: Fundacja Zeszytów Literackich, 2006), 32; Bohdan R. Bociurkiw, "Shpetytskyi and the Ukrainian Greek Catholic Church under the Soviet Occupation of 1939–1941," in *Morality and Reality*, ed. Magosci, 103, 112; Serhyi Bohunov et al., eds., *Likvidatsiia UHKTs (1939–1946): Dokumenty radianskykh orhaniv derzhavnoi bezpeky* (Kyiv: PP Serhiychuk, 2006), 1:101 (doc. 13), 103 (doc. 14).

42 Bonusiak, "Sowietyzacja kultury Lwowa," 570.

43 The złoty-ruble exchange rate, 3.30 : 1.00 before the war, was fixed at 1 : 1 by the invaders. The abolition of the złoty was implemented suddenly in December 1939. As Ivan Serov reported, the timing was particularly harmful because many employers had paid out cash salaries days before. Despite the threat of severe punishment for currency speculation, a black market for strongly discounted złoty developed; they were still legal tender in the German zone of occupation (Bonusiak, "Sowietyzacja kultury Lwowa," 569; Hryciuk, *Polacy we Lwowie*, 67–68, 91–92; Danylenko et al., *Radianski orhany*, 280 [doc. 156]).

them "overnight into beggars."[44] Peasants, meanwhile, did not expect the new money to last. They would only barter or sell for gold, dollars, and złoty, anticipating the latter's return after an anticipated German invasion.[45] Inflation was relentless across all currencies. Prices "were increasing constantly and the market was being saturated with our underwear and clothes," a Lviv inhabitant noted.[46] Some plundering was expert; 262 especially trustworthy Soviet banking officials were sent to Western Belarus and Western Ukraine to count spoils, including nearly 10 million złoty, other foreign currency, precious metals worth more than 1.5 million rubles, and twenty-six thousand valuable objects.[47]

Provisions for Lviv improved in the spring of 1940, with privileges decreed for the city of the same priority as Moscow and Leningrad and semiofficial references to it as the "favorite of Comrade Stalin."[48] In 1940, according to Hryshchuk, Lviv received goods worth more than 18 million rubles.[49] Fresh embezzlement, however, curtailed public benefit. In November 1940, the Kyiv authorities found they were *delivering* more goods-per-head to the western than to the eastern oblasts, but fewer actually *arrived*.[50] Real-Socialist trading was creative; 1 million rubles worth of coffee was sold from Lviv to eastern oblasts and then resold to Lviv for 400,000 rubles.[51] Throughout Lviv's first Soviet occupation, a worker's daily wage did not buy two pounds of butter, and the living expenses of a working-class family were always "significantly higher" than the monthly salary.[52]

In February 1941, Hryshchuk still deplored that local production was down, with pre-Soviet workshops idle in new enterprises. Not only tools were wasted, he implied, but people. On arriving in Lviv, he and other Soviet officials had appreciated the standards of Lviv's craftsmen. Almost eighteen months later, he warned that it was time to husband human resources and find all remaining artisans to "exploit their experience and technical knowledge."[53]

44 Dov Levin, *The Lesser of Two Evils: Eastern European Jewry under Soviet Rule, 1939–1941* (Philadelphia: The Jewish Publication Society, 1995), 185.

45 TsDAHOU 1, 20, 7441: 11.

46 Wanda Ossowska, *Przeżyłam: Lwów-Warszawa 1939–1946* (Warsaw: Oficyna Przeglądu Powszechnego, 1990), 29.

47 RGASPI 82, 2, 779: 81–84.

48 DALO P-3, 1, 4: 121; Hryciuk, *Polacy we Lwowie*, 69–72, 76.

49 DALO P-3, 1, 12: 8.

50 TsDAHOU 1, 1, 627: 197–99.

51 DALO P-3, 1, 17: 9–10.

52 Hryciuk, *Polacy we Lwowie*, 64. In August 1940, Hryshchuk noted new bread lines, while a contemporary recorded spending hours on finding food every day (DALO P-3, 1, 12: 109–10; Hryciuk, *Polacy we Lwowie*, 76).

53 DALO P-3, 1, 17: 14. On the background of the suppression and marginalization of Soviet artisans in the 1930s, see Sheila Fitzpatrick, *Everyday Stalinism: Ordinary Life in Extraordinary Times. Soviet Russia in the 1930s* (New York: Oxford University Press, 1999), 44–45.

Dislocation

Soviet state terrorism was extended immediately to the new territories, where Ivan Serov primed his men to expect "the fiercest enemies" in the shape of "Polish, Ukrainian, and other counterrevolution[aries]." Lists of individuals to be repressed in case of a Soviet attack westward had been in preparation since at least 1925.[54] Once the invasion was underway, Serov quickly reported 5,972 arrests in Western Ukraine, including 1,482 in Lviv oblast.[55] By 27 September 1939—ten days into the Soviet invasion—a task force, whose area of operations included Lviv, had made almost a thousand arrests and recruited ninety-four informers.[56] Soon there were 130 informers for Lviv alone.[57] Those arrested included its mayor, members of his administration, and politicians and prominent citizens.[58] A special arrest wave targeting Polish officers produced 570 fresh victims from Western Ukraine in one night, including 226 in Lviv.[59] A Kyiv Politburo decree of 20 December 1939 assigned seven thousand additional party and Komsomol members to NKVD duty in the conquered territories.[60] In January 1940, the arrest of several left-wing Polish intellectuals was made into a terrifying public event.[61] Arrests remained a constant feature of Lviv's Soviet occupation, with the city's main prisons always overcrowded.[62] By June 1941, on the eve of the German invasion, the Lviv oblast office of the secret police alone would report having processed 20,540 arrestees since the beginning of 1940, with special task forces from Moscow and Kyiv sent in to help.[63]

Repression was a mass phenomenon beyond its immediate victims and perpetrators. The Polish writer Jan Kott remembered it as a "kind of terror" in "the air, slowly infecting everyone" with a "widespread belief in the omniscience and

54 Prusin, *Lands Between*, 141.

55 Danylenko et al., *Radianski orhany*, 264 (doc. 148).

56 Ibid., 199 (doc. 107). This task force was one of five operating in Western Ukraine. Within weeks after the Soviet attack, they had arrested almost four thousand Polish state functionaries (Prusin, *Lands Between*, 141).

57 Weiner and Rahi-Tamm, "Getting to Know You," 14.

58 Hryciuk, *Polacy we Lwowie*, 36.

59 Danylenko et al., *Radianski orhany*, 283 (doc. 158); Hryciuk, *Polacy we Lwowie*, 36.

60 Bilas, *Represivno-karalna systema*, 1:126; Serhiychuk, *Ukrainskyi zdvyh*, 3:23.

61 Marci Shore, *Caviar and Ashes: A Warsaw Generation's Life and Death in Marxism, 1918–1968* (New Haven: Yale University Press, 2006), 166–72.

62 Hryciuk, *Polacy we Lwowie*, 36–37, 41. On the general background of arrests and emprisonment in the former Polish territories, see Catherine Gousseff, "'Kto naš, kto ne naš': Théorie et pratiques de la citoyenneté à l'égard des populations conquises. Le cas polonais en URSS, 1939–1946," *Cahiers du monde russe* 44 (2003): 527; and Gross, *Revolution from Abroad*, 144–86.

63 GDA SBU 16, 34, 16: 161–62.

omnipresence of the NKVD."[64] Fears and denunciation were nationalized. One Pole felt better about informing because he denounced mainly Ukrainians and they, he decided, deserved it.[65] Accusations that Jews served the occupier were widespread. For Kott, traitors were Ukrainian. He felt "watched" by them after they had "changed overnight from nationalists to the most rabid Communists."[66]

Mass migrations, entirely or partly compulsory, were a key tool of Stalinist governance.[67] In the new territories, they came in four main waves and were partly entangled with policies to demonstrate superiority over capitalism by liquidating unemployment.[68] In December 1939, the city had nearly 27,500 registered unemployed, including almost 10,700 refugees. Over a ferocious winter, unemployment had risen to almost thirty-eight thousand by the beginning of 1940. Yet within three months more than 19,000 persons got jobs in Lviv, while 15,500 went east, mainly to the Donbass (in Ukrainian, Donbas) industrial region but also to Siberia, many of them Jewish refugees.[69] Though categories were fuzzy and not everybody passed through Lviv, the total figure for refugees and unemployed arriving in eastern Ukraine in the last quarter of 1939 alone is estimated at more than forty-five thousand.[70] Officially, labor migration was voluntary, but in practice, it was to some extent compulsory. In January 1940, a western obkom secretary instructed his staff that everybody had to leave and their task was not "to hire but remove," with the "formalities" to be settled later.[71] At least initially, however, work migrants were frequently still able to quit their new jobs. By Soviet estimates more than 80 percent of those sent to the Donbas returned to Lviv—with or without permission.

This compulsory labor migration contributed to an important pattern, with Soviet authorities viewing workers from the new West as poorly disciplined and ideologically contagious. In December 1939, the NKVD officer Romanchuk reported on problems with refugee workers at construction sites near Kyiv. The

64 Jan Kott, *Still Alive* (New Haven: Yale University Press: 1994), 35.

65 Motyka, *Ukraińska partyzantka*, 75.

66 Kott, *Still Alive*, 35.

67 Generally on Soviet deportations, see Pavel Polian, *Against Their Will: The History and Geography of Forced Migrations in the USSR* (Budapest: Central European University Press, 2004).

68 For a concise survey of the four deportation waves in the former Polish territories, see Gousseff, "'Kto naš,'" 528–29. As an example of Soviet claims to have liquidated unemployment, see O. Tsybko, "Vyzvolnyi pokhid chervonoi armii v zakhidnu Ukrainu ta vozziednannia zakhidnoi Ukrainy z radianskoiu Ukrainoiu," in *Trista rokiv vozziednannia Ukrainy z Rosiiu* (Lviv: Vydavnytstvo Lvivskoho universytetu, 1954), 204.

69 Levin, *Lesser of Two Evils*, 189–91.

70 Hryciuk, *Przemiany narodowościowe i ludnościowe*, 175.

71 Ibid., 175n61.

absence of water and warm apparel, scant food, and irregular pay were provoking "mass flight" and collective complaints. Serov seconded Romanchuk's call for improvements. The report was also packed with denunciations portraying the refugees as "contaminated" by hostile "elements." In a toxic sample of incriminating refugee statements—with authors identified by name, social background, and nationality—some were quoted saying they would prefer the Germans, others that Poland had been a better place than the Soviet Union. Romanchuk warned of their influence on other workers and Serov agreed that they needed "active *agentura* processing," which meant surveillance and repression.[72] Meanwhile, in Lviv, returnee tales led to fewer volunteers.[73] Differences between voluntary mobility and deportation finally collapsed in June 1940, with most refugees deported, officially for not getting a Soviet passport and a job. At the end of the same year, unemployment was declared over.[74]

This deportation, however, was only one of four operations. In February 1940, the first deportation in the new territories targeted mostly the countryside and the Polish settlers, vilified together with landowners as the "most fanatic enemies of the Ukrainian population" and accused of engaging in "banditism."[75] With Soviet statistics showing a Western Ukrainian total of more than 95,000 deportees, 142 families were taken in Lviv and loaded into box cars at the city's Kleparów train station.[76]

Deportees were to be resettled under secret police supervision in twelve main areas, with no more than five hundred families in the same place.[77] The general deportation direction was northeast, into inhospitable woods and steppe; many

72 Danylenko et al., *Radianski orhany*, 274–78 (doc. 154)

73 Hryciuk, *Polacy we Lwowie*, 62–63. The Donbas generated rumors: when the famously proletarian and Ukrainian husband of the elite Polish Communist writer and Soviet collaborator Wanda Wasilewska was killed, some of the city's inhabitants surmised that he had been murdered by the authorities for having talked too openly about the realities of work in the Donbas (Nakonechnyi, *"Shoa" u Lvovi*, 68–69).

74 Pohl, *Nationalsozialistische Judenverfolgung in Ostgalizien*, 29–30.

75 I. M. Premysler, "Revoliutsiyna borotba proty polskoho panuvannia v Zakhidniy Ukraini," in *Zakhidna Ukraina: Zbirnyk*, ed. Oleksandr Ohloblin (Kyiv: Vydavnitstvo Akademii Nauk URSR, 1940), 87; S. M. Belousov, "Rozpad polskoi derzhavy i ziednannia velykoho ukrainskoho narodu v iedniy ukrainskoi derzhavy-URSR," in *Zakhidna Ukraina*, ed. Ohloblin, 103.

76 Śtanisław Bizuń, *Historia krzyżem znaczona: wspomnienia z życia Kościoła katolickiego na Ziemi Lwowskiej 1939–1945*, ed. Ks. Józef Wołczański (Lublin: Wspólnota Polska, 1993), 79. Even before the first deportation of civilians, the inhabitants of Lwów had witnessed Polish officer POWs being loaded onto railroad cars. See Irena Grudzińska-Gross and Jan T. Gross, eds., *"W czterdziestym nas matko na Sibir zesłali. . ." Polska a Rosja 1939–1942* (Cracow: Znak, 2008), 114.

77 Bilas, *Represivno-karalna systema*, 1:139; Hryciuk, *Polacy we Lwowie*, 37; Kosytskyi, *Entsyklopediia Lvova*, 2:39. The "colonists" [*osadniki*] were classified mostly as "special resettlers" or "spetspereselentsy" (Bilas, *Represivno-karalna systema*, 2:129–34).

deportees were assigned to the Soviet Forest Commissariat. Locked into cattle cars in freezing temperatures, victims faced a lethal threat, complicating fine distinctions between murderous intent and murderous neglect. Deportation also meant harsh forced labor; all deportees aged sixteen to sixty (men) or fifty-five (women) had to work, under often punishing conditions and for negligible compensation.[78]

Although deportations were a mass trauma, the probability of being deported was significantly different for Poles, Jews, and Ukrainians. In the former eastern Galicia alone, Poles made up about 80 percent of the 125,000 deportees; the rest were split almost evenly between Ukrainians and Jews, the latter often refugees.[79] The absolute number of Jewish deportees was smaller than that of Poles, but measured by their share of the total population, Jews were overrepresented, while Ukrainians were least affected. Out of the total of nearly thirty thousand deportees from Lviv, an estimated 70 percent were not prewar inhabitants but refugees from western and central Poland.[80]

Deportations facilitated plunder and screening for arrests and killings. Deportees were forced to leave most of their property behind, and what they were allowed to pack was often confiscated at the internal border that had replaced the former Polish-Soviet one.[81] Screening, along with infiltration and torture, managed to "crush the Polish underground" of Lwów and forced the Ukrainian underground to concentrate its forces outside Lviv.[82] In February 1941, the Soviet secret police reported arresting 520 suspected nationalist operatives in Lviv oblast, four-fifths of them in a single operation, called the "December Smashing."[83]

Deportations increased contact between the new and old inhabitants of the Soviet Union. Thus, in Moscow in 1940, Fyodor Mochulsky, then a hopeful young graduate of the Railroad Transport Engineering Institute, was first offered an assignment in "as we said in those days 'the liberated region of Western Ukraine.' "[84]

78 On deportation conditions, see Joachim Schoenfeld, *Holocaust Memoirs: Jews in the Lwow Ghetto, the Janowski Concentration Camp, and as Deportees in Siberia* (Hoboken: Ktav, 1985), 202–5; and Instytut Pamięci Narodowej, ed., *Deportacje obywateli polskich z Zachodniej Ukrainy i Zachodniej Białorusi w 1940 roku* (Warsaw: Instytut Pamięci Narodowej, 2003), 26. Deportations in the summer often exposed their victims to scorching heat and dehydration (*Deportacje obywateli polskich*, 28).

79 Hryciuk, *Przemiany narodowościowe i ludnościowe*, 186.

80 Kosytskyi, *Entsyklopediia Lvova*, 2: 41.

81 Prusin, *Lands Between*, 144.

82 Instytut Pamięci Narodowej, *Deportacje obywateli polskich*, 25; Serhiychuk, *Ukrainskyi zdvyh*, 3:26–27; Danylenko et al., *Radianski orhany*, 313–19 (doc. 171), 328.

83 Danylenko et al., *Radianski orhany*, 329 (doc. 178).

84 Fyodor Vasilevych Mochulsky, *Gulag Boss: A Soviet Memoir*, trans. and ed. Deborah Kaple (Oxford: Oxford University Press, 2011), 5.

Yet he went east instead to become a young Gulag perpetrator in camps beyond the Arctic Circle. He still got to meet the new western subjects, forcing them to work in the "stylish" clothes in which they had been deported, lethally inadequate to their destination. Those slow at loading bricks in permafrost found that food was viciously linked to speed; going slow to avoid exhaustion meant starvation. Mochulsky displayed a special resentment against Poles. Even his post-Soviet memoirs, while mildly regretting his Gulag career, are still self-confidently cruel about these deportees' need to lose their "noble Polish conceits."[85]

In the new West, deportations also increased local interethnic tension.[86] In Lwów, a Polish victim would recall the armed men coming to deport him and his family as including a "Soviet officer" and "a Ukrainian policeman."[87] The Roman-Catholic priest Stanisław Bizuń was certainly not the only Pole to wrongly blame local Ukrainians.[88] Some Polish underground publications even denounced Sheptytskyi for Soviet deportations.[89] Orders, however, came from Moscow. Yet with Ukrainian nationalist activists infiltrating village meetings and even the Soviet police, deportation probably did provide one of the first opportunities for some de facto, if tacit, cooperation between Ukrainian nationalists and Soviet authorities when Poles were targeted—a model with a bright, brutal future.[90]

A second, much larger deportation afflicted Lwów in April 1940. Its official aim was to "cleanse" the new territories of unreliable subjects. In March, the Moscow Politburo decided to murder more than twenty-one thousand Polish prisoners, mostly reserve officers, in several locations, the most infamous of which is now Katyń. Many of the victims had relatives in the annexed territories, who were deported following proposals by Khrushchev.[91] Targets of the April deportation, however, were not only the families of Polish prisoners of war (POWs) and of those already repressed but also virtually all remaining significant former representatives of the Polish state. Nearly 90 percent of the seventy-two hundred deported inhabitants of Lviv were ethnic Poles.[92]

85 Ibid., 17–18.

86 Gross, *Revolution from Abroad*, 201–2; Bilas, *Represivno-karalna systema*, 1:139; Grünberg and Sprengel, *Trudne sąsiedztwo*, 548.

87 Grudzińska-Gross and Gross, *W czterdziestym nas matko na Sibir*, 115.

88 Bizuń, *Historia Krzyżem Znaczona*, 78.

89 Zięba, "Sheptytskyi in Polish Public Opinion," 389–90.

90 On local OUN infiltration, see Serhiichuk, *Ukrainskyi zdvyh*, 3:21–23; and Gross, *Revolution from Abroad*, 54.

91 Hryciuk, *Polacy we Lwowie*, 37; Instytut Pamięci Narodowej, *Deportacje obywateli polskich*, 716–19; Grünberg and Sprengel, *Trudne sąsiedztwo*, 548–49; Gousseff, "'Kto naš,'" 528–29.

92 Grünberg and Sprengel, *Trudne sąsiedztwo*, 549; Hryciuk, *Polacy we Lwowie*, 37–39; Kosytskyi, *Entsyklopediia Lvova*, 2:39. According to NKVD reports, the total number of deportation victims on this occasion was nearly sixty thousand for Western Ukraine and western Belarus together (Instytut Pamięci Narodowej, *Deportacje obywateli polskich*, 414–546, esp. 546).

At the end of June 1940, the third and largest deportation from Lwów mostly targeted refugees, about four-fifths of them Jewish. A preceding Soviet-German refugee exchange helped identify targets for the June deportation: between February and May, about sixty-six thousand refugees left the Soviet zone for the German one, while about thirty-four thousand went in the opposite direction. Other refugees, however, were not allowed to leave for the German zone. Jewish refugees, applying in numbers that astonished German and Soviet observers, had almost no chance of success.[93] In March, the Soviets decided to deport those not leaving for the German zone.[94] It is plausible that a refusal to return to the German zone served as a trap for deportation east, as contemporaries suspected.[95] Soviet documents indicate about twenty-two thousand deportees from Lwów that June.[96] Adding to the terror of this operation's unprecedented scale, as Jan Gross has pointed out, was the fact that these were the first public roundups in Lviv's streets.[97] Mass state violence produced urban spectacle, with victims, as one of them later recalled, "in carts" (*furami*) or walking "on foot," with "crying, wailing, [and] shouts."[98]

Almost one year later, at the end of May 1941, a third deportation, aiming mainly at Ukrainians, removed several hundred inhabitants from Lviv and about two thousand from its surroundings. Another deportation of "counterrevolutionary, anti-Soviet, and socially alien elements" was ordered on 21 June, but the German attack the next day foiled it.[99]

Soviet deportations had lasting and far-reaching effects beyond the circle of their immediate victims. Witnesses recalled a "general terror," with rumors about trucks and boxcars on standby.[100] In April 1940, Leon Weliczker-Wells, later one of the very few Holocaust survivors from Lviv, was hiding out of fear of Soviet

93 Gross, *Revolution from Abroad*, 205–7; Hryciuk, *Przemiany narodowościowe i ludnościowe*, 78. The cases of Jewish refugees trying to return to German-occupied areas should not be overemphasized. Ivan Serov reported that the "attitude of the local population, especially of Jews, toward the Germans [i.e., the members of the resettlement commissions]" was "sharply negative," with some locals jeering Germans in the streets (Danylenko et al., *Radianski orhany*, 281 [doc. 156]).

94 Hryciuk, *Przemiany narodowościowe i ludnościowe*, 174–75; Edyta Czop, *Obwód lwowski pod okupacją ZSRR w latach 1939–1941* (Rzeszów: Wydawnictwo Universytetu Rzeszowskiego, 2004), 78.

95 Gross, *Revolution from Abroad*, 202–6.

96 Hryciuk, *Polacy we Lwowie*, 41; Kosytskyi, *Entsyklopediia Lvova*, 2:40. On the background of this deportation as part of a general drive to remove Jewish refugees, see Levin, *Lesser of Two Evils*, 194–96.

97 Gross, *Revolution from Abroad*, 207.

98 Hryciuk, *Polacy we Lwowie*, 40–41.

99 Ibid., 41; Kosytskyi, *Entsyklopediia Lvova*, 2:40; Grünberg and Sprengel, *Trudne sąsiedztwo*, 549; Jolluck, *Exile and Identity*, 15–16.

100 Bereza, *Lwowskie pod okupacją*, 167; Nakonechnyi, "*Shoa*" *u Lvovi*, 80.

deportation.[101] Officially, children who excelled at school were told that their honor diplomas, decorated with portraits of Lenin and Stalin, guaranteed special Soviet care. Rumor interpreted this as a promise that they would not be taken away.[102] Despite official propaganda, deportation also opened a window on a terrifying East. Once at their destinations, some deportees sent letters to those left behind, describing a world of scarce food, devastating cold, disease, death, and grueling work.[103]

Interlocking: Soviet Passportization, Nazi New Ethnic Order

Deportations were linked to Soviet "passportization," the imposition of identity papers, introduced in Moscow and Leningrad in 1932–1933. Passportization was also an instrument of purging and expulsion.[104] In the new Soviet West, it produced, in Catherine Gousseff's words, an "authentic climate of inquisition."[105] In Lviv, passportization was mostly complete by May 1940.[106] Beginning in June, there were repeated police sweeps to catch offenders against the passport regime, with 766 suspects arrested in five months.[107] Deportations increased demand for passports, believed to offer some protection. Yet acquiring a passport could also trigger dislocation through a restricted document, banishing the holder from major cities.[108] Moreover, passports became a resource for a pilfering bureaucracy. Some apartment owners were threatened via passport discrimination to seize their places. A massive bribe could buy a passport free of incriminating entries.[109]

101 Leon W. Wells, *Ein Sohn Hiobs* (Munich: Heyne, 1963), 33; Wells, "Interview," Visual History Archive Online: USC Shoah Foundation Institute, Wells Leon, 23410, http://vhaonline.usc.edu/viewingPage.aspx?testimonyID=25727&returnIndex=0.

102 Czekanowska, *Świat rzeczywisty*, 109.

103 Jacob Gerstenfeld-Maltiel, *My Private War: One Man's Struggle to Survive the Soviets and the Nazis* (London: Valentine Mitchell, 1993), 31–32; Helen C. Kaplan, *I Never Left Janowska* (New York: Holocaust Library, 1989), 33; Nakonechnyi, *"Shoa" u Lvovi*, 73; Leszek Dzięgiel, *Lwów nie każdemu zdrów* (Wrocław: PTL, 1991), 86.

104 On the emergence and rationale of Soviet passportization, see Nicolas Werth, *Cannibal Island: Death in a Siberian* Gulag (Princeton, NJ: Princeton University Press, 2007), 15–22. On passportization as collecting *kompromat*, see Weiner and Rahi-Tamm, "Getting to Know You," 16. For Soviet expulsion and deportation operations in cities and border zones in the 1930s, see Oleg V. Khlevniuk, *The History of the Gulag: From Collectivization to the Great Terror* (New Haven: Yale University Press, 2004), 87–89.

105 Gousseff, "'Kto naš,'" 524.

106 Ibid., 525; Bilas, *Represivno-karalna systema*, 1:123. The process of registering the newly acquired subjects did not stop; by 15 September 1940, the NKVD had registered 1,514,342 persons (Bilas, *Represivno-karalna systema*, 1:123).

107 Danylenko et al., *Radianski orhany*, 324 (doc. 174).

108 Gousseff, "'Kto naš,'" 526.

109 Hryciuk, *Polacy we Lwowie*, 57–59.

Locally and compared with the refugee exchange and the deportations, the resettlement of ethnic Germans from the Soviet to the German zone seemed a minor and relatively quiet operation, lasting in Lviv from December 1939 to January 1940.[110] It affected a fraction of the population, with 7,563 registering and slightly more than 6,600 leaving.[111] Descent from parents regarded as German was crucial, generally overriding weak knowledge of the German language. Gender was treated asymmetrically, with the non-German wives of ethnic German men eligible for resettlement if they had assimilated to German identity; the test was how German they were considered to be in terms of raising their children.[112] Although a relatively small operation, the resettlement of Soviet Lviv's Germans was still a special moment: part of Hitler's new "ethnographic" order, implemented by Heinrich Himmler, head of the SS and Reich Commissioner for the Strengthening of German Ethnicity, it was the first explicitly ethnic and virtually complete resettlement in Lviv.[113]

110 Ibid., 168–69. Comparatively less openly violent, the German resettlement operation was inextricably tied to the destructiveness of the Nazi enterprise as a whole—at this point, in Christopher Browning's words, evolving as a "grandiose program of demographic engineering based on racial principles"—and especially the Holocaust. Consolidating "Germandom," demoting non-Germans, and killing Jews converged in the broad aim of deep racist transformation. The majority of those resettled from the Soviet zone of occupation were given farms taken from recently expelled Poles. Others, initially resettled as ethnic Germans but then screened out as Ukrainian, ended up in camp guard units. By 1942, with the Holocaust at its peak, Himmler designated resettlers as recipients of Jewish property. By the end of the war, resettlers had to flee or were expelled westward. See Valdis O. Lumans, "A Reassessment of *Volksdeutsche* and Jews in the Volhynia-Galicia-Narew Resettlement," in *The Impact of Nazism: New Perspectives on the Third Reich and Its Legacy*, ed. Alan E. Steinweis and Daniel E. Rogers (Lincoln: University of Nebraska Press, 2003), 91–97; Christopher R. Browning and Jürgen Matthäus, *The Origins of the Final Solution: The Evolution of Nazi Jewish Policy, September 1939–March 1942* (Lincoln: University of Nebraska Press, 2004), 27–30, 66, 108; Browning, *Remembering Survival: Inside a Nazi Slave-Labor Camp* (New York: W. W. Norton, 2010), 114; and Röskau-Rydel, "Galizien," 193–94, 212.

111 Hryciuk, *Przemiany narodowościowe i ludnościowe*, 169. According to a German report, the number of resettlers from Lemberg was ten thousand (against initial expectations of four thousand) and an additional three thousand left in the summer of 1940 as part of a general operation to return refugees from the Soviet zone of occupation to the German zone of occupation (BA R 186, Band 4, MF 1: 1629). Diverging figures may be due to differences between the city of Lemberg and Lemberg region. Once on German-controlled territory, the resettlers were instructed to avoid "Jewish" names for their children, such as "Jakob," and use "German" ones, such as "Adolf." See Kurt Lück and Alfred Lattermann, eds., *Die Heimkehr der Galiziendeutschen* (Posen: Historische Gesellschaft Posen, 1940), 54–73.

112 BA R 186, Band 4, MF 1: 1622.

113 Röskau-Rydel, "Galizien," 192. For the general background and implementation of all 1939–1941 resettlements of ethnic Germans into German-controlled territories, setting these operations in the overall context of Nazi ethno-spatial thinking and for the specific resettlement from Volhynia and Galicia, see Browning, *Origins of the Final Solution*, 12–89, especially 22–23, 30, 46–72, 93–101. See also Lumans, "Reassessment," 85.

Poles rightly suspected ethnic bias in Soviet deportations, but they were not chiefly or officially ethnically targeted. It was the smaller German resettlement that explicitly introduced ethnicity as a key criterion. It also demonstrated that this crucial ethnicity was considered both primordially non-negotiable *and* subject to officials' personal discretion. All members of the mixed selection commissions, German and Soviet, had the power to refuse resettlement applications.[114]

Soviet officials, according to a German report, prevented the resettlement of some experts even when ethnic criteria would have permitted it.[115] For German officials, being what they considered a good citizen and having a clean criminal record played a role. Some functionaries among the resettled were given special influence.[116] Sepp Müller, himself a Galician German, served as an ethnic doorkeeper with insider knowledge, rejecting those who, in his judgment, had betrayed their German identity. Yet he knew that some of those he cast out actually did belong by racist criteria of descent, while some of those accepted for resettlement did not.[117] In fact, the operation also served as cover to take some politically useful Ukrainians to the German zone.[118]

Thus, the resettlement of Lviv's Germans was the city's first encounter with the "combination of cumbersome bureaucracy and simple arbitrariness," with which Germans looking for more Germans would impose delusions of race and clarity.[119] What was special about Lviv in 1940 was that this encounter took place in a Soviet city and in open cooperation with a Soviet power building up its own local record of de facto if implicit ethnic discrimination. All differences notwithstanding, how could contemporaries fail to think that

114 Lumans, "Reassessment," 88–89.

115 BA R 186, Band 4, MF 1: 1629.

116 Ibid., 1623.

117 Sepp Müller, *Von der Ansiedlung bis zur Umsiedlung: Das Deutschtum Galiziens, insbesondere Lembergs 1772–1940* (Marburg: Johann Gottfried Herder-Institut, 1961). After the war, Müller wrote two long reports on his experience as an occupation official, responsible initially for resettlement of Germans from Lemberg, then for Polish cooperatives under German occupation, sharply criticizing the arrogance of the incoming Reich Germans against the ethnic Germans as well as what he now deplored as German brutality against the Slavic "Ostvölker" (*Galizien und sein Deutschtum: Eine Dokumentation aus Sepp Müller's Nachlaß ergänzt durch Unterlagen des Hilfskomitees der Galiziendeutschen 1948–1951 [bearbeitet von Erich Müller]*, 1: *Heimatbuch der Galiziendeutschen Teil V* [Stuttgart: Hilfskomitee der Galiziendeutschen, 1999], 3.2, 3.3). He believed that the key *Reich* German mistake regarding the *Volksdeutsche* had been to rely too much on strictly racist criteria, whereas "quality selection [*qualitative Auslese*]" by "attitude [*Gesinnung*]" would have been preferable (*Galizien*, 3.8, 3.10).

118 Gross, *Revolution from Abroad*, 31. According to Alexander Prusin, the total of those who left the Soviet-controlled areas as Germans was 124,000, including 55,000 from western Ukraine, while official statistics indicated only 40,000 Germans there (*Lands Between*, 136).

119 Doris L. Bergen, "The Nazi Concept of 'Volksdeutsche' and the Exacerbation of Anti-Semitism in Eastern Europe, 1939–45," *Journal of Contemporary History* 29 (1994): 572–73.

ethnicity, in the hands of bureaucrats serving both of these allied conquerors, was fateful as well as malleable? Yet when German antisemitism entered this constellation, the difference became obvious. Although some non-Germans, even when identified as such, left as if ethnically German, "no known Jews slipped through."[120]

The Ethos of Sovietization

The meaning of the conquest on the western periphery went to the heart of the Bolshevik project because Soviet discourse put it there. For the conquerors, the backwardness of the conquered was not a cynical propaganda device but an "authentic metaphor," a way of speaking about themselves to one another.[121] None of this excluded traditional pride in land grabbing. At the Fifteenth Congress of the Communist Party of Ukraine in 1940, a speaker hailed the "liberation" for ending "centuries of capitalist slavery," while exulting in the territorial and population gains for "our glorious country."[122]

In the September 1939 issue of *Bilshovik Ukrainy*, the "theoretical and political monthly" of the Kyiv Central Committee, a programmatic article, "The Manifesto of Victorious Communism," followed Soviet Foreign Minister Viacheslav Molotov's speech on the recent agreement with Germany. With the "Stalin Constitution of Socialism" in place and "Socialism built in its foundations," it was time to "catch up with and overtake" the capitalist countries of Europe and the United States. A "new epoch of world history" demanded that the "cultured, educated, highly conscious builders of Socialism" shed the last mental "survivals of capitalism." A "specter" in the original Communist Manifesto, Communism was now embodied in Soviet power advancing toward a global "triumph of Communism."[123] Soviet "Socialist humanism" was described as superior to earlier humanism, born in the Renaissance, since it could build the new world even with those "raised" and "spoiled" by capitalism. *Bilshovik*'s next issue, which opened

120 Lumans, "Reassessment," 90. According to Dov Levin, however, "a few hundred Jews" did manage to leave the Soviet occupation areas through the German-Soviet resettlement process, although not all of them were allowed to then cross to the German side (*Lesser of Two Evils*, 193). Apart from the small size of this exceptional group, the decisive difference remained that German representatives accepted some non-Jewish non-Germans knowingly, while the small number of Jews who managed to pass their scrutiny did so by deception.

121 For the concept of an "authentic metaphor," see Richard Slotkin, *Gunfighter Nation: The Myth of the Frontier in Twentieth-Century America* (Norman: University of Oklahoma Press, 1998), 3.

122 TsDAHOU 1, 1, 603: 147.

123 V. Berestnev, "The Manifesto of Victorious Communism," *Bilshovik Ukrainy*, September 1939, 39–53.

with Molotov announcing the Soviet attack on Poland, editorialized on the "Liberation from the Lordly Yoke" of Polish rule and called Soviet intervention an "act of great Socialist humanism." Khrushchev was quoted implying that only Socialism, by means of revolution or "liberation," made subjects into full human beings.[124] According to *Izvestiia*, the Soviet advance was removing a "border between two worlds." The "liberated" were jubilant and ignorant, amazed at kolkhoznik peasants with trucks and asking questions which "to us, Soviet people, appear childishly naïve." Their "culture and everyday life" was promptly exhibited at the Ethnography Museum in Leningrad.[125]

Destroyed Poland served as a foil to praise the superiority of Soviet nationality policy. The top Soviet jurist Ilia Trainin spotted the roots of Polish defeat not in two crushingly strong enemies conspiring but in the Polish failure to consolidate "a multinational state."[126] On the twenty-second anniversary of the Great October Revolution, *Bilshovik* reminded readers that the latter had begun humankind's "liberation." Bolsheviks going west were a "glorious detachment," gaining a "new world-historic victory."[127] They were part, as the writer-politician Oleksandr Korniychuk explained in May 1940, of the inevitable downfall of capitalism as a civilization and the making of a new era by Lenin's followers.[128]

Like Habsburgs of an earlier era, Bolshevik enlighteners imagined Lviv as both marginal and central, backward and crucial: a potential proving ground for their cutting-edge modernity. On the first anniversary of the "liberation," *Bilshovik* summarized "A Year of Social Reconstruction of the Political and Economic Life in the Western Oblasts of Ukraine." The key point was Stalin's insistence on "liquidating that backwardness (economic, political, cultural) of the nationalities that we have inherited from the past, giving the backward peoples

124 V. Paukova, "On Socialist Humanism," *Bilshovik Ukrainy*, September 1939, 54–72; "Liberation from the Lordly Yoke" (unsigned), *Bilshovik Ukrainy*, October 1939, 5–16. On Stalinism's positive if condescending reading of Renaissance humanism against bourgeois utility, see Clark, *Moscow, the Fourth Rome*, 131–32.

125 "The Population of Western Ukraine and Western Belarus Meets the Red Army with Enthusiasm," *Izvestiia*, 20 September 1939, 1; 21 September 1939, 1.

126 Ilia Trainin, *Natsionalnoe i sotsialnoe osvobozhdenie Zapadnoi Ukrainy i Zapadnoi Belorussii* (Moscow: Gosudarstvennoe sotsialno-ekonomicheskoe izdatelstvo, 1939). Rationalizing the Soviet conquest of Polish territory by attaching a failed-state label to the militarily weaker nation was also projected backward: within a few years, a Soviet historian called for more skepticism regarding nineteenth-century Polish risings in view of Poland's "unviability." See David Brandenberger, *National Bolshevism: Stalinist Mass Culture and the Formation of Modern Russian National Identity, 1931–1956* (Cambridge, MA: Harvard University Press, 2002), 121-22.

127 "The 22nd Anniversary of the Great Socialist Revolution in the Soviet Union" (unsigned), *Bilshovik Ukrainy*, November 1939, 1–7; "The 25th Congress of the Communist Party (Bolsheviks) of Ukraine," *Bilshovik Ukrainy*, May 1940, 42–45.

128 TsDAHOU 1, 1, 602: 48–49.

the opportunity to catch up with central Russia." Accordingly, Maria Soliak from Lviv wrote a "Letter to the Future," addressing Western Ukraine's "liberators" from a dark past about to pass.[129]

The Soviet director Mikhail Romm, already decorated with an Order of Lenin, called his 1940/1941 film about a dark interwar Lwów of unemployment and oppression *The Dream*.[130] It follows its characters through ceaseless rounds of struggle and humiliation. The main protagonist finally achieves redemption when she moves to the Soviet Union. At the end of the film, she returns to just "liberated" Lviv and confirms that she is now "from over there." In fact, the Soviet Union appears only once in the film and then indirectly, in a picture of a factory with a Lenin poster, but "over there" was central even if reduced to a single image. Lviv, read as the footprint of what Hryshchuk called twenty years of Poland's now "unmasked colonial" policy, was really all about the superiority of "over there."[131]

In a similar vein, at a 1940 Kyiv Central Committee plenum, Khrushchev insisted that mountaineers of the Carpathian range in Ukraine's new West had seen "a car for the first time" when "the Red Army arrived."[132] Not only technology but plain size mattered, with Korniychuk boasting of a "Red Armada" of huge modern war machines, impeded only by throngs of the jubilant "liberated" and Lilliputian local roads—yet still so fast that hidebound Polish generals could not believe their eyes.[133] Droning on about Polish aggression, the conquerors also staged an exhibition of captured Polish arms, inviting viewers to laugh at a Polish cannon, "decommissioned forty years ago from the arsenal of tsarist Russia."[134]

Religion was read as a special marker of backwardness and superiority. *Izvestiia*'s Red Army soldiers encountering nuns were disciplined enough to turn away and superior enough to laugh at their dress.[135] In the Soviet writer Viktor

129 *Bilshovik Ukrainy*, September 1940, 11–22. For Soliak's "Letter," see *Nam partiia sylu dala: Z istorii Komsomolskoi orhanizatsii Lvivskoho derzhavnoho universytetu im. Ivana Franka* (Lviv: Vydavnytstvo Lvivskoho universytetu, 1960), 25.

130 *Mechta* (1941), directed by Mikhail Romm—not to be confused with Abram Room's *The Wind from the East* (Veter s Vostoka/Viter zi Skhodu) of 1940, which also depicted interwar Poland's eastern territories as sites of oppression and exploitation and featured several scenes in Lviv. However, it focused on Ukrainian peasants as victims and Polish landowners as villains, not on city dwellers.

131 TsDAHOU 1, 1, 602: 40, for Hryshchuk. Probably because of propaganda policy shifts caused by increasing tensions with Germany, *The Dream* was not shown for two years; it was released only when Soviet policy again sought to stress its claim to the territories it seized from Poland. See Peter Kenez, "Black and White: The War on Film," in *Culture and Entertainment in Wartime Russia*, ed. Richard Stites (Bloomington: Indiana University Press, 1995), 164.

132 TsDAHOU 1, 1, 627: 119.

133 Oleksandr Korniychuk, "The Red Armada [originally published in 1939]," in *Zolotyi veresen* (Kyiv: Dnipro, 1979), 47-48.

134 Nikita Petrov, *Pervyi predsedatel KGB Ivan Serov* (Moscow: Materik, 2005), 25.

135 "Dykhanie mira," *Izvestiia*, 6 October 1939, 3.

Shklovsky's long reportage, "Tales about Western Ukraine," Galicia was a "remote corner" and "natural preserve of religion," especially Christianity and Judaism. Depicting clergy and believers in a distanced, pseudoethnographic mode, he mused about exotic confession booths, forelocks, and a cunning ideological enemy, fielding the "artillery and tanks" of rites and art.[136]

Moscow's *Bezbozhnik* journal, peddling a philistine atheism, targeted Lviv's synagogues, with the special correspondent Kryvelev reconnoitering these many fortresses, as he called them, of superstition. At the famous Golden Rose Synagogue, "talmudists," recognizable by sidelocks and dress more reminiscent of "1640 than 1940," seemed as "overgrown with moss" as the premises. Kryvelev also dismissed the modern looks of believers at the Temple, Lviv's major reform synagogue, who shaved and wore jackets but were, he warned, "essentially not more advanced."[137] Clearly, modernity, under Soviet eyes, was not a matter of appearance only.

Although an opportunity to ascribe backwardness and superiority, the conquest was also rife with disturbing contradictions. Quantities were impressive. By November 1940, more than forty thousand cadres had gone west, and the Cadre Department of the Kyiv Central Committee stressed the operation's unprecedented scale. Yet quality suffered from haste and cheating, with eastern offices shedding inferior staff. Almost half of the cadres deployed were quickly recalled as too weak. The new Soviet West, in effect, turned into a fickle mirror, provoking vanity as well as self-hatred. For Khrushchev, the eastern oblasts had sent "some sort of rubbish." An eastern cadre who committed suicide "should have shot himself ten years ago" but not now, not in the new West. Under observation there, "Soviet man" must not die as "demoralized trash."[138] Yet, in fact, cadres sent west received special privileges, often receiving party membership simply for going there, which led to admission for "absolutely everybody" and a "rush" into the party. Documentation was neglected, mostly due to drunkenness.[139] As Włodzimierz Bonusiak has shown, for most leading cadres going west meant further promotion.[140] The Soviet West was a career. Ivan Serov's rise was representative, if especially steep: fresh from organizing mass deportations in western Ukraine and massacring Polish officers, he was made a candidate member of the Soviet Union's Politburo.

136 Viktor Shklovsky, "Rasskazy o Zapadnoi Ukraine," *Znamia*, no. 2 (1940): 11.

137 I. Kryvelev, "Dukhovnye kreposti," *Bezbozhnik*, 13 October 1940, 2.

138 TsDAHOU 1, 1, 627: 129, 150, 217–19, 223.

139 TsDAHOU 1, 1, 627: 173–76.

140 Włodzimierz Bonusiak, *Polytika ludnościowa i ekonomiczna ZSRR na okupowanych ziemiach polskich w latach 1939–1941: "Zachodnia Ukraina" i "Zachodnia Białoruś"* (Rzeszów: Wydawnictwo Universytetu Rzeszowskiego, 2006), 73–74.

In 1940, at the first oblast party conference in Lviv's history, the city was presented as an "outpost" of the "blossoming Soviet fatherland." Hryshchuk emphasized the "great honor" of being a Sovietizer. Yet "moral failure" also occurred, in the form of drinking, embezzlement, and deals, especially between Communists and the impoverished wives of arrested Polish officers. Moreover, there were "many cases" of male Communists having sex with local women. A worker liked an official's speech on the Paris Commune but not that "he comes to our women." Communists were also warned not to be arrogant or neglect "local comrades." Yet a factory director openly complained that locals were generally unable to work.[141]

The Experience of the Conquered: "In the Paws of Humanists"

Arms decided who would rule; they did not settle old struggles over who should. The distinction between a "civilized Europe" and a "barbaric Asia" was deeply rooted in the European Enlightenment, whose binary opposition of East and West, "barbaric" and "civilized," "Asia" and "Europe" became a dominant dichotomy of modern thought.[142] These narratives about a cultural gradient between "Europe" and "Asia" were diverse and versatile: they could be inverted and even caricatured, but it was impossible to abandon them. On the Soviet side, the Red Army, often the first representative of Soviet power encountered on the ground, was meant to appear as a "progressive, cultured, and political force."[143] Viktor Shklovsky wrote of the "Red Fighter," his quintessential Soviet Man. While some locals held on to the conquerors as "frightened children cling to their mother's skirt," the Soviet soldier was "like an adult, who takes children across the road." Personally modest, he was proud "because he had earned the right to direct history." His ability to look to the future made him the "man of Socialism."[144]

Yet many of the conquered saw simple people in poor uniforms. The Greek Catholic priest and theologian Havril Kostelnyk noted "the 'proletarian look' of the Bolshevik troops," their "very modest dress," and what he saw as their "unintelligent, uncultured faces and simple-minded movements."[145] Poles mocked Soviet troops as "rabble."[146] For Shklovsky, however, superior modern arms were the

141 DALO P-3, 1, 4: 72, 167, 170.

142 Larry Wolff, *Inventing Eastern Europe: The Map of Civilization on the Mind of the Enlightenment* (Stanford, CA: Stanford University Press, 1994).

143 TsDAHOU 1, 1, 603: 13.

144 Shklovsky, "Rasskazy o Zapadnoi Ukraine," 24–25, 27, 31–32.

145 Milena Rudnytska, *Zakhidna Ukraina pid bolshevykamy, IX 1939–VI 1941* (New York: Naukove tovarystvo im. Shevchenka v Amerytsi, 1958), 18.

146 Aleksandr Klotz, *Zapiski konspiratora 1939–1945*, ed. Grzegorz Mazur (Cracow: Księgarnia Akademicka, 2001), 60–61, 74.

payback for the conquered's arrogance. Challenged about his shabby uniform, his Red Army man pointed to Soviet riches in tanks.[147]

Although many arrivals were not uniformed, easterners and locals often recognized each other, with signals encoded not only in language but also in appearance, manner, gait, posture, and gestures. Lviv's first Communist conquerors were no urban elite. Hryshchuk admitted that one of their problems was a lack of city experience.[148] Locals saw the Soviet easterners as simple and impoverished: dressed in "rags," unfamiliar with the use of toilets, and rude.[149] When Soviet soldiers told the Lviv mathematician Hugo Steinhaus that mathematics, too, was a "class science," he felt he was dealing with "liars and quarter-intellectuals duped by them."[150] He also noted their ambivalence between feeling superior and inferior. When in a more forgiving mood, he infantilized them; they could not be considered adults.[151]

Contempt for the occupiers was a blunt weapon of the weak, its use provoked even more by the Soviet desire to be exactly the opposite: politically, culturally, and technologically superior and prosperous. The Polish writer Stanisław Lem, then a seventeen-year-old Lwówian, would recall the Soviets as both ridiculous and terrifying: while "the Germans evoked only fear, at the Soviets you could also laugh." For Lem, quoting Osip Mandelstam, they resembled "a terrible, gigantic ape," with Lwów helpless in the "paws of humanists."[152] Among those suddenly thus seized, many reactions were similar. More portentous, however, were responses further dividing Lviv.

The Polish Encounter

The meeting between the Soviet Union and Lwów's Poles was shaped by the special meaning of Lwów for Poles and of Poland for the Soviet and especially Russian imagination. Soviet interwar attitudes to Poland were generally hostile and in the later 1930s Soviet mass culture had emphasized this enmity.[153]

During Lviv's first Soviet occupation, the policy toward Poles went through two main phases: from the fall of 1939 to the summer of 1940, it blended shrill denunciation of "Polish lords," stressing nation as well as class. Initially, local

147 Shklovsky, "Rasskazy o Zapadnoi Ukraine," 32.

148 DALO P-3, 1, 4: 43–44, 67–69.

149 Hryciuk, *Polacy we Lwowie*, 149–50.

150 Steinhaus, *Wspomnienia i zapiski*, 170–71.

151 Ibid., 173–75.

152 Stanisław Lem, *Świat na krawędzi: Ze Stanisławem Lemem rozmawia Tomasz Fiałkowski* (Cracow: Wydawnictwo Literackie, 2000), 41.

153 Brandenberger, *National Bolshevism*, 227–28.

Ukrainians assaulted Poles in the countryside and were only infrequently stopped by Soviet officials.[154] Soviet policy temporarily facilitated bloody "revenge" for real and imagined interwar injustice. Lviv's new Soviet and Ukrainian-language local newspaper, *Vilna Ukraina*, denounced "Polish settlers" as "fierce enemies of the toilers of Western Ukraine" and warned of "Polish gangs" stashing weapons.[155] Although Lwów was generally not directly affected by this wave of violence, news about it did spread.[156] Even in Lviv, some Polish military or police officers were abused or killed by local inhabitants.[157]

At the same time, Polish Lwów's civil society was obliterated by the same blast that hit Ukrainians and Jews. Associations, media, and institutions were dismantled. With the number of Polish schools reduced and the remaining ones transformed, Polish history and geography were abolished, and non-Polish speaking teachers from the East were hired. Schools were sites for spreading a key element of the Stalinist way of life to the young: children were encouraged to report on their parents' talk at home.[158] Direct abuse also occurred: in November 1940, the Kyiv Central Committee deplored that students were being beaten in Lviv's decrepit and dirty schools; an orphanage director sneered at freezing children to ask Piłsudski for boots and stoves.[159]

Soviet words and deeds signaled a conflation of class and ethnicity in the discrimination against Poles. This happened not only because Lwów's Poles had lost a state that had privileged them, but also through the Soviets' specific measures of turning Lwów into Ukrainian Lviv. Hryshchuk was proud that, as of April 1940, more than 13,000 employees in Lviv had lost their jobs, including nearly 10,900 railway staff. He also demanded further "Ukrainization" of the railways: under Poland, 95 percent of employees had been Poles, and at present only 34 percent were Ukrainians. "By far" not all hostile elements had been dismissed, he insisted. When discussing aid for workers victimized in interwar Poland, Hryshchuk mentioned only "Ukrainians and Jews." It would have been hard to imagine a clearer, if implicit, statement that, when it came to Poles, ethnicity trumped class. At this point, "hostile elements" meant Poles, even among the working class.[160]

154 Gross, *Revolution from Abroad*, 35–41.

155 *Vilna Ukraina*, 1 October 1939, 4; 5 October 1939, 3.

156 Karolina Lanckorońska, *Wspomnienia wojenne* (Cracow: Znak, 2003), 19.

157 Hryciuk, *Polacy we Lwowie*, 17.

158 Lili Chuwis Thau, *Hidden: Only the Leaves Bore Witness to Her Secret* (Austin, TX: Groundbreaking Press, 2012), 85.

159 TsDAHOU 1, 1, 627: 141–42.

160 DALO P-3, 1, 4: 74, 95–96.

In prewar Lwów, academia had been a bastion of Polish predominance. A few select left-wing Polish intellectuals were courted for collaboration, but in general Soviet rule brought a radical break along both class and ethnic fissures. Initial promises of dual Polish-Ukrainian higher education were not kept.[161] Under the Habsburgs, the Polonization of Lwów's academic institutions had been a key part of Polish ascendancy.[162] Lwów's interwar university had been a site and symbol of national discrimination; Ukrainian secret university activities, while short-lived, had resonated with a sense of persecution and mission. Ivan Krypiakevych recalled teaching in "the catacombs."[163]

Soviet rule quickly made Ukrainian a mandatory subject for all students.[164] The Polish professor Ryszard Gansiniec's request that the new University Statute, in Ukrainian and Polish, should be edited into correct Polish was granted; his demand for a chair in Polish history was not.[165] Lviv's now Soviet university was Ukrainianized and renamed—under Khrushchev's direct tutelage—after a nineteenth-century Galician Ukrainian writer, Ivan Franko, with his early sympathy for socialism forged into a national and proto-Soviet liberation hero legend.[166] The newly appointed rector, the eastern cadre Mykhailo Marchenko, responded to Polish protest with a violent speech, claiming that in Soviet Ukraine there would only be exclusively Ukrainian universities.[167]

At least eighty faculty members were purged, around forty arrested, and some killed. Of the thirty-six hundred Polish students at the time of the Soviet invasion, within three months only sixteen hundred remained. At the Polytechnic, according to a Soviet report, two thousand out of thirty-six hundred students left in a process called "natural," although it coincided with beatings of

161 Shklovsky, "Rasskazy o Zapadnoi Ukraine," 31. This is what a Polish contemporary remembered, too (Hryciuk, *Polacy we Lwowie*, 128; DALO R-163, 2, 78: 26–31, repr. in *Kulturne zhyttia*, 1:52–57). Generally, on the Soviet uses for some Polish left-wing intellectuals, see Shore, *Caviar and Ashes*, 153–94.

162 Jadwiga Suchmiel, *Działalność naukowa kobiet w Uniwersytecie we Lwowie do roku 1939* (Częstochowa: WSP, 2000), 30–36, 242–43.

163 Grünberg and Sprengel, *Trudne sąsiedztwo*, 366–68; Krypiakevych to Stepan Tomashivskyi, 8 June 1922, repr. in Isaievych, *Ivan Krypiakevych u rodynnii tradytsii*, 397–400 (here 398).

164 Adam Redzik, *Wydział Prawa Uniwersytetu Lwowskiego w latach 1939–1946* (Lublin: TN KUL, 2006), 124.

165 Dalo R-119, 3, 64: 16–17.

166 TsDAHOU 1, 1, 602: 68. With bitter perceptiveness, a Polish observer remembered the "Ukrainian writer Ivan Franko" who "enjoyed great Soviet esteem (because he was no longer among the living)" (Jerzy Węgierski, Bardzo różne życie: we Lwowie, w sowieckich łagrach, na Śląsku [Katowice: J. Węgierski, 2003], 117). Ivan Franko's real relationships with socialism, nationalism, and Polish culture were more complex than the Soviet retelling.

167 Hryciuk, *Polacy we Lwowie*, 43.

students accused of right-wing politics or antisemitism.[168] While the numbers of Polish students plummeted, those of Ukrainians and Jews rose fast. Soviet policy offered genuine opportunities, demonstrating its power to conflate social equality and ethnic liberation and to discriminate against Poles on both grounds.

Yet Poles continued to provide the core of Lviv's faculty. According to later German calculations, under the Soviet occupation, Ukrainians and Poles each accounted for 40 percent of Lviv's academics. But among the elite bearing the rank of full professor, there were fifty-two Poles, twenty-two Ukrainians, and eight Jews.[169] Whereas the Polish auto-stereotype of cultural superiority was thus reinforced, the Soviet occupation added the feel of a beleaguered enclave. The head of a kafedra of Polish literature, a Polish diarist noted, maintained a "truly Polish atmosphere," as if "there were no war, no enemies, and no terrible deportations to Siberia."[170] In Shklovsky's view from above, Polish academics were even "more tied to the past than Jewish traders."[171]

Ironically, it was fear of allies abroad that changed attitudes toward "hostiles" at home. In May 1940, Soviet Marshal Semen Timoshenko wrote to Stalin about a German request to take a look at the Mannerheim defense line recently taken by the Soviet Union in its war against Finland.[172] In return, Timoshenko suggested, the Germans should let Soviet officers inspect the French Maginot Line recently taken by Nazi Germany.[173] Courtesies aside, the rapid defeat of France made the Soviet leadership fear Germans more and look differently at Poles.

By mid-June 1940, Khrushchev was mauling a Lviv Bolshevik for agitating Poles in Ukrainian, stressing that Poles had to be addressed in Polish.[174] In early July, Stalin blamed the abuse of Poles on local authorities and ordered changes. Secretly, the Kyiv Central Committee rebuked the Lviv authorities for engaging in corruption, snatching apartments, and denying jobs and passports to Poles. In Lviv, the Polish-language local newspaper grew, and a new Polish highbrow

168 Grzegorz Hryciuk, "Politechnika Lwowska w latach 1939–1941 w świetle sprawdzan kierownika katedry Marksizmu-Leninizmu F. S. Koczergi," in *Politechnika Lwowska: Macierz Polskich Politechnik*, ed. Ryszard Sroczynski et al. (Wroclaw: Wroclawskie Towarzystwo Naukowe, 1995), 73–74; Redzik, *Wydział Prawa Uniwersytetu Lwowskiego*, 227.

169 Hryciuk, *Polacy we Lwowie*, 130.

170 Ibid., 133–34.

171 Shklovsky, "Rasskazy o Zapadnoi Ukraine," 31.

172 The Winter War, started by the Soviet Union in November 1939 and ended in March 1940, reverberated in Lviv, where initial Soviet blunders inspired hopes among the occupied and it seemed to some that Soviet troops practiced skiing in the city's parks (Czekanowska, *Świat rzeczywisty*, 79).

173 RGASPI 82, 2, 801: 45.

174 TsDAHOU 1, 1, 623: 304.

journal, *Nowi Widnokręgi*, started publication. Two stridently anti-Polish rectors were replaced. A group of academics, including many Poles, visited Moscow, which produced rumors about new policies; and some Polish deportees were allowed to return to Lviv. The gesture with the most publicity was the celebration, in late 1940, of the anniversary of the Polish national poet Adam Mickiewicz's death.[175]

Some Polish intellectuals, like the writer Aleksander Wat, hoped that Lwów could be turned once more into a shelter of Polish culture, a "kind of cultural Piedmont," if "on the sly."[176] The greatest symbol for such hopes was the "National Ossoliński Institute," or Ossolineum, a large complex combining a library, museum, and publisher. Founded in the early nineteenth century, it took on features of a de facto national library before the reestablishment of a Polish state in 1918. Ukrainian attacks only added shine to this Polish national emblem.[177] The underground Polish Home Army in Soviet-occupied Lwów considered the Ossolineum "one of the most brilliant achievements of our culture," which was at risk of becoming "the basis for dreams about a Polish Bolshevism" and of "a Soviet Poland."[178]

In reality, the Ossolineum's founder, Count Ossoliński, had been an enlightenment elite patriot and not a modern nationalist, quite capable of reconciling Polish and Habsburg loyalties.[179] Yet Poland's "fourth partition" in 1939 between a German Reich, including Prussia and Austria, and a Soviet Union dominated by Russia could not but evoke the Ossolineum's myth as a fortress of national

175 Hryciuk, *Polacy we Lwowie*, 44–49.

176 Aleksander Wat, *Mój wiek* (Warsaw: Czytelnik, 1990), 1:273; Tomas Venclova, *Alexander Wat: Life and Art of an Iconoclast* (New Haven: Yale University Press, 1996), 136. There were about two hundred writers among the refugees from the German zone of occupation (Hryciuk, *Polacy we Lwowie*, 99). Especially after the end of Poland's postwar Communist regime, Polish intellectuals who worked for Soviet institutions, showed loyalty to the Soviet order (especially by publicly welcoming the "unification of Ukraine"), and enjoyed privileges in wartime Lwów have become the object of controversies about collaboration. See, in particular, Jacek Trznadel, *Kolaboranci: Tadeusz Boy-Żeleński i grupa komunistycznych pisarzy we Lwowie 1939–1941* (Komorów: Wydawnictwo Antyk Marcin Dybowski, 1998); and Barbara Winklowa, *Nad Wisłą i nad Sekwaną: Biografia Tadeusza Boya-Żeleńskiego* (Warsaw: Iskry, 1998), 182–202; and her earlier edited volume *Boy we Lwowie: Antologia tekstów Tadeusza Żeleńskiego (Boya) we Lwowie* (Warsaw: RYTM, 1992).

177 Maciej Matwijów, *Zaklad Narodowy imienia Ossolinskich w latach 1939–1946* (Wrocław: Towarzystwo Przyjaciól Ossolineum, 2003), 333–34; Wolff, *Idea of Galicia*, 82–85; Röskau-Rydel, *Galizien, Bukowina, Moldau*, 44; Prokopovych, *Habsburg Lemberg*, 135–41. From 1946 on, the Ossolineum has been in Wrocław, where about one-third of its Lwów holdings were moved under a Polish-Soviet-Ukrainian agreement.

178 AAN 203/XV-47: 41 (MF 2400/9).

179 Prokopovych, *Habsburg Lemberg*, 135–37.

identity, especially when, in their occupation zone, Germans targeted Poland's elites with mass murder.[180]

Yet, in the end, hopes for a Communist Polish "Piedmont" were disappointed. Instead the Ossolineum was Ukrainianized and transferred to the newly founded Lviv branch of the Ukrainian Academy of Sciences.[181] The latter, in turn, was the Sovietized former National Shevchenko Society, a center for Ukrainian scholarship since the late nineteenth century.[182] As a nationalizing symbol it resembled the Ossolineum. Giving the latter's library to the Ukrainian Academy of Sciences had obvious implications.

The failure of dreams of a Soviet Polish Piedmont was especially difficult for left-wing intellectuals. The first Soviet-appointed Ossolineum director, Jerzy Borejsza, a writer and prewar Polish Communist, was demoted.[183] His inability to preserve a Polish Ossolineum sharply delineated the lower position of Polish culture in Soviet Lviv and, in conjunction with the Mickewiecz anniversary, the limits of the pro-Polish turn of 1940. Borejsza, after all, had pitched the Ossolineum as a potential center of a Polish and Soviet culture, to be headed by a Marxist with knowledge of Polish culture, quite possibly himself.[184] His failure showed that even the most Soviet interpretation of perhaps the most signally Polish secular institution had no place in Soviet Ukrainian Lviv. Later, Polish Lwów would have to disappear, preferably without a trace. Borejsza's defeat adumbrated this possibility.

If the Ossolineum's fate restricted the space for Polish identity, the Mickiewicz anniversary showed what could still fit. The Soviet aim was to lay a claim to

180 Jacek Chrobaczyński, "Kraków i Lwów 1939–1945: Funkcje miast w systemie okupacyjnym i w konspiracji," *Lviv: Misto, suspilstvo, kultura* 3 (1999): 614; Lanckorońska, *Wspomnienia*, 23–24. Large-scale German "extermination operations" against a broadly defined Polish intelligentsia took place during and after the initial invasion in September 1939, continuously escalating until the so-called General Pacification operation of March 1940. See Christoph Kleßmann, *Die Selbstbehauptung einer Nation: NS-Kulturpolitik und polnische Widerstandsbewegung im Generalgouvernement 1939–1945* (Düsseldorf: Bertelsmann, 1971), 12, 43–45. Alexander Rossino has estimated that about fifty thousand Polish civilians had been killed by December 1939 (*Hitler Strikes Poland* [Lawrence: University Press of Kansas, 2003], 234–35). While not comparable on the whole, for contemporaries there was another reference point. Lithuanian higher education policies in Vilnius looked more radical in their de-Polonization measures than those that Soviet education brought to Lwów. See Sławomir Kalbarczyk, *Polscy pracownicy nauki: Ofiary zbrodni sowieckich w latach II wojny światowej* (Warsaw: Neriton, 2001), 45.

181 Matwijów, *Zaklad Narodowy imienia Ossolinskich*, 63–64, 67.

182 For the Sovietization of the Shevchenko Society, see Tsentralnyi Arkhiv Akademii nauk U[krainskoi] SSR, 251, 1, 75: 171–75, 190, repr. in *Kulturne zhyttia*, 1:65–68.

183 Some ethnic Poles resented Borejsza's Jewish background, in addition to his youth, ambition, and Marxism. A Home Army communication derided him as the center of "that whole Bolshevik-Russian-Jewish mixture." See Maciej Matwijów, *Walka o lwowskie dobra kultury w latach 1945–1948* (Wrocław: Ossolineum, 1996), 23; and AAN 203/47 (AK): 41 (MF 2400/9).

184 Matwijów, *Zaklad Narodowy imienia Ossolinskich*, 63.

Mickiewicz's legacy and prestige.[185] In 1940, Korniychuk had denounced Polish prewar elites for going on about "humanism" and "culture" but abandoning Mickiewicz manuscripts "in the dirt" as they fled Lwów.[186] Thus, the Soviet Mickiewicz anniversary of 1941 made Lviv the scene of a salvaging and appropriation gesture that was a key feature of Socialist Realism, as Boris Groys and Katerina Clark have shown. Soviet spokesmen claimed that they "honored the works of a rival state's culture more than that state did."[187] Picking up Mickiewicz from the "dirt," the Soviet invaders blended metaphorical and physical conquest, proudly seizing a high-culture symbol they had forced the defeated to abandon.

The Mickiewicz celebration also took its cues from the recent Soviet Pushkin anniversary. The main festivities took place in late November 1940: the library of the Lviv branch of the Ukrainian Academy of Sciences (the former Ossolineum) put on an exhibition; the Lviv Opera, recently site of the Popular Assemblies dramatizing Poland's end, staged a Mickiewicz evening, attended by the oblast party-state elite.[188] Lwów's public loudspeaker system transmitted Mickiewicz in Polish, Ukrainian, Russian, and Yiddish. Wreaths were laid at the Mickiewicz monument, and multiple events were held at cultural institutions.[189]

Officially, the celebrations were considered a success. In 1944, the Kyiv Central Committee prepared a pamphlet citing the anniversary as "brilliant evidence of the attitude of Soviet power to Polish national culture."[190] According to the Polish psychologist and diarist Tadeusz Tomaszewski, however, the Polish response was not enthusiastic, and few showed up for the university meeting.[191] But for the diarist Jan Rogowski, Poles had appropriated the event for their own national purposes.[192] At a meeting held at the opera house, a speaker invoked the immortality not only of Mickiewicz but also the Polish people; the newspapers omitted the statement.[193]

Neither Soviet nor Polish interpretations could really decipher the odd spectacle of the Polish national poet celebrated in Soviet and officially "ancient Ukrainian" Lviv. There was an obvious Soviet attempt to take over Mickiewicz. Poles noted a welcome decrease of terrifying pressure, and an increase of pressure on

185 Ibid., 59–60.

186 TsDAHOU 1, 1, 602: 50.

187 Boris Groys, *The Total Art of Stalinism: Avant-Garde, Aesthetic Dictatorship, and Beyond* (London: Verso, 2011), 40–41; Clark, *Moscow, the Fourth Rome*, 11 (emphasis in the original).

188 Hryciuk, *Polacy we Lwowie*, 48–49.

189 Ibid.

190 TsDAHOU, 1, 70, 157: 51–52, repr. in Volodymyr Serhiychuk, *Poliaky na Volyni u roky druhoi svitovoi viiny: Dokumenty z ukrainskykh arkhiviv i polski publikatsii* (Kyiv: Spilka, 2003), 41–42.

191 Tadeusz Tomaszewski, *Lwów: Pejzaż psychologiczny* (Warsaw: WIP, 1996), 42–44.

192 Hryciuk, *Polacy we Lwowie*, 49.

193 Ibid., 48, 105.

Ukrainians. The preceding Polish demotion was not fundamentally reversed, however. In Lwów, the single institution most symbolizing the Polish claim to supremacy via high culture, the Ossolineum, was and remained Ukrainianized. Conversely, the Mickiewicz anniversary also marked a historic if passing moment, when Soviet policy congealed around having a Soviet Ukrainian Lviv and its Poles, too—if in a new, subordinate role.

The Ukrainian Encounter

Only Ukrainians were offered a combination of ostensible national liberation and unification. Ivan Nimchuk was the editor of prewar Lwów's leading Ukrainian newspaper, *Dilo*. When it was shut down and replaced by *Vilna Ukraina*, he noted fellow Ukrainians in Lviv viewing this as a sign of Soviet promotion of Ukrainians, notwithstanding *Vilna*'s inferior quality.[194] The Soviet authorities boasted of increasing Western Ukraine's urban population "mostly on account of Ukrainians."[195] Yet the occupiers also insisted that local Ukrainians were backward. Bolshevism, one of them told Sheptytskyi, was a global force and "all the Western Ukrainians . . . still droning on about 'their' national question" were "late by one hundred years."[196] Western Ukrainians met eastern Ukrainians, or, in terms often used, "Galicians" encountered "Great Ukrainians" and for once, a stereotype came true. They met the Other and it was them—or, in both nationalist and Soviet terms, it ought to have been.

For some, this meeting was deeply unsettling. Soviet rule turned out to be much more oppressive than Polish rule. The rich world of Ukrainian publications in Polish Lwów, for instance, was gone in Soviet Ukrainian Lviv, and with it many journalism jobs, as Nimchuk observed.[197] Likewise, in 1940, Osyp Nazaruk, eager to take Poles hostage in 1918, fled to German-occupied Warsaw. Initially, he had welcomed what he saw as the Soviets' eradication of Polishness.[198] After his flight, though, he personified confusion; he had worked his "whole life for the unification of the Ukrainian people" but ran when it happened.[199]

Although Havril Kostelnyk felt superior to primitive Soviet troops, he was also shaken, his knees trembling "from shame in the face of the Poles," as this was

194 Ivan Nimchuk, *595 dniv sovietskym viaznem* (Toronto: Vydavnytstvo Vasilian, 1950), 30–31.

195 *Bilshovik Ukrainy*, September 1940, 19.

196 Serhiy Kokin et al., eds. *Mytropolyt Andrei Sheptytskyi u dokumentakh radianskykh orhaniv derzhavnoi bezpeky, 1934–1944 rr.* (Kyiv: Ukrainska vydavnycha spilka, 2005), 178 (doc. 33).

197 Nimchuk, *595 dniv sovetskym viaznem*, 31.

198 Myroslava Diadiuk, ed., *Milena Rudnytska: Statti, listy, dokumenty* (Lviv: Misioner 1998), 437.

199 Osyp Nazaruk, *Zi Lvova do Varshavy: 2–13 Zhovtnia 1939 roku* (Lviv: NTSh, 1995), 13.

"the army of the state" to which Ukraine belonged.[200] Were these victorious yet dismal troops more Soviet or Ukrainian? Clearly, for Kostelnyk they were Ukrainian enough to make him feel vicarious disgrace before Lviv's defeated Poles.

On the whole, initial Ukrainian reactions ranged from radical rejection to hopeful welcome. While others fled, many Ukrainian elite representatives stayed, some at least welcoming the demotion of Poles or complaining about imagined preferences for Jews. In reality, Ukrainians predominated among locals given positions in Soviet institutions in Lviv oblast, accounting for two-thirds (4,909) of 6,822 locals promoted by the middle of 1940.[201] Party admissions showed a similar pattern. Between April and June 1940, a total of 265 new party members or candidates were admitted in Lviv oblast, including 171 Ukrainians, 61 Russians, 27 Jews, 5 Belarusians, and 1 Pole.[202]

Some local Ukrainians acknowledged their promotion by the Soviet authorities.[203] Kost Pankivskyi's response was telling. Appointed head of a centralized pharmacy administration, he still found that "Jews predominated," although he also thought that "Ukrainization was flourishing."[204] He praised Soviet rule for breaking "the narrow circle of our petty Galician-Ukrainian concerns" to impose all-Ukrainian perspectives.[205] The new rector of Lviv University, Marchenko, flaunted its Ukrainization, hardly mentioning Communism or the Soviet Union and emphasizing the triumph in the "Ukrainian people's" struggle against "Polish masters." The large library—Marchenko omitted that almost all its books were in Polish—now had a Ukrainian director, Bohdan Barvinskyi, unemployed "under Polish-feudal rule."[206]

200 Rudnytska, *Zakhidna Ukraina pid bolshevykamy*, 18.

201 DALO P-3, 1, 4: 69.

202 Czop, *Obwód lwowski pod Okupacją*, 66. "Ukrainians" in these statistics included locals and eastern Ukrainians. Nevertheless, the promotion of some local Ukrainians was a reality, even if it is hard to gauge its dimensions precisely. A similar pattern, moreover, prevailed in Western Ukraine as a whole. By the summer of 1941, nearly two-thirds of the thirty-seven thousand or so party members and candidates in Western Ukraine were Ukrainians, almost one-fifth Russians, and less than one-sixth Jews. Poles were included in "other nationalities," together not quite 5 percent of the total (ibid.).

203 Kostiantin Kondratiuk and Ivana Luchakivska, "Zakhidnaukrainska intelihentsiia u pershi roky radianskoi vlady (veresen 1939—cherven 1941)," *Visnyk Lvivskoho universytetu*, no. 33 (1998): 178.

204 Pankivskyi, *Vid derzhavy do komitetu*, 23–24.

205 Ibid., 26–27.

206 DALO R-119, 3, 24: 1–2. Marchenko had a complex career. Born in a village near Kyiv in 1902, he owed his advance to Komsomol and party activism and his training in Ukrainian history at a Red Professors institute (Redzik, *Wydział Prawa Uniwersytetu Lwowskiego*, 139). Having also been in some trouble during a purge in the 1930s, he was later arrested again for "Ukrainian nationalism" in the summer of 1941. Marchenko's grandson became a Ukrainian dissident and died under arrest and medical neglect (M. V. Koval, "Polityka proty istorii: Ukrainska istorychna nauka v druhii svitovii viini i pershi povoyenni roky," *Ukrainsky istorychny zhurnal*, no. 1 [2002], 14). Two years later, Barvinskyi reported to the new German authorities that working under Soviet rule had meant living between "Scylla and Charybdis," but he still stressed that he had been the first Ukrainian director of the library (DALO R-1295, 1, 13: 4–5).

The university also was a site where some local and eastern Ukrainians advanced together: Marchenko arrived in Lviv without a higher academic decree, as a political-administrative cadre with the Soviet forces.[207] New academic positions for Lviv's Ukrainian elite were well paid, at least for important scholars, and their satisfaction was publicized.[208]

Yet intra-Ukrainian differences could not simply be abolished, even by Stalinist fiat. On the contrary, the power differentials of unification by conquest made latent differences acute. For some, Galicia belonged to a culturally superior Europe, while Soviet power appeared "Asian" and backward. Yet Galicia's privileged association with Europe was inseparable from Habsburg and Polish dominance, which both Soviet and Ukrainian nationalist discourses condemned as foreign "occupation" or "colonialism." Moreover, superior ties to Europe had become an "article of faith in Ukrainian national ideology" in general.[209] This touched on long-standing issues of the relationship between Ukraine and Russia, while Galician Ukrainians also had a tradition of insecurity about their own place, preceding and independent of Soviet discourses of backwardness.[210]

From an eastern perspective, by 1945 Soviet film director Oleksandr Dovzhenko was lamenting what he called the tragedy of the liberation and unification of 1939, when, in effect, the "Ukrainian people" had "played no role at all," being split by diverging aims and "six hundred years of different foreign lands," making them "pray [and] think differently."[211] Dovzhenko, the maker of the most important Soviet propaganda documentary on the 1939 campaign against Poland, was skeptical in private.[212] He was afraid of the effects of eastern "Asiatic" clumsiness on Western Ukraine, with easterners carrying west "our boorishness, tactlessness," and "lack of culture."[213] Yet Dovzhenko still celebrated Ukrainian unification, because now all Ukrainians would be the same, with easterners no longer despising "Galicians for being better and more cultivated" and Galicians

207 Tamara Marusyk, *Zakhidnoukrainska humanitarna intelihentsia: Realii zhyttia ta diialnosti* (Chernivtsi: Ruta, 2002), 37–38; Redzik, *Wydział Prawa Uniwersytetu Lwowskiego*, 140.

208 *Pravda*, 3 January 1940, 4.

209 Roman Szporluk, "The Making of Modern Ukraine: The Western Dimension," *Harvard Ukrainian Studies* 25 (2001): 73.

210 In a private correspondence of 1922, Ivan Krypiakevych had admitted to not expecting too many interesting publications from a Galicia too stuck in its provincialism (Isaievych, *Ivan Krypiakevych u rodynnii tradytsii*, 39).

211 Cited in *Kulturne Zhittya*, 1:309–10.

212 On Dovzhenko's *The Liberation of the Ukrainian and Belarussian Lands from the Yoke of the Polish Masters and the Unification of Fraternal Peoples into a Single Family* as part of a war-induced revitalization of the Soviet documentary genre, see Jay Leyda, *Kino: A History of Russian and Soviet Film: A Study of the Development of Russian Cinema from 1896 to the Present*, 3rd ed. (Princeton, NJ: Princeton University Press, 1983), 357–59.

213 Danylenko et al., *Radianski orhany*, 1073–74 (doc. 457), 1152 (doc. 483), 1172 (doc. 490).

not fearing easterners for being "big and tough, 'non-independent' people."[214] Between West and East, insecurities collided no less than swaggering claims.

Unlike Dovzhenko, Milena Rudnytska, a longtime member of the interwar Polish parliament and an activist for women's issues and moderate Ukrainian nationalism, did lose hope. Initially she tried to work for the Soviet authorities, welcoming Soviet measures that expropriated Jewish trade.[215] Yet she soon fled to the German zone and wrote to her fellow refugee Nazaruk that twenty "years of fighting with Poland" had not exhausted her "as much as three weeks of 'cooperation' with the Bolsheviks."[216]

Rudnytska was most frightened by the possibility that Soviet rule was, in fact, reshaping Ukrainians. "Getting to know the compatriots from Greater Ukraine" was among her "most shameful experiences." The fact that they spoke "excellent Ukrainian" only made it worse. Ironically, the absence of any literal language barrier revealed that they were "so foreign to us" that no "common language at all" seemed possible.

Rudnytska had believed in the manifest destiny of a "Galician Piedmont." For her, Soviet Ukrainians had been a potential target of Western Ukrainian nationalizing tutelage, but she felt that their Soviet miseducation had already become irreversible. Reporting these fears to Nazaruk, she challenged his convictions. Nazaruk's 1936 publication "Galicia and Great Ukraine" had argued that Galician Ukrainians, the "organizationally highest type" among Ukrainians, must not mix, socially or sexually, with the disorganized eastern types, lest they drown in their "Ukrainian chaos."[217]

Nazaruk was an ordinary European racist of his time, believing in Aryans and other tribes. His racist distinctions between Ukrainians, articulated in an idiom of organization and culture, elevated the Galician Ukrainians to a "human Gulf Stream," destined to nurture the nation, and dismissed easterners as

214 Oleksandr Dovzhenko, *Ukrainy v ohni: Kinopovist, shchodennyk* (Kyiv: Rad. pysmennyk, 1990), 238, 251.

215 Rudnytska had no record of Soviet sympathies. In the early 1930s, during the murderous famine in Soviet Ukraine, Rudnytska condemned the Soviet Union for a policy of "Russian imperialism" and the "physical destruction of the Ukrainian people," denouncing its admission to the League of Nations as a "humiliation of Western culture." See R. Kushnezh, "Uchast ukrainskoi hromadskosti Polshi v dopomohovykh ta protestatsiinykh aktsiiakh proty holodomoru v Ukraine," *Ukrainsky istorichny zhurnal*, no. 2 (2005): 138. Christoph Mick underlines that Rudnytska "did not agree with the general accusation of collaboration levelled against Jews." At the same time, she also thought that Soviet employment of Jews was due to the fact that "with the exception of them [the Bolsheviks] often have nobody else on whom they can depend" (Mick, "Incompatible Experiences," 345). She still stereotypically assumed that only Jews were loyal to Soviet rule and others not.

216 Diadiuk, *Milena Rudnytska*, 590–92.

217 Osyp Nazaruk, *Halychyna i Velyka Ukraina* (Lviv: Nova zoria, 1936), 37, 42–43, and 46.

contaminated "Creoles." Thus, his fear of pollution and longing for purity defined the most important Other of Galician Ukrainians as not Russians or Poles or Jews but other Ukrainians. But he found hope in his ideas about gender. Distinguishing between Galician Ukrainian men and women, he concluded that males must never marry east, while females could. Honey-trapped males, he reasoned, were so weak they would descend to the level of their new eastern niche. Females, however, fortified by Greek Catholicism, would lift their family up to western order.[218]

After her experience under Soviet rule, Rudnytska homed in with devastating precision on Nazaruk's last great Galician hope, explaining why eastern Ukrainians were irredeemably Soviet. She warned that they would not "stop being themselves" to "become the kind of people we are." The Bolsheviks had, after all, made a difference. In principle, a Ukrainian Galician woman, Rudnytska agreed, could improve an Eastern Ukrainian man, but only if he were "of the pre-Bolshevik period." Out of a Soviet Eastern Ukrainian man, she insisted, "even ten Galician women won't make anything." Rudnytska's crisis of national belief engendered fantasies not only of polygamy but also of extermination, making her ask "with terror" if it would "not be necessary to wipe out thousands" of "compatriots, mainly the young generation" since "it was as "impossible to reeducate them" as "to tolerate them the way they are."[219] It was not Soviet terror but apparent Soviet success that made Rudnytska despair over nationalism's axiom that national identity was the deepest identity, if not the only one. To her, being Soviet no longer appeared as exogenous to Eastern Ukrainians, but rather ingrained beyond reprieve. Rudnytska argued that Soviet Eastern Ukrainians' "completely different mental education" made them "more foreign to us than any other European people." Like Nazaruk's hope, her fear was, ultimately, racist, with Eastern Ukrainians evoking "African savages" and "a zoo." Soviet rule, she concluded, had "pulled the country, *including Ukraine*, two hundred years into the past," with its "isolation from Europe."[220]

Dovzhenko would find the solution to his personal Europe/Asia dilemma in making Eastern Ukrainians a third group between Europe and Asia, while Soviet Ukrainian unification propelled Rudnytska in the opposite direction. Instead of trying to save national unity from the Europe/Asia polarity, she radically acknowledged that polarity: Ukraine would now be entirely Soviet and Asian. Crediting Bolshevism with the power to remake Ukrainians, she was ready to give up on the nation.

218 Ibid., 152.
219 Diadiuk, *Milena Rudnytska*, 591.
220 Ibid., 594–95 (my emphasis).

The Jewish Encounter

Generally, Soviet conquest brought massive disruption to the shtetl, still a key site of Jewish life in the newly conquered territories.[221] At the same time, Jewish reactions to the Soviet occupation of eastern Poland included relief at not facing Germans and hopes inspired by the end of interwar antisemitic Polish policies.[222] Moreover, especially for the poor and the young, the Soviet regime did offer some genuine opportunities.[223] In Lviv, Joachim Schoenfeld, a Jewish refugee, already past his first Soviet arrest as a "spy," still appreciated that his son could now enter the Polytechnic, formerly infamous for its antisemitic incidents.[224] Marian Pretzel's family lived in fear of deportation; his father was demoted from business owner to salesman. Yet, as a Jew, Marian also remembered prewar antisemitism and restrictions on his prospects of higher education. By March 1940, Soviet statistics showed almost seven hundred Jewish students at Lviv University, the largest single group out of a total of 1,835.[225] In Pretzel's experience, "the Russians" ended discrimination and opened a path to personal independence. Leon Weliczker-Wells, too, while temporarily hiding from deportation, would remember that it was under Soviet rule that he first thought of higher education.[226]

The Jewish encounter with Soviet rule was complex, however. One challenge was a meeting between different ways of being Jewish, not entirely unlike the one between Western and eastern Ukrainians. Historically, there had been not only cultural affinity between Jews in Habsburg Galicia and those in the Russian Empire but also mutual condescension for what was perceived as the other's backwardness or lack of piety or proper Yiddish.[227]

In important respects, the Soviet authorities treated their new Jewish subjects differently from Ukrainians and Belarusians. The conquest of Western Ukraine increased Soviet Ukraine's Jewish population from 1.5 million to 2.35 million or from 5 to 6 percent of the total.[228] Yet only Ukrainians and Belarusians were slated for both national and social "liberation." In other ways, however, Soviet rule treated Lviv's Jews like its Poles and Ukrainians, depriving them of a rich

221 Ben-Cion Pinchuk, "Sovietization of the Shtetl of Eastern Poland, 1939–1941," in *Essays on Revolutionary Culture and Stalinism*, ed. John W. Strong (Columbus, OH: Slavica, 1990), 73.

222 Levin, *Lesser of Two Evils*, 31–47, 59.

223 A contemporary recalled that shtetl youth "bloomed" and was echoed "by many others" (Pinchuk, "Sovietization of the Shtetl," 74).

224 Schoenfeld, *Holocaust Memoirs*, 30.

225 Redzik, *Wydział Prawa Uniwersytetu Lwowskiego*, 205.

226 Marian Pretzel, *Portrait of a Young Forger: A Memoir of Wartime Adventures* (St. Lucia: University of Queensland Press, 1993), 33–36; Wells, "Interview."

227 Wolff, *Idea of Galicia*, 345, 354.

228 Dieter Pohl, "The Murder of Ukraine's Jews under German Military Administration and in the Reich Commissariat Ukraine," in *The Shoah in Ukraine: History, Testimony, Memorialization*, ed. Brandon and Lower, 24.

array of political and social leadership and institutions.[229] Jews of all political backgrounds were arrested and deported.[230] Like Ukrainians, Lviv's Jews were exposed to a local show trial of young underground activists.[231] Lviv's Gmina (Kehile) Jewish religious community organization was dissolved, its property confiscated, forcing Jews, as the Lwów legal scholar Maurycy Allerhand later had to explain to the Germans, to "gather around individual synagogues."[232]

While some Ukrainians and Poles denounced a special relationship between Jews and Communism, some Soviets were constructing special relationships between local Jews and backwardness. Interwar Soviet propaganda had devised the image of a "new Jew," characterized by "hardened . . . body and intellect" and "en route to the Soviet version of a modern, renovated humanity.[233] In Viktor Shklovsky's reporting, Lviv's Jews, frantic with street trade, represented "the old world." Becoming Soviet and modern meant becoming unrecognizable as a Jew. Shklovsky's local Jews asked why Soviet Jews had faces with a "non-Jewish expression." The Soviet Jewish drivers, tank crews, doctors, and soldiers, with their "quiet tenderness, patient and forgiving talk, the absence of abrupt intonation" were, according to Shklovsky, "for the local people Jews and, again, not."[234]

While Lviv's Poles were facing oscillating demotion and its Ukrainians conditional promotion, its Jews were confronted with the most confusing blend of Soviet demands and offers: to achieve full equality in a deeply unequal, unfree, and bafflingly sui generis polity of citizen-subjects, one of whose principal obligations was to pretend that all were equal and free. This official Soviet narrative juxtaposed an age of Polish darkness with Soviet liberation, a crude myth that could not accommodate the reality of Jewish experiences. In interwar Poland, Jews had been citizens of a state becoming increasingly authoritarian and antisemitic. Especially in the first and last years of interwar Poland, discrimination was widespread; by the 1930s, Poland's public space was marked by open antisemitism, in the form of assaults, economic boycotts, exclusion, and state policies aiming at

229 Ezra Mendelsohn, "Introduction: The Jews of Poland between Two World Wars—Myth and Reality," in *The Jews of Poland between Two World Wars*, ed. Yisrael Gutman et al. (Hanover, NH: University Press of New England, 1989), 16.

230 Jones, *Żydzi Lwowa w okresie okupacji*, 27–28, 38–42.

231 Ibid., 42, for the March 1941 show trial of seven Hashomer Hatsair activists. For two Lviv trials of Ukrainians accused of nationalist activity in 1940 and 1941, and another mass trial in neighboring Drohobych, producing, together, about fifty state killings, see Motyka, *Ukraińska partyzantka*, 85–86. On the 1941 trial in Lviv, see also Liuba Komar, *Protses 59-ty* (Lviv: Naukove tovarystvo im. Shevchenka, 1997).

232 ŻIH 229/4: 2 (USHMM RG-15.069).

233 Jonathan Dekel-Chen, "'New' Jews of the Agricultural Kind: A Case of Soviet Interwar Propaganda," *Russian Review* 66 (2007): 446.

234 Shklovsky, "Rasskazy o Zapadnoi Ukraine," 31.

large-scale emigration.[235] By 1937, the government was working toward depriving Jews of their citizenship.[236] In the 1930s, Poland's Jews were pauperized more than Poland's population as a whole, not only from the Great Depression but also from targeted discrimination and a severe tax burden.[237]

On the eve of the Second World War, antisemitism had left fresh scars in Lwów.[238] Its Polytechnic was the first Polish university to impose "ghetto bench" segregation in lectures.[239] Most restrictions on Jewish admissions to higher education were not law but operated de facto. Between the early 1920s and the late 1930s, the share of Jewish students at Polish universities decreased from a quarter to less than a tenth.[240] The introduction of segregation by "ghetto benches" brought a further "drastic decrease."[241]

Yet Polish Jews did not lose their citizenship or political representation before Poland lost its state. Whereas the German Nuremberg Laws of 1935 found a "positive echo" in Poland, attempts at local racial ordinances failed.[242] In interwar Poland, Yisrael Gutman argues, antisemitism "did not destroy Jewish social and cultural activities."[243] Lwów remained an important center

235 Levin, *Lesser of Two Evils*, 26. On growing antisemitism in the interwar years in general and in Warsaw, see Israel Gutman, *Resistance: The Warsaw Ghetto Uprising* (New York: Houghton Mifflin, 1994), 14–48; and Emanuel Melzer, "Antisemitism in the Last Years of the Second Polish Republic," in *Jews of Poland*, ed. Gutman et al.

236 Yfaat Weiss, *Deutsche und polnische Juden vor dem Holocaust: Jüdische Identität zwischen Staatsbürgerschaft und Ethnizität 1933–1940* (Munich: Oldenbourg, 2000), 108–12; Szymon Rudnicki, "Anti-Jewish Legislation in Interwar Poland," in *Antisemitism and its Opponents in Modern Poland*, ed. Robert Blobaum (Ithaca, NY: Cornell University Press, 2005), 160–61.

237 Ezra Mendelsohn, *The Jews of East Central Europe Between the World Wars* (Bloomington: Indiana University Press, 1983), 74; Antony Polonsky, *The Jews in Poland and Russia* (Oxford: The Littman Library of Jewish Civilization, 2012), 3:95.

238 A Jewish defendant's trial in Lwów for an assassination attempt on the Polish president was the occasion for antisemitic demonstrations in 1924; the defendant was acquitted. In 1929, Polish local and central authorities suppressed what Antony Polonsky has called a "failed pogrom" ("A Failed Pogrom: The Demonstrations in Lwów, June 1929," in *Jews of Poland*, ed. Gutman et al., 109–25). In 1935–1938 a fierce campaign to introduce separate seating (so-called ghetto benches) for Jews at Lwów University and the Polytechnic succeeded. In 1938 and 1939, six Jewish students were murdered (Pohl, *Nationalsozialistische Judenverfolgung in Ostgalizien*, 26–27).

239 Levin, *Lesser of Two Evils*, 26; Rudnicki, "Anti-Jewish Legislation," 165.

240 Bauer, *Death of the Shtetl*, 17.

241 Weiss, *Deutsche und polnische Juden*, 113.

242 Ibid., 114. Jewish representation in the Polish parliament was in effect curtailed by a constitutional reform and electoral changes in 1934 (Levin, *Lesser of Two Evils*, 26). In 1938, the Polish government made an ominous breach in the citizenship status of Polish Jews when it deprived some of them who were living in Germany of it (Pohl, *Nationalsozialistische Judenverfolgung in Ostgalizien*, 27). Yet the practice was not extended to Poland itself.

243 Yisrael Gutman, "Polish Antisemitism between the Wars: An Overview," in *Jews of Poland*, ed. Gutman et al., 103–5.

for Jews with, on the eve of the war, the third-largest Jewish population in Poland.[244]

In the German zone, Nazi occupation "wrought a transition from an era of human troubles to one of inhumanity and destruction."[245] In the Soviet zone, however, outcomes were different. The party-state, rather than systematically marginalizing or murdering the Jews, suppressed the richness of Jewish identity. Forced to pretend that they were citizens for the first time, in reality Jews found their autonomy and self-expression violently reduced.

Soviet simplifications proved a bad fit for Lviv's complexities, with no room for combined Polish-Jewish identities. The Holocaust survivor Kurt Lewin, victimized by German as well as Ukrainian and Polish antisemitism, would still remember Lviv's prewar Jews as the "greatest support" of its Polishness.[246] Yet when forced to write a memorandum for the *Gestapo* during the German occupation, Maurycy Allerhand, defining himself as Polish by nationality, described "assimilationists, that is, Jews declaring Polish nationality" as a "minority on the point of vanishing."[247] It was true: the mid-nineteenth-century elite project of a synthetic Jewish-Polish identity had mostly failed.[248]

But in an essentializing Soviet world, with Jews forced to use "progressive" Yiddish and not "reactionary" and "Zionist" Hebrew, those who would have preferred Polish did not matter.[249] For some Jewish authors and artists, already expressing themselves in Yiddish, the Soviet occupation brought opportunities. There were Yiddish radio broadcasts; Dov Levin has identified Soviet-occupied eastern Galicia as a "hotbed of Jewish theater activity."[250]

244 Wolfdieter Bihl, "Die Juden," in *Die Habsburgermonarchie 1848–1918*, 3, pt. 1: *Die Völker des Reiches*, ed. Adam Wandruska and Peter Urbanitsch (Vienna: Verlag der Österreichischen Akademie der Wissenschaften, 1980), 937; Mazur, "Skic do dziejów stosumków polsko-żydowskich," in *Świat niepożegany*, ed. Jasiewicz, 401.

245 Gutman, *Resistance*, 48.

246 Lewin, *Przeżyłem*, 32.

247 ŻIH 229/4: 3 (USHMM RG-15.069).

248 Theodore R. Weeks, "The Best of Both Worlds: Creating the *Żyd-Polak*," *East European Jewish Affairs* 34 (2004): 16.

249 On the relationship between Hebrew/Aramaic, modernizing Hebrew, and modernizing Yiddish from the Middle Ages up until a modern Yiddish language was installed as the one and only legitimate national Jewish language in the Soviet Union at the beginning of the 1920s, see David Shneer, *Yiddish and the Creation of Soviet Jewish Culture, 1918–1930* (Cambridge: Cambridge University Press, 2004), 30–41.

250 Levin, *Lesser of Two Evils*, 131–45. Behind the scenes, however, hierarchy mattered and even official Soviet Jewish culture ranked low. Initially, Lviv's Ukrainian opera and theater and its Polish theater were put in the second tier of Soviet theater salaries and funding; the Jewish theater in the third. Making their 1940 Polish turn, the Soviet authorities upgraded the Polish theater to tier one, then considered it politic to do the same for Ukrainians; the Jewish theater's rank was not even discussed (RGASPI 17, 125, 313: 7–9).

Yet much of the Soviet-Jewish encounter occurred in the everyday life of schools. Modern school systems create deep interactions between individual subjectivity and the state.[251] In interwar Poland, in particular, education had been at the "core of Jewish activity."[252] Over the whole area occupied by the Soviet Union between 1939 and 1941, half the "members of the [school] system (students, teachers, parents, and families) were Jewish."[253]

In the interwar Soviet Union, the school system had been the "initial site of contested Jewish language politics," with the suppression of Hebrew and the compulsory ascendancy of Yiddish shaping official Soviet Jewish identity.[254] At the same time, in interwar Poland's last census in 1931, 88 percent of all Polish Jews identified Yiddish as their native language, but in the region of Lwów only 65 percent did.[255] In general, the census figures should not eclipse what contemporary observers noted: that "the new Jewish generation was at least to some extent becoming culturally Polonized."[256] In the former Galicia in particular, Polish influences were, if anything, stronger.[257] During his interwar trip in Poland, Döblin had noted that in Lwów Polish was the language of the "Jewish intelligentsia and upper classes."[258] Döblin may just have been traveling through, but his observation coincided with the experience of those growing up in interwar Lwów, such as Marian Pretzel and his sister Giza, who learned Polish and no Yiddish.[259] Shimon Redlich recalled "growing up in Polish" in a small town fifty miles from interwar Lwów. Polish, replacing German, was turning into "the second language of the younger generation," with "Galician Jewry . . . the most Polonized part of the Jewish population in Poland before the Second World War."[260]

Thus the Soviet demand to abandon Polish in education hit many Jews especially hard. Lwów's prewar Jewish community had three Jewish secondary schools with teaching in Polish.[261] The Soviet authorities, however, imposed Yiddish-language teaching on them and on the city's Jewish teacher-training institutions. By 1940, about a third of all Jewish children in Lviv oblast attended schools

251 Catherine Wanner, *Burden of Dreams: History and Identity in Post-Soviet Ukraine* (University Park: Pennsylvania State University Press, 1998), 79–80, 90.

252 Yitzhak Arad, *The Holocaust in the Soviet Union* (Lincoln: University of Nebraska Press: 2009), 27.

253 Levin, *Lesser of Two Evils*, 89.

254 Shneer, *Yiddish and the Creation of Soviet Jewish Culture*, 41, 46.

255 Pohl, *Nationalsozialistische Judenverfolgung in Ostgalizien*, 24.

256 Mendelsohn, *Jews of East Central Europe*, 67.

257 Sean Martin, *Jewish Life in Cracow, 1918–1939* (London: Vallentine Mitchell, 2004), 244.

258 Quoted in Martin, *Jewish Life in Cracow*, 51.

259 Pretzel, *Portrait of a Young Forger*, 10.

260 Shimon Redlich, *Together and Apart in Brzezany: Poles, Jews, and Ukrainians, 1919–1945* (Bloomington: Indiana University Press, 2002), 38, 35, 41.

261 Polonsky, "Introduction," in *Private War*, ed. Gerstenfeld-Maltiel, xi.

officially teaching in Yiddish, which was an "enormous increase in the number of schools with Yiddish as the teaching language."[262]

Yet the manner in which Yiddish was introduced in Jewish schools was at least as important as its new official status. A Soviet official explained that the Polish state and its language were gone, while in the Soviet Union Yiddish was equal to other languages.[263] Yet most teachers did not know Yiddish well; in reality, teaching was only partly in Yiddish and partly still in Polish. Thus, teachers and pupils who wanted Polish were not only made to use a language they did not know well or at all but to agree that this language was their own. Moreover, Hebrew was also suppressed. First, Soviet authorities decided that their new subjects must be liberated from Polish to be authentic in their own culture. Second, within that culture, they decided what exactly was authentic—that is, Yiddish but not Hebrew.

This Soviet message played in reverse, too. Enforcing Yiddish implied that a preference for Polish was inauthentic, even a betrayal. The Soviet authorities insisted that Lwów's Jews adapt in the present; they also cast a shadow over their pasts, making Polish a sign of a lack of self-assertion, while suppressing a sacred language with significance second to none in Jewish identity. Finally, at the end of the 1940 school year, the same authorities reduced Yiddish to one subject among others. Officials explained that the schools were in a city on Ukrainian territory and pupils now had to switch to Ukrainian.[264]

Soviet rule did not merely impose its own restrictive idea of Jewish identity. Inevitably, while robustly set against open antisemitism, the Soviet interaction with its local variant proved complex. As if under a magnifying lens, the case of Natalia S. showed how Lviv's ethnic tension and antisemitism intersected with Soviet social transformation and repression. In November 1940, Natalia appealed against her recent deportation to Central Asia, arguing that it was "the result exclusively of the fact that I am Jewish," and "my neighbors [in Lviv were] Poles."[265] She presented her own biography in detail. Her family was poor, her father had died eight years before, and her mother was an invalid. In interwar Poland, she and her brother had had no access to higher education or state employment because they were Jewish. Twenty-six years old, she had been working in different jobs for nine years but, she insisted, never as a prostitute, an allegation that may have featured in denunciations of her.

262 Jones, *Żydzi Lwowa w okresie okupacji*, 31.

263 Andrzej Żbikowski, ed., *Archiwum Ringelbluma: Konspiracyjne Archiwum Getta Warszawy*, 3: *Relacje z Kresów* (Warsaw: PWN, 2000), 792–96 (document no. 42). According to the editors of the "Ringelblum Archive" volumes, the author of this report was probably Stanisław Różycki.

264 Jones, *Żydzi Lwowa w okresie okupacji*, 32; Żbikowski, *Archiwum Ringelbluma*, 3:792–96 (document no. 42).

265 DALO-R 221, 1, 247: 239–43, for Natalia S.'s letter.

Claiming she had studied the Stalin Constitution before the war, she recalled her great expectations of Soviet rule, feeling "for the first time . . . a member of society with equal rights," convinced that "a bright shining life had begun." Having worked as a Soviet trade inspector and then a translator at an NKVD passport office, she epitomized the sudden visibility of Jews in the lower Soviet bureaucracy, which interacted with traditional stereotypes and prejudice.[266] While working for or with Soviets was inevitable, ordinary, and widespread, many observers perceived it through a prism of stereotypes when it involved Jews.[267]

Natalia thought that her non-Jewish neighbors' denunciation and her subsequent deportation were due to such prejudice but had been triggered by Soviet forced redistribution. When she had received a room in a "Polish quarter," Natalia's new neighbors failed to welcome her, because, she wrote, she was "Jewish and proletarian."[268] There was no heating in her room. Yet the winter of 1939/1940 was harsh, with firewood prices shooting up thirteen times.[269] Sleeping on the floor, she fell ill and was hospitalized. While she was away, the frozen pipes in her rooms burst, and she dated her neighbors' denunciations from the flooding.

At this point, Natalia was hit not only by the contingency of a fierce winter but also by a combination of local prejudice and an essential practice of Soviet social transformation: the redistribution of residential space.[270] Claims to receive this "living space" and to see others deprived and humiliated were inseparable in newly Soviet Lviv. At a 1940 oblast party meeting, an officer complained that many military men were still living in tents while priests and "some sort of scientific workers" kept "seven-room" apartments, although they should be "resettled

266 Jan T. Gross, "A Tangled Web: Confronting Stereotypes concerning Relations between Poles, Germans, Jews, and Communists," in *The Politics of Retribution in Europe*, ed. Deák et al., 98; Yosef Litvak, "The Plight of Refugees from the German-Occupied Territories," in *The Soviet Takeover of the Soviet Eastern Provinces, 1939–1941*, ed. Keith Sword (London: Macmillan, 1991), 61–62; Michael C. Steinlauf, *Bondage to the Dead: Poland and the Memory of the Holocaust* (Syracuse, NY: University of Syracuse Press, 1997), 36; August Grabski, *Działalność komnistów wśród Żydów w Polsce, 1944–1949* (Warsaw: Trio, 2004), 30–35, esp. 34; Pohl, *Nationalsozialistische Judenverfolgung in Ostgalizien*, 31.

267 Osyp Nazaruk, for instance, was indignant at a Red Army soldier he guessed to be Jewish harassing civilians, shouting more than "all the other Red Army soldiers taken together" (Nazaruk, *Zi Lvova do Varshavy*, 22–25, 36). Excluding Jews from national solidarity, some Polish underground activists approached their Soviet enemies with an offer to exchange a prisoner for information not just about any speculators, but Jewish ones (Wnuk, *"Za pierwszego sowieta,"* 111).

268 DALO-R 221, 1, 247: 239–43.

269 Hryciuk, *Polacy we Lwowie*, 83.

270 Julia Obertreis, *Tränen des Sozialismus: Wohnen in Leningrad zwischen Alltag und Utopie 1917–1937* (Cologne: Böhlau, 2004), 35. In fact, forced redistribution of residential space was the topic of the first Soviet feature film, which premiered for the first anniversary of the October Revolution (ibid.).

in the basement."[271] One year into "liberation," *Pravda* boasted that, in Lviv, Soviet rule had broken down "the invisible yet firm barriers between the center and the outskirts, between Polish, Ukrainian, and Jewish quarters," claiming ethnic as well as social redistribution.[272] Announced in the local press, the redistribution of apartments, with the partial or complete eviction of inhabitants and compulsory assignment of new ones, was bound to be interpreted in ethnic as well as class terms. Where the social was so clearly punitive, moreover, the ethnic took on a similar aspect, meshing with local stereotypes and tensions. A Polish diarist believed that he recognized "a Jewish or Jewish-Ukrainian 'commission'" in those taking the buildings.[273]

Natalia, seeing herself as a victim of antisemitism and class prejudice, also generalized, telling the Soviet authorities that her constant harassment by Polish fellow deportees during their long train trip east was "characteristic of the attitude of Poles to Jews." They had taunted her: "There, you Jews welcomed the Red Army with flowers, and look, what Soviet power has done to you—deported you . . . just like us." Natalia's petition produced an order to review her case.[274]

Soviet rule did not bring antisemitism to its new borderlands. Yet if Natalia's interpretation was correct, Soviet power could end up unintentionally implementing local antisemitism with specific methods not yet seen in Lviv. Prewar Poland had simply not offered the option of having individual Jews deported thousands of miles to Central Asia through a well-targeted denunciation. Simultaneously instrumentalizing and benefiting Natalia by giving her a room in a "Polish quarter," Soviet rule not only permitted the intrigue and denunciation that led to her deportation from the city but also created a world in which neighbors could denounce one another for deportation. Locked up in their boxcar, the deportees then kept fighting along ethnic lines. Polish passengers harassed an essentialized Jew, and at the end of the trip, a Jewish deportee denounced essentialized Poles in general.

271 DALO P-3, 1, 12: 85.

272 D. Kosov, "Sovetskii god vo Lvove," *Pravda*, 29 August 1940, 4. In reality, the Soviet confiscation practice was by no means generally favorable to Jews. Włodzimierz Bonusiak has found that most complaints about the confiscations of premises came from Jews because they were often heavily affected by being deprived of business as well as residence premises ("Sowietyzacja kultury Lwowa," 566).

273 Hryciuk, *Polacy we Lwowie*, 80.

274 DALO R-221, 1, 247: 239–43. The outcome of her case is not clear from the record. In a terrible manner she could not have foreseen, in the end Natalia was lucky if her request to return to Lviv was not granted. According to Thomas Sandkühler's estimate, "probably 30,000 Jews," deported from the occupied Polish territories as a whole, died in Soviet camps or on the way there. But the deportations also offered a chance of survival for another 90,000–100,000 Jewish deportees, who might otherwise have fallen into Nazi hands after the German invasion of 1941 (Sandkühler, *"Endlösung" in Galizien*, 62).

Natalia's promotion, denunciation, deportation, and complaint also traced a Soviet power invisible to her and her fellow deportees. She thought that her new Soviet living space triggered conflict with her new Polish neighbors. She could not know that one explicit yet internal purpose of deportation was to make room for Soviet officials.[275] Thus, she could see her deportation literally only as due to an assault by her neighbors, "from below," as it were. In this way, pre-Soviet tensions and the visible and invisible modes of Soviet power reinforced each other. The Soviet story held, and the shock of Soviet violence led to even more confrontation among its new subjects.

What happened in and to Lviv between the fall of 1939 and the summer of 1941 was one of the first instances of Sovietization during the Second World War. This would have been literally unthinkable—first of all, to the Sovietizers themselves—without their vision of Soviet modernity and Lviv's backwardness. The conquered, meanwhile, often responded by negating Soviet claims of superiority and pointing to Soviet backwardness.

During the first Soviet occupation of Lviv, the conquering party-state was dealing with three main ethno-religious or national groups: Poles, Jews, and Ukrainians. In stark contrast to the situation after 1944, there were three local ethnic identities and no attempt to remove any of them. During Lviv's first Soviet occupation, the party-state was ruling a borderland city with its traditional multiethnic population fundamentally intact, even if terribly battered.

Soviet policies demoted Poles but did not destroy or remove them; they offered the local Ukrainians ascendancy in return for adopting Soviet Ukrainian identity; they imposed a Soviet Jewish "emancipated" identity on Jews. Lviv was, in fact, becoming a microcosm of the recently developed Soviet concept of the "Friendship of the Peoples," which accorded an indispensable, if subordinate and historically transitory, role to a primordially understood national identity.[276]

It is important to note, that in this early version of Soviet Lviv, this idea of a multinational Soviet body politic seemed to fit local circumstances. There was an unpeaceful meeting of minds: Polish-Ukrainian rivalry had focused on institutions and symbols of culture long before the Soviet arrival, and using culture for national policy came easily to the Soviet conquerors, too. While specific outcomes of preference and discrimination were at the center of contention, the *principle* of demoting and promoting the culture of national groups via institutions of

275 Hryciuk, *Polacy we Lwowie*, 37; Litvak, "Plight of Refugees," in *Soviet Takeover*, ed. Sword, 60. For the relevant Soviet decrees, see Instytut Pamięci Narodowej, *Deportacje obywateli polskich*, 354–66, esp. 356, 364, 716–18.

276 Martin, *Affirmative Action Empire*, 444–48.

higher education and science or language policies, for instance, seemed simple and obvious to many. For a moment, it seemed as if the tensions of prewar Lwów and the Soviet nationality policy in the new Lviv could converge—given enough compulsion, perhaps the only resource never scarce under Stalinism.

Yet could there really be a lasting Friendship of the Peoples in one city, when two of the peoples in that city regarded it as one of their prime and exclusive national symbols? Could the Soviet nationality-policy paradigm solve what neither Habsburg nor interwar Polish policy could? Could a Soviet Lviv based on the simultaneous demotion and presence of the formerly ascendant Poles be stable? Could Galician Ukrainians become Soviet Ukrainians, while Lviv remained a demographically non-Ukrainian city with a non-Ukrainian majority? It was only the German attack on the Soviet Union in June 1941 that turned these questions into counterfactuals.

CHAPTER THREE

The Lemberg of Nazism

German Occupation, 1941–1944

Early Soviet rule in Lviv began to end on 22 June 1941 with Germany's attack on the Soviet Union. Within six days, after killing prisoners and destroying documents, Soviet forces and authorities fled Lviv.[1] On 30 June, Germans and their Ukrainian nationalist auxiliaries arrived, welcomed by crowds. The German occupation, which began with a pogrom and a Ukrainian nationalist attempt to found a state—de jure sovereign, de facto a Nazi client—brought fresh ruptures, most devastatingly the genocide of the city's Jewish population. German rule also reignited local conflicts that predated the war and extended the effects of Soviet occupation. In this regard, the crucial question is not whether Soviet and German motivations and policies were similar or dissimilar. Notwithstanding the massive violence of Soviet deportations and massacres, in Lviv the German occupation brought forms and extremes of violence that the Soviet occupation had not: Germans did, solicited, and allowed things that were unprecedented and remained unique. Yet in the experience of a society reshaped by both forces in quick succession Stalinist and Nazi methods inevitably interacted. They also interacted in the eyes of the new occupiers: for Germans, thinking and talking about what they thought of as Lemberg's Bolshevik legacies became one way of imagining the city and their own role in it. This chapter traces ruptures, continuities, and interactions under German occupation.

Ruling Lemberg: Fantasies and Strategies

Lviv was renamed "Lemberg," and many streets and squares got new, German names. The city's main boulevard was named after Adolf Hitler and a granite

1. On the massacres, see below; on the destruction of the records, see the obkom's postwar report to Moscow (DALO 3, 1, 208: 46).

Figure 3.1 German troops in Lviv, 30 June 1941. Bundesarchiv, Bild 146-1975-081-25. Photographer: König.

block plunked down in his honor in front of the Habsburg Opera House.[2] The designation "Western Ukraine" was prohibited. A Distrikt Galizien was established, largely covering the former eastern Galicia.[3] On 1 August, the Distrikt joined the Generalgouvernement under the Nazi lawyer Hans Frank. A vague, violent construct, the Generalgouvernement was the de facto German occupation regime for most of those parts of Poland not annexed to Germany.[4]

2. Isaievych et al., *Istoriia Lvova*, 3:210. According to postwar obkom figures, 80 percent of Lviv oblast party members, as of 1941, volunteered for Soviet forces (DALO P-1, 183, 170: 3). Not everybody's conduct was exemplary, however. In 1988, the oblast party archive reported that reliable information on Leonid Hryshchuk's war and postwar fate was largely missing but, according to "unconfirmed documents and information," he had dropped out of the fighting in 1941 somewhere around Kyiv to lie low in a village until the Soviet return, when he was expelled from the party. He then worked as head of a *domoupravlenie* building administration in Kyiv until his death at the end of the 1950s (DALO P-1, 1, 319: 13). Lviv's first Communist leader, it seemed, was better forgotten.

3. Werner Präg and Wolfgang Jacobmeyer, eds., *Das Diensttagebuch des deutschen Generalgouverneurs in Polen 1939–1945* (Stuttgart: DVA, 1975), USHMM Acc.1999.A.0194, Reel 4: 672, 687.

4. It was not an occupation regime in the sense by then usual in international law, which would have implied fundamentally recognizing the continuing sovereignty of the occupied state. Instead, having decided not only to conquer but to abolish Poland, the Germans insisted that, with respect to the Generalgouvernement "any reference to 'the occupied territories'" should be avoided (Mazower, *Hitler's Empire*, 76–77).

Lemberg also entered an imaginary space, mixing German fantasies of backwardness and transformation through mass murder. In 1941, with German troops marching east, Frank told fellow Nazis to stand by their slogans with pride.[5] Frank, like Molotov before him, felt that he had capital-H History on his side. The Germans saw their opponents as "dying representatives of doomed epochs."[6] They sought to occupy the past while brutally changing the present: in 1942, Frank would claim Lemberg as regained ancient German territory even as he praised "German fists" for transforming the "old Jew-nest" and "homestead of Polacks."[7] By 1943, with the city's ghetto razed and its Jews murdered, Germans were searching for deep traces of German influence to rename its quarters.[8] The Lemberg branch of the Institut für Deutsche Ostarbeit, a Nazi think tank based in Cracow, researched the early modern German contribution to "Lemberg's economic development" and the "history of German law in Poland and Ukraine in connection with German settlement and trade."[9]

Hitler quickly declared that ultimately the Distrikt would belong to the Reich.[10] The Generalgouvernement's Pressedienst news agency explained his

5. Präg and Jacobmeyer, *Das Diensttagebuch*, USHMM Acc.1999.A.0194, Reel 4: 646.

6. Ibid., 647. This sense of "historic" triumph was not restricted to conquest in Eastern Europe. In the West, too, the same Nazi "euphoria" accompanied victories over "protectors of a dying epoch" (Mazower, *Dark Continent*, 143). Generally Communism played a special role for Germans. Moreover, German warfare and occupation rule in "the East" escalated in deliberate brutality. Yet in the Nazi imagination, Communism, liberal democracy, and the international order—political, legal, and economic—associated with Versailles had in common that all were dismissed as a past on the verge of necessary extinction.

7. Präg and Jacobmeyer, *Das Diensttagebuch*, 532–34.

8. In his quest for Germany's past and future in Lemberg, the German Stadthauptmann, however, had to ask the Polish scholar and archivist Karol Badecki for help (TsDIA 755, 1, 13: 1–3).

9. AUJ IDO 37 Oddział lwowski (Zweigstelle Lemberg). Korespondencja wychodząca 1942–1943, Letter to Erwin Hoff, Institut für Deutsche Ostarbeit, Sektion Geschichte, 20 February 1942, and "Arbeitsgegenstand des Instituts für Rechts- und Vefassungsgeschichte," no pagination, undated. The institute contributed to everyday practice as well as grand theory: it conducted research projects for the military, using eighty "Russian research assistants"; it helped purge Lemberg's street names of some Polish and all Jewish references; it dispatched the Ukrainian Police to confiscate buildings and evict their inhabitants; it ordered menial labor services from the Labor Office of Lviv's Judenrat and, at the peak of the Holocaust in Lemberg, systematically plundered Jewish books for purposes of "Jew Research" (AUJ IDO 37 Oddział lwowski [Zweigstelle Lemberg]. Korespondencja wychodząca 1942–1943, Letter to Stadthauptmann von Lemberg. Deutsches Wohnungsamt, 27 October 1943; letter to Institut für Deutsche Ostarbeit, Herrn Dr. Sommerfeldt, Krakau of 21 September 1942; letter to Stadthauptmann of 21 September 1942; letter to Institut für Deutsche Ostarbeit of 17 September 1942; letter to Jüdisches Arbeitsamt of 30 June 1942; letter to Ukrainische Hilfspolizei of 22 June 1942 and AUJ IDO 38 Oddział lwowski [Zweigstelle Lemberg]. Korespondencja wychodząca, 1941–1942, letter to Institut für Deutsche Ostarbeit [Lviv branch] of 19 December 1942, no pagination).

10. Pohl, *Nationalsozialistische Judenverfolgung in Ostgalizien*, 97. For Hitler's hesitations, however, about making "Galicia" part of the Reich immediately, see Czesław Madajczyk, *Die Okkupationspolitik Nazideutschlands in Polen 1939–1945* (Berlin: Akademieverlag, 1987), 80.

picture on its stamps as "unequivocally" expressing this belonging.[11] Meanwhile, like Soviets, Germans saw Lviv as a forward position: for its new conquerors, Lemberg was as a "bulwark" or "pillar in the quay wall of Europe."[12] The Generalgouvernement as a whole was imagined in a "cultural gradient" zone between a backward Slavic Eastern Europe and a superior German-dominated *Mitteleuropa*.[13] For Lviv's new, German-controlled, Ukrainian daily *Lvivski visti*, Lemberg's *Mitteleuropa*-past guaranteed its future. Although "Bolshevik Asians" had defiled its "European look," it still was a "city of the West."[14] Frank promised that German rule would link Lemberg to a "European cultural community."[15]

Yet Lemberg irritated its new rulers by blending the "German" with a hostile Other. The Generalgouvernement would, Frank foresaw, eventually be home to hundreds of thousands of German veteran families, "settling in nice and comfy." Other inhabitants, especially Jews, would have to disappear, so the Generalgouvernement would become the most "Aryan" area of the future Reich.[16] In March 1942, with the Holocaust in Lviv reaching a peak, Frank confirmed that Germanizing the Generalgouvernement would mean "gradually removing . . . Poles and Ukrainians."[17] German master-plan fantasies of reshaping through genocide, expulsion, and resettlement assumed the absence of Jews and almost

11. Präg and Jacobmeyer, *Das Diensttagebuch*, USHMM Acc.1999.A.0194, Reel 4: 759; DALO R-35, 6, 155: 13 (USHMM Acc.1995.A.1086, Reel 7); R-35, 6, 34: 1 (Yad Vashem Microfilm M-37).

12. Pressedienst des Generalgouvernements, 3 July 1942, DALO R-35, 6, 158: 50 (USHMM Acc.1995.A.1086, Reel 7); Präg and Jacobmeyer, *Das Diensttagebuch*, USHMM Acc.1999.A.0194, Reel 4: 654.

13. Max Freiherr Du Prel, ed., *Das Generalgouvernement: Im Auftrage und mit einem Vorwort des Generalgouverneurs Reichsminister Dr. Frank* (Würzburg: Konrad Triltsch Verlag, 1942), 16.

14. *Lvivski visti*, 13 August 1941, 4 and 29 August 1941, 3. According to the Ukrainian writer Ostap Tarnavskyi, who contributed to its culture pages, *Lvivski visti* was meant to be a popular publication with mass appeal. Like the Polish-language *Gazeta Lwowska, Visti* was under German censorship and control. However, its editorial offices in Lviv—on premises taken over from prewar Polish newspapers—were staffed by Ukrainian journalists and enjoyed, as Tarnavskyi claimed later, more editorial independence under the Germans than under the Soviets (Ostap Tarnawski, *Literacki Lwów 1939–1944: Wspomnienia ukrainskiego pisarza* [Poznan: Bonami, 2004], 139–44, 155). On *Lvivski visti* in general, see Kostiantyn Kurylyshyn, *Ukrainska lehalna presa periodu nimetskoi okupatsii (1939–1944 rr.)* (Lviv: Stefanyka, 2007), 1:514–54. This is plausible as it resembles the situation at *Krakivski visti*, which was an even more important outlet of German as well as Ukrainian nationalist propaganda (John-Paul Himka, "Ethnicity and the Reporting of Mass Murder: *Krakivs'ki visti*, the NKVD Murders of 1941, and the Vinnytsia Exhumation," in *Shatterzone of Empires*, ed. Bartov and Weitz, 379).

15. *Lvivski visti*, 21 October, 1941, 1.

16. Präg and Jacobmeyer, *Das Diensttagebuch*, USHMM Acc.1999.A.0194, Reel 4: 655–57 (the odd English reflects Frank's odd German).

17. Regierungssitzung des Generalgouvernements, 11 March 1942; Präg and Jacobmeyer, *Das Diensttagebuch*, BA R52II/242: 8–10.

two-thirds of the non-Jewish population in what had recently been the core of Western Ukraine.[18]

Except regarding Jews, however, these aims were mostly not realized.[19] Removing Poles and Ukrainians, Frank thought, would take decades. Yet it remained the goal: war meant delay, not retreat. Meanwhile, the Generalgouvernement would retain millions of Ukrainians and Poles, their labor "needed for the war," with a "certain camouflaging of our final political intentions," so as to promote Polish-Ukrainian antagonism in a "tilting game of ethno-political conflict."[20] The genocide of Jews, by contrast, would not be delayed. The antisemitism of the Holocaust made total destruction a priority, quickly overriding even war needs.

Ruling Lemberg also meant facing a Soviet legacy. The Distrikt joined a Generalgouvernement earmarked for full Reich accession, making it a special case: the planned absorption of a former part of the Soviet Union into the future Nazi empire's core. The Institut für Deutsche Ostarbeit investigated both past German influence on Lemberg and its recent Soviet administration, emphasizing the negative influence of the latter.[21] A German report stressed that Lemberg's "German face" could hide legacies of "Bolshevik disintegration" as well as of despised Poland.[22] Although Lemberg's military commandant quickly recommended taking its unemployed for work in the Reich, SS leader Heinrich Himmler was initially wary of new subjects who were contaminated, he feared, by Soviet influence.[23]

18. Pohl, *Nationalsozialistische Judenverfolgung in Ostgalizien*, 97; Sandkühler, *"Endlösung" in Galizien*, 90.

19. All Jews had to die, but in a perverse twist, for some German occupation officials some of their artifacts should be saved. In September 1941, the head of the SS and police in the Generalgouvernement received a German official's request for the protection of the synagogue in the town of Husiatyn, since it would be "an original enrichment of the cultural monuments in the 'Reich.' [The synagogue's] destruction would be regrettable." The answer was that the synagogue had already "been destroyed by artillery during the fighting for [Husiatyn]" (DALO R-35, 12, 239: 32–33; R-35, 12, 247: 17).

20. Regierungssitzung des Generalgouvernements, 11 March 1942; Präg and Jacobmeyer, *Das Diensttagebuch*, BA R52II/242: 8–10.

21. Redzik, *Wydział prawa Uniwersytetu lwowskiego*, 242.

22. Yad Vashem M-37; DALO R-35, 13, 21: 1.

23. DALO R-31, 1, 1: 81 (USHMM Acc.1995.A.1086, Reel 5); Maria Wardzyńska, ed., *Deportacje na roboty przymusowe z Generalnego Gubernatorstwa 1939–1945* (Warsaw: Instytut Pamięci Narodowej, 1991), 87.

Ruling Lemberg: The Practice of Incompetence and Corruption

In de facto continuity with the Soviet occupation, the German regime in Distrikt Galizien often consisted of especially incompetent and corrupt staff.[24] By September 1942, a total of not quite 14,400 Reich Germans, including dependents, were ruling a population of about 4.5 million in a manner aptly characterized by Dieter Pohl as "totalitarian colonial." In Lemberg, with the highest concentration of occupiers, they made up barely 1.5 percent of the population.[25] With the Generalgouvernement said to attract the especially corrupt, Distrikt governor Otto Wächter, unwittingly echoing Khrushchev's complaints of 1940, soon railed against German bureaucracies unloading their worst on his Galizien.[26] In 1942, the SS killed or forced into suicide Wächter's predecessor Karl Lasch, in an effort to use Lasch's corruption against Frank. Lasch's death made no difference. A year later, another SS investigation found pervasive embezzlement and corruption rampant in the Distrikt.[27] A site of ambitious German fantasies of racial purification and eastern mission, at the same time Nazi Galizien soon appeared to its own leaders as a gathering of German profiteers in search of an "Eldorado," in the SS's own terms a "Gegenauslese"—a counterselection, with all the Social-Darwinist overtones of that term—among the putative master race.[28]

Pogrom and Ukrainian Nationalism

For Lemberg's Jews, the German occupation brought the unprecedented: the murder of virtually all. Estimates of the Jewish population in the former eastern Galicia at the start of the German occupation range from 540,000 to 650,000, about a tenth of the total population and probably, in absolute numbers, a little more than that of Germany in 1933.[29] From western Ukraine, a larger area, an estimated forty thousand to fifty thousand initially managed to flee east; how

24. On professional incompetence, corruption, cruelty, and narratives of a "German mission in the East," see Bernhard Chiari, *Alltag hinter der Front: Besatzung, Kollaboration und Widerstand in Weißrußland, 1941–1944* (Düsseldorf: Droste, 1998), esp. 59–63.

25. Pohl, *Nationalsozialistische Judenverfolgung in Ostgalizien*, 94–95; Sandkühler, *"Endlösung" in Galizien*, 87.

26. DALO R-35, 13, 21: 21–22; Yad Vashem M-37 (1992.A.0069).

27. Dieter Schenk, *Der Lemberger Professorenmord und der Holocaust in Ostgalizien* (Bonn: Dietz, 2007), 154–57.

28. Sandkühler, *"Endlösung" in Galizien*, 77.

29. For discussion of these estimates, see Pohl, *Nationalsozialistische Judenverfolgung in Ostgalizien*, 43–44.

many of them later fell into German hands is unclear.[30] In the end, almost a tenth of all Holocaust victims came from what had once been eastern Galicia.[31]

In 1939, there were about 104,000 Jews in Lwów, almost a third of the total population of about 333,500. The next two years brought refugees and Soviet deportations of thousands of them. Of the Jewish population of Lemberg in the summer of 1941, four-fifths were dead by the end of 1942, almost all by the end of 1943.[32] The exact number of survivors in the city is not known. It is certain that it was minuscule, with about thirteen hundred Jews in the city in August 1944, shortly after the Soviet reconquest.[33]

Unlike its long postwar neglect, the crucial importance of the Holocaust is not a matter of later memory choices. There may be, as Mark Mazower has argued, aspects of "cultural obsession" in the current memory of the Holocaust, which should not eclipse other experiences.[34] Yet, in Lviv, as in many other cities and places, the rapid annihilation of an ethnically targeted large share of its population was the deepest, most visible, and most dramatic change wrought by Lemberg's German occupation, whether immediately—or later—recognized as such or not. Moreover, as Jan Gross has recently emphasized, generally the implementation and effects of the Holocaust cannot be understood without fully taking local agency into account.[35] In Lviv, urban genocide began as a public

30. Dieter Pohl, "Schauplatz Ukraine: Der Massenmord an den Juden im Militärverwaltungsgebiet und im Reichskommissariat 1941–1943," in *Der deutsche Krieg im Osten 1941–1944: Facetten einer Grenzüberschreitung*, ed. Christian Hartmann et al. (Munich: Oldenbourg, 2009).

31 Pohl, *Nationalsozialistische Judenverfolgung in Ostgalizien*, 9. About every fourth victim of the Holocaust came from Ukraine. See Dieter Pohl, "Schlachtfeld zweier totalitärer Diktaturen—die Ukraine im Zweiten Weltkrieg," *Österreichische Osthefte* 42 (2000): 349.

32. In October 1941, after the German attack on the Soviet Union and after a first wave of pogroms and killings, yet before the peak mass murders of 1942, there were an estimated 111,000 to 119,000 Jews in Lemberg (Hryciuk, *Polacy we Lwowie*, 50). For slightly higher minimun estimates, see Frank Golczewski's contribution on Poland in *Die Dimension des Völkermords: Die Zahl der jüdischen Opfer des Nationalsozialismus*, ed. Wolfgang Benz (Munich: Oldenbourg, 1991), 411–97, esp. 445. By the summer of 1943, virtually all remaining Jewish inmates of camps and ghettos were murdered (Pohl, "Schlachtfeld zweier totalitärer Diktaturen," 349; Pohl, *Nationalsozialistische Judenverfolgung in Ostgalizien*, 139–51).

33. Hryciuk, *Polacy we Lwowie*, 50. Philip Friedman counted 823 survivors in Lwów at the time of the Soviet reconquest and later estimated their number, including survivors emerging from hiding in the city or returning from the countryside outside Lwów, at over 2000 (Benz, *Dimension des Völkermords*, 484, 491). According to Eliyahu Jones, there were thirty-four hundred Jews in Lwów and its surrounding areas as of 21 September 1944 (*Żydzi Lwowa w okresie okupacji*, 123). This number for Jewish survivors is likely to have already included some Jews who did not survive in Lwów but returned to it.

34. Mazower, *Salonica, City of Ghosts*, 9.

35. Jan T. Gross, "A Colonial History of the Bloodlands," *Kritika: Explorations in Russian and Eurasian History* 15 (2014): 595.

spectacle, when the Germans arrived together with Ukrainian nationalist auxiliaries, the OUN-B-dominated Nachtigall battalion and other activists, translators, guides, and informers. Immediately, an estimated four thousand to eight thousand Jews were murdered in a pogrom that peaked on 1 July. Since Ukrainian nationalists declared a state at the same moment, this pogrom, in Alexander Prusin's apt phrase, "took place under the specter of national statehood," linking killing Jews in public with "national purification."[36]

The pogrom was encouraged by the propagandistic use of the preceding Soviet massacre of thousands of Lviv prison inmates.[37] Omitting Jewish victims of this Soviet killing spree, German and Ukrainian-nationalist propaganda blamed the massacre on "Judeo-Bolshevism," calling for collective revenge on Jews.[38] With Germans filming the pogrom, propaganda boss Joseph Goebbels raved about "textbook" footage of "Bolshevik atrocities"; Hitler praised it too.[39] German and Ukrainian nationalist intentions converged in this matter: some nationalist intellectuals

36. Prusin, *Lands Between*, 156–57. Similar combinations of antisemitic violence and nationalist self-assertion occurred in Lithuania and Latvia.

37. On the pogrom, see John-Paul Himka, "The Lviv Pogrom of 1941: The Germans, Ukrainian Nationalists, and the Carnival Crowd," *Canadian Slavonic Papers/Revue canadienne des slavistes* 53 (2011): 209–43; and Kai Struve, "Tremors in the Shatterzone of Empire: Eastern Galicia in Summer 1941," in *Shatterzone of Empires*, ed. Bartov and Weitz, 463–84. For the estimate of the number of Jewish pogrom victims, see Mick, "Incompatible Experiences," 349. Regarding the victims of the preceding NKVD massacres: according to Grzegorz Motyka, the NKVD murdered at least 5,387 prisoners on the territory of the former eastern Galicia, the majority of them ethnic Ukrainians (*Ukraińska partyzantka*, 87). This did not mean that there were no Poles or Jews among those killed (Motyka, *Ukraińska partyzantka*, 87; Pohl, *Nationalsozialistische Judenverfolgung in Ostgalizien*, 56). The number of prisoners massacred in Lviv was probably close to twenty-five hundred (Brandon and Lower, *Shoah in Ukraine*, 20n20). On the NKVD massacres in western Ukraine's prisons but also farther east in the summer of 1941, see Hryciuk, *Polacy we Lwowie*, 186–91 (in more detail and with slightly higher estimates of the number of victims than Motyka); Pohl, *Nationalsozialistische Judenverfolgung in Ostgalizien*, 55–56; and Karel C. Berkhoff, *Harvest of Despair: Life and Death in Ukraine under Nazi Rule* (Cambridge, MA: Harvard University Press, 2004), 14–16.

Motyka, *Ukraińska partyzantka*, 97; Hryciuk, *Przemiany narodowościowe i ludnościowe*, 201; Pohl, *Nationalsozialistische Judenverfolgung in Ostgalizien*, 58–67, especially for direct German involvement behind the scenes as well as on the ground.

38. On the public call by Ukrainian nationalists to "destroy" Jews and other "enemies," see John-Paul Himka, "Metropolitan Andrey Sheptytsky and the Holocaust," *Polin Studies in Polish Jewry* 26 (2014): 339. The fact that the Soviets perpetrated a cruel slaughter did not keep others from manipulating the evidence: the corpses of Jewish victims of the Soviet massacre were concealed; moreover, there is some evidence that the Germans and their auxiliaries disfigured the corpses of other massacre victims so as to enhance the traumatic effect (Prusin, *Lands Between*, 157).

39. Pohl, *Nationalsozialistische Judenverfolgung in Ostgalizien*, 59; Philipp-Christian Wachs, *Der Fall Theodor Oberländer (1905–1998): Ein Lehrstück deutscher Geschichte* (Frankfurt am Main: Campus, 2000), 79–81; Ivan Himka [John-Paul Himka], "Dostovirnist svidchennia: Reliatsiia Ruzi Vagner pro Lvivskii pohrom vlitku 1941 r.," *Holokost i Suchanist*, no. 2 (2008): 43–65. The initial pogrom in Lviv reappeared several times in Soviet wartime publications. Although the Soviet

Figure 3.2 German military propagandists shooting footage of the pogrom, 1941. Yad Vashem Photo Archive, Signature 4613/581.

saw the Soviet prison massacre as an opportunity to, as one of them wrote, attract international attention, produce "moral capital," and defeat long-standing attempts by an international "Jewish mafia" to keep Ukraine down and out in the "world press"; now, the "national name" had appeared again on the front pages.[40]

Germans were present and active but not alone. Ukrainian nationalists, a Ukrainian volunteer force on its way to becoming the Ukrainian Police of Lemberg, and segments of the local population participated. Marching east, Germans sought to incite pogroms while stressing local "self-cleansing." Once again a conqueror sought to temporarily turn war into "civil war," as a German official put it.[41] Along with German instigation, however, local initiative contributed not only to the Lemberg pogrom but also to a wave of assaults from the Baltic to the Black

authorities knew that part of the local population had participated in the violence, this fact was consistently omitted (Karel C. Berkhoff, *Motherland in Danger: Soviet Propaganda during World War II* [Cambridge, MA: Harvard University Press, 2012], 226; Tarik Cyril Amar, "A Disturbed Silence: Discourse on the Holocaust in the Soviet West as an Anti-Site of Memory," in *The Holocaust in the East: Local Perpetrators and Soviet Responses*, ed. Michael David-Fox, Peter Holquist, and Alexander M. Martin [Pittsburgh: University of Pittsburgh Press, 2014], 158–83). This policy continued during the postwar period (Amar, "Disturbed Silence," 179).

40. Himka, "Ethnicity and the Reporting of Mass Murder," 382–84.

41. Babette Quinkert, *Propaganda und Terror in Weißrussland, 1941–1944: Die deutsche "geistige" Kriegführung gegen Zivilbevölkerung und Partisanen* (Paderborn: Schöningh, 2009), 56–57; Pohl, "Schauplatz Ukraine," 160; Struve, "Tremors," 468–70.

Sea.[42] In the former eastern Galicia alone, thirty-five such pogroms have been identified, with the number of those killed estimated at above twelve thousand.[43] In Lemberg, a German Sonderkommando mass murder squad and the local German military and civil administration arrived after the pogrom had begun.[44] A central element of the latter, known later as the "prison *aktsiia*," was to force Jews to recover corpses left after the Soviet prison massacres and to torture and murder them at the same time. The initiative for this violent performance was unclear. The German army, at any rate, gave orders to continue it, and the civilian Stadthauptmann later boasted of levying more "Judenkommandos" for this task.[45]

The Polish Home Army reported local pogrom perpetrators as Ukrainian and Polish "scum."[46] Some Jewish witnesses exclusively blamed Ukrainians from the lower classes.[47] After the pogrom of 1918, a Polish official had tried to deny his military's responsibility by presenting pogromists as criminals playing soldiers.[48] After the 1941 pogrom, Kost Pankivskyi continued this developing tradition of denial by insisting that this pogrom was the work of a Polish "rabble" playing Ukrainians.[49]

Eyewitness accounts, a key source for facts about the pogrom, tell another story.[50] Maurycy Allerhand observed that "Ukrainians were beating Jews with sticks and whips" and pulled them from houses whose doors were shut to those

42. Motyka, *Ukraińska partyzantka*, 97.

43. Hryciuk, *Przemiany narodowościowe i ludnościowe*, 201; Pohl, *Nationalsozialistische Judenverfolgung in Ostgalizien*, 58–67; Bauer, *Death of the Shtetl*, 33; Struve, "Tremors"; and Wendy Lower, "Pogroms, Mob Violence, and Genocide in Western Ukraine, Summer 1941: Varied Histories, Explanations, and Comparisons," *Journal of Genocide Research* 13 (2011): 217–46. According to Pohl, the number of victims may have been "much higher" (*Nationalsozialistische Judenverfolgung in Ostgalizien*, 64, 67n159). For a number of leading German Holocaust perpetrators, such as Friedrich Jeckeln or Paul Blobel, the summer of 1941 in the former eastern Galicia marked one stage of their murderous path (Struve, "Tremors," 467). The Soviet invasion of 1939 also triggered some Ukrainian nationalist violence against Jews, if on a far smaller scale than the German attack of 1941 (Prusin, *Lands Between*, 130).

44. Pohl, *Nationalsozialistische Judenverfolgung in Ostgalizien*, 56, 58–59, 62–64.

45. Sandkühler, *"Endlösung" in Galizien*, 116; DALO R-35, 2, 67: 38 (USHMM Acc.1995.A.1086, Reel 6). Wendy Lower has shown that such "prison actions" occurred in several locations ("Pogroms, Mob Violence, and Genocide").

46. *Armia krajowa w dokumentach*, 6:200.

47. Mick, "Incompatible Experiences," 350.

48. Mick, *Kriegserfahrungen in einer multiethnischen Stadt*, 250.

49. Pankivskyi, *Vid derzhavy do komitetu*, 35. Nakonechnyi's memoirs continued this tradition into the post-Soviet period (Himka, "Debates in Ukraine," 354). On the implausibility of relativizing the pogrom as a "spontaneous combustion" of mob violence, see Himka, "Lviv Pogrom of 1941," 235.

50. John-Paul Himka has shown the high degree of accuracy of one account ("Dostovirnist svidchennia"). On the importance of testimony for the history of the Holocaust, see Omer Bartov, "Communal Genocide: Personal Accounts of the Destruction of Buczacz, Eastern Galicia, 1941–1944," in *Shatterzone of Empires*, ed. Bartov and Weitz, 400–401.

trying to flee. He identified the perpetrators as Ukrainian by their blue-yellow armbands and the language in which they swore.[51] Wendy Lower has found local elite leadership for pogroms across the former Galicia, if not directly for Lviv, and that in general "all sections of society participated."[52] It makes no sense to imagine Lemberg as an exception, especially given evidence of its pogrom's public, even "carnival" character.[53]

The 1941 pogrom would have been impossible without Germans. They created its preconditions, watched, sometimes speechified on Jewish "guilt," and murdered.[54] A German report, referring to only a fraction of the victims, showed seventy-three Jews killed by German forces as alleged Soviet collaborators and another forty denounced by the local population and killed. At the same time, the Germans prevented the murder of some craftsmen and specialists.[55] They had the power to stop the pogrom and eventually did. They also started forcing Jews to do backbreaking, lethally dangerous work, sometimes killing them right afterward.[56]

In Lviv, as in smaller places, an emerging Ukrainian militia force, consisting of nationalists and former Soviet police, who were changing sides, played an important role.[57] Jeffrey Burds has identified individual militia members in pogrom pictures.[58] According to the survivor J. Berman, some members joined the pogrom while "still in civilian dress."[59] He was beaten and forced to shout the

51. ŻIH 229/22: 1 (USHMM RG-15.069).

52. Lower, "Pogroms, Mob Violence, and Genocide," 222–24.

53. Himka, "Lviv Pogrom of 1941," 211–12. In this respect, the pogrom of 1941 resembled that of 1918. Then, too, violence was "symbolically charged" in a "brutal street drama," with "carnivalesque elements" (William W. Hagen, "The Moral Economy of Popular Violence: The Pogrom in Lwów, November 1918," in *Antisemitism and Its Opponents*, ed. Blobaum, 143, 147). The 1941 pogrom was liminal, linking pre-Holocaust forms of antisemitic violence with the Holocaust; it was part of both, and drawing a sharp line between them would be ahistorical.

54. Struve, "Tremors," 465.

55. Jones, *Żydzi Lwowa*, 48.

56. Himka, "Lviv Pogrom of 1941," 238–40; Wells, *Ein Sohn Hiobs*, 47–48.

57. On the Ukrainian militia's role in pogroms in settlements other than Lviv, see Pohl, *Nationalsozialistische Judenverfolgung in Ostgalizien*, 60. The OUN had made systematic attempts to infiltrate the Soviet police (Pohl, *Nationalsozialistische Judenverfolgung in Ostgalizien*, 6; Serhiychuk, *Ukrainskyi zdvyh*, 3:22–23). In general, participating in violence against Jews could also serve as a perverse form of compensation for prior collaboration with Soviets and was explicitly recommended as national atonement by at least one Ukrainian nationalist leader (Prusin, *Lands Between*, 158).

58. Himka, "Dostovirnist svidchennia," 63–64.

59. The militia (*milits*) was the forerunner of collaborating Ukrainian police units. Whereas Lviv's Ukrainian police needed a little longer to be fully institutionalized, the militia was emerging even before the German arrival (Pohl, *Nationalsozialistische Judenverfolgung in Ostgalizien*, 61).

nationalist "Glory to Ukraine" salutation.[60] Some who had arrived with the preceding Soviet occupation may also have taken part in the pogrom. Klara Rosenfeld remembered a "Russian" pianist from the East, staying behind under German occupation to become a Ukrainian nationalist, while his Jewish wife and their child moved to the ghetto.[61] Local perpetrators, however, scarred survivors' memory in a special manner. In a postwar deposition, Fryderyka Bratspiel called them "Haidamaks," a historic term for Ukrainian social bandits infamous for their pogroms. Their viciousness stood out for her "because they were locals and often a neighbor led his neighbor to death."[62]

Among Germans, there were individual cases of reluctance to face the murderous reality that their invasion was spreading.[63] Hugo Steinhaus witnessed a Ukrainian man kicking a Jew and a German officer intervening.[64] One Jewish witness reported that a German noncommissioned officer tried to protect some Jews, shouting that "we are not Bolsheviks, after all"; another survivor of the pogrom described a similar, perhaps the same, scene.[65] Appeals to Germans by Jews who had served in Habsburg forces, however, were futile.[66] Maurycy Allerhand's son initially got some protection from German soldiers before he was severely abused by both Ukrainians and Germans.[67] An acquaintance of Allerhand was told that now he was "not a brother-in-arms but a Jew."[68]

The Ukrainian militia's involvement in the pogrom implicates Ukrainian nationalists, especially Bandera's OUN-B. There was a covert nationalist plan for using the "chaos and confusion" of a German attack to assault Jews and others, defined as enemies in ethnic and political terms. The plan featured "liquidation," "terror," and expulsions.[69] With a history of proud lethal extremism, the OUN-B also called for a dictatorship that would be "terrible" for its enemies, prominently including Jews.[70] Ukrainian nationalists viewed Soviets and Jews as allied

60. ŻIH 229/26: 1, 4 (USHMM RG-15.069).

61. Klara Rosenfeld, *From Lwów to Parma: A Young Woman's Escape from Nazi-Occupied Poland* (London: Vallentine Mitchell, 2005), 48.

62. YIVO RG 720, Box I, folder 37: 1.

63. Pohl, "Schauplatz Ukraine," in *Der deutsche Krieg*, ed. Hartmann, 160; ŻIH 229/52: 2 (USHMM RG-15.069); Pohl, *Nationalsozialistische Judenverfolgung in Ostgalizien*, 59.

64. Steinhaus, *Wspomnienia i zapiski*, 211.

65. ŻIH 229/54: 4 (USHMM RG-15.069); Pohl, *Nationalsozialistische Judenverfolgung in Ostgalizien*, 66.

66. ŻIH 229/24: pagination illegible (USHMM RG-15.069).

67. ŻIH 229/8: 1–2 (USHMM RG-15.069).

68. ŻIH 229/20: 1 (USHMM RG-15.069).

69. Marco Carynnyk, "Foes of Our Rebirth: Ukrainian Nationalist Discussions about Jews, 1929–1947," *Nationalities Papers* 39 (2011): 329–32; Struve, "Tremors," 469.

70. Anatolii Kentii, *Zbroinyi chyn ukrainskykh natsionalistiv 1920–1956: Istoryko-arkhivni narysy* (Kyiv: TsDAHOU, 2005), 1:222; Pohl, *Nationalsozialistische Judenverfolgung in Ostgalizien*, 57; Motyka, *Ukraińska partyzantka*, 96.

adversaries: targeting "Moscow" as the main opponent did not decrease their hostility toward Jews. On the contrary, while Moscow was a distant and strong enemy, Jews were near, vulnerable, and denounced as loyal to the Soviet regime.[71] Even before the war, in 1938, Yaroslav Stetsko, a top nationalist leader and antisemite, called for the liquidation of "Russia and Bolshevism," defined as "the main present-day instrument of the Jewish danger."[72] "Judeo-Bolshevism" was an important part of nationalist ideology.[73] After the 1926 killing of exiled Ukrainian anti-Bolshevik leader Symon Petliura, Dontsov had specifically demanded the collective punishment of Jews.[74] During the Lviv pogrom, the nationalist leader Ivan Klymiv (called "Lehenda") issued public calls for the destruction of "Moscow, Poland, Hungarians, and Jewry" and for collective national liability.[75] Nationalist publications blamed "all Jews" for "Russifying and Polonizing" and hence destroying Ukraine.[76] During the Soviet occupation, nationalists told villagers that Communists made "Jews with whips rule over Ukrainians."[77] On 28 July, the Lviv OUN-B reported that "our *milits*, together with the German authorities, is now conducting numerous arrests of Jews."[78]

Nachtigall legionaries did not participate in the Lviv pogrom as an organized military unit, as long claimed by Soviet propaganda. Yet they may have taken part individually as they were allowed to look for relatives among the prison massacre

71. An OUN-B resolution of April 1941 has sometimes been misread as rejecting antisemitism. In reality, the resolution warned not to let pogroms distract attention from Moscow as the main enemy. At the same time, it identified Jews in general as its supporters. Subsequently, the warning against pogroms remained a dead letter, while the practice of targeting Jews as agents of Moscow was fully implemented. For a concise discussion of this resolution, its meaning, and context, see Struve, "Tremors," 469–70.

72. Carynnyk, "Foes of Our Rebirth," 338. On Stetsko's antisemitism, see also Himka, "Lviv Pogrom of 1941," 222–23. During the Cold War, Stetsko reinvented himself as an antitotalitarian freedom fighter. His widow would return to post-Soviet Ukraine to public honors. Before the Second World War, Stetsko had fiercely attacked another prominent nationalist because of his Jewish wife and castigated Jews as "fleecers" and "corrupters," who "demoralize and corrupt the nations of the world." Before the German attack on the Soviet Union, he coauthored the OUN-B's secret guidelines on the use of the fog of war for mass terror (Carynnyk, "Foes of Our Rebirth," 327–29, 336; Per A. Rudling, "The OUN, the UPA, and the Holocaust: A Study in the Manufacturing of Historical Myths," *Carl Beck Papers in Russian and East European Studies*, no. 2107 [Pittsburgh: University of Pittsburgh, 2011], 8–9).

73. Motyka, *Ukraińska partyzantka*, 96; Taras Kurylo and Ivan Khymka [John-Paul Himka], "Iak OUN stavylasia do ievreiv? Rozdumy nad knyzhkoiu Volodymyr Viatrovycha," *Ukraina moderna*, no. 13 (2008), 257–58; Rudling, "The OUN, the UPA, and the Holocaust," 5–7.

74. Motyka, *Ukraińska partyzantka*, 45.

75. Struve, "Tremors," 465. In 1943, Klymiv-Lehenda was killed by the Gestapo, which made no difference to his victims of 1941.

76. Carynnyk, "Foes of Our Rebirth," 317; Kurylo and Khymka, "Iak OUN stavylasia," 264.

77. Serhiychuk, *Ukrainskyi zdvyh*, 3:33.

78. Franziska Bruder, *"Den ukrainischen Staat erkämpfen oder sterben!" Die Organisation Ukrainischer Nationalisten (OUN) 1929-1948* (Berlin: Metropol, 2007), 147; Carynnyk, "Foes of Our

victims.[79] Thus, they were present at sites of the mass torture and murder of Jews, where a delusional script of revenge for imagined Jewish-Bolshevik collusion was enacted with fantastic brutality. A Nachtigall veteran later claimed that the de facto commander Roman Shukhevych expressly prohibited taking "revenge on our enemies the Poles and Jews, because it is not our business to take care of this."[80] This statement, if correct, hardly speaks for Nachtigall innocence; it may indicate plausible denial as a goal from the beginning.[81] Nachtigall legionaries later served Germany in Belarus, where "antipartisan" warfare blended into the massacre of civilians and the Holocaust.[82] German police squads, assisted by the Ukrainian Auxiliary Police emerging from the militia, recorded shooting between twenty-five hundred and three thousand Jewish men in the first days of July.[83]

German killings also targeted the Polish elite. In July 1941, forty-five Polish academics, family members, and friends were murdered, thirty-eight of them in one initial massacre. Lists were prepared in advance, possibly with help from Ukrainian nationalists.[84] Roman Volchuk later remembered them collecting information on Polish professors; Germans demanded directions to their residences.[85] Further victims included the Polytechnic professor and former prime minister Kazimierz Bartel as well as students.[86]

Rebirth," 337. Kai Struve has found that, by comparison with publications by Lithuanian nationalists, Ukrainian ones were somewhat less explicit in their antisemitism. This, however, made no difference to the fact that "the OUN's rank-and-file members embarked on anti-Jewish violence on a large scale, and when they did so, they were far from ignoring the political program or the instructions of the leadership; on the contrary, they found encouragement in them" (Struve, "Tremors," 470).

79. Ivan Patryliak, "Dialnist Romana Shukhevycha v Ukrainskomu Lehioni," *Ukrainskyi vyzvolnyi rukh*, no. 10 (2007): 192.

80. For this statement, see Patryliak, "Dialnist Romana Shukhevycha," 193. Shukhevych, like Stetsko, was a co-author of the OUN-B's secret war guidelines.

81. For Nachtigall's role in 1941 and the issue of Soviet falsification, see Himka, "Lviv Pogrom of 1941," 225–26. John-Paul Himka's discussion is exemplarily precise, but I am more skeptical about Nachtigall's role and the claims in its favor made by the Nachtigall veteran Myroslav Kalba and their uncritical use by the Lviv historian Ivan Patryliak.

82. On antipartisan warfare in occupied Belarus, mixing plunder, atrocities—sometimes deliberately committed in disguise to compromise the enemy—hard drinking, torture, murder, and chaos, see Christian Gerlach, *Kalkulierte Morde: Die deutsche Wirtschafts- und Vernichtungspolitik in Weißrußland 1941 bis 1944* (Hamburg: Hamburger Edition, 1999), 859, 870–909, 914–16; and Chiari, *Alltag hinter der Front*, 181–94.

83. Pohl, *Nationalsozialistische Judenverfolgung in Ostgalizien*, 69; Struve, "Tremors," 467; Hryciuk, *Przemiany narodowościowe i ludnościowe*, 202 (with slightly different figures).

84. Schenk, *Der Lemberger Professorenmord*, 115–29, 258–60.

85. Hryciuk, *Polacy we Lwowie*, 193; Roman Volchuk, *Spomyny: Z peredvoiennoho Lvova ta voiennoho Vidnia* (Kyiv: Krytyka, 2002), 89.

86. Zygmunt Albert, *Lwowski wydział lekarski w czasie okupacij Hitlerowskiej, 1941-1944* (Wrocław: Zakład Narodowy im. Ossolińskich, 1975), 25; Albert, "The Extermination of the Lwów Professors in July 1941," in his *Kaźń profesorów lwowskich, lipiec 1941: studia oraz relacje i*

Holocaust: Devastation, Plunder, Involvement

The German occupation meant mass plunder as well as mass murder. Heinrich Himmler fantasized about killing without greed. Yet, in reality, genocide was also a historic robbery, profiting both private and state perpetrators.[87] Germans strove to monopolize the looting, but those under occupation also had opportunities.[88] During the initial pogrom, there was widespread looting, and Jews were robbed as well as killed.[89]

Subsequently, for years the robbery of tens of thousands of households was the dark white noise of genocide, as German agencies preyed on Jewish institutions and sites. Jewish genealogical records were looted, synagogues and prayer houses demolished, documents destroyed, and cemeteries despoiled and razed.[90] German looting in the East was generally more ad hoc than in the West, with constant face-to-face robbery.[91] In Lemberg, too, a legalistic Confiscation Decree went together with "spontaneous expropriations."[92] The 1943 SS investigation finding abundant corruption among Distrikt Germans also pointed to "Jew goods [*Judengut*]" as their main enrichment source, with personal slavery added in the form of the "house and court Jew."[93] Plundering included scavenging the dead. Even remains, dug up again and burned to obliterate traces, were searched for valuables.[94]

dokumenty (Wrocław: Wydawnictwo Uniwersytetu Wrocławskiego, 1989), 91–93; Schenk, *Der Lemberger Professorenmord*, 133–41; Hryciuk, *Polacy we Lwowie*, 193.

87. For Himmler's ideas about the "duty" to kill a people while taking "not so much as a fur" or "a cigarette" for personal gain, see Weiner, *Making Sense of War*, 25.

88. For this phenomenon in the occupied East in general, see Martin Dean, *Robbing the Jews: The Confiscation of Jewish Property in the Holocaust, 1933–1945* (Cambridge: Cambridge University Press, 2008), 173–221.

89. Himka, "Dostovirnist svidchennia," 47–48.

90. Patricia Grimsted, *Trophies of War and Empire: The Archival Heritage of Ukraine, World War II, and the International Politics of Restitution* (Cambridge, MA: Harvard Ukrainian Research Institute, 2001), 205–6; Iakub Khonigsman, *Katastrofa evreistva zapadnoi Ukrainy: Evrei vostochnoi Galitsii, zapadnoi Volyni, Bukoviny i Zakarpatiia v 1933–1945 godakh* (Lvov: s.n., 1998), 125; DALO R-35, 13, 146: 20; Sandkühler, *"Endlösung" in Galizien*, 198; Wells, *Ein Sohn Hiobs*, 141, 163; Gabriele Kohlbauer-Fritz, "Judaicasammlungen zwischen Galizien und Wien: Das Jüdische Museum in Lemberg und die Sammlung Maximilian Goldsteins," *Wiener Jahrbuch für Jüdische Geschichte, Kultur und Museumswesen* 1 (1994/95): 133; Andrzej Mężýński, ed., *Biblioteki naukowe w Generalnym Gubernatorstwie w latach 1939–1945: Wybór dokumentów źródłowych* (Warsaw: LTW, 2003), 135–37.

91. Dieter Pohl, "The Robbery of Jewish Property in Eastern Europe under German Occupation, 1939–1942," in *Robbery and Restitution: The Conflict over Jewish Property in Europe*, ed. Martin Dean et al. (New York: Berghahn Books, 2007), 72–73.

92. For surveys of German looting, see Pohl, *Nationalsozialistische Judenverfolgung in Ostgalizien*, 299; and Sandkühler, *"Endlösung" in Galizien*, 198.

93. Schenk, *Der Lemberger Professorenmord*, 154, 168.

94. Wells, *Ein Sohn Hiobs*, 171.

The Germans established a Judenrat. Its officials were in a categorically different position from that of non-Jews; yet, in everyday Jewish perception, German looting could form a continuum with that committed by local non-Jews and by parts of the Judenrat bureaucracy. Initially German and Soviet plunder appeared similar. As a Jewish victim put it in January 1942, the Soviets had "introduced their system" and the Germans were "continuing the expropriation of the Jews."[95]

Non-Jews could welcome opportunities and overlook causes. More than ten years after the war, Kost Pankivskyi recalled Jews and Poles in the pharmacy administration vanishing "into obscurity" on their own initiative, while "we," Ukrainians, "were convinced that the office" would "remain in our hands."[96] But the "stepping aside" of 70 Jewish pharmacists out of a total of 181 was a German purge of the so-called "Judaization" of pharmacies.[97] Not just opportunism, cast as national interest, but also a "desire for revenge for experiences of failure," as Tomaszewski observed, lay at the heart of antisemitic acts.[98] Ukrainian nationalists explained how "Jews and faithful agents of Moscow" had taken all the best positions.[99] Lviv's German-controlled press, in both Polish and Ukrainian, kept up a propaganda barrage against Jews.[100] The Ukrainian-language *Lvivski visti* accused them of denouncing Ukrainians to the Soviets, bringing about the Bolshevik revolution and the war, creating a "Soviet Judea," and severing Ukraine from Europe.[101] According to *Visti*, the public welcomed suppressing Jewish trade because a "red Jewish-Communist clique" had kept shops and goods for Jews. Under Soviet rule, everybody had been "stew[ed] in a Jewish-international pot," with Jews and "Moskals" (a pejorative term for Russians) replacing Ukraine's cultural elite. Jewish malfeasance, in *Visti*'s reading, had deep roots, too: medieval Polish conquest had degraded Ukrainians to "proletarian" status through a "Jewish invasion."[102]

Visti was produced under German control but with significant local input, and its appeals overlapped with local discourses.[103] A fragmentary 1941 "Report

95. ŻIH 212/61: 1 (USHMM RG-15.069).

96. Pankivskyi, *Vid derzhavy do komitetu*, 26, 29 (my emphasis).

97. DALO R-35, 9, 353: 49.

98. Tomaszewski, *Lwów*, 67, 75–76.

99. Carynnyk, "Foes of Our Rebirth," 339–41.

100. On Lemberg's Polish-language occupation newspaper *Gazeta lwowska*, see Lucjan Dobroszycki, *Die legale polnische Presse im Generalgouvernement, 1939–1945* (Munich: Institut für Zeitgeschichte, 1977), 117. More generally, on the prominence of antisemitism and "Judeo-Bolshevism" in the Ukrainian press in the Generalgouvernement, see Himka, "Ethnicity and the Reporting of Mass Murder."

101. *Lvivski visti*, 17/18 August 1941, 1; 19 August 1941, 1.

102. *Lvivski visti*, 11 August 1941, 2; 12 August 1941, 1–4; 17 September 1941, 3; 12/13 October 1941, 3.

103. On the relationship between German and local input into *Lvivski visti*, see Henry Abramson, "Nachrichten aus Lemberg: Lokale Elemente in der antisemitischen Ikonographie der NS-Propaganda in ukrainischer Sprache," *Jahrbuch des Fritz Bauer Instituts* 6 (2002): 252–53.

on the Jewish Question in Lemberg," clearly written by a non-native speaker of German, accused Jews of serving the Soviets, robbing non-Jews, and even of plundering shops after the German arrival. "Masters" under the Soviets, they had seized everything, especially residences; "gold, jewels, and so on" were now "exclusively owned by Jews." In retribution, the author demanded armbands, forced labor, and killings and insisted that paying jobs must go only to non-Jews. He also accused the Jews of shouting "murderer" and "robber" at soldiers and the Ukrainian Police.[104] Jews were thus presented as guilty of a dual crime: both exploitation and collaboration with the Soviets. This became a rationalization of both murder and pillaging: the guilty would face punishment and their former victims enjoy both justice and profit. These delusions meshed with the German tendency, described by Frank Bajohr, to cultivate self-pity while looting Jews.[105] Here was an opportunity for the occupiers and some of the occupied to share both gains and rationalizations. *Lvivski visti* was not writing into a void when it announced that Germans would bring a new, fairer life and exclude Jews.[106]

Words and practices intersected. Peaks of violence came with formalized German exploitation and multiple opportunities for grassroots creativity, greed, and brutality for Germans and non-Germans. The father of Janina Hescheles, a young girl who would survive the Holocaust but lose her family, disappeared in the pogrom at the beginning of July. Her mother was quickly targeted by swindlers pretending to be able to get news from him for a fee of three thousand dollars.[107] On 28 July 1941, the last day of the so-called Petliura Days pogrom, the German authorities extorted a large "contribution" from Lviv's Jews, but the pogrom also featured much looting by plunderers from the countryside.[108] The line

104. DALO R-35, 6, 250:1–2 (USHMM Acc.1995.A.1086, Reel 7). This fragment may be part of a similar document cited by Thomas Sandkühler, who identifies the temporary head of the Lviv city administration, Yuriy Polianskyi, as the likely author.

105. Frank Bajohr, "Die wirtschaftliche Existenzvernichtung und Enteignung der Juden. Forschungsbilanz und offene Fragen," *Terezin Studies and Documents (Theresienstädter Studien und Dokumente)*, 13 (2006), 357.

106. *Lvivski visti*, 12 August 1941, 4.

107. Ianina Hesheles [Janina Hescheles], *Ochyma dvanadtsiatyrichnoi divchynky* (Kyiv: Dukh i litera, 2011), 33. Hescheles was highly exceptional in that she survived the Holocaust in Lviv. Her memoirs of this time show that manifold schemes to defraud, blackmail, and sell out Jews were not exceptional but widespread.

108. Sandkühler, *"Endlösung" in Galizien*, 126–27; Jones, *Żydzi Lwowa w okresie okupacji*, 52–53; Pohl, *Nationalsozialistische Judenverfolgung in Ostgalizien*, 65; Mick, "Incompatible Experiences," 351–52. The Ukrainian exile leader Symon Petliura had been assassinated on 25 May 1926. Nonetheless, the assault at the end of July 1941 received its name from the perpetrators in an attempt to depict it as "retaliation" for his killing. According to Pohl, the SS leader Heinrich Himmler visited Lviv shortly before the Petliura Days, and a special role may have been played by a German

between grabbing and exchanging was blurred. For Jews, raising the "contribution" often meant selling off things at depreciated prices. According to David Kahane, news of the "contribution" spread quickly; "peasants from the villages around Lviv" arrived looking for a good deal.[109] Local and German profiteering meshed; formalized and face-to-face robbery too. German bureaucrats, later trying to account for the "contribution," found scant records, showing that the Distrikt governor, the Stadthauptmann, and the Stadtbaudirektor had refurbished their residences.[110]

Opportunities proliferated. Warned of an impending arrest, Benedykt Munk fled and survived, but the acquaintance who warned him did not return his valuables.[111] Grabbing furs from Jews in the streets preceded an official plunder operation.[112] Searching Jewish homes to confiscate winter apparel turned into an opportunity to steal anything else as well and extort bribes for not snatching people.[113] When Leontyna Goldblatt was threatened with arrest, the Germans released her for a bribe while telling her that her mother, also seized, would die anyhow.[114] Some Ukrainian Police officers reported Jewish attempts to bribe them, delivering the bribes and the victims.[115] Others were ready to trade.[116] Even sadism and mercy could coincide: one Ukrainian policeman, after swearing in Yiddish while terrorizing a group of Jews, professed his gratitude for his home town's rabbi and let them go.[117]

Put on starvation rations and vitally dependent on prohibited exchange, Jews had to sell off whatever they still had and pay inflated prices for food. Janina Masłowska later remembered a potato soup for five, paid for with a valuable tablecloth, and many "traders" buying up Jewish property "for nothing" during the *Aktion* (an official operation or organized pogrom) of August 1942.[118] Jews were helpless when cheated, even by the standards of these unequal deals.[119] At the

Sonderkommando, while Ukrainian militia involvement was clear and OUN-B involvement likely (*Nationalsozialistische Judenverfolgung in Ostgalizien*, 65).

109. David Kahane, *Shchodennyk Lvivskoho hetto* (Kyiv: Dukh i litera, 2003), 51–52.

110. Jones, *Żydzi Lwowa w okresie okupacji*, 52–53; AAN 362/224: 94–96 (USHMM RG-15.007M, Reel 16).

111. YIVO RG 720, box 2, Benedykt Munk: 3.

112. Dzięgiel, *Lwów nie każdemu zdrów*, 138.

113. ŻIH 229/36: 3 (USHMM RG-15.069); Chuwis Thau, *Hidden*, 114–15.

114. ŻIH 229/8: 4, 229/20: 2 (USHMM RG-15.069).

115. USHMM MF 1995.A.1086 (Reel 3), DALO R-12, 1, 37: 16–20.

116. DALO R-58, 1, 30: 13 (USHMM Acc.1995.A.1086, Reel 10).

117. Pretzel, *Portrait of a Young Forger*, 95–98.

118. Michal Grynberg and Maria Kotowska, eds., *Życie i zagłada Żydów polskich 1939-1945: Relacje Świadków* (Warsaw: Oficyna Naukowa, 2003), 275, 280.

119. Rosenfeld, *From Lwów to Parma*, 23.

same time, one of the first initiatives of the Stadthauptmann was to blame Jews for "wild street trade" and exclude them from it. When systematic German massacres began again in the fall of 1941, the pretext was the need to suppress the black market.[120] Both Nazi state power and initiatives from below produced relentless plunder.

At the same time, newspapers warned non-Jews against adopting "Jewish habits" of "getting rich at others' expense."[121] This was another Soviet-German continuity with a twist. Despite differences in their attitudes toward private property and the market, both regimes made illicit exchange practically inevitable in Lviv while stigmatizing it as speculation and the black market. Only the Germans, however, made it state policy to externalize this offense onto a publicly abused other, defined in racist terms as below the human and slated for rapid total removal. Illicit exchange, irreconcilable with the rampant ethos of nationalism and authoritarianism, was denounced as a crime of the Jews, the one group most vitally dependent on, most victimized by, and most excluded from it.

Holocaust: Killing and Living Space

The Holocaust fundamentally reconfigured Lviv as a place to kill and die as well as a place to live. The new conquerors rapidly took over several of the best streets to set up a special area for themselves.[122] The Stadthauptmann used Hausverwalter janitors to survey residential space, especially for two kinds of apartments, those already vacant and those still inhabited by Jews. Noting that about 80 percent of the city's janitors were Ukrainian, Kost Pankivskyi complained to the Germans about their deploying a new group of about two hundred overseers—"almost exclusively Poles."[123] By April 1942, Ukrainian nationalists lamented that Poles had taken over Lemberg's janitorial power structure.[124] Lemberg's living space became a national resource to be fought over among non-Jews.

120. Sandkühler, *"Endlösung" in Galizien*, 75; DALO R-35, 2, 67: 35 (USHMM Acc.1995.A.1086, Reel 6).

121. Zhanna Kovba, *Liudianist u bezodni pekla: Povedinka mistsevoho naselennia skhidnoi Halychyny v roky "ostatochnoho rozviazannia ievreiskoho pytannia,"* 3rd rev., exp. ed. (Kyiv: Dukh i litera, 2009), 106.

122. Philip Friedman, *Zagłada Żydów lwowskich* (Łódż: Centralna Żyd. Komisja Historyczna w Polsce 1945), 10.

123. DALO R-37, 7, 42: 111–12 (USHMM Acc.1995.A.1086, Reel 28); Wasyl Veryha, *The Correspondence of the Ukrainian Central Committee in Cracow and Lviv with the German Authorities, 1939–1944* (Edmonton: Canadian Institute of Ukrainian Studies, University of Alberta, 2000), 1079–80.

124. Volodymyr Viatrovych, ed., *Polsko-ukrainski stosunky v 1942–1947 rokakh u dokumentakh OUN ta UPA* (Lviv: Tsentr doslidzhen vyzvolnoho rukhu, 2011), 1:152 (doc. 4). Generally, Volodymyr Viatrovych's work is politically biased by his committed national history activism and is used here only where plausible.

Expulsion escalated quickly.[125] At the beginning of November 1941, the Germans ordered about eighty thousand Jews to move into a ghetto, largely identical with the poorer Zamarstynów (Zamarstyniv) quarter. About twenty-five thousand Jews were already living there; non-Jews had to leave.[126] In effect, at least a third of Lemberg's total population had to move. Several thousand Jews were murdered during this ghettoization.[127] Germans forced Jews to pay non-Jews for new inferior residences while producing legalistic contortions to prevent Jews from actually owning what they paid for. To prevent "Aryans" from paying higher rents for new housing, Jews had to cover any difference.[128] Although we know little about their fate, later some Roma were also forced into Lviv's ghetto.[129]

Ghettoization brought more face-to-face looting, too. To David Kahane it even seemed as if its main purpose was to "deprive the Jews . . . of their property."[130] Only non-Jews could take their belongings with them; Jews kept little or nothing.[131] Some non-Jews informed Germans about Jewish households to plunder. Here was another public performance of the Jews' new role, with carts of pillaged Jewish goods filling the streets.[132] The ghetto's reduction after peaks of mass murder brought further residential shifts, with 3,350 vacant apartments and 416 vacant shops reported in November 1942.[133] In 1941, Germans made lists of spoils, including cash, furniture, jewelry, and bed linen. The Stadthauptmann took the money; his employees, German policemen, and the SS took the things.[134] Plunder could be gendered; household items were distributed to German officials' wives.[135] Some loot was to be released at low prices to the rural population for meeting food delivery quotas.[136]

125. Internally, the German authorities did use the term "ghetto," especially after its area was shrunk and closed in November 1942. See DALO R-37, 4, 140: 36; and R-35, 9, 667: 16 (USHMM Acc.1995.A.1086, Reel 24).

126. On the thousands of forced relocations even before ghettoization, see the Judenrat's letter of 10 November 1941, DALO R-35, 2, 155: 4 (USHMM Acc.1995.A.1086, Reel 6).

127. Pohl, *Nationalsozialistische Judenverfolgung in Ostgalizien*, 159–60.

128. DALO R-37, 4, 140: 38 (USHMM Acc.1995.A.1086, Reel 25).

129. Pohl, *Nationalsozialistische Judenverfolgung in Ostgalizien*, 114.

130. Kahane, *Shchodennyk Lvivskoho hetto*, 65.

131. DALO R-35, 2, 155: 6, 30 (USHMM Acc.1995.A.1086, Reel 6); ŻIH 229: 53 (USHMM RG-15.069).

132. Kahane, *Shchodennyk Lvivskoho hetto*, 52.

133. Jones, *Żydzi Lwowa w okresie okupacji*, 113–14; DALO R-37, 4, 140: 23 (USHMM Acc.1995.A.1086, Reel 25); R-35, 9, 667: 17 (USHMM Acc.1995.A.1086, Reel 24).

134. DALO R-37, 4, 941: 31, 37–39 (USHMM Acc.1995.A.1086, Reel 26).

135. Sandkühler, *"Endlösung" in Galizien*, 158–59. In Germany's constructed "East" of war and genocide, German women joined in plunder and mass murder. One police official's wife ran a shop to trade in booty; a Lemberg camp commander's wife became as infamous as her husband for the way she killed for fun (Wendy Lower, *Hitler's Furies: German Women in the Nazi Killing Fields* [New York: Mariner Books, 2014], 101–2, 133–63, 187–88).

136. DALO R-35, 12, 69: pagination illegible (USHMM Acc.1995.A.1086, Reel 25).

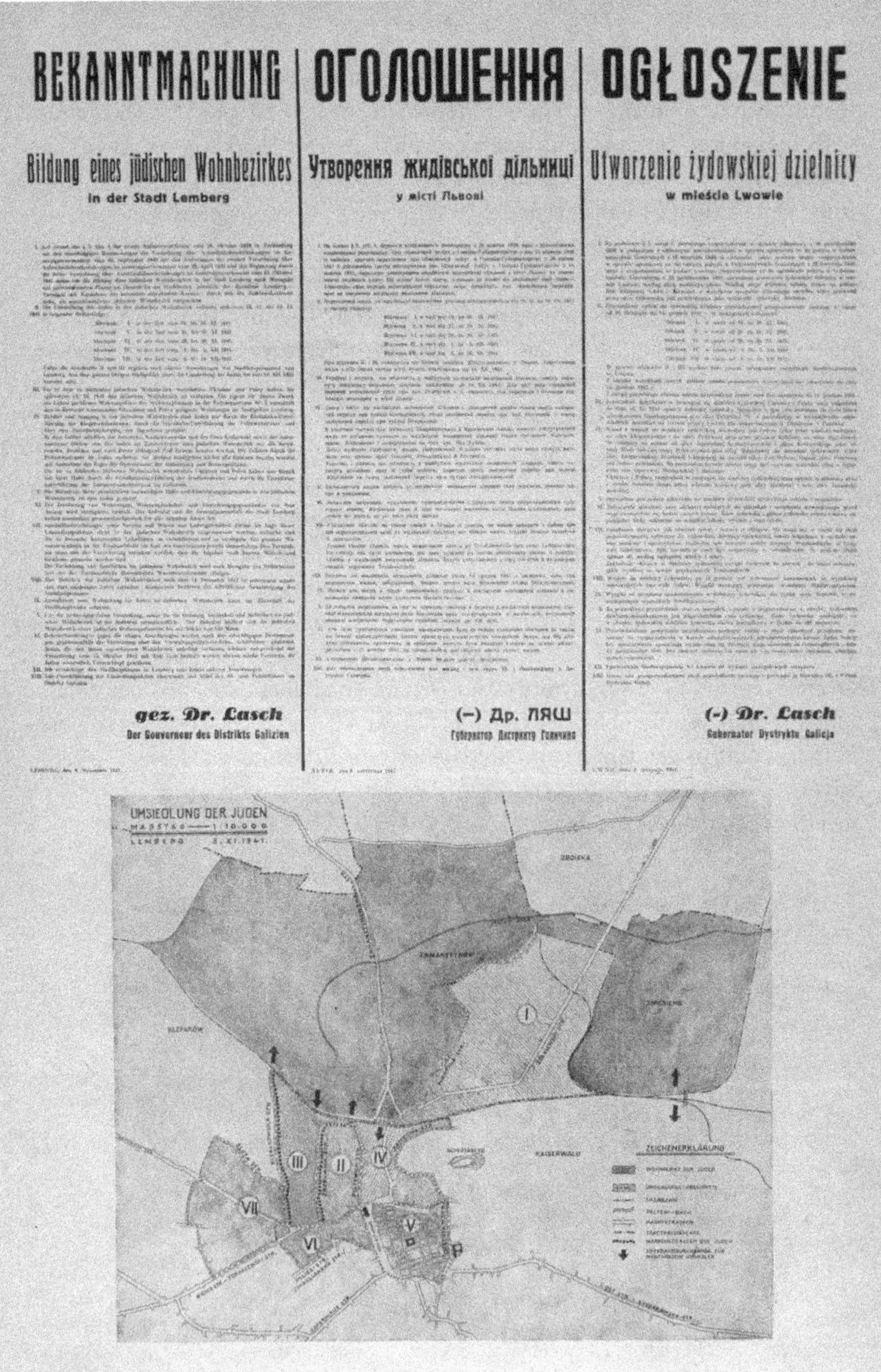

BEKANNTMACHUNG

Bildung eines jüdischen Wohnbezirkes

in der Stadt Lemberg

gez. Dr. Lasch

Der Gouverneur des Distrikts Galizien

ОГОЛОШЕННЯ

Утворення жидівської дільниці

у місті Львові

(–) Др. ЛЯШ

Губернатор Дистрикту Галичина

OGŁOSZENIE

Utworzenie żydowskiej dzielnicy

w mieście Lwowie

(–) Dr. Lasch

Gubernator Dystryktu Galicja

Figure 3.3 German ghettoization order for Lviv, 1941. Bundesarchiv, Poster Plak 003-037-085.

Like the initial pogroms, ghettoization was a public urban event; crowds formed to lay claims on Jewish apartments.[137] Petitions for living space featured arguments about social need as well as losses through Soviet expropriations.[138] Addressing requests for living space to Germans also constituted material incentive to speak "Judeo-Bolshevism" to power, a way to share and adopt stereotypes; and asking for restitution did not exclude seeking fresh gains. Thus, one petitioner described how the Soviets had deported her daughter, imprisoned her son-in-law, and confiscated two of her three rooms. These had been assigned first to a *komandir*, then, according to the petitioner, to a Jewish family. Now, the petitioner argued, she had no room for her daughter and her husband when they returned from "Bolshevik hell," so she requested another apartment.[139] Non-Jews who succeeded in taking the place of Jews had an incentive to rationalize their removal.[140] The new inhabitants of Marian Pretzel's disappeared parents' apartment blamed the war and their son's death on "the bloody Jews" who had "brought it" on themselves.[141] Not for the first or the last time, Lviv's "living space" was a discrimination and cooptation resource second to none in its pervasive reach into the everyday.

For the German occupiers, displacing everybody was an obvious entitlement. As late as July 1944, on the eve of the Soviet reconquest, a city administration secretary was arguing with Lemberg's German Labor Office. The office wanted her apartment; she objected. She had been among the first Germans to move into the building in the fall of 1941, she wrote, and after the gradual removal of "native" inhabitants there were still three "natives" left in the building. She felt that, "as a *Reichsdeutsche*," she should move only after they did.[142] Here was occupation as occupancy, internalized into German subjectivity, an everyday self-training in belonging to a "master race," its future cut short only by defeat.

Holocaust: Traps and Exceptions

Some non-Jews saved Jews, at great risk to themselves. Metropolitan Sheptytskyi's hiding of more than one hundred Jews through a conspiracy inside his Greek

137. Kahane, *Shchodennyk Lvivskoho hetto*, 43.

138. DALO R-37, 7, 35: 19, 20.

139. DALO R-37, 7, 35: 9.

140. For a detailed study of similar and related phenomena in postwar Poland, see Jan T. Gross, *Fear: Anti-Semitism in Poland after Auschwitz. An Essay in Historical Interpretation* (New York: Random House, 2007), esp. chap. 2.

141. Pretzel, *Portrait of a Young Forger*, 81–82.

142. AAN 540, I, 191: 48–50.

Catholic Church is the best-known case.[143] But there also were other organized rescue attempts, including those by a branch of the Polish Żegota network and Franciscan monasteries.[144]

In some cases, assistance arose from employment relationships. Zofia Tyran, a Ukrainian servant, helped her former employer Henryka Trauber, until Trauber obtained papers proclaiming her an "Aryan."[145] Anna Romaniuk, another Ukrainian servant, was caught hiding her former employers; she argued that she had done it not for money but because they had protected her from deportation to Siberia during the "Bolshevik period."[146] What the Germans did to Romaniuk is not clear but, in general, by the summer of 1942, those who attempted to help Jews were liable to be punished "like the Jews themselves"—that is, by death. A German Sondergericht (special court) in Lemberg provided the formalities, as in the cases of Michalina Merska, Josef Bernartowicz, and Władysław Korbecki (or Wladimir Korpyczki), whose judicial murders were publicized.[147]

Compassion sometimes took surprising forms. Samuel Drix remembered an exceptional Ukrainian policeman sparing his grandfather, although most Ukrainian police were "even worse than the SS men."[148] A "simple peasant" tried to console Maurycy Allerhand.[149] On another occasion, a woman saved him during an *Aktion*, holding his arm to hide the armband and leading him away.[150] Strangers sometimes helped, while intimacy could be treacherous. Helpers could face denunciation or blackmail by neighbors, who might demand a share of assumed profits. Self-preservation could converge with antisemitism and greed, leading some to deliver Jews directly to Germans.[151] Janina Hescheles would remember a

143. Shimon Redlich, "Sheptytskyi and the Jews during World War II," in *Morality and Reality*, ed. Magosci, 156–57; Kahane, *Shchodennyk Lvivskoho hetto*; Lewin, *Przeżyłem*.

144. For Żegota activities, see Joseph Kermish, "The Activities of the Council for Aid to Jews ('Żegota') in Occupied Poland," in *Rescue Attempts during the Holocaust: Proceedings of the Second Yad Vashem International Historical Conference*, ed. Yisrael Gutman and Efraim Zuroff (Jerusalem: Yad Vashem, 1974), http://www1.yadvashem.org/yv/en/righteous/pdf/resources/activites_zegota.pdf. On convents, see Nahum Bogner, "The Convent Children: The Rescue of Jewish Children in Polish Convents during the Holocaust," *Yad Vashem Studies* 27 (1999): 235–85, http://www1.yadvashem.org/yv/en/righteous/pdf/resources/nachum_bogner.pdf. On individuals in Lviv and other places, see Kovba, *Liudianist u bezodni pekla*, 166–220.

145. YIVO RG 1258, Box 48, Folder 853, Henryka Trauber: 4–5.

146. DALO R-77, 1, 1111: 19 (USHMM Acc.1995.A.1086).

147. DALO R-24, 1, 389: 2; R-77, 1, 504: 2–13; R-77, 1, 851: 36–41; R-77, 1, 1198: no pagination (USHMM Acc.1995.A.1086, Reels 21, 29, and 34).

148. Samuel Drix, *Witness to Annihilation: Surviving the Holocaust. A Memoir* (Washington: Brassey's, 1994), 42.

149. ŻIH 229/20: 1–2 (USHMM RG-15.069).

150. ŻIH 229/17: pagination illegible (USHMM RG-15.069).

151. Schoenfeld, *Holocaust Memoirs*, 30.

scheme that involved making Jews pay to escape from Lviv and then delivering them to the Germans for a reward.[152]

Money again played an important role. Non-Jews frequently demanded payment for helping Jews. A Polish couple hid Józef Menker for more than a year. Menker paid 3,000 złoty per month and deposited valuables with them. Yet after the death of one partner in June 1944, the other turned Menker out.[153] The desire to extort money from Jews, combined with fear of German punishment, could lead to murder. In a 1942 investigation, Lviv's Criminal Police suspected two brothers of first hiding, then robbing and murdering three Jews.[154] Leszek Dzięgel would remember rumors about a man in his neighborhood who was said to have first hidden a Jew for money, then killed him.[155] Yet not every payment necessarily meant profit. Korbecki/Korpyczki, a poor father of seven, took money from two Jewish women and a child and later said that he had not asked for a particular sum but took what was offered to buy food. The Germans executed him.[156] Some ran disinterested risks. When Josef Bernartowicz took over a house in March 1942 and found nine Jews hiding in the basement, he let them live there until they and he were arrested together six months later. His defense that he had sought no profit did not save his life; his widow got three years imprisonment for abetting her husband's "crime" of *Judenbeherbergung* (harboring Jews).[157]

Helpers—whether they collected money or not, much or little—were in danger of denunciation. Threats made Jula temporarily send away her former employers.[158] Henryka Trauber felt that her neighbors had not denounced her only because of a priest's reassuring visits.[159] Korbecki/Korpyczki, too, got frightened and sent his lodgers away. After Rebeka Kuryniec arrived in Lwów as a refugee from Vilnius in 1940, a man hid her and her family until he was denounced by a relative who thought hiding Jews meant a fortune and resented not getting a

152. Hesheles, *Ochyma dvanadtsiatyrichnoi divchynky*, 70–71.

153. DALO R-77, 1, 1160: 2, 19 and several illegible paginations (USHMM Acc. 1995.A1086, Reel 33). A week later, the Ukrainian Police caught Menker, beat him into "confessing" to being Jewish and telling who had helped him, then sent him to a camp. Menker's statements assigning all the "blame" for hiding him to the deceased partner could have been an attempt to protect the one still alive.

154. DALO R-77, 1, 343: 32 (USHMM Acc.1995.A.1086, Reel 29).

155. Dzięgiel, *Lwów nie każdemu zdrów*, 64–65. Dzięgel implied that these rumors were implausible. Yet they are important in any case because the idea as such of hiding and murdering Jews was, in fact, not implausible in Lviv during the Holocaust.

156. DALO R-77, 1, 504: 25–28 (USHMM Acc.1995.A.1086, Reel 29).

157. DALO R-77, 1, 1327: 1–2 (USHMM Acc.1995.A.1086, Reel 29).

158. Nava Ruda, *Zum ewigen Angedenken: Erinnerungen eines Mädchens aus dem Ghetto Lwow. Jüdische Familiengeschichte 1899–1999*, ed. Erhard Roy Wiehn (Konstanz: Hartung-Gorre, 2000), 29, 35.

159. YIVO RG 1258, Box 48, Folder 853, Henryka Trauber: 4.

share.[160] Helping Jews was always risky. Beyond that it could be heroic, opportunistic, profitable, disinterested, or exploitative.[161] But, whatever the individual motivations, the cumulative effect of rescue was to add another layer to the Holocaust as massive expropriation. The few who managed to escape—temporarily or for good—lost their last belongings in the process.

Holocaust: Interaction

Jewish women were sexually exploited, sometimes while receiving assistance, sometimes in conjunction with betrayal, incarceration, and murder. While incarcerated, the survivor Marceli Lubasz met a Polish Criminal Police officer, also imprisoned, who bragged about blackmailing some Jewish women for sex while delivering others to the Germans.[162] Despite draconian laws against sex with Jews, the German also combined murder with rape. Over a period of eighteen months, the Sondergericht in Lemberg tried thirteen cases of "racial defilement," meting out three death sentences and five prison terms against the German partners, while the Jewish women had already been "resettled"—that is, killed. Such cases were not brought against Lemberg's camp personnel, protected by unwritten codes of misconduct and the easy killing of victims and witnesses.[163]

German authorities knew that killing Jews deprived them of laborers, yet murder quickly became more important to them than exploitation. In the Generalgouvernement and its Distrikt Galizien, Hans Frank and Otto Wächter agreed in 1941 that exploitation was not the "finally inevitable" and "radical solution" of the "Jewish question."[164] In Lemberg, SS leader Friedrich Katzmann and civilian authorities pondered tensions between slavery and speedy mass murder.[165] They

160. YIVO RG 1258, 853: 3.

161. This complexity was not unique. Omer Bartov's detailed study of the smaller town of Buczacz/Buchach, for instance, has shown a similar mix of behaviors and motives ("Communal Genocide," 409–17).

162. YIVO RG 720, Box II, folder 115 (Marceli Lubasz), 4. As Omer Bartov has pointed out, the traces of sexual victimization are especially faint ("Communal Genocide," 406). Klara Rosenfeld, working for Italian soldiers in Lviv, thought that some Jewish women had sex with them (*From Lwów to Parma*). Although the character of these relationships was inevitably vague in her account and perhaps ambiguous in reality, the women clearly had no genuine choice.

163. Schenk, *Der Lemberger Professorenmord*, 156–57.

164. Pohl, *Nationalsozialistische Judenverfolgung in Ostgalizien*, 77–78.

165. Jones, *Żydzi Lwowa w okresie okupacji*, 153–54; Pohl, *Nationalsozialistische Judenverfolgung in Ostgalizien*, 332, 335. By comparison with other Generalgouvernement districts, the Galizien administration left particularly few traces of debating the question of the uses of extended exploitation versus quick mass murder. See Karsten Linne, "Arbeiterrekrutierungen in Ostgalizien 1941 bis 1944: Zwischen Freiwilligkeit und Menschenjagden," *Jahrbücher für Geschichte Osteuropas* 62 (2014): 69.

gave political priority to killing in accordance with general German policy.[166] Stanisław Lem, then working at the Lviv Rohstofferfassung works, later recalled that its remaining Jewish employees were taken with the comment that "politics has precedence over the economy."[167]

As long as they lasted, employment opportunities underscored the differences between Jews and non-Jews. Almost everybody under occupation was highly dependent on some official form of employment, which granted access to food (even if often insufficient). By also offering tenuous protection against deportation, German labor exploitation also appeared to echo Soviet patterns. Yet the Jewish experience sharply underscored the differences; it was both exceptional and liminal. Under German occupation, Jewish dependency on certified work was decisively different, with Jews "essentially only work[ing] to have a work document," which offered nothing but a temporary reprieve from murder.[168] A market in such working documents, for which Jews had to pay, showed that this difference was generally understood.

The segregation between Jews and non-Jews also existed in the workplace, which became an extension of the black market, with Jews charged high prices for food and goods they could not buy elsewhere.[169] In forced labor details combining Jews and non-Jews, solidarity was an exception. As Samuel Drix would remember, among camp inmates, the few non-Jewish prisoners and the many Jews usually stayed apart.[170]

More than two hundred thousand Jews from the former eastern Galicia were deported to death camps and murdered out of sight.[171] But local implementation of the Holocaust also took the form of mass shootings close to the victims' homes.[172] A large part of Lemberg's Jewish population was deported, while an estimated thirty-five thousand to forty thousand victims—not exclusively from the city—were killed in the Yanivska/Janowska labor and mass murder camp. While some Yanivska victims were non-Jews, the overwhelming majority was Jewish.[173] Although located in the city's outskirts, Yanivska was still close to its

166. Jones, *Żydzi Lwowa w okresie okupacji*, 154–55; Browning, *Origins of the Final Solution*, 410.

167. Lem, *Świat na krawędzi*, 44.

168. Kahane, *Shchodennyk Lvivskoho hetto*, 81.

169. Gerstenfeld-Maltiel, *My Private War*, 81–82, 166; Rosenfeld, *From Lwów to Parma*, 63.

170. Drix, *Witness to Annihilation*, 85–86.

171. Pohl, "Schlachtfeld zweier totalitärer Diktaturen," 360.

172. Pohl, *Nationalsozialistische Judenverfolgung in Ostgalizien*, 9–10.

173. Pohl, *Nationalsozialistische Judenverfolgung in Ostgalizien*, 335, 338. As Dieter Pohl and Grzegorz Hryciuk have pointed out, the original Soviet estimate of two hundred thousand victims murdered in the Yanivska Camp is too high (Pohl, *Nationalsozialistische Judenverfolgung in Ostgalizien*, 335, 338; Hryciuk, *Przemiany narodowościowe i ludnościowe*, 213n43). This conclusion

center. Walking from the Habsburg Opera House to the largest single Holocaust camp on what is now Ukrainian territory would have taken about thirty minutes.

As it shifted from pogroms to ghettoization and camps, Lemberg's Holocaust remained urban and public. As Yevhen Nakonechnyi recalled, the camp's murderous purpose was generally known "to the whole city." By the fall of 1942, "the majority of Lvivians" had "no doubts" that the Germans sought the destruction of all Jews, with frequent talk about this among non-Jews "at home and outside."[174] During roundups, open streetcars and trucks crammed with victims crossed the town, the captives pleading with passersby to tell relatives.[175] Some Jews who tried to escape these transports were shot in full public view.[176] In January 1943, a publication by Lviv's small Communist underground stressed that German mass murder of Jews was now moving into "the city itself," concluding from the killings in its streets that Hitler's threat to kill all Jews in Europe was being realized.[177] After an *Aktion*, according to a German report, two "adult male Jews and a child lay shot dead" on a busy street.[178]

Non-Jewish reactions to this public violence were diverse. Children were particularly feared as denouncers.[179] Some had already played a cruel role in the pogrom at the beginning of the German occupation.[180] David Kahane reported that the destruction of synagogues attracted crowds, some apparently indifferent, others satisfied or even joining in.[181] When members of the Judenrat and of the Jewish Ordnungsdienst ghetto police were publicly hanged, crowds came to watch. Fryderyka Bratspiel recalled that some spectators cut off small pieces of rope as souvenirs.[182] Yet the German authorities also reported that the violent *Aktionen* angered the non-Jewish population, damaging the "German reputation."[183]

does not diminish either Yanivska's principal role as a combined terror, forced labor, and killing complex, compared by Pohl—in its kind if not size—to Auschwitz and Maidanek or the total number of Jews killed in eastern Galicia or Lviv. More of the victims died either close to home in mass executions or—often after passing through Yanivska—after deportation to the Bełżec death camp.

174. Nakonechnyi, *"Shoa" u Lvovi*, 219, 222.

175. Gerstenfeld-Maltiel, *My Private War*, 132; YIVO RG 720, 37, 128 (deposition of Benedykt Munk): 2.

176. Dzięgiel, *Lwów nie każdemu zdrów*, 140.

177. DALO P-183, 1, 10: 49.

178. DALO R-35, 13, 115: 17 (USHMM Acc.1995.A.1086, Reel 22).

179. Kovba, *Liudianist u bezodni pekla*, 95–96.

180. Himka, "Lviv Pogrom of 1941," 234.

181. Kahane, *Shchodennyk Lvivskoho hetto*, 54–55.

182. YIVO RG 720, 37: 2.

183. DALO R-35, 13, 115: 17; R-35, 6, 32: 49 (USHMM Acc.1995.A.1086, Reels 7, 22).

A City without Jews

In July 1943, during the "final liquidation" of the ghetto, the Germans burned it and massacred its remaining inhabitants.[184] The fire and smoke were widely visible; the smell penetrated homes far and wide.[185] They then declared Lemberg "free of Jews." In November, with the Yanivska Camp also "liquidated," the city was declared "cleansed of Jews," reaching the final stage of official genocide completion.[186] Nevertheless, Germans, the Ukrainian Police, and the Polish Criminal Police continued to hunt Jews and their helpers, with rewards per victim caught and careful accounting for the ammunition fired at those allegedly resisting.[187]

The threat of denunciation remained constant. At the end of 1943, a Ukrainian acquaintance delivered Marceli Lubasz to the Criminal Police, who handed him over to the Gestapo, assuring them that, in spite of his fake papers, he was Jewish. Between beatings, Lubasz had as a cellmate a Polish Criminal Police officer, who, although also imprisoned, still tried to make him "admit" to being Jewish.[188] Jews fleeing to the countryside often faced hostility, as in the case of a local official asking the Germans to clear his area of remaining Jews.[189]

With only few hunted survivors left, German genocide had transformed modern Lemberg into something it had never been: a historic metropole of Jewish culture was now reduced to the nightmare utopia of European antisemitism, a city without Jews.[190] With the Germans eventually driven from Lviv, this was a moment that would not last. Still, it marked the most extraordinary, pervasive, and consequential change they had brought. Poles and Ukrainians were now alone with the German occupier in a city over which they could not stop fighting. The fate of the Jews kept reverberating among the three groups. In 1942, a

184. Jones, *Żydzi Lwowa w okresie okupacji*, 121.

185. Dzięgiel, *Lwów nie każdemu zdrów*, 140.

186. Jones, *Żydzi Lwowa w okresie okupacji*, 121–22. Very few Jews, about one hundred, were still imprisoned in the Yanivska Camp until the German retreat from Lwów in July 1944, when they were forced to accompany the Germans (ibid., 174). A small number of members of the so-called Sonderkommando 1005—Death Brigade, set up to exhume and burn corpses—escaped in November 1943; some of the escapees survived. Lemberg's Sonderkommando 1005 was the first implementation of a general German strategy to obliterate the traces of genocide (ibid., 176–79).

187. DALO R-36, 1, 6: 90–91, 123, 137, 140, 147; R-77, 1, 309: 2–8; R-77, 1, 1227: 1; R-77, 1, 1258: 14; R-77, 1, 1279: 2, 12 (USHMM Acc.1995.A.1086, Reels 9 and 29). Lviv's labor administration kept functioning as a genocide co-organizer, filtering out Jewish women who tried to escape by applying for work in Germany (Linne, "Arbeiterrekrutierung in Ostgalizien," 71).

188. YIVO RG 720, Box 2, Folder 115, Marceli Lubasz: 4–5.

189. DALO R-24, 1, 123: 128 (USHMM Acc.1995.A.1086, Reel 20).

190. On the central importance of "the fate of the modern city" for postemancipation antisemitism, see Hillel J. Kieval, "Antisemitism and the City: A Beginner's Guide," in *People of the City: Jews and Urban Challenge*, ed. Ezra Mendelsohn (Oxford: Oxford University Press, 1999), 14–15.

Ukrainian Police report denounced Jews and Poles as stubborn enemies of Germany, whereas Ukrainians were, "as always, deutschfreundlich" and believed in Germany's victory.[191] When a Pole was found hiding a Jew, Ukrainian Police Commander Pitulei reported to the Germans a case of "cooperation of Poles with Jews."[192] When a Polish builder murdered a Jewish woman, Lemberg's Sondergericht found mitigating circumstances in his support for German policy and his need to carry a knife because of frequent Polish-Ukrainian fights at construction sites. Still, having shown too much initiative by intruding in "official measures," he got seven years of imprisonment.[193]

Echoing Bolshevik pride in bringing Ukrainians to cities, in 1941 *Lvivski visti* had hailed German occupation as a historic opportunity to create a Ukrainian *mishchanstvo* (urban middle class), brimming with national consciousness, and to give "our cities" their "real face."[194] In 1943, a German-licensed Ukrainian publisher released Olena Stepaniv's *Contemporary Lviv*, which noted that now, "after the deportation of the Jews," the former Jewish quarter was "Aryan."[195] Ukrainians were not alone in blaming flawed modernization and lack of national upward mobility on the Jews; this idea appeared in Polish Home Army reporting, too.[196] While disagreeing radically on the real face of Lemberg/Lwów/Lviv, Germans and significant numbers of Ukrainians and Poles did agree that none of it must be Jewish. In a city without Jews, they kept struggling and making plans.

Immiseration and Exploitation

A POW camp for Soviet prisoners was located in Lemberg's nineteenth-century Habsburg Citadel, bringing the Germans' mass starvation, killing, exploitation, and abuse of these prisoners close to the city center.[197] The city's non-Jewish civilians were not subjected to systematic starvation policies, but many still suffered

191. USHMM MF 1995.A.1086, Reel 2, DALO R-12, 1, 41: report dated 28 February 1942 and *Monatsmeldung* 30 March 1942, no pagination.

192. DALO R-58, 1, 71: 18 (USHMM Acc1995.A.1086, Reel 10).

193. DALO R-77, 1, 574: 2–6 (USHMM Acc.1995.A.1086, Reel 29).

194. *Lvivski visti*, 12/13 October 1941, 3.

195. Olena Stepaniv, *Suchasnyi Lviv* (Cracow: Ukrainske vydavnytstvo, 1943), 87.

196. Mick, "Incompatible Experiences," 354; Omer Bartov, "Eastern Europe as the Site of Genocide," *Journal of Modern History* 80 (2008): 576.

197. Pohl, *Nationalsozialistische Judenverfolgung in Ostgalizien*, 112–13. Lemberg's mental asylum was another historic Habsburg landmark turned into a site of German mass murder: before it became a field hospital in 1942, almost all its patients were systematically starved to death (ibid., 115–16.). After Italy's exit from the Axis in 1943, the Citadel also served as a camp to incarcerate Italian troops. While such de facto prisoners were generally subject to German abuse, exploitation, individual killings, and, in other locations, several massacres, a mass killing of Italian officers in

severely. In postwar retrospect, even a strictly anti-Bolshevik Ukrainian nationalist felt that Germans fed Lviv worse than Soviets.[198] In November 1942, German officials, both military and civilian, reported losing out in comparisons with the "Russian period." With "not a single gram of fat" and hardly any meat or sugar officially available for six months, non-Germans had to starve or buy on the black market.[199] A German manager reported that his employees received on average two hundred złoty per month. With a loaf of bread costing thirty, they embezzled, fainted at work, or stayed away to search for food.[200] When Frank visited Lemberg again in 1943, Germans found Ukrainian participation listless because of "increasing food scarcity."[201]

The German practice of shipping Distrikt inhabitants away for forced labor affected Lviv directly and indirectly.[202] Initially, some labor recruiting was voluntary.[203] David Kahane remembered such volunteers coming through Lemberg on their way to the Reich and taking the opportunity to assault Jews.[204] Compulsion soon prevailed and escalated quickly from obligatory registration to manhunts.[205] In line with general German policy, a German expert identified labor as the key resource of the backward Generalgouvernement.[206] In June 1942, a visit by the Reich's chief exploiter of foreign labor, Fritz Sauckel, produced instructions for

Lviv seems not to have taken place. See Gerhard Schreiber, *Die italienischen Militärinternierten im deutschen Machtbereich, 1943 bis 1945: Verraten, verachtet, vergessen* (Munich: Oldenbourg, 1990), 547–48 and passim.

198. Nakonechnyi, *"Shoa" u Lvovi*, 140, 156.

199. NARA RG-242, T 501, Reel 214: frames 001239, 001399; reel 215: frames 000098, 000761f, reel 225: frames 001191, 001422f and DALO R-35,13,115: 11, 16 (USHMM Acc.1995.A.1086, Reel 22)

200. DALO R-35, 6, 32: 49 (USHMM Acc.1995.A.1086, Reel 7); R-35, 9, 646: 29; R-35, 13, 115: 16 (USHMM Acc.1995.A.1086, Reel 22, 24)

201. Schenk, *Der Lemberger Professorenmord*, 145.

202. The term "forced labor" here refers to a spectrum of systematic but varied exploitation practices, involving noneconomic compulsion, lack of choice, special policing, repression, segregation and discrimination regimes, and lack of or insufficient compensation. In occupied Europe as a whole, forcible dislocation and the prohibition against returning home were elements of German forced labor for millions of its victims; it should be borne in mind that others, also numbering in the millions, suffered forced labor without deportation. For a discussion of various practices and concepts of forced labor under German occupation, see Ulrich Herbert, "Zwangsarbeit im 20. Jahrhundert. Begriffe, Entwicklung, Definitionen," in *Zwangsarbeit in Hitler's Europa. Besatzung, Arbeit, Folgen*, ed. Dieter Pohl and Tanja Sebta (Berlin: Metropol, 2013), 23–36.

203. In 1943, collaborating Ukrainian officials reminded the German authorities that there had been a "rather high number" of volunteers from Distrikt Galizien in 1941 and 1942, so that the "healthy, more intelligent, and more ambitious" persons had left (Veryha, *Correspondence of the Ukrainian Central Committee*, 1254).

204. Kahane, *Shchodennyk Lvivskoho hetto*, 55.

205. Linne, "Arbeiterrekrutierung in Ostgalizien," 83.

206. Du Prel, *Das Generalgouvernement*, 16, 25. On the German economic policy of using the Generalgouvernement primarily as a labor reservoir, see Karsten Linne, "Struktur und Praxis der

Galizien to speedily send 100,000 additional laborers on top of the 150,000 already delivered. According to Wächter, the Distrikt Galizien and its "human riches" were crucial. With only the young and fit to be taken, older and weaker workers were to stay, "disturbances" to the Distrikt's economy accepted, and force used in a manhunt off main roads and railway lines, probably to reduce resistance.[207] In Lemberg in August 1942, Heinrich Himmler also demanded more labor from the Distrikt.[208]

Those considered racially Germanic enough, "ethnic Germans" and those "of German descent," were exempt, with Lemberg a future "outpost" of Germanization.[209] Yet, given their 1940 extraction of ethnic Germans, German officials now felt that the remaining population of the Distrikt by 1942 was "racially inferior." Especially in Lemberg, they deplored a "racially extraordinarily poor" set of volunteers applying for the status of "German descent," often speaking Polish or Ukrainian and offering no "desirable addition" to the German people. Nevertheless, in the Distrikt, their racist screening still affected about twenty-four thousand persons. In 1942, German planners noted that those claiming German descent had to come forward voluntarily. At the same time, they broadened their trawl for humans as racial raw material, explicitly seeking to put "race" above "ethnicity": Those judged valuable should be Germanized, especially by targeting children, even if their German descent was "very minor." The underlying strategy implied a zero-sum delusion by also aiming to "deprive the enemy" of what was "racially" best. Incarcerations and the kidnapping of children resulted.[210] In 1943, labor and rationing records identified fifteen thousand people in Lemberg with putative German names.[211] Friedrich Katzmann, charged not only with murdering Galizien's Jews but also with fostering its (proto-)Germans, willing or not, explained that they must *not* leave, even voluntarily, for the Reich.[212]

By the middle of 1943, the labor shipments had mostly ended.[213] On the whole, about 325,000 of the Distrikt's estimated 4.5 to 5.1 million inhabitants, as of 1941, were made to leave, including an estimated 230,000 Ukrainians and 95,000

deutschen Arbeitsverwaltung im besetzten Polen und Serbien 1939–1944," in *Zwangsarbeit*, ed. Pohl and Sebta, 43. The Distrikt Galizien's other significant contribution to the German war economy was oil from the area around Boryslav (Linne, "Arbeiterrekrutierung in Ostgalizien," 64).

207. DALO R-54, 1, 2: 5, 8.

208. BA NS 19, 1695: 1.

209. Czesław Madajczyk, ed., *Vom Generalplan Ost zum Generalsiedlungsplan* (Munich: Saur, 1994), 124. Also see the map in Martin Dean, "Soviet Ethnic Germans and the Holocaust in the Reich Commissariat Ukraine, 1941–1944" in *Shoah in Ukraine*, ed. Brandon and Lower, 264.

210. BA R 186, Band 4, MF 1: 1629–1634; Sandkühler, *"Endlösung" in Galizien*, 92, 95.

211. DALO R-35, 12, 44: 123–25.

212. DALO R-54, 1, 16: 3.

213. Sandkühler, *"Endlösung" in Galizien*, 99.

Poles.[214] Nearly thirty thousand are estimated to have come from Lviv.[215] While there was some voluntary labor migration, genuine choice was rare.[216] Thus, by June 1942, most of one village's harvest had been devastated by a storm, a Ukrainian official reported. Only 23 of 130 horses had survived the winter. With Germans refusing to lower delivery quotas, 350 villagers left for work in Germany to "escape starvation."[217] From the fall of 1942 on, there were public manhunts for labor deportation in Lemberg itself.[218] Soon, however, Wächter was complaining about delays. His Distrikt had to send 46,000 fresh workers by the middle of December but only 12,411 had been levied, with a third of those initially caught rejected as too ill; collecting the "young and fit" went badly with imposing deprivation.[219]

There were vicious cycles even within the viciousness. With peasants bringing produce to Lemberg, according to German reports, "caught ruthlessly" for deportation, urban supplies dwindled further. A German official estimated that about sixty thousand non-Germans went without even their official rations in order to hide from labor deportation. Army workshops incentivized their local workers with better rations and strong spirits, granted from the beginning with the intention to later withhold them as punishment.[220]

Nazis felt the urge to compete with Stalinists. Germans told one another they would only be taken seriously if they met Soviet standards of compulsion.[221] In fact, they were surpassing them. By 1943, Ukrainian nationalists reported growing discontent among peasants and widespread flight due to German labor deportations, especially since they were accompanied by crippling agricultural levies, brutal raids, and plunder.[222] Still, by comparison with German occupation further east, in the Reichskommissariat Ukraine under Erich Koch and the eastern Ukrainian territories under military administration, Lemberg's Ukrainians, especially articulate urban elites, were mostly better off and also had more opportunities to collaborate. They were also treated better than the Poles, the city's major other non-Jewish ethnic group.

214. For estimates of Distrikt Galizien's population and the dimensions of labor deportation, see Hryciuk, *Przemiany narodowościowe i ludnościowe*, 203–10; and Pohl, *Nationalsozialistische Judenverfolgung in Ostgalizien*, 43–44. For varying, also higher figures, see Linne, "Arbeiterrekrutierung in Ostgalizien," 83.

215. Kosytskyi, *Entsyklopediia Lvova*, 2:41.

216. Linne, "Arbeiterrekrutierung in Ostgalizien," 67.

217. TsDAVOU 3959c, 2, 83b: 17–21.

218. Kosytskyi, *Entsyklopediia Lvova*, 2:41; Hryciuk, *Polacy we Lwowie*, 262; Linne, "Arbeiterrekrutierung in Ostgalizien," 71–74.

219. DALO R-54, 1, 2: 14–15.

220. DALO R-62, 1, 26: 3, 75, and 95 (USHMM Acc.1995.A.1086, Reel 11).

221. Yad Vashem M-37; DALO R-35, 13, 21: 3.

222. GDA SBU 13, spr. 376, tom 71: 76.

Winning a Losing Game: *Collaboration afin d'état*

Germans did not offer Ukrainian elites the option of what Yohanan Petrovsky-Shtern and Antony Polonsky have termed "high-level . . . polititcal collaboration."[223] Yet in the Generalgouvernement, they did offer substantial opportunities for lower-level collaboration not only but especially to Ukrainians.[224] It bears emphasis that the relationship between statehood and collaboration was complex: as Robert Paxton has observed with great precision, German-dominated France, a defining case of collaboration, is best compared not with other West European countries but with "formerly stateless peoples like the Croats of Yugoslavia and the Slovaks of Czechoslovakia for whom Hitler's destruction of the . . . status quo meant the chance for ethnic statehood."[225] Grasping this chance was a key aim of Ukrainian collaborators too, as Kost Pankivskyi remembered.[226] The difference was that Germany never rewarded them with a satellite state, while the collaborating strategy aiming to first utilize German power against Poles and Jews, then exploit a German collapse, achieved the desired results only in part.[227] But their motivations and actions are inexplicable if their drive for national statehood is omitted: where the collaborating elite of an established but defeated nation-state could opt for a *collaboration d'état*—a collaboration citing as its justification state preservation and a "national revolution" of reactionary transformation, the ambitious elites of stateless nationalism were practicing what we can call *collaboration afin d'état*, collaboration to achieve a state under German hegemony. Their tragedy was that the Germans never fully accommodated them but gave them just enough perks and hope to maintain their cooperation.[228]

223. Yohanan Petrovsky-Shtern and Antony Polonsky, "Introduction," in "Jews and Ukrainians," special issue, *Polin: Studies in Polish Jewry* 26 (2013): 46.

224. The term "collaboration," as we use it now, is a product of the history it describes. This feature—shared with other key notions of modern history such as fascism, communism, totalitarianism, or Cold War—does not diminish its usefulness as a reflected historical category, even if it can still inspire reflexes of denial.

225. Robert O. Paxton, *Vichy France: Old Guard and New Order, 1940–1944* (New York: Columbia University Press, 1972), 139.

226. Grzegorz Rossoliński-Liebe, Stepan Bandera: The Life and Afterlife of a Ukrainian Nationalist. Fascism, Genocide, and Cult (Stuttgart: ibidem, 2014), 180–81.

227. Recognizing that collaborators attempted to use German power for their own purposes does *not* imply that Germans did not have their own extremely destructive policies or that German responsibility is somehow lessened.

228. Even in this respect, differences between a "state" and a "nonstate case," between Western and Eastern Europe were real but not absolute. Vichy's "National Revolutionaries," despite having their state (at least for a while), also had to live with the fact that Hitler "ignored or scorned" much of their program, even though German occupation "did shape the National Revolution" (Paxton, *Vichy France*, 143).

Frank expected Ukrainians to submit "forever as a labor force," rejecting any "Great-Ukrainian" aspirations. For him, they were both "friends of the German people" and "not trusted by it."[229] Once the Ukrainian-nationalist attempt to found their own client state had been suppressed, OUN-B leaders were arrested. Ukraine was not the only country where Germans were too shortsighted to benefit from what fascist nationalists offered—proxy rule and serving Nazi Germany "under the leadership of Adolf Hitler," as the OUN-B promised.[230] Still, the OUN-B staked out its claim to nationalist leadership: it did not simply declare a state; it declared *its* state, one that would belong to authoritarian nationalists and fascists because Germans would back them, except—they did not.[231]

After German rejection, Ukrainian nationalists continued to look for opportunities to cooperate, occasionally stressing common hostility to Bolsheviks and Jews.[232] A report of unclear authorship, preserved in German files, mentions a nationalist offer to settle for a western Ukrainian protectorate excluding central

229. Motyka, *Tak było w bieszczadach*, 74.

230. On other cases of unrequited collaboration, see Mazower, *Dark Continent*, 148–49. On the Ukrainian nationalist case, see Serhiychuk, *Ukrainskyi zdvyh*, 3:98, 112; and Kentii, *Zbroinyi chyn*, 215. The German authorities initially handled the Ukrainian nationalist attempt to establish a state with comparative restraint. German suppression of the OUN became much more violent and pervasive by September and November 1941 (Armstrong, *Ukrainian Nationalism*, 83, 97, 106–8). Yet many nationalist activists remained in occupation offices (Motyka, *Ukraińska partyzantka*, 93). Even later, the German treatment of incarcerated Ukrainian nationalists remained ambiguous. Sixteen out of 48 nationalists sent to Auschwitz between 20 July and 8 August 1942 died in the camp. At the same time, as a group they seem to have received some preferential treatment, such as labor assignments with higher odds of survival and in several cases releases, which were extremely rare in Auschwitz. See Franziska Bruder, "'Der Gerechtigkeit zu dienen': Die ukrainischen Nationalisten als Zeugen im Auschwitz-Prozess," in *Im Labyrinth der Shuld: Täter—Opfer—Ankläger*, ed Irmtrud Wojak und Susanne Meinl (Frankfurt am Main: Campus, 2003), 153–55.

231. Ukrainian nationalism in the Second World War had both "integral nationalist" and fascist features. It is ahistorical to impose a misleading dichotomy here. For a detailed discussion of the fascist characteristics of both the OUN-B and the (weaker and smaller) OUN-M, see Rudling, "The OUN, the UPA, and the Holocaust" 2–7; Bruder, *Den ukrainischen Staat erkämpfen*, 51; Gregorz Rossoliński-Liebe, "The Ukrainian National Revolution of 1941: Discourse and Practice of a Fascist Movement," *Kritika: Explorations in Russian and Eurasian History* 12 (2011): 83–114. Oleksandr Zaitsev's recent and important study of Ukrainian nationalism in the 1920s and 1930s illustrates the inconsistency of attempts to magnify differences where similarities prevailed. Showing what he calls the "parallels" with fascism in great depth and detail, Zaitsev's insistence on a rigid dichotomy of "fascism" and "integral nationalism" is inconsistent with his own findings (*Ukrainskyi intehralnyi natsionalism, 1920–1930-ti roky* [Kyiv: Krytyka, 2013], 426).

232. Kentii, *Zbroinyi chyn*, 218, 220–21, 227, 234, 253–54, 258. As Grzegorz Motyka has argued, the German suppression of the Stetsko government may, in the long run, have saved the OUN-B from itself. If its state had lasted longer, "it would doubtlessly have had a fascist character" and its leaders would have been "considered collaborators," sharing "the fate of Vidkun Quisling, Andrei Vlasov, and Josef Tiso" (Motyka, *Ukraińska partyzantka*, 90–92). Stetsko, if he had had his will in 1941, might have failed to be received by Ronald Reagan in 1983.

and eastern Ukraine.[233] In 1942, for the first anniversary of its state declaration—also a peak moment of the Holocaust—the OUN-B issued a declaration that rejected German and Soviet imperialism, blaming the latter on Jews.[234] The "Moscow-Jewish" enemy was identified as the worse of the two, so confronting Germans was to be avoided.[235] By the end of the year, a regional OUN report declared that the national situation had changed "in our favor, most of all thanks to the complete liquidation of the Jewish element."[236]

For some Ukrainian activists, the incorporation of Distrikt Galizien into the Generalgouvernement, a German occupation regime for parts of Poland, was a signal disappointment, apparently integrating Galizien with occupied Poland.[237] Even as the German army's Oberfeldkommandatur office in Lemberg noted Ukrainian discontent, it found older Ukrainians ready to recognize dependency on "German experience."[238]

The German preference for Ukrainians had diverse effects, including mundane but substantial privileges and opportunities to serve in auxiliary units, especially the Waffen-SS Galizien Division set up in 1943. More than eighty thousand volunteered; thirteen thousand were eventually recruited.[239] Up to thirty-seven thousand Ukrainians from the Distrikt ended up in German auxiliary service.[240] Not all were volunteers and choices were restricted, but the incentives were real. In 1941, German Order Police head Kurt Daluege sent instructions to Lemberg that Ukrainian auxiliaries' relatives receive "protection against measures by German offices" and additional food, especially not less than the Polish Police.[241]

233. Yad Vashem M-37, DALO R-35, 13, 102: 3.

234. Volodymyr Serhiychuk, *Stepan Bandera: U dokumentakh radianskykh orhaniv derzhavnoi bezpeky (1939–1959)* (Kyiv: PP Serhiychuk, 2009), 1:154.

235. Ibid., 155, 157.

236. GDA SBU 13, spr. 376, tom 30: 8.

237. Präg and Jacobmeyer, *Das Diensttagebuch*, USHMM Acc.1999.A.0194, Reel 4: 930. Referring to Galicia's Ukrainians as "Austrian Ukrainians" or "Rutheno-Ukrainians," Germans insisted on using the border between the Distrikt Galizien and the eastern Reichskommissariat Ukraine to prevent Galician-"Piedmontese" contagion in the latter. See Volodymyr Kosyk, *Ukraina i Nimechchyna u Druhii svitovii viini* (Paris: Naukove tovarystvo im. T. Shevchenka u Lvovi, 1993), 133–34, 138; Yad Vashem M-37; DALO R-35, 13, 102: 3.

238. NARA RG-242, T501, Reel 214: frames 001042–43, 001238–39, 001399–400; Reel 215: frames 000316-17, 000494-95, 000760–62.

239. Frank Golczewski, "Shades of Grey: Reflections on Jewish-Ukrainian and German-Ukrainian Relations in Galicia," in *Shoah in Ukraine*, ed. Brandon and Lower, 136. On the Waffen-SS Galizien Division as a form of collaboration, the context of its creation, and its legacies, see Olesya Khromeychuk, *"Undetermined" Ukrainians: Post-War Narratives of the Waffen SS "Galicia" Division* (Bern: Lang, 2013), 170–72.

240. Hryciuk, *Przemiany narodowościowe i ludnościowe*, 211.

241. DALO R-35, 12, 18: 2 (USHMM Acc.1995.A.1086, Reel 8)

Sometimes, joining the Waffen-SS has been rationalized as patriotism. In a reductionist yet persistent view, it was merely a tactical concession to weakened post-Stalingrad Germans, desperate for fresh soldiers, with its only real purpose to create the core of a future Ukrainian army to gain independence once Nazi Germany and the Soviet Union both collapsed. Yet the Galizien Division was "the result of a complex combination of factors, rooted in the specificity of Ukrainian nationalism and the changing situation throughout Europe."[242]

In reality, no neat line separated supposed patriotic pragmatism from German aims. Initially, Metropolitan Sheptytskyi publicly welcomed German "liberation" from Bolshevism. Yet Sheptytskyi's position cannot be reduced to his response to the trauma of Soviet occupation; his aims were more ambitious. In letters to Hitler, Sheptytskyi expressed "great hopes" that the latter's "genius statesmanship" would "deliver a lethal blow to Bolshevism." With God putting Ukraine in Hitler's hands, the metropolitan prayed for German victory over "the destroyer of European Christian culture."[243] The enemy extended beyond Bolshevism: the "smashing of Russia"—a country, nation, and empire, not an ideology—would offer Ukraine an "opportunity to integrate" into Europe. Ukrainian leaders were ready for "closest cooperation," he promised, if Germany would respect Ukrainian interests.[244] A new order would also open the East for the Greek Catholic Church. Sheptytsky wrote in this vein not only to the Germans but also to the papal nuncio in Budapest.[245] In sum, at this point Sheptytskyi expected Hitler to deliver a crusade where the Habsburgs had failed.

Sheptytskyi, however, was ready to learn from experience. He was aware of antisemitic and other forms of violence from the beginning.[246] While greeting the Germans, he had publicly called for "consideration" for "the needs and welfare of all citizens . . . without regard to . . . faith, nationality, and social stratum."[247] Sheptytskyi shared some traditional Christian prejudice against Jews; he believed in a special link between Jews and Communism and had no sympathy for the latter.[248] Yet, by 1942, he found German rule "perhaps even more evil" than Soviet power and "almost diabolical." He recognized Jews as the "primary victims" of a "regime of truly unbelievable terror and corruption."[249] In general, in 1942 and

242. Khromeychuk, *"Undetermined" Ukrainians*, 171.

243. Serhyi Bohunov et al., eds., *Likvidatsiia UHKTs (1939–1946): Dokumenty radianskykh orhaniv derzhavnoi bezpeky* (Kyiv: PP Serhiychuk, 2006), 1:179–80.

244. Hansjakob Stehle, "Sheptyts'kyi and the German Regime," in *Morality and Reality*, ed. Magosci, 129–30; Bohunov et al., *Likvidatsiia UHKTs*, 1:184–86 (doc. 38).

245. Himka, "Metropolitan Andrey Sheptytsky," 343.

246. Ibid., 342.

247. Ibid., 339.

248. Ibid., 344, 353–54.

249. Redlich, "Sheptytskyi and the Jews," 155.

1943, Sheptytskyi objected to the Holocaust in various, if usually indirect or confidential, forms.[250] By 1944, Soviet intelligence confirmed that he had abandoned all "Germanophilism."[251] He initiated Polish-Ukrainian secret talks and issued a pastoral letter threatening anathema for murder. Yet, in 1943, he still supported the Waffen-SS division with chaplains and a special service. He may have believed in the priority of training Ukrainian soldiers; unusually, he saw their future task not in fighting Poles or Soviets, but in keeping order until the latter reasserted their rule, which, it seems, he came to prefer to "anarchy."[252]

Others besides Sheptytskyi embraced diverse motives for supporting the division in addition to anti-Bolshevism or material incentives.[253] For some division volunteers, it seems to have been the alternative to labor mobilization, as an internal OUN report of May 1944 indicated.[254] Moreover, memories of the First World War inspired hopes that the second one would also end with the collapse of several empires. Later, during the Cold War, some Ukrainians adopted the preferred memory of having even-handedly fought against both Nazis and Soviets. But the facts never fit this simplistic antitotalitarian myth. Zenon Vrublevskyi, one of the youngest Galizien Division volunteers, recalled expectations not of German-Soviet collapse but of German victory, with a "piece of Ukraine" for German allies, even if only as a "protectorate."[255] Although Vrublevskyi's memories express the views of one individual, they are still more plausible than hindsight interpretations that fail to recall the full context of 1943. In sum, the most realistic explanation for Ukrainian support of the Germans is a combination of individual motives with the strategic desire to preserve *all* options: to fight all comers, especially the Poles, in a potential power vacuum, *and* to accumulate casualties against the Soviet Union to serve as negotiating chips in case of German victory.

The Galizien Division was a comparatively late phenomenon, even if Lemberg was the central stage of its making. Schutzmannschaft auxiliaries, also recruited

250. Himka, "Metropolitan Andrey Sheptytsky," 345–53.

251. Bohunov et al., *Likvidatsiia UHKTs*, 1:216–17 (doc. 41).

252. Budurowycz, "Sheptyts'kyi and the Ukrainian National Movement," 63–64; Stehle, "Sheptyts'kyi and the German Regime," 134–38. On Polish-Ukrainian talks, Sheptytskyi's role in them, and his pastorals as well as letters attacking murder and "demoralization," see Torzecki, "Sheptyts'kyi and Polish Society," 92–94; and Stehle, "Sheptyts'kyi and the German Regime," 131–36.

253. On benefits for the division soldiers and their family members, see Veryha, *Correspondence of the Ukrainian Central Committee*, 1233–34.

254. GDA SBU 13, spr. 376, tom 35: 174–75. The same report, critical of German initiatives, including the division, also registered the case of 120 Ukrainians who had first fought for nationalist forces in Volyn and then joined the division.

255. Oksana Tovarianska, "Usni istorii kolyshnykh voiakiv dyvizii 'Halychyna': Interviu s Zenonom Ivanovychem Vrublevskym," *Skhid/Zakhid*, no. 11–12 (2008): 320.

in the Distrikt Galizien, were mostly used outside it.[256] Lemberg's Ukrainian Police had a longer, local history. The Distrikt had by far the greatest concentration of Ukrainian Police officers anywhere. In Lemberg, their pay and benefits were comparatively good, to encourage cooperation. Most policemen were volunteers.[257] The writer Arkadyi Lubchenko fantasized their "preponderant majority" as patriots eager to double as future national army cadres.[258]

Initially, many rank-and-file members of what was originally called the Ukrainian Auxiliary Police, the Hilfspolizei, were nationalist militia members; its leaders included older men, some of whom had served in the Polish police.[259] For the Distrikt as a whole, the Ukrainian police grew from thirty-four hundred members in April 1942 to forty-one hundred in 1943.[260] In the spring of 1942, in the adjacent Distrikt Krakau, roughly corresponding to former Habsburg western Galicia and with a Polish population majority, the majority of local police, 3,383 out of 4,231, were Polish.[261] In Distrikt Galizien, roughly corresponding to Habsburg eastern Galicia, with a Ukrainian majority and a total of about 4,100 policemen, Lemberg had the highest concentration of Ukrainian police, with an official roster of 860 in July 1943 and another 434 in the surrounding area.[262]

The Ukrainian Police were officially meant to control the "native population," fight the so-called black market and criminal gangs, and to join the struggle

256. Sandkühler, *"Endlösung" in Galizien*, 477n122.

257. Golczewski, "Shades of Grey," 138–39; DALO R-135, 6, 155: 173–76 (USHMM Acc.1995.A.1086, Reel 7).

258. Iuriy Lutskyi, ed., *Shchodennyk Arkadiia Liubchenka. 2/XI-41–21/II-45 p.* (Lviv: M. P. Kots, 1999), 140. Frank Golczewski has stressed that higher officers of Lemberg's Ukrainian Police were, at least in some cases, members of the elite, including veterans of the Polish-Ukrainian conflict in 1918, not merely "criminal elements" ("Shades of Grey," 138–39). Their collaboration and Holocaust participation cannot be relativized as socially marginal.

259. Hryciuk, *Polacy we Lwowie*, 218. Also see the case of Polizei-Obermeister Krawczyk, AAN 540, I, 3: 3. The policemen were ordered to wear green armbands, expressly not in the Ukrainian national colors, labeled in German and Ukrainian. In early German documents, the term *Hilfspolizei* was sometimes replaced by "Ukrainian Police" and its leader signed as "Commander of the Ukrainian Police." See DALO R-35, 2, 58: 1, 6, 19 (USHMM Acc.1995.A.1086, Reel 6); and R-58, 1, 71: 18 (USHMM Acc.1995.A.1086, Reel 10).

260. Pohl, *Nationalsozialistische Judenverfolgung in Ostgalizien*, 92. See also Gabriel N. Finder and Alexander V. Prusin, "Collaboration in Eastern Galicia: The Ukrainian Police and the Holocaust," *East European Jewish Affairs* 34 (2004): 105.

261. Präg and Jacobmeyer, *Das Diensttagebuch*, USHMM Acc.1999.A.0194, Reel 4: 671; Finder and Prusin, "Collaboration in Eastern Galicia," 105.

262. Finder and Prusin, "Collaboration in Eastern Galicia," 105. German documents show some divergence between projected and actual strength. In August 1943, the official roster for the city of Lviv included 840 men; in reality there were only 680. See DALO R-58, 1, 30: 12 (USHMM Acc.1995.A.1086, Reel 10).

against Bolshevism. They assisted in the Holocaust by helping guard, terrorize, exploit, and raze ghettos and catch and kill Jews.[263] The Ukrainian Police also facilitated rural-urban social mobility, since many young volunteers had been born in small villages.[264] Poles lampooned Ukrainian policemen in rhymes about cow herding; some Lviv Ukrainians did the same.[265] Here was a form of rural-urban social mobility that came with mockery and murder.

The Germans tolerated the Greek Catholic Church and allowed Generalgouvernement Ukrainians to expand their education system.[266] Educating under a German umbrella meant opportunities for nationalizing the masses—Ukrainian kindergartens served 70 percent of the villages that nationalists considered Ukrainian—and thousands of jobs for local Ukrainian intelligentsia, who also benefited from almost sixty Ukrainian periodicals and a Ukrainian publishing house.[267]

A 1942 German report on the first year of the new Distrikt emphasized the "better cooperation [*Mitgehen*] of the local population," compared with mostly Polish districts. The report noted 150,000 workers registering for labor in the Reich by May 1942, "nearly exclusively voluntarily," and the good performance of the local Baudienst, a drafted construction service, praised for reaching almost German standards. Germans felt that Lemberg's population was more difficult than the "naïve . . . rural" one.[268] Official segregation remained evident. When Frank visited Lemberg in the summer of 1942, schoolchildren greeted him "divided by ethnicity," as Germans, Ukrainians, and Poles.[269]

263. Golczewski, "Shades of Grey," 127; Mick, *Kriegserfahrungen in einer multiethnischen Stadt*, 502–6, 518. For assignments beyond Lemberg, see DALO R-58, 1s, 32: pagination illegible (Der Kommandeur der Ordnungspolizei im Distrikt Galizien, Lemberg, den 16.8.1943); R-58, 1, 30: 12 (USHMM Acc.1995.A.1086, Reel 10); and Sandkühler, *"Endlösung" in Galizien*, 106.

264. Veryha, *Correspondence of the Ukrainian Central Committee*, 1249; DALO R-16, 1, 11: pagination illegible (USHMM Acc.1995.A.1086, Reel 20).

265. Hryciuk, *Polacy we Lwowie*, 219; Nakonechnyi, *"Shoa" u Lvovi*, 149.

266. By the end of 1943, Ukrainian educational institutions included nearly 430 kindergartens, more than 3,000 primary schools, 10 elite high schools (gymnasia), more than 65 professional and commercial schools, and about 200 agricultural schools. About two thousand Ukrainians were enrolled in quasi-academic *Fachkurs* training in Lemberg (Veryha, *Correspondence of the Ukrainian Central Committee*, 1274–78). For even higher figures for Ukrainian schools, see N. V. Antoniuk, *Ukrainske kulturne zhyttia v "Heneralnii hubernii," 1939–1944 rr.: Za materialamy periodychnoi presy* (Lviv: Stefanyka, 1997), 169–71.

267. Antoniuk, *Ukrainske kulturne zhyttia*, 169–71.

268. Yad Vashem M-37; DALO R-35, 13, 21: 12–13.

269. AAN 111, 1, 1430: 20. Frank was accompanied by seven train cars of flags, masts, stage elements, and a "Hoheitsadler" as well as expert staff from a specialized Hamburg company to set up this roadshow of Third Reich pomp (ibid.: 60–61, 80).

With the OUN-B suppressed, the main institutional partner for co-opting Ukrainians in the Generalgouvernement was the Ukrainskyi Tsentralnyi Komitet (UTsK), or Hauptausschuss, located in Cracow.[270] Under its head Volodymyr Kubiiovych, the UTsK strongly supported the Waffen-SS division, trying to parlay its assistance into German concessions, such as the release of Ukrainian prisoners of the Germans or access to additional media outlets for propaganda purposes.[271] Its ambitions went beyond such pragmatism. The "politically reliable Ukrainians," the Hauptausschuss explained to the German authorities, were *deutschfreundlich*, unlike the unreliable Poles, and should be employed to help eliminate "hostile saboteurs and concealed Communists" and "break the influence" of Jews and Poles.[272] When asking for the release of Ukrainians, the UTsK argued that they were victims of Polish and Jewish denunciation.[273] Appealing to German claims of defending Europe against Bolshevik barbarism, Kubiiovych and his Hauptausschuss declared that, as an "outpost of European culture," Ukrainians had started a "fight to the death" against Bolshevism as early as 1917.[274]

Despite the existence of rationalizing memoirs and Soviet condemnations, there is still no history of this important institution. Its purpose was collaboration, or "legal cooperation," as Kost Pankivskyi, the head of the Lviv Hauptausschuss branch, described it in 1943. He demanded a full commitment to Germany, leaving no ambiguities. Those wanting "to part ways with the Germans should leave" immediately because "we must conduct German policy."[275] Kubiiovych would insist for the rest of his life that the German rule he had served had been "incomparably easier" than further east, implying that it had been right to serve such putatively moderate Nazis, perhaps even contributing to their lack of ferocity.[276] For Lviv, Kost Pankivskyi made the same argument.[277]

270. This body was called both "Ukrainskyi Tsentralnyi Komitet" (UTsK) and "Hauptausschuss" in German. To avoid confusion with the Central Committee of the Communist Party of Ukraine, Kubiiovych's committee will be referred to as UTsK or "Hauptausschuss."

271. Veryha, *Correspondence of the Ukrainian Central Committee*, 542, 551–55, 1185–88, 1201–2, 1254–67, 1270–73.

272. TsDAVOU 3959c, 2, 83b: 12; Veryha, *Correspondence of the Ukrainian Central Committee*, 241.

273. Veryha, *Correspondence of the Ukrainian Central Committee*, 552, 1220–21.

274. Ibid., 1201.

275. TsDAVOU 3959c, 2, 40: 112.

276. Golczewski, "Shades of Grey," 126, 134; Olesa Lysiak, ed., *Brody: Zbirnyk statei i narysiv* (Drohobych-Lviv: Vidrodzhennia, 2003), 6. Kubiiovych, it has been claimed, also rescued some victims from Nazi persecution. According to Ryszard Torzecki, he "provided Poles and Jews, threatened by the [German] occupier, with about three hundred documents of various types, which saved these people" (*Polacy i Ukraińcy*, 242).

277. Kost Pankivskyi, *Roky nimetskoi okupatsii* (New York: Kliuchi, 1965), 12.

Regarding Ukrainians, much of both men's work did concern social welfare and culture. By 1942, Pankivskyi's Lemberg Committee was organizing more than 8,000 contributing members in six district branches as well as various professional associations and institutions, including eighteen professional schools with 1,638 trainees. Over seven months, it had provided welfare services for about seventy thousand Ukrainians.[278] The Hauptausschuss also criticized Germans when they victimized Ukrainians. By 1942, Germans reported that "about everything" had been gotten out of Distrikt Galizien, all the while taking more.[279] Within a year, they were worried that recent labor manhunts and neglect were alienating the population.[280] Kubiiovych, too, decried "wild manhunts." Delays in the restitution and redistribution of property seized under the Soviet occupation produced rumors about German plans for "a large operation to resettle the Ukrainians from Galicia to the East." Yet the Hauptausschuss was not merely about welfare. It had policies and its existence was inevitably political, institutionalizing a form of *collaboration afin d'état*, an attempt to instrumentalize Nazi power for Ukrainian national aims, including the creation of a state. It would be an anachronistic dichotomy to contrast the UTsK's nationalist politics with its social and cultural activities. Even Kubiiovych's criticism of some German actions was embedded in his strident nationalism. He denounced Poles to Germans, complaining that Ukrainians had expected better treatment than Poles, who "actively fought against Germany." Yet Germans treated "all peoples of the East" the same.[281] Ivan Krypiakevych would later describe Kubiiovych to Soviet authorities as driven by ambition, personal resentment, and hatred of the Soviet Union and Poles.[282] In any case, Kubiiovych's ruthless national self-assertion included the denunciation of others to a lethally dangerous conqueror.

An expert in geography and demography, he interpreted "autonomy for the Ukrainian ethnic group" as preference in employment and local administration. He sought the "removal of . . . Polish and Jewish elements" from areas he claimed for Ukrainians, "a complete separation" between Poles and Ukrainians, and population transfers to create "pure Ukrainian territories."[283] His positions also

278. TsDAVOU 3959, 1, 30: 128–29, 185.

279. Yad Vashem M-37; DALO R-35, 13, 21:12, 20.

280. Yad Vashem M-37; DALO R-35, 13, 21: 41. On German manhunts for labor, see Mick, *Kriegserfahrungen in einer multiethnischen Stadt*, 493–94.

281. Veryha, *Correspondence of the Ukrainian Central Committee*, 598; TsDAVOU 3959c, 2, 131: 2–8.

282. Inna Zabolotna, "Roky nimetskoi okupatsii na zakhidnii Ukraini za spohadamy I. P. Krypiakevycha," *Ukrainskii arkheohrafichnyi shchorichnyk*, n.s., no. 7 (Kyiv: M. P. Kots, 2002), 405–6.

283. Golczewski, "Shades of Grey," 127; Volodymyr Kubiiovych, *Ukraintsi v Heneralnii Hubernii, 1939–1941: Istoriia Ukrainskoho Tsentralnoho Komitetu* (Chicago: Vydavnytstvo Mykoly Denysiuka, 1975), 420.

depended on the course of the war. In June 1941, with Germany on the attack, Kubiiovych advocated a nationalist, authoritarian, single-leader Ukraine, occupying unprecedentedly large *Lebensraum*, preserving "the purity of the Ukrainian race," and defending a German-dominated new Europe from Asia and its leader, Russia.[284] There is no reason to assume that this was mere opportunism or tactics. If Kubiiovych was "speaking Nazi," his proposals delineated a shared grammar of nationalism and authoritarianism.

Its rules applied not only to Poles and Jews but also to other Ukrainians, sorted along an assumed East-West divide of national consciousness. One month after the German attack, the UTsK explained that many Soviet POWs were "nationally unconscious" and indoctrinated against the Reich's "new Europe" and asked for access to POWs to segregate the "great mass of Ukrainian men" for "ideological and national retraining."[285] Meanwhile, the UTsK was also visiting German POW camps and correctly reporting their conditions as "a true Dantean hell" now "raised to a modern degree of pure monstrosity."[286] Yet it also wanted nationalist triage, asking for only Western Ukrainians, already "nationally conscious," to be released immediately.[287] At this point, the UTsK thus asked Germans to retain eastern Ukrainians as a literally captive audience for indoctrination by nationalist intellectuals: the hell of German POW camps, it seemed, might be just the right purgatory for fellow Ukrainians lost to the nation. Once again, nationalism plus arrogance equaled not solidarity but nationalist self-othering.[288]

The face Kubiiovych presented to the Germans was that of a kindred spirit, an up-to-date right-wing *völkisch* totalitarian, aware of the opportunities offered by a new order. The question of which Kubiiovych was truer (or perhaps preferable to himself in hindsight), the fluent speaker of Nazi or one who was just lying in it, is moot. What is pertinent is that it was possible to effectively speak Nazi to Nazis and then become an "innocent nationalist" during the Cold War. Kubiiovych's truth, if any, was that he mastered both.

Pragmatism and brutality thus meshed seamlessly. For Kubiiovych, developing the Ukrainian cooperative system under Germans would not only strengthen the Ukrainian economy but also protect Ukrainian peasants from Jewish

284. Veryha, *Correspondence of the Ukrainian Central Committee*, 220–30.

285. TsDAVOU 3959c, 2, 83b: 38.

286. TsDAVOU 3959c, 2, 84a: 2.

287. TsDAVOU 3959c, 2, 83b: 40.

288. By 1943, when helping the Germans recruit for the Waffen-SS Division, the UTsK sought the release of Ukrainians not only as political prisoners but also as POWs from the Soviet army (Veryha, *Correspondence of the Ukrainian Central Committee*, 1220).

exploitation.[289] In June 1942, during the peak of the Holocaust *Aktionen* in Lemberg, its Hauptausschuss branch pointed out that commercial training would enable Ukrainian youth to occupy "areas of economic life" formerly "reserved almost exclusively for Jews."[290] Sometimes even taking over the Jews' place was not good enough. In the fall of 1942, Kubiiovych complained that the exploitation of Ukrainian peasants could turn them into landless "proletarian[s] eking out a miserable existence in some city between the bleak walls of a former Jew house."[291] He decried German humiliations of Ukrainians both by beating them and by ordering a Jew to search a Ukrainian woman, which "the Jew did, in a manner offending human and female dignity"; he blamed Jews, Poles, and escaped Soviet POWs for provoking German retaliation against Ukrainians.[292] Ruthlessly wielding the weapons of the weak against the weaker, Kubiiovych also knew what to do with weapons received from the strong. As Christoph Mick has pointed out, when the Waffen-SS Galizien Division was being recruited, Kubiiovych called on volunteers to continue the Ukrainian independence struggle and to help "exterminate the Jewish-Bolshevik pestilence."[293]

Another sharp line missing in reality and drawn thickly in memory was that separating Ukrainian national self-realization from German interests and ideology. *Nashi dni*, a Ukrainian paper published in Lviv, focused on culture but also featured antisemitic articles.[294] Initially, the Ukrainian historian Ivan Krypiakevych, like Sheptytskyi, saw Germans not merely as liberators from the Bolsheviks but as offering opportunities for Ukrainians, especially Western Ukrainians. In a November 1941 letter to his fellow historian Oleksandr Ohloblyn, just appointed the figurehead mayor of German-occupied Kyiv, Krypiakevych recommended adapting "to the German way of thinking," emphasizing German-Ukrainian relationships, and the fight against Bolshevism and Russification. Ukrainians should show their "organizational and creative forces" to

289. Golczewski, "Shades of Grey," 126.

290. Veryha, *Correspondence of the Ukrainian Central Committee*, 388.

291. Ibid., 1176.

292. TsDAVOU 3959c, 2, 131: 2–8; Veryha, *Correspondence of the Ukrainian Central Committee*, 552; TsDAVOU 3959c, 2, 131: 2–8. Kubiiovych's addressee and the context of this correspondence need to be taken into account. But it bears emphasis that he was not shy about strong criticism of German treatment of Ukrainians, while adding accusations against Poles and Jews, when both groups were suffering from severe, if also radically different forms and degrees of persecution. Kubiiovych's retrospective statements, moreover, should be no less contextualized.

293. Mick, *Kriegserfahrungen in einer multiethnischen Stadt*, 509. On the UTsK's role in the making of the Galicia Division, see also Michael O. Logusz, *Galicia Division: The Waffen-SS 14th Grenadier Division, 1943–1945* (Atglen: Schiffer, 1997), 59–76.

294. Myroslav Shkandrij, *Jews in Ukrainian Literature: Representation and Identity* (New Haven: Yale University Press, 2009), 179–81.

prove that they deserved a state, with "Galicians" as advanced mediators with the Germans. These occupiers, Krypiakevych believed, had a positive attitude toward Ukrainians, placing Poles and Russians far lower in their racist hierarchy. He suggested exploiting Soviet-German continuities, Ukrainians having enjoyed "great privileges as against Poles" during the Soviet occupation. Fearing "Russophiles" among the Germans, Krypiakevych still thought that Ukrainans were "natural allies of the Germans in their hostility to Poles and Russians." This outlook made it possible to hope for a Ukrainian state.[295]

Collaboration in One City

If not a state, perhaps a city; when Lemberg's municipal administration was quickly taken over by a German Stadthauptmann, much of its staff remained Ukrainian. Crediting Soviets with having "achieved their aim" of an impoverished and lethargic population, Germans found it encouraging that Ukrainians welcomed them. "Professional deficiencies" were blamed on prior discrimination.[296] This German view made a difference: preference for administrative employment meant better access to food and heating fuel and protection against eviction.[297] Distrikt Governor Lasch, however, soon complained that letting Ukrainians have positions led to "devastating" results, ordering his staff to denounce them in case of failure or sabotage.[298] Still, a 1942 German report proudly noted that the lower levels of local administration were largely staffed by Ukrainians, successfully improved by training.[299] By demoting Poles and promoting Ukrainians, the Germans, in effect, continued Soviet policy. Lemberg's street names advertised German preferment. In late 1942, while removing some Polish and all Jewish references, the Stadthauptmann's office sought to replace them not

295. Liubomyr Vynar, "Lysty Ivana Krypiakevycha do Oleksandra Ohloblyna z 1941–1943 rokiv," in Isaievych, *Ivan Krypiakevych u rodynnii tradytsii*, 173–74. Krypiakevych was clutching at fantastic straws: occasionally, Hitler took blond children he spotted in Ukraine as evidence of some potential for "re-Germanization" (Mark Mazower, *Hitler's Empire: Nazi Rule in Occupied Europe* [London: Allen Lane, 2008], 206). Yet racist hatred of Slavs was decisive. Months before Krypiakevych's letter to Ohloblyn, Hitler, speaking to a small audience, stated his views on Ukrainians and Russians, deriding the former as "every bit as idle, disorganized, and nihilistically asiatic as the Greater Russians." Both, Hitler insisted, needed "the whip" (Ian Kershaw, *Hitler 1936–1945: Nemesis* [London: Penguin, 2000], 401).

296. DALO R-35, 2, 41: 2, 6, 9 (USHMM Acc.1995.A.1086, Reel 6).

297. DALO R-37, 4, 3: 31 (USHMM Acc.1995.A.1086, Reel 10).

298. Yad Vashem M-37; DALO R-35, 6, 34: 4.

299. Yad Vashem M-37; DALO R-35, 13, 21: 8; NARA RG-242, T501, Reel 214, Frame 001042–43.

only with German and Austrian but also with Ukrainian names "to make the Ukrainian national element too appear clearly in the streetscape."[300]

Some quickly understood the new opportunities. A former Ukrainian student of the mathematician Hugo Steinhaus spiked his—apparently at least partly successful—application for a teaching position in Lemberg with references to his love of German culture, his family's persecution in interwar Poland, and a long tale about harassment by the "baptized Jew" Steinhaus and his "race comrades."[301]

By murdering Lemberg's Jews, the Germans also changed the population balance between Poles and Ukrainians. In March 1943, a census counted 153,066 Poles and 81,593 Ukrainians, in a city also inhabited by 20,722 Jews then still alive and engaged in forced labor, 19,013 Germans, and 8,998 "others."[302] Even if partly distorted by politics, these statistics show the nearly complete annihilation of Lemberg's Jewish population, a significant decrease in Poles, and a strong increase for Ukrainians.[303] This increase, generally slower in cities than in villages, affected Lemberg the least. While the share of Ukrainians in the city rose to nearly 29 percent, Poles still constituted 54 percent.[304] This persistence of the Polish urban presence in the area's key city coincided with an absolute increase in Lviv's number of Ukrainians and an absolute decrease in the number of Poles. The new balance between Poles and Ukrainians was most influenced not by anything happening to either of them but by the mass murder of the Jews.

300. AUJ IDO 38 Oddział lwowski (Zweigstelle Lemberg). Korespondencja wychodząca, 1941–1942, letter to Institut für Deutsche Ostarbeit (Lviv branch) of 19 December 1942, no pagination.

301. AAN Państwowy Wyżse Kursy, 105: 59–62.

302. Hryciuk, *Przemiany narodowościowe i ludnościowe*, 223.

303. Ukrainian leaders saw the census as an opportunity to maximize Ukrainian numbers. During the first Soviet occupation, one of them had predicted that the number of Ukrainians in Lviv would increase because those who had formerly denied their own national identity would acknowledge it. Poles later accused Ukrainians of "fabricating 'Volks-Ukrainians' or 'Ukrainians-by-ethnic-descent'" following "hitlerite examples." German data of September 1942 indicated 2,240 *Volksdeutsche* in Lemberg. Poles were more likely to register as *Volksdeutsche* in the Distrikt Galizien than in other parts of occupied Poland (Nazaruk, *Zi Lvova do Varshavy*, 17; Hryciuk, *Przemiany narodowościowe i ludnościowe*, 219–34; Mick, *Kriegserfahrungen in einer multiethnischen Stadt*, 495). According to the March 1943 census, eastern Galicia had a total population of 4,233,071, including 3,262,840 Ukrainians (77.08 percent), 799,428 Poles (18.86 percent), 87,466 Jews (2.07 percent), and 67,303 Germans. Establishing comparability by applying the confessional nationality criteria of the Polish 1931 census to the results of the ethno-racist March 1943 census, Grzegorz Hryciuk has concluded that the March 1943 figures indicated a decrease of slightly more than 40 percent in the counted Polish population of eastern Galicia as compared to 1931, while the counted Ukrainian population increased by more than 14 percent (Hryciuk, *Przemiany narodowościowe i ludnościowe*, 221). Regional variations were significant.

304. Hryciuk, *Przemiany narodowościowe i ludnościowe*, 223, 227. A major extension of Lviv's territory and population caused by integrating twenty smaller municipalities added more than

In this context of violent demographic loss, ethnic nationalism, gains, claims, and threats, German manipulations in recruiting were especially toxic. Ukrainians felt that they were "on the rise" while Poles felt threatened, both meanwhile observing that the city's now fatal ethnic balance could be radically changed as never before. Competing for the state's local jobs, perks, and power was not new, but doing so in an environment fundamentally changed by genocide was. This was Frank's ethno-political "tilting game" played out in an everyday life reshaped by mass murder.

The stakes were significant and kept growing, as even rudimentary statistics on administrative position show: by the end of 1941, the city administration had 759 employees, including only 20 Germans, 432 Ukrainians, and 307 Poles. Top positions were occupied by Germans in conjunction with twenty-six Ukrainians and eight Poles. The staff of the city's communal enterprises consisted of 74 Germans, 2,909 Poles, and 1,040 Ukrainians. By early 1944, it included almost five thousand Ukrainians and seven thousand Poles.[305] Toward the end of German rule, the Distrikt administration had 1,471 employees and the Lviv city administration 9,359. The total number of employees in companies and bureaucracies receiving some kind of support was higher, 16,983.[306]

The Oberfeldkommandatur was too optimistic when it claimed in 1942 that Lemberg's Poles were "generally ready for cooperation" to recover positions.[307] Yet, when prosecuted after the war, a Polish collaborator did claim he had worked with Germans but for Poland, so as to save Lwów from drowning in what he referred to as a Ukrainian wave.[308] In the Distrikt, the Polish underground noted with satisfaction that Poles held majorities "on the railways, in treasury offices, [and] in the Criminal Police," pushing aside Ukrainians. Ukrainian nationalists lamented this victory of Polish "intrigue."[309] The Ukrainian Police complained about "Polish chauvinists," camouflaged as *Volksdeutsche*,

forty-two thousand inhabitants but made no significant difference in the ethnic composition of the city's population, which was joined by about nearly twenty-three thousand Poles, more than eighteen thousand Ukrainians, and eleven hundred Jews (DALO R-58, 2, 6: 22).

305. Hryciuk, *Polacy we Lwowie*, 216–17.

306. AAN 689, 231: 24.

307. NARA RG-242, T 501, Reel 215: Frames 000760–62.

308. Dobroszycki, *Die legale polnische Presse*, 240n249.

309. Motyka, *Ukraińska partyzantka*, 302, 304. For a German salary roster of 166 Lviv Criminal Police Officers with mostly Polish names and mostly not *Volksdeutsche*, see AAN 362/224: 68–84 (USHMM RG-15.007M, Reel 16). Moreover, SD auxiliary branches (*Aussenposten*) were "nearly completely" manned by Polish Criminal Police officers, commanded by a few SS officers (Sandkühler, *"Endlösung" in Galizien*, 81).

infiltrating the administration, while Polish employers still "harassed" Ukrainian employees by making them speak Polish.[310]

At first, the Germans intended simply to deny higher education to Slavs. Whereas Soviet rule had made Lviv's higher education a site of social and national promotion, demotion, and a transformed competition, the Germans shut it down. Especially with a view to the "loss" of Jewish medical practitioners, however, both Lasch and Wächter soon called for some higher education for non-Jews.[311] The so-called State Professional Courses, Staatliche Fachkurse, were to provide higher training without academic degrees. As German authorities insisted, they were not to go beyond what was needed to form "assistance structures for the German administration in Galizien."[312]

The initial German intention had been to open the courses only to Ukrainians. In reality, out of a total Fachkurs faculty of 1,240, only 326 were Ukrainians and 868 were Poles. Among the students, the proportions were reversed. Out of a total of 2,840 students, 2,101 were Ukrainians and 723 Poles.[313] In reality, Polish and Ukrainian were both widely used. By 1942, Roman Volchuk, having entered the Polytechnic under Soviet rule, was a student of the technical Fachkurse, which he saw as the Polytechnic by another name. Though mainly taught by Poles, his class now consisted entirely of Ukrainians.[314] The Fachkurse produced some Soviet-German continuity in education opportunities for Ukrainians.[315]

310. NARA RG-242, T501, Reel 215: frames 000097–98 and 000316–17 and USHMM MF 1995.A.1086, Reel 2, DALO R-12, 1, 41: report dated 28.2.1942 and *Monatsmeldung* 30 March 1942, no pagination.

311. Kleßmann, *Die Selbstbehauptung einer Nation*, 60; Yad Vashem M-37, DALO R-35, 6, 34: 5; R-35, 2, 67: 17 (USHMM Acc.1995.A.1086, Reel 6).

312. AUJ IDO 37 Oddział lwowski (Zweigstelle Lemberg). Korespondencja wychodząca 1942–1943, "Akten-Niederschrift. Termin bei Herrn Generalgouverneur Dr. Frank" of 20 March 1943, no pagination.

313. Christoph Kleßmann and Wacław Długoborski, "Nationalsozialistische Bildungspolitik und polnische Hochschulen," *Geschichte und Gesellschaft* 23 (1997): 551. The *Fachkurse* were quantitatively significant, as a comparison with Polish underground higher education shows: there 6,300 students, about 13 percent of the prewar student total, were taught by nearly 750 academics, about half the prewar number. Another estimated 5,800 students were trained in semi-underground vocational schools (ibid., 553–54, 557). According to earlier Polish research, the number of Polish students studying officially in Lwów under German occupation was especially high (Ryszard Zabłotniak and Jerzy Kubiatowski, "Polacy na studiach we Lwowie w latach okupacji hitlerowskiej," *Przegląd historyczno-oświatowy*, no. 4 [1979]: 535).

314. Volchuk, *Spomyny*, 99.

315. This continuity was persistent in postwar Soviet Lviv too, though denied. In 1960, a draft obkom report noted that "almost a quarter" of the institute's then teaching staff "entered training or studied or worked at the Medical Institute [i.e., were officially enrolled in the *Fachkurse*] during the period of the fascist occupation." This paragraph, however, was crossed out, while a preceding one, denouncing the elevated "class" background of the staff was not (DALO P-3, 8, 45: 34). "Class," it seems, was a handy, simple political cudgel; continuity with Germans and their institutions was not.

Despite Frank's efforts, Ukrainians perceived the Fachkurse as higher education. In the spring of 1942, the Ukrainian Police reported that Ukrainians deeply appreciated the opening of a "university" for them and called for Poles to be excluded.[316] At the same time, a German observer at the Institut für Deutsche Ostarbeit denounced the fact that the staff and students at the Fachkurse openly presented them as institutions of higher education.[317]

Ivan Krypiakevych felt that Ukrainians were winning the struggle for positions, including as Fachkurs faculty.[318] With German as the Fachkurs "language of administration," after the war Kost Pankivskyi still insisted that "the administration was in our hands" because the "character" of the Fachkurs was Ukrainian. Overlooking Soviet contributions, he credited the German occupation with "perhaps the greatest changes in the sphere of higher education"; to him, the Fachkurs system marked a breakthrough in "Ukrainian national culture and education."[319] The student Roman Volchuk, however, recalled that many of the new Ukrainian students were driven by the need to make a living and evade the risky black market or German labor service, while showing little interest in national mobilization.[320]

The Ukrainian-Polish struggle also invaded the Fachkurse in the form of direct violence. Two professors, one Polish and one Ukrainian, were assassinated. A heart attack killed a third who was hiding at Metropolitan Sheptytskyi's residence. At least one professor fled Lviv; students organized bodyguard details.[321] The Hauptausschuss appealed to the Germans for "energetic intervention" against Polish "banditism."[322] Ukrainian nationalists suspected Polish Fachkurs participants of doubling as an anti-Ukrainian fighting force.[323]

316. USHMM MF 1995.A.1086, Reel 2; DALO R-12, 1, 41: *Monatsmeldung* 30 March 1942 (no pagination) and *Monatsmeldung* 28 April 1942: 32.

317. AUJ IDO 37 Oddział lwowski (Zweigstelle Lemberg). Korespondencja wychodząca 1942–1943, letter to the "Direktor des Institutes für Deutsche Ostarbeit" of 15 May 1942, no pagination.

318. Krypiakevych, "Spohady," in *Ivan Krypiakevych u rodynnii tradytsii*, ed. Iaroslav Isaievych, 429.

319. Pankivskyi, *Roky nimetskoi okupatsii*, 364, 366.

320. Volchuk, *Spomyny*, 101, 109.

321. A detailed report on the circumstances of Professor Mariian Panchyshyn's heart attack was produced by Oleksandr Barvynskyi for the obkom and probably Khrushchev (DALO P-3, 1, 78: 27–30). Panchyshyn had been a delegate to the Supreme Soviet under the first Soviet occupation, and Soviet news had introduced him to the Soviet public as "one of the most popular personalities" of Western Ukraine (Sergej Drobaschenko and Manfred Hagen, *Sowjetische Filmpropaganda zur Westexpansion der UdSSR, 1939–1940: Ausgewählte Berichte der Staatswochenschau "Sojuskino-schurnal"* [Göttingen: Institut für den Wissenschaftlichen Film, 1999], 32). Later he had figured as designated minister of health in the Banderite attempt at a state. He was involved in organizing the medical *Fachkurse*.

322. Veryha, *Correspondence of the Ukrainian Central Committee*, 1:626.

323. Viatrovych, *Polsko-ukrainski stosunky*, 286 (doc. 76).

Possession

In addition to positions and knowledge, there was property or, at least, possession. Germans controlled Lemberg's important enterprises through trust-like structures. Business control and wealth were also redistributed among the occupied. Ukrainian collaborators aimed not just to reclaim Ukrainian property confiscated under Soviet rule but also to acquire more. In August 1941, Kubiiovych urged Hans Frank to consider that "a very significant part of confiscated Jewish wealth" should go to Ukrainians.[324]

Like the report writer of July 1941, deploring the suffering of the "poor Aryan" population against the backdrop of a pogrom, Kubiiovych, too—if on a grander historic scale—blamed Jews. Arguing that the "whole Jewish property" had "originally . . . belonged to the Ukrainian people," who had been deprived of it by Jewish "malfeasance," he pleaded that Ukrainians should get Jewish things. He also insisted that "resettlers to the Soviet Union," here clearly referring to Poles deported by the Soviets, had left behind "property, especially land," that needed to be secured so it would not be taken by Poles arriving from western and central Poland.[325]

Clearly, such demands aimed to use Soviet and German power to expropriate Jews and Poles, not to restore the prewar status quo. Such aims were partly realized. By the spring of 1942, the Lemberg Hauptausschuss branch estimated that the share of the city's businesses in Ukrainian hands had increased from 7.4 percent during "the Polish period" to nearly 44 percent.[326]

Especially when replacing Jews in trade, Ukrainians were preferred. Engaging in a perverse form of social policy, Germans assigned formerly Jewish shops to Ukrainians especially harmed by Soviet rule, as well as invalids.[327] Social assistance could be juxtaposed with murder. At the end of March 1942, the Ukrainian Police reported handing over 4,805 Jews during three days of an *Aktion*, continuing to report daily "catches" and munitions fired through April.[328] Meanwhile, its men could claim new special assistance for reasons including a large family and "economic indigence stemming from" Soviet rule."[329]

324. Golczewski, "Shades of Grey," 134–35. On the OUN's aim to use "all opportunities" to take over trade, production, and administration, see Motyka, *Ukraińska partyzantka*, 101.

325. TsDAVO 3959c, 2, 83b: 35; Veryha, *Correspondence of the Ukrainian Central Committee*, 342; Golczewski, "Shades of Grey," 134–35.

326. TsDAVOU 3959, 2, 39: 128. The now Ukrainian-owned enterprises included those under trusteeship.

327. Hryciuk, *Polacy we Lwowie*, 202.

328. USHMM MF 1995.A.1086 (Reel 3); DALO R-12, 1, 37: 9, 13; R-12, 1, 38: 16; R-12, 1, 40: 54, 56, 64. On the March *Aktion*, see also Pohl, *Nationalsozialistische Judenverfolgung in Ostgalizien*, 185–88.

329. AAN 540, I, 3: 5.

In retrospect, for Kost Pankivskyi, it was only Bolshevik and Nazi cruelty that "fostered a feeling of indifference for the other's fate" and "obtuseness."[330] Yet he knew this obtuseness from personal experience. In May 1942, with Lemberg's Jews rounded up in public, he demanded higher wages for Ukrainians because the war had impoverished everybody "except the Jews."[331] In August 1943, with the Jews gone, he reported that German officials had challenged him about growing "anarchy." Taking some responsibility for young Ukrainians deserting the police and Baudienst units, he drew the line when the Germans criticized the Ukrainian Police for shooting Poles. Pankivskyi explained that what was "eating" Ukrainians was "first of all the matter of the deserters and not the fact that fifty Poles have been killed." He also told the Germans that they were falling for "Polish propaganda"; Ukrainians would "not get hysterical."[332] It is crucial to understanding the effect of collaboration that this did, in fact, shut up Pankivskyi's German interlocutors. Verbally, he had matched their demonstrative brutality.

The End of Lemberg

The German occupation effectively ended on 23 July 1944, after more than three years, when Germans retreated and the Polish Home Army took over part of the city. A year before, the Distrikt had already been declared a "Bandenkampfgebiet" counterinsurgency zone, marking the brittleness of German rule in the countryside and a further escalation in killings.[333] By February 1944, German Bezirksämter district administrations reported rising "panic" and refugees heading west.[334] In March, Sheptytskyi expected the Bolsheviks back within days and reported widespread fear of Soviet retribution for cooperation with the Germans.[335]

At the same time, Ukrainian policemen murdered young Poles to steal their papers, and the Polish underground assassinated Ukrainian policemen.[336] The Germans, according to the Home Army, displayed "very diverse" attitudes. The

330. Pankivskiy, *Roky nimetskoi okupatsii*, 61.

331. Veryha, *Correspondence of the Ukrainian Central Committee*, 1134.

332. TsDAVOU 3959, 2, 40: 112.

333. Sandkühler, *"Endlösung" in Galizien*, 96.

334. AAN 540/I, 209: 1–12.

335. Bohdan R. Bociurkiw, *The Ukrainian Greek Catholic Church and the Soviet State, 1939–1950* (Edmonton: Canadian Institute of Ukrainian Studies Press, 1996), 62.

336. Grzegorz Hryciuk, *"Kumityt" Polski Komitet Opiekuńczy Lwów Miasto w latach 1941–1944* (Toruń: Marszałek, 2000), 73; Jerzy Węgierski, *W lwowskiej Armii Krajowej* (Warsaw: PAX, 1989), 98; Motyka, *Tak było w bieszczadach*, 126. The German authorities also suspected—but did not prove—that a Lviv OUN-B group which they destroyed in April 1944 had systematically killed Poles after checking their identity papers (DALO R-36, 1, 11: 16–17 [USHMM Acc.1995.A.1086, Reel 9]). The group's case was complicated, apparently combining political and financial motivations. German investigations obviously have to be handled very cautiously.

army was reluctant to engage Ukrainian nationalists, who mostly left it alone. Wächter said he considered the "ceaseless massacre of Poles" by Ukrainian nationalists a "severe blow to German authority"; he found Poles "more energetic and disciplined" than Ukrainians but "also more dangerous."[337]

Germans kept exploiting the Polish-Ukrainian conflict. Wächter refused Polish requests to establish militias "even under German command," recommending that "young and strong" Poles seek safety through labor in the Reich, while the "old and weak" should flee to bigger towns. According to the Home Army, at least one German officer nevertheless supported Polish militias; others clearly assisted Ukrainian fighters.[338] According to the Home Army, Ukrainian units linked to the SS Division Galizien participated in attacks on Polish villages.[339]

With the end of German occupation impending, expectations about the war's outcome remained complex. The question of whether Soviet rule would return and what would happen when it did worried Lemberg's inhabitants. German propaganda exploited the memory of Soviet terror. Among Generalgouvernment Polish-language newspapers, *Gazeta Lwowska*, with its local background of a city having already undergone Soviet occupation, had a special line in anti-Soviet propaganda.[340]

At the same time, Tadeusz Tomaszewski observed, German actions led to a preference for Soviet rule, and news about the mass graves of Katyń, where Soviets had massacred Polish officers, was initially received skeptically. Yet when Lwów's Poles found names they knew in victim lists published by the Germans, Katyń "spoiled the shadow of sympathy" for the Bolsheviks. As Soviet military success grew, the agonizing about whether Germans or Soviets were worse never ceased.[341]

In February 1944, Lwów Home Army sources predicted that all Poles would flee to the West "and no propaganda will help." This was too pessimistic. Yet some Poles did flee, remembering 1939. Villagers and the poor urban population complained that as Polish elites had "fled in 1939, leaving us to perish," they were also "fleeing now." With "Ukrainian gangs" threatening villages, Polish leaders were

337. Motyka, *Ukraińska partyzantka*, 224–25.

338. AAN 203/XV-14: 136–37. For a March 1944 Ukrainian nationalist report, describing in detail a case of local German-nationalist cooperation, involving an exchange of German arms for nationalist de facto occupation support in an area depleted of German troops as well as the use of those weapons to massacre 450 Poles, many of them civilians and refugees from Volhynia, see GDA SBU 13, spr. 376, tom 68: 244–45.

339. AAN 203/XV-14: 47; Motyka, *Ukraińska partyzantka*, 181, and on the case of the village Huta Pieniacka, 383–84.

340. Dobroszycki, *Die legale polnische Presse*, 118.

341. Tomaszewski, *Lwów*, 164, 172, 177.

telling "us to defend" Poland in the borderlands, while they themselves were "sitting quietly in the city."[342] Such Polish responses did not fit nostalgic categories of national perseverance. By June, there were rumors that Germans would draft Ukrainians compulsorily, with Poles to be "abducted and liquidated like Jews."[343]

Toward the end of German rule, Lemberg's German propaganda office proved relentless, staging a widely advertised exhibition on the "Jewish World Pestilence."[344] Once more illustrating the fantastic nature of the Judeo-Bolshevism complex, German propaganda, with almost all Jews murdered, portrayed local Jews as instigating a "Jewish rule of terror" wherever Soviet forces returned.[345] Heinrich Himmler made his last appearance in Lemberg in May 1944. Addressing officers of the Waffen-SS Galizien Division, he congratulated them on their "beautiful homeland" Galicia, even more beautiful since German initiative had removed its Jews.[346] Two policemen claimed their rewards for arresting Józef Menker.[347] Kurt Lewin remembered a devastated city with an empty former ghetto.[348] Stanisław Lem would not forget the "Klondyke"-like hammering there from the search for treasures Jews were believed to have left behind.[349]

When the Germans left in July, the Polish Home Army fought them, trying to implement the local part of the Polish exile government's Burza plan and liberate the city before the arrival of the Soviets. There were clashes between the Home Army and Ukrainian nationalists. Soviet troops took the city center on 27 July, relying on Home Army assistance.[350]

By the time the Soviets returned, the German occupation had changed the city fundamentally, most of all by murdering its Jews. But some things had not changed. German occupation had not modernized the city. In the spring of 1943, a German survey of the Vereinigte Eisen- und Metallwarenbetriebe (VEM), one of Lemberg's major metalworking enterprises, indicated that all eleven of its

342. AAN 203/XV-14 (1944): 1–3; 203/XV-15: 102, 140; 203/XV-18: 132–33 (MF-2400/3).

343. DALO R-35, 9, 128: no pagination; Der Stabsamtsleiter, Fernschreiben no. 347 (USHMM Acc.1995.A.1086, Reel 8); *Karta* 13 (1994), 3, from the diary of Alma Heczko.

344. DALO R-35, 9, 184: 1; R-35, 9, 241: 6, 29, 41–42 (USHMM Acc.1995.A.1086, Reel 8).

345. DALO R-35, 9, 127: no pagination; Gouverneur Galizien. Der Beauftragte des Pressechef [sic] der Regierung, Fernschreiben no. 24; DALO R-35, 12, 18: 95 (USHMM Acc.1995.A.1086, Reel 8).

346. Sandkühler, *"Endlösung" in Galizien*, 108.

347. DALO R-77, 1, 1160: 2 (USHMM Acc. 1995.A1086, Reel 33).

348. Lewin, *Przeżyłem*, 166–67.

349. Lem, *Świat na krawędzi*, 48.

350. Węgierski, *W lwowskiej Armii Krajowej*, 99–101; Motyka, *Tak było w bieszczadach*, 128; Oleksandr Lutskiy and Kim Naumenko, "U roky svitovoi viiny," in *Lviv: Istorychni narysy*, ed. Iaroslav Isaievych et al. (Lviv: Instytut ukrainoznavsta im. I. Krypiakevycha, 1996), 504.

Figure 3.4 German propaganda, in Ukrainian, for the Waffen-SS Galizien Division, 1943. Bundesarchiv, Poster Plak 003-025-059.

workshops were "based on primitive means," exploiting mostly individual "craft skills." Jews still provided half of this labor, and the report's author knew that soon they were likely to be put to "other uses." To replace them with Poles and Ukrainians, however, would be difficult because too many had been taken away.[351] The grandiloquent VEM was really a technologically primitive array of dispersed sites, where Jews did slave labor for the railways and the army. Once the Jews were murdered, the enterprise would be out of labor, too. In general, the whole Distrikt Galizien was of only minor significance for the German war industry.[352]

Polish-Ukrainian conflict escalated but remained unresolved. By the spring of 1943, German setbacks signaled unpredictability. By September, the writer Arkadyi Lubchenko noted panic among Lemberg's Ukrainian elite—some fleeing west, and some refugees arriving from the eastern areas reoccupied by Soviet forces.[353]

Feelers for cooperation between the Polish underground and the Ukrainian nationalists were failing.[354] By September 1943, a Polish delegate, remonstrating with Sheptytskyi over Greek Catholic clergy involvement in attacks on Poles, found that Sheptytskyi was saddened but would not publicly intervene.[355] Yet in April 1943, a Polish Home Army report still found that while the traditional "conciliationist" Ukrainian politicians of the past were hardly noticeable, there were "very many opportunists" seeking some sort of "reinsurance for a future with Poles." Though put bluntly, this was merely realistic, as was the same report's observation that Poles had "got used quickly to the use of the Ukrainian language in official institutions."[356]

On 17 July 1944, with the Soviets' return clearly imminent, a denunciation to the Ukrainian Police displayed another kind of foresight. A Ukrainian woman, Antonia, accused her Polish neighbor, Helena, of constantly calling her a "Ukrainian swine." Antonia had put up with it "since the arrival of the Germans" and was finally denouncing Helena because the latter was adding threats that the Bolsheviks were close and would send Antonia to Siberia.[357]

351. AAN 689, 192: 139–46. In fact, much of this report was based on information provided by the "former Jewish chief accountant" of the VEM (ibid., 139).

352. Sandkühler, *"Endlösung" in Galizien*, 97–98.

353. Lutskyi, *Shchodennyk Arkadiia Liubchenka*, 169.

354. Torzecki, *Polacy i Ukraińcy*, 1:241–81: Grzegorz Motyka, "Der polnisch-ukrainische Gegensatz in Wolhynien und Ostgalizien," in *Die Polnische Heimatarmee: Geschichte und Mythos der Armija Krajowa seit dem Zweiten Weltkrieg*, ed. Bernhard Chiari and Jerzy Kochanowski (Munich: Oldenbourg, 2003), 537, on the 1943 project.

355. Torzecki, *Polacy i Ukraińcy*, 1:283.

356. Ibid., 123, 129.

357. DALO R-16, 1, 1: 10 (USHMM Acc.1995.A.1086, Reel 4).

Why did Antonia wait for three years before striking at her neighbor? If she was lying, why did she bother to pretend that she had been waiting? Perhaps the reticence overcome in her last-minute denunciation was due to a bad conscience. Perhaps it really was an attempt to eliminate a perceived threat from her Polish neighbors before the Bolsheviks returned to help them and with the Ukrainian Police still there to destroy them: not getting your retaliation in first, almost last might also work. Maybe it was only the anticipated next regime change that tipped the balance toward denunciation.

The German occupation produced an unambiguous and irrevocable effect when it murdered the city's Jews. With the struggle between Poles and Ukrainians remaining open, it was still a time of learning, or simply using, the other's language and taking out "reinsurance"—be it through opportunism, waiting for years with a denunciation, or by finally launching it against its target.

CHAPTER FOUR

After Lemberg

The End of the End of Lwów and the Making of Lviv

When Soviet forces reconquered Lviv in July 1944, the city had 150,000 to 160,000 inhabitants—less than half its prewar population—including about 108,000 Poles.[1] By 1955, its 380,500 inhabitants included slightly more than 2 percent—less than 8,600 individuals—identified as Poles.[2] By 2001, Poles were as rare in the city of Lviv as in its surroundings. Lviv oblast registered 18,900 Poles, less than 1 percent of its population—nearly 95 percent of whom were Ukrainian—and the city of Lviv counted about 6,000 Poles, less than 1 percent of its population of about 725,000.[3] The key event producing this historic change was the population exchange between Poland and Soviet Ukraine of 1944–1946/1947, during which Lviv became the central site of the expulsion of the Polish majority from Western Ukraine. The Ukrainian Soviet republic and the Polish Committee of National Liberation (the PKWN, core of the future Polish satellite government), agreed to this exchange in Lublin on 9 September 1944. Ethnically defined Ukrainians from Poland—as newly defined by Soviet hegemony—moved to Soviet Ukraine, while Poles in the western Soviet Union, partly covering what had been eastern Poland, went to Poland.[4] In the resettlement,

1. Hryciuk, *Przemiany narodowościowe i ludnościowe*, 334.

2. Halyna Bodnar, "Mihratsiia silskoho naselennia do Lvova v 50–80-kh rokakh XX stolittia," Candidate of Sciences (History) diss. (Lviv: Ivan Franko University, 2007), appendix (dodatok) M.

3. Hryciuk, *Przemiany narodowościowe i ludnościowe*, 319; Stepan Davymuka, *Lvivshchyna na porozi XXI stolittia: sotsialnyi portret* (Lviv: Natsionalna akademiia nauk Ukrainy, Instytut rehionalnykh doslidzhen, 2001), 48 ; and State Statistics Committee of Ukraine, http://2001.ukrcensus.gov.ua/eng/results/general/nationality/. Although Soviet and post-Soviet statistics need to be used critically, the general picture is clear.

4. The agreement was one of three. The other two were concluded between the PKWN and Soviet Lithuania and Soviet Belarus respectively. Thus, the PKWN-Soviet-Ukrainian agreement was part of a general removal of Poles from the new Soviet western territories first conquered in 1939 and 1940. For more information, see Yosef Litvak, "Polish-Jewish Refugees Repatriated from the Soviet Union at the End of the Second World War and Afterwards," in *Jews in Eastern Poland*

prewar citizenship was a criterion for resettlement but trumped by formalized ethnic identity.[5] As a result, documents deciding individual fates in a population exchange between authoritarian socialist regimes were, ironically, often issued by religious or German authorities. Marriages were treated asymmetrically: if a man had to leave Ukraine, his wife went with him, but if a woman was recognized as Polish but her husband not, he had to stay.[6] The exchange was supposedly voluntary, but compulsion was pervasive.

Expulsion, Degradation, and Legitimation

Lviv oblast was one of the areas most affected by the so-called "evacuation" of ethnic Poles and Jews from Western Ukraine. By the end of 1946, a total of about eight hundred thousand people, the vast majority ethnic Poles and about thirty thousand Polish Jews, had left for Poland.[7] About a quarter of them came from Lviv oblast, including almost 105,000 from Lviv itself.[8] The expulsion meant that the Polish presence in eastern Galicia "practically ceased." For Western Ukraine as a whole, the Soviet expulsion completed the ethnic cleansing of Poles by Ukrainian nationalists begun in 1943 (although the methods were now much less bloody, if still brutal).[9]

and the USSR, 1939–46, ed. Norman Davies and Antony Polonsky (London: St. Martin's Press, 1991), 228; and Theodore R. Weeks, "Population Politics in Vilnius, 1944–1947: A Case Study of Socialist-Sponsored Ethnic Cleansing," *Post-Soviet Affairs* 32 (2007): 81. Weeks brings out many similarities between the Vilnius and Lviv cases of postwar expulsion, in particular its uses as a de facto meeting point between Soviet and nationalist interests.

5. Litvak, "Polish-Jewish Refugees," in *Jews in Eastern Poland*, ed. Davies and Polonsky, 228. On the Soviet authorities' prioritizing of ethnicity over citizenship when deciding which Poles would be freed from various forms of detention, including POW camps and special settlements, and—eventually—might have a chance to escape from the Soviet Union as part of the renewed diplomatic relationships with the exile Polish government in London, see Gousseff, "'Kto naš,'" 534–35.

6. Grzegorz Hryciuk, "Die 'Evakuierung' der polnischen und jüdischen Bevölkerung aus den Ostgebieten der Zweiten Polnischen Republik in den Jahren 1944–1947," *Zeitschrift für Geschichtswissenschaft* 55 (2007): 727.

7. S. A. Makarchuk, "Pereselennia poliakiv iz zakhidnikh oblastei Ukrainy v Polshchu 1944–1946 rr.," *Ukrainsky istorychnyi zhurnal*, no. 3 (2003): 104–5. A Soviet report of 15 September 1946 listed as "evacuated Polish citizens" 746,993 Poles, 30,408 Jews, and 12,581 others, mostly persons from mixed families and some "Polish Gypsies" (*tsygany*) (TsDAHOU 1, 23, 2610: 192–93.). These figures were almost complete.

8. Of the nearly 105,000 people expelled from Lwów, nearly 99,000 were non-Jewish Poles, nearly 3,500 were Jewish (Hryciuk, *Przemiany narodowościowe i ludnościowe w Galicji*, 334; Makarchuk, "Pereselennia poliakiv," 104). After the expulsion, more Poles were left in Ukraine than Soviet figures indicated, but their numbers were still very small. Soviet estimates indicated about 77,000 remaining Poles, while about 170,000 seems a more likely figure (Hryciuk, "Die 'Evakuierung,'" 731).

9. Hryciuk, "Die 'Evakuierung,'" 741.

The significance of the expulsion exceeded its numbers. It meant the end of the last major Polish city on territory settled by a majority of Ukrainians. Moreover, in the national myth of Poland's eastward expansion, the fourteenth-century acquisition of Lwów was a founding moment. The last Soviet history of Lviv would also identify it as the beginning of Polish expansion in "Ukrainian lands."[10] Across national and ideological divides, everybody agreed: departure from Lwów meant Poland's final retreat from its eastern ambitions.

The expulsion of Lwów's Poles also completed the violent ethnic simplification of the Second World War and shaped the city's first Ukrainization. As Stanisław Lem later recalled, for Lwów's Poles, this was the end of the end of a world destroyed in stages, initially "after the [first] arrival of the Soviets, then after the arrival of the Germans, and finally—when we had to leave Lwów."[11] The Polish expulsion demonstrated that—crucial differences notwithstanding—the Germans, Soviets, and Ukrainian nationalists all pursued policies of "ethnic unmixing." Here was another complex continuity with a deep past and a long future.

Postwar Soviet Lviv became a key site of the next round in the struggle over hegemony between eastern and western Ukrainian elites. Whereas nationalists from western Ukraine had sought to carry eastward their version of Ukraine, authoritarian and in deference to Nazi Germany, eastern Ukrainians in postwar Lviv helped impose a version of Ukraine that was Stalinist and subordinate to a Russian "elder brother." Nazaruk's "creoles" were back with a Soviet vengeance after surreptitious "Galician" attempts to play German-backed "Prussia" to them. In postwar Lviv, more important than any Russification tendencies was the ongoing struggle between Ukrainians over who was "liberator" and who was "backward." With Poles and Jews gone and Moscow committed to "ancient Ukrainian Lviv"—something neither Vienna nor Warsaw ever came close to—this conflict entered a new phase.

Ironically, for a brief time before the expulsion of Poles from Lwów, the city became more Polish than ever. Ukrainian nationalist assaults on the rural Polish population had driven refugees to the city. As the proud Ukrainian nationalist Yevhen Nakonechnyi would recall, German-occupied Lemberg "kept its Polish-speaking character," in "the street" and "on the market."[12] Also due to the murder of Lwów's Jews, by 1944, the relative Polish share in the city's population was unprecedentedly high. Lwów, in this sad sense, had never been as ethnically Polish as when it was about to be replaced by Ukrainian Lviv.

10. Sekretariuk et al., *Istoriia Lvova*, 29.

11. Lem, *Świat na krawędzi*, 49.

12. Nakonechnyi, *"Shoa" u Lvovi*, 36–37.

When the Polish underground reasserted itself, it inadvertently aided Soviet rule by reminding Ukrainians of Polish claims. In the fall of 1943, a Ukrainian nationalist report quoted a Pole's promise never to give up Lviv "since there are 80 percent of us there, and 29 percent Ukrainians."[13] A later report described the first day of the Soviet reconquest as the "culminating point" of Polish success, with armed Polish groups taking over parts of Lviv, including the precincts of the Ukrainian Police and the warehouses of the UTsK, and arresting and killing dozens of Ukrainians. Within days, however, Soviet power surged, and Ukrainians started to "quietly compete with the Poles" for key positions.[14] Within the first year after reconquest, Soviet authorities arrested about 1,500 suspected Polish underground members in Lviv oblast.[15]

Lwów's Poles were a young population. As of October 1944, more than 12,600 of the city's roughly 17,000 school pupils were Polish and 4,184 Ukrainian, whereas, in the oblast as a whole, 121,450 Ukrainian pupils outweighed 24,371 Poles. There was also hardly anyone else left. Before the Germans, Lviv had had a total of 43,924 young people in school.[16] Much of the difference was due to the Holocaust.

At the moment when the Germans left and the Soviets returned, the contrast between the Polish majority in the city of Lwów and the lack of Poles in the surrounding countryside had never been so pronounced. Soviet authorities and local Ukrainians now largely agreed on removing the Poles; the latter sometimes blamed expulsion on Ukrainians alone. They were wrong, but there was significant local Ukrainian support for it.[17] In August 1944, a month before the Lublin Agreement, Lviv's new obkom head, Ivan Hrushetskyi, reported to Khrushchev on a meeting of the local Ukrainian elite. A philology professor pleaded that "Lviv must be settled by Ukrainians" and be "Ukrainian not only in form" but also "in substance."[18] One year later, representatives of the Ukrainian intelligentsia complained that a Soviet-Polish treaty confirming Poland's eastern losses was not severe enough and painted the Soviet Union as a victim of "pressure" by cunning Poles, who were "more impertinent than the Jews."[19] Some Ukrainians were also

13. GDA SBU 13, spr. 376, tom 74: 22; tom 30: 32. The numbers were slightly wrong, but the point was clear.

14. Viatrovych, *Polsko-ukrainski stosunky*, 575–76 (doc. 255), 577 (doc. 256).

15. Isaievych et al., *Istoriia Lvova*, 3:254.

16. DALO P-661, 1, 6: 13–14. One month later, the contrast was even more pronounced, with a total of 19,528 pupils in the city of Lviv, including 15,251 Poles and 3,688 Ukrainians (DALO P-66, 1, 31: 51).

17. Makarchuk, "Pereselennia poliakiv," 108–9.

18. DALO P-3, 1, 78: 31.

19. RGASPI 17, 88, 451: 55.

fearful, with memories of being targeted by Poles during the German retreat. For two Ukrainian railway workers only the rapid deportation of all Poles could prevent "national hostility and killings."[20]

Thus, unsettling and resettling Lviv were not mere side effects of a population exchange meant to neutralize ethnic conflict or secure a border zone; rather, these moves were part of making Ukrainian again an "ancient Ukrainian" but Polonized city. Cultural Ukrainization—of schools, street names, and monuments—was to follow.[21] This approach was fundamentally different from that taken by the Soviets before 1941, when Poles were demoted but expected to stay. The brutal political and cultural hegemony of that time was now replaced with a massive expulsion.

By Ukrainizing the key city of western Ukraine, the Soviet authorities also deprived the Poles of leadership. Polish urban elites, decimated and deprived of institutions, had already been reduced to conspiracy. In destroying the Polish underground—that is, the conspiracy as a para-state institution—for a moment, the Soviet authorities inevitably if unintentionally increased the Polish intelligentsia's symbolic importance. Hrushetskyi reported to Khrushchev a Polish history lecturer's claim that Lwów was "a Polish city and the leading role in all of Galicia belongs to the intelligentsia of this city"; even if there was a "preponderant majority of Ukrainians" around it, it should still be part of Poland.[22]

A Soviet report of 1951 noted that Lviv's oblast's remaining Poles, now often collectivized peasants, were loyal to Soviet power, frequently Stakhanovites, "active," "honest," and "conscientious."[23] By 1956, a visiting Polish journalist observed that the few Poles left in Lviv were mostly from the proletariat, with small numbers of intelligentsia cultivating "illusions" in lonely apartments.[24] By 1959, only 1.4 percent of Poles in Ukraine were listed as having a higher education. In 1970, four-fifths of all Poles in Ukraine were manual laborers. In Lviv oblast in 1979, the share of Poles of the total population was 7.5 percent; only 395 of them had completed a secondary education.[25] In sum, the expulsion of Western Ukraine's Poles between 1944 and 1946 not only removed Poles but also socially

20. RGASPI 17, 88, 450: 31.

21. DALO P-3, 1, 63: 14–16.

22. DALO P-3, 1, 68: 85. Stochek's name here transcribed from a document written in Cyrillic.

23. DALO P-3, 4, 170: 25.

24. *Kulturne zhyttia*, 2:223–24.

25. Aleksandra Matiukhina, *W Sowieckim Lwowie: Życie codzienne miasta w latach 1944–1990* (Cracow: Wydawnictwo Uniwersytetu Jagiellońskiego, 2000), 150. Twenty years after the Soviet Union's demise, an inhabitant of Lviv recalled the postwar years as a time when elderly Poles were still around—in semi-basements. From an interview with Yuryi Bosov, taken by Halyna Bodnar, Lviv, 22 February 2012.

degraded those who remained. Interwar Soviet policies had similarly placed Poles in "a rural, poor, and largely illiterate context."[26]

Emerging from War: A Cluttered Void

Although its Poles were expelled, Lviv quickly acquired a new population of Ukrainians, Russians, and Soviet Jews. Out of the city's about 380,000 inhabitants in 1950, about 145,000 were counted as Ukrainian, 90,000 as Russian, and 19,000 as Jewish.[27] In postwar Lviv, the majority of the population had not been there before 1939. It was almost nobody's original home, but a new home for many.

Lviv's new inhabitants produced new identities. "Locals" or "natives" were commonly distinguished from "eastern" inhabitants. The Lviv miskom, reporting a murder in 1945, emphasized that the victim was an "arrival from the East."[28] There were other important categories, such as party membership or its lack; social status in Soviet terms: poor, middle, *kulak/kurkul* in the countryside and worker, employee, or intelligentsia in the cities; those with a past on German-occupied territory and those without; army veterans; believers and nonbelievers; categories of age and gender; and, of course, ethnic distinctions: Russian, Ukrainian (east and west), Jewish and Polish. In postwar Lviv, this was all interwoven with the division into "locals" and "easterners."

Local Stalemate, Imperial Opportunities: Ukrainian Failure, Polish Intransigence

The importance of Lwów for Poles and Lviv for Ukrainians was charged with extreme urgency as of the midsummer of 1943, when Ukrainian nationalist ethnic cleansing moved west and south, reaching the former eastern Galicia in early 1944.[29] By the end of March, Ukrainian nationalists had killed between seventy-five hundred and ten thousand Poles in this area.[30] Nationalist orders demanded "permanent" attacks on Poles "until their extermination from these territories," while some nationalist leaders started deliberate memory manipulation by blaming what had "happened up until now . . . on the Germans, Bolshevik partisans," and "the war."[31]

26. Kate Brown, *A Biography of No Place: From Ethnic Borderland to Soviet Heartland* (Cambridge, MA: Harvard University Press, 2004), 28.

27. Isaievych et al., *Istoriia Lvova*, 3:259.

28. DALO P-4, 1, 58: 174.

29. Motyka, *Ukraińska partyzantka*, 220, 366–90.

30. Motyka, *Tak było w bieszczadach*, 126.

31. Motyka, *Ukraińska partyzantka*, 377–80 (my emphases).

It is not clear how many Polish refugees reached Lwów, but the number was substantial. Ukrainian observers noted that the news from Volyn was inspiring Poles with "hatred" for Ukrainians and "the desire for retaliation."[32] In 1943, Tadeusz Tomaszewski found Lwów's Poles talking much about the massacres; its Polish Committee assisted about twenty-five thousand refugees, who became a Polish public cause.[33] With Poles also launching attacks on Ukrainians in the countryside, Lviv became a refuge for the latter as well. Echoing a long history of national rivalry and jealousy, the local Hauptausschuss branch complained about a shoddy camp for refugee Ukrainians, while the Polish Committee, the Ukrainian functionaries noted, took "good care of its refugees."[34]

Poles feared Ukrainian policemen, feeling such "hatred of Ukrainians" that some Germans received a good word by comparison.[35] For Alma Heczko, with her building barricaded and refugees sheltering inside, Ukrainians aimed to destroy.[36] Yet Polish resistance stalled Ukrainian forces.[37] When Soviet rule returned, Ukrainian nationalists had driven many Poles from the countryside, but not from Lwów. In fact, their killing spree in the countryside reinforced Lwów's role as a Polish stronghold.

Poles and Ukrainians had long agreed that cities were decisive for the appropriation of contested territory and Lwów/Lviv was decisive among cities. Moreover, historically, Bolshevism had had particular success in forging revolution in cities. Here the long arcs of nationalism and Bolshevism met with German occupation and genocide, and nationalist ethnic cleansing. By 1944, all strategies and fantasies intersected in Lwów/Lviv. Soviet reconquest entered a perfect storm geared to ride it.

Only Soviet intervention secured the most important prize for Ukrainian nationalism in Western Ukraine. It was the Soviet party-state, not the Ukrainian nationalists, to which the philologist and head of the Museum of Ukrainian Art Ilarion Sventsytskyi addressed his postwar complaint about Poles still "working in the shops" and offending him "as a Ukrainian" by pretending not to understand his language.[38]

32. GDA SBU 13, spr. 376, tom 71: 4.

33. Tomaszewski, *Lwów*, 163; Hryciuk, *"Kumityt" Polski Komitet*, 62–63 and 77–78. The Ukrainian City Committee was also assisting "its" refugees, some of whom came from eastern and central Ukraine and some from Lviv's surroundings. Hryciuk, *"Kumityt" Polski Komitet*, 87.

34. TsDAVOU 3955, 1, 30: 34.

35. Tomaszewski, *Lwów*, 164–66.

36. *Karta* 13 (1994), 3, from the diary of Alma Heczko.

37. The Polish-Ukrainian fighting, expulsions, and massacres—especially in Volhynia and later in Galicia—was extensive. According to Grzegorz Motyka, the best estimate is that the conflict was responsible for up to a hundred thousand Polish and ten thousand to twenty thousand Ukrainian casualties (*Tak było w bieszczadach*, 128; *Ukraińska partyzantka*, 411–12.).

38. O. S. Rubl'ov and Iu. A. Cherchenko, *Stalinshchyna i dolia zakhidnoukrainskoi intelihentsii* (Kyiv: Naukowa dumka, 1994), 231–32; DALO P-3, 1, 320: 23, repr. in *Kulturne zhyttia*, 1:292–94.

Polish resilience, no less than Ukrainian nationalist failure, fed Soviet power. The Home Army's aim was to liberate and reconquer all territories of interwar Poland, including the eastern areas inhabited by a majority of non-Poles and annexed by the Soviet Union in 1939.[39] By 1942, the Polish underground in Lwów was exploring a "solution to the Ukrainian question" by deporting Ukrainians.[40]

This, however, presupposed a successful Polish reconquest of the borderlands, with Lwów still the most important prize. The Home Army anticipated a long fight against Ukrainians, to be won, as in 1918, by reinforcements from central Poland. Expecting a Ukrainian uprising to "occupy cultural positions and create . . . legends of heroism and ownership," the Home Army intended to "make a public showing to stress the Polishness of these territories and especially of Lwów."[41] Toward this end, it flew Polish flags on Lwów's streets during Soviet reconquest.[42]

With the Soviet reports of Poles arresting and, "in individual cases," killing Ukrainians, Ukrainian fears mirrored Polish hopes: the city might become Polish again, and Ukrainians would face retaliation.[43] Soviet troops, friendlier toward Poles than Ukrainians, according to the Home Army, nurtured those fears and hopes.[44] Initially, some Soviet officials expected Poles to stay, reporting their Soviet sympathies and "deep hatred" of Germans and Ukrainian nationalists. A Polish woman noted that German brutality made Lwów "alien and terrible like a prison"; she viewed the Soviet tank crews as "savior-angels."[45] In August 1944, the Ukrainian deputy head of government and writer Mykola Bazhan told a meeting at the Lviv History Museum about the need for harmony between Ukrainians and Poles.[46]

39. Motyka, *Tak było w bieszczadach*, 104.

40. Mick, "Incompatible Experiences," 360.

41. Motyka, *Ukraińska partyzantka*, 300–301; Motyka, "Der polnische-ukrainische Gegensatz in Wolhynien und Ostgalizien," in *Die Polnische Heimatarmee*, ed. Chiari and Kochanowski, 535; Chrobaczyński, "Kraków i Lwów," 622. The last Polish underground structure in the Lviv area, an isolated cell, was destroyed in the autumn of 1948. See Łukasz Kamiński et al., *Opór społeczny w Europie Środkowej w latach 1948–1953 na przykładzie Polski, NRD i Czechosłowacji* (Wrocław: ATUT, 2004), 54; AAN 203/XV-48 (AK 1944): 48 (MF 2400/9); 203/XV-15 (AK 1944): 103 (MF 2400/3); and Węgierski, *W lwowskiej Armii Krajowej*, 199.

42. *Karta* 13 (1994), 4, from the diary of Alma Heczko; *Karta* 17 (1995), 135, reproducing DALO 3, 1, 63: 69–70.

43. *Operacja "Sejm," 1944–1946: Polska i Ukraina w latach trzydziestych-czterdziestych XX wieku* (Warsaw: Archiwum Ministerstwa Spraw Wewnţrznych i Administracji Rzeczypospolitej Polskiej, 2007), 6:232–34 (doc. 15); TsDAHOU 1, 23, 703: 30–36, repr. in Volodymyr Serhiychuk, *Desiat buremnykh lit: Zachidnoukrainski zemli v 1944–1953 rokakh* (Kyiv: Dnipro, 1998), 91–94.

44. AAN 203/XV-15: 18; 203/XV-16: 230–31.

45. DALO P-4, 1, 15: 14.

46. DALO R-2591, 1, 7: 2.

Figure 4.1 Monument to tank guard troops "who fell in the battles for the freedom and independence of the Great Soviet Fatherland," overlooking Lviv and pointing its gun at the city's center. Collection: Central State Kinofotofono Archive of Ukraine, Kyiv.

A Kyiv Central Committee report of 1944 deplored that Poles were leaving Lviv. Noting their anti-Soviet attitude and estimating sixteen thousand Poles taking orders from the government in exile in London, the report nevertheless recognized that Poles had helped fight Germans and obeyed the first Soviet local call-up no less than Ukrainians. A page praising Poles for welcoming Soviet forces, repairing city facilities, and raising occasional shouts of "Long live Stalin," was crossed out, however.[47] Crossing-out prevailed, and ethnic transformation meshed with Soviet fear of Poles. Engineer Baranov from Russia, visiting Lviv's Gas Works in early 1946, reported that the enterprise was still "entirely in the hands of" a "close collective of Poles." Although they maintained it well, he believed they would not "peacefully abandon 'their' Lvov" but would blow it up. Alarmed, Lviv's authorities found no evidence of any plot.[48] By early 1947, there

47. Of the 3,644 men called up in the city, 2,975—about 80 percent—turned up. A Soviet breakdown by nationality showed no major differences between "Poles," "Ukrainians," and "Others." All turned up at a rate of between 80 and 85 percent. This rate subsequently fell. Of the 2,202 called up in the city in mid-August 1944, only 70 percent showed up. Compliance elsewhere was much lower: for the villages the report noted "serious difficulties," meaning strong resistance to and evasion of the draft. See TsDAHOU 1, 46, 809: 158–60, 169, 172–73, 174.

48. DALO P-3, 1, 427: 50–57.

was no need to fear sabotage. With Lviv plagued by electricity, food, water, and gas shortages, the obkom noted that everybody now in charge of the gas system was ignorant of how it worked.[49]

Leaving Lwów, Slowly

It was a key aspect of Lviv's remaking that the expulsion of the Poles took time. Three-quarters were gone by the end of 1945, but the expulsion was complete only by the summer of 1946.[50] Soviet documents declared it over as of 1 September 1946; a protocol, signed by Soviets and Poles, officially terminated it on 6 March 1947.[51]

Polish mistrust of the Soviets, bureaucratic complications, transport scarcity, and wartime uncertainty prolonged the expulsion. According to the Lviv obkom, by December 1944, 946 Poles had left Lviv, with 84,681 still to go. Those who had left were "mainly single persons who arrived during the German occupation."[52] Thus, their removal made no dent in the demographic substance of Polish Lwów. Meanwhile, the Polish evacuation plenipotentiary for Lviv oblast was requesting delays for families.[53] Soviet authorities suspected their Polish counterparts of surreptitiously encouraging Poles to stay.[54] Ironically, the presence of Soviet forces encouraged some Poles to remain or even return after fleeing from Ukrainian nationalists.[55]

After the Soviet reconquest of Lwów, the protracted disappearance of Lviv's Poles shaped the city's postwar identity. Post-German, post-Holocaust, postwar Lviv was a place where displacement continued, overriding the distinction between peace and war.

49. DALO P-3, 2, 84: 7.

50. Ther, "Chancen und Untergang," 143.

51. TsDAHOU 1, 23, 2610: 191–96, repr. in Volodymyr Serhiychuk, *Deportatsiia poliakiv z Ukrainy: Nevidomi dokumenty pro nasylnytske pereselennia bilshovytskoio vladoiu polskoho naselennia z URSR v Polshu v 1944–1946 rokakh* (Kyiv: Ukrainska vydavnycha spilka, 1999), 170–74, here 171.

52. DALO P-3, 1, 239: 10. According to Philipp Ther, many more Poles (7,142) had left Lwów by the end of 1944 ("Chancen und Untergang," 142). There is no obvious explanation for these diverging figures, both based on sets of official documents. It is possible that the Polish authorities, when receiving those expelled, for an unknown reason, counted more than the Soviet authorities sending them off. The obkom may also have been wrong, and not necessarily unintentionally. Even the higher figures found by Ther do not substantially alter the conclusion that the expulsion took off slowly.

53. DALO P-3, 1, 239: 10.

54. TsDAHOU 1, 23, 2610: 191–96, repr. Serhiychuk, *Deportatsiia poliakiv*, 170–74.

55. RGASPI 17, 88, 451: 35.

Social Decapitation: The Removable and the Redeemable

On the day of the Lublin agreement, Hrushetskyi reported that Lviv's Polish intelligentsia had been opportunistic and treacherous under German occupation. Polish organizations, supported by the United States and Great Britain, would make "imperialist demands," especially for Lviv. Now its Polish intelligentsia displayed a "sharply critical attitude toward Soviet people," preferring them to leave and "take all the Ukrainians with them."[56] Hrushetskyi also reported on the cooperation of Lviv's Ukrainian intelligentsia with the Germans, but with a quite different conclusion: its "most progressive part" was going to "work for the good of its socialist motherland" in Lviv.[57]

At an intelligentsia meeting in early December, several speakers stressed Slavic solidarity against Germans, but this did not decrease the need for Poles to leave. Hrushetskyi demanded that they "understand that Lviv was, is, and will be a Soviet city, and once that is so, there will be Soviet order." There would be no repetition of the "playing-around" of 1939–1941. Instead, Poles would be "mobilized" with the same rigor as Ukrainians, including for work in the "eastern oblasts." "Soviet programs and Ukrainian language" would be the only way. Soviet policy would be "national in form and socialist in content" in the name of the Ukrainian majority. All "honest Poles" could "voluntarily choose [their] state," with "the free will to decide their fate" by, as Hrushetskyi clearly implied, leaving. Meanwhile, deportations eastward would target those not working or hoping for a return of the pre-1939 status quo, those "parasites" who "walk dogs on the streets and spoil the air in Lviv."[58] Informed by Hrushetskyi about a "reserved" Polish response to his disquisitions on free will and clean air, Khrushchev reported to Stalin that Lviv's Poles, "mostly intelligentsia," still questioned the loss of eastern Poland and the "need to leave."[59]

Shortly afterward, Poles saw an arrest wave as aimed not only at the Polish underground but also at breaking resistance to expulsion. The Soviet secret police agreed that an increase in registrations was linked to arrests.[60] By mid-March 1945, it reported 7,064 "reactionary Polish elements" arrested in all of Western Ukraine,

56. DALO P-3, 1, 63: 17–21. Clearly, in this case, Hrushetskyi meant *local* "Ukrainians." Signally, he still saw them and "Soviet people" no less as distinct categories than did the Poles he denounced.

57. DALO P-3, 1, 63: 22–28.

58. DALO P-3, 1, 59: 282–83, repr. in *Kulturne zhyttia*, 1:231–33 (doc. 100).

59. DALO P-3, 1, 63: 69–74; TsDAHOU 1, 23, 790: 137–39, repr. in Serhiychuk, *Desiat buremnykh lit*, 168–69 (doc. no. 64).

60. Grzegorz Hryciuk, "'Ciężkie Dni Lwowa.' Akcja masowych aresztowań we Lwowie w styczniu 1945 r.," in *Studia z historii najnowszej*, ed. Wojciech Wrzesiński (Wrocław: Gajt, 1999), 26, 30; DALO P-3, 1, 239: 8–9; Isaievych et al., *Istoriia Lvova*, 3:256.

including 21 leaders of the Home Army.[61] When the Home Army leadership was subjected to a show trial in Moscow in June 1945, the obkom noted that the black market price of Lwów's still existing but scarce Soviet Polish-language newspaper, *Czerwony Sztandar*, shot up, with Poles desperate for information on the trial.[62]

At meetings, people asked if refusal to leave meant deportation to Siberia. *Czerwony Sztandar* confirmed the resonance of such rumors by denouncing them.[63] Some may have wanted to leave but feared entrapment as in 1940.[64] Hrushetskyi reported Polish suspicions that the Soviet authorities would try to destroy all "Poles and Jews" by sending them to Germany.[65] Some refused to sign a declaration of gratitude to Stalin because the signature list might facilitate expulsion.[66] The memory of deportation had become paralyzing and, for Soviet plans, counterproductive. Potential "evacuees" did fear deportation to the Donbas or Siberia if they did not register to go west, but they were also afraid that registering for moving west might take them east or too far west.[67]

Some Poles insisted that they would never leave.[68] Encouraged by the Polish underground press, they doubted Soviet stability.[69] As late as December 1945, Professor Ryszard Gansiniec noted that "there still is a war atmosphere": there was an expectation of a new war and Soviet defeat.[70] Others hoped for a Soviet civil war.[71] Some Poles assumed that the Western allies would not let the Soviet Union keep Lwów. Yet, in reality, Western leaders saw "ethnic unmixing" as a means to stability: Churchill, in 1944, welcomed a "clean sweep" to end the "mixture of populations" that had caused "endless troubles."[72]

Yet hope died hard. After the First World War, Zofia Romanowiczówna had staked her last hopes on "English troops."[73] After the Second World War, a Polish

61. A. F. Noskova, *Iz Varshavy: Moskva, tovaryshchu Beriia. Dokumenty NKVD SSSR o polskom podpole, 1944–1945 gg.* (Moscow: Rossiiskaia akademiia nauk, 2001), 120 (doc. 31), reproducing GARF 9401, 2, 94: 49–56. On the details of deceiving and suppressing the Lwów Home Army leadership, see Tomasz Balbus, "Sowieci i żymierski a Lwowska AK 1944," *Biuletyn Instytutu Pamięci Narodowej*, no. 12 (2004): 67–68.

62. RGASPI 17, 88, 451: 26–29.

63. DALO P-4, 1, 2: 26–27; Hryciuk, "'Ciężkie Dni Lwowa,'" in *Studia z historii najnowszej*, ed. Wrzesiński, 23.

64. RGASPI 17, 88, 451: 35; Serhiychuk, *Deportatsiia poliakiv*, 68 [no archive reference]; Drix, *Witness to Annihilation*, 233.

65. DALO P-3, 1, 63: 43–50.

66. DALO P-3, 1, 319: 87; P-3, 1, 114: 18.

67. DALO P-3, 1, 63: 43–50.

68. TsDAHOU 1, 23, 892: 109–20, repr. in Serhiychuk, *Deportatsiia poliakiv*, 53–60, here 55.

69. Hryciuk, "'Ciężkie Dni Lwowa,'" 23; RGASPI 17, 88, 451: 21.

70. Ryszard Gansiniec, *Notatki Lwowskie, 1944–1946* (Wrocław: Sudety, 1995), 70.

71. RGASPI 17, 88, 451: 35.

72. Ther, "Chancen und Untergang," 141.

73. Romanowiczówna, *Dziennik lwowski*, 2:302.

inhabitant of Lwów saw British grand strategy in the "evacuation" itself: once in Poland, the evacuees would, "with the assistance of England," force the Soviets to leave and "return to Lwów."[74] President Roosevelt's death also encouraged some Poles.[75] For Stanisław Lem's father, faith in the "allies, who will save Lwów" ceased only when he faced a stark choice of leaving or taking Soviet citizenship.[76] By March 1945, there were eight hundred to twelve hundred registrations for "evacuation" every day. The Home Army reported that the Polish population was "breaking."[77] Pressure was relentless, with dismissals, passport confiscations, police orders, forced-labor harassment, and persistent rumors about deportations east.[78]

There was symbolic as well as violent resistance. On 1 November 1944, thousands gathered at the historic Łyczaków Cemetery to celebrate the anniversary of the 1918 "Defense of Lwów" with patriotic songs and shouts of "Death to the Bolsheviks."[79] The assassination of Zdisław Belinski on 8 February 1945 was the most prominent case of violence. Belinski, who served as Lwów deputy head of the ZPP, a Soviet Polish organization that propagandized the evacuation, publicly welcomed the Soviets and attacked the Polish exile government.[80] According to the obkom, he wanted Poland to become a Soviet republic.[81] Because he was involved with pro-Soviet underground activities during the German occupation, Khrushchev received him immediately after the Soviet reconquest of Lviv. According to an internal wartime report, Belinski, on the eve of the Soviet reconquest, had provided Soviet agent Kurylovych with ten names and addresses of "Ukrainian and Polish nationalists . . . opposed to Soviet power."[82] Between his covert marking of targets for Soviet repression and his public statements, Belinski could not have been short of enemies. He was killed by a letter bomb; his wife was badly injured; three Poles were arrested.[83] Beria reported the assassination to Stalin as one of several "terrorist acts," intended, he thought, to inspire Poles to stay.[84]

74. On hopes for British assistance, see TsDAHOU 1, 23, 892: 109–20, repr. in Serhiychuk, *Deportatsiia poliakiv*, 53–60, here 58.

75. TsDAHOU 1, 46, 759: 25–28.

76. Lem, *Świat na krawędzi*, 52.

77. *Karta* 17 (1995), 139, reproducing TsDAHOU 1, 23, 1466: 33–46; DALO P-3, 1, 239: 45. This figure probably refers to the whole oblast of Lviv. Some Polish officials working on the evacuation in Lviv were not only dismissed but arrested by the Soviet authorities (Isaievych, *Istoriia Lvova*, 3: 254; *Armia Krajowa w dokumentach*, 6:459).

78. Nakonechnyi, *"Shoa" u Lvovi*, 140–41; Gansiniec, *Notatki Lwowskie*, 128–30, 149, 157–59, 161, 165–67, 173–74, and 180–81.

79. Makarchuk, "Pereselennia poliakiv," 107.

80. TsDAHOU 1, 46, 809: 168–69.

81. DALO P-3, 1, 63: 21.

82. DALO P-183, 1, 175: 21, 34; P-183, 1, 179: 43–44.

83. DALO P-3, 1, 240: 29, 31.

84. Noskova, *Iz Varshavy*, 117 (doc. 31), reproducing GARF 9401, 2, 94: 49–56.

The obkom cited alleged statements from four Poles, clearly selected for spin. Two academics, an accountant, and a janitor all praised the killing, which implied that the struggle against the Polish underground was a struggle against the Poles in general, sampled as socially diverse, intelligentsia-led supporters of "terrorism."[85] The report made the Polish intelligentsia's authority work only one way: when nationalist, it had broad support, but when pro-Soviet, not. The "Polish street," to use an anachronistic term, appeared nationalist and bloodthirsty; the Polish intelligentsia could only incite it, not restrain it. The obkom had found a way to combine maximum blame of the Polish intelligentsia with minimum hope for it.[86]

Legacies

Removing Polish traces took much longer than removing Poles. In 1950, Hrushetskyi would reprimand a party audience for street names still commemorating Polish "colonizers" and "saints."[87] Saints mattered, not just religiously but nationally. For the Soviet authorities, as for many Poles, Roman Catholicism was an essential element of Polish identity. The expulsion of its clergy from Lwów peaked between April and June 1946, with three major transports leaving the city.[88] Petro Kucheriavyi, Lviv's plenipotentiary for matters of religious cults, expected that only "fifteen thousand to eighteen thousand believing Poles" and twenty-three priests would remain in his oblast. For Kucheriavyi, Pole and Roman-Catholic were synonyms and each one left behind was one too many: they should all "go and leave our motherland in peace."[89] His Kyiv superior, Ukraine's Plenipotentiary for Matters of Religious Cults Petro Vilkhovyi, conceded that some Roman Catholics would remain, but only with priests "more or less progressive (that is loyal to Soviet power)."[90]

By the beginning of 1947, according to Kucheriavyi, the number of Polish/Roman Catholic priests in Lviv oblast had decreased to eight, with no monks, no monasteries, four nuns, and seven functioning churches left.[91] Kucheriavyi estimated the number of Roman Catholic believers in the oblast at sixteen thousand, concentrated mostly in Lviv, which had "rid itself of unnecessary elements hostile to Soviet power." Remaining Roman Catholics behaved "loyally toward the Soviet state."[92]

85. DALO P-3, 1, 240: 29–30.

86. The city authorities identified Belinski's killers as "Polish-German nationalists" and awarded to his family the modest assistance of 1,000 rubles as well as support in getting their apartment repaired (DALO 3, 1, 219: 302).

87. DALO P-4, 1, 346: 150–51.

88. DALO R-1332, 2, 6: 48–50.

89. DALO R-1332, 2, 6: 42–44.

90. DALO R-1332, 2, 6: 25–26.

91. DALO R-1332, 2, 6: 57.

92. DALO R-1332, 2, 6: 57–59, 62, and 87.

Yet buildings remained. Kucheriavyi strove to curtail despolation of former church property, as a matter of political significance.[93] Official appropriations were a different matter. In May 1946, he reported that the Ukrainian Academy of Sciences was lifting "a library out of the monasteries," but, he warned, it was written "in foreign languages." When the members of the clergy were expelled west, two boxcars of books went east.[94]

The material legacy of the Roman Catholic Church was only part of the cultural artifacts at stake during the expulsion. Which cultural artifacts—such as pictures, books, or opera scores—would leave with Lwów's Poles? The Lublin agreement did not mention this issue and Polish Communists accorded it low priority until the spring of 1946, when it was spun for propaganda.[95] Some Poles wanted to remove whole libraries and archives.[96] Yet most artifacts remained in Lviv. In 1969, the Lviv obkom estimated that there were "more than four hundred thousand works of art, history, and culture" in Lviv's museums alone, with only 6 percent of them on continuous display.[97]

This legacy caused fears of contamination. After the expulsion, the oblast censors estimated that Lviv's Poles had taken more than six hundred thousand books with them. All had been checked and fifty-thousand confiscated.[98] Yet in 1947, the Kyiv Central Committee fretted over the "enormous" amounts of literature in foreign languages left in Lviv, an estimated 1.5 million works at the former Ossolineum alone, all in need of screening. Removing them from circulation had merely contained these hazardous remains.[99]

From 1949 to 1951, tens of thousands of works were purged at Lviv's libraries and museums. The anti-Soviet matter stockpiled in Lviv's stacks had many faces, including fascist, Soviet but heterodox, Russian but anti-Soviet, and Ukrainian nationalist. Polish things were still prominent, including books left behind by Polish "repatriates," portraits of Piłsudski, or works on the Polish defense of Lwów in 1918. Even with ongoing purges and one whole library shipped to Moscow, the task of cultural cleansing remained Sisyphean, especially since the supply of proper Soviet works was slow.[100] Thus, postwar Lviv was literally crammed full with a past that had no place in the Soviet present. This was partly and ironically due to Soviet intransigence. The new Poland got only about a quarter of the Ossolineum's possessions, a small selection of monuments and other artifacts.[101]

93. DALO R-1332, 2, 6: 46–47 and 120–21.
94. DALO R-1332, 2, 6: 48–50.
95. Matwijów, *Walka o lwowskie dobra kultury*, 54, 81–93.
96. Ibid., 69.
97. DALO P-3, 13, 142: 11–15, as reproduced in *Kulturne zhyttia*, 3:295.
98. DALO P-3, 2, 139: 185.
99. TsDAHOU 1, 23, 4501: 1–4.
100. DALO P-3, 4, 159: 50–74.
101. Matwijów, *Walka o lwowskie dobra kultury*, 80, 84–85, 89–93, 114.

"Ancient" as well as Soviet Ukrainian Lviv acquired not only the pervasive Habsburg and Polish presence of its architecture but also holdings of Polish cultural heritage second to none.

It should be noted, however, that Polish identity in Lwów had historically been imagined as immovable, tied to the city's site and its buildings' stones. Now Poles were forced to reimagine Polish Lwów's past as a movable memory. The fate of Janusz Witwicki, a Polish engineer and historian of architecture, and his model of eighteenth-century Lwów crystallized in miniature the paradoxical future of the Polish past. Only the central part of Witwicki's ambitious City Panorama of Lwów ever approached completion.[102] Having survived German occupation, Witwicki was murdered on 16 July 1946, just before he would have left for postwar Poland.[103]

What made Witwicki's City Panorama special was the fact that it was a movable representation of that immovable past of Lwów about to be abandoned, potentially linking a city to be left in the past and in Soviet Ukraine with a memory in a new Poland. Yet the Soviet authorities did not want to lose this emphatically Polish work and spent much energy much energy trying to keep it.

Habsburg bureaucrats had despised Lwów's "baroque" backwardness, which they wanted to replace with progressive neoclassicism.[104] Witwicki, in turn, strove to demonstrate Lwów's persisting Polishness, disparaging the Habsburgs' "pseudoclassicism." Even with 80 percent of architecturally significant pre-Habsburg buildings remaining in interwar Lwów, this authentic cityscape was still threatened by a modern (i.e., Habsburg) "sea of houses," punctuated by "barracks, hospitals, or businesses." His City Panorama would resist this monotony by deploying spotlighting, periscopes, and movable viewing platforms. It would occupy Lwów's historic and pre-Habsburg Powder Tower.[105] A technologically modern City Panorama with a historic mission would thus take the place of arms.

102. There were two important panoramas in Lwów, and both had a complicated history during the war and afterwards. The Racławicka Panorama was a large 360-degree mural painting of a key battle of Polish history, displayed in a specially constructed rotunda. Witwicki's Panorama was a three-dimensional scale-model of Lwów. I refer to Witwicki's Panorama as the City Panorama.

103. His killers may have been three unknown visitors, pretending, according to the obkom, to be correspondents of a Moscow newspaper. See Michal Witwicki, ed., *Plastychna Panorama davnoho Lvova: Janusz Witwicki/Panorama plastyczna dawnego Lwowa. Janusz Witwicki 1903–1946* (Lviv: s.n., 2003 or 2004), 5, 26; and DALO P-3, 1, 445: 36.

104. Prokopovych, *Habsburg Lemberg*, 83–93, 276.

105. DALO R-35, 12, 251: 24. Having already constructed his model old city center, Witwicki asked the Germans for funding. In 1942, the Stadthauptmann office supported Witwicki's request for access to archival documentation. See DALO R-35, 12, 251: 21–25; and TsDIA 755, 1, 160: 3.

After the 1944 Soviet reconquest, Khrushchev himself paid a visit to Witwicki's workshop, praised his work as of "great significance," and offered support, although from "a political point of view" this was "difficult."[106] When Khrushchev refused to sign the visitors' book, Witwicki tried to persuade him by stressing differences between the Germans and the Soviets as well as the power of architecture. It was "the stone, the raw material for propaganda." Khrushchev agreed, but he refused to be measured against the Germans and reminded Witwicki that Lviv was "contested territory" as well as "ours." Witwicki's work was "not convenient in that respect."[107]

Several months later, the Lviv obkom recommended to Khrushchev that the City Panorama project should continue, but as a state institution and with its emphasis on Lviv's Polish past reduced.[108] The party wanted a more Ukrainian "model of historic Lviv."[109] In June 1945, the Ukrainian Academy of Architecture took over the workshop, making Witwicki the deputy of a new director while recognizing his authorial rights.[110] When Witwicki decided to leave for Poland together with most of his work, equipment, and staff, a "compulsory sale" was considered.[111] In April 1946, his models were declared state property and he was told that he lacked "a Soviet psychology."[112] Work on the City Panorama was frozen; Poles about to leave were barred from access.[113] Witwicki noted that, at least in Lwów, the story of the City Panorama was over.[114]

106. In May 1946, Witwicki submitted these notes to the local party authorities to support his request to leave for Poland with his City Panorama and the contents of his workshop by claiming Khrushchev's general favor (DALO P-3, 1, 445: 35). Witwicki was signing his name to his version of what the most powerful man in Ukraine had said. To hand such a document to a bureaucracy that was likely to submit it, in turn, to Khrushchev would have been inadvisable if it had not been accurate.

107. DALO P-3, 1, 445: 52.

108. DALO P-3, 1, 281: 58–59.

109. DALO P-3, 1, 445: 47.

110. Matwijów, *Walka o lwowskie dobra kultury*, 121–22.

111. The Ukrainian government passed a decree facilitating a forced sale in February 1946 (ibid., 122).

112. DALO P-3, 1, 445: 47–48. The Soviet position was summarized in a report on the April 1946 negotiations of a specially charged commission with Witwicki (DALO P-3, 1, 445: 39–41). Witwicki explained his point of view in a letter to Khrushchev of 8 May 1946: he promised that what he offered to leave behind could be completed by Soviet experts. He announced that he would also continue working on his project, writing that to "leave the work of my whole life unfinished would be an irremediable blow for me. . . . Knowing how the Soviet government encourages the artist, I ask [you] to grant my request [i.e. to leave for Poland with substantial parts of his work], and I will remember with gratitude for my whole life the assistance which has already been given to me in the years 1939–1941 and 1944–1946" (DALO P-3, 1, 445: 45–46).

113. DALO P-3, 1, 445: 48.

114. DALO P-3, 1, 445: 49.

After submitting petitions to Khrushchev and Stalin, Witwicki obtained permission to leave with his work.[115] This decision caused alarm in Lviv. In June 1946, the City Panorama's director urgently reminded Hrushetskyi that Witwicki was about to remove his creation. The Ukrainian Academy of Architecture wanted it retained.[116] According to the Soviet writer Vladimir Beliaev, the director was present when the Lviv oblast censorship department, obllit, seized Witwicki's belongings shortly before he was abducted and killed.[117] After the murder, Beliaev suggested that the obkom exploit it for propaganda. He knew that two arrests had already been made. Yet he was worried about rumors that "the enemies" of Soviet rule were "strong, cunning, and well-concealed, whereas we are weak"; he reported that many locals blamed the killing on the "Bolsheviks." He called on Hrushetskyi to "imagine ourselves in the situation of a native inhabitant." Beliaev implied that the Soviet City Panorama director had acted against Moscow's decision to let the panorama go. Then, a sinister "third force" had had Witwicki killed to create a "martyr." Beliaev fantasized that it was the British "intelligence service" pulling the strings. The City Panorama would now become a reminder of a "myth" of his killing by the Soviets. Witwicki's death had "state significance" and required a major show trial to unmask the immediate perpetrators and distant instigators, with international coverage through the Sovinformburo news agency and, clearly, its Lviv correspondent, who happened to be Beliaev.[118]

Yet a show trial over Witwicki's murder never materialized. After his death, his wife Irina was allowed to take the City Panorama to Poland, where it only gradually returned to the public eye toward the end of Communist rule.[119] Local authorities in Lviv did remember and make claims. In 1954, one of their

115. Matwijów, *Walka o lwowskie dobra kultury*, 122–23.

116. DALO P-3, 1, 445: 38.

117. DALO P-3, 1, 445: 57. Beliaev's career combined Stalinist propaganda for the young in 1937, war writings that a post-Stalinist Soviet dictionary would cite as examples of mendacious kitsch, attacks on Ukrainian nationalism where due and where not, a brutal antisemitic speech against "those Shmuelsons and Gordons organically alien to us," delivered in Lviv during the "anti-cosmopolitan" campaign of 1949, and a long afterglow writing on "antifascist" and Great Fatherland War themes. In 1955, Beliaev explained himself to an elite readership at the Higher Komsomol School at the Komsomol Central Committee in Moscow. Witnessing killings of Communists during a Civil War childhood, young Beliaev later started writing at a local newspaper "to unmask teachers" as reactionary. He saw his life's greatest challenge in meeting postwar Lviv's Ukrainian nationalism. Warning of its dangers became his mission (TsDAMLM 780, 2, 23: 5–6, 70–71). Beliaev's position in Lviv, however, was both influential and precarious. Hrushetskyi shared his distrust, feeling that the "local population" was marked more deeply by the past and especially the German occupation than people in the eastern oblasts. Yet he also denounced Beliaev's recent publications as vulgar and his "incorrect and often unprincipled" behavior as harming the "cause of the political education of the local intelligentsia." See DALO P-3, 1, 418: 35; P-3, 1, 236: 74.

118. DALO P-3, 1, 445: 57–58 for all references to Beliaev's letter.

119. Witwicki, *Plastychna Panorama davnoho Lvova*, 27–28.

representatives argued that the City Panorama should be returned to, as she wrote in Russian, "Lvov, where it belongs." She failed to mention Witwicki's aim of rescuing Lwów's pre-Habsburg Polishness and depicted him as creating a model of "Lvov, the central city of Western Ukraine."[120] Less than ten years after his murder, Witwicki's attempt to create a permanent model of an ancient Polish Lwów was officially forgotten by Poland, while claimed as local heritage in Lviv itself, by an official calling the city by its Russian name and locating it within Western Ukraine. The memories of the panorama and of Witwicki himself both bore the imprint of dislocation and reappropriation.

Resettling Lviv: From Above and from the East

With the city's Jews and Poles gone and most of its buildings still standing, the gap between the prewar and the postwar populations was filled rapidly by immigration. As early as July 1946, the Kyiv Central Committee put Lviv's population at 352,013, slightly above 1939 levels.[121] Three years later, Hrushetskyi estimated that more than 70 percent of Lviv's inhabitants had arrived from the east.[122] In 1951, the party-state counted an officially registered population of 383,000, while reprimanding Lviv's police for not removing illegals; clearly, the real figure was higher.[123]

During the first years after the reconquest, a new urban elite arrived. Lviv was the most important destination for a vast restaffing operation that brought 49,000 eastern cadres, including 22,400 Communists to Western Ukraine by 1945 alone.[124] Within less than a year after the Soviet reconquest, the Kyiv Central Committee and Ukrainian Narkomat ministries had sent nearly 7,000 top cadres to Lviv—including about 2,000 for industry, communications, and transport; more than 1,200 for the secret police, the courts, and prosecutors' offices; and 115 for key party positions.[125] Lviv's plenipotentiary from the central economic planning agency, Gosplan, reported a peak of immigration in 1945 and 1946, when a "mass movement" drew on cadres "from the central and eastern regions of the Soviet Union" and demobilized soldiers. By 1947, this extraordinary influx was abating and the situation "more or less stabilized."[126]

120. DALO R-1660, 2, 58: 13.

121. TsDAHOU 1, 23, 4575: 16–37. The same report counted 1,003,122 inhabitants of Lviv oblast as a whole (including the city).

122. DALO-P 3, 2, 481: 88.

123. DALO-P 3, 4, 507: 28, 31.

124. Weiner, *Making Sense of War*, 92.

125. Isaievych et al., *Istoriia Lvova*, 3:252.

126. DALO P-3, 2, 533: 113.

Figure 4.2 A demobilized Soviet serviceman on Lenin Street in Lviv, 1949. Lenin Street is now Lychakiv Street again. Collections: Volodymyr Rumiantsev and Center for Urban History of East Central Europe, Lviv.

In western Ukraine and Lviv, postwar eastern immigration was a tsunami rather than a tide, overlapping with the expulsion of Poles. The change in urban elites was particularly dramatic. The newcomers went into administration, exploitation, repression and surveillance, and the key project of Lviv's industrialization. In October 1944, fifty-seven out of seventy-three directors of major industrial enterprises were easterners. Locals, by contrast, landed jobs of lesser rank: managerial positions in smaller enterprises or minor leadership roles in obedient trade unions.[127] The postwar hierarchy, with locals subordinated to an imported Soviet eastern elite, thus shared some similarities to Lviv's earlier situation, when a Polish urban elite dominated both the city and the largely non-Polish countryside.

127. DALO P-4, 1, 156: 29; P-4, 1, 4: 10. According to this document, sixty-four of the sixty-nine heads of smaller *promartil* workshops were locals.

Many in the new urban elite were demobilized military personnel, and almost all were party members. By May 1948, the obkom counted nearly 56,500 demobilized in the oblast, including about 25,200 in Lviv. In the Soviet Union veteran officers were celebrated as modernizers of the countryside, but in Lviv, they usually had the privilege of staying in the city, accounting for almost twenty-two thousand, more than four-fifths of all the demobilized living there.[128] Party members also had better chances of landing a place in the oblast center. While their combined total in the oblast amounted to nearly 11,400, more than 9,500 stayed in Lviv. Demobilized soldiers clustered in "economic" and "industrial" jobs and provided considerable numbers of party, Komsomol, agriculture, and transport cadres.[129] Many entered academic institutions. In 1947, a fifth of Lviv's students were veterans.[130]

Privilege was only relative, however. Most officers were not from senior ranks. Halyna Abigalova, the daughter of a Soviet and Russian lieutenant who moved to Lviv in 1946, would later remember feeling hungry as she watched her mother bake goods not for the family to eat, but to sell on the black market to pad the family budget.[131]

Few officers arriving in Lviv came from rural backgrounds..[132] Halyna Abigalova's father did come from a village in central Russia; he had graduated from a *tekhnikum*. Lviv meant an urban apartment with gas but no bathroom.[133] It also meant continuing upward mobility. The de facto rule of providing officers with the privilege of city living space established a lasting pattern. Out of 3,548 reserve and retired officers settling in Lviv oblast between April 1953 and April 1957, 3,106 stayed in its central city. About 70 percent of them were party members; hundreds took part in political and public life.[134] Out of 161 reserve and retired officers demanding residence in Lviv oblast between 1960 and 1967, 156 would stay in its center.[135]

128. Weiner, *Making Sense of War*, 49.

129. DALO P-3, 2, 481: 127. The demobilized soldiers reaching Lviv were overwhelmingly male (52,714). Only 798 of them left for Poland.

130. *Nam partiia sylu dala*, 35.

131. Interview with Halyna Agibalova conducted by Halyna Bodnar, Lviv, 2 February 2012.

132. Only 428 of the 5,575 officers in Lviv by November 1946 were listed as having worked in agriculture. For those who had, going to Lviv was a virtually certain way into the city. Of all the officers in the oblast, including the city and its rural surroundings, only 488 had been in agriculture. Thus, only sixty, or about 12 percent, of all officers with a prewar rural professional past who came to the oblast did not move to the city after the war (DALO P-3, 1, 421: 116).

133. Interview with Halyna Agibalova conducted by Halyna Bodnar, Lviv, 2 February 2012.

134. DALO P-3, 6, 84: 114, 118–19.

135. DALO P-3, 10, 241: 1.

Figure 4.3 The market behind the Habsburg Opera House (in the background), 1947. It was central and crucial to early postwar Soviet Lviv and existed, in this place, until circa 1960. The Soviet propaganda aerostat hovering over it shows that the picture was probably taken on an important Communist holiday, when, clearly, the market was open. Collections: Volodymyr Rumiantsev and Center for Urban History of East Central Europe, Lviv.

The demobilized were not necessarily easterners, but the demobilized locals were granted fewer privileges.[136] Locals were less likely to be party members or officers, and most of them ended up in the countryside outside Lviv. This was a potential problem, with Hrushetskyi expecting demobilized servicemen in the villages to fight Ukrainian nationalists.[137]

The authorities made special efforts to accommodate the needs of officers and Communists, who were mostly easterners.[138] Demobilized officers could not go unemployed, Hrushetskyi insisted: they had to replace the "crooks and cheats . . . hired during the war"; officers left without work might, ironically, themselves turn to "speculation" and the "bazaar."[139]

Mobilization and demobilization also contributed to the removal of Poles from Lviv. In early 1945, *Vilna Ukraina* ran articles on "thousands" of Lvivians,

136. DALO P-3, 2, 211: 9.
137. DALO P-3, 1, 209: 156.
138. DALO P-4, 1, 187: 51–52; P-4, 1, 162: 73.
139. DALO P-3, 1, 361: 238.

ethnically neutrally termed *zemliaki*, joining the fight against Germany after their city's "liberation." Hrushetskyi, however, did not see these soldiers as Lviv inhabitants with a right to return, but as Poles who should stay away when demobilized.[140]

If Poles were out, who was in? There is some evidence on the ethnic background of the easterners. In the fall of 1946, the secret police provided the obkom with some statistics: between January and July 1946, a total of 32,010 immigrants had been registered; 22,167 were classified as Ukrainian, 5,704 as Jewish, 2,816 as other, and 1,323 as Polish, with the Ukrainian category thus making up more than 69 percent of the total.[141]

In leadership positions, it was easterner cadres who predominated. The obkom criticized open discrimination, as in the case of a rural official refusing to employ a local Communist because he would not "select from among locals."[142] Yet the new elite remained deeply eastern. By August 1947, the total of all occupied nomenklatura positions in the oblast, including the obkom as well as all miskoms and raikoms, was 9,869. There were only three locals in leading positions at the obkom level, 1,213 at all miskoms and raikoms, and another 2,316 at a level described as that of "lower village work." Locals were thus included, but in clearly inferior positions.[143] In Lviv, the share of locals in raion leadership positions was also very low: 7 out of 288 nomenklatura members in Zheleznodorozhnyi raion and 9 out of 291 in Stalinskyi raion.[144] In the city, unlike the countryside, locals were rare even at the base of the power structure.

In July 1948, less than 15 percent of miskom nomenklatura positions were held by locals, none of whom held either party or security positions. The largest concentration of locals clustered in the less sensitive culture and science positions, and even there 29 locals were eclipsed by 154 easterners.[145] By 1949, Lviv oblast's Society for the Spreading of Political and Scientific Knowledge, de facto the largest single propaganda organization in the oblast, had 1,872 lecturers, of whom only 342 were locals.[146] Inevitably, most of its nearly forty-nine hundred events in 1949 meant easterners literally lecturing locals.

It is important not to confuse the local western Ukrainians with Ukrainians in general. The latter were represented much more strongly in Lviv's new elite.

140. *Vilna Ukraina*, 2 February 1945, 6, and 4 February 1945, 5; DALO P-3, 1, 282: 59–60.

141. DALO P-3, 1, 523: 88.

142. DALO P-3, 1, 469: 20.

143. DALO P-3, 2, 214: 249.

144. DALO P-3, 2, 211: 10.

145. DALO P-4, 1, 251: 377. The discrepancy in the figures regarding nomenklatura in these documents probably occurred because the July 1948 data excluded all positions that were also part of the obkom nomenklatura.

146. DALO P-3, 3, 363: 25–30. Only four hundred lecturers, however, were actually lecturing.

In January 1948, of 2,444 obkom nomenklatura positions, only 299 were occupied by locals, who were thus slightly more underrepresented than women, with 330 positions. With 1,575 nomenklatura positions, Ukrainians nonetheless held a clear majority.[147] Likewise, of 10,733 engineering-technical workers, 1,547 were locals, 4,407 were Russians, and 5,023 Ukrainians.[148]

In the spring of 1945, the Lviv oblast party organization had 5,613 members, "basically [working] on the railways and in the organs of the NKVD and NKGB." The latter, at the same time, made special efforts to purge the railways of "hostile elements." The Ukrainian Komsomol had sent west 4,533 leading eastern cadres.[149] By 1949, about 70 percent of railway staff would be counted as ethnically Ukrainian.[150]

Resettling Lviv: From Below

Two important groups of new settlers are rarely considered. Illicit migration to the city was significant. In 1946 and 1947, Lviv was a destination for internal refugees fleeing a postwar famine: although its existence was denied, an estimated one million people starved to death.[151] In early 1947, Lviv was running low on bread; the obkom feared a "collapse" of supplies.[152] It prohibited the use of freight cars for individual transport, increased controls at train stations, and removed dystrophy cases from the streets, "in view of the specific traits" of this disease.[153]

The police reported that "arrivals from other cities" of the Soviet Union were infested with fleas spreading infectious diseases, and rats were disfiguring corpses at the morgues. Carts stacked high with corpses were driven to the cemetery during daytime, producing "hostility" and talk among a population described as mesmerized by the spectacle.[154] Kyiv instructed Hrushetskyi to use Lviv's train station to screen and hospitalize infected passengers, especially street children.[155] This experience marked another important moment in the real unification of Ukraine. Alongside the powerful and victorious, another kind of easterner came into view: hungry refugees. Stalin's realm brought home to Lviv its vertiginously paradoxical nature: it could beat Nazi Germany *and* let its own people starve.

147. DALO P-3, 2, 211: 5.

148. DALO P-3, 2, 211: 32.

149. TsDAHOU 1, 45, 570: 1–6, 79–80. For railway purges, see RGASPI 17, 88, 450: 31–33. By mid-March 1945, 13,500 railway staff had been checked; nearly 400 were labeled "hostile."

150. Borys Lewytzkyj, *Die Sowjetukraine 1944–1963* (Cologne: Kiepenheuer und Witsch, 1964), 43.

151. Volodymyr Baran, *Istoriia Ukrainy, 1945–1953* (Lviv: Instytut ukrainoznavstva im. I. Krypiakevycha, 2005), 67–69.

152. DALO P-3, 2, 139: 69–70.

153. DALO P-3, 2, 134: 1, 23, 38.

154. DALO P-3, 2, 134: 3–6.

155. DALO P-3, 2, 134: 7–8.

Higher education helped repopulate Lviv: large numbers of students quickly arrived. In the 1944/1945 academic year, there were 2,200 freshmen, including 945 from "the eastern oblasts." Studying in Lviv was not necessarily voluntary. In 1944, a student from Kharkiv wrote that, with the conditions there "terrible," many students were sent to Lviv; those refusing were assigned "to rebuild factories" instead.[156]

Locals were not excluded from higher education, however. In the 1946–1947 academic year in Lviv, there were 3,056 locals in a total of 10,559 higher education students.[157] By 1950, 44.5 percent of Lviv's students were "western oblast natives."[158] While locals faced distrust *as locals*, Soviet admission policy was geared toward not excluding but co-opting them. Higher education in Lviv was a mixed experience, helping and compelling locals to find their way in a new authoritarian order, combining repression with opportunity.

Not all fresh inhabitants of the city came from the East or western Ukraine. The new arrivals included returnees from German forced labor deportation and Ukrainians driven from Poland. Nearly five hundred thousand Ukrainians—mostly peasants—were expelled from Poland. Moreover, an estimated eighty thousand inhabitants had left Lviv oblast for mostly compulsory work in Germany. The Lviv oblast Repatriation Department expected that substantially fewer would return; still, by December 1946, it counted 3,551 returnees in Lviv and 26,808 in its oblast.[159]

In general, Lviv oblast was a major Soviet transit point, with nearly 350,000 repatriates passing through its nine screening camps by October 1945.[160] In the same month, Hrushetskyi obtained from Kyiv permission to select, with secret police assistance, 15,000 repatriates for Lviv's factories; Moscow was to be petitioned to leave permanently in the city 6,400 "repatriates and former POWs"

156. TsDAHOU 1, 23, 871: 210–12.

157. DALO P-3, 2, 181: 35.

158. DALO P-3, 3, 351: 91, 156.

159. DALO R-221, 2, 911: 2, 14.

160. DALO P-3, 1, 319: 64. In Lviv oblast, by October 1945, about eighteen thousand inmates were still in these camps, according to this document. At the beginning of 1946, central Soviet authorities put the number for all repatriates to the Soviet Union at 4.2 million. They were generally considered a security problem, and all underwent filtration—that is, verification by the Soviet intelligence agencies. A "filtration file" was produced for each repatriate. The number of those who were given permission to return directly to their former places of residence or other nonpunishment destinations was 2.4 million, mostly women and children, who then underwent another round of verification at their places of residence and often, even if cleared again, continued to be stigmatized. Different outcomes for the remainder included 800,000 conscriptions, mostly into punishment battalions; 600,000 assignments to labor battalions, usually for two years; and nearly 273,000 confinements to camps or punitive special settlements. See Baran, *Istoriia Ukrainy*, 18–19. For a slightly higher number of repatriation camps in Lviv oblast and its general role in Soviet repatriation, see Pavel Polian, *Zhertvy dvukh diktatur: Zhizn, trud, unizhenie i smert sovetskikh voennoplennykh i ostarbaiterov na chuzhbine i na rodine* (Moscow: Rosspen, 2002), 363.

already temporarily assigned to its industry.[161] By the second half of 1945, at the Lviv city branch of the oblast construction trust, out of 613 workers, 113 came from Lviv and 492 from the transit camps.[162] Communal and construction enterprises urgently demanded another three thousand repatriates.[163] At least two important plants supplied themselves exclusively from a resettlement point.[164]

What was it like for future and some former Lvivians to enter or reenter the Soviet Union through the screening camps? The obkom's extensive reports depicted impoverishment, violent crime in collusion with Soviet authorities, suspicions of treason, interrogations, and discrimination. As of August 1945, none of the camps had real shelters, and inmates lived in stables and yards.[165] One such camp was situated in the small town of Rava Ruska. During the Holocaust, trains to German death camps had left its station; it had also been the location of a German camp. Now on the Ukrainian side of the border, by 1945, it had the biggest Soviet repatriation camp in the oblast. By late October, nearly a third of those transiting the oblast had passed through it.[166]

In Rava Ruska, even indoctrination was scarce, with movies rare and no radios or loudspeakers for a long time, and the staff insisting that they conducted interrogations rather than propaganda.[167] There was no fuel for heating or cooking; the inmates scavenged wood, antagonizing the local population; food was a problem. Soldiers in collusion with "speculators" harassed and robbed the inmates.[168] The troops also abused them, employing such epithets as "traitors to the motherland" or "strangers-Banderites."[169] In its Rava Ruska window on the East, no worse than in other oblast camps, Stalinist civilization appeared in minimalist guise, stripped down to essentials: screening, scarcity, crime, and punishment.[170]

Despite initial Soviet plans to move expelled Ukrainians from Poland to eastern and southern Ukraine, most of them—nearly 323,000—were resettled in western Ukraine, including almost 60,000 in Lviv oblast.[171] Few were allowed to

161. DALO P-3, 1, 208: 107.
162. DALO P-4, 1, 61: 50–51.
163. DALO P-4, 1, 62: 38.
164. DALO P-4, 1, 66: 48.
165. DALO P-3, 1, 319: 50.
166. DALO P-3, 1, 319: 64.
167. DALO P-3, 1, 319: 47.
168. DALO P-3, 1, 319: 39.
169. DALO P-3, 1, 319: 62.
170. DALO P-3, 1, 319: 39.
171. Baran, *Istoriia Ukrainy*, 40; Orest Subtelny, "Expulsion, Resettlement, Civil Strife: The Fate of Poland's Ukrainians, 1944–1947," in *Redrawing Nations: Ethnic Cleansing in East-Central Europe, 1944–1948*, ed. Philipp Ther and Ana Siljak (Lanham, MD: Rowman and Littlefield, 2001), 156, 165; Witold Sienkiewicz and Gregorz Hryciuk, *Wysiedlenia wypędzenia i ucieczki 1939–1959: Atlas ziem Polski* (Warsaw: Demart, 2008), 211.

settle in urban centers. By October 1946, out of 16,010 expellee households in Lviv oblast, 14,596 were in the countryside and 1,128 in Lviv.[172] The resettling of Ukrainian expellees from Poland was primarily a phenomenon of the immediate postwar years. By 1950, the total of repatriates and Ukrainians expelled from Poland officially settled in Lviv approached twelve thousand, less than 4 percent of the population.[173] For 1951, the authorities registered only sixty-six new repatriates for the whole oblast.[174]

Yet the small numbers of "resettlers" or returnees registered officially in Lviv were deceptive. By 1950, oblast secret police head Maistruk and Hrushetskyi saw "resettlers" and "repatriates" as security risks and potential nationalists.[175] Often residents of the suburban outskirts, repatriates worked in and were part of the city.[176] They were not a small group. Hrushetskyi deplored that, with Lviv's population at above 378,000, a total of 30,000 were resettlers from Poland.[177] In postwar Lviv, the experience of being driven from Poland was present in the personal and family memories of almost one-tenth of the city's de facto inhabitants. Being a resettler, literally on the margins of Lviv, could be precarious. Denied a place on the Komsomol honor guard after Stalin's death, a student complained about not being trusted because she was a resettler. The Komsomol then made her point by expelling her.[178]

Mutual expulsion may have forced ethnic conflict out of the everyday sphere and into the realm of memory, but it remained there, well preserved. Fifteen years after the Soviet reconquest, when Polish parents complained about their children's treatment at a school in Lviv, they were told to leave for Poland if they did not like it in Lviv; another official reminded them that "we Ukrainians" had had to leave Poland "naked and barefoot."[179]

Purity in One City: Purging, Projection, and Vicarious Contamination

Postwar Lviv was the theater of a Soviet-nationalist struggle, but its eastern immigrants also brought with them biographies that, by Soviet standards, were broken. Here was a commonality between East and West that divided the city's

172. DALO P-3, 1, 443: 150.
173. Isaievych et al., *Istoriia Lvova*, 3:259.
174. DALO R-221, 2, 957: 20.
175. DALO P-3, 3, 460: 47; P-4, 1, 334: 183; RGASPI 17, 88, 794: 17.
176. Bodnar, "Mihratsiia silskoho naselennia," 61.
177. DALO P-3, 3, 460: 47.
178. DALO P-3, 3, 692, reproduced in *Kulturne zhyttia*, 2:26.
179. DALO P-4, 1, 180: 411–12.

inhabitants rather than uniting them: easterner fears of "going native" were exacerbated by the anxiety of having too much in common in an immediate past overshadowed by Germans. The difference between locals and easterners was not, in reality, between those who had survived under the Germans and those who had not, since many easterners had done so too. A special western Ukrainian census in the spring of 1945 aimed at "labor deserters," the illegally armed, those lacking identity papers, and those suspected of helping Germans or Ukrainian nationalists. The campaign was aimed at easterners no less than locals and nationalists, and the locals seem to have been only one of several categories of suspects.[180] Similar operations occurred throughout Ukraine, west and east.[181] The difference was one of interpretation, not screening: in his reporting from Lviv, Hrushetskyi simplified the operation's targets by calling them nationalist "bandits."[182]

In 1947, Lviv's Medical Institute reported a total of 2,541 students. Half of them were locals, whereas four-fifths had been under German occupation, so over half of the eastern students had shared that experience.[183] In 1948, the obkom identified seven of twenty-two directors, forty-nine of seventy-six leading cadres, and eleven of twenty-one *apparat* staff at the city's Masloprom food trust as having survived German rule under suspicious circumstances. All four cases discussed in detail were from the East.[184] In the same year, Hrushetskyi reported that 558 members of Lviv's 1,626 academic staff had lived under German occupation, including 137 who "collaborated actively." Again, a "significant share" of these suspect cadres was from the East.[185]

In 1950, Maistruk concluded that Lviv was a hiding place for both local nationalists and for some who had collaborated with Germans in eastern Ukraine.[186]

180. Baran, *Istoriia Ukrainy*, 21–22. For some incomplete statistics on this campaign, see RGASPI 17, 88, 450: 31–38. By the beginning of April the total of suspects identified in Lviv oblast was 3,405. These, however, included only 244 putative nationalists or their supporters, while the number of those either dodging the draft or illegally obtaining an exemption was 1,592 (ibid., 37–38).

181. Tetiana Pastushenko, "'Die Niederlassung von Repatriierten ist verboten . . .': Die Wiedereingliederung von ehemaligen Zwangsarbeitern in die sowjetische Gesellschaft nach dem Krieg," in *Zwangsarbeit*, ed. Pohl and Sebta, 356.

182. Baran, *Istoriia Ukrainy*, 21–22. A police operation in September 1945 took a snapshot of a place, where sometimes even the dead returned to haunt Soviet security. Netting 2,351 "anti-Soviet elements," Lviv's police found—in addition to a Kharkiv student accused of killing and robbing her landlady, Polish Home Army members, and unofficial "resettlers"—a suspect, who was described in the files as having been executed for spying in 1941 (TsDAHOU 1, 46, 809: 46–58; DALO P-3, 1, 183).

183. DALO P-3, 2, 96: 9–14.

184. DALO P-3, 2, 425: 136–44.

185. TsDAHOU 1, 23, 5078: 3–4.

186. DALO P-4, 1, 334: 184.

Hrushetskyi also considered Lviv a rallying point for those with "dark affairs" to hide. Cadre records were a mess made worse by "nepotism," without proper documents or background checks of prior lives in "the Urals or in Kiev."[187] In the same year, the party organization of the Lviv Instrument Factory reported that one of its candidate members had committed suicide, "fearing the unmasking" of her wartime stay in Austria, her liberation by British and American troops, and the Soviets' arrest of her brother for having worked for the Germans.[188] Despite the shared reality of the past, however, it was the locals who were stereotyped as nationalists and collaborators, while easterners were not.

Its prewar population decimated, its new population resettled from above and below and from east and west, Lviv preserved its capacity to provoke special ambitions and anxieties among its inhabitants and rulers. When Soviet "quicksand society" on the march met a Central European borderland city in a moment of war, genocide, ethnic cleansing, and competitive totalitarian conquest, yet another fantasy of a bulwark emerged in which challenges domestic and foreign clashed in a theater of contamination, purification, and delimitation.

Lviv Unsettling: Under Soviet Eyes

In October 1945, Vladimir Beliaev produced a long description of Lviv just after the peak of the expulsion of its Poles.[189] His letters to Khrushchev and the Central Committees in Moscow and Kyiv triggered detailed investigations that confirmed his allegations.[190] For Beliaev, Lviv was a strategic base "for the Soviet order in the West" and a site for "great state experiments," but it was "very difficult ground, saturated not only with international espionage but by age-old hatred . . . for everything Russian," and a "very dark" place for us, the "people arriving from the eastern oblasts."[191]

With "the technology of forgery" locally developed "beyond measure," it was easy to buy fake documents such as a visa for the United States or ration cards. Beliaev recommended a complete reregistration of all inhabitants. He suggested that Lviv was the center of the Ukrainian nationalist underground.[192] Worse, in his urban jungle fantasy—in which everybody, for money, was able to seem what

187. DALO P-3, 3, 412: 48–49.

188. DALO P-3, 3, 409: 3.

189. TsDAHOU 1, 46, 752: 62–67.

190. TsDAHOU 1, 46, 809: 46–58.

191. TsDAHOU 1, 46, 752: 62–67. At about the same time, Biliakevych, the rector of Lviv University, described his institution as the oldest university in Ukraine as well as a "forward position [*forpost*] of Soviet culture and science" (DALO R-119, 6, 10: 7). Beliaev had no monopoly on the sense of being at the cutting edge of manifest destiny Soviet style.

192. TsDAHOU 1, 46, 752: 62–67.

they were not and claim what they should not—the locals were liars: Beliaev accused the local Ukrainian intelligentsia of assisting Ukrainian nationalists while signing Soviet loyalty declarations. Moreover, they were duplicitous because they were "closer to" the nationalists "than to us 'Soviets.'" These suspicions inspired calls for the creation of a janitorial surveillance network.[193] Janitors were a formidable surveillance force, a source of denunciation and favors under both Soviet and German rule.[194] Beliaev proposed removing locals from all janitorial positions and replacing them with party members "free of old links to the local population." Encapsulating a fundamental paradox of the ideal easterner's role, he demanded that the new janitors be both perfect outsiders and perfect insiders who would never divide the world between locals and easterners. The Soviet authorities shared Beliaev's concern over the janitors' strategic position, although there was no single great purge of them. At a 1946 janitors' meeting in Shevchenko raion, all 130 participants were locals.[195] Yet leading janitorial positions were easternized by August 1949, at least, with the miskom counting 48 locals out of a total of 280.[196]

Turning the janitors into "a Soviet eye in every house," Beliaev argued, would also help end "speculation."[197] Demanding better eastern cadres, he blasted those arriving as corrupt speculators and draft dodgers. By denouncing "gesheftemakher," he added an antisemitic twist.[198] Yet he also blamed Lviv itself for spoiling these eastern arrivals. He described crippled Soviet war veterans begging from local "fine ladies." Helping his wife sell pork, a uniformed NKVD sergeant "cut the meat, borrowed weights from the neighboring trader-Poles, weighed the goods," and "handed out change." Beliaev was horrified by this case of historic devolution and going native in front of the natives, the "open 'grafting [*vrastanie*] of an NKVD employee onto capitalism' under the eyes of the Lviv public at the bazaar."[199] It is beside the point that Beliaev's insinuation that such corruption occurred only in Lviv was absurd. His Lviv was a magic mirror permitting the externalization of the abhorred. If the Sovietizers would not Sovietize the city,

193. A city consisted of houses, often inhabited by several parties. In February 1946, Hrushetskyi reported to Moscow 6,280 buildings under Lviv's *zhilfond* living-space administration. There were 1,170 *domoupravlaiushchii* janitors or house wardens, each responsible for several buildings (DALO P-4, 1, 111: 50).

194. Gerstenfeld-Maltiel, *My Private War*, 28, 35; Rosenfeld, *From Lwów to Parma*, 19; Nakonechnyi, *"Shoa" u Lvovi*, 228; Wells, *Ein Sohn Hiobs*, 250.

195. DALO P-3, 1, 488: 45.

196. DALO P-4, 1, 331: 34.

197. TsDAHOU 1, 46, 752: 62–67.

198. Ibid.

199. Ibid. Beliaev's use of the term *vrastanie* was probably ironic. In the 1920s, it had been used in official Bolshevik discourse to refer to a transition to socialism.

Beliaev implied, it would de-Sovietize them. The reverse of fear, however, was relief; the un-Soviet had a place—marginal, contained, and ready for transformation.[200]

The residential buildings of Lviv became sites of temptation and corruption, and their maintenance collapsed. Although the first Soviet and the German occupation damaged many structures, by 1947, some of their new easterner inhabitants admitted feeling ashamed for not "restoring but ruining" them. In a closed meeting, Lviv's *Radianska pravda* correspondent, bitter at still receiving his gas bill in the name of his Polish predecessor, called it "demagogy" to blame the German occupation.[201] Even Lviv's degraded buildings were highly attractive. By expelling the city's Poles, the Soviet authorities reinforced the shifts in residential space begun in 1939 and boosted by the Holocaust. The new wave of Soviet cadres joined the struggle for "living space," making Beliaev quip that if they were as keen on work as on apartments, the Soviet order would already have arrived. Lviv's Gosplan plenipotentiary reported that construction organizations tasked with building factories were renovating private apartments instead.[202]

In fact, the corruption Beliaev decried was as essential to the real Soviet order as his own systemic and conformist criticism. Although Lviv's population had been more than halved by the war and the Holocaust, many apartments became available only after the Soviet reconquest, when yet more residents were removed. The expulsion of Lviv's Poles fed into both the ongoing uprooting of the city's society and followed a traditional Soviet pattern, summarized by Julia Obertreis for prewar Leningrad: the expulsion of "people from their residential space to provide others with it."[203]

Expulsion also exposed the contradictory but essential role of the real-existing market in Soviet civilization. In principle, Lviv's Poles could not sell the apartments they had to abandon; the city administration, in the form of the city executive committee (ispolkom in Russian, vykonkom in Ukrainian) was to

200. Beliaev's complaint could also be read in a longer as well as less direct perspective: a Russian elite tradition of fascination and corruption anxiety over cities representing Western alternatives, as recently described by Victor Taki. In that sense, Soviet-imagined Lviv, mutatis mutandis, may have shared some features with Königsberg and Paris in the eighteenth- and nineteenth-century Russian imperial imagination. On Königsberg and Paris, see Victor Taki, "The Horrors of War: Representations of Violence in European, Oriental, and 'Patriotic' Wars," *Kritika: Explorations in Russian and Eurasian History* 15 (2014): 265–67.

201. DALO P-3, 2, 84: 39, 5–7.

202. TsDAHOU 1, 46, 752: 62–67; RGAE 4372, 45, 134: 51. At the same time, at least one Lviv factory party organization was complaining that official apartment repairs for its staff were extremely shoddy because builders avoided this type of work as insufficiently lucrative (DALO P-2638, 1, 7: 6. Clearly, in some ways postwar Lviv was a builders' nonmarket.

203. Obertreis, *Tränen des Sozialismus*, 148–49.

dispose of them. Yet by November 1945 the Kyiv Central Committee found "mass speculation with apartments" in Lviv, fueled by the expulsion.[204] The obkom noted that "hundreds of middlemen" were taking 2,000–3,000 rubles in brokerage fees, and prices were rising rapidly in a market that should not have existed. Whereas a furnished apartment had formerly cost an average of 6,000–10,000 rubles, by the summer of 1945 it cost between 15,000 and 40,000.[205]

Expulsion also led to fleecing. Riszard Gansiniec noted that getting his books packed could cost up to 14,000 rubles, while his monthly professorial income was at first 1,200, then 2,000 rubles.[206] He estimated that, in general, leaving took approximately 6,000–7,000 rubles, more than many Poles had.[207] While driving Poles out, Soviet officials extorted bribes for documents.[208] By 1947, the Moscow agency of State Control (Goskontrol) reported widespread privatized plunder from those expelled.[209]

Little wonder then that, according to the obkom, the Lviv vykonkom joined the living space "speculation" too. Vykonkom Chairman Boyko claimed that only furniture was traded, but his assertions were dismissed. "Not one Pole," the obkom maintained, gave "up his apartment before the 'buyers of the furniture' " had moved in.[210]

Soviet veterans complained about corruption: "If you grease it, all's fine. For money you can buy a great apartment and position," and Communists did.[211] The obkom counted two thousand eastern cadres without shelter; Hrushetskyi complained that there were three hundred Soviet elite science cadres and even generals unable to find lodgings, making it hard to keep them interested in Lviv.[212] Even after almost all the Poles were expelled, he still blamed them for "circumventing the evacuation conditions."[213] The apartments went not only to those making deals with Poles but also to those bribing "our organizations." Bribes need takers as well as givers; yet Hrushetskyi demanded an end to "this outrage from the Poles."[214]

204. TsDAHOU 1, 46, 809: 46–58.

205. DALO P-3, 1, 183: 60–65.

206. Gansiniec, *Notatki Lwowskie*, 46, 49, 59, 65, 72.

207. Ibid., 149.

208. Jadwiga Złotorzycka, *Dwugłos pokoleń* (Wrocław: Wydawnictwo Uniwersytetu Wrocławskiego, 1996), 26.

209. DALO P-3, 2, 134: 230–31.

210. Boyko himself was also accused of being involved in shady deals with apartments, as another obkom file of November 1945 shows. He got rapped on the knuckles when he assigned an apartment earmarked for a Lviv Komsomol secretary to an accountant, classifying the latter as a "deserving artist of the republic" (DALO P-3, 1, 183: 60).

211. DALO P-3, 2, 126: 17–18.

212. DALO P-3, 2, 103: 88–93.

213. DALO P-3, 1, 239: 49.

214. DALO P-3, 2, 103: 88–93.

Jews became the other ethnic scapegoat. Illicit trading of apartments and "speculation" came with antisemitism among Soviet officials. The obkom's language combined traditional and specifically Soviet postwar prejudices, decrying those "robbing the toilers of the home front" with their "sinister business." The bad example singled out had a profession and a name stereotypically Jewish, the dentist Shtein from Dnipropetrovsk, accused of bribing his way to a place in Lviv.[215] Here was a pattern with support at the top and a long future. In 1947, an obkom report denounced the official Kalynychenko for illicitly issuing residence permits for a family—"all Vulfovny by patronymic," implying that they were Jewish. "That fact," goes the grim comment, "will sufficiently answer Comrade Hrushetskyi's question how these Vulfovny get to Lviv and mess up the trade here." Clearly, antisemitism was well rehearsed at the core of Soviet power in postwar Lviv.[216] In 1950, Hrushetskyi blamed his obkom buro staff for the failure of Lviv's trade system and insisted that it must "represent . . . the national composition . . . of the oblast." Otherwise "corrections" would be needed and officials who failed to implement such measures would be "expelled from the party." Without explicitly mentioning Jews, Hrushetskyi made his meaning clear by concluding, "We won't build socialism [in Lviv] with people who have arrived from Tashkent [and] Alma-Ata," alluding to Soviet stereotypes of Jews as shirkers who had sat out the fighting in Central Asia. Hrushetskyi insisted that the "people from Alma-Ata" were preventing the promotion of Ukrainian locals.[217] In the context of latent Soviet antisemitism, speaking up for the local could also mean denigrating Jews.

At the same time, in postwar Lviv, official claims by Holocaust survivors were not welcome. When one of them demanded her property, she was turned down.[218] A decorated Soviet veteran and party member, however, who had first come to Lviv before 1941, did obtain an apartment and furniture.[219] Samuel Drix noted that apartments were assigned to eastern cadres, while "Jews who had found a home here after the Germans had fled were now forced by the Soviet authorities to leave."[220] Denouncing both "speculation" and illegal arrivals in ethnic terms, blaming Poles on the way out and arriving Jews, while de facto upholding the dispossession of the Holocaust, the obkom marked change as well as continuity in a history of prejudice.

215. DALO P-3, 1, 183: 63–65. On widespread and high-placed pre-Bolshevik yet modern Russian stereotypes casting Jews as "speculators" and exploitative middlemen, see Peter Holquist, *Making War, Forging Revolution: Russia's Continuum of Crisis, 1914–1921* (Cambridge, MA: Harvard University Press, 2002), 19–20.

216. DALO P-3, 2, 13: 43–50.

217. DALO P-3, 3, 412: 49–51.

218. DALO R-6, 2, 44: 125.

219. DALO R-6, 2, 44: 126–28.

220. Drix, *Witness to Annihilation*, 222, 230.

In September 1949, *Vilna Ukraina* described what should have happened to Lviv's living space. Focusing on one three-story building, the newspaper introduced the former doorman Zalinskyi, the "building's living chronicle." He recalled its prewar tenants' exploitation by the owners, called Polovtser, who were Polish and "alien to the people." *Vilna* credited "Soviet power" with sweeping them "from Lviv as if by the wind," freeing its best apartments for workers. By 1949, the building housed a sample of exemplary and grateful "simple Soviet people," including a "hero mother," a "famous Stakhanovite," an "old soldier," and the "young heroes of the Five-Year Plan."[221]

In reality, the Soviet authorities effectively if grudgingly, oversaw a process in which the best living space of the city was distributed not by criteria of Soviet "social justice" but by "speculation," favoring easterners and relegating locals to second place. By 1951, the obkom found at least ninety-nine cases of top—usually eastern—cadres who kept apartments in Lviv although they had been reassigned to work elsewhere.[222] A year later, the obkom buro noted that these elite holders of living space were also selling apartments to one another. Acquaintance and bribes were, according to the report, still decisive in settling the "question of living space." The military served themselves as they liked, and the milits (Soviet police) registered all who paid up.[223]

An obkom resolution of January 1952 had no effect, the obkom buro found nine months later. There was still an illicit market in living space, with its own rates and prices as well as known trading spots.[224] Some in the local Soviet elites were turning into absentee landlords living far from Lviv, and corruption was widespread. Yet in 1956, according to the vykonkom, more than nine thousand inhabitants were officially registered as waiting for an assignment of living space.[225]

The easterners' rush for apartments came just in time to leave Poles with fresh bad memories as they departed for a new Poland slated for Soviet hegemony: their last impression of the Soviets was one of discrimination, expulsion, and plunder, not liberation from the Germans. In April 1945, Roza Cieszyńska, the widow of a Polish professor murdered by the Germans, asked Vladimir Beliaev to protect her from an easterner who offered her 47,000 rubles, officially for her "furniture" and in reality for her apartment. The man had then failed to secure vykonkom confirmation and demanded his money back. Cieszyńska told him that she had already

221. Mykola Mykhailov, "Pid dakhom odnoho budinku," *Vilna Ukraina*, 6 September 1949, 3.
222. DALO P-3, 4, 94: 42–56.
223. DALO P-3, 4, 415: 17–18.
224. DALO P-3, 4, 440: 11, 17–20.
225. DALO P-3, 5, 410: 90.

spent it to settle her debts. When he did not receive it, he threatened to have her and her son deported to Siberia.[226]

A Very Wild West: The Brutalization of "Liberation"

As Cynthia Hooper has argued, at the end of the war, the Soviet military was a major source of violent crime, especially in the western Soviet Union.[227] For Lviv, this violence was formative. Postwar Soviet Lviv was not merely often a lawless city, but one where, as Beliaev's complaint showed, disorder and crime were inseparable from the representatives of Soviet power.

Officially, the memory of the second historic meeting between the Soviet forces and Lviv was reduced to a bland screen of "liberation," covering pervasive experiences of abuse, fear, and humiliation. In 1948, a thesis presented at the law department of Lviv's university was scrapped when its author found that the Great Fatherland War had produced hooliganism and theft.[228]

Soviet servicemen viewed Lviv as a conquered enemy city. Deploring the harm this did to Sovietization, Beliaev demanded that the troops be told to see themselves as liberators and reject the "widely held view" that there was no difference between the German city of "Dresden and Lviv."[229] Lviv also fell victim to the stereotype that Ukrainians were traitors, having welcomed the Germans and then waited for liberation by their "elder brothers," the more steadfast Russians. When a bystander tried to prevent two officers from abusing a woman by pointing out that the woman was not Polish but Ukrainian, the officers replied that that was even worse because "Ukraine betrayed us."[230]

The Soviet army in Lviv was a violent and arrogant as well as an everyday presence. In May 1945, a city park was restored with two thousand hours of manpower; in July, the army destroyed it by turning it into pasture for a

226. TsDAMLM 780, 2, 28: 10–11. Beliaev left an impression of influence and some readiness to help with others too. Leon Weliczker-Wells remembered him as very powerful; he also recalled his advice to leave for the West. See Leon Wells, "Interview," Visual History Archive Online: USC Shoah Foundation Institute, Wells Leon, 23410, Segment 193http://vhaonline.usc.edu/viewingPage.aspx?testimonyID=25727&returnIndex=0.

227. Cynthia Hooper, "A Darker 'Big Deal': Concealing Party Crimes in the Post-Second World War Era," in *Late Stalinist Russia: Society between Reconstruction and Reinvention*, ed. Juliane Fürst (New York: Routledge, 2006), 145.

228. DALO R-119, 6, 48: 145.

229. TsDAHOU 1, 46, 752: 62–67. It was not the first time or only under the Soviets that these borderlands challenged the troops' ability to tell friend from enemy. During the First World War, Habsburg commanders fighting off a Russian imperial attack had had to remind their soldiers that they were *not* in enemy territory there (Prusin, *Lands Between*, 44).

230. TsDAHOU 1, 46, 752: 62–67.

thousand horses and a car park.[231] One month later, the central "Liuks" restaurant complained about soldiers brawling, stealing, and beating the female staff. Most regular offenders lived in Lviv, and neither the city's military commander nor military patrols attempted to stop them; the patrols, too, were often dangerously drunk and extorted bribes.[232] Late into the night, the city's streets and restaurants were full of drunken officers and soldiers having public shoot-outs.[233] A "strange habit" of driving cars through parks and on pavements produced, in two months alone, thirty-four car accidents that left fourteen dead and fifteen wounded.[234] The Lviv Polytechnic reported that soldiers were devastating its teaching farm, harassing female students, and beating up the farm's staff. When faculty members complained to the officers, they were beaten in front of servicemen shouting that "the civilian bastards" should "be exterminated."[235] Ryszard Gansiniec wrote in his diary about the night of 6–7 November (the anniversary of the October Revolution), describing it as a macabre peak performance, when the morgue had received "forty bodies of Moskals, who killed one another when drunk. Usually [it] receives five to seven bodies of killed soldiers per night."[236] At the beginning of December 1945, he noted that over the preceding month 350 bodies of victims "killed in the street" had been delivered to the morgue and that the soldiers were robbing "in broad daylight." He knew about the recent arrest of "a big gang made up of high-ranking officers," and about a woman killed by a soldier, who pushed her under a truck when she resisted being robbed.[237]

The Kyiv Central Committee amplified such allegations, attributing the majority of crimes against public order to Soviet soldiers. In September 1945, 8,238 of them were arrested for offenses such as drunkenness, robbery, rape, and murder; only 282 were arrested for infringements of military discipline. Twenty days in October netted 3,940 arrests, with 1,206 for robbery, theft, and murder.

One case of murder and robbery involved much premeditation and cooperation between airport officers and the NKVD Political Department. Rioting soldiers killed a policeman at a market; officers formed a gang of "robber-killers"; a drunken soldier fired on a crowd without provocation, killing two and wounding five civilians, including two children. A long list of similar incidents concluded with the statement that such "examples can be multiplied, as Comrade Beliaev writes in his letter, to infinity."[238] The Soviet police and secret police were also

231. DALO P-4, 1, 60: 120.
232. DALO P-4, 1, 60: 56–59.
233. TsDAHOU 1, 46, 809: 46–58; RGASPI 17, 125, 310: 36.
234. TsDAHOU 1, 46, 809: 46–58.
235. DALO P-3, 1, 242: 169.
236. Gansiniec, *Notatki Lwowskie*, 49.
237. Ibid., 62.
238. TsDAHOU 1, 46, 809: 46–58.

involved in violent and profitable crime. In 1948, the obkom buro discussed the case of the oblast head of police. A hard drinker, who met his lover—politically suspect—in a conspiratorial apartment and was threatened with murder by one of his raion police heads for raping the man's wife, he was recommended for a combined lateral-vertical transfer to another oblast and a lower position.[239]

The police largely consisted of eastern cadres. By the middle of 1948, only five hundred of the twenty-two hundred police officers were locals. Hrushetskyi criticized his obkom officials for requesting "easterners" instead of employing "proven" locals, such as Komsomol or rural militia members with a record of fighting Ukrainian nationalists.[240] In the first half of 1948, two-fifths of those expelled from the party for various offenses were police and secret police officers. The reasons for expulsion included torture and rape, while a high-ranking officer was sentenced for robbing a bank and killing another police officer.[241]

The countryside around Lviv was despoiled no less than the city. According to two Kyiv Central Committee reports in early 1945, the deportations of "Banderite families, and very often also of families who should not have been subject to deportation," were welcome opportunities for the raion elites to take the deportees' property, while those peasants who remained faced systematic plunder and beatings to feed the elites' dining halls with vodka and geese.[242]

At the end of 1947, the secret police in Lviv was still reporting that crime was "systematic and threatening," causing the local population to feel "mistrust . . . and anger toward all military units."[243] Postwar crime abated in 1948, however. A Lviv milits report on 1948 showed that crime, at least in the city, was decreasing, with 1,401 cases in 1947 and 759 in 1948 and the number of murders down from 37 to 19.[244]

Yet some violence persisted. As late as 1951, the head of Lviv's kafedra of forensic medicine was shifted to another oblast because of his habit of wildly shooting a gun from his car in the countryside under the pretext of "bandit" attacks, as well as using his trips for extramarital sex. For some members of the Soviet elite, the West remained liberatingly wild for years.[245] In the same year, the Lviv secret police reported a case of an officer drinking himself into a stupor, walking into a village soviet, calling somebody a "bandit," and shooting him dead, while a whole gang of soldiers, also drunk, beat to death a "local youth" and knifed a party member.[246]

239. DALO P-3, 2, 383: 231–32.
240. DALO P-3, 2, 424: 22.
241. DALO P-3, 2, 424: 131.
242. Serhiychuk, *Ukrainskyi zdvyh*, 3:289–93.
243. DALO P-3, 2, 461: 1–2.
244. DALO P-3, 2, 480: 169.
245. DALO P-3, 4, 174: 207–8.
246. DALO P-3, 4, 170: 35–36.

Speaking Bolshevik in a Local Idiom

Differences between the Soviet self-image and reality were not the most important aspect of the encounter between easterners and locals. The relationships between them were also characterized by confrontation, counterdistinction, and cooperation.

Not content with occupying the best living space in Lviv, elite easterners also established a system of food privileges. In post-reconquest Lviv, the continuity with German practices could be disturbing. In 1951, Kuzma Pelekhatyi, a key actor among promoted locals, told the obkom buro that the city administration had the best cafeteria in town; the first to set up dining facilities there had been the Germans.[247] Generally, there were forty-nine cafeterias in Lviv, organized in a *trest*; one was headed by a local. In January 1950, Hrushetskyi denounced what he considered the anti-Soviet practice of excluding locals from promotion. He demanded precise statistics on the national and regional backgrounds of all employees in the trade system, since "locals . . . are mostly working as cleaners and watchmen."[248] In restaurants and shops, the relationship between the locals, often rural immigrants, and the "easterners" was on clear display.

Even extreme cadre scarcity did not reduce these interactions and the mutual perceptions they created. While postwar reconstruction and the ambitious Soviet industrialization project for Lviv did cause an objective need for more experts, the *meaning* of the newcomers' arrival from the East was an ideological construct. Lviv, for instance, had lost many medical practitioners in the Holocaust and the war, with the head of Lviv's Polyclinic for Dentistry, Mykytok, singling out his discipline as the one that had "suffered the most."[249] At that moment, there were only twenty dentists in Lviv, which was "a catastrophe." Yet Mykytok did not call for new cadres from the East, instead asking the authorities *not* to send "young doctors" because they had received their degrees in "Buriat-Mongolia" and still needed to be trained, for which there was no time in Lviv. Not denying that the eastern dentists were poorly trained, the oblast health department head, Trehub, demanded that Lviv provide them with further training, with Mykytok as an old expert having a special obligation to help.[250]

In Lviv, speaking fluent Bolshevik came to include a special idiom about locals and easterners. In December 1944, two hundred students from Lviv's Soviet Trade Institute wrote to Khrushchev. Reminding Khrushchev of their personal

247. DALO P-3, 4, 87: 11.

248. DALO P-3, 3, 434: 23.

249. At the same meeting, a Ukrainian Central Committee representative put the number of doctors killed by the Germans in Lviv at about four hundred (DALO R-312, 2, 3: 115).

250. DALO R-312, 2, 3: 42–44.

loyalty to him, they had come west to "study and grow . . . when you called." Yet as "arrivals from the eastern oblasts" they had encountered prejudice and resistance. Their dorm had wet walls and no heating or kerosene. The gas was turned off. Some students were not attending lectures for lack of clothing. Many were sick.

There was nothing exceptional here, with dorm inhabitants often living in stark poverty. Even two years later, in November 1946, nine main dorms of Lviv's three principal institutions of higher education—Lviv's university, the Polytechnic, and the Medical Institute—lacked window panes, sewerage, furniture, and heating. At the Polytechnic's dorms, there were rats and mice. At the Medical Institute, many students were sick from sleeping on cold floors.[251] Yet the Trade Institute's students specifically blamed their misery on the fact that they were easterners and on the institute's director, "a local" who "does not yet know what Soviet means." Barely two months later, Hrushetskyi himself reported to Khrushchev that the students were right and measures were being taken.[252]

Appeals couched in terms of eastern/local antagonism became a pattern. In 1947, a group of students of the Dentistry College complained to *Lvovskaia pravda* about cold dorms; they also denounced the director of the school, Myketiuk (i.e., Mykytok), as "a local" who "does not care about us." The students presented themselves as "Soviet," clearly seeing themselves as easterners and implying that "Soviet" and "local" were antagonistic categories. In their view, it was "*because* he is a local" that Mykytok harassed them with hard living conditions.[253]

The rhetoric of local/eastern difference permeated Lviv down to the family level. In January 1945, Lidia Ukolova petitioned for permission for her mother to come to Lvov. Ukolova herself had arrived from Tashkent with her husband and two small children. The Ukolovs were quintessential eastern cadres, employed in strategic offices, she at the railways and her husband in the secret police. Ukolova's job required frequent nightshifts; she also spent much time on party work, and needed someone to look after the children. Yet the Ukolovs could not "take a servant from the local population [*prisluga iz mestnogo naseleniia*] in connection

251. DALO P-3, 1, 483: 123–27.

252. DALO P-3, 1, 281: 16–17. On the ground, there were limits to the effect of even Khrushchev's intervention. In mid-September 1946, nearly two years after the initial complaint, Director Parasiuk wote to the obkom that it was impossible to make Lviv factories produce any furniture for a Lviv higher education establishment. The obkom had ordered two factories to provide furniture for his institute but nothing happened until representatives of the institute made a trip to the factories to establish personal contact. The two factories then came to an "agreement" (in quotation marks in the original). More twists and turns followed while furniture remained elusive and "normal work at the institute [is] not possible." Supplying the institute had turned into a bitter lesson in Soviet trade (DALO P-3, 1, 527: 64).

253. DALO P-3, 2, 264: 36 (my emphasis).

with the fact that my husband works at the NKGB." Hence, a traditional arrangement to have the grandmother look after the children was cast in terms of local-easterner distrust and hierarchy.[254]

Left Behind: The Making of the Postwar Local

The term "local" became a synonym for those Ukrainian inhabitants of western Ukraine who had not been Soviet before 1939 and needed to catch up on Soviet civilization.[255] The categories of local and easterner were central to making sense of Soviet rule in Lviv and of Lviv in the Soviet Union. Within only a few years after the Soviet reconquest of 1944, they became ubiquitous. A typical 1947 report from the party organization of the city's Veterinary Institute found that the difference and distance between "local westerners" and "incoming easterners" persisted. Even when living together in the same dorm rooms, the two groups kept apart.[256]

Yet the definition of the local as synonymous with Ukrainian also marked a crucial excision in Lviv's postwar memory, erasing both Poles and Jews. A Russian girl who arrived in 1946 with her typical "easterner" family in Lviv—and would remember her life in fluent, locally inflected Ukrainian—found it natural that her playmates came in three mutually exclusive types: easterners like herself, locals (i.e., Ukrainians), and the children of a few remaining Poles.[257] As a category, Poles had been physically and literally expelled from Soviet/Ukrainian Lviv. And it was child's play to understand it.

Yet Poles had once been locals too. In early 1945, according to Hrushetskyi, Lviv's Marxism-Leninism University had 203 participants from the "local population," including 79 Poles.[258] In May, the obkom praised two "local Poles" for contributing to a state loan.[259] Even in November, with the expulsion in full swing, the obkom counted not only 1,782 Ukrainians but also 879 Poles among the 2,661 members of the "*local* population," who had been promoted into "leading work."[260]

In December 1944, Soviet Polytechnic director Yampolskyi described the ideological struggle as between Poles and easterners, without mentioning local

254. DALO R-6, 2, 105: 399.

255. In Soviet statistics, the term "local population" did sometimes include non-Ukrainians. However, in Soviet usage, locals were clearly and pervasively identified with local *Ukrainians*.

256. DALO P-3, 2, 264: 279–81. The report is undated but can be dated by context and file to 1947.

257. Interview with Halyna Agibalova conducted by Halyna Bodnar, Lviv, 2 February 2012.

258. DALO P-4, 1, 31: 26.

259. RGASPI 17, 88, 450: 40.

260. DALO P-3, 1, 319: 15.

Ukrainians. He denounced the past Polytechnic as a stronghold of Polish nationalism and capitalism.[261] He charged local Poles with backwardness, treason under German occupation, and a long, lingering history of nationalism. These same features would be ascribed to Ukrainians from western Ukraine for years after most Poles had left.

In the spring of 1947, the "evacuation" of western Ukraine's Poles was declared complete. In 1948, Hrushetskyi reported that Lviv no longer needed a Polish-language newspaper. With its subscription down to 508, *Czerwony Sztandar* was to be replaced by a new youth paper in Ukrainian.[262] Anomalies kept disturbing this neat picture. In September 1947, a representative of the Central Committee of Ukraine's Komsomol complained about some Lviv students from the "local Ukrainian population" making a point of speaking only Polish.[263] There is no way of knowing if these students were really Poles rebelling against their role as local Ukrainians or if they really were the latter but found Polish useful for rebellion and counterdistinction.

At any rate, they were young. Something, it seemed, refused to die and seemed even to surreptitiously reproduce. Lviv would remain a place where one could not always tell who was who and who remembered what. Expulsion, however devastating a weapon, was also blunt. Effective at mass disruption, it could not prevent the past from seeping into the fissures in the foundations of the new Lviv.

For years after the Soviet reconquest in 1944, Lviv was a city where massive displacement and resettlement occurred simultaneously. Official Soviet memory constructed a neat exchange of Poles leaving and easterner cadres arriving, with the latter then harmoniously developing the city along with the locals. In reality, this period was violent and chaotic as well as formative.

In reserving much of Lviv for new eastern elites, Soviet Ukrainization actually undermined local Ukrainians. The Soviet-Western Ukrainian relationship in Lviv was ambiguous from its second beginning. Yet historic Lwów, now the center of Ukrainian Lviv, also constituted a reminder or a disturbance of memory, as Witwicki's fate showed.

Perhaps the most important way in which Lwów's past continued to shape Lviv's Ukrainian present was hidden in plain sight, articulated pervasively if indirectly, through the local/eastern dichotomy. This division was a surrogate, employed in part to assign quasi-national traits to western Ukrainians, and was used to censure stereotypical features of Poles as well as western Ukrainians.

261. DALO P-380, 1, 1: 16.
262. DALO P-3, 2, 484: 76, reproduced in *Kulturne zhyttia*, 1:516 (doc. 218).
263. DALO P-66, 1, 206: 85.

The Soviets saw and practiced a clear difference between Poles and local Ukrainians: Poles had to leave, local Ukrainians to stay and become Soviet. Yet both were once "locals," a fact not acknowledged in Soviet "unification" or Ukrainian nationalist fantasies. Soviet narratives had no room for anything that questioned Soviet expansion, and nationalism was incapable of facing the limits of national unity.

In a Ukraine united under Soviet conditions, western Ukrainians started out as alien as Poles. By 1948, the Lviv Writers' Union party buro noted that Vladimir Beliaev had once actively criticized Polish nationalism; after the Poles left, he simply turned his pen against "Ukrainian-German nationalism."[264] The difference was not in the otherness but in the fact that western Ukrainians could stay but must become less "other," while Poles could remain "other" but must leave. In the postwar Soviet Union, the expelled Pole and the western Ukrainian local were born twins.

264. DALO P-3808, 1, 12: 4.

CHAPTER FIVE

The Founding of Industrial Lviv

Factories and Identities

Postwar Lviv became the hub and symbol of the Sovietization of Western Ukraine. Signaling its special position, Lviv was immediately industrialized, unlike the western Belarusian city of Grodno, comparable to Lviv as a new Soviet conquest from the Second World War, but like Minsk, the *capital* of the Belarusian Soviet Republic. This process continued into the 1960s, but its formative inception occurred in the immediate postwar years, the focus of this chapter.[1]

Lviv's industrialization produced not only factories, workers, and the things they made but also some of the key stories and symbols of Sovietization. In 1950, the Lviv obkom noted the three "fundamental issues" of the postwar years: the industrialization of Lviv, the collectivization of its countryside, and "ideological work," meaning the battle against Ukrainian nationalism and the education of toilers [*trudiashchie*] to follow the "party of Lenin-Stalin."[2] In 1951, the second secretary of the Kyiv Central Committee, Oleksyi Kyrychenko, rhetorically asked a Lviv oblast party conference if "this city, with its many centuries of history," had ever seen "such machines, as they are now being produced in its plants and factories." He also meant this literally: an open-air exhibition of new "complex machines" made in Soviet Lviv was at that very moment next to the city's Habsburg Opera House.[3]

It is unlikely that the juxtaposition was accidental. Lviv's postwar newspapers blamed its backwardness on neglect by Habsburg and Polish rulers and celebrated its takeoff into Soviet modernity. In 1947, this was a principal theme of the first

1. On Grodno, see Felix Ackermann, *Palimpsest Grodno: Nationalisierung, Nivellierung und Sowjetisierung einer mitteleuropäischen Stadt, 1919–1991* (Munich: Harrassowitz, 2010), 238–40. On Minsk, see Thomas M. Bohn, *Minsk—Musterstadt des Sozialismus: Stadtplanung und Urbanisierung in der Sowjetunion nach 1945* (Cologne: Böhlau, 2008), 149–51.

2. DALO P-3, 3, 448: 1.

3. TsDAHOU 1, 24, 1550: 3–4.

major postwar exhibition of Lviv artists.[4] Likewise, Olga Barkova's *Every Day* and Boris Buryak's *Taras Zhurba*, the first postwar Soviet novels about Lviv, focused on industrialization.[5] In Barkova's story, Khrushchev identified rapid industrialization in the "new Soviet territories" as proof of the Soviets' "experience" and "highly developed technology."[6] Once again, the new West was viewed as a test and triumph of the Soviet achievement as a whole.

Lviv's postwar industrialization shaped its reality and image for decades. In 1989, a Lviv University scholar complained that the postwar history of Western Ukraine remained rigidly structured by a "Stalinist triad" of "industrialization, collectivization, [and] cultural revolution."[7] At the same time, the obkom head Pohrebniak admitted that Lviv could not bear more industry; nearly forty projects had recently been canceled.[8] Yet, when demonstrators challenged the party-state's view of the "unification" and "liberation" of 1939, Pohrebniak, while admitting to repression, insisted that nobody could deny its achievements in terms of modernization and historic justice.[9]

Industrialization stood at the core of this modernization. In the long run, it had to compensate for something that did not happen. Ambitious and detailed Soviet plans to raze and rebuild Lviv's center into an assembly of a giant square and Stalinist architecture were drawn up but not realized.[10] Industrialization also symbolically linked Lviv to the Soviet Union's center. Stalin himself, postwar propaganda stressed, watched over this "leap from backwardness to progress."[11] In

4. Volodymyr Badiak, *U leshchatakh stalinshchyny: Narys istorii Lvivskoi orhanizatsii Spilky khudozhnykiv Ukrainy, 1939–1953 rr.* (Lviv: SKIM, 2003), 102.

5. O. Barkova, *Kazhdyi den: Povest* (Moscow: Sovetskii pisatel, 1950). In Barkova's novel Lviv is called Levandovsk but is easily recognizable.

6. Ibid., 329. There was an intriguing continuity that Soviet discourse seems to have failed to acknowledge. Even before the First World War, Russian writers had used Galicia's poverty to highlight what they touted as "the benevolent and progressive effects of Russian rule" in the parts of Poland which then had belonged to Romanovs and not Habsburgs. See Weeks, *From Assimilation to Antisemitism*, 120.

7. P. Lekhnovskyi, "Vozzednalis bratty: Notatky z respublikanskoi naukovoi konferentsii," *Vilna Ukraina*, 30 September 1989, 2.

8. DALO P-3, 62, 476: 38.

9. "Pro potochnu politichnu obstanovku v oblasti," *Vilna Ukraina*, 6 October 1989, 1.

10. Sofia Dyak, "Tvorennia obrazu Lvova iak rehionalnoho tsentru Zakhidnoi Ukrainy: Radianskii proiekt ta ioho urbanistych vtilennia," *Schid-Sakhid*, nos. 9–10 (2008): 75–86; Bohdan Tscherkes, "Stalinist Visions for the Urban Transformation of Lviv, 1939–1955," in *Lviv: A City in the Crosscurrents of Culture*, ed. John Czaplicka (Cambridge, MA: Harvard University Press, 2005), 205–22. There is no archival evidence to explain the fortunate failure to realize full Soviet urban renewal in postwar Lviv. Costs and the personal preferences of easterner decision makers appreciating the comforts of Lviv are likely to have played a role. Postwar Vilnius also saw a combination of quick postwar industrialization and ambitious rebuilding plans that failed to materialize (Weeks, "Multi-Ethnic City in Transition," 167–68).

11. TsDAVOU 2, 7, 4340: 87–89.

Western Ukraine, the aim was clearly defined: to "catch up in economic and cultural terms with the eastern oblasts [of Ukraine] in the nearest future," as Komsomol Secretary Chyrva put it at Lviv's second postwar Komsomol conference.[12] Thus, industrializing postwar Lviv inscribed the city in both the teleology of Soviet modernity and the continuing competition between western and eastern Ukraine.

Lviv's Soviet industrialization, too, was a site of paradoxes: marked by acute and latent violence, it was also the city's main arena of peaceful interaction between easterners and locals. Driven by an ideology of superior urban modernity, Soviet modernization brought peasants to the city as never before. Extraordinarily harsh in its conditions, it also offered genuine opportunities for personal improvement, especially by comparison with a harsher countryside. Although wasteful and inefficient, it effected historic change.

Making a Difference: Transformation and Catching-Up

The Soviet industrialization of Lviv combined staggering waste with historically unprecedented ambitions, mobilization, and state capabilities. Resolutions and decrees passed between 1943 and 1945, as well as the first postwar five-year plan, which demanded the transformation of "Lvov into a large industrial center of Ukraine," bound the city into what Stefan Plaggenborg has aptly characterized as the great imaginary chain of planning, sequencing the way to the Communist future since 1929.[13]

Notwithstanding imperfect statistics, the general trends are clear. According to Hrushetskyi, before the German attack, Lviv had had more than five hundred mostly small enterprises with a total of 36,600 workers and 5,150 employees.[14] By the end of 1945, more than four hundred industrial enterprises were running again, and several new factories had started production.[15] By 1947, Lviv's Gosplan plenipotentiary Goltvianskii reported 608 enterprises in the city.[16] Three years later, the oblast's industrial production was more than double that of 1941.[17]

12. DALO P-66, 1, 101: 11.

13. B. K. Dudykevych et al., eds. *Narysy istorii Lvova, 1256–1956* (Lviv: Knyzhkovo-zhurnalne vydavnytstvo, 1956), 163, 176, 184. For the five-year plans as "temporal chains" integrating Bolshevik modernization into teleological time, see Stefan Plaggenborg, *Experiment Moderne: Der sowjetische Weg* (Frankfurt am Main: Campus, 2006), 90.

14. DALO P-4, 1, 31: 45.

15. Dudykevych et al., *Narysy istorii Lvova*, 183. Some of their equipment came from defeated Germany, with Hrushetskyi making detailed requests. He also tried, in the same way, to acquire goods from Warsaw (DALO P-3, 1, 242: 68–71, 118).

16. RGAE 4372, 47, 145: 76.

17. DALO P-3, 4, 80: 62–63.

Lviv's industrial workforce also grew rapidly, with almost twenty-six thousand "workers, engineer-technical staff, and employees" in the oblast in 1945 and nearly fifty-six thousand in 1950. In that year, by Soviet criteria, workers made up 20 percent of the city's population, as compared to 5 percent in 1938.[18] From a Soviet perspective, which associated modernity with large enterprises, an important factor was that many postwar factories had between a thousand and twenty-five hundred workers.[19] There was also a significant link between Lviv's new industry and its party. Although not all of them were workers, almost a quarter of the oblast party members and candidates belonged to the 341 primary party organizations in Lviv's industry.[20] In 1967, there were 138 major factories in Lviv. Since 1955, their workforce had grown from 67,100 to 142,800 people.[21] By 1984, more than 529,000 of Lviv's 753,000 official inhabitants were employed, including 265,200 in industry and another 124,000 in building, transport, and trade.[22] Growth came with concentration. By 1958, more than half of the total value produced in Lviv oblast came from enterprises employing more than five hundred people. More than half of the oblast's labor force worked in such large plants, which made Soviet Lviv superior to the Polish Lwów of the past, according to Soviet propaganda.[23]

Since large enterprises were responsible for housing, social services, and, especially inititally, food distribution, the industrialization of Lviv meant central control: many new enterprises belonged to Moscow-based, not Kyiv-based, ministries. In 1945, the share of such centrally controlled plants in Lviv oblast increased from under 8 percent to 40 percent.[24] The oblast planning commission foresaw an increase of total production by 1950 of more than 2,000 percent. Republic, oblast, and raion enterprises were to increase production by 330 to 390 percent, but those at the union level by more than 3,200 percent.[25] Regardless of the results, party-state priorities were clear. Many workers in Lviv worked and lived under the direct control of central Moscow bureaucracies. Only an administrative reform in 1957 reduced the number of workers employed in the oblast by union-level plants to less than 6 percent.[26]

18. Dudykevych et al., *Narysy istorii Lvova*, 190; DALO P-3, 4, 80: 63.
19. DALO P-3, 3, 448: 28.
20. DALO P-3, 3, 448: 30, 62.
21. DALO P-3, 10, 115: 54–55.
22. Sekretariuk et al., *Istoriia Lvova*, 315.
23. L. I. Horozhankina, ed., *Lvivshchyna industrialna: Dokumenty i materialy* (Lviv: Kameniar, 1979), 99, 101, repr. of DALO R-335, 1, 864: 6–19.
24. DALO P-3, 1, 403: 6.
25. DALO R-335, 1, 52: 2.
26. Horozhankina, *Lvivshchyna industrialna*, 102, repr. of DALO R-335, 1, 864: 6–19.

Lviv's industrial output was touted to confirm its place in the Soviet order. By the end of the 1950s, its factories produced large shares of many goods made in Soviet Ukraine, such as four-fifths of Ukrainian forklifts and almost two-thirds of buses and televisions.[27] At the heart of postwar industrial Lviv was the manufacture of modern machines and consumer goods. Between 1946 and 1958, the oblast's industrial production increased more than tenfold, while machine building, metalworking, and textile production increased by between forty and fifty times. With almost 37,000 workers, machine building had the largest single share of the oblast's nearly 142,000 workers.[28]

It was an essential Soviet claim that economic growth was faster in Western Ukraine than the Soviet average: erasing the backwardness of the periphery meant being faster than the center.[29] In reality, catching up with Soviet industry also entailed acquiring its flaws. In 1961, the Kyiv Central Committee complained about severe underinvestment in every sector of Ukraine's economy, leading to obsolescence and delays. Ukraine was still far from realizing the often invoked aim of liquidating simple manual labor. In industry nearly half and in construction more than two-thirds of the labor force were using muscle, not complex machines.[30] Lviv was no exception. At about the same time, a report found that the roughly ten thousand workbenches at Lviv's metalworking enterprises were already outdated, many of them more than twenty years old.[31] In 1962, Hrushetskyi complained to his obkom buro that in "a whole series of enterprises and industry branches" 50–60 percent of the work was manual labor.[32]

This was a failure to achieve essential Soviet goals, since technology symbolized Soviet modernity. Barkova's novel of Lviv's industrialization, *Every Day*, depicted pristine plants filled with gleaming new workbenches.[33] As a speaker at a 1952 meeting put it, "where there used to be wastelands, new factories have emerged, equipped with our state-of-the-art Soviet technology."[34] Yet clearly much equipment brought to Lviv during its postwar industrialization was not new. Ironically, the same speaker also praised a worker innovator for his deft use of "trophy" materials captured in the war to make special fittings for Lviv's construction machines.[35] In 1949, the new Bus Factory received machinery from a

27. Ibid., 100, repr. of DALO R-335,1, 864: 6–19.
28. Ibid., 103–6, repr. of DALO R-335, 1, 864: 6–19.
29. Sekretariuk et al., *Istoriia Lvova*, 273.
30. RGANI 5, 40, 161: 53–56.
31. RGANI 5, 31, 144; 118.
32. DALO P-3, 8, 391: 27.
33. Barkova, *Kazhdyi den*, 74.
34. TsDAHOU 1, 46, 6469: 45.
35. TsDAHOU 1, 46, 6469: 47.

Figure 5.1 The construction of the Lviv Bus Factory, 1948. A key project of the Soviet industrialization of Lviv, the Bus Factory was built between 1945 and 1950. Collection: Central State Kinofotofono Archive of Ukraine, Kyiv.

plant in Minsk, but its party buro worried that the latter tried to "keep the best for itself."[36] In hindsight, one generation after Sovietization began, Lviv, in fact, was catching up with an economy on its way to deep stagnation.

In postwar Lviv, however, catching up specifically meant beating the Polish past. By the early 1960s, Soviet publications claimed that the city had almost twenty times more workers and employees than under interwar Poland, while the total industrial production of the western oblasts was twenty times greater, so that the region's daily output now nearly equaled its monthly one before 1939.[37] The occasional admissions of straggling blamed poor performance on lingering effects of the past.[38]

By the 1980s, official publications stressed Lviv's integration into the Soviet economy, with links to the Urals, Central Asia, and the Caucasus, Moscow,

36. DALO P-2638, 1, 9: 12.

37. S. Stefanyk, *Dva svity—dvi demokratii* (Lviv: Knyzhkovo-zhurnalne vydavnytstvo: 1962), 28; *Torzhestvo istorychnoi spravedlyvosti* (Lviv: Vydavnytstvo Lvivskoho universytetu, 1968), 697. Strictly speaking, the "western oblasts" included areas that had been in Poland before the war and others that had been in the Soviet Union. This complication, however, was not addressed in official triumphalism, the gist of which came through loud and clear.

38. Iuriy Slyvka et al., *Stanovlennia i rozvytok masovoho ateizmu v zakhidnykh oblastiakh Ukrainskoi RSR* (Kyiv: Naukova dumka, 1981), 40.

Leningrad, and Kyiv.[39] Most networks did not survive the end of the Soviet Union, but the imprint of industrialization did. Even with most large plants closed, by 2004 over half of Lviv oblast's value-measured production was still industrial; machine building and metal processing were still the most important branches, attracting most of the oblast's foreign direct investment.[40]

Urbanization proceeded apace. By 1959, in Lviv oblast, it matched the average for the republic as a whole, with 46 percent of the inhabitants of Ukraine as well as of the oblast categorized as living in urban settlements; by 2001, nearly 60 percent of the oblast's population lived in towns or cities.[41] Conversely, the numbers of those working in agriculture decreased, with 5,000,000 employed in 1938 in the agricultural sector of what was to become Western Ukraine and only 920,000 in 1976.[42]

Grand Strategies, Global Stakes, and Local Needs

Lviv's industrialization was much more than postwar reconstruction. It aimed, in Hrushetskyi's words, at "changing the social face of our city, to make it, in the full sense of the word, our Ukrainian Soviet city."[43] As he and the prominent local writer Yaroslav Halan explained in *Vilna Ukraina*, under Poland's "colonial" rule Lviv could have had neither Ukrainian culture nor modern industry. The new Soviet Lviv would feature advanced industries with local workers.[44] Its industrialization was also an instrument of "Lenin-Stalin nationality policy," part of the universal Soviet project of liquidating periphery—*okraina*—backwardness, as generally announced by Stalin in 1923, year one of the Soviet Union.[45]

Wars, hot and cold, also mattered. In his widely acclaimed 1945 Lviv speech against Ukrainian nationalism, Dmytro Manuilskyi, then commissar of foreign affairs of Soviet Ukraine, stressed that the Soviet victory had proven economic as well as moral and military superiority.[46] A beacon of this superiority, Lviv would

39. Sekretariuk, *Istoriia Lvova*, 315.

40. Davymuka, *Lvivshchyna na porozi XXI stolittia*, 21, 40.

41. Lewytzkyj, *Die Sowjetukraine*, 231; Davymuka, *Lvivshchyna na porozi XXI stolittia*, 22–23.

42. Slyvka, *Stanovlennia i rozvytok masovoho ateizmu*, 35.

43. DALO P-4, 1, 31: 60.

44. Horozhankina, *Lvivshchyna industrialna*, 38–42, repr. from *Vilna Ukraina*, 7 February 1945, and *Vilna Ukraina*, 1 January 1945, 7.

45. DALO P-3, 3, 448: 26; *Narysy istorii Lvivskoi oblasnoi partinoi orhanizatsii*, 2nd rev., exp. ed. (Lviv: Kameniar, 1969), 176; M. Chernysh, "Borotba lvivskoi miskoi partorhanizatsii za provedennia v zhyttia rishen partii i uriadu pro industrializatsiiu mista Lvova," in *Trista rokiv vozziedannia Ukrainy z Rosiiu* (Lviv: Vydavnytstvo Lvivskoho universytetu, 1954), 214. In later texts, the nationality policy would be "Leninist" alone.

46. RGASPI 17, 125, 351 for the speech.

be a bulwark in the Cold War, too, with Hrushetskyi putting its industrialization in the context of two of its rhetorical opening salvoes, Stalin's speech of 9 February and Winston Churchill's Fulton speech of 5 March 1946.[47]

Sovietization, modernization, and Ukrainization went together, and all three needed workers, so the "essence of the Stalin task to industrialize Lvov" consisted in "creating a working class" from locals.[48] Lviv was also expected to provide industrial cadres for other western oblasts.[49] The rising political consciousness of Lviv's new workers, as Bohdan Dudykevych said, would spread regionally and socially, imbuing collectivized peasants and the intelligentsia.[50] Even if such hopes were one-sided, industrialization was the most important, large-scale, and long-term party-state strategy to shape Soviet Lviv and its mostly new population. In conjunction with collectivization in the countryside, industrialization also played an important role in the Manichean war against Ukrainian nationalism. In September 1950, Leonid Melnikov, Khrushchev's successor as Ukrainian party head, reminded a Lviv party-state elite audience that collectivization was depriving the "enemy" of "all economic roots": whereas nationalists had hoped to realize their idea of Ukraine on the back of the private peasant, the Bolsheviks had "struck down that horse" from under them. Melnikov also insisted that local workers were easy to recruit due to local land scarcity.[51] In this scenario, nationalist resistance only raised the stakes. At Lviv's first postwar Komsomol conference, a Komsomol secretary had already warned that nationalists were trying to prevent village youth from joining Lviv's industry.[52] Getting rural youth into industry thus meant defeating nationalism.

This double strategy of rural collectivization and urban industrialization aimed much higher than simply depriving the nationalist insurgents of rural recruits. The making of a Lviv proletariat from local rural-urban migrants would mark a historic Soviet triumph over nationalism because the peasantry stood at the core of nationalism's idea of Ukraine.[53] For Stalin, too, "the national question was in essence a peasant question."[54] And there was no Ukrainian peasantry considered more national/ist—by nationalists as well as Stalinists—than that of Western Ukraine. Making these peasants into Soviet urban proletarians in Western Ukraine's key city—which was, in turn, made Ukrainian as never

47. DALO P-3, 1, 403: 2; *Vilna Ukraina*, 3 April 1946, 1–2.
48. DALO P-3808, 1, 16: 75.
49. DALO P-4, 1, 280: 13.
50. DALO P-4, 1, 537: 174.
51. TsDAHOU 1, 24, 255: 47, 74.
52. DALO P-66, 1, 101: 71.
53. Weiner, *Making Sense of War*, 298–99.
54. Snyder, *Bloodlands*, 44.

before—would be a devastating blow to both Ukrainian nationalism's manpower base and its beliefs.

Conversely, this change would vindicate Soviet views of modernity and urbanization as projects not only of repression, but also of reshaping and participation. At the core of the Soviet phenomenon was the fantasy of a perfect revolutionary will accelerating a fully understood universal History to achieve socialist transformation in a largely precapitalist country. Essential to this ambition was the transformation of backward peasants—or, in some areas, pastoralists—into modern urban proletarians.[55] All of this was also true for Lviv, where peasants were refashioned into proletarians and locals into Soviet Ukrainians.

The Ferocity of Rural Life: Exploitation, Insurgency, and Counterinsurgency

While the Soviets often viewed them as opposites, the city and the countryside were not isolated from each other. Many rural migrants to Lviv brought with them memories of violence not only from the war: postwar western Ukraine also went through a repetition of the violent social remaking of the prewar Soviet Union, with nationalist insurgency and party-state counterinsurgency added to a devastating mix of expropriation and collectivization.

In his September 1950 speech to Lviv's party-state elite, Melnikov explained that the "dignity of man" applied to peasants too. The "kolkhoznik of the western oblasts" was not "some*thing* second-rate." Gratuitous threats of "fifteen years" in the camps were mistaken. Melnikov was serious, but the audience laughed, clearly appreciating the burlesque Bolshevik fun of driving rustics a touch roughly.[56]

For decades dissatisfaction with life in Western Ukraine's countryside was the most widespread motivation for moving to Lviv.[57] Soviet taxation of Western Ukraine's collective farms was crushing, imposing "unbearable" burdens, as Lavrentii Beria admitted in 1953. Initially the state also appeared both innumerate and incomprehensible: 235 out of its 704 tax agents lacked "the most elementary arithmetic" and knew only Russian.[58] Wages remained miserable, amounting to less than a kilogram of grain, forty grams of potatoes, and less than a ruble per

55. David L. Hoffmann, *Peasant Metropolis: Social Identities in Moscow, 1929–1941* (Ithaca, NY: Cornell University Press, 1994), 2. Bolshevism was special in its terror, violence, and authoritarianism, but not outside history or modernity. As David Ekbladh has recently shown, it had no monopoly on the belief in modern technology's power to transform whole societies rapidly, pervasively, and—perhaps most important—as planned (*Great American Mission*).

56. TsDAHOU 1, 24, 750: 11–14, 34, 45 (my emphasis).

57. Bodnar, *Lviv*, 41.

58. RGAE 4372, 45, 134: 46–47.

workday. At the end of the year, peasants could end up earning two rubles per month or even owing money. With collective farms functioning as poverty traps, some peasants recalled that life had been better "under Poland" or wondered if it would improve if "Poles, Austrians, or Germans" returned.[59] Even if villagers had money, there was little to buy in the villages, because of pervasive corruption as well as planned deprivation. In 1948, the obkom noted that goods intended for the countryside, such as cloth, shoes, or soap, ended up being "realized" in the towns or raion centers.[60] At least initially, the postwar party-state was much better at reaching its quasi-serfs for taking than for giving.

Likewise, the rural infrastructure remained miserably inadequate for years. In 1951, the oblast health department reported a failure to spread health care to the villages or even to understand its political importance as well as a refusal to treat sick villagers when they made it to the city. On an inspection tour, a rural hospital turned out to be the "worst house" in the village. Its all-purpose medic (*feldsher*) slept in the same room in which he saw his patients and had no medication for them. To obtain medication or x-rays, peasants had to go to Lviv, where they faced difficulties.[61] Improvements came, but slowly. In 1951, child mortality was 60 percent higher in Lviv oblast's villages than in its towns; by 1956, the difference had been reduced to 35 percent. The first year in which all rural raions had some kind of permanent access to pediatric care was 1957.[62]

In 1956, a memorandum for the Kyiv Politburo, then called the Presidium, admitted that agriculture in the western oblasts was less productive than before 1939 because of the "very many" mistakes made by Soviet authorities, such as the indiscriminate transfer of techniques and plants from eastern Ukraine and the mindless destruction of traditional drainage systems.[63] Soviet technology disrupted traditional methods but was bad at bringing improvements. Also in 1956, only a fifth of the collective farms of the western oblasts had electricity, and most power stations were so weak they could not be used to drive machines.[64] For peasants in postwar western Ukraine, Soviet Lviv meant the hope of sharing in twentieth-century modernity as well as in earlier historic transitions from barter to money and from precarious subsistence to stable exploitation.

In western Ukraine, moreover, for years rural poverty was accompanied by violence or the threat of it. Soviet collectivization went hand in hand with the

59. RGASPI 17, 88, 450: 13. What the party-state learned then, Halyna Bodnar's interviewees also told her after its demise (*Lviv*, 43). For some, at least, Soviet power had a way of inducing rueful, deeply heterodox, and lasting what-ifs about other rulers.

60. DALO P-3, 2, 393: 43.

61. DALO R-312, 2, 107: 264, 270–72.

62. DALO P-3, 6, 84: 156–63.

63. TsDAHOU 1, 24, 4350: 4–5.

64. TsDAHOU 1, 24, 4350: 17.

destruction of Ukrainian nationalism. As one report stressed in 1947, collective farms were expected to help bring about, not merely to follow, the defeat of nationalist resistance.[65] Plunder and beatings of peasants were widespread, and others besides the Soviets took part.[66] The nationalist underground lived off the land and its inhabitants—recruiting their sons and daughters, demanding food and obedience, and killing and torturing locals as well as easterners.

The Soviet authorities, meanwhile, systematically recruited locals to fight and denounce other locals. This policy, together with scores left unsettled from the recent past, added to the cruelty. With some operations killing 142 "bandits" while capturing only 20, this war increasingly took no prisoners.[67] As Alexander Statiev has pointed out, the reports of Soviet security forces resembled those of German ones on the Eastern Front "in the disparity between the two sides' casualties and the number of killed versus captured."[68]

Often overlooked in this context, the Soviet-nationalist war was, in fact, the first major Soviet policy to take root successfully among the locals in western Ukraine. In another continuity between war and a postwar lacking in peace, a civil war went native before literacy campaigns or Komsomol organizations. Some Soviet combat groups consisted of former nationalist "bandits." The obkom proudly reported that some locals fought nationalists "mercilessly" to avenge family members, and it provided special aid in the form of "tools, apartments, [and] wood" to victims of nationalists.[69] In 1951, Lviv oblast's nationalism-fighter-in-chief Maistruk lauded the example of a local father who handed over his own "bandit" son, demanding his destruction as an "enemy . . . of the whole kolkhoz, the whole village." Here, Maistruk admonished the obkom buro, was the heart of the matter: the need to "know the secret of the inner hatred of Soviet people."[70]

By recruiting locals, Soviet authorities also made them targets. By one count, nationalist postwar killings produced at least 30,676 victims. Half of them were peasants and collective-farm members, preponderantly locals.[71] For the nationalists, no less than for the Soviet authorities, here was a society that must be partially destroyed in order to be saved.

65. TsDAHOU 1, 75, 62: 40.

66. TsDAHOU 1, 23, 4258: 5; 1, 23, 4205: 25.

67. RGASPI 17, 88, 450: 26. On the "exterminatory" Soviet combat style in the fight against nationalist insurgents, which contributed to producing a "war with no prisoners," see Weiner, *Making Sense of War*, 172–82.

68. Alexander Statiev, *The Soviet Counterinsurgency in the Western Borderlands* (Cambridge: Cambridge University Press, 2010), 285. See also Serhiy Kudelia, "Choosing Violence in Irregular Wars: The Case of Anti-Soviet Insurgency in Western Ukraine," *East European Politics and Societies* 27 (2013): 149–81.

69. RGASPI 17, 88, 450: 22–27.

70. DALO P-3, 4, 101: 118–19.

71. P. S. Sokhan et al., eds. *Litopys Ukrainskoi Povstanskoi Armii*, n.s., 7 (Toronto: Litopys UPA, 2003): 68–69.

Rural hardships and comparative urban opportunities, produced in the Soviet case by the same party-state, were complementary. For a rural population cajoled, exploited, and left behind, Lviv's industry offered a genuine chance of social improvement. Migrants recalled that going to Lviv meant finding employment less harsh than fieldwork, earning real money, and even having some time left for leisure.[72] Only the Soviet authorities, however, represented the state in ambitiously totalizing charge, jealous as well as powerful, expecting loyalty and irreversible transformation. In an inadvertently biblical vein, exemplary young locals, as presented in Lviv's *Vilna Ukraina*, knew that for a new worker there was no looking back "at the village," to a former "piece of land," now "socialized in the *kolhosp*."[73]

In reality, things were more complex. For Padalka and Hryhoryi Martynyshyn land would not have been the only thing to look back to. According to an obkom report of 1953, their mother had five adult children; their sister lived in the same *kolhosp* as she did, whereas one brother served in the Soviet military and another spent ten years in the camps for Ukrainian nationalism.[74] Clearly, newcomers came to Lviv with entangled local experiences.

Locals had much to forget. In 1951, the obkom buro confirmed that a kolkhoz head, in collusion with the local militia and the village soviet (*silrada*), was beating, kicking, raping, and pillaging the peasants, when not busy with heavy drinking. Earlier complaints had been ignored. The obkom also realized that the kolkhoz had fulfilled its plan by less than 17 percent and during the war its head and de facto tyrant had collaborated with the Germans—not, incidentally, in western but in eastern Ukraine.[75]

Such an abysmal concentration of treason, failure, and brutality was unusual. Yet violence as such was neither exceptional nor short-lived. A 1947 Kyiv Central Committee report attacked the Lviv obkom and Hrushetskyi personally for the violence in the countryside, including mass arrests, beatings, and shootings.[76] Six years later, during the 1953 spell of Soviet self-criticism, complaints about violence at collective farms still featured large at official meetings. The head of the Stalin Kolkhoz admitted that, following his superiors' example, he beat kolkhozniks and "resettled" them by leveling their houses.[77] Five years later, an investigation confirmed a complaint from Lviv oblast about a kolkhoz head's verbal and physical assaults, worthy of "English colonizers."[78] In 1966, the obkom

72. Bodnar, "Mihratsiia silskoho naselennia," 47–48, 51.
73. "Velyki Zminy," *Vilna Ukraina*, 27 August 1950, 3.
74. DALO P-3, 4, 837: 2.
75. DALO P-3, 4, 105: 7, 24–30.
76. TsDAHOU 1, 23, 4258: 5–6.
77. DALO P-3, 4, 794: 43–48.
78. DALO P-3, 6, 262: 53–56.

explicitly prohibited beating kolkhozniks, while it also counted about forty thousand workers commuting daily into Lviv from the surrounding villages and deplored their "hooliganism" and lack of political education.[79] Clearly, rural people who had been beaten and their kin could be unruly urbanites. In 1968, the censors were still suppressing stories about collectivization driving peasants off the land or a woman bartering sex for hay, while the obkom found widespread physical abuse in the countryside, including whippings with belts as well as pervasive corruption, arbitrary fines, and expulsions.[80] Even in 1979, thirty years after the completion of collectivization in Western Ukraine, the village and its supply of workers remained a necessity as well as a problem. By then, fifty thousand workers were commuting from villages into Lviv. Yet, according to the obkom, in "view of their special features," they needed "constant party influence."[81]

Working Together: Locals and Easterners

Factors driving rural migration and dislocation, however, took time to work. After the war, Lviv's new factories needed workers urgently. While aiming at locals, the party-state also drew heavily on easterners. Labor was scarce as well as illicitly mobile everywhere in the postwar Soviet Union.[82] But in Lviv, expelling those initially available, the city's Poles, made things worse. In April 1945, Hrushetskyi pleaded for cadres: the Elektrokombinat Power Station needed 1,505 employees but had only 743, with 699 about to leave for Poland.[83] Half a year later, Hrushetskyi warned that Lviv should have a working population of nearly sixty thousand but had less than forty thousand, including almost a third, who were Poles already registered for departure. Even among the non-Polish workforce, six thousand were repatriates and demobilized soldiers, also on their way out, albeit for the Donbas. In Lviv's vital enterprises providing water, gas, power, and transport, 80 percent of the staff was Polish. Hrushetskyi feared a collapse of urban infrastructure.[84]

Later references to thousands of eastern cadres assisting with reconstruction glossed over the chaotic replacement operation in a city, where streetcars, the most important public transport, had 826 specialized staff, including 776

79. DALO P-3, 9, 225: 70.

80. DALO P-3, 10, 212: 38–41; P-3, 10, 208: 69–74.

81. DALO P-3, 43, 118: 15.

82. Deborah A. Kaple, *Dream of a Red Factory: The Legacy of High Stalinism in China* (Oxford: Oxford University Press, 1994), 21–26.

83. DALO P-4, 1, 60: 7.

84. DALO P-3, 1, 282: 59–60.

Figure 5.2 Employees of the Lviv power station, c. 1945–1953: posing for a photograph in front of a Stalin portrait on the crossing of (then) Pushkin and Stalin Streets (now named after the nationalist Second World War leaders Chuprinka (Shukhevych) and Bandera). Collections: Andriy Knysh and Center for Urban History of East Central Europe, Lviv.

Poles.[85] By December 1946, when most Poles were gone, the director of the *tramtrust* admitted that inexperienced replacements had "put the rolling stock out of commission." Former passengers were now walking long distances—a special hardship in view of a recent surge in robberies.[86]

Given this combination of expulsion and industrialization, Lviv's authorities had high ambitions but few short-term options. Hrushetskyi identified Lviv's badly needed labor force as the "main issue" for the party while decrying failure. At the end of 1945, labor scarcity brought several plants to a standstill.[87] In 1946, Gosplan reported a deficit of more than forty-two thousand workers and seventeen thousand employees. According to Hrushetskyi, Lviv already had over twice as much factory equipment as in 1939, but almost half of it stood idle because of the labor deficit. Discipline, moreover, was "extremely low." A fifth of employed workers were not even showing up.[88]

85. DALO P-4, 1, 2: 26–27.
86. DALO P-3, 2, 84: 32, 38.
87. DALO P-4, 1, 87: 23, 28
88. RGAE 4372, 46, 127: 22–23; DALO P-3, 1, 403: 6, 8, 10.

Thus, at the beginning, most of Lviv's new labor did not come from the western Ukrainian countryside but from the East. Between 1945 and 1948, the towns and cities of Lviv oblast received more than a hundred thousand official immigrants from the Russian Socialist Republic alone. Most of them came from urban environments in central Russia. Some, such as Vasyl and Klavdiia Antonov, were veterans not only of the Great Fatherland War but also of pioneer projects of prewar Stalinist industrialization, such as Magnitogorsk.[89]

Between 1946 and 1950, out of an incomplete total of twenty thousand skilled workers and two thousand engineering-technical staff sent to Western Ukraine from the biggest industrial centers of the Soviet Union, nearly sixteen thousand joined industrial enterprises in the city of Lviv.[90] The local press feted them as carriers of Soviet progress: for example, the workers Stepan Abramian, Mykola Bobykin, and Arkadii Sakharov helped found Lviv's flagship plant for agricultural machinery Lvivsilmash, while Leningrad engineers drew up its blueprints.[91] Boasting of the multinational Soviet assistance to Lviv, Soviet reports also underlined the leading role of the "great Russian people."[92]

Here was another foundational moment. For the easterners, building industry and guiding locals confirmed Lviv as their new home. Modernization was presented as a continuation of "liberation." In 1945, *Vilna Ukraina* celebrated twenty-two Russian women, former anti-aircraft gunners, who had fought their way from Stalingrad to Lviv and then formed a key brigade in the new and pivotal Electric Lamp Factory. Now they could write to their former homes—and to the public of their new home city—speaking for "us here in Lviv."[93] *Vilna Ukraina* also hailed Viktor Vasiliev, another employee at the Electric Lamp Factory. An accomplished "engineer-practician," Vasiliev combined technological skill and experience from Moscow with war service and exemplary innovations for speeding up production. In gratitude, *Vilna Ukraina* declared, the workers nominated him for Lviv's oblast soviet.[94] The tutelary role offered to easterners integrated the discourse of local newspapers, acclamatory pseudoelections, the everyday experience of the workplace, and the Soviet Union as a whole. Thus, in 1950,

89. Roman Lozynskyi, *Etnichnyi sklad naselennia Lvova* (Lviv: Vydavnychnyi tsentr LNU imeni Ivana Franka, 2005), 195–96. On the Antonovs, see H. Podoliak and L. Shlemkevych, *Robitnyk—tse zvuchyt hordo* (Lviv: Kameniar, 1965), 34. On Magnitogorsk, see Kotkin, *Magnetic Mountain*.

90. O. A. Kirsanova, *Rozvitok suspilno-politychnoi aktyvnosti trudiashchykh zakhidnykh oblastei URSR u protsesi budivnytstva osnov sotsializmu* (Kyiv: Naukova dumka, 1981), 83. For similar figures, see also Podoliak and Shlemkevych, *Robitnyk*, 34.

91. Horozhankina, *Lvivshchyna industrialna*, 50 (doc. 22).

92. Ibid., 58 (doc. 26); DALO P-3808, 1, 3: 46.

93. *Vid maisternia do veletnia* (Lviv: Kameniar, 1975), 19–20.

94. "Novator," *Vilna Ukraina*, 14 December 1950, 3.

at the aviation plant Factory no. 87, an impending increase in local workers meant the need, according to its party buro, to teach them their Soviet "rights and, above all, obligations" and to integrate them into the "social-political life of our factory" and "of the country." The party buro emphasized that this political education should involve a broad section of the factory's staff and institutions. Special lectures "On Some Peculiarities [of] and Mass-Political Work Methods with Workers from the Local Population" were to be held for the party secretaries, foremen, and Komsomol and trade union organizers.[95]

The speed of the first resettlement wave would never again be matched. Lviv had less than 186,000 inhabitants in 1945, almost 411,000 in 1959, and about 787,000 in 1989. Whereas the population more than doubled between the end of the war and the end of the 1950s, it grew by more than a third in the 1960s, by a fifth in the 1970s, and by nearly another fifth in the 1980s. Net immigration accounted for almost three-quarters of new Lvivians between 1945 and 1959, but in the thirty years between 1959 and 1989, it contributed only about 60 percent of Lviv's 376,000 new inhabitants.[96] Locals provided an ever larger share of the immigrants. By 1958, as Lviv newspapers reported, forty thousand young workers had arrived from Western Ukrainian villages.[97] By the 1959 census, nearly a third of Lviv's total population of approximately 411,000 consisted of Ukrainians from the territory of the former Galicia but not from Lviv.[98]

In the long term, a short but high-cresting wave of immigration by easterners was succeeded by longer and flatter waves of local immigration. However, locals did in fact play a significant role in immigration even during the years right after the war. Party-state rhetoric can be misleading in this respect: in 1950, Leonid Melnikov berated Lviv's authorities for the "stupidity" (*tupoumie*) of hiring easterners rather than locals for the city's factories and construction sites.[99] The local writer Petro Kozlaniuk complained that there was much talk about promoting locals, just as with "local fuel, peat, or . . . coal. Everybody talks about it and nobody wants . . . it."[100] Yet in reality, locals quickly joined easterners in the making of industrial Lviv. According to Lviv's Komsomol, by 1948, six thousand young people had come from the "oblast's villages" to work in Lviv's plants; at one of

95. TsDAHOU 1, 24, 615: 90–91.

96. Bodnar, "Mihratsiia silskoho naselennia," 29–31 and appendix (dodatok) Z.1 (in part, my own calculations).

97. *Vilna Ukraina*, 27 July 1949, 2.

98. Lozynskyi, *Etnichnyi sklad naselennia*, 212.

99. TsDAHOU 1, 24, 255: 46–47.

100. DALO P-3, 3, 351: 140–41, repr. in *Kulturne zhyttia*, 1:644 (doc. 282).

Lviv's biggest plants, the majority of young workers were from the countryside.[101] In 1950, even an angry Melnikov admitted that 25–35 percent of Lviv's workers came from local areas.[102] His figures may have been low: also in 1950, a group of city party activists was told that nearly 63 percent of the workers in Lviv were locals.[103] Whatever their precise share, there was no doubt that, within five years after the war, locals constituted a substantial part of Lviv's emerging industrial workforce. This is significant because the construction sites and factories of postwar Lviv became crucibles of the local-easterner encounter, despite the massive influx of easterners, local resistance, and the inequality between them. Like a bad marriage, postwar Soviet Lviv was an unequal yet intimate co-production from the beginning.

Locals featured prominently in the city newspapers celebrating the creation of its "new working class," their lives depicted as a mixture of painful memories of an inequitable, Polish-dominated past and the redemption of a Soviet present, shaped by advanced leaders from the East, order, cultured leisure, and a "new morality" of "building Communism." Visiting their former home villages, these workers, as presented by *Vilna Ukraina*, found their admiring neighbors recognizing them just enough to acknowledge change beyond recognition; they were Stakhanovites whose speech was marked by constant reference to "our plant" and its "collective," which made them "human beings in the full sense of the word."[104] For these idealized locals the passage from "teenager" to "adult worker" came when they saw their names on their factory's board of honor for the first time. Those who had been exposed to the old world of capitalism and Poland were reformed and policed each other's work norms, while working in a plant they now recognized as "ours."[105] The best Lviv Stakhanovites were sent on excursions to factories in Moscow, Leningrad, and Kyiv.[106] In 1949, the tenth anniversary of "unification" was celebrated by grateful double shifts.[107]

101. DALO P-66, 1, 296: 11, 28.

102. TsDAHOU 1, 24, 255: 47.

103. DALO P-4, 1, 361. Even according to more conservative figures in a later official history, 56 percent of all Lviv workers were already "natives of the western oblasts" (H. I. Kovalchak, *Rozvytok promyslovosti v zakhidnykh oblastiakh Ukrainy za 20 rokiv radianskoi vlady, 1939–1958 rr.* [Kyiv: Naukova dumka, 1965], 46).

104. As Alexander Etkind has pointed out, (almost) achieving unrecognizability is a classical trope of conclusive transformation (*Warped Mourning: Stories of the Undead in the Land of the Unburied* [Stanford, CA: Stanford University Press, 2013], 46).

105. "Os vin, robitnychnyi klas industrialnoho Lvova," *Vilna Ukraina*, 12 July 1949, 2; "Litopys slavnoho desiatyrichchia," *Vilna Ukraina*, 10 September 1949, 2; Barkova, *Kazhdyi den*, 206.

106. DALO P-3, 3, 448: 29.

107. P. D. Melnychuk, "Uchytysia u velykomu rosiskomu narodu," *Vilna Ukraina*, 6 August 1949, 2.

The Theory and Practice of Local Transitions

In reality, the transition from the local countryside to Lviv's industry was less straightforward. Although Soviet and Ukrainian nationalist pressure made the village a place to escape, Lviv's industry was not initially a welcome alternative. In 1947, at Lviv's emerging Bus Factory, one of Lviv's new top plants, the party organization found it hard to deal with locals. For instance, it worked hard to change Comrade Semeniuk, but he still showed "a great longing [to go] home to the village." His absenteeism had been punished, but the official urge to educate him persisted.[108] Despite such ambivalent beginnings, by 1952 half of the fourteen hundred workers at the Bus Factory were locals, and over half of them still lived in villages close to the city.[109]

Comrade Semeniuk was not an isolated case, and his motives were not hard to understand. The party-state realized that its key industrialization project in western Ukraine lacked grassroots appeal. Inevitably, in a postwar environment of both scarcity and rapid industrialization, the city failed to "show the toilers of Lviv cultured socialist enterprises," as Hrushetskyi would admit in 1950. Most of the new factories were still using preliminary facilities, making for "difficult production and living conditions."[110] One year later, the obkom buro believed that workers' dining facilities were terrible because they were staffed by people who viewed them as a penal assignment.[111] Yet blaming the staff—instead of larger issues of planning and priorities—was myopic at best. Two years later, the Bus Factory was still "unfinished." Its dining hall had been planned for a maximum of five hundred workers, but the plant actually had more than 2,200.[112]

Komsomol leaders blamed rural reluctance to embrace industrial work on nationalist propaganda. The latter did equate Soviet professional schools with forced labor in mines and with the "physical extermination of the nation."[113] Yet Soviet hiring efforts were also counterproductive, sometimes resembling German manpower hunts: in 1953, a Komsomol secretary explicitly equated some Soviet recruitment drives with German occupation methods.[114]

In February 1945, the head of the Labor Reserve Administration of Lviv oblast, Riadchenko, complained that 70 percent of those mobilized were Polish

108. DALO P-2638, 1, 4: 22 (At this point, the Bus Factory was still called the Auto-Assembly [*avtozborochnyi*] Factory).

109. DALO P-2638, 1, 16: 61; P-2638, 1, 20: 33.

110. DALO P-3, 3, 448: 2, 33.

111. DALO P-3, 4, 87: 7.

112. DALO P-2638, 1, 22: 75, 159.

113. GDA SBU 13, spr. 376, tom 41: 174 (a nationalist 1948 leaflet).

114. DALO P-66, 1, 100: 72; P-3, 3, 692: 3–194, repr. in *Kulturne zhyttia*, 2:10–47 (doc. 3), here 24.

youth; he demanded local Ukrainians instead.[115] Yet collectivization had barely begun, and rural Ukrainians were reluctant to leave for the city.[116] One month later, Riadchenko criticized the brutality with which workers were mobilized; sometimes they were not allowed to say good-bye to their parents.[117] In 1946, the obkom reported on a specific recruitment drive in the countryside. Instead of two hundred new workers each, the wood-processing obllespromsoiuz and the light-industry oblmestprom, for instance, received twenty-two and thirty-five, respectively. Another expedition, marching its recruits under armed guard to the village soviet, was besieged by their families. Finally, four girls were driven off on a truck; one tried to jump off, then cut her face with a broken bottle. The truck stopped, the girls escaped, and the recruiters were left without a single future worker. Villagers, the report explained, feared bad conditions in the city. Those who went to the city often returned home. Fifteen villagers were quickly driven away by a diet of boiled potatoes without fat or salt.[118] This fact, however, also implied opportunities: in 1946, Hrushetskyi praised the Enerhokombinat for fulfilling its recruitment plan by an exceptional 50 percent. It had treated new workers well and attracted additional manpower.[119]

Mobilization problems persisted. In May 1947, Riadchenko reported that nine hundred youth should have been mobilized by March. The real number recruited, however, was 291, including at least 180 who were not locals but originally from the eastern oblasts. The drafts for 1945 and 1946 had also been ineffective.[120]

A system of professional training schools, however, was quickly set up in Lviv.[121] In 1950, Hrushetskyi told the obkom buro that Lviv's industrialization depended on these schools' success with local recruits. At the same meeting, however, the schools and the Komsomol were subjected to severe criticism for their failure to politically educate local youth.[122] In general, these Soviet professional schools were a key channel for inducting rural labor into industry.[123] At the beginning of 1946, there were thirteen of them in Lviv, with 1,787 trainees; one

115. DALO P-4, 1, 31: 91–92.

116. In 1945, of the 222 collective farms that had been established in Lviv oblast before the German occupation, only 1 had been set up again; by 1946 there were 12, and by 1947, 45 (RGASPI 17, 138, 9: 86).

117. DALO P-6[6], 1, 44: 267–69, repr. in *Kulturne zhyttia*, 1:252–53.

118. DALO-P 3, 1, 469: 60–64.

119. DALO P-3, 1, 403: 27.

120. DALO P-3, 2, 139: 150.

121. DALO P-66, 1, 100: 107.

122. DALO P-3, 4, 417: 12–19.

123. Donald Filtzer, *Soviet Workers and Late Stalinism: Labour and the Restoration of the Stalinist System after World War II* (Cambridge: Cambridge University Press, 2002), 37.

year later there were twenty-two and 4,255, respectively; by 1952, following Soviet trends, their number had decreased again to ten with 2,134 trainees.[124] Many of these trainees, however, were easterners, not locals. In 1950, Melnikov berated Lviv's authorities for filling more than two-thirds of their professional schools with easterners.[125]

Yet mobilizing rural youth into the schools was difficult. In the spring, out of 3,000 planned new trainees, only 1,318 were found. Evasion was a "mass" phenomenon, which Goltvianskii blamed on nationalist agitation and "backward psychology."[126] By 1950, Hrushetskyi was still complaining that over seven rural raions had not sent a single trainee.[127] Many schools were unappealing, even by postwar standards, with bad nutrition, dirt, and solitary confinement. Frequently, the trainees responded with despair and rebellion, drinking, gambling, and black marketeering.[128]

Moreover, the schools failed to transmit Soviet ideology. They did not bring the Komsomol into the life of young locals or take religion out of it. As a Komsomol official complained, trainees kept prayer books under their pillows.[129] Although there were eighteen hundred Komsomol members at the schools in 1947, only three hundred of them were locals.[130]

Corruption was rife. In 1949, the obkom demanded the dismissal of the head of the oblast's Labor Reserve Administration for years of embezzling the schools' food and money while inflating the number of trainees.[131] In 1950 and 1951, obkom surveys of the professional schools still found weak propaganda, harsh living conditions, old equipment, and lack of discipline. In 1952, the obkom suspected professional-school trainees of organizing a riot against the seizing of church bells.[132]

124. DALO P-3, 1, 419: 27; 66, 4, 51: 104. As of 1952, Lviv's professional schools included six trade (*remeslennye*), two factory (FZO), and six railway (*zheleznodorozhnye*) schools. All were under the Ministry of Labor Reserves, but trade and railway schools tended to offer better skills and conditions, while factory schools provided only rudimentary preparation and basic skills. For details of the professional schools as what amounted to a state system of indentured labor, see Filtzer, *Soviet Workers and Late Stalinism*, 34–39.

125. TsDAHOU 1, 24, 255: 49.

126. DALO P-3, 2, 534: 111–12, repr. in *Kulturne zhyttia*, 1: 555–57 (doc. 239); RGAE 4372, 48, 250: 94.

127. DALO P-3, 3, 433: 29.

128. DALO P-4, 1, 42: 73–74.

129. DALO P-66, 1, 100: 107.

130. DALO P-3, 3, 403: 12–23.

131. DALO P-3, 3, 71: 70–76. The purpose of "dead-soul" trainees may have been not only enrichment but also the creation of an accounting "reserve" to compensate for turnover (Filtzer, *Soviet Workers and Late Stalinism*, 35).

132. DALO P-3, 4, 439: 2–3. The riot was significant in size. According to one obkom estimate, it involved about five thousand people, who shouted and hurled stones and bottles, and led to two

In the factories, management and older workers often exploited trainees. In the schools, many teachers were unqualified and "inspired no confidence" politically. Their offenses included hooliganism, alcoholism, collaboration with the Germans, and printing religious books. The obkom also declared it inadmissible that teaching was in Russian when the majority of the trainees were locals.[133]

Despite harsh conditions and inadequacies, the professional school system was nonetheless a life-changing institution and a site of real power. If there were hidden prayer books under pillows, then the schools were a place where they could be found; if corruption overshadowed ideology, then that was an important aspect of Soviet socialization. In the Soviet West, the professional school system had an additional use: in 1948, Hrushetskyi told the obkom buro that urban youth who had been trained in Lviv should go east because they were "better worked-over [*obrabotana*]," while local "youth from our villages" should go to professional schools in Lviv. The drafting of students in and out of Lviv thus became a revolving-door mechanism. While undermining the creation of a stable proletariat in Lviv, this approach dispersed local youth and helped cripple nationalist resistance. It is not clear how effectively it was implemented. Ironically, in 1950, the obkom found that local youth "deserting" Donbas mines for home were using amnesty offers meant for nationalist fighters as a cover.[134]

In a signature Soviet way, doing things crudely and wastefully had little to do with lack of power or effects. Despite resistance and inefficiency, results were impressive: over fifty-two thousand workers—and another thirteen thousand skilled foremen and white-collar employees—were trained in Lviv between 1947 and 1950. While more than thirty-seven thousand of them acquired their new skills not in the professional schools but on the job, by 1957 the Lviv Labor Reserves Administration had channeled forty-five thousand young people into industry. Many more had come to factories directly from villages.[135] In 1948, Goltvianskii reported that many rural locals were taking construction jobs in Lviv, despite harsh conditions.[136]

Yet socialization by literally building Stalinist socialism did not necessarily produce the desired results. Villagers came to Lviv to work in construction, but some openly stated their particular dislike of construction sites.[137] They were

militia members being hurt. It was also due to a misunderstanding: the bells were meant to be transferred from a closed church to a working one, but the protesters thought that "the Soviets need the bells for smelting." See DALO P-3, 4, 439: 1–8.

133. DALO P-3, 3, 417: 13–14, 34–39; P-3, 4, 94: 35–39.

134. DALO P-3, 3, 460: 36–37.

135. DALO P-3, 4, 168: 82; P-3, 3, 113: 4.

136. RGAE 4372, 48, 250: 94.

137. DALO P-4, 1, 87: 4.

unlikely to experience the construction industry as the authorities would have liked: in 1950, the obkom found that construction work was poorly paid and construction enterprises lacked basic equipment.[138] If building modern Lviv was not an experience shaped by modern technology, it was also not always very explicitly Communist. In 1950, the Lviv branch of the Ministry of Enterprise Construction employed about one thousand builders, yet its party organization had only nineteen members and its Komsomol sixty-four. Its construction sites also employed prisoners, who provided, for instance, more than nine-tenths of the builders of the Electric Lamp Factory. At the building site of the Forklift Plant there were sixty to seventy prisoners among the two hundred workers. There was no party organization and only six Komsomol members.[139] Six years after the Soviet reconquest of Lviv, a construction site where the city's largest construction organization was building one of its most hyped new plants was actually a meeting point of young locals and prisoners, while the party was virtually absent. This phenomenon was neither unusual nor short-lived. In 1952, the obkom found that construction enterprises had failed at political indoctrination and labor discipline remained poor.[140]

While work in construction enterprises was often transitory, the party-state's difficulties extended farther. In 1946, a Kyiv Central Committee report found that trade union work in Lviv, as in all western oblasts, had failed to improve labor discipline, quality of life, or political education.[141] In 1951, seven years after the Soviet reconquest, Lviv's obkom noted that trade union work, which looked as if it had just begun, was still neglecting the political education of young workers and failing to have any effect on "everyday life," including the workers' spare time, which, in one of Lviv's major parks, was filled with "nothing but boozing." Only two of the thirty-two oblast trade union organizations were headed by locals, while thirteen thousand workers in the oblast were not even members.[142]

In the same year, the Kyiv Central Committee reported that local workers remained at the bottom of the work hierarchy in Lviv's machine-building plants despite instructions to promote them. There was not a single local in higher managerial or party positions, and few even in minor qualified positions (only 25 of 282 foreman were locals; only 18 of 245 held midlevel *tekhnolog* and *konstruktor* positions). Hiring and firing practices disadvantaged locals. In 1951, all plants together hired 737 locals but fired 905.

138. DALO P-3, 3, 422: 32.
139. DALO P-4, 1, 366: 116.
140. DALO P-3, 4, 665: 88, 124.
141. TsDAHOU 1, 75, 210: 133–35.
142. DALO P-3, 4, 102: 17–18.

The party organizations of five out of ten plants had no local members. Out of eight hundred party members across all plants, sixteen were locals. The trade unions had eighty-nine local members. Of a total of nearly 1,300 Komsomol members, 304 were locals, and even exemplary locals turned out wrong. Comrade Vantuk was a young, well-paid Stakhanovite. Yet he refused to join the Komsomol because it opposed his going to church.[143]

Getting workers was only the beginning. Keeping them was equally important, as Hrushetskyi insisted, and difficult.[144] For Lviv's Soviet industrializers, beating labor fluctuation was not only a practical necessity but also a self-imposed marker of progress.[145] Already in 1940, the Soviet authorities tried to fight what they saw as widespread "absenteeism" (*progul*) with mass arrests of peasants arriving for day labor and then "deserting."[146] After a German occupation in which knowing how to escape labor drafts became an even more precious skill, workers remained hard to pin down. In 1952, according to an obkom report, the monetized loss from worker absenteeism, legitimate and illicit, equaled the annual production of Lvivsilmash, one of the city's biggest new factories.[147]

For a substantial share of the new workers, learning to be part of Lviv's new industry meant learning to escape it. *Progul* was as much part of Sovietization as "speculation." Out of 1,769 young workers finishing Lviv's professional schools in 1946, only 978 were to be found at their assigned place of work at the beginning of 1947.[148] During the rest of the year, more than two-thirds of all school trainees quickly disappeared from their jobs because of "inadmissible work and living conditions," as Gosplan plenipotentiary Goltvianskii noted.[149] Many workplaces also had high rates of absenteeism, such as 25 percent at Lviv's railways and 45 percent at several construction sites.[150]

Draconian laws, unevenly implemented, failed to deter many offenders. At the end of 1947, there were over one thousand cases pending against labor "deserters" in Lviv's courts, but, as Hrushetskyi lamented, the police were not even trying to catch offenders, who went "unpunished."[151] Here the experience of Soviet police was similar to that of the collaborating Ukrainian Police under

143. DALO P-3, 4, 154: 8–11.

144. DALO P-4, 1, 87: 4.

145. In retrospect, a 1975 Soviet history of a Lviv factory characterized lack of plant loyalty as a flaw of the past, when local workers viewed Lviv's factories merely as places to earn money (*Vid maisternia do veletnia*, 105).

146. TsDAHOU 1, 1, 627: 84; DALO P-3, 1, 12: 85–87.

147. DALO P-4, 1, 607: 4.

148. DALO P-4, 1, 180: 147–49.

149. RGAE 4372, 48, 252: 24.

150. TsDAHOU 1, 23, 4577: 2.

151. DALO P-3, 2, 461: 63.

German occupation, also blamed for allowing mass labor "desertion" to grow into "anarchy."[152] The two police forces may have been after the same unwilling workers, now very skilled at evading the urban-based state on the prowl.

Germans were still present in post-reconquest Lviv, though in a new role. In 1945, the party organization of the Bus Factory, still a construction site at this point, demanded that residences for its workers be built by German POWs.[153] Yet the spoils of victory destabilized Lviv's emerging workforce: workers were subject to wage cuts by managers with access to a literal "reserve army" of labor. In 1947, Goltvianskii deplored the general preference for inefficient *spetskontingent* labor (POWs and other prisoners). At Lvivsilmash, construction workers received 13.40 rubles per hour—that is, only two-thirds of their pay-by-plan—and faced decrepit accommodation and wage delays of up to three months; some survived only by stealing coal from the railways and selling it on the black market.[154] At the Electric Lamp Factory, hourly pay was 9.08 rubles.[155] Yet *Spetskontigent* workers fulfilled only 25–35 percent of their work norms, causing a "breakdown" in the construction schedule of Lviv's new factories.[156] In 1946, priority projects, such as the power station and the Bus and Electric Lamp Factories, relied on *spetskontingent* workers for most of their construction labor, while all workers on Lviv's war memorial were prisoners.[157] In May 1947, there were still 3,188 POWs working on Lviv construction projects, and their "extraordinarily low" productivity was blamed on management's "criminal-negligent" attitude.[158] Stern internal demands to stop the "trade" in POW labor implied corruption.[159] The extensive use of forced labor depressed wages and undermined the creation of a permanent work force. In 1951, the Lvivsilmash plant was reprimanded for "systematically" using *spetskontingent* workers while downsizing the regular workforce, and the Electric Lamp Factory's party buro claimed to have stopped relying on *spetskontingent* labor but blamed its delays on the loss of this labor.[160]

Even when the free labor force grew, it did not stabilize. The abolition of wartime rationing and the postwar currency reform increased Lviv's labor supply

152. TsDAVOU 3959c, 2, 40: 112.
153. DALO P-2638, 1, 1: 22.
154. DALO P-4, 1, 172: 61.
155. DALO P-3, 2, 533: 126–27.
156. TsDAHOU 1, 23, 4577: 3.
157. TsDAHOU 1, 23, 4577: 3; DALO P-4, 1, 124: 26.
158. DALO P-3, 2, 183: 13. By August of that year, the same official claimed that the POWs were becoming Stakhanovites and should be supplied with equipment to encourage this sudden trend (ibid., 59–62).
159. DALO P-3, 1, 418: 9; P-3, 1, 419: 33.
160. DALO P-3, 4, 99: 20; TsDAHOU 1, 24, 1413: 180.

but also led to managers neglecting their workers, again undermining stabilization.[161] The plenipotentiary estimated that around 30 percent of the new workers had come from villages, and most had little or no industrial experience. Despite improvement in trainee retention, he also found high rates of fluctuation, with more than eighty-five hundred workers leaving and about half of that number infringing labor discipline. Goltvianskii blamed Lviv's managers for offering no incentives, such as better pay and conditions.[162]

Moreover, reliance on *spetskontingent* labor was "backward," the obkom noted, and sometimes workers lacked the most basic tools.[163] This was a problem of Soviet legitimacy as well as efficiency. The party-state had staked its reputation on being both best *and* first at industrializing Lviv. Initially it was, at least as far as large-scale plants were concerned: nothing comparable had been attempted under the Habsburgs, Poles, or Nazis. But brute size was not all; the experience of the laborers inside those big plants was equally important. In 1951, the Soviet authorities noted that Lviv's enterprises lacked new equipment and were dirty and unsafe; Lvivsilmash alone had six thousand accidents over nine months.[164]

Persisting Difference

The categories of easterners and locals continued to be seen as mutually exclusive. In 1946, Hrushetskyi explained that celebrating a "local Stakhanovite," if a "Communist" was not also feted, could make it seem as if "we had no Communists" overfulfilling the plan. Clearly, behind closed doors, "local" and "Communist" were still categorically different. For Hrushetskyi, "Communists"—that is, here also implicitly easterners—had to play "the avant-garde role" in production.[165] There was a pervasive if mostly implicit and diffuse hierarchy linking easterners and locals. It is an unacknowledged fact of great importance that party-state reporting considered easterners the norm, while to be a local meant to be specified as a *local*. Leaders, in Soviet reports, were easterners by default. If locals did become leaders, as Soviet policy officially urged, such promotions were carefully noted.[166]

In industrializing Lviv, Communists were usually easterners, while locals joined the party and Komsomol slowly. With easterners predominant in more

161. RGAE 4372, 48, 250: 95.
162. DALO P-3, 2, 533: 113–16.
163. DALO P-3, 2, 533: 131.
164. DALO P-3, 4, 134: 23–25.
165. DALO P-3, 1, 398: 77.
166. For two examples from 1949, see DALO P-3, 3, 140: 1–2, 21. Local and Ukrainian were not the same. Thus *kolhosp* women leaders could be described as either "Ukrainian" (i.e., from pre-1939 Soviet Ukraine) or "Ukrainian/local" (DALO P-3, 3, 140: 1–2).

qualified work and locals occupying more manual jobs, the party failed to be a party of workers or locals. In November 1946, Hrushetskyi complained that sixteen primary party organizations at industrial enterprises had made no efforts to recruit locals. Seventy workers had been admitted, but 663 employees [*sluzhashchie*]. Lviv's Zheleznodorozhnyi and Shevchenko raions, with high concentrations of industry, provided only 17 percent of the oblast's admissions.[167]

Several enterprises, including major employers such as the gas and water works and prestige projects such as Lvivsilmash, had entirely stagnant party organizations. Of 150 primary party organizations in Stalinskii raion, 46 were not growing at all.[168] In Krasnoarmeiskii raion, only ten out of eighty-six admissions in 1946 were workers; even fewer, six, were locals.[169] By the spring of 1952, the obkom found a plant with 34 party members but not a single local; another had 191 party members, including 3 locals.[170] At meetings, workers rarely spoke, especially local workers. In 1950, at all—strictly Russian-language—meetings at Lvivsilmash, then employing more than five hundred locals, only one local spoke.[171] Two years later, at another factory with about four hundred local workers, six of the thirty-two speakers at a meeting were workers, two of them locals.[172]

Reaching the growing local workforce with Soviet ideology therefore remained difficult. In 1949, an obkom official complained that the primary ideology school of Lviv's primary industrial raion had no chairs or water and was freezing cold; attendance was at 40 percent; preparation and participation were lousy. Lower down, the raion's *kruzhki*—basic indoctrination circles—were also dysfunctional. In Krasnoarmeiskii raion, also highly industrialized, reports about agitators featured impressive numbers and sophisticated breakdowns by nationality but were fabricated. Across the city, attendance in agitator-training groups hovered between 20 and 30 percent. Central Committee instructions were similarly divorced from reality. The important Shoe Factory no. 3 required twenty-four agitator seminars in half a year; there had been six. How, the exasperated official asked, could people who had no preparation agitate others; how could they guide newspaper reading if they themselves failed to read newspapers? Then again, not many were interested anyhow; at the flagship Forklift Factory, 115 of the 1,115 employees subscribed to newspapers.[173]

167. DALO P-3, 1, 361: 11–12.
168. DALO P-3, 1, 361: 53.
169. DALO P-3, 1, 361: 87; P-3, 3, 409: 4.
170. DALO P-3, 4, 422: 44–45.
171. DALO P-3, 3, 415: 131.
172. DALO P-3, 4, 423: 47–49.
173. DALO P-4, 1, 280: 9–12.

At Lvivsilmash, in 1951, there was no propaganda planning, speeches by management, or party agitation "in the workshops," and wall newspapers were scanty. The results of "socialist competition" were poorly publicized. In June 1951, one workshop displayed those of June 1949.[174] This was typical. Propaganda was poor in many plants, partly due to language barriers: at the power station, not a single agitator knew Ukrainian.[175]

Shop-floor agitation was also rare because Communists avoided production work, sticking to managerial positions instead. In 1947, the Kyiv Central Committee found that only nine out of the fifty-eight Communists at Lvivsilmash worked in production; this was "representative," the report emphasized, of "many other plants" in Lviv.[176] In 1951, Hrushetskyi criticized the Communists for concentrating in the offices and shunning the night shifts.[177] A system of privilege and inequality was obvious and embedded in everyday work.

Some locals did advance in the immediate postwar years, but their advancement depended on how easterners saw them relative to other locals. Thus, in 1950, the Lvivsilmash party buro discussed the party admission of the local worker Vasilii Kh., an "example," working hard and doing well in political education, "disregarding the difficulties." He had two sisters in a neighboring town but explained that he had no correspondence with them and that they had not been arrested. His past as a Habsburg army lieutenant and in German-occupied Lviv was mentioned but little discussed. He was asked if he would not be "embarrassed by some party tasks" or be "afraid before the locals." He replied that he would be neither embarrassed nor afraid.[178]

Locals could find that the rewards for success were disappointing. At the Forklift Factory, by 1952, the local worker Fliak had made it into the party buro, yet he complained that there was much talk but little action about promoting locals, although the factory had been founded with a special brief to raise the number of local cadres. In spite of his own promotion, he felt ignored: "I am a member of the party buro, but I am . . . not even noticed. I am a member of the party raikom, but the raikom does not invite me to its meetings."[179] Fliak did learn, however, to make practical demands. He complained not only that nobody took "care of my political growth," although the party ought to pay

174. DALO P-3, 4, 99: 21–22.
175. DALO P-3, 4, 91: 28; P-3, 4, 134: 25–26.
176. TsDAHOU 1, 23, 4257: 3.
177. DALO P-3, 4, 80: 32–33.
178. DALO P-266, 1, 10: 1.
179. TsDAHOU 1, 24, 2422: 74–75.

"maximum attention" to "us local Communists," but also about not receiving an apartment.[180]

Women and the New Lviv

In postwar Lviv, being local was not the only reason for having to catch up. Being a woman, especially a local woman, produced a similar party-state response. Almost half of Lviv's postwar workforce came to consist of women. Women were of special significance for the Soviet imagination of modernity and backwardness. Overcoming their supposed weaknesses—perceived as gender-specific as well as malleable—was seen as a touchstone of successful Soviet modernization. At the same time, women were considered a special danger; their backwardness needed to be cured lest it contaminate Soviet modernity via their pervasive influence on men and children, and thus on the labor force and the future.[181]

This typical Soviet (and not only Soviet) gendering of modernization was reproduced in the new Soviet West. In early 1945, Hrushetskyi demanded special efforts to "radically" improve political work among women, "especially" in Lviv, where before Soviet rule, he claimed, women had not been drawn into "socially useful work."[182] At the same time, he had only two things to say about women at a party gathering. First, a recent women's meeting had confirmed that women had the same rights as men; second, some women had "incorrect thoughts about the churches," mistaking a wartime truce with religion for a permanent change, whereas in reality there could "not be [any] compromise." Instead science had to be deployed against the church and superstition.[183] Arguably, much of the meaning of the statement was in its isolation and juxtaposition, since this was all the oblast's ruler had to say about women: a generality about equality that was no news and a specific, gendered reprimand.

The urgency with which the party-state approached policies toward women in Lviv and western Ukraine needs to be contextualized. It was not comparable in

180. TsDAHOU 1, 24, 2422: 75.

181. Elizabeth Wood, *The Baba and the Comrade: Gender and Politics in Revolutionary Russia* (Bloomington: Indiana University Press, 1997); Wendy Z. Goldman, *Women at the Gates: Gender and Industry in Stalin's Russia* (Cambridge: Cambridge University Press: 2002), 22, 49–50. Women were also key symbols in Western mass culture productions critical of the Soviet Union. Several of Hollywood's first anti-Bolshevik movies featured women as victims; the major production often considered a cinematic Cold War opening shot, Ernst Lubitsch's *Ninotchka*, was famously built around a female commissar, played by Greta Garbo, who abandons Bolshevik severity and the Soviet Union under the influence of Western consumer culture and romance. See Tony Shaw, *Hollywood's Cold War* (Amherst: University of Massachusetts Press, 2007), 14–23.

182. DALO P-4, 1, 31: 35.

183. DALO P-3, 2, 106: 161.

importance to the central projects of industrializing Lviv, collectivizing western Ukraine's countryside, or fighting Ukrainian nationalism. Yet gendered and ungendered aims were still complementary. "Work among women," as the party-state called the whole of its activities in this area, was subordinate yet contributed to more central party-state strategies.[184] To achieve the Soviet modernization of women in the new West would serve as evidence of both female backwardness and the Soviet ability to overcome it. Although Bolshevik suspicion of women's backwardness was universal, certain regions were viewed as especially problematic, such as "the East," as the Moscow Central Committee put it in 1930.[185] There issues of ethnicity, social position, and geography converged to make women a special challenge and opportunity for Bolshevik modernizers. As Yoshie Mitsuyoshi has shown, Soviet policies toward women in postwar Western Ukraine can be understood as a telescoping of those prewar Soviet policies.[186]

The large influx of women into the city and its plants immediately made a difference. By the summer of 1950, more than 800 of the 1,066 workers at the Electric Lamp Factory were women, mostly "former peasant women, who have come from all corners of the western oblasts [of Ukraine], and now they have perfectly mastered the most difficult special skills."[187]

By 1951, there were forty-two thousand women in Lviv's industry—including almost sixteen thousand Stakhanovites; there had been fifteen hundred in 1939—and the majority were local. Some women held high positions, with 7 female factory directors, 5 chief engineers, 119 workshop heads, and 174 forewomen. At the same time, women were underrepresented in party leadership positions.[188] For most local women, the urban encounter with easterners and the party-state took place on the shop floor.

Yet their real experiences diverged from Soviet ideals. In 1952, Maria Kikh, a local and head of the obkom's Department for Work among Women, found that party and trade union bodies failed to provide elementary health care and basic services, while women workers were also harshly exploited. At Lviv's Tricotage Plant, 673 out of 831 workers were women. Yet the plant offered no support for pregnant women or women with children, while forcing some women to work up

184. On the interwar historical background of this subordination of policies especially in and about women's interests to other party-state goals, see Goldman, *Women at the Gates*, 33–68.

185. Ibid., 60.

186. Yoshie Mitsuyoshi, "Public Representations of Women in Western Ukraine under Late Stalinism: Magazines, Literature, and Memoirs," *Jahrbücher für Geschichte Osteuropas* 54 (2006), 21. See also her "Gender, Nationality, and Socialism: Women in Soviet Western Ukraine, 1939–1950," (PhD diss., University of Alberta, 2004).

187. TsDAHOU 1, 24, 611: 47; DALO P-3, 4, 193: 10.

188. DALO P-3, 4, 193: 51–52, 71.

to twelve hours and delaying salary payments. At the Bus Factory, with 418 women among its 2,026 workers, at least one woman had been subjected to a routine work load of fourteen to sixteen hours and threatened with discharge when she protested. At the meat processing Miasokombinat, working over eight hours but getting paid for only eight was common. The low salaries were also not fully paid. At the Lviv *tramtrust*, with 694 women employees, turnover was high, with 282 hired in 1952 and 253 discharged. At a textile factory, 904 of the 1,049 workers were women, but the plant still offered no facilities for children. In general, factories often had inadequate cafeterias (if any), offering a monotonous diet, sometimes little more than bread.[189]

While this discrepancy between ambitious public aims and a reality of postwar scarcity and Soviet inefficiency was not limited to women's experiences, there were gender-specific issues. To be an easterner usually meant higher status as well as an expected role of exemplar and teacher; to be a local generally meant lower status and the role of follower. We see this pattern in Barkova's novel on Lviv's postwar industrialization and in Romm and Gabrilovich's earlier movie on "liberation," discussed in chapter 2. Barkova's local women characters tended to be workers and followers, while the eastern women tended to be experts and leaders. In Romm and Gabrilovich's work, one local woman did become a leader, but only because she had traveled over "there"—to the Soviet Union—and returned to teach others. What these stories shared was a focus on the intersection of two types of backwardness as imagined by the Soviets: female and local.

In Lviv's factories, being a local woman in a position of responsibility led to heightened scrutiny and criticism.[190] At Sewing Factory no. 1, the mostly female workers "heavily criticized" the chair of its women's organization, Koval, for having "detached" herself from the workers and not "wanting to grow." In so doing, they emphasized her identity as a local. Brigade Leader Zhelezniakova, a Stakhanovite, scolded Comrade Koval directly: "We have a duty [to help you] as a local person [*kak mestnomu cheloveku*] but not to work in your place without end. You must not hide behind others' backs; it's time to learn to work."[191] Judging by her name and the position she took, Zhelezniakova was probably an easterner. The "we" in her warning was ambiguous. It may have been a reference to all easterners who helped the locals but were fed up with their failures, or it may have referred to the factory workers as a whole. At any rate, Koval was pilloried not simply as lazy but as a lazy local—in need of much tougher love.

189. DALO P-3, 4, 438: 29–32.
190. DALO P-3, 1, 488: 52, 55.
191. DALO P-3, 4, 151: 8–9.

Life in Lviv

In Lviv as elsewhere in the Soviet Union, postwar destitution was made worse by Soviet preference for heavy industries over consumer production. In April 1946, while claiming rapid growth over the prewar production of machinery, the obkom head Hrushetskyi declared that pre-1939 levels in food production would be reached only between 1947 and 1950, while the 1946 levels of production in consumer and food products hovered between 38 and 70.5 percent of prewar levels.[192] At the beginning of 1950, Hrushetskyi noted that Lviv's light industry was floundering: everything it should produce had to come from plants in Leningrad, Moscow, and Kyiv.[193]

Urban infrastructure developed slowly, especially in quarters with high concentrations of workers and industry, contradicting a key claim of Soviet superiority: everyday life in Lviv became evidence of Soviet flaws. At the city's first oblast party conference in 1940, the obkom head Hryshchuk had denounced pre-Soviet Lviv for providing modern infrastructure and amenities only in the city center, while neglecting—"like all capitalist cities"—the poorer outskirts.[194] Yet, according to a 1949 *Vilna Ukraina* reader's complaint, the water in two Lviv workers' suburbs, Bohdanivka and Levandivka, was contaminated with dirt and industrial lubricants. The Ministry of Transportation had declared this water too dirty for industrial use, and the Vodokanal Waterworks had reassigned it from machines to people. Probably inspired by the antisemitic anti-cosmopolitan campaign then in full swing, the letter's author took care not to blame institutions but to scapegoat "Doctor Comrade Berman" from the oblast health department.[195]

With more than 600 million rubles assigned for building major factories in 1950 and 1951 alone, postwar Lviv did not lack development.[196] Priorities, however, turned out to resemble Hryshchuk's "capitalist" ones. A City Plan Commission was founded in November 1944, but by April 1948, a check-up found that its work was "extremely unsatisfactory" and that it had not even really existed.[197] In 1950, the miskom complained that the outskirts offered their worker population little in terms of dorms or health care, having "essentially been turned into garbage heaps," leaving their inhabitants to turn to drinking and hooliganism.[198]

192. DALO P-3, 1, 403: 22.
193. DALO P-3, 4, 82: 85.
194. DALO P-3, 1, 4: 97.
195. See V. Pershyn's letter in *Vilna Ukraina*, 6 July 1949, 3.
196. See TsDAHOU 1, 24, 2690: 5 for the figure of 600 million rubles.
197. DALO R-335, 113, 1: 34.
198. DALO R-406, 2, 140: 20; DALO P-4, 1, 334: 66.

Hrushetskyi wrote to Moscow that Lviv urgently needed more hospitals, with Lviv's Shevchenko raion and the city's worker suburbs having none.[199]

Trade was also part of public infrastructure in the Soviet Union. In 1950, Hrushetskyi noted that Lviv's postwar Soviet trade network arose spontaneously, by liquidating private traders and their reprehensible commercial goals and reducing the number of trade outlets in the city center. Yet no new trade network was created in the suburbs and the collectivization of 1949/1950 reduced agricultural deliveries to the city.[200] Hrushetskyi also reprimanded his obkom buro because the whole city was served by a total of six buses.[201] The union-level ministries had "completely" neglected to build living space or infrastructure such as clubs, hospitals, or polyclinics, thus worsening the living and working conditions of their workers.[202] Out of a city total of eighteen nursery schools and kindergartens, two were in the outskirts, only recently opened.[203] While industry and population exceeded prewar levels, the city's communal infrastructure had been left at those levels.[204] Given wartime disruption alone, it must really have been worse. Lviv's streetcars failed the needs of its workers, as the city's new factories were far away from their stops. There were seven public baths, all located in the city center.[205] Likewise, almost all the city's seventeen cinemas—key sites of entertainment as well as propaganda—were in the center, prompting a Kyiv official to demand that one of the few surviving synagogue buildings be turned into into a cinema.[206]

The worker settlements represented a stark contrast between Soviet claims and realities. Change was slow. At the beginning of 1952, the city's outskirts still needed forty kilometers of water mains and sixty kilometers of sewers, and worker settlements lacked water, power, baths, roads, and pavements. The industrial ministries were criticized for neglecting the infrastructure needs of their workers and Lviv's population in general.[207] In the same year, the second secretary of the Kyiv Central Committee, Oleksyi Kyrychenko, told a Lviv obkom plenum that Levandivka—home to three-quarters of Lviv's railway personnel—had been neglected and had a club without chairs or heating.[208] The obkom, in turn,

199. DALO P-3, 3, 460: 77.
200. DALO P-3, 3, 412: 43–45.
201. DALO P-3, 4, 82: 85.
202. DALO P-3, 4, 80: 64, 66–67; P-3, 3, 448: 34–35.
203. DALO R-406, 2, 131: 95.
204. DALO P-3, 3, 448: 35.
205. DALO P-3, 4, 80: 64, 66–67.
206. DALO P-3, 3, 351: 278.
207. DALO P-3, 4, 80: 67; P-3, 4, 458: 74–76.
208. TsDAHOU 1, 24, 2690: 12.

found that seemingly sound indicators of improvement only concealed "complete disruption."[209]

One year later, Bohdan Dudykevych described his visit to the "most remote" *agitpunkt* station for local elections in Shevchenko raion. Next to the *punkt*, he found a "small hut," home to a mother and her seven "half-naked" children, receiving very little support. More was out of the question, an official had explained, since she had arrived only two years before. Two of the children went to school, but the director merely made the children catch his runaway pigs.[210]

The Local as Hero

The making of industrial Lviv was accompanied by the creation of local heroes who epitomized the ideal merger of the workers' western Ukrainian roots and Soviet transformation. Its most popular representative in Lviv was the lathe operator Volodymyr Hurhal.[211] He was born in 1925 and spent most of his first twenty years in very modest circumstances, but in postwar Lviv he became a famous worker; specialist in high-velocity machining; writer of manuals, memoirs, and travelogues; and deputy of the Supreme Soviet of Ukraine. In 1952, Lviv's Komsomol named him first on a list of "new young Stakhanovites"; four years later he was selected to represent Lviv's workers at its seven hundredth anniversary celebrations.[212]

Hurhal's story represented not only the Soviet worker-hero, who achieves plan overfulfillment and self-improvement, but also Ukrainian "liberation" from both Polish rule and Nazi occupation. In 1962, Hrushetskyi invoked Hurhal's call for acceleration toward "high-speed Communism," while criticizing "some comrades" for diminishing Western Ukraine. By now, Hrushetskyi declared, it had caught up with the rest of Soviet Ukraine and become an integral, "irremovable part of the Ukrainian nation [*natsiia*]." With all Soviet Ukrainian large buses, forklifts, light bulbs, and telegraph equipment now produced in Lviv as well as 85 percent of the television sets, the "artificial" division into "locals" and "easterners" had become

209. DALO P-3, 4, 655: 71–72, 120.

210. DALO P-3, 4, 907: 22.

211. Hurhal's importance was reflected in a large number of publications, including Volodymyr Hurhal, *Na velykykh shvydkostiakh* (Lviv: Knyzhkovo-zhurnalne vydavnytstvo, 1953); Hurhal, *Dvadtsiat dniv za okeanom* (Lviv: Knizhkovo-zhurnalne vydavnytstvo, 1962); Hurhal, *Druzia moi stanochnyky!* (Moscow: Izdatelstvo VTsPS Profizdat, 1963); Hurhal, *Storinky robitnykoho zhyttia* (Kyiv: Derzhavne vydavnytstvo politychnoi literatury URSR, 1963); Hurhal, *Ya robitnyk* (Lviv: Knyzhkovo-zhurnalne vydavnytstvo, 1964); and Eduard Kalinovskii, *Vremia, kotoroe on obgoniaet: Geroi sovetskoi rodiny. Dokumentalnyi povest* (Moscow: Izdatelstvo politicheskoi literatury, 1973).

212. DALO P-66, 4, 51: 95; P-4, 1, 720: 146.

unacceptable.[213] Hurhal thus symbolized Lviv's and Western Ukraine's defeat of backwardness and Ukraine's integration into the Soviet way of life.

The most specific feature of Hurhal's public self was his relationship to time. The title of his biography by Eduard Kalinovskii, published in Moscow in 1973, was emblematic. At the beginning of the first Soviet occupation of Lviv, *Izvestiia* had explained that its locals had a slower understanding of time. Time was measured in industry: whereas the locals expected Lviv's factories to take two years to return to full capacity, comrades from the East told them that with "Soviet speed" they would need only two months.[214] Written thirty-four years later, Kalinovskii's *The Time He Overtakes* (Vremia, kotoroe on obgoniaet) was a hymn to changing times. Kalinovskii's version of Hurhal was a local from a poor worker-peasant background. In his wartime apprentice years in a Lviv factory he had experienced both the terrors of fascism and capitalism.[215] In postwar Lviv he shone with his extraordinary skill as a lathe operator and aggressive pursuit of political education to make up for lost time.

Asked where he found enough time to read so much, Kalinovskii's Hurhal gave a Faustian response: "I have an agreement with time: I borrow years from the future."[216] In a picture caption he was the man who had said goodbye to "the twentieth century in the mid-fifties," when he had overfulfilled the century's plans so that his further production had to be booked under the year 2000. He explained to a doubting friend how tricky time was, as it would "not forgive delay." Hesitating for a second would leave you behind by hours. "Look at our Lvov. Over two Soviet decades, it has grown more intensely than in the eighty preceding years." How had such acceleration been possible? "Because progress has permeated everything, it has become each and everybody's need to create."[217] Hurhal embodied the local's internalization of the mission to liquidate backwardness. He also embodied generational change. Just old enough to attest to pre-Soviet oppression, he was also young enough to represent the young and idealistic workers in opposition to the old and cynical.[218] He not only worked in the year 2000, but he also hectored others to speed up toward the future: "to overcome" the chasm of the past "we must stubbornly learn and work."[219]

213. DALO P-3, 8, 420: 10–68, 72–76. The minutes contain an error, showing Hrushetskyi using the infinitive form of the verb *nazdohnaty* (to catch up), instead of the past tense. The latter, however, is the most plausible reading here.

214. "Dykhanie mira," *Izvestiia*, 6 October 1939, 3.

215. Kalinovskii, *Vremia, kotoroe on obgoniaet*, 3–18.

216. Ibid., 50.

217. Ibid., 64–65.

218. Ibid., 48.

219. Ibid., 61–62.

Figure 5.3 Employees of Lviv's streetcar network in the 1950s posing in front of a Line One car. Line One ran on a circular line from the Central Railway Station (one of the largest and, at the time, most modern structures built during the Habsburg Empire and rebuilt after the Second World War) to the city center and back, via Stalin, Red Army, and Dzerzhinsky Streets (all renamed now). Collections: Andriy Knysh and Center for Urban History of East Central Europe, Lviv.

Hurhal came to symbolize the local as he or she should have been remade through the industrialization of Lviv. Yet Hurhal's story of acceleration and success was based on the dislocation of the postwar years. Lviv's industrialization replicated key features of Soviet civilization. Lviv was disrupted by war, genocide, expulsion, and resettlement, then by the transposition of the quicksand society of Stalinist rapid industrialization, as Moshe Lewin has aptly termed it. In postwar Lviv, for years beyond the end of the war and as under the prewar first five-year plans, labor fluctuation did not prevent quantitative expansion.[220] Massive waste went with massive if lopsided growth, cruel regimentation with widespread anarchic individualism, modern large plants with primitive and hazardous technology—the grand strategies of the state, in Stephen Kotkin's words, with the little tactics of the habitat. All of this was part of becoming Soviet. In the short run at least, none of it diminished Soviet power.

220. Kotkin, *Magnetic Mountain*, 77–80; Dietmar Neutatz, "Zwischen Enthusiasmus und politischer Kontrolle: Die Arbeiter und das Regime am Beispiel von Metrostroj," in *Stalinismus: Neue Forschungen und Konzepte*, ed. Stefan Plaggenborg (Berlin: Berlin-Verlag, 1998), 191.

CHAPTER SIX

Local Minds

After the Soviet return to Lviv in 1944, the city's pre-Soviet Ukrainian intelligentsia came to symbolize the transformation of the local population as a whole. In some nationally invested post-Soviet accounts, this intelligentsia has now been depicted as the "avant-garde" of the nation, its "uninterrupted evolution" lending legitimacy even to Stepan Bandera's ethnic nationalism.[1] But in reality things were more complex. What the Soviets often referred to as the old local intelligentsia comprised academics, writers, and artists whose careers dated to before 1939 and had begun and unfolded outside the Soviet Union. Many of them were subject to various forms of pressure and persecution.[2] The most prominent trial of members of the old local intelligentsia targeted the Barvinskyi family.[3] Yet to understand the old intelligentsia's role in the shaping of the local, we have to focus on how some of its key representatives were turned into the most prominent exemplars of Sovietization as personal transformation. Unlike the Polish majority, western Ukraine's Ukrainians stayed—and with them their pasts. They were seen and urged to see themselves as liberated from Polish "colonialism" and Nazi occupation but also as contaminated and underdeveloped, having missed out on the "great school of Socialism building" of the interwar Soviet Union. Ukrainian locals had to transform themselves in order to participate in the Soviet order and this change was expected to be a challenge. Hrushetskyi felt that Soviet

1. Eleonora Narvselius, "The 'Bandera Debate': The Contentious Legacy of World War II and Liberalization of Collective Memory in Western Ukraine," *Canadian Slavonic Papers/Revue canadienne des slavistes* 54 (2012): 481.

2. For a comprehensive survey of postwar repression against the intelligentsia of Western Ukraine, and, mostly, Lviv, see Marusyk, *Zakhidnoukrainska humanitarna intelihentsia*, 66–172.

3. Ibid., 124; Tarik Cyril Amar, "A Disturbed Silence: Discourse on the Holocaust in the Soviet West as an Anti-Site of Memory," in *The Holocaust in the East: Local Perpetrators and Soviet Responses*, ed. Michael David-Fox, Peter Holquist, and Alexander M. Martin (Pittsburgh: University of Pittsburgh Press, 2014), 175–77.

propaganda talked too much about what Socialism could do for locals; it needed to tell them what locals could do for Socialism, what they must "lay on the altar" of building the new Lviv.[4] The performance staged with the old local intelligentsia dramatized the process of overcoming the corrupt past. Ironically, the old local intelligentsia's identity was new.

New Sacred Duties

A May 1946 *Lvovskaia pravda* article by the writer Iryna Vilde, a prominent representative of the old local intelligentsia, detailed the Soviet expectation that this group would play an exemplary role in the making of Soviet Western Ukraine. According to Hrushetskyi, Vilde had been "the first to come to the Bolsheviks . . . with the desire to work for the well-being of the people together," and she admitted her past mistakes.[5] She hit the right tone, too. Hrushetskyi praised her blend of criticism of Soviet bread lines with praise for delivering more than German occupiers.[6]

Tellingly, Vilde's article "The Sacred Duty of Our Intelligentsia" had less to say about this duty's actual meaning than about the sins of the "Ukrainian-Galician," clinging to narrow "Galician patriotism" and "political separatism." She contrasted "Galician small houses and smoke stacks" with Soviet "grandiosity." Her "Ukrainian-Galicians"—"figures," as in a play or the Soviet lexicon of suspicion and contempt—were laggards. Offered the bracing vigor of Soviet progress, they longed for provincial somnolence. Their defining flaw was not being slow but refusing to catch up, still yearning for their lost city of "holiday . . . cafés" and "imported goods." In Vilde's view, the old local intelligentsia would have to find its place in a future shaped by what she invoked as, in effect, an all-Soviet General Will sanctified by the blood sacrifice of the war. It would have to serve in what Jochen Hellbeck has aptly called the Stalinist "factory of the soul" by helping train "our peasants," arriving in town to become workers, to develop a "Soviet psychology." Only a genuinely Soviet intelligentsia could fulfill this role. Otherwise, the "simple people" would reply: "Doctor, heal yourself."[7] This was a special demand as well as a promise of privilege.[8]

4. DALO P-3, 3, 410: 8.

5. DALO P-3, 1, 401: 329–31.

6. DALO P-4, 1, 31: 57–58.

7. *Lvovskaia pravda*, 19 May 1945, 5. For "factory of the soul," see Jochen Hellbeck, *Revolution on My Mind: Writing a Diary under Stalin* (Cambridge, MA: Harvard University Press, 2006), 165.

8. Vilde's article signaled that Soviet post-reconquest policy toward Lviv's local intelligentsia would follow the classical Bolshevik pattern, as identified by Stuart Finkel: rewards for exemplary behavior and political obedience and quiescence. See Stuart Finkel, *On the Ideological Front: The Russian Intelligentsia and the Making of the Soviet Public Sphere* (New Haven: Yale University Press, 2007), 3.

Not Indispensable yet Crucial

Despite Vilde's promising threats, the Soviet authorities hardly needed Lviv's old local intelligentsia. In reality, the majority of the city's actual pre-Soviet intelligentsia (Poles and Jews) was gone by 1946, killed or expelled. Subsequently, the old intelligentsia left in Lviv was almost exclusively Ukrainian, small, and overshadowed by new Soviet arrivals. By 1953, 1 of the 37 heads and deputy heads of Lviv oblast's academic institutions, 2 of the 43 deans, and 42 of the 275 kafedra heads were locals. The obkom put the total of the city's intelligentsia at 13,337, including 2,774 "locals," with only 561, however, labeled "old."[9] In sum, this was a small group of mostly older men. Their qualifications tended to be high, but they were not irreplaceable.

Nonetheless, the Soviet authorities put the local intelligentsia in the limelight by persistently targeting it. A 1944 obkom degree on Lviv concerned food, transport, and the intelligentsia.[10] A top representative of the old local intelligentsia, the composer Vasyl Barvinskyi, was chosen to speak at the main "liberation" celebration.[11] Yet the outlines of future conflict also emerged quickly. Hrushetskyi warned of the intelligentsia's submission to "Austro-Hungarian barons."[12] In July 1945, the Kyiv Central Committee deplored the limited influence of Marxism-Leninism, which touched only an "insignificant" number of Lviv's intelligentsia, while many remained under nationalist influence.[13] Five years later, an especially important Moscow Central Committee Orgburo resolution identified three decisive issues for Lviv: the intelligentsia, industry, and agriculture. Its first section dealt with the local intelligentsia.[14] In May 1953, shortly after Stalin's death, Minister of State Security Lavrentii Beria revised Soviet policy in Western Ukraine. Again, the old local intelligentsia of Lviv was a main concern: when Ukraine's First Secretary Leonid Melnikov confessed his errors to the Kyiv Politburo, he noted that his "greatest mistake" was not to trust Western Ukraine's—by which he meant mostly Lviv's—local intelligentsia.[15] In the wake of Beria's initiative, a Lviv obkom plenum in June 1953 also assailed Soviet policies in Western Ukraine for failing "most of all the local intelligentsia," especially "its older generation."[16] Clearly, in postwar Lviv, the local intelligentsia was a priority, but also a paradox: it was not indispensable, but the authorities focused on it relentlessly. In the process, they showed—as if under a magnifying glass—what "local" meant.

9. DALO P-3, 4, 861: 173.
10. DALO P-3, 1, 40: 46, 48.
11. DALO P-3, 1, 42: 3–7.
12. DALO P-4, 1, 31: 10–11 and 21.
13. TsDAHOU 1, 6, 878: 52–61.
14. TsDAHOU 1, 24, 1614: 1–8.
15. TsDAHOU 1, 6, 1878: 43–72.
16. DALO P-3, 3, 692, repr. in *Kulturne zhyttia*, 2:11, 13 (doc. 3).

Not all members of the local intelligentsia were treated as opponents. In 1946, some were praised for working harder on Marxism-Leninism than truant Komsomol and party members.[17] In 1947, Hrushetskyi noted that there was a group of friendly old local intelligentsia, including the museum director Bohdan Dudykevych and the writers Yaroslav Halan and Petro Kozlaniuk, who were former members of the prewar Communist Party of Western Ukraine (KPZU) and reliable supporters of Soviet rule. He saw "many other" members of the local intelligentsia genuinely struggle toward Marxist-Leninist transformation.

Yet Hrushetskyi also accused Lviv's old intelligentsia of systematic deception, privately denouncing those assisting Soviet power as mercenary traitors, resisting criticism and going "deeper underground." In such cases, arrest was the only solution.[18]

Soviet policy in an imagined triangle of the willing, the unwilling, and the undecided was mutable. In 1950, Bohdan Dudykevych decried it as "oscillating by a wide amplitude between complete liberalism and," as he delicately put it, "the other extreme."[19] Another local speaker counted eleven regime changes in Western Ukraine between 1914 and 1944 and deplored that under "such conditions, even the wise can turn stupid, not to speak of the dim." Postwar Soviet policies, he made clear, were no better. Lifting some people "on the shield" in 1945 and 1946 to then harshly criticize them publicly, it produced "complete chaos" and "uncertainty in the ranks of the intelligentsia."[20] Leonid Melnikov supported this view, noting the local intelligentsia's "complicated path"; changing its "psychology" would require considerable time.[21]

Getting Started on the Past: The Anti-Hrushevskyi Campaign

By 1950, the local intelligentsia's "complicated path" included years of Soviet experience. The first great postwar campaign in 1946 targeted the present through the past by attacking the persistent "school" of the historian Mykhailo Hrushevskyi. It involved Lviv University, as well as Lviv's newspapers, public spaces, and authorities. The main targets of the anti-Hrushevskyi campaign were four scholars: one dead and three still alive. In a phenomenon resembling an exorcism, the ghost was central: post mortem vilification turned Mykhailo Hrushevskyi into a haunting specter. Alive he had been one of the most important

17. DALO P-4, 1, 86: 78–79.
18. DALO P-3, 2, 181: 33–37.
19. DALO P-3, 3, 351: 148.
20. DALO P-3, 3, 351: 170–71.
21. TsDAHOU 1, 24, 255: 54.

historians of Ukraine and, for a short period during the postrevolutionary civil wars, a well-known political figure. In his paradigm-shifting contribution to Ukrainian history he had contested Russian claims to the legacy of Kievan Rus′, instead embracing a narrative of Ukrainian national origins. Presenting Galicia as "a crucial link in the Ukrainian historical continuum from Kievan Rus′ to the present," he had also sometimes endorsed Galicia as Ukraine's Piedmont of national rebirth. Lecturing on Ukrainian history in Lwów before the First World War, he became an object of suspicion.[22]

By the mid-twentieth century, he symbolized a repressed yet fundamental challenge to the Russian imperial and Soviet idea of Ukrainian identity and to a key claim of Soviet conquest—that Soviet rule was the one and only way for western Ukraine. From a Soviet perspective, there could be nothing worse.

Moreover, Hrushevskyi's death in 1934 epitomized the brutal limits of Soviet interwar Ukrainization. Having returned to Soviet Ukraine from exile, he was initially celebrated. Then his teaching and disciples were repressed and his daughter deported. Not formally charged but persecuted in conjunction with an alleged Ukrainian nationalist conspiracy, he died a sick old man and under unclear circumstances.

The postwar anti-Hrushevskyi campaign focused on his "nationalist" scheme of Ukrainian history, which depicted a classless Ukrainian people struggling against national more than social oppression. This was unacceptable, since a nation without classes was incapable of Marxist revolution, while national oppression implied oppressors not only Polish and Habsburg but also Russian.[23] Moreover, Hrushevskyi had depicted Ukraine as more advanced than Russia.[24] As Yaroslav Halan complained, Hrushevskyi had tried to "include Ukraine in the orbit of Western European culture."[25] Such tinkering with the continually embattled East-West cultural gradient was especially odious during frantic Soviet postwar campaigns against subservience to the West.

A 1945 Moscow Central Committee report noted another reason why Hrushevskyi was so irritating: he had little competition. Speaking Bolshevik, there was no telling Ukraine. For once, Bolsheviks found they had little to say. For years,

22. Magocsi, *Galicia*, 55–56, 136. On Hrushevskyi's appointment to a chair of Ukrainian History in Habsburg Lemberg, see Hillis, *Children of Rus′*, 106–7.

23. According to Serhii Plokhy, however, "For all the accusations of his Soviet critics," the real Hrushevskyi had never argued that Ukrainians lacked social stratification: on "the contrary he rejected the 'plebeian myth' of Ukraine as a peasant nation, with no elites or rulers of its own, that was promoted by populist historiography and picked up by Soviet historians of the 1920s and 1930s" (*Unmaking Imperial Russia*, 419).

24. Ibid., 417.

25. DALO P-66, 1, 206: 31.

the Soviet alternative to Hrushevskyi's narrative about the second most important Soviet republic's past and its titular nationality's relationship to Russia was a yawning void. When it came to the "most important questions of the history of Ukraine," there was, according to the experts in Moscow, "no Marxist literature in Ukraine at all."[26]

Nearly a decade later, Oleksandr Korniychuk, then deputy head of Ukraine's Council of Ministers, still found that "up until now, we do not have a history of Ukraine," with Soviet historians too afraid to produce one and youth left alone with Hrushevskyi's temptations.[27] While the postwar campaign against Hrushevskyi's legacy claimed superior modernity, it was also a frustrated assault on a more productive story of the past.

The most prominent living victims of the campaign in Lviv were the historian Ivan Krypiakevych and the philologists and literature scholars Mykhailo Vozniak and Mykhailo Rudnytskyi, all of them members of the old local intelligentsia. Vozniak mostly studied Ukrainian literature, and Rudnytskyi mostly Western European literature and languages.[28] Most of the campaign in Lviv was a public hounding of these men, beginning in 1946 and lasting, in recurring fits, through the early 1950s.

Three easterners led the attack: the new rector of the University, Ivan Beliakevych; the dean of its history department, Volodymyr Horbatiuk; and the head of its kafedra on the history of the Soviet Union, Vasyl Osechynskyi.[29] They were all about the same age. Beliakevych, born in 1905 in Kherson, had spent most of his prewar academic career in Odessa.[30] Vasyl Osechynskyi, born in 1904,

26. RGASPI 17, 125, 310: 24.

27. Dalo P-3, 3, 692, repr. in *Kulturne zhyttia*, 2:46 (doc. 3).

28. There were further victims from Lviv and western Ukraine of campaigns focused on Hrushevskyi's legacy and accusations of nationalism, such as, for instance, historians Myron and Omelian Terletskyi. Krypiakevych, Vozniak, and Rudnytskyi, however, would turn out to be the recurring campaign's core set of victims. For the anti-Hrushevskyi campaign, see also Serhy Yekelchyk, *Stalin's Empire of Memory: Russian-Ukrainian Relations in the Soviet Historical Imagination* (Toronto: University of Toronto Press, 2004), 60–62; and Marusyk, *Zakhidnoukrainska humanitarna intelihentsia*, 70–73.

29. Iaroslav Isaievych, *Instytut ukrainoznavstva imeni Ivana Krypiakevycha natsionalnoi akademii nauk Ukrainy: Naukova diialnist, struktura, pratsivnyky* (Lviv: Instytut ukrainoznavstva im. I. Krypiakevycha, 2001), 159; Marusyk, *Zakhidnoukrainska humanitarna intelihentsia*, 194; DALO P-92, 1, 297: 301.

30. DALO R-119, 6, 11: 1–16. A party member from 1926 who encountered trouble ten years later, he had been readmitted during the war. Initially, Biliakevych's postwar career in Lviv was very successful, but it ended in demotions and soft landings, punctuated by scandals over plagiarism and credentials. In 1948, after his public two-day drinking bout at the university dining hall with a Ministry of Education representative, his long decline began, with the obkom finally finding his administrative, political, and moral failings and fake degree intolerable. In the early 1970s, he would roar again in the worst Stalinist fashion to purge the ideologically suspect (DALO P-3, 2, 395: 137–40).

a party member since 1926, had come to Lviv during the first Soviet occupation to lead the kafedra on the history of the Soviet Union and the university party buro.[31] He stayed in Lviv during the German occupation, where he may have had Soviet orders to collect information.[32] Volodymyr Horbatiuk was the youngest of the three. Born in 1912, he had spent much of his prewar career in Odessa, in the university's Komsomol and history department. During the war, he had been taken prisoner, escaped, then joined the Soviet underground; he had a military decoration.[33]

In July 1946, the Moscow Central Committee's culture warfare journal *Kultura i zhizn* attacked Krypiakevych and others for still teaching "in the spirit of Hrushevskyi."[34] An initial peak phase, defining main features of the anti-Hrushevskyi campaign lasted until the fall, when Krypiakevych and several other scholars agreed under pressure to move to Kyiv, while several of the Lviv branches of the Ukrainian Academy of Sciences were shut down, marking a

31. In 1940, Osechynskyi took student excursions to Moscow and Leningrad. One year later, he stayed in Lviv when the Germans arrived. After Soviet rule returned, he was rapidly cleared of any suspicion of collaboration, although, as officially noted, he had done nothing to help the underground resistance, "the Red Army or the Soviet government." His failure to leave was explained by being wounded when trying. His long stay in a Lviv hospital, the destruction of his party card, and work for a Ukrainian cooperative legal under German occupation were not challenged. Instead, he got his party card back (DALO P-4, 1, 41: 51–52; P-3, 1, 168: 79). See also Yu. V. Babko, *Istoriia Leninskoi komunistychnoi spilky molodi Ukrainy* (Kyiv: Molod, 1979), 29, on Osechynskyi's leading student excursions. He received a decoration in 1946, on which see Yaroslav Dashkevych, "Borotba z Hrushevskyim ta ioho shkoloiu u Lvivskomu universyteti za radianskykh chasiv," in *Mykhailo Hrushevskyi i ukrainska istorychna nauka*, ed. Yaroslav Hrytsak and Dashkevych (Lviv: Instytut istorychnykh doslidzhen Lvivskoho derzhavnoho universytetu im. Ivana Franka, Instytut ukrainskoi arkheohrafii ta dzhereloznavstva im. Mykhaila Hrushevskoho NAN Ukrainy, Lvivske viddilennia, 1999), 262.

32. There is evidence of at least one such mission in Lviv, when the NKVD sent the wife of a Ukrainian national activist, a woman they had recruited to their cause, to Lviv in 1940 to infiltrate the Ukrainian nationalists and ordered her to stay behind in 1941 to collect information on them under German occupation. However, she ended up being accused of collaboration with the Germans and the Ukrainian nationalists herself until she was formally rehabilitated in 1965 (DALO P-3, 9, 107: 221).

33. DALO P-3, 4, 172: 111–12. Horbatiuk lost his party membership between 1948 and 1951 and was demoted to a minor lecturer rank. He seems to have suffered from penury and alcoholism, which perhaps contributed to his early death in 1953. His wife recalled that he was under constant pressure because of his past in German captivity and suspicions of collaboration (Dashkevych, "Borotba z Hrushevskyim," 257–61; DALO P-92, 1, 297: 308).

34. Cited in Dashkevych, "Borotba z Hrushevskyim," 235. The article published some results of a verification of ideological work in Ukraine for the Moscow Central Committee. The resulting internal report of 1 July 1946 faulted the local authorities in Lviv and the Kyiv Central Committee for protecting "open nationalists" and collaborators with the Germans (RGASPI 17, 125, 405: 38–39, repr. in *Kulturne zhyttia*, 1:340–41).

hiatus in the campaign.[35] By 1948, Ukrainian Komsomol leader Vladimir Semichastnyi complained that the purge of the members of the Hrushevskyi school was producing complacency at Lviv University as if "bourgeois nationalism" was no longer a problem.[36]

In the anti-Hrushevskyi campaign, Lviv served unique purposes of vicarious purification: Kyiv academics were also caught up in the campaign, which was related to the broader Soviet postwar attack on intellectuals and artists known as the Zhdanovshchina.[37] Yet a 1946 Kyiv Central Committee report found it self-evident that "disclosing hostile ideas" had "special significance" in Lviv.[38] Only there, public space was turned into the stage of the campaign.[39] In Kyiv, the campaign took place at the Academy of Sciences; in Lviv, it peaked at a meeting at the city's main theater in September 1946.[40]

In the postwar Soviet imagination two peculiarities of Lviv reinforced each other. Hrushevskyi's disciples there had not been persecuted during the first Soviet occupation, but after the war against Germany, both nationalism and collaboration with Germans were blamed on his influence. In 1945, a Moscow Central Committee report found that publications by Krypiakevych and other Lviv historians under German occupation had a "pogrom-fascist" character and viewed them as clear expressions of Hrushevskyi's ideas.[41] Guilt by association, moreover, worked both ways. According to this logic, Krypiakevych and other Lvivians were bad because they stood for Hrushevskyi, while Hrushevskyi was even worse because he was tarred with collaboration in a war he had not lived to see. The Soviet authorities also turned his memory into a caricature of treason on behalf of first the Austrians then the Nazi Germans and, by equating him with the fascist Dmytro Dontsov, of racist "zoological nationalism."

35. This was a compulsory change of residence but not a deportation. It was possible to refuse the demand to relocate to Kyiv. Mykhailo Vozniak did so and was treated no worse than others. Although the relocated scholars were compelled to accept inferior residences and humiliatingly minor positions, they were neither forced to abandon their subjects completely nor to spend all their time in Kyiv. Ivan Krypiakevych, for instance, spent 120 days of 1947 in Lviv. He was permitted to return to Lviv for permanent residence in May 1948 (Rubl'ov and Cherchenko, *Stalinshchyna i dolia*, 329n28).

36. DALO P-66, 1, 296: 204.

37. On the Zhdanovshchina as an antinational campaign everywhere in the Soviet Union outside Russia, see Yekelchyk, *Stalin's Empire of Memory*, 54.

38. Cited in Rubl'ov and Cherchenko, *Stalinshchyna i dolia*, 215–16.

39. DALO P-3, 1, 401: 329–31. The obkom also designated the campaign as the most important task for the local newspapers.

40. Dashkevych, "Borotba z Hrushevskyim," 229; Marusyk, *Zakhidnoukrainska humanitarna intelihentsia*, 72.

41. RGASPI 17, 125, 310: 20–24.

The campaign blended images of West and East while straddling the porous line between the Great Fatherland War and the Cold War. While purging a multilayered past in the present, it also laid the groundwork for a future mobilization and for unity in a war that never materialized. At Lviv's first postwar Komsomol conference in 1946, Krypiakevych was denounced for the "blasphemy" of asserting the influence of the West and Germans on Ukraine against the backdrop of Nazi destruction.[42] At a meeting of the anti-Hrushevskyi campaign on 9 September 1946, the Ukrainian deputy head of the government and writer Mykola Bazhan attacked the Nazis, Churchill's recent "Iron Curtain" speech, and several Ukrainian scholars for making racist distinctions between Eastern and Western Ukrainians. Bazhan decried Hrushevskyi's work as a "repository for the enemies of the Ukrainian people." Borrowing from Stalin, Bazhan also dismissed Hrushevskyi as irredeemable: once a slave of the bourgeoisie, always so.[43] If generalized, this statement implied that there might already be no way back—or forward, or out—for Lviv's old intelligentsia. Yet Bazhan also conceded that Krypiakevych was at least "starting on our way."

Adding to the Cold War backdrop, Yaroslav Halan insisted that any talk about independent Ukraine was only a ploy to reestablish prewar Poland. Asking why all the fuss about Hrushevskyi, when a Soviet atom bomb was already being whispered about, he explained that brute power was no match for dangerous minds. As long as Hrushevskyi had followers, his ideas would linger like a contagious disease. The plague, Halan warned, was still oozing from the historian's former office and needed to be "snuff[ed] out," before affecting youth.[44]

Thus, while nationalism was being fought everywhere in Soviet Ukraine, its newly conquered territories served to localize it in a double sense. Its worst form was contained for extirpation in a specific place on the spatial and temporal fringe, for the past of which, implicitly, Kyiv authorities had less responsibility than for areas longer under their control. Nationalism's transitory nature was stressed by projecting it on "backward" locals—and Western Ukraine was the place where Soviet Ukraine should prove it could handle it by handling them. This first postwar campaign with a special focus on Lviv signaled that the city would remain a paradoxically marginal yet central site of ideological challenge and response. It also turned its old local intelligentsia into convenient and disproportionately prominent scapegoats.

42. DALO P-66, 1, 101: 29.
43. DALO P-3, 1, 414: 6–39.
44. DALO P-3, 1, 414: 48–54.

By the same token, however, the party-state unwittingly reinforced the traditional conceit of Lviv's *Sonderweg* as nationalism's Piedmont. By vigorously stomping out nationalist salvation, the Soviet authorities confirmed a unique capacity for temptation. This was Lviv's hardy *Doppelgänger* in the making: *Bandershtat*. Together they would form a sort of fetish surviving Soviet rule, a place of contested obsession, abject but absorbed, abhorred but desired.[45] A term of abuse in the Soviet lexicon, connoting nationalism, Bandera, savage gangs (*bandy*), Habsburgs and Germans (*Stadt*), and Kipling's devious and anarchic as well as arrogant monkeys, *Bandershtat* would also be appropriated as a proud self-designation.

In the anti-Hrushevskyi campaign, persecutors and persecuted rehearsed roles they would play for years, in a conflict that continually seemed to be on the brink of escalating into naked state terror: the Kyiv Central Committee repeatedly reported the victims' fear of deportation.[46] But, in these prominent cases, this escalation did not occur. Instead, the case of Ivan Krypiakevych, one of the most prominent representatives of the old local intelligentsia, was more typical.

Born in 1886, young Krypiakevych had spent a formative decade under Hrushevskyi's supervision. Soviet rule coopted Krypiakevych in 1939 and again after the Soviet return. In 1945, Hrushetskyi, the obkom head, proudly noted that he was among the first students at Lviv's Marxism-Leninism University, the city's top institute for remedial indoctrination.[47] Yet the authorities never trusted him. An early internal report denounced him as "clearly compromised under German occupation" and, mistakenly, for a "pro-Polish orientation."[48] He was reported as equating the Soviet Union and Nazi Germany. While Hitler had destroyed Germany, Krypiakevych maintained, the Soviet leadership had killed millions of Ukrainians during collectivization. The Soviet people were obeying only because they were ignorant and Hitler had left them no alternative.[49]

But cooptation prevailed. By 1955, Krypiakevych was the main editor of Lviv's first comprehensive Soviet history, with Dudykevych as his deputy and probably supervisor.[50] By 1956, ten years after the beginning of the campaign, Krypiakevych represented Lviv's intelligentsia at the official celebrations of the city's seven hundredth anniversary, held, like the popular assemblies of 1939, where he had also

45. On fetishization in Soviet culture, see Lilya Kaganovsky, *How the Soviet Man Was Unmade: Cultural Fantasy and Male Subjectivity under Stalin* (Pittsburgh: University of Pittsburgh Press, 2008).

46. TsDAHOU 1, 70, 570: 12–13, cited in Rubl'ov and Cherchenko, *Stalinshchyna i dolia*, 218; TsDAHOU 1, 23, 4559: 1–4, repr. in *Kulturne zhyttia*, 1:423–26 (doc. 188), here 425.

47. DALO P-4, 1, 31: 26.

48. TsDAHOU 1, 70, 887: 4–6.

49. DALO P-3, 1, 69: 93–95, repr. in *Kulturne zhyttia*, 1:221–23 (doc. 94), here 222.

50. DALO P-4, 1, 697: 60.

served, in Lviv's Habsburg Opera House.[51] One year later, with the authorities worried about disquiet driven by the Thaw, Krypiakevych was a safe choice, selected to be a principal speaker at a big public meeting "For the Power of the Soviets."[52] In 1966, the Academy of Sciences of Ukraine nominated him for the Order of the Red Banner, citing his public commitment not only to Soviet aims after the unification of 1939 but also to revealing the "national and social oppression" of Ukrainians under Habsburgs and Poles.

His past was not simply omitted. He was officially praised for his pre-1939 activities in popular education, the Shevchenko Society, and Lviv's Ukrainian secret university. Since his earlier failures at Marxism-Leninism and his publications under Germans were also mentioned, that part of the past was clearly no obstacle to receiving one of the highest decorations of the Soviet Union. Krypiakevych's training by Hrushevskyi was, however, left out: Germans, yes; Hrushevskyi, no.

What mattered was his postwar history writing: having mastered Marxism-Leninism, he stressed links between Ukrainians and Russians. His study of the seventeenth-century Ukrainian Cossack leader Bohdan Khmelnytskyi was particularly significant: here was the leading Soviet historian from western Ukraine—his biography laboriously reclaimed from foreigners, nationalism, and collaboration, just like the area as a whole—writing the life of a key eastern figure of the Soviet Ukrainian historical pantheon, who was venerated for driving Polish magnates from Ukraine to unite it with Russia.[53] Khmelnytskyi's rising was one of the few pre-twentieth-century events that received a monument in Soviet Lviv.[54]

None of this, however, was inevitable. In 1948, the Lviv oblast publisher denounced Krypiakevych's work on Khmelnytskyi as a hypocritical attempt to wrap bourgeois nationalism in ultrarevolutionary phraseology.[55] Yet, in 1959, at a meeting of what was by then his institute, Krypiakevych mused about how "extraordinarily interesting" it would be to explore "all the Galicians" who had played important roles "in building Bolshevism."[56]

51. DALO P-4, 1, 720: 146.

52. See DALO P-3, 6, 91: 81–87; and P-3, 6, 91: 42–47, on unrest at factories, including a strike in Chervonohrad in Lviv oblast. See DALO P-3, 6, 97: 94–97; and P-3, 6, 91: 88–94, on rebellious questions, including about the famine of 1932/1933, among participants of political education circles and even in elite party schooling.

53. DALO P-3, 9, 228: 21–23, for official praise of Krypiakevych's Khmelnytskyi.

54. On the monument, erected in 1954 to coincide with the general celebration of Ukraine's putative historic union with Russia, effected on the Cossack side by Khmelnytskyi three hundred years earlier, see Oleksandr Shyshka, "Pamiatnyky i memorialni znaky Lvova (do 1991 roku)," *Halytska Brama*, nos. 6–7 (2010): 16.

55. DALO P-3, 2, 606: 68–78, repr. in *Kulturne zhyttia*, 1:568 (doc. 244).

56. *Kulturne zhyttia*, 3:747 (doc. 212).

Krypiakevych's career does not diminish the real humiliation and pain that Soviet campaigns inflicted on him and other victims or contradict the fact that other members of Lviv's old local intelligentsia were deported, arrested, and subjected to show trials. Yet key protagonists in the performance of cleansing the old local intelligentsia's past were neither deported nor arrested. Instead, a small, important group was granted special prominence by the party-state and subjected to years of harassment, followed by rehabilitation and careers.

This group's reactions were not homogeneous. Krypiakevych adopted a submissive position, quickly abandoning attempts to reconcile Hrushevskyi with Marxism. He publicly condemned Hrushevskyi and himself, then declared his desire to change by studying Lenin and Stalin.[57] Mykhailo Rudnytskyi, then the head of the university's philology department, had a history of expressing no sympathy for Socialism and defending what he saw as art without politics. When admitted to the new Lviv branch of the Writers' Union in 1940, he had been sternly reminded that his past would never be forgotten.[58] "Hostile to the Soviet order" and "closely linked to several Ukrainian nationalists," according to Soviet reports, he was also suspect for defending Krypiakevych, considering leaving the Soviet Union, spending time in Western Europe, having siblings in exile, and doing little for *Vilna Ukraina* during the first Soviet occupation. Describing his mother as "Ukrainian (allegedly of Jewish nationality)," the authorities doubted that he had been forced to hide from the German occupiers.[59] Under attack in 1946, Rudnytskyi tried to secure a future by writing articles against Hrushevskyi and by appealing to interwar western Ukrainian backwardness, when only a little Soviet literature was available.[60] His Soviet persecutors, however, reprimanded him for pretending that backwardness alone gave rise to nationalism.[61] Clearly, local backwardness was not for locals to claim. They must overcome it, not hide behind it.

Also targeted for praising Hrushevskyi, Mykhailo Vozniak refused to write self-incriminating articles.[62] At the same time, he was the only member of the old intelligentsia who was both a party candidate and a target of the campaign. He had joined the university party organization in November 1945. His advanced

57. Mykhailo Nechytaliuk, *"Chest pratsi!" Akademik Mykhailo Vozniak u spohadakh ta publikatsiiakh* (Lviv: Lviv University, 2000), 57, 60–61; Dashkevych, "Borotba z Hrushevskyim," 235–37.

58. Mykola Ilnytskyi, *Drama bez katarsysu: Storinky literaturnoho zhyttia Lvova pershoi polovyny XX stolittia* (Lviv: Misioner, 1999), 1:26, 42.

59. DALO P-3, 1, 238: 29–30. The German authorities did, in fact, have dangerous doubts about Rudnytskyi's "Aryan descent" (DALO R-1295, 1, 5: 479).

60. Nechytaliuk, *"Chest pratsi!"* 57; Dashkevych, "Borotba z Hrushevskyim," 238; DALO P-3, 1, 114: 108–9.

61. Cited in Dashkevych, "Borotba z Hrushevskyim," 238.

62. Nechytaliuk, *"Chest pratsi!"* 38–39.

age, it was hoped, would make him epitomize the way forward even for those heavily encumbered by a pre-Soviet past. Vasyl Osechynskyi stressed his good record of cooperation with Soviet authorities and testified that Vozniak had not "befouled himself" under Germans.[63] Vozniak was exceptional: although the university party organization had eighty-two members by 1948, Vozniak was one of only two locals among them.[64]

Even as a party candidate, however, Vozniak remained suspect. Although he agreed to be paraded on a lecture tour for local peasants, reportedly he said in private that he was not trying to help Bolsheviks but to protect "the Ukrainian people from annihilation" and that Lviv had only been "a really Ukrainian city" under the Germans.[65] Vozniak, according to a report for Khrushchev, was "a Ukrainian nationalist, having been in Lvov during the period of German occupation."[66]

Irrelevant yet Crucial, Naïve yet Evil, Ours yet Treasonous: Dmytro Manuilskyi's Local Intelligentsia

Dmytro Manuilskyi delivered the most brutal public verdict on the old local intelligentsia in a speech before a Lviv intelligentsia meeting in the summer of 1947.[67] It displayed a relentless obsession with a group he derided as marginal and continuing ambiguities about locals as both one's own and a defining Other.

As Soviet Ukraine's deputy head of the government and minister of foreign affairs, Manuilskyi in effect served as one of Ukraine's most prominent ideological enforcers.[68] On 24 July 1947, he delivered a devastating attack on Lviv's old local intelligentsia.[69] In "the former Galicia," he charged, there were those standing "aside" from "Socialism Building." Contrasting "our Soviet people" and even simply the "Ukrainian people" with the inhabitants of Western Ukraine, he threatened its so-called survivals from the pre-Soviet past with a purge to "clean the streets of Lviv of all that capitalist dirt." He depicted the old local intelli-

63. DALO P-92, 1, 284: 31–32.

64. DALO P-3, 2, 610: 4–5, repr. in *Kulturne zhyttia*, 1:554 (doc. 238).

65. DALO P-3, 1, 238: 60–61.

66. TsDAHOU 1, 23, 1605: 33–43, repr. in *Kulturne zhyttia*, 1:267–76 (doc. 116), here 273.

67. TsDAHOU 1, 30, 614: 37–80.

68. Manuilskyi was also a historian and a member of the Academy of Sciences of Soviet Ukraine. His academic output was meager, but he knew foreign languages and had some experience with international academia. See Rubl'ov and Cherchenko, *Stalinshchyna i dolia*, 220; and A. D. Skaba, ed., *Radianska entsyklopedia istorii Ukrainy* (Kyiv: Hol. red. Ukr. rad. entsyklopedii, 1969), 3:80. Manuilskyi's position as Soviet Ukraine's minister of foreign affairs was decorative, as Soviet Ukraine had no independent policies.

69. TsDAHOU 1, 70, 1782: 18–31.

gentsia as both backward and benefiting from generous Soviet patience, since "we understand that you have not gone through the same school as our Soviet citizens." Old sins had been forgiven when "in 1939 and 1944, Soviet power and the Ukrainian people wiped out the whole past, as with a sponge." Yet, he made clear, the deceitful Galicians were failing to change. The time had come to abandon the duplicity that Galician locals had learned from Habsburgs and Poles. He treated deception itself as a symptom of backwardness, a corrupting heritage, naïve and futile. Manuilskyi ridiculed Krypiakevych as a simpleton, not fooling an ambiguous "we," standing for the party-state or simply Ukraine or even just Eastern Ukraine. There was no hiding; even "when you are silent, we understand the meaning of that silence."

Manuilskyi heaped up examples of Galician treachery, including glorifying Hrushevskyi and collaborating with Germans during two world wars. He almost implied that Western Ukrainians had let the Germans loose on Eastern Ukrainians. Nothing, it turned out three years after the Soviet reconquest, was over: "We remember what you thought and did"; the past could "be forgiven but not forgotten."[70]

Expelled but Not Deported, Unbearable but Not Expelled: Rudnytskyi and Vozniak

In late 1947, after Manuilskyi's speech, two purges coincided: a major deportation from Lviv in October and the expulsion of two representatives of the old local intelligentsia from the Lviv Writers' Union branch in November. Both Rudnytskyi and the poet Petro Karmanskyi had been among Manuilskyi's main targets. Shortly afterward, Hrushetskyi publicly attacked Rudnytskyi as a "rotten soul," declaring that any attempt to cure such a "chronically diseased" case would be useless.[71]

In effect, Hrushetskyi was delineating the limits of the old intelligentsia's dramatic-pedagogical usefulness. But Halan still believed in it; having supported Rudnytskyi's admission to the Writers' Union in 1940, seven years later he argued that Rudnitskyi should write confessional memoirs exposing the nationalist past. In sum, Hrushetskyi and Halan differed on a key issue. Was Rudnytskyi still useful for the performance of intelligentsia reconstruction? Even Hrushetskyi did not question the principle of self-reconstruction; he simply deplored a lost opportunity. Properly guided, perhaps Rudnytskyi would "have understood that he must write or it will end badly for him."[72] Rudnytskyi's fate, however, did not

70. See DALO P-3, 2, 80: 1–21 for all of Manuilskyi's statements at the meeting of 24 July 1947.
71. DALO P-3, 2, 7: 68–69.
72. Ilnytskyi, *Drama bez katarsysu*, 42; DALO P-3, 2, 7: 70.

end as badly as it could have, although he was terrified. Despite Hrushetskyi's threats, he was not deported, when that was a real possibility: between 21 and 22 October, the Lviv obkom implemented a mass deportation of "nationalists" and their families. Part of a larger operation in all western oblasts and striking a total of nearly 71,000 individuals, the Lviv deportation removed 15,774 people from the oblast's rural raions and 275 families from Lviv.[73] Shortly before this operation, Hrushetskyi mentioned Rudnytskyi as a local whom locals should criticize.[74] After the deportation, a Lviv party activists' group decried his hypocrisy. In November, a meeting of the Ukrainian Writers' Union Presidium attacked the "bourgeois nationalists" Karmanskyi and Rudnytskyi for "treason"; both were expelled.[75] Yet Rudnytskyi was not deported or arrested.

Whereas Karmanskyi was generally believed to have written poetry praising Hitler, Rudnytskyi's case was different.[76] According to a report by Mykhailo Parkhomenko, a member of the Lviv Writers' Union, all nonparty members of the Lviv branch of the union reacted negatively to Rudnytskyi's expulsion. Parkhomenko had already warned that Rudnytskyi should not be accused of "Ukrainian-German nationalism," since he had "Jewish blood."[77] Parkhomenko also pointed out that Rudnytskyi had not, as charged, edited a collaboration paper. According to Vladimir Beliaev, Rudnytskyi had been a reliable supporter of Soviet power from 1939 on. Beliaev, promising to raise the issue in Moscow, also argued that many perceived Rudnytskyi as "taking a Soviet position," with his expulsion appearing to be unfair "revenge for the past" before 1939. Locals also remembered that "Rudnytskyi, being half-Jewish, had to hide" under the Germans and now saw him as "being slandered."[78]

Parkhomenko advised even more caution concerning Mykhailo Vozniak, also under discussion for possible expulsion from the Writers' Union. Nationalists, Parkhomenko explained, considered Vozniak a traitor, and Vozniak argued that his party candidacy was already proof of his "break with the past."[79] A Kyiv Central Committee report noted that a "significant part" of Lviv's local

73. Oleg V. Khlevniuk et al., *Politburo TsK VKP(b) i Sovet ministrov SSSR 1945–1953* (Moscow: Rosspen, 2002), 248 (doc. 216). Some of the perpetrators of this deportation were decorated for their performance, which was publicized (ibid., 248; DALO P-3, 2, 116: 96–102, repr. in *Kulturne zhyttia*, 1:473–81 [doc. 211]).

74. DALO P-3, 2, 96: 27–32.

75. Rubl'ov and Cherchenko, *Stalinshchyna i dolia*, 228–29.

76. Behind closed doors, local party officials also condemned Karmanskyi for having talked about the mass Soviet famine of the early 1930s (DALO P-3, 2, 126: 169–75).

77. DALO P-3808, 1, 8: 11.

78. TsDAHOU 1, 70, 693: 1–16, repr. in *Kulturne zhyttia*, 1:497–506 (doc. 214), here 502–4.

79. Ibid., 504–5.

intelligentsia, including pro-Soviet representatives Vilde, Kozlaniuk, Halan, and Pelekhatyi were preparing a letter in support of Vozniak.[80] Caution was needed; expulsion from the Writers' Union would trigger expulsion from the party. Yet prior praise for Vozniak's joining meant that expulsion would demonstrate "our inability to reeducate." Put differently, if not Vozniak, who *could* the party-state change? Parkhomenko stressed that expulsion would make nationalists crow over a "creep and traitor" getting what he deserved. This would be a bizarrely self-defeating spectacle: the party-state punishing, as nationalists saw fit, one of the most coopted members of the old local intelligentsia. Moreover, Soviet publicity had made sure that the performance would resonate widely: even the "rank-and-file masses" saw Vozniak as "faithfully . . . striving to serve Soviet power" and the current official hostility toward Vozniak was "perceived as . . . injustice even by Western Ukrainians," who were "sympathetic to Soviet power."[81] In short, if harassment was the reward of cooperation, why try?

Willing yet Incapable: Vilde, the Local Insufficient

Whereas the cases of Rudnytskyi, Vozniak, and Krypiakevych turned on the themes of deception, hypocrisy, and backwardness, for the writer Iryna Vilde the focus was insufficiency, another defining feature of the Soviet imagination of the local.

Born in 1907 in postwar Lviv, Vilde wrote for the oblast publisher. In 1948, its chief editor defended her work in a report for Hrushetskyi. Her main task as an editor, she explained, was to educate local writers with "maximum Bolshevik vigilance" and a "delicate psychological approach." Even those willing and with "progressive" pre-Soviet biographies were unable to articulate the right messages. Worse, local writers could "not understand what is happening now in the Western Ukrainian village" or the "heroism of Stakhanovite labor." Petro Kozlaniuk, a "talented writer-Communist" with "Soviet views" who was also the head of the Lviv Writers' Union, remained a local and thus unable "to fully grasp what is going on around him." A visit to a collective farm had left him with the non-impression that there was nothing exceptional to see there. The editor had "to literally read out" to him "a lecture on the advantages of the kolkhoz system, based on Lenin's works."[82]

80. TsDAHOU 1, 23, 4255: 13–14.
81. TsDAHOU 1, 70, 693: 1–16, repr. in *Kulturne zhyttia*, 1:497–506 (doc. 214), here 505–6.
82. DALO P-3, 2, 606: 68–78, repr. in *Kulturne zhyttia*, 1:566–70.

Vilde served as an example of how hard it was for local writers to learn to treat "contemporary topics." Well known for her "narrowly national" and "bourgeois" works under "feudal Poland," Vilde's local fame was still valuable. Initially, she had been told "to tell the truth" about life in Poland, which she had, accepting all "corrections of an idea-political kind." The second topic assigned had been "the friendship of the peoples." By 1948, Vilde was working on a large work called *The Richynskyi Sisters* that aimed to show the rottenness of the Polish prewar petty bourgeoisie and the rise of a young rebellious and pro-Soviet generation in interwar Western Ukraine. Requiring a laborious but rewarding process of writing and editing, it was "her diploma work for the right to consider herself a Soviet writer."[83] Vilde showed that local insufficiency could be overcome, with much Soviet help.

In sum, the anti-Hrushevskyi campaign of 1946 created much of the cast and the conventions of the transformation drama of the old intelligentsia. Manuilskyi's assault delineated Lviv's old intelligentsia as an evil Other, treacherous to both the Soviet order and eastern, that is authentic Ukraine. Manuilskyi also threatened to end opportunities for self-transformation. Locals must either stop pretending and genuinely change or face punishment. The deportation of October 1947 exemplified such punishment. Mykhailo Rudnytskyi's and Petro Karmanskyi's expulsion from the Writers' Union showed that even punishment did not end transformation and spectacle. The failure to expel Vozniak and the work on Vilde's inability to correctly understand the Soviet world as well as her own revealed the limits to Soviet pressure. Vozniak was a symbol of adaptation, and precisely for that reason to crush him would have been self-defeating. Vilde needed much remedial training but, given Soviet assumptions of widespread backwardness, to lose those willing yet weak would have left few followers, as the oblast publisher's editor illustrated, pointing out that even Kozlaniuk and Halan could not fully grasp Soviet Socialism when it was in action around them. By the late 1940s, the relationship between the Soviet authorities and the old local intelligentsia remained an open-ended site of party-state strategies, local tactics, frustration, ambition, careers, and ambiguities.

A Killing

Yaroslav Halan's murder on 24 October 1949 marked an unprecedented escalation and the convergence of two struggles, over the old intelligentsia and youth. Halan's killers were young; one of them, Ilarion Lukashevych, was a student in Lviv. His two brothers, Aleksandr and Myron, accused of assisting him, were also

83. DALO P-3, 2, 606: 46–64.

Lviv students.[84] Thus, Halan's assassination fed Soviet fears that the nationalist underground was attracting a new generation and infiltrating future elites. This fear pointed to a persisting counterinsurgency problem, while striking deep at Soviet self-understanding: in 1939, Molotov had boasted that Socialist Humanism could build a new world with those spoilt by the old. Yet having the added prestige of triumph in the Great Fatherland War and despite massive postwar police and propaganda efforts, it seemed to be failing to win over even those not yet spoilt. As a Kyiv Central Committee memorandum noted in 1947, Soviet authorities felt that local youths were joining the nationalist movement not merely out of fear but out of ideological conviction. Without "liberating" the young from nationalist influence, the counterinsurgency struggle could not be won conclusively.[85]

Four years later, however, oblast secret police head Maistruk told the obkom buro that his forces still encountered "youngsters" among the nationalists, "born in, for instance 1934, who have not known any other systems than the Soviet." Communist education had failed.[86] From the beginning, Soviet authorities had stressed both the need to suffuse the western Ukrainian countryside with Komsomol structures to fight "for every young man or girl" under nationalist influence and the failure to do so.[87] In zero-sum mode, they also identified their own failure with nationalist success. "Where we work poorly, our enemies will work better," a Lviv Komsomol secretary warned in typical fashion in 1946.[88]

But the Komsomol faced an unacknowledged, though not unique, dilemma: how to reconcile conquering hearts and minds with destroying bodies. In postwar western Ukraine, the Komsomol had two main aims, as one of its Lviv oblast leaders put it in 1946: to help western Ukraine catch up with the "advanced eastern oblasts" and to fight the nationalist "gangs."[89] Here, the Komsomol served as a combat force in a bloody tit-for-tat. A 1979 Soviet history put the number of Komsomol fighters in postwar antinationalist destroyer battalion militias in three western oblasts alone at almost ten thousand.[90] In early 1945, Lviv oblast

84. Strictly speaking, at the time of the assassination Ilarion Lukashevych, who did not strike the fatal ax blows but was crucial in gaining access to Halan, was already a *former* student of Lviv's Agriculture Institute using his recent relegation as a pretext to ask Halan for help (GDA SBU 13, spr. 372, tom 47: 204). But, tellingly, in the campaign following the murder, he was overwhelmingly identified as a student. On Aleksandr and Myron and for more detail on the secret police version of the murder, see GDA SBU 13, spr. 372, tom 93: 1–10.

85. TsDAHOU 1, 75, 62: 34–35.

86. DALO P-3, 4, 101: 115–16.

87. RGASPI 17, 88, 671: 34–41; DALO P-66, 1, 100: 60.

88. DALO P-66, 1, 100: 70.

89. DALO P-66, 1, 100: 51.

90. Babko, *Istoriia Leninskoi komunistychnoi spilky*, 469–70.

Komsomol members killed nearly three hundred and captured almost fifteen hundred nationalists.[91] Those who killed their way to a high body count "on their tally," in obkom parlance, were honored and decorated. Having killed "ten bandits," a Komsomol member could end up joining the Interior Ministry troops.[92]

Nationalists responded in kind—by killing six out of fifteen participants at a rural Komsomol meeting, for instance. At their funeral, Dykalo—the head of the village Komsomol, one of whose sisters had been killed and another wounded—vowed to "pay the bandits back."[93] On the ground, it could get personal between young people with guns.[94] In the reconquered Soviet West, the rural Komsomol started as a fighting and an extraction force.

Thus, winning over local youth, rather than killing or being killed by them, remained difficult. At the end of 1944, the deceased Metropolitan Sheptytskyi's brother Klimentyi had led a Greek Catholic delegation on a mission to Moscow. Ivan Polianskii, head of the Soviet government's Council on Matters of Religious Cults, recommended taking advantage of the church's offer to help detach western Ukrainian youth from militant nationalism—which, according to Klimentyi Sheptytskyi's sober assessment, had imbued the young with hatred for their neighbors rather than fostering love for the fatherland.[95]

Polianskii's good advice marked a turn not taken. With the Greek Catholic Church brutally crushed, Klimentyi Sheptytskyi was arrested in 1947 and died in prison in Russia in 1951. Also in 1947, Lviv's Gosplan plenipotentiary reported that collecting grain from peasants was very hard with nationalist resistance rising.[96] Hrushetskyi, meanwhile, noted the contradiction: Soviet reeducation was essential for transforming the "human material" of local students into Soviet specialists, yet those same students became "loudspeakers" of nationalist propaganda on trips to their home villages.[97] Halan admonished Lviv University's Komsomol that "our youth" included "many masked nationalists," to be fought "mercilessly."[98]

Two years later, his own murder seemed to show that neither repression nor indoctrination was working. A high Soviet official noted that the nationalists were "recruiting youth" in Lviv's academic institutions. Clearly, Soviet education

91. RGASPI 17, 88, 450: 18.

92. DALO-P 3, 1, 487: 67–68; RGASPI 17, 88, 450: 29. The Komsomol also kept long lists of the fallen (DALO P-66, 3, 9: 4–12).

93. DALO P-66, 3, 9: 2–3.

94. DALO P-66, 1, 100: 110.

95. RGASPI 82, 2, 501: 21–24.

96. RGAE 4372, 47, 145: 59.

97. RGASPI 17, 88, 450: 17–20; DALO P-3, 2, 96: 27–32.

98. DALO P-66, 1, 206: 34.

was failing at the "fight for every soul of a young girl or . . . man."[99] Militarily, however, the nationalists, although lavishly sacrificing the young as well as killing "traitors," never had a chance. By the time of Halan's murder, the Soviet authorities were easily winning a counterinsurgency war they could not lose.[100] Unwittingly, however, by resisting beyond Soviet mission-accomplished delusions, their opponents did hurt Soviet arrogance.

The Victim

Halan's obituary described his death as "tragic" but did not mention that it was violent.[101] Later it became the basis for a carefully pruned martyr cult. Halan, however, had had a complicated life. Born in 1902 in Habsburg Galicia, he became an interwar left-wing writer and activist in Polish Lwów. He tried but failed to emigrate to Soviet Ukraine. His first wife, Anna, was admitted to a medical institute there, but the Soviet secret police reinvented her and Yaroslav, at that time beyond its reach in a Polish jail, as anti-Soviet subversives. She was executed in 1937; officially at least, Halan never found out how she died, despite repeated inquiries.[102]

Returning to Lviv in 1945, after a career as a Soviet war correspondent, he became the most prominent local propagandist, launching public attacks on Ukrainian nationalism and the Greek Catholic Church in covert coordination with the secret police. The police later saw those attacks, together with Halan's condemnation of the fugitive nationalist leader Stepan Bandera, as the main reason nationalists wanted to assassinate Halan.[103]

As explained in internal Soviet communications, Halan's polemics against Greek Catholicism were especially valuable: by publishing under a pseudonym, he wrote not as the "progressive Soviet fighter-atheist" he really was but as an indignant local believer, in order to, in effect, speak down to "those backward parts of Western Ukraine's peasantry infected" by religion. Halan, simultaneously Soviet and local, knew how to "talk to backward people within the limits of

99. TsDAHOU 1, 23, 5864: 63.

100. Jeffrey Burds, "AGENTURA: Soviet Informants' Networks and the Ukrainian Underground in Galicia, 1944–48," *East European Politics and Society* 11 (1997): 123, 126.

101. *Vilna Ukraina*, 25 October 1949, 3.

102. *Kulturne zhyttia*, 1:531 (doc. 226); Aleksandr Bantyshev and Arzen Ukhal, *Ubiistvo na zakaz: Kto zhe organizoval ubiistvo Iaroslava Halana?* (Uzhhorod: Gorodskaia tipografiia, 2002), 50–52.

103. For a secret police report on Halan's writing as part of "a process of implementation of a plan of measures regarding the Greek-Catholic Church," see Bohunov et al., *Likvidatsiia UHKTs (1939–1946)* 2:29 (doc. 164). For secret police assessments of the killing's motives, see GDA SBU 13, spr. 372, tom 47: 205; 13, spr. 372, tom 93: 3.

their conservative worldview."[104] Here was a tested Soviet propagandist understanding locals like the local he was; even better, here was a tested local speaking Bolshevik in a local patois.

As rediscovered in the perestroika period of the 1980s, Halan was a muckraker as well as a local who knew locals. In 1990, a Lviv publisher praised him, in a language truly Halanian in its blend of the loyally rebellious with an acute sense of the permitted, as revealing "negative phenomena of the administrative-bureaucratic system—corruption and swindling, vulgarity and heartlessness."[105]

Halan used his local status to cover his muckraking. At a 1947 meeting, presenting himself as an "old inhabitant" of the city as well as a "Soviet person," he deplored what he characterized as the tragedy of Lviv's decay occurring, as he stressed provocatively, after the Soviet return: the "ruination" of streets, buildings, parks, sewage systems, pavements, and flower beds by "hooliganism," neglect, and corruption.[106] In the same year, he denounced Lviv's university with implications of graft, calling it a "pigsty." Halan's fulminations converged with official concerns. At the same time, the Kyiv Central Committee produced a damning report on higher education, and Lviv featured as the worst in a bad field.[107]

Not all muckraking was welcome. Halan had reported from the Nuremberg Trials, but, once back in Lviv, his work on Nazi crimes was not appreciated. In 1948, Hrushetskyi reprimanded him: it was time to stop mentioning the war, or at least the Nazis, and to produce something positive and contemporary.[108] Halan's plays against Ukrainian nationalists and in favor of collectivization in Western Ukraine initially had no success with the bureaucracy. Also in 1948, he lost his position as correspondent of *Radianska Ukraina* and was harassed by Soviet police officers.[109]

When Halan applied for party membership through the Lviv branch of the Writers' Union in 1949, Vladimir Beliaev, as secretary of its party organization,

104. RGASPI 17, 132, 397: 322.

105. Yaroslav Halan, *Z neopublikovanoho: Feiletony. Statti. Vystupy. Lystuvannia. Shchodennyk* (Lviv: Kameniar, 1990), 2.

106. DALO P-3, 2, 84: 20–27.

107. *Kulturne zhyttia*, 1:364–65; TsDAHOU 1, 23, 4530: 3. Halan also complained—not publicly—about low local admission figures for academic training in Lviv and the replacement of Ukrainian by Russian on movie posters (*Kulturne zhyttia*, 1:623).

108. DALO P-3, 2, 7: 63–64, 70.

109. Rubl'ov and Cherchenko, *Stalinshchyna i dolia*, 332, 337; Halan, *Z neopublikovanoho*, 77. These harassment incidents should not be overrated as evidence of conspiracy. Soviet officials had a long record of arbitrary violence of the type that Halan encountered. The same is true, mutatis mutandis, for an obkom's 1947 report about a Ukrainian anti-Soviet underground organization planning to assassinate Halan (Marusyk, *Zakhidnoukrainska humanitarna intelihentsia*, 143).

warned him that flogging nationalists was no longer enough; it was time to write about the "heroes of our day, exemplary builders of socialism." Halan would have to limit his muckraking "indignation" to "party channels." Beliaev and Halan knew each other from occasional common assignments and had spent Crimean holidays together in 1948. Halan remembered those holidays as windy, boring, and vulgar; Beliaev did not like Halan either. In 1947, he complained in private correspondence that Halan accused him of "trying to make money out of German atrocities." Halan was admitted as a party candidate.[110] His diary during this period combined midlife crisis anxiety with vague political references. Although publishing became harder, he was still invited to Moscow and Kyiv; one month before his murder, he was made head of the oblast's art department. His nonconformist attacks on bureaucratism were removed from display in Lviv's Halan Museum in 1962.[111]

A Bolshevik Fortress

The background of Halan's assassination has remained unclear. He was bludgeoned to death with an ax by two young nationalists, Mykhailo Shtakhur and Ilarion Lukashevych, a student of the Lviv Agriculture Institute and the son of a Greek Catholic priest respectively.[112] Both were sentenced to death at trials in Lviv in 1951. The authorities also punished several putative co-conspirators and ideological sympathizers, including Ilarion's father and his two brothers Oleksandr and Myron, both sentenced to death—not for directly participating in the murder but for assisting in its preparation.[113] In 1953, the nationalist organizer of the killing, Roman Shchepanskyi, aka "Bui-Tur," was caught and sentenced to death.[114] Rumors that the killing was provoked by Soviet infiltration of the nationalist underground emerged quickly and have neither died down nor been confirmed.

Stressing their "enormous political significance," the Ukrainian Politburo ordered the use of show trials (open trials) for individual members of "bandit-terrorist groups" in Lviv oblast less than a month before Halan's killing. Lviv's military

110. DALO P-3, 2, 257: 22–25. Beliaev and Halan knew each other from occasional common assignments and had spent Crimean holidays together in 1948. Halan remembered them as windy, boring, and vulgar; Beliaev did not like Halan either. In 1947, he complained in private correspondence that Halan accused him of "trying to make money out of German atrocities." For Halan's bad Crimea trip with "Volodia Beliaev," see Halan, *Z neopublikovanoho*, 76.

111. Halan, *Z neopublikovanoho*, 5, 73–80.

112. On Lukashevych and Stakhur, see Dmytro Viedienieiev and Hennadiy Bystrukhin, *Dvobii bez kompromisiv: Protyborstvo spetspidrozdiliv OUN ta radianskykh syl spetsoperatsii, 1945–1980-ti roky* (Kyiv: KIS, 2007), 111–12.

113. Bantyshev and Ukhal, *Ubiistvo na zakaz*, 46–48, 60.

114. Vieniedieiev and Bystrukhin, *Dvobii bez kompromisiv*, 114.

tribunal was to try defendants selected by the obkom; trials should be held in Ukrainian.[115] The authorities carefully monitored the response of Lviv's population to the reintroduction of the death penalty for traitors, spies, and subversives, noting complaints that Communist reeducation should make the death penalty superfluous.[116] Maistruk pointed out that the death penalty made nationalist surrender less likely.[117]

In contrast to its causes, the consequences of Halan's murder were obvious. It provided the occasion for the most comprehensive single postwar wave of repression of students, youth, and the local intelligentsia in Lviv. Although the official reaction to the killing was quick, with all three Lukashevych brothers arrested within less than three weeks, the signal for a wider crackdown was a visit by Khrushchev to Lviv at the end of November. According to Maistruk, Khrushchev, "in a very trenchant" manner, ordered the "Bolsheviks of Lvov" to turn the city into a fortress and to make "the ground burn" under the nationalists' feet. One week after Khrushchev's visit, Maistruk oversaw another "deportation of hostile elements" from Lviv.[118]

Halan's assassination and Khrushchev's call for more militancy coincided with a fresh push for collectivization.[119] At the end of 1947, Hrushetskyi reported that collectivization in his oblast had not yet reached the low, pre-German-occupation levels, with 98.5 percent of farms still in private hands.[120] One year later, one-fifth of all peasant households had joined collective farms.[121] By the fall of 1949, this share had increased to a third, Khrushchev reported to Stalin.[122] In sum, collectivization was still far from complete. Moreover, Moscow received reports of the Lviv obkom cheating and making up collective farms.[123] At the beginning of 1949, the Sixteenth Congress of the Communist Party of Ukraine demanded faster collectivization.

In western Ukraine, collectivization was about strategy as much as hamlets. Although the nationalist insurgency was a rural phenomenon, Lviv was deeply

115. Serhiychuk, *Desiat buremnykh lit*, 737–38. The trial of one of Halan's killers, however, was based on a similar decree issued in October 1951.

116. DALO P-3, 3, 460: 32.

117. DALO P-4, 1, 334: 190.

118. DALO P-4, 1, 334: 182–83, 191.

119. This was part of a larger regional pattern. As Romuald Misiunas and Rein Taagepera pointed out, "the percentage of Baltic, Moldavian, and western Belorussian and Ukrainian farms collectivized grew in a similar way, with a very sharp increase in 1949" (*The Baltic States: Years of Dependence, 1940–1980* [Berkeley: University of California Press, 1983], 95).

120. RGAE 4372, 47, 145: 76.

121. RGASPI 17, 138, 9: 87.

122. RGASPI 17, 138, 98: 6.

123. RGASPI 17, 138, 9: 96–101.

Figure 6.1 Monument to Yaroslav Halan: unveiled in 1972, it dominated one of Lviv's important squares and traffic junctions, also named after him. The monument was removed and the square renamed after Ukrainian independence. A writer and publicist, Halan was a local who identified with Soviet rule and launched public attacks on Ukrainian nationalism and the Greek Catholic Church. His assassination by nationalists in 1949 triggered a wave of repressions targeting in particular the intelligentsia and academia. Collection: Central State Kinofotofono Archive of Ukraine, Kyiv.

embedded in an embattled countryside. The Soviet authorities were continually afraid of nationalists infiltrating the city with false documents. In 1945, a city raion official warned that "alien elements," including Banderites from "the forests," were constantly trying to sneak into Lviv.[124] In April 1946 alone, twenty-eight were caught.[125]

The decline of nationalist resistance in the countryside only increased Soviet fears of urban subversion: in "mortal agony," according to a Komsomol speaker, nationalists were still trying to manipulate youth. With Lviv University's

124. DALO P-4, 1, 66: 2–3.

125. RGASPI 17, 88, 794: 16. For more details on various arrests of suspected nationalist underground members in Lviv in the immediate postwar years, see Isaievych et al., *Istoriia Lvova*, 3:259–67 and, for a specific case in 1948, DALO P-3, 2, 480: 168–69.

Komsomol featuring 21 locals among a total membership of 636, nationalists had opportunities.[126] In 1949, Maistruk explained that nationalists were abandoning guerrilla warfare in rural areas, so as to move to cities and forge innocuous biographies, with Lviv's academic institutions among the best covers available.[127]

Maistruk warned that nationalists were also eager to spread their "influence east." Khrushchev had read out a passage from a captured nationalist leadership document, identifying "youth from the East" as a top priority.[128] With some young people from eastern Ukraine, nationalists might succeed, Maistruk warned.[129] Clearly, this was an intolerable effect of the Soviet unification of Ukraine.

Parting Shots: Khrushchev's Last Meeting of Party Activists in Lviv

On the surface, the meeting of party activists held on 30 November and 1 December focused on Lviv's academic institutions and was hosted by the city party committee. In fact, it was attended by everybody who mattered in the oblast party and state elite, and its real leader was Khrushchev. The first major meeting dedicated to the consequences of Halan's killing, it featured an ominous minute of silence to commemorate the fifteenth anniversary of the Leningrad party boss Sergei Kirov's 1934 assassination, associated with the interwar purges. This was Khrushchev's final personal intervention in Lviv before leaving Ukraine for Moscow. He stayed for seven days and appeared at several additional meetings.[130]

Deeply involved in the Sovietization of Western Ukraine since 1939, Khrushchev became concerned with the fight against Ukrainian nationalism. This involvement brought out his most brutal side. In a November 1944 letter to Stalin, Khrushchev argued that it was not enough "terror" to shoot "bandits." Instead they should be hanged and the local population forced to watch, which meant copying German methods—a point he failed to mention. He also called for such emergency instruments as reestablishing the rapid-sentencing squads known as troikas for fast-track detention, incarceration, deportation, and judicial murder. Although these measures were not adopted, the existing system proved capable of

126. DALO P-66, 1, 100: 26, 38.

127. DALO P-3, 2, 427: 16.

128. DALO P-3, 3, 75: 130–31.

129. This was a large group to worry about. The number of village teachers alone, mostly young, sent west has been given by Ukrainian historians as forty-four thousand (Rubl'ov and Cherchenko, *Stalinshchyna i dolia*, 211).

130. DALO P-3, 3, 75: 9; *Vilna Ukraina*, 3, 4, and 7 December 1949; *Vilna Ukraina*, 28 January 1950.

producing public hangings, with spectator response carefully reported.[131] In 1945, Khrushchev repeatedly called for higher body counts and increasing repression of the families of suspected resistance fighters.[132] In April 1949, Maistruk noted that Khrushchev's insistent order to use bloodhounds was being implemented and the twenty dogs which he personally had had sent were a success.[133] Between 1944 and 1949, Khrushchev kept returning to Lviv for meetings with the party, police, and military elite to issue instructions in a frustrating war on nationalism that he clearly expected to be much shorter and easier, promising Stalin as early as April 1946 that the final blow was near.[134] On the ground, he incited his subordinates to destroy whole villages and take a "hundred of them for one of ours."[135] Khrushchev was a micromanaging insurgency fighter, confidently speculating on the psychological effects of the end of the war or the demobilization of Soviet forces and ordering the use of locals in Soviet militias and as informers.[136]

Khrushchev's statements at the 1949 activists' session echoed through subsequent party, student, and Komsomol meetings, serving to escalate attacks on alleged nationalists and their sympathizers. For the head of the student department

131. Iurii (Yuri) Shapoval, "The Ukrainian Years, 1894–1949," in *Nikita Khrushchev*, ed. William Taubman, Sergei Khrushchev, and Abbott Gleason (New Haven: Yale University Press, 2000), 37–38; Serhiychuk, *Ukrainskyi zdvyh*, 3:274–75.

132. For explicit orders by the Central Committee of Ukraine to apply and then "decisively increase" repression against families, see the key decrees of 10 January and 26 February reprinted in Serhiychuk, *Desiat buremnykh lit*, 198, 243, from TsDAHOU 1, 23, 1674: 2–11 (10 January) and 1, 16, 29: 138–54 (26 February). "According to some sources," as Karel Berkhoff has noted, Stalin himself, in his general urge to exterminate "traitors," seems to have recommended reprisals against families (*Harvest of Despair: Life and Death in Ukraine under Nazi Rule* [Cambridge, MA: Harvard University Press, 2004], 279).

133. DALO-P 3, 3, 81: 8, 16, 50.

134. RGASPI 82, 2, 897: 122. This was not only a result of Khrushchev's ebullient temperament and wishful thinking but a systemic fault. He was not alone in facing the frustrations of a mission unaccomplished. Generally, early Soviet predictions had been recklessly optimistic. In April 1944, with Soviet forces barely reentering western Ukraine, the Central Committee of Ukraine admitted that reestablishing local Soviet rule was "somewhat" harder there because of nationalism, but it also maintained that the local population was already shifting allegiances to Soviet rule, while nationalist groups were falling apart (RGASPI 17, 88, 351: 8). Learning took time, too. Nearly one year later, in February 1945, the Central Committee of Ukraine set 15 March 1945 as the deadline for the "final liquidation" of nationalist formations (quoted in Serhiychuk, *Desiat buremnykh lit*, 247, from TsDAHOU 1, 16, 29: 138–54). At a major meeting of the western Ukrainian party and secret-police elite in Lviv on 15 May, Khrushchev announced that the war was virtually over, with "only a few isolated major groups" and some "small bandit groups" of nationalist fighters remaining in the field. All that was left to do was mopping up these diehards and putting more pressure (through collective liability and punishments) on the rural population to hand them over (TsDAHOU 1, 23, 1670: 1–7, as reproduced in Serhiychuk, *Desiat buremnykh lit*, 295–98).

135. Weiner and Rahi-Tamm, "Getting to Know You," 41.

136. RGASPI 82, 2, 897: 106–15, 120–22.

of Lviv's Komsomol organization, Khrushchev's statements "must become the ABC of the class struggle."[137]

In his introductory speech, Miskom Secretary Bondar reviewed the threatening international situation and the successes of Soviet higher education. Much more vigilance was needed, he argued. He reprimanded higher education party organizations for only making "parade noise," with most students beyond party or Komsomol influence.[138] Weakness was bound to be exploited by the enemy; the Agriculture Institute, where Ilarion Lukashevych had studied, was the "obvious example." Lukashevych's involvement in Halan's murder foreshadowed what would happen sooner or later, Bondar warned, at the much bigger university and Medical Institute. The Communists at the Agricultural Institute, as well as its director and party secretary, had failed and were writing self-serving reports.[139] Even after Halan's murder, they took "no measures at all."[140] Moreover, this failure was representative. Cyanide and guns had been found in the university's chemistry department. Students avoided the Komsomol because of pressure from their home villages. Antireligious propaganda was weak, with some students, known as religious, receiving excellent grades in Marxism-Leninism. The University Club was organizing "Western European dances." One student declared pragmatically that building Communism made no sense because the imperialists were "preparing a nuclear war" anyhow.[141] At the Medical Institute, agitation was conducted frivolously, sometimes in the anatomy theater and with "catcalls and ironical applause." A student and daughter of an intermittently rebellious institute professor with a left-deviationist past said that Stalin's Nature Transformation Plan was a topic fit only for kolkhozniks. Voitok, the leader of the Lviv Komsomol, later pointed out bitterly that she was "by the way from the East." Another female student had married in church. For the oblast Komsomol head Chyrva, the wedding made this student a "future enemy."[142]

Lack of political engagement pervaded the student body, especially the Komsomol; the purge of one student for nationalism looked like an inevitable result of widespread Soviet deficiencies, not an exception.[143] Chyrva quantified the Komsomol failure with local youth: of about 9,000 nonlocal students, 5,453 were in the Komsomol, about 60 percent. But of all local students, only 20 percent

137. DALO P-3, 3, 268: 70.
138. DALO P-4, 1, 285: 119.
139. DALO P-4, 1, 285: 133–41.
140. DALO P-4, 1, 285: 141–44.
141. DALO P-4, 1, 285: 146–47.
142. DALO P-4, 1, 285: 75, 95; P-3, 3, 268: 70.
143. DALO P-4, 1, 285: 148–49.

had joined.[144] The student group to which one of Halan's assassins had belonged consisted of twenty-six students, six of whom belonged to the Komsomol, just one of them a local.[145]

Moreover, resistance to the Komsomol could be disturbingly open. A local student was expelled from the Polytechnic for picking on a fellow local because of his Komsomol badge.[146] Komsomol members were shy about their membership. A "daughter of a big landowner" in hiding said of a fellow student she had dated that if she had known he was in the Komsomol, he would not have got "as far as my doorstep." Although she was denounced and "chased from the institute," the fact remained that she had been more assertive about her dislike of the Komsomol than her suitor had been about his membership in it.[147]

University Rector Savyn's moderate self-criticism was not enough. Khrushchev made it clear that there was pre-Halan and post-Halan. The first secretary publicly humiliated the rector by telling him that he had failed to find the class enemy only because he was not looking. Savyn admitted that ideological mobilization at the university was poor. The "predominant mass" of the students failed to show "vigilance" and report on fellow students. The crucial kafedras of Marxism-Leninism, Ukrainian history, and the history of the Soviet Union and the student groups were not, as required, transmission belts of ideological training.[148]

The main message of the activists' meeting was clear: Halan's murder was no coincidence but a symptom of the inadequate ideological education of students, especially locals. In response, Bondar insisted they "escalate the class struggle" in Lviv's academic institutions "to force the enemy into the open." Unreliable students should be forced to give talks at meetings on "collectivization, industrial-

144. DALO P-4, 1, 285: 79. Central Committee of Ukraine Secretary Ivan Nazarenko put the number of local Komsomol members even slightly lower, at 980 (TsDAHOU 1, 23, 5864: 69). The proportions of the problem, however, were the same.

145. DALO P-4, 1, 285: 151–56.

146. DALO P-3, 3, 250: 104.

147. DALO P-4, 1, 285: 151–56.

148. DALO-P 4, 1, 285: 14–18. At the meeting, Khrushchev also developed a spontaneous theory of collective irresponsibility that anticipated his situation during post-1956 de-Stalinization: a university party buro member criticized the head of the buro for terrorizing its members by making constant allusions to secret service connections. A voice from the audience challenged the speaker by asking why he and other members had allowed this to happen. Khrushchev commented that when "one member of a party buro criticizes another and for this is interrupted by criticism . . . what have you done [then]? That means . . . to stifle criticism . . . so to speak: if you also are . . . linked to these insufficiencies, then better be silent" (DALO P-4, 1, 285: 39–40). After his Secret Speech of 1956, attacking select parts of Stalinism, the party leadership would face the same conundrum on an all-Soviet scale (Polly Jones, *Myth, Memory, Trauma: Rethinking the Stalinist Past in the Soviet Union, 1953–70* [New Haven: Yale University Press, 2013], 53–54; William Taubman, *Khrushchev: The Man and his Era* [New York: W. W. Norton, 2003], 273, 514).

ization, and nationalism." Meetings, however, should be called only when a student majority was ready to support a "purge." First, a smaller group of "comrades" was to be primed to "squeeze the enemy against the wall and force him to acknowledge his guilt." The purge would be a purge from above *and* from below, mobilizing "the preponderant mass of the students."

Khrushchev's visit launched a vicious campaign against suspected nationalists. He also solicited criticism of some Soviet institutions and cadres. Shortly afterward, Lviv's student Komsomol organizers practiced this double approach. With many local officials in attendance as well as Vladimir Semichastnyi representing the Central Committee of Ukraine's Komsomol, Valentyn Malanchuk, the head of Lviv University's Komsomol, gave the first speech. For him the post-Halan campaign was his real graduation. Born in 1928 in Soviet Ukraine, he entered the party and was appointed head of the Lviv oblast Komsomol in 1950. After graduating from the university's history department, he went on to a successful career based on fighting Ukrainian nationalism taking him, by the early 1970s, to the Kyiv Central Committee.[149] In 1949, his explanation of the Komsomol's failure in Lviv turned on the peculiarities of Western Ukraine: he insisted that Lviv's Komsomol performance should be different from elsewhere in Ukraine, since Western Ukraine was special, the site of "fierce class struggle."[150]

The social composition of the student body made this failure crucial. In 1949, out of 2,671 students at the university 858 were locals, including 544 from peasant families. Only 122 of the latter had already entered a kolkhoz, 70 of them as late as 1949.[151] At the Polytechnic, the Komsomol put the number of local students at one thousand, among them seven hundred children of peasants; only two hundred had tried to persuade their parents to enter a kolkhoz.[152] The Komsomol failed to make itself attractive to locals; locals failed to make collective farms attractive to their parents. Malanchuk explained that the Komsomol was ineffective at recruiting local youth because it was no fun, leaving the "local comrades" to "find entertainment in hostile groups." After Halan's death, however, the emphasis clearly had to shift to force. Malanchuk accused the university Komsomol of failing to react to the murder: "If we had acted the way the party has taught us, with three blows for one, then we would have had many results."[153]

149. On Malanchuk, see *Nam partiia sylu dala*, 88.

150. DALO P-3, 3, 268: 6. The impact of the 1950 collectivization escalation was immediate and devastating. As the obkom knew from its internal reports, child mortality in Lviv oblast increased by 3.3 percent during that year. While nearly 20.9 percent of all deaths in 1950 ended the life of children, in some rural raions, this share was as high as 31 percent (DALO P-3, 4, 507: 21).

151. DALO P-3, 3, 260: 281.

152. DALO P-3, 3, 268: 59.

153. DALO-P 3, 3, 268: 34.

Khrushchev's successor as first secretary, Leonid Melnikov, brought a fresh whiff of frank brutality. At a large Lviv meeting of the party-state elite of all western oblasts on 9 December 1949, with several ministers and Central Committee members from Kyiv attending, he insisted that the "class struggle" in Lviv's higher education called for violent, even lethal measures. "Hostile elements" should be thrown out of third- or fifth-floor windows. He praised hardy peasants for cutting off, on their own initiative, the heads of several "bandits"; this was not a vigilante lynching, he stressed, but a "wonderful patriotic incident."[154] Lviv's authorities should have mobilized hatred, but they had not. Lviv was still the "most backward oblast," and the city of Lviv had been "transformed into a center of OUN propaganda." This was a fantasy, but it was articulated as reality by the most powerful man in Soviet Ukraine. Lviv, once again, was central. And at the center of this imagined Lviv was academia, accused of sheltering Ukrainian nationalism like no other institution.[155]

Central Committee Propaganda and Agitation Secretary Ivan Nazarenko scolded local officials for neglecting their two main tasks, collectivization and "the national question in the western oblasts," invoking Khrushchev's recent appearances in "tough" villages, where peasants failed to collectivize. Khrushchev had given them a choice to "either destroy the bandits and set up a kolkhoz" or "we will deport you all to Siberia."[156] Within a decade, a history of the university Komsomol would glorify the contribution of Lviv's academic institutions to collectivization.[157] Yet in 1950, Nazarenko was decrying inertia. It should be "so very easy to argue with nationalists," he felt. "Nationalists are for the bourgeois nation and we are for the Socialist one: the bourgeois nation—that is landowners and kulaks," but "with us—[it is] without landowners, without kulaks."[158] For Western Ukraine in 1949, where—often Polish—landowners were gone, the difference between Socialism and the bourgeois world was defined as the absence or presence of—usually local Ukrainian—kulaks or of full collectivization. Applying Stalinist lessons meant the "liquidation of the kurkul as a class," as Hrushetskyi would put it.[159] Khrushchev, Nazarenko also explained, had talked to the arrested killers, who had told him "that nobody worked with them," which meant that nationalist agitation was stronger than Soviet efforts.[160] In sum, Nazarenko constructed a fundamental link between the youth of Halan's assasins, the failure of

154. TsDAHOU 1, 23, 5864: 32–35.
155. TsDAHOU 1, 23, 5864: 174.
156. TsDAHOU 1, 23, 5846: 54–58.
157. *Nam partiia sylu dala*, 71–77.
158. TsDAHOU 1, 23, 5864: 70.
159. DALO P-3, 3, 448: 22.
160. TsDAHOU 1, 23, 5864: 71.

Lviv's higher education and collectivization, and the fight against nationalism. Yet the emphasis on who had the more effective agitation did not diminish demands for more purging. Purges and agitation formed a whole in Stalinism's dialectic of pervasive violence and violent persuasion.

Avalanches Roll Downward

Purging became self-purging; self-purging came with manipulation and control from above. Mobilizing students for purging was an education—perhaps as much for the purgers as for the purged. In each purge meeting, a majority of students was effectively obliged to vote for expelling a fellow student. Within a few months, by March 1950, 2,000 such meetings had happened, purging 110 students.[161] Between March 1950 and January 1951, fifty-nine university teachers were also dismissed, including eight for not inspiring "political trust."[162] By the spring of 1950, we can estimate that almost 1 percent of Lviv students had been expelled because of the post-Halan campaign.[163] By 1951, 1–2 percent of Lviv's students had been arrested and/or expelled.[164] Each expulsion had significant multiplier effects: to expel one student, many had to vote. The meetings also featured intense questioning and attacks. This process left its mark on those "merely" threatened with expulsion, too. Zhikharev, a student in the law department, was, it seems, not expelled, but his belief that there were "no principal differences between Christianity and Communism" was exposed and ridiculed. After being subjected

161. DALO P-4, 1, 377: 60.

162. DALO P-3, 4, 84: 79.

163. DALO P-3, 4, 172: 37–43. The number of arrests of students and staff in October and November 1949 was officially put at 103. The number of expulsions was most likely higher. In 1951, the secret police reported that it had uncovered eight underground youth groups and made eighty-two arrests in connection with these cases over 1950 and 1951 (Isaievych et al., *Lviv: Istorychni narysy*, 513). There may be a significant overlap between these figures, and different sets of them are not always consistent. Thus, an obkom report of late 1949 put the number of arrested students at the Agricultural Institute at thirty-two, those of students "unmasked" after the meeting at nineteen. Yet another obkom report lists only fifteen students as expelled at the institute, and another thirteen for whom the "question of expulsion" had been raised (TsDAHOU 1, 23, 5666: 97; 1, 24, 196: 30). Arrests were not restricted to academic institutions: in the first half of 1950, sixty of Lviv's almost three thousand trainees in special professional schools were arrested (DALO P-3, 3, 417: 36).

164. In some cases, students who were expelled were later readmitted. In others, students were expelled from the university's full-attendance courses but shifted into the distance-learning (*zaochnyi*) department. For examples of such cases, see DALO P-3, 4, 83: 60 and P-92, 1, 136: 7. Quantitatively, it is difficult to assess what difference reinstatements made. By 1951, Brahinets explained at the obkom that, in the preceding year, the university had expelled fourteen students and reinstated three. At the same time, he announced that another twenty-two students would soon be expelled. A reinstatement carried some risk for those permitting it: in 1951, the obkom buro criticized such leniency toward two students (DALO P-3, 4, 83: 60, 68–69).

to "pertinent work" and "helped to acknowledge" his mistakes, he joined the Komsomol.[165]

In March 1950, the obkom criticized Lviv Polytechnic party secretary Aleksandr Malyshev for doing too much of a good thing when making his student groups expel a student that the obkom wanted left alone.[166] Malyshev described his purging in a January 1950 report. He started the process in a few select student groups "where we had an assured majority by the composition of the student body and the number of Komsomol members." Expulsion decisions by these select student groups were then used to shape larger meetings. He was proud of using fear as a tool for recruitment and disintegration. After the expulsion of 11 students and some academic staff, the Komsomol acquired 153 new local members in about three months, whereas admissions for the whole preceding year had been 32.[167] After several expulsions of those accused of concealing their family backgrounds, students began denouncing parents and siblings, and locals denounced locals, as someone underlined in Malyshev's report.[168]

The minutes of the Polytechnic student Shur's expulsion illustrated the purge process. Shur was accused of threatening to hang a Komsomol member "on the next tree" if they should ever meet "in the forest."[169] A student invoked Khrushchev's instruction to "show the enemy force again." Shur's fate was clear. It remained to be seen whether his two friends, the locals Fedushak and Trushkevych, would also be expelled. Their fellow students insisted that the two were not "sincere"; it was impossible to "know who is sitting with us in this auditorium, our friends or enemies." In his own defense, Trushkevych pointed out that after arriving in Soviet Ukraine from Poland in 1946, he had become Soviet especially recently. Admitting he had no "ability to think politically," he depicted himself as not hostile but only "incompetent." His religion was a product of his past. In sum, he pleaded his own underdevelopment.[170]

165. DALO P-92, 1, 136: 7.

166. Malyshev was a Stalinism promotee: born in Ufa in 1902 in a working-class family, Russian, and a party member since 1925, he graduated from the Stalin Komvuz military academy in 1932 and headed a Marxism-Leninism kafedra and agitation and propaganda departments at gorkoms for several years. After serving as a political officer during the war, in 1946 he became party secretary and lecturer in Marxism-Leninism at the Lviv Polytechnic. He had four decorations, and the obkom wanted a fifth one for him. A former student remembered him as vindictive: he ordered his students to explicitly renounce religious belief; if they refused, he gave them a failing grade, not only a low one, like other lecturers. See Anna Fastnacht-Stupnicka, *Zostali we Lwowie* (Wrocław: Sator Media, 2010), 196–97.

167. DALO P-3, 3, 250: 104–6. On the number of expelled students and staff the document is not absolutely precise.

168. DALO P-3, 3, 250: 106.

169. DALO P-3, 3, 250: 107.

170. DALO P-3, 3, 250: 109.

These arguments were rejected: his dithering was the way "Mensheviks talked." There was, he was told, "no middle ground, as little as there are third forces." It was time to make up his mind whether he lived "in the Soviet Union or in old Poland." The meeting decided to exclude Shur and to require Trushkevych and Fedushak to give monthly political talks. Their fellow students planned to visit their homes to investigate the causes of their delayed development.[171]

The Old Intelligentsia and the Post-Halan Campaign

While expulsions and Komsomol recruiting gathered speed, a fresh drive against the old intelligentsia was launched. At an obkom meeting in January 1950, Hrushetskyi discussed a letter by Ivan Krypiakevych, to be published in *Vilna Ukraina*, in which Krypiakevych was "flogging himself [*bichuietsa*] for his past mistakes" and declared his desire "to work honestly." His example should be followed. Melnikov had demanded that authors go "to the kolkhoz" to speak about their old "bourgeois" and new Soviet selves. Hrushetskyi was turning director: at such meetings, Hrushetskyi demanded, nothing should be left to accident. Speakers should be instructed one on one and told "perhaps against their will at which worker [and] kolkhoznik meetings they must appear, what kind of speech they must make." The equally captive audiences were to be prepared in advance so that "the workers, the kolkhozniks," would speak up and "ask Krypiakevych, what made him agree to the Germans publishing his works."[172] Scripting the old-intelligentsia roles as well as the worker-kolkhoznik choir's intermissions, Hrushetskyi was, in effect, making the obkom talk to itself in a new season of the old-intelligentsia-scourging-and-redemption reality drama.

Yet not all performers were the same. At a February obkom meeting, Andriy Brahynets, the dean of the university, explained why Mykhailo Vozniak was still a hopeless case. The audience laughed when Brahynets mentioned reports about whether Vozniak was "reconstructing himself or not." Everybody seemed to agree that Vozniak was "too settled in his head." He was independently studying Marxism-Leninism, yet he still failed. Thus, he was not simply denounced as stubborn. He was a local who tried, but a hopeless case.[173]

Iryna Vilde turned out to be unreliable. One of the students accused of involvement in Halan's killing was the son of a Greek Catholic priest. Investigators found out that Vilde had visited his father in 1949 to have her marriage—to a husband with twenty-five years of party membership—sanctified by a secret church wedding. In May 1950, she was brutally attacked at a meeting of the party

171. DALO-P 3, 3, 250: 108–12.
172. DALO P-3, 3, 434: 13.
173. DALO P-3, 1, 251: 71.

organization of the Lviv Writers' Union.[174] The sincerity of old intelligentsia conversion was at stake. Her fellow writer Lozovyi pointed out that "our enemies" now could say that Vilde's writings were due to compulsion, while in her soul she remained pious. Several speakers warned of religion as a cover for nationalism and subversion. They also suspected that Vilde had protected another writer, Olha Duchyminska—a very serious allegation, because Duchimynska had been arrested. Although she denied any involvement in the Halan killing, she was sentenced to twenty-five years in the camps.[175] Vilde called Duchyminska "psychologically not normal."[176] Beliaev warned that the enemy was fighting "not only with bombs but with hypocrisy and flattery." Vilde defended herself by pleading, in effect, that her true lies were for other locals. She had gone through "the parody of a wedding" merely to please her mother. Now, even the most deserving past could become a burden: in post-Halan Lviv, even the fact that Vilde's former husband had been killed by the Germans was turned against her; she was told that she had ideologically joined his killers.[177] There were calls to make an example of her.[178] Yet Vilde survived the campaign, probably because, as a Writers' Union colleague complained, she resorted to "political blackmail."[179] A women's activist who was sent for ten years to the camps later reported that during her interrogations she had to list acquaintances with nationalist views. When she mentioned Vilde, an officer had her name omitted.[180]

Trials of Locals, Tests of Conversion

The three Lukashevych brothers and a further suspect, the worker Tymofei Chmil, confessed to Halan's murder. In 1951, all were sentenced to death. Chmil pleaded that nationalists had misled him. The Lukashevych brothers asked forgiveness not only for killing Halan but also for western Ukraine and its past. Myron stressed the "romantic" attraction of conspiracy for youth; Oleksandr addressed the "causes of the emergence of nationalism in Galicia": Germanization under the Habsburgs, too much clericalism, and too little Marxism. He had finally understood, he claimed, the vacuity of nationalism. His brother Ilarii, the only one who had actually been in Halan's presence during the murder, admitted

174. DALO P-3808, 1, 16: 12–24.

175. Bantyshev and Ukhal, *Ubiistvo na zakaz*, 72. Duchymynska demanded a review of her case several times, until she was finally released in 1968.

176. DALO P-3808, 1, 16: 14–15.

177. TsDAHOU 1, 24, 36: 399–408 (the minutes of the Lviv Writers' Union meeting with Vilde's letter attached).

178. DALO P-3808, 1, 16: 38.

179. DALO P-3808, 1, 16: 37.

180. Marusyk, *Zakhidnoukrainska humanitarna intelihentsia*, 234.

that he had wasted the opportunities granted by Soviet power. Mykhailo Stakhur had struck the lethal blows. He was caught in July 1951; his show trial was held in October in the "overcrowded hall of the Railway Workers' Building of Culture."[181] Nine months earlier, his parents, Mariia and Vasilii, had been sentenced to deportation and the camps. For killing Halan and his involvement in seven other murders, Mykhailo was sentenced to death on 16 October and executed immediately.[182] His trial was only one of a series of show trials against putative Ukrainian nationalists, most of whom were executed.[183]

The trials tested both Stalinist jurisprudence and the locals. Whereas two years earlier local witnesses at similar trials had tried to stay neutral, now the majority of the witnesses—"kolkhozniks, village intelligentsia"—came forward as "furious" denouncers of the OUN "bandits."[184] Although the trials were a controlled staging of Soviet crime and punishment, local responses were still read as reliable indicators of progress.

In Stakhur's case, Maistruk was upbeat about the "largely positive" popular response. He reported no doubts about the sincerity of a seventy-eight-year old writer and "close friend of Ivan Franko" finding hanging too good for the "reptile"; better to throw him to the public, "and we would have torn him to pieces." A library worker, "local, Ukrainian, nonparty," recommended the publication of Prosecutor Rudenko's speech, "a historic document for us, natives of the western oblasts of Ukraine." Letting his famous erudition shine, Mykhailo Rudnytskyi remarked that the Catholic Church had always employed assassins. Generally, Maistruk felt, all went well before an audience of nine hundred, including a majority of Lviv "workers, students, and intelligentsia," with a few kolkhozniks thrown in.[185] Another report, with precise figures on the social composition of the audience showed that, in Lviv, it had been carefully calibrated toward the intelligentsia.[186] Maistruk's choices, too, reflected Lviv's status as an intelligentsia center, with twelve of those quoted in support of Stakhur's punishment from its higher education.[187]

181. See Bantyshev and Ukhal, *Ubiistvo na zakaz*, 47–48, 78; Beliaev and Yolkin, *Yaroslav Halan*, 275; and GDA SBU 13, spr. 372, tom 93: 1–10 for a detailed 1960 secret police report on Stakhur's capture, showing that it was the result of a combination of long-term use of an informant, whose loyalties were ambiguous but sufficient, and the forced resettlement of a hamlet's population, which restricted nationalist provisioning options.

182. Bantyshev and Ukhal, *Ubiistvo na zakaz*, 80, 83–84. For the seven other killings, see GDA SBU 13, spr. 372, tom 93: 8–10.

183. The report on this trial series by a military prosecutor for internal security forces is not quite clear on the number of cases. Although eleven are mentioned at the beginning of the document, a later statement seems to imply there were nine (TsDAHOU 1, 24, 874: 378–81.

184. TsDAHOU 1, 24, 874: 378–81.

185. DALO P-3, 4, 170: 13–14.

186. DALO P-3, 4, 170: 17–20.

187. DALO P-3, 4, 170: 4–12.

Show trials coincided with counterinsurgency victories. In the summer of 1951, Maistruk reported success in "shattering" half of the nationalist organizations active in Lviv oblast in 1949. Clearly referring to the killing of the nationalist leader Roman Shukhevych, Maistruk saw a turning point.[188] Purging and fighting were supplemented by preemption. During admissions in 1950, special teams, sent into all western oblasts to "check on the ground the political face of every high-school graduate," eliminated thirty-six applicants.[189]

Yet despite trials, military success, Komsomol growth, and purges, the Soviet authorities soon had fresh doubts. Soon after the Shtakhur trial, the university party found some students arguing that "bandits" were bandits, but "nationalists" were something else altogether, which was the precise opposite of the Soviet position.[190] A fundamental dilemma came to the fore, since the Komsomol drive entailed a forced conversion. In 1950, the Polytechnic student Marmush was the last of six non-Komsomol students in his group; all others had joined. Marmush was about to do the same, "if they apply pressure." After all, he reasoned, his fellow student Paikut had joined, and he hated Soviet power and the Komsomol. Pressure meant recruiting the unwilling and hostile. Worse, the obkom feared that nationalist infiltrators would join the Komsomol drive, and its officials were especially suspicious of locals who joined in a deliberate and apparently sincere way: sincerity could mask perfidy.[191] In June 1950, the Soviet authorities captured an underground group planning the assassination of Bohdan Dudykevych, the head of the city's freshly opened Lenin Museum. A third-year law student at Lviv University, an active Komsomol member, was accused of leading the group.[192] The more pressure local subjects underwent, the less reliable they were.

The Halan campaign happened at a time when there was an established pattern not only for campaigns but also for their failure.[193] In March 1951, Maistruk warned of a "calming down" mood at the university.[194] At about the same time, obkom reports indicated that almost all recent measures concerning higher education had stalled. Twenty of twenty-nine miskom decrees on higher education had not been implemented.[195] Student groups were still not well mobilized.[196]

188. DALO P-3, 3, 418: 18.

189. DALO P-3, 3, 494: 88.

190. DALO P-92, 1, 190: 328.

191. DALO P-3, 3, 494: 66–69.

192. Oleksandr Ishchuk, *Molodizhni orhanizatsii OUN, 1939–1955 rr.* (Toronto: Litopys UPA, 2011), 113.

193. For an example of turning "into a campaign" as implying failure and routine, see *Vilna Ukraina*, 8 January 1950, 3.

194. DALO P-3, 4, 83: 70–71.

195. DALO P-3, 4, 306: 34–36, 42–43, 48–49.

196. DALO P-92, 1, 489: 27.

Seminars for student group agitators, as required by Central Committee resolutions, were not taking place; seminars for faculty met only infrequently.[197] Meanwhile, Bukhalovskaia, an obkom official, critiqued the purge of faculty, accusing the university of keeping "compromised people" while discharging "young, capable, truly Soviet pedagogues, on the grounds of mendacious, subjective evaluations." She suspected that the university had purged some purgers.[198]

Officials complained that Komsomol recruitment efforts, after a peak between February and March 1950, soon declined. The peak was a clear reflection of the post-Halan campaign, after which momentum was lost: monthly admissions for 1950 had averaged out at nearly 300; in the first nine months of 1951, the corresponding figure was just above 150.[199] Yet overall results were effective.[200] A sudden increase in Komsomol membership among local students at Lviv's university did occur from 1949 to 1951. By 1951, nearly 90 percent of them would be in the Komsomol, and by the late 1950s almost all.[201]

But what was this new, bigger Komsomol? At the beginning of September, the obkom buro castigated it. Nazarenko, investigating, found that his student interlocutors still "tried to start discussing" religion, invoking the national poet Taras Shevchenko's authority.[202] The university Komsomol meeting announcing the huge increase in Komsomol membership called for "vigilance," denouncing unreliable Komsomol members. For instance, in the history department, a Komsomol representative for ideological education from a family accused of underground activity failed to denounce a fellow student who had served in the SS-Galizien Division. The Komsomol representative for political education could not be relied on either; his father, a veteran of Polish forces loyal to the London government, was sending him parcels from Britain.[203]

Ukraine's Komsomol Central Committee reported to Melnikov that "vigilance" was sagging in Lviv. At the university, thirteen "enemies of the people" had been "removed by the organs of state security" in March and April 1952. Ten of them had been Komsomol members "and two even made their way onto the staff of faculty and section Komsomol buros." The deputy secretary of the Polytechnic Komsomol committee had shared an apartment with an "OUN bandit."[204]

The purges continued. Students denounced and "chased away" those accused of nationalism or secretive about relatives. "Komsomol member-natives of the

197. DALO P-92, 1, 489: 30.
198. DALO P-3, 4, 306: 6.
199. DALO P-3, 4, 109: 62 (in part, my calculations).
200. DALO P-3, 4, 109: 61.
201. *Nam partiia sylu dala*, 46.
202. DALO P-3, 4, 109: 8; P-3, 3, 260: 144.
203. DALO P-3545, 9, 365: 131–32.
204. TsDAHOU 1, 24, 1626: 80–81.

western oblasts" helped. Young subjects learned fear. At the university alone, fifty students confessed their relatives' misdeeds.[205] Their party-state confessors also learned something new that they would not unlearn: unlike before the post-Halan campaign, the local remained suspect even when fully mobilized and terrorized.

Doubts continued. Two years before Halan's murder, Hrushetskyi had warned that local students returned to their villages not as Soviet but as nationalist propagandists. Ten years later, in 1957, a party official speaking at an obkom plenum noted that the true allegiance of Komsomol members was still suspect, although 95 percent of Lviv students were members. In the city they did not attend church, but only because "they are afraid." When they arrived at their home "village, then perhaps they do what they should not. About this we do not know."[206] And they never would.

Despite uncertain results, Khrushchev's 1949 appearance became a locus classicus in its own right. At a major 1962 meeting of ideology cadres from Western Ukraine, the Central Committee representative Skaba quoted extensively from Khrushchev's 1949 performance, concluding that "unfortunately, today, too, we must talk about many of the faults," pointed out thirteen years before.[207]

Adaptation and Redemption

Krypiakevych, Vozniak, Rudnytskyi, and Vilde all survived Stalin. In September 1950, a little less than a year after Halan's murder, Melnikov himself signaled that the distrust of the Lviv authorities had gone too far. Vozniak, if not "left in the camp of enemies," could be useful; Krypiakevych also had much Soviet experience and needed help rather than rejection.[208] Even Vilde's clerical wedding could not dampen Melnikov's conciliatory mood. Instead of attacking her, he ridiculed her attackers: "Good God, let her have a wedding, or were you getting jealous [of it?] . . . One person changes very fast, another more slowly. Help is what's needed."[209] He also accused Beliaev, Vilde's fiercest persecutor, of being a self-important panic monger who carried three guns, and a pompous "orthodox" expert "in questions of national policy," who should not be feared at the Writers' Union or receive body guards from Maistruk.[210]

Hrushetskyi also confessed that Lviv's party authorities had been excessively suspicious.[211] By November, he found that Vozniak had started working "honestly";

205. TsDAHOU 1, 24, 1626: 81–85.

206. DALO P-3, 6 (obkom plenum 26 July 1957): 122.

207. DALO P-3, 8, 420: 54–55.

208. TsDAHOU 1, 24, 750: 16–18.

209. TsDAHOU 1, 24, 255: 60. Literally translated, Melnikov said, "God with her" (*Bog s nei*), not "Good God," but the effect was the same, if not even more pronounced.

210. TsDAHOU 1, 24, 255: 61–62.

211. DALO P-3, 3, 433: 114.

not printing his works meant failure to make the intelligentsia participate.[212] By March 1951, Vozniak was a speaker at an intelligentsia meeting to celebrate the reopening of an official branch of the Academy of Science in Lviv. Before an audience with a majority of locals, counted and reported with relentless precision, Vozniak declared that never before had science and culture in Ukraine had such great perspectives; the "unification of the Ukrainian people in a single Ukrainian socialist soviet state" had "annihilated forever" centuries of "social and national oppression." Krypiakevych condemned Hrushevskyi's "'school'" and praised Stalin as well as the "opportunity to revise our former views, condemn our errors, and correct [our] flaws." He promised to justify the "great trust" that the new Academy of Sciences branch symbolized. Rudnytskyi underlined the help Ukrainians received from Russians and condemned Ukrainian nationalists.[213]

From 1951 on, both Vozniak and Krypiakevych were heads of institutes at the new branch. Vozniak died in 1954. By 1975, a monumental Soviet history would quote his 1944 promise to ideologically reconstruct himself as evidence of progress among Western Ukraine's intelligentsia.[214] Krypiakevych died in 1967; from 1953 to 1962 he directed the Institute of Social Sciences. Mykhailo Rudnytskyi died in 1975, but his fortunes began to change in 1950, with the post-Halan campaign still raging. In a letter to the Lviv Writers' Union in that year, Rudnytskyi admitted "the great damage" he had done in the pre-Soviet past but argued that now he had also done much to compensate for it.

Clearly inspired by the anti-cosmopolitan campaign then underway, Rudnytskyi blamed his expulsion on the "cosmopolitan" literary critic Ilia Stebun. Rudnytskyi accused Stebun of spitting on "Ukrainian Soviet literature," while Rudnytskyi had defended it and thus been denounced. Rudnytskyi also emphasized his useful status as a local: "For people dizzy from nationalist propaganda, the word of a local person" knowing both "the circumstances of the war" and "the population" had more "influence than any other."[215]

He was readmitted to the Writers' Union in September 1950, and despite later incidents of persecution his status kept rising.[216] In November 1952, he admitted that the older generation felt challenged to keep up with Soviet transformation but stressed its gratitude for the opportunity to "be reborn" and transformed.[217] By 1955, he was singled out for praise at the Higher Komsomol School at the Moscow

212. *Kulturne zhyttia*, 1:646 (doc. 283).

213. DALO P-3, 4, 193: 125–28.

214. I. Nazarenko et al., eds., *Ukrainskaia SSR v Velikoi Otechestvennoi Voine Sovetskogo Soiuza*, 3 vols. (Kyiv: Izdatelstvo politicheskoi literatury Ukrainy, 1975), 3:258.

215. TsDAMLM 780, 2, 24: 24–25. Perhaps unwittingly, Rudnitskyi's term for the "dizzy" (*zapomorochenyi*) sensation that nationalism could induce was the same word used in the Ukrainian version of Stalin's famous title "Dizzy with Success."

216. For the 1951 criticism, see *Kulturne zhyttia*, 1:659 (doc. 292).

217. DALO P-3, 4, 465: 53.

Komsomol Central Committee. Rudnytskyi's cooperation with Beliaev in publishing works against Ukrainian nationalism was particularly commended in view of the "load" of the past he was bearing.[218] The past, although a burden, was now also a currency.

After Stalin's death, the attacks were clearly limited. Although the rhetoric could be similar, stakes and outcomes were different. To push Rudnytskyi out of his position as dean of the philology faculty, for instance, colleagues denounced his unwillingness to understand the necessity of political education at universities. Yet however severe this reproach in principle, it led only to Rudnytskyi making room for another dean while keeping the chair of English literature, a far cry from the sanctions at stake earlier.[219]

Despite harassment in 1951, Vilde's Soviet career proved equally robust. In 1952, she declared that more than a decade had passed since the "sun of freedom" had risen in 1939. Back then, she admitted, locals had needed special mentoring, not yet "politically steady on [their] legs." Now, however, the locals had "grown up": "[We], so to speak already old Soviet citizens, had to start talking about duties before the party, the people, and the Soviet state." Especially "our intelligentsia" was "in great debt before the party."[220] She had come full circle since her 1946 *Lvovskaia pravda* article, when she had decried the old intelligentsia's unwillingness to change; now she found that all locals had changed. What remained the same was her emphasis on the need for loyalty to the Soviet system: "Today, the measure of patriotism can only be the answer to the question . . . what have we all together done for the building of Communism."[221]

She succeeded Petro Kozlaniuk as head of the Lviv Writers' Union and was made a deputy of Lviv's oblast rada as well as Ukraine's Supreme Soviet. In later Soviet publications she was depicted in stereotypically laudatory fashion: she was a good citizen, her work a "shining page of Ukrainian Soviet literature."[222]

The post-Halan campaign was the last major Stalinist intelligentsia campaign specific to Lviv and western Ukraine. Its uneven outcomes did not challenge Soviet power, but it was also the last major Soviet attempt to make the local vanish, and in this sense it failed. Once the Stalinist party-state decided to break local reticence, it did, but ambiguity was not replaced by certainty. Transformation was achieved, but it was interlaced with fear, opportunism, and distrust. Locals changed, but what they changed into was a new iteration of the local.

218. TsDAMLM 780, 2, 23: 50.
219. DALO P-3, 6, 110: 15–16.
220. DALO P-3, 4, 465: 25.
221. DALO P-3, 4, 465: 26.
222. *Kulturne zhyttia*, 3:50 (doc. 7).

CHAPTER SEVEN

Lviv's Last Synagogue, 1944–1962

Before the Holocaust, Lviv had been an important center of Jewish life. The virtually complete destruction of its prewar Jewish population brought this part of the city's history to a terrible end. Moreover, Soviet postwar memory had little room for Lviv's Jewish past. There was, however, one institution that bridged the prewar and postwar periods: Lviv's only surviving synagogue. Reopened after the war, this synagogue, built in the 1840s and then known as the Jakob Glasner Shul, was close to the city center as well as the old Jewish cemetery, which had been razed by the Germans. Its postwar history was marked by frequent and complex conflicts with the party-state that culminated in the early 1960s, when it was shut down. This chapter focuses on the two most significant conflicts, in 1949–1950 and 1961–1962. Together they delineated the relationship between the party-state and the last officially recognized and public institution that constituted if not a link with then a reminder of Lviv's prewar Jewish history. The postwar fate of Lviv's synagogue was shaped by general Soviet policies toward religion and Jewish national identity. Its fate was decisively influenced by factors that had little to do with its reality. Instead it was made to function as a symbol of traditional and specifically Soviet stereotypes, and it served as a scapegoat for the inequality, corruption, and industrialization problems of Soviet Lviv.

Generally, in the postwar Soviet Union, two main factors shaped the relationship between the Soviet authorities and the synagogue. As a place of worship, it was a target of antireligious policies and the only public site where one could evade, subvert, or resist those policies. As a site of Jewish community life, the synagogue became a crossroads of Soviet policy and Jewish identity.[1] Historically, challenges

1. Shneer, *Yiddish and the Creation of Soviet Jewish Culture*, 10; Frank Grüner, "Jüdischer Glaube und religiöse Praxis unter dem Stalinistischen Regime in der Sowjetunion während der Kriegs- und Nachkriegsjahre," *Jahrbücher für Geschichte Osteuropas* 52 (2004): 534; Katrin Boeckh, "Jüdisches Leben in der Ukraine nach dem Zweiten Weltkrieg. Zur Verfolgung einer Religionsgemeinschaft im Spätstalinismus (1945–1953)," *Vierteljahrshefte für Zeitgeschichte*, no. 3 (2005): 421–24; Yaacov Ro'i, "The Role of the Synagogue and Religion in the Jewish National Awakening," in *Jewish Culture and Identity in the Soviet Union*, ed. Ro'i and Avi Beker (New York: New York University Press, 1991), 112.

from Jewish socialists had influenced Lenin's and Stalin's thinking about the nation and about Jews.[2] Both Bolshevik founding figures rejected Bundist concepts of how to reconcile socialism and the nation. Stalin concluded that Jews must assimilate, and Lenin felt that any "Jewish 'national culture'" was hostile to the interests of the proletariat, leaving vague room for Jewish Marxist contributions to an international working-class culture.[3] Attempts to foster a secular and socialist Yiddish-language Jewish Soviet culture mostly ended in the 1930s, while modernization and urbanization encouraged assimilation into Russian culture.[4]

The Holocaust reduced the number of registered Jewish religious communities in Soviet Ukraine from 657 to virtually none.[5] Immediately after the war, however, among the survivors, the social assistance and network role of the synagogues persisted, and Jewish self-identification increased.[6] Synagogues were crowded on major Jewish holidays and for special services for the victims of the Holocaust.[7] Later, as Zvi Gitelman has found, Jewish Soviet war veterans remembered fighting not "as Jews but as Soviet citizens." Yet the Holocaust amplified their sense of Jewish identity.[8]

The later 1940s brought the closing of the last Jewish cultural institutions during the strongly antisemitic anti-cosmopolitan campaign.[9] By 1952, there were only thirty-nine registered communities; by 1964, only fifty to sixty synagogues were left in the whole Soviet Union, about half of them in the Caucasus and Central Asia, then home to only about 10 percent of Soviet Jews.[10] Although the Holocaust was clearly the main cause of disappearing Jewish religious communities, Soviet policy also contributed to it, by shutting synagogues and allowing few new

2. Shneer, *Yiddish and the Creation of Soviet Jewish Culture*, 16.

3. Ibid., 17.

4. Ibid., 18, 219.

5. Boeckh, "Jüdisches Leben in der Ukraine," 429. According to Katrin Boeckh, there were 5.1 million Jews inside Soviet borders as of June 1941, of whom 2.8 million were killed through the combined effects of the Holocaust, military casualties, and civilian casualties that were not part of the German genocide campaign against Jews (ibid., 425). These figures do not include Jewish victims who were outside Soviet borders in June 1941.

6. Grüner, "Jüdischer Glaube und religiöse Praxis," 535. Katrin Boeckh has observed that by the end of the 1930s, "the Jewish population of Soviet Ukraine, in its majority, was assimilated and acculturated" ("Jüdisches Leben in der Ukraine," 424).

7. On the Soviet authorities' temporary and geographically uneven encouragement of such memorial services, see Mordechai Altshuler, "Jewish Holocaust Commemoration Activity in the USSR under Stalin," *Yad Vashem Studies* 30 (2002), 277–79.

8. Zvi Gitelman, "Internationalism, Patriotism, and Disillusion: Soviet Jewish Veterans Remember World War II and the Holocaust," in *The Holocaust in the Soviet Union: Symposium Presentations*, ed. Center for Advanced Holocaust Studies (Washington, DC: Center for Advanced Holocaust Studies, United States Holocaust Memorial Museum, 2005), 97, 110–13.

9. Ro'i, "Role of the Synagogue," 112.

10. Ibid., 131.

registrations.[11] The founding of Israel in 1948 intensified Soviet distrust of Jews, now regarded as potentially loyal to another state.[12]

In postwar Lviv, there were two public representatives of Soviet antireligious policy. The plenipotentiary for matters of the Russian Orthodox Church monitored the Russian Orthodox Church and the underground Greek Catholic Church. All other denominations were supervised by the plenipotentiary for matters of religious cults, Petro Kucheriavyi, who oversaw Jehovah's Witnesses, Jews, Muslims, Protestants—a category including different groups—and Roman Catholics.[13] Both plenipotentiaries were representatives of central government offices under the Council of People's Commissars, later Ministers, in Moscow.

The Council for Matters of the Russian Orthodox Church and the Council for Matters of Religious Cults were created during the war to control religion and maintain contact with its representatives. The party-state saw what may appear as concessions to religion as a sign of its submission. As an early Religious Cult Council document insisted, the establishment of the councils did *not* signal a major change in Soviet policy.[14] Wartime favors, moreover, were distributed unevenly, and Judaism received comparatively little.[15]

The first head of the Council for Matters of the Russian Orthodox Church, Georgii Karpov, was also a colonel and a secret police department head on religious affairs. The Council for Matters of Religious Cults, too, was under the control of secret police colonels—first K. Zaitsev, then Ivan Polianskii. In Ukraine, the republic plenipotentiaries, Khodchenko and Petro Vilkhovyi, were both writers and, according to a 1945 secret police report, not "our employees" and suffering "from deficiencies." In 1945, Vilkhovyi was criticized for allowing several synagogues to open without coordinating with either the secret police or his superiors.[16] During the suppression of the Greek Catholic Church, Vilkhovyi and Khodchenko therefore needed special secret police "direction," provided by the operative Karin, working under cover as Danilenko and publicly pretending to speak for the Ukrainian Council for Matters of Religious Cults.[17]

11. Boeckh, "Jüdisches Leben in der Ukraine," 430.

12. Ro'i, "Role of the Synagogue," 114.

13. Kucheriavyi, born in 1902, was officially identified as Ukrainian. He had some form of higher education and had joined the party in 1927, while working at a mine in the Donbas (DALO P-3, 4, 439: 9; P-4455, 1, 23: 61).

14. Cited in Yaacov Ro'i, *Islam in the Soviet Union: From the Second World War to Gorbachev* (New York: Columbia University Press, 2000), 14–15.

15. Grüner, "Jüdischer Glaube und religiöse Praxis," 540.

16. Bohunov et al., *Likvidatsiia UHKTs*, 2:46–47 (doc. 167).

17. Ibid., 2:41–46; Bociurkiw, *Ukrainian Greek Catholic Church*, 67–69; Marusyk, *Zakhidnoukrainska humanitarna intelihentsia*, 301. On links to the secret police in general, see also Ro'i, *Islam in the Soviet Union*, 16–17.

Officially, the plenipotentiaries were to make believers obey Soviet laws on religious practice and to suppress unregistered, in the Soviet view illegal, religious communities. There were some gray areas. The head of the Religious Cult Council in Moscow, Polianskii, saw advantages in sometimes tolerating unregistered communities because they were especially vulnerable.[18] Yet for the most part Lviv's plenipotentiaries were deeply involved in harassing believers and clergy. In 1948, Vilkhovyi explained how to drive unofficial communities, especially of Jews and Jehovah's Witnesses, into "self-liquidation" through punitive taxes. Vilkhovyi believed that the few who would not obey the "moral power of Soviet law" would be driven underground, to be "utterly miserable and the object of the special organs' attention."[19]

Lviv's Postwar Jewish Community

In early 1946, a little more than six thousand Polish Jews returned to Lviv from the eastern territories of the Soviet Union. About five thousand had attended the one synagogue that reopened after the war. Most of the original members of this first postwar Jewish community left Lviv for Poland before the end of 1946, frightened by blood libel rumors and a near-pogrom in Lviv in June 1945.[20] A new Jewish population arrived from the eastern oblasts, and by 1949 Kucheriavyi estimated that 95 percent of all Jews in Lviv were easterners. Only a hundred to four hundred regularly attended the synagogue, but on religious holidays up to twenty-five hundred showed up. This post-1946 Jewish population lived preponderantly in the city of Lviv, not its rural surroundings, partly out of fear of Ukrainian nationalist attacks.[21]

The community requested additional premises for synagogues, which Kucheriavyi initially supported but then refused.[22] He reported that the official community kept engaging in activities that he tried to suppress.[23] In early 1946, the community's office was "visited daily by up to one hundred Jews," some to "give money for poor Jews," and others looking "for lost members of their families" or seeking aid. The synagogue served as a shelter for hundreds leaving for Poland.[24]

18. Ro'i, *Islam in the Soviet Union*, 29–30.

19. DALO R-1332, 2, 9: 18–19.

20. Iakub Khonigsman, *Liudi, gody, sobytiia: stati iz nashei davnei i nedavnei istorii* (Lvov: Lvovskoe obshchestvo evreiskoi kultury im. Sholom Aleikhema, 1998), 109–12; DALO R-1332, 2, 2: 8.

21. DALO R-1332, 2, 15: 26, 63, 82, 116.

22. DALO R-1332, 2, 9: 126–27; R-1332, 2, 2: 3.

23. DALO R-1332, 2, 13: 29; R-1332, 2, 6: 27.

24. DALO R-1332, 2, 6: 95; Mikhail Mitsel, *Obshchiny iudeiskoho veroispovidannia v Ukraine: Kiev, Lvov: 1945–1981 gg.* (Kyiv: Sfera, 1998), 162, 166.

Kucheriavyi complained of "dirt everywhere," and warned that "there must be no strangers."[25] During this period, Kurt Lewin remembered that some Soviet soldiers tried to help Jewish survivors but that the Soviet authorities were "indifferent."[26]

Kucheriavyi combined traditional prejudice with specifically Soviet resentment. In 1946, Aleksandr Shtakelberg, a member of the synagogue council, had demanded payment and quit when it was denied. Kucheriavyi added that the head of the *trest* where Shtakelberg had worked called him a "son of a bitch" who had "run away somewhere." Kucheriavyi also generalized that "the Judaic community" had several leading members "interested only in material advantage." Stressing that Shtakelberg was a party member and war veteran, he implied that even a Jew with party and veteran credentials could not be trusted.[27]

Soviet reports also accused the first post-reconquest head of the synagogue community, Sobol, of "Jewish nationalism" and spying for the United States.[28] After Sobol left for Poland, Kucheriavyi reported that he and Lev Serebrianyi, Sobol's successor, agreed to reject all requests for permission to stage Jewish cultural events, especially at the synagogue, and to prevent Jewish artists from earning money for the community.[29] The "Judaic religious community," Kucheriavyi wrote, "must be firmly restricted within the bounds of a religious cult."[30] From a Soviet perspective, Serebrianyi appeared more cooperative than Sobol, but some Soviet reports characterized him as an "active Zionist."[31] In the spring of 1947, he was arrested and accused of links with foreign intelligence, to be rehabilitated only in 1956.[32]

Before his arrest, Serebrianyi challenged Soviet restrictions by publicly stressing mutual aid, a "cult of good works," and international support. He did not shy away from talking publicly about the Holocaust. By 1947, according to Kucheriavyi, the community had received twelve thousand inquiries from abroad about missing relatives. It had sent Victory Day parcels to all veteran officers, Jews and non-Jews, and organized help for Jewish war veterans in general as well as non-Jews who had saved Jews. Serebrianyi had unsuccessfully tried to publish a collection of Holocaust survivors' testimonies and argued for a memorial to Jews

25. DALO R-1332, 2, 6: 95.
26. Lewin, *Przeżyłem*, 172–73.
27. DALO R-1332, 2, 6: 95.
28. Viktor Voinalovych, *Partiino-derzhavna polityka shchodo relihii ta relihiinykh instytutsii v Ukraini 1940–1960-kh rokiv: Politolohichnyi dyskurs* (Kyiv: NAN Ukrainy, 2005), 580.
29. DALO R-1332, 2, 6: 48–50.
30. DALO R-1332, 2, 6: 84.
31. Voinalovych, *Partiino-derzhavna polityka*, 580.
32. Mitsel, *Obshchiny iudeiskoho veroispovidannia*, 149.

murdered by the Germans.[33] As Amir Weiner has pointed out, the postwar party-state decried such efforts to commemorate Jewish losses as a "pretext for stirring up separatist nationalist sentiments." Shortly after Serebrianyi's arrest, Kucheriavyi reported that synagogue attendance was falling. The new community head, Yakov Makhnovetskyi, was no longer raising funds for social purposes; parcels from abroad had ceased to arrive, and most letters were handed over to the authorities. The community was still requesting assistance for a number of needs, including a ritual bath, a second synagogue, and the protection of the remains of the old Jewish cemetery, devastated by the Germans and now being turned into a market. But these requests were denied.[34] Warning of "harmful talk" and problems with sanitation, Kucheriavyi supported only the community's complaint against using part of the cemetery area as a public convenience and leaving disinterred human remains.[35]

Yom Kippur, 1949

This repressive calm did not last, however. The founding of Israel in 1948 led to a celebration at the Lviv synagogue, attended by many young people, which stirred Soviet paranoia and repressive reflexes.[36] Vilkhovyi singled out the activities at Lviv's synagogue as especially dangerous and denounced a service in Chernivtsi as a nationalist meeting for which Lviv's community had set the tone.[37]

The year 1949 was marked by the escalating anti-cosmopolitan campaign, for which, in Soviet Ukraine, a *Radianska Ukraina* article in the fall of 1948 served as a public starting signal. At the beginning of 1949, fiercely antisemitic speeches were delivered at the Sixteenth Congress of the Ukrainian Communists—by Dmytro Manuilskyi among others—and in the spring the republic branch of the Writers' Union called for a "final smashing of kinless cosmopolitanism." In Lviv, 1949 brought two major antisemitic persecutions. A group of ten or eleven high school students were sentenced to long terms for alleged Jewish nationalism.[38] At

33. Mitsel, *Obshchiny iudeiskoho veroispovidannia*, 164–65, 168; I. B. Krayzman, "Poslevoennye repressii lvovskoi iudeiskoi obshchiny," in *Materialy konferentsii (Kiev, 8–9 dekabria 1994 g.): Evreiska istoriia i kultura v Ukraine*, ed. Assotsiatsiia iudaiki Ukrainy, http://www.jewish-heritage.org/eu94a26r.htm, 2; Altshuler, "Jewish Holocaust Commemoration Activity," 274, 283.

34. DALO P-3, 2, 256: 33–34; Weiner, *Memory*, 182.

35. DALO R-1332, 2, 9: 55.

36. Yaacov Ro'i, *The Struggle for Soviet Jewish Emigration, 1948–1967* (Cambridge: Cambridge University Press, 1991), 26.

37. Boeckh, "Jüdisches Leben in der Ukraine," 432; TsDAHOU 1, 23, 5667: 62–64, repr. in Mikhail Mitsel, *Evrei Ukrainy v 1943–1953 gg.: Ocherki dokumentirovannoi istorii* (Kyiv: Dukh i litera, 2004), 231.

38. Ro'i, *Struggle for Soviet Jewish Emigration*, 46.

Lviv University, an international law jurist and law department party buro head was purged under the same accusation, along with several Jewish students.[39] Kucheriavy reported that Lviv synagogues in Kharkiv, Odesa, and Chernivtsi "had been closed for breaking the law" and emphasized its own compliance with Soviet regulations to avoid a similar outcome.[40]

Against this background, a sharp conflict between Kucheriavyi and the Lviv synagogue began on Yom Kippur in 1949. It was not publicized, but it provoked interventions from the authorities in both Kyiv and Moscow. According to Kucheriavyi, on 3 October 1949, the eve of Yom Kippur, the synagogue was so crowded that worshippers gathered outside it. He estimated the crowd to be about fifteen hundred "people of the Jewish population," "more than half" in breach of "labor discipline."[41] When a peasant was in danger of being beaten up by this crowd, Kucheriavyi tried to protect him, but the crowd spat at him, and "one Shlepak, Boris Khaimovych," later identified as a Soviet police officer, threatened to shoot him, saying, "You have only come to protect the Ukrainian." In a report to Khrushchev in Kyiv and Polianskii in Moscow, Vilkhovyi and Kucheriavyi accused Shlepak of having led a "crowd of fanatical Jewish believers." After the incident, Kucheriavyi disbanded the synagogue council and closed the synagogue until further notice.[42] He began a campaign to replace the synagogue in the center with a smaller one in Lviv's outskirts, admittedly not big enough for the city's Jews, which "would be just right, too."[43]

In the end, he failed to move the synagogue, and by early 1950 it was reopened in central Lviv. But during this time Kucheriavyi escalated his denunciations, interlaced with traditional antisemitic stereotypes. The first Soviet occupation had already brought extensive press campaigns against "speculation."[44] Local stereotypes and traditional prejudice could converge with Soviet self-presentations, even where there was little common ground on any other issues. Thus, Metropolitan Sheptytskyi, who later rescued some Jews during the Holocaust, blamed speculation not on the Soviets, whom he abhorred as godless Communists and enemies of Ukraine, but on Jews, who had "invaded economic life in prodigious numbers" with "sordid avarice."[45] Subsequent German antisemitism also exploited and reinforced stereotypes of Jews as illicit and unfair traders.

39. DALO 92, 1, 78: 43.
40. DALO R-1332, 2, 15: 75–76 (my emphasis).
41. DALO R-1332, 2, 15: 115.
42. DALO R-1332, 2, 15: 79–87; Mitsel, *Obshchiny iudeiskoho veroispovidannia*, 193.
43. DALO R-1332, 2, 15: 142; R-1332, 2, 13: 70.
44. Levin, *Lesser of Two Evils*, 272.
45. Cited in Shimon Redlich, "Metropolitan Sheptyts'kyi and Ukrainian-Jewish Relations," in *Bitter Legacy: Confronting the Holocaust in the USSR*, ed. Zvi Gitelman (Bloomington: Indiana University Press, 1997), 66.

In Kucheriavyi's terminology, the Soviet term "speculation," the suppressed but pervasive private exchange of goods and services, served also to refer to Jews: Jews were "speculators," and "speculators" were Jews. Against the backdrop of the anti-cosmopolitan campaign, Kucheriavyi's picture of Lviv's synagogue combined the economic and the political, the criminal and the national. He decried the infringement of labor discipline to attend Yom Kippur and the "nationalism" of believers. In his view, the synagogue's location "in the center of town, on the Krakyvskyi Market" was leading to "a concentration of . . . speculators and merchants," gathering to make deals. Only moving it would stop this "detrimental concentration of elements of Jewish nationality."[46]

Kucheriavyi explicitly denounced "the preponderant majority of those attending synagogue" as "out-and-out nationalists and cosmopolitans," with the synagogue the site of nationalism and illicit commerce.[47] Less than ten years after the peak of the Holocaust in Lviv, Kucheriavyi argued for purging Lviv's center of the Black Market by relegating its synagogue to the margins. This rhetoric was not a call to mass murder, and the difference was crucial. Yet it would be ahistorical not to see Kucheriavyi's campaign in its real context, deeply shaped by the mass murder that had taken place so recently: ideological difference, even fundamental difference, did not exclude interaction, even where neither intended nor recognized.[48] Vilkhovyi, too, denounced Lviv's synagogue to Khrushchev as a "nationalist . . . profit enterprise for all kinds of crooks from nonreligious elements." In his version of the Yom Kippur incident, Shlepak had threatened to "shoot [Kucheriavyi] like a dog," and the Jewish crowd had shouted that Kucheriavyi should be beaten. Vilkhovyi demanded a "revolutionary tribunal for Shlepak."[49] He also denounced the "nationalist tendencies" of "some circles of Jewish society" for monopolizing mass graves as places where "only Jews were killed by the Germans."[50] For both, Kucheriavyi and Vilkhovyi, when it came to disobedience to a Soviet official, individual and collective responsibility merged seamlessly. Collective mourning was viewed as offensive as a form of national egotism.

To close down a registered religious community, local authorities had to obtain permission from the Council for Matters of Religious Cults in Moscow.[51] But

46. DALO R-1332, 2, 15: 116.

47. DALO R-1332, 2, 13: 69–70.

48. Kucheriavyi's attacks on trade in the synagogue also echoed a classical element of the Christian tradition.

49. TsDAHOU 1, 23, 5667: 326–31.

50. TsDAHOU 1, 24, 12: 86, 146. On the making of the Soviet imposition of "hierarchical heroism" combined with "universal suffering" on the memory of the Second World War/Great Fatherland War, see Amir Weiner, "When Memory Counts: War, Genocide, and Postwar Soviet Jewry," in his *Landscaping the Human Garden: Twentieth-Century Population Management in a Comparative Framework* (Stanford, CA: Stanford University Press, 2003), 177–82.

51. Ro'i, *Islam in the Soviet Union*, 22.

Polianskii was wary of his subordinates. Calling the Yom Kippur incident "unprecedented" and in need of a "thorough investigation," he criticized Kucheriavyi and Vilkhovyi for the scanty information they had provided. He found that "the behavior of the unnamed peasant" had remained "completely unexplained." In particular, he did not exclude the possibility that the peasant had "behaved provocatively." He sounded skeptical that the crowd was so electrified by nationalist elements that it "tried to beat up a man guilty of nothing only because he belonged to another nationality." Polianskii rejected the "demand to put Shlepak before a revolutionary tribunal" and criticized the course of action Kucheriavyi had already taken in Lviv. Only further information, Polianskii argued, could show if the incident was the fault of a few individuals or if the whole community was "infected with nationalist anti-Soviet attitudes," which he found "entirely unlikely." Although Polianskii let the decisions made by Kucheriavyi and Vilkhovyi stand, he also warned them that all further measures would have to be cleared first with Moscow.[52]

Polianskii's reticence was atypical. The Council on Matters of Religious Cults only rarely protected religious communities from local authorities, instead usually shutting them down, with 1,237 religious communities deregistered between 1948 and 1954 alone. But appearances were also taken into account: in December 1949, Polianskii warned against deregistration en masse, in campaign-style, as he put it.[53]

In Lviv's case, Polianskyi's reticence prevailed. By 1951, Kucheriavyi had accepted that the synagogue would remain in Lviv's center. Yet he was also satisfied with Soviet repression, following the "attack on me." The "most glaring speculators" had been arrested and "nationalist elements" stopped. Khrushchev, moreover, helped Kucheriavyi go after Shlepak. Polianskii may have mocked calls for a revolutionary tribunal, but in 1951, a military tribunal sentenced Shlepak to six years.[54] By comparison with Passover in 1950, synagogue attendance was down

52. DALO R-1332, 2, 15: 143.

53. Ro'i, *Islam in the Soviet Union*, 24, 34–35.

54. According to a report of early 1950, Shlepak's case was already under investigation by the Special Inspection Department of the Ministry of State Security, Kucheriavyi was right, and Shlepak had been absent without leave when clashing with Kucheriavyi (TsDAHOU 1, 23, 5667: 345–46; DALO R-1332, 2, 19: 70–72). There happens to be good evidence to assess the importance of "me" in Kucheriavyi's drive for retaliation. Shortly after the Yom Kippur incident, on 12 November 1949, Kucheriavyi, in his capacity as the head of the party buro of the oblast executive committee (not to be confused with either the oblast party committee or the oblast executive committee itself) presided over a case in which the victim had been mistreated similarly, if worse, than Kucheriavyi by Shlepak: a party member and oblast executive committee administration-management head had beaten his landlady with a pistol and kicked her when she prevented him from shooting her husband during an argument over living space. Kucheriavyi severely reprimanded the offender, telling him that he should lose his party card. Yet considering he was a "young Communist," he could keep it (DALO P-4455, 1, 17: 11–12; P-4455, 1, 23: 5).

by a third. In sum, in the first quarter of 1951, there were "no nationalist phenomena" in the synagogue.[55]

Intimidation was not persistently effective. Even before the death of Stalin in 1953, both attendance on the high holy days and voluntary financial contributions increased, with about a thousand to eleven hundred believers attending Yom Kippur in 1952 and twenty-three hundred to twenty-five hundred in 1955. While partly explaining these trends by increasing numbers of Jews in Lviv, Makhnovetskyi, the head of the community, considered diminished fear more important.[56] Even worse, from the plenipotentiary's perspective, was the widening rift in the community by 1956–1957: the "opposition," labeled Hasidic by the authorities, almost succeeded in taking over the community leadership. Kucheriavyi's successor, Dryl, reported that most of the synagogue community was in open rebellion. During this time, the authorities observed increased activity in Ukraine across all religions. A meeting of plenipotentiaries in Kyiv in April 1957 blamed the "propaganda of religious activists" and "fanatics," but also democratization and the "strengthening of legality," by which they meant Khrushchev's Thaw.[57]

In Lviv, the synagogue community temporarily slipped away from guided voting and elected a new leadership without Dryl's vetting. The opposition denounced what it saw as Makhnovetskyi's financial irregularities, links to the secret police, and dictatorial tendencies, while Makhnovetskyi reported "infringement of Soviet laws," and accused his opponents of "seizing power" to "drag the synagogue into the Middle Ages." Dryl refused to register the new council, keeping Makhnovetskyi in place *faute de mieux*.[58]

Khrushchev's Thaw also increased Soviet sensitivity to international reactions. By 1957, Dryl asked for one bakery to produce matzos since a complete prohibition might provoke believers and make "nationalist elements" launch international protests against the "oppression of the Judaic religion." Foreign visitors to Lviv, he underlined, showed a special interest in the position of the city's Jews.[59]

By 1958, Dryl reported that the opposition had "apparently fallen apart." But the community was more, not less, active. Attendance at Sabbath services increased from 100 in 1953 to 186 in 1957, while attendance on holy days doubled in the same period.[60] On Yom Kippur the numbers went from thirty-eight hundred

55. DALO R-1332, 2, 19: 70–72.

56. DALO P-3, 5, 249: 195.

57. DALO R-1332, 2, 25: 96–97. Kucherivayi lost his position and party membership in 1952, when the obkom held him responsible for causing a riot in Lviv over the seizing of church bells (DALO P-3, 4, 439: 9–11).

58. DALO R-1332, 2, 25: 76.

59. DALO R-1332, 2, 25: 63.

60. DALO R-1332, 2, 26: 7, 82.

in 1957 to forty-three hundred in 1959. In 1957, the synagogue collected 80,000 rubles in donations; in 1959, 115,000. Only the number of burials fell slightly. In 1959, the synagogue completed a women's section and a ritual bath. In October, an Israeli embassy official and his wife visited. Dryl suspected them of distributing "nationalist Zionist literature" and believed that Israeli representatives were "enlivening the . . . religious community" and encouraging "a certain part of believers" to attend.[61] On Yom Kippur in 1960, according to Yaacov Ro'i, "the street outside the Lviv synagogue was packed."[62] With or without an organized opposition, during the 1950s, the synagogue was expanding and under increased suspicion.

Yet a 1960 Kyiv Central Committee report showed official satisfaction with the situation in Ukraine, noting that the number of communities of "Judaic believers" had been reduced from thirty-seven to twenty-three, mostly managed "smoothly." There were fewer visits by Israeli diplomats; tourists were still denounced for going to the synagogue to talk politics, but community leaders had been told how to deal with them. The report counted eighteen unofficial Jewish religious communities, with a total of one hundred for all denominations. Protestants and Catholics received more attention.[63]

Closing Lviv's Last Synagogue

At the beginning of the 1960s, the Lviv community was active and dynamic, while the party-state was suspicious yet generally self-satisfied. By the end of 1962, however, the Lviv synagogue had been closed. What had not happened under Stalin, despite Kucheriavyi's best efforts, did happen under Khrushchev.

Clearly, there were continuities from the antisemitic antispeculation campaign of late Stalinism to Khrushchev's attacks on speculation and the second economy.[64] In Lviv, the theme of speculation was central in both postwar attacks on the synagogue. Kucheriavyi had fused it with nationalism, and that theme persisted. In 1952, the obkom buro attacked the managers of a plant for "Jewish bourgeois nationalism" in their hiring practices, which was turning the factory into a "Jewish synagogue," provoking "anti-Soviet activity" that might even lead to strikes.[65] The obkom also noticed that workers, female and local, were exploited

61. DALO P-3, 8, 120: 81–85.

62. Ro'i, *Struggle for Soviet Jewish Emigration*, 317.

63. TsDAHOU 1, 24, 5297: 84–87.

64. Benjamin Pinkus, *The Soviet Government and the Jews 1948–1967: A Documented Study* (Cambridge: Cambridge University Press, 1984), 201–7; Sheila Fitzpatrick, *Tear off the Masks! Identity and Imposture in Twentieth-Century Russia* (Princeton, NJ: Princeton University Press, 2005), 298.

65. DALO P-3, 4, 451: 8–9.

by twelve-hour shifts and "suppression of criticism."[66] Here, scapegoating Jews disguised some of the cost of Soviet catch-up industrialization as well as the tensions between locals and easterners. Yet the permanent closing of the synagogue in Lviv requires a more sophisticated interpretation than reference to continuity, be it general or locally specific: why in 1962, if not in 1949?

Context provides part of the answer to this question. The 1962 attack on Judaism in Lviv was also part of a larger antireligious campaign, which originated with Khrushchev. In Lviv oblast, which had 1,169 sites of religious worship (of all denominations), 109 were deregistered and 281 "stopped working" between the beginning of 1961 and March 1962.[67] Between 1959 and 1963, 309 Orthodox and 7 Roman Catholic places of worship and 6 communities of evangelical Christians had been suppressed.[68] Part of this larger campaign consisted of 1961 legislation empowering local authorities to shut down religious institutions without appeal to the center.[69]

Where Jews were concerned, this antireligious campaign coincided with official support for antisemitic stereotypes. Trokhym Kychko's 1963 *Judaism without Embellishment* was a loud signal, seeking to show Zionism's roots in Judaism and vilify both.[70] Especially significant for western Ukraine was the publication in *Literaturna Ukraina* of a poem by the canonized "progressive" pre-Soviet writer Ivan Franko, pillorying Jewish innkeepers for exploiting Ukrainian peasants. Contemporary relevance was underlined by juxtaposition: the poem was printed together with a piece depicting contemporary Jews in Kyiv as criminals and black marketeers.[71]

According to a November 1962 report, "the Jewish religious network" had been reduced from forty-four communities in 1959 to fifteen in 1962, with only thirteen synagogues.[72] Campaigns against synagogues, resembling the one staged in Lviv, were conducted in several major Soviet cities, including Chernivtsi, Minsk, and Smolensk.[73] Yet Lviv played a special role among assaults on Jewish

66. DALO P-3, 4, 451: 8–23.

67. Mitsel, *Obshchiny iudeiskoho veroispovidannia*, 214–18.

68. RGANI 5, 31, 237: 42.

69. Vladislav Zubok, *Zhivago's Children: The Last Russian Intelligentsia* (Cambridge, MA: Harvard University Press, 2009), 128.

70. On Kychko, see Weiner, "When Memory Counts," 171–72; Lewytzkyj, *Politics and Society*, 42–43; and F. Ia. Gorovskii et al., *Evrei Ukrainy: Kratkii ocherk istorii* (Kyiv: Ukrainsko-finskii instytut menedzhmenta i biznesa, 1995), pt. 2, 196–97. In Lewytzkyj's summary, Kychko's main messages, in addition to the quasi-identity of Judaism and Zionism and the accusation of working for American imperialism, were that Jews were engaging in the crimes of underground religious activity, illegal assembly, and illicit economic activities (Lewytzkyj, *Politics and Society*, 42.)

71. Lewytzkyj, *Politics and Society*, 70.

72. TsDAHOU 1, 24, 5488: 231–34.

73. Nora Levin, *The Jews in the Soviet Union since 1917: Paradox of Survival* (New York: New York University Press, 1988), 624–25.

communities. The Kyiv Central Committee praised the Lviv authorities as exemplary for closing down the city's synagogue and for exposing the synagogue as "a meeting place of out-of-town speculators and currency speculators." Publicizing these allegations in the local media, they had split the community, with believers "falling away" until it "finally ceased to exist." They had demoralized its leadership through the "deft use of compromising materials" for "active atheist work among believing Jews," forestalling any protests. They had delivered a "powerful blow" not only against the "position of Judaism among the Jewish population of the western oblasts," but also against "the intelligence service of Israel." The report recommended that Lviv's lessons should be applied to the Jewish communities of Odesa and Kyiv, the most important synagogues remaining in Ukraine.[74]

There was an unspoken implication to the 1962 attack on the Lviv synagogue: it diverted local discontent, as the obkom's internal documentation shows. In Lviv, as elsewhere in the Soviet Union, the early 1960s were marked by a crisis of scarcity, with lines even for basic foodstuffs, including bread.[75] Moreover, in 1962 the party-state worried about an increase in "mass hooligan phenomena," crime, and unrest. There were fears of "anti-Soviet elements" exploiting disaffection over housing, food, and salary issues.

At the same time, the economy underwent large-scale reform. New production associations or complexes were introduced, with some decentralization and more local responsibility. The first Ukrainian enterprise representing this new approach was opened in Lviv in 1961. By the end of 1962, there were twenty-six of them. Yet official attacks on too much localism in the economy also signaled retrenchment.[76]

Between 1961 and 1963, against this background, several extensively publicized trials of economic crimes took place in Soviet Ukraine, ending with harsh sentences and executions. Jews were overrepresented among the accused and the punished. Although constituting only about 2 percent of Ukraine's population at the time, they made up 83 percent of those sentenced.[77]

It was not unusual that synagogues were dragged into these campaigns against speculation.[78] But Lviv's case shed special light on the relationship between the antispeculation drive and the attack on Judaism: in Lviv the latter can be shown to have been not simply a cover for closing the synagogue; it

74. TsDAHOU 1, 24, 5488: 231–34.

75. Bodnar, *Lviv*, 109.

76. Volodymyr Baran, *Ukraina: Novitnia istoriia, 1945–1991 rr.* (Lviv: Instytut ukrainoznavstva im. I. Krypiakevycha, 2003), 153–54, 170–72.

77. Mitsel, *Obshchiny iudeiskoho veroispovidannia*, 151. For slightly different but substantially similar figures and shares, see Pinkus, *Soviet Government and the Jews*, 202–4.

78. Pinkus, *Soviet Government and the Jews*, 207.

was genuine and preceded the attack on the synagogue. What was not genuine was the Soviet authorities' propagandized belief that the synagogue was a major center of speculation. By combining the campaign against the shadow economy with the closing of the synagogue, the authorities distracted Lviv's population from the party-state's corrupt ostentation against a background of scarcity and social inequality.

"1937" or a "Pogrom"? The Manipulation of Fear and Prejudice

At the center of the storm that struck Lviv from 1961 to 1962 was a purge of alleged participants in the shadow economy and their contacts *inside* the party-state's own elite. In early 1962, Obkom head Hrushetskyi invoked the memory of Stalin's Great Purges, telling his obkom buro that there were "rumors that this is 1937; many people with prominent positions are being imprisoned [and] expelled from the party."[79] He also mentioned rumors circulating about himself, with "much talk . . . about . . . Hrushetskyi and [the head of the oblast KGB] . . . Shevchenko," who "supposedly, want to pile up kudos for themselves over people's dead bodies" and were "organizing terror against honest people." Hrushetskyi stressed that "simple people" should know that there was no way out for "crooks," who would be fought not "by half-measures but to the end."[80] The most powerful man in the oblast, moreover, stoked such fears. In his view, Lviv's problem was that it was shot through with corruption, and the general public knew that the responsibility for its corruption rested with the party elite.[81] Serious political harm had been done, he felt, since the arrest of some party members for corruption made the public conclude that "they are all like that."[82]

What was needed in response, Hrushetskyi demanded, was to "seriously cleanse" the apparat.[83] Those who adhered to old habits of profiteering, negligent oversight, or bribe taking should be warned that "measures" would be used against them, akin to those applied, "at a certain stage . . . against the enemies of Soviet power."[84] Whereas in 1950 he had identified Lviv's outskirts as a hiding place for nationalist subversives, by 1962, he warned that "all sorts of scoundrels"

79. DALO P-3, 8, 374: 114.
80. DALO P-3, 8, 383: 87.
81. DALO P-3, 8, 374: 149–50.
82. DALO P-3, 8, 384: 25–26. Hrushetsky's term for "harm" was *vred*, which to a Soviet listener would have evoked the "harming" (or, as it is usually translated into English, "wrecking" [*vreditelstvo*]) accusations of Stalinism. In reality, "1937" was a massive exaggeration as an analogy to Lviv in 1962. Yet the point was that the city's boss clearly rather liked its undertones.
83. DALO P-3, 8, 383: 90.
84. DALO P-3, 8, 382: 8.

were gathering there.[85] It was against this background that the KGB and the Lviv obkom took "measures . . . to compromise the aktiv of the Jewish religious community among the believers."[86]

These measures focused on Lviv's light industry, especially textile production, which had already been investigated in 1955.[87] At that time, Lviv was singled out for criticism by Kyiv Central Committee Chairman Mykola Pidhornyi (Nikolai Podgornyi).[88] At the end of 1961, Hrushetskyi wrote to him that the obkom was receiving denunciations about "some persons" becoming "millionaires by dishonest means" and complaints that nobody was stopping them. The KGB arrested two brothers accused of smuggling gold, and through them uncovered those it called "the millionaires" of Lviv, corruption among high officials, and black market production at several factories, especially at Textile Factory no. 1, with about a third of output being diverted for illicit sale and whole workshops being traded. Integrated operations went far beyond Lviv, large sums were flowing, and "bribery had become a system," with the majority of those involved in these schemes being party members. Substantial amounts of gold, precious stones, and dollars were confiscated. Forty-four people were arrested, with many stereotypically Jewish names among them (Sheikhet, Kogan, Akselrud), indicating bias. At this point, however, the synagogue was not linked to the case.[89]

Although the involvement of party members was already clear, later reports more precisely focused on officials, such as Lviv's police. Crime was increasing, while many cases remained unsolved. The Criminal Investigation Department and the Department for the Fight against the Embezzlement of Socialist Property were passive, facilitating economic crime. The obkom demanded more action, particularly in industries supplying, or not, consumer goods to the local population.[90]

At the same time, the obkom buro aggressively questioned several high-ranking officials, and Hrushetskyi and Lviv KGB head Shevchenko personally interrogated them. The Kyiv Central Committee also sent representatives. In January 1962, the obkom buro reprimanded Migalin, the head of Lviv's State Control Commission (Goskontrol). His office, "the eye of the party," was blind, failing to act against "major currency speculation" and production "on the left," to the tune of an estimated ten million rubles at Textile Plant no. 1, while "this state factory was

85. DALO P-3, 8, 383: 90. By the 1960s—at the latest—an illicit if regular market and a repertory of complex if unofficial practices for settling in Lviv's outskirts semilegally had been established (Bodnar, *Lviv*, 55–56).

86. Mitsel, *Obshchiny iudeiskoho veroispovidannia*, 218–19.

87. DALO P-3, 6, 84: 17–29.

88. DALO P-3, 8, 225: 32.

89. TsDAHOU 1, 24, 5503: 3–16.

90. DALO P 3, 8, 348: 45–50.

producing only half of the workday" for the state and the other half for "those embezzlers." Management positions sold for tens to hundreds of thousands of rubles. Migalin was accused of taking large bribes, as were other high officials, including the oblast prosecutor. There was no mention of the synagogue.[91]

By mid-February, the number of arrests exceeded sixty. According to the KGB, currency speculators and embezzlers were carving out their own "workshops and even whole companies." Several high-ranking members of the oblast local industry department, including its head Spyrydon Bondarchuk, were reportedly getting hefty bribes for covering up these operations. Conveniently, Hrushetskyi also blamed Lviv's industrialization problems on Bondarchuk, accusing him of single-handedly mismanaging the entire priority project of Lviv's industrial development, although he occupied a relatively humble position. Here was a convenient scapegoat for what, from a Soviet point of view, appeared to be Lviv's persistently lopsided focus on small-scale industry to the detriment of heavy industry.[92]

By March 1962, Bondarchuk's deputy and other party-state elite members were also expelled from the party for having taken bribes to cover up production "on the left."[93] Pressure was growing. The prosecutors and the KGB had fifty-six investigators on the case. The prosecutor's office was working on about thirty cases, involving three hundred or so suspects across several institutions and plants. One hundred of them were from the Administration of Light Industry; others from trade organizations, plants, and Lviv's psychiatric hospital. The KGB had arrested eighty-five people. Together, the KGB and the prosecutor's office confiscated money and valuables worth more than 57 million rubles.[94] The Kyiv Central Committee especially mentioned Lviv in a March 1962 decree, "On Facts of Major Embezzlement of Socialist Property and Corruption, Uncovered in Lviv and Several Other Oblasts of the Republic." On 29 March, the Moscow Central Committee sent out a circular: "On Intensifying the Fight against Corruption and Embezzlement of People's Property." Shortly before, the Kyiv Central Committee had found that in Lviv "bribing . . . the staff of economic, administrative and other organs" had become "widespread." Graft had not only shielded a local shadow economy but also invaded the state economy to its core, with "even plan raw materials and equipment" available "on time often only for bribes," paid to central planning officials in Kyiv and Moscow as well as local bureaucrats.[95]

91. DALO P-3, 8, 374: 60–94, esp. 61, 67, 83.
92. DALO P-3, 8, 374: 182–85, 207.
93. DALO P-3, 8, 383: 73–78.
94. DALO P-3, 8, 383: 85–86.
95. TsDAHOU 1, 24, 5503: 24–29 (repr. in Mitsel, *Obshchiny iudeiskoho veroispovidannia*, 152).

For purposes of longitudinal comparison, it is important to note that this kind of crisis was not entirely unprecedented. In 1947, a Kyiv Central Committee report had detailed pervasive corruption involving Lviv oblast's party-state elite, especially Hrushetskyi.[96] In 1958, a Moscow Central Committee report had also detailed corruption in Lviv and the city party elite's "immodest behavior," provoking "much talk among the population."[97] In 1962, however, the consequences were much more severe. A number of leading cadres in Lviv were arrested; after his dismissal for embezzlement, the former first secretary of the miskom Petro Ovsianko committed suicide. Again "provocative rumors" were circulating, with some Communists speaking up at meetings to demand the dissolution of the Lviv miskom or even the Higher Party School in Moscow because, they suspected, it was training "dishonest party workers."[98]

At the same time, a June 1962 obkom report registered popular discontent with increasing prices and food scarcity producing loaded questions, such as why there were no strikes as in France and the United States, or where in the "classics of Marxism-Leninism" it said that "under socialism the leaders have salaries twenty times higher than the average worker."[99] Explicitly to calm angry meetings at grassroots party organizations, the obkom was conducting a "cleansing" (*ochyshchenniu*) of trade staff, discharging six hundred by the end of May 1962.[100] Expelling Migalin from the party, Hrushetsky told him that there was no explaining his misbehavior "before the people" who would say that "the head of Goskontrol is a crook himself."[101]

While the obkom buro was targeting trade personnel as well as the local elite, Lviv's press began a public attack on the synagogue, starting on 16 February 1962 with a *Lvovskaia pravda* article by I. Berman and E. Volfson, "Prayer and Speculation." The article opened with a sensationally vivid scene of conspiracy and fraud in the synagogue, complete with direct speech and tsarist gold currency. Two members of the synagogue council were denounced for currency speculation, and Makhnovetskyi, the head of the council, was accused of living off believers' donations. All of the council members, the article charged, got along too well with visiting foreigners, particularly Israeli diplomats.[102] This text was also

96. TsDAHOU 1, 23, 4258: 6–7.

97. RGANI 5, 31, 98: 184–85.

98. TsDAHOU 1, 24, 5503: 24–29. On Ovsianko's career from director of Lviv's Tank Repair Works via the city executive committee to the city party committee, his suicide—apparently at least in part provoked by Hrushetskyi's personal hounding—and his instant night-time burial, see Isaievych et al., *Istoriia Lvova*, 3:308; and Bodnar, *Lviv*, 160.

99. DALO P-3, 8, 436: 83–85.

100. DALO-P 3, 8, 436: 79.

101. DALO P-3, 8, 374: 86.

102. *Lvovskaia pravda*, 16 February 1962, 4.

broadcast on local radio stations. According to official reports, "Prayer and Speculation" evoked a "very active response" among the public.[103]

In another newspaper piece on a currency speculation trial in March, *Lvovskaia pravda* denounced the "common language" between speculators and Jewish religious community leaders. Whereas its first article had appealed to workers' "just indignation" and claimed that "many Jewish workers" had no use for a synagogue, the second article explicitly attacked it as a "place of criminal deals," doing "serious harm to our country." Receiving long sentences, "criminals got what they deserved."[104]

At the end of March, *Lvovskaia pravda*'s "Scandal in the 'House of God'" reported Makhnovetskyi's resignation and noted that attendance at the synagogue was "completely insignificant." Depicting a violent brawl and a humiliating trial of synagogue "activists" for "petty hooliganism," *Lvovskaia pravda* claimed widespread demands to close the synagogue, citing a letter by twenty-six textile factory workers.[105]

This public smear campaign was thoroughly coordinated from above. Behind the scenes, Dryl was liasing with the KGB to achieve maximum damage to the synagogue. In February 1962, he reported Makhnovetskyi's suggestion to remove both alleged offenders from its council. Yet Dryl, consulting with, as he wrote, the "neighbors," foiled this plan.[106] Clearly, Dryl and the "neighbors" were intentionally preventing Makhnovetskyi from protecting the synagogue as a whole by dissociating it from specific speculation accusations: the party-state publicly dragged the synagogue into an anticorruption purge that was really about itself and made sure that the synagogue would not get out again.

The operation to smear the synagogue with the "speculation" scandal was also supervised by Dryl's immediate superior, Soviet Ukraine's religious cult plenipotentiary Polonnyk. Paying a ten-day visit to Lviv in March, he met with the obkom secretary and the department head for propaganda and agitation, a KGB representative, the editors of *Vilna Ukraina* and *Lvovskaia pravda*, the head of the oblast radio committee and the—new—public prosecutor. Using a pejorative term with special antisemitic connotations, Polonnyk directed the newspaper campaign to continue displaying demands by "Jewish workers" to close the synagogue as a "nest of gesheftmakher." Additionally, one or two articles by academics—"obligatorily Jews"—were to demonstrate the "reactionary essence of Judaism" and "shatter the ideas of the Judaic confession." The campaign against

103. Mitsel, *Obshchiny iudeiskoho veroispovidannia*, 214–18.
104. *Lvovskaia pravda*, 9 March 1962, 4.
105. *Lvovskaia pravda*, 31 March 1962, 4.
106. DALO P-3, 8, 436: 52.

this specific synagogue was also a campaign against Judaism as such. The Komsomol was charged with mobilizing Jewish children to make their parents write public letters to renounce the synagogue and "castigate" its "black deeds."[107]

In public at least, formalities went smoothly. After the deregistration of the synagogue council, its new acting head petitioned the obkom to be relieved of his responsibilities and to transfer the synagogue's premises to administration by the pertinent city raion. Praising the obkom for its "great work" in the "disintegration" (*rozklad*) of the religious community, Polonnyk called for continuing the mobilization of "Jewish workers," especially against expected international criticism.[108]

Behind the scenes, however, there was some friction and resistance, even within the party. It provoked a telling if nonpublic response from Hrushetskyi. In March 1962, at the height of the assault on the synagogue, he instructed the obkom buro to "differentiate" its "explanatory work" aimed at Jews: "If we say that many among the criminals are . . . of Jewish nationality . . . we mean the criminals but not the whole Jewish population." Yet, he warned, "Jewish criminals" (*prestupniki-evrei*) were trying to suggest that "there is a pogrom underway against Jews." In Hrushetskyi's reality, however, "if we are dealing with an honest person of Jewish nationality, we won't allow any offense to be done to him [*my v obidu ne dadim*], but crooks, whatever nationality they may have, including Jews, will get what they deserve." He also reminded the obkom buro that the party's "internationalism" needed more explaining, since several "Jewish Communists" (*evrei-kommunisty*) had refused to support the attack on the synagogue.[109]

In sum, Hrushetskyi knew that the people of Lviv, whether in fear or with approval, regarded his operation as a purge; he also knew that Jews—and possibly non-Jews, too—associated the same operation with a pogrom. His disquisitions on the finer points of Soviet internationalist antisemitism were unsurprisingly callous. Their implications, however, were ominously meaningful: by emphasizing that *even* Jews would be punished if guilty, he implied that complaints of fear were nothing but a devious attempt to secure a special immunity and thus illicit advantages for Jews. While ostensibly rejecting antisemitic bias, Hrushetskyi displayed and incited even more of it.

The lease for the synagogue premises was officially canceled on 26 March 1962; subsequently it became a sports facility and library.[110] One day earlier, Hrushetskyi

107. TsDAHOU 1, 24, 5488: 57–69, repr. in Mitsel, *Obshchiny iudeiskoho veroispovidannia*, 211–13.

108. Ibid.

109. DALO P-3, 8, 383: 89.

110. TsDAHOU 1, 24, 5488: 57–69, repr. in Mitsel, *Obshchiny iudeiskoho veroispovidannia*, 214–18.

sent a fresh report to Podgornyi (Pidhornyi), covering the preceding year. More than twenty groups of alleged embezzlers with a total of 350 members had been exposed in his oblast, including many who were also active in currency speculation. By now, the list of things confiscated included sixty-four cars, sixty houses, and much more. Embezzling, the report explained, was pervasive in light industry, food processing, and—achieving, in effect, vertical integration—collective farms. Many of the suspects denounced had stereotypically Jewish names, such as Shapirshtain, Akselrud, and Katsman. Whatever Hrushetskyi's obkom buro musings on honesty, nationality, and internationalism, a loud antisemitic undertone had swollen to a noisy crescendo.

Yet at the peak of the campaign against the synagogue, Hrushetskyi, in an important internal communication, said nothing to link the synagogue to speculation and embezzlement.[111] Although it was the target of a fierce propaganda campaign, in a serious communication among powerful men in the know, the synagogue was not worth mentioning. A report from Hrushetskyi to Pidhornyi half a year later followed the same pattern; again there was no mention of the synagogue.[112]

Thus, these communications between the most powerful man in Lviv and the most powerful man in the Ukrainian republic cast an important difference in sharp relief. There is no doubt that Hrushetskyi and Pidhornyi genuinely believed in the corruption and embezzlement charges and probably shared traditional and Soviet prejudices associating Jews with illicit trade. Yet their silence indicates that the synagogue was either irrelevant or unimportant to Soviet Lviv's threatening and thriving second economy; they are likely to have known that using the campaign against speculation for the specific purpose of closing a synagogue was a pretext.

At the same time, the Soviet authorities continued to monitor the effect of the synagogue's closing in terms that they associated with its recent real activity: that is, religious observance and the visits of foreign diplomats.[113] In late June 1962, Shevchenko sent a report to Hrushetskyi about a *Lvovskaia pravda* article, "It Won't Work Out, Gentlemen," which aimed at "the [propaganda] activities" of foreign diplomats visiting the closed synagogue. Only one Jewish worker, Shevchenko reported, had called the article slanderous. Since the worker also complained about food prices, he was put under observation.[114]

111. TsDAHOU 1, 24, 5503: 65–73.

112. TsDAHOU 1, 24, 5503: 90–94. The report also showed that the criminal machinations reportedly involving Lviv embezzlers had reached Moscow, Kyiv, Omsk, Kokand, and Vilnius. The number of arrests was raised to 240, with 100 persons charged and 41 sentenced, including 4 death sentences.

113. For instance, on a visit to the closed synagogue by a US and a Japanese diplomat, see DALO-P 3, 8, 446: 87.

114. DALO-P 3, 8, 437: 62–65.

After the Last Synagogue

The closing of the synagogue did not mean the end of all Jewish religious life in Lviv. Underground groups persisted. In 1979, Cherpak, the head of the Lviv oblast KGB, reported that Lviv had twenty-six thousand Jewish inhabitants, three thousand of whom corresponded with "capitalist countries"; an increasing number planned to emigrate. Two illegal minyans had recently been shut down. Cherpak denounced Jewish visitors from abroad who still caused trouble, especially among Jews denied emigration.[115] In 1985, a miskom list of "negative" groups and places in Lviv also featured ten "concentrations of persons of Jewish nationality, refuseniks, [and] emigration-minded persons" and two former and one current underground minyans.[116]

Petitions to open a synagogue preceded the end of the Soviet Union. In 1987, a group of "citizens of Jewish nationality" demanded the registration of a religious community and the return of the synagogue's premises, invoking general perestroika democratization and the expectation of Jewish tourists.[117] A Jewish religious community was registered in late 1989. In October, *Vilna Ukraina* published "The Return of the Lviv Synagogue." The new head of the community, Filipp Niukh pointed out that there had been many Jews in Lviv before the German occupation and that the last remaining synagogue of the city had been closed down by Soviet authorities, forcing believers into underground religious services. He explained that the central authorities in Moscow had expressed support for reopening the synagogue, while local authorities had obstructed such plans. Niukh was not aware of it, but in a sense the synagogue was back in the position where it had been during its first major postwar crisis in 1949/1950. Local resistance was overcome with the help of the Soviet Ukrainian poet and Supreme Soviet deputy Rostyslav Bratun; the synagogue obtained premises and was collecting funds for their repair. In 1989, too, Jewish holidays began to be legally celebrated again in Lviv.[118]

115. Cherpak's long report of 10 September 1979 was leaked to anti-Soviet politicians and reproduced in the post-Soviet local newspaper *Vysokyi zamok*, 16 January 1992, 2.

116. DALO P-4, 41, 41: 2.

117. DALO P-3, 62, 985: 16–17.

118. K. Chabaha, "Povernennia Lvivskoi synahohy," *Vilna Ukraina*, 4. The article featured two pictures, one providing a look through a round aperture into a vague interior space viewed through a lens of secretive curiosity, the other showing two elderly men holding open books with one wearing Soviet veterans' decorations. The premises were not the same as those taken away in 1962.

CHAPTER EIGHT

A Soviet Borderland of Time

Post-Soviet memory has become an issue of scholarly and public interest.[1] At the same time, we know less about how the Soviet past was remembered during the Soviet period.[2] This imbalance is due, as Polly Jones has shown with special reference to post-Stalinism, to the "conviction that 'real' memory had been silenced, even killed, throughout the Soviet period," reinforcing the notion of a rigid "public-private memory divide in state socialism." Yet a rigid dichotomy between "official memory" on one side and "communicative" and "counter" memories on the other fails to accommodate the dynamic interplay between them.[3]

This chapter addresses the making and development of two important Soviet narratives: one about the interwar Communist Party of Western Ukraine (KPZU); and the other about a Communist underground in German-occupied Lviv, the so-called Narodna Hvardia imeni Ivana Franka or Ivan Franko People's

1. There is an extensive literature on memory in general, which cannot be recapitulated here. The literature is rich, even for Ukraine alone. Contributions with a special focus on Lviv and Western Ukraine include Omer Bartov, *Erased: Vanishing Traces of Jewish Galicia in Present-Day Ukraine* (Princeton, NJ: Princeton University Press, 2007); Tarik Cyril Amar, "Different but the Same or the Same but Different? Public Memory of the Second World War in Post-Soviet Lviv," *Journal of Modern European History* 9 (2011); Wolff, *Idea of Galicia*, 411–19; Yaroslav Hrytsak, "Historical Memory and Regional Identity among Galicia's Ukrainians," in *Galicia: A Multicultured Land*, ed. Hann and Magocsi, 185–209. On topics beyond Western Ukraine, see Wanner, *Burden of Dreams*; John-Paul Himka, "Encumbered Memory: The Ukrainian Famine of 1932–33," *Kritika: Explorations in Russian and Eurasian History* 14 (2013): 411–36; Georgii Kasianov, "The Holodomor and the Building of a Nation," *Russian Social Science Review* 52 (2011): 71–93; and Andriy Portnov, "Post-Soviet Ukraine Dealing with Its Controversial Past," *Journal of Modern European History* 8 (2010), 152–55.

2. The major exception to this pattern with reference to Ukraine is Yekelchyk, *Stalin's Empire of Memory*. With reference to individual cities in Central and Eastern Europe, several studies have addressed history and memory under authoritarian state socialism. See, e.g., Gregor Thum, *Uprooted: How Breslau Became Wrocław during the Century of Expulsions* (Princeton, NJ: Princeton University Press, 2011), 389–408; Peter Oliver Loew, *Danzig und seine Vergangenheit, 1793–1997: Die Geschichtskultur einer Stadt zwischen Deutschland und Polen* (Osnabrück: fibre, 2003), 494–522.

3. Jones, *Myth, Memory, Trauma*, 10.

Guard. Together they constituted a Soviet history of the present, to borrow a phrase but not its meaning, which connected Lviv's past not only to a general Soviet Marxist account of universal history but also to the specific teleology of the postwar Soviet Union, anchored in the key myths of the Great October Revolution and the Great Fatherland War. Thus for Lviv and Western Ukraine, a few twentieth-century phenomena were joined in a special relationship with the unfolding Soviet present, forming a hinge between a deep past before 1917 and the Soviet present and future.

From a Soviet perspective, the liberation and modernization of Lviv initiated its Soviet Ukrainian future. In Olga Barkova's roman à clef *Every Day*, the building of Lviv's first postwar factories marks the beginning of the city's "new history."[4] Yet this new history in a Soviet Ukrainian present aimed at the past as well as the future. It was not surprising that an official Soviet culture of memory produced a new, more or less usable past that united universally Soviet features with locally specific ones. A regime with, in Catherine Wanner's apt summary, an "unwavering commitment to control historical representation and public discourse about historical events," did more of the same in Lviv.[5]

Lviv's new Soviet history reached back over the whole period of the city's existence. In the late 1940s, both Vladimir Beliaev, the quintessential easterner, and Kuzma Pelekhatyi, a representative local, called for popularizing King Danylo Halytskyi, Lviv's medieval founder and, as Pelekhatyi stressed, fighter against "foreign invaders," in this case the Poles.[6] For Corresponding Member of the Soviet Union's Academy of Architecture S.V. Bezsonov, the history of Western Ukraine under Polish rule was a clash of "diametrically opposed" cultures embodied in classes, between the "old Slavonic" and ethnically "Russian" ways of life of the people and the "European" habits of the elites.[7]

According to the second and last Soviet history of Lviv, published in 1984, Lviv's initial development in the Halyts-Volyn Principality had prepared it to preserve its "eastern Slavonic" character even under the "yoke of foreign feudalists" imposed by Polish and Roman-Catholic expansionism. Lviv's Orthodox Ukrainians had embodied an "organic continuation" of Kyiv Rus, the "common source"

4. Barkova, *Kazhdyi den*, 42.

5. Wanner, *Burden of Dreams*, 35. It was also not surprising that, in the official view, only "Marxist historiography"—here really meaning just Soviet post-1939 publications—offered a "scientific" history of Lviv, which, driven by political and ideological priorities, was highly restrictive but neither unchanging nor free of inconsistencies. For an example of the Soviet view of Marxist history and the latter's exclusive claim to science, see Sekretariuk, *Istoriia Lvova*, 6.

6. DALO P-3808, 1, 8: 21; P-3, 3, 85: 13–14.

7. S. V. Bezsonov, *Arkhitektura Zapadnoi Ukrainy* (Moscow: Izdatelstvo Akademii arkhitektury SSSR, 1946), 49–51.

of Russian, Ukrainian, and Belarusian history. In this inter/nationalized legend of common eastern Slavonic origins, Ivan Fedorov, a persecuted sixteenth-century Russian printer who came to settle in Lviv, shone as a brilliant symbol of Ukrainian-Russian union.[8] The period of Habsburg rule, by contrast, was caricatured as one of backward decline and the deliberate deprivation of modernization.[9] The party-state was especially touchy about nostalgia for the Habsburgs or Galicia. In 1951, the obkom buro lamented that some local intelligentsia representatives fondly remembered the Habsburgs. As for the "question of Galicia," there was no reason anymore to refer to it as "a separate organism."[10]

A History of the Present

Initially, the relationship between the Soviet present and Western Ukraine's non-Soviet past had appeared simple: from the Soviet perspective, backwardness and progress mapped neatly onto the geography of conquest and liberation. In 1940, traveling in the new borderlands, Romm and Shklovsky felt as if they were on a trip from a radically better future into a bad past, crossing a sharp line in space that seemed to correspond to a clear break in teleological time.[11]

Yet in the postwar period, the Soviet practice of recounting Lviv's recent history created its Soviet history of the present, a new liminal space between the pre-Soviet past and the Soviet present, notwithstanding the simultaneous use of universal Soviet periodizations into feudalism, capitalism, and the Soviet era.[12] Ironically, this liminal area in historical time resembled a traditional borderland.

8. Sekretariuk, *Istoriia Lvova*, 28, 32, 50–56. The Soviet legend about Ivan Fedorov illustrated themes of Russian-Ukrainian unity and claims of Russian cultural superiority. It also offered a sort of alternative Gutenberg Galaxy expanding from Moscow into what was to become Western Ukraine. Already in 1945, Lviv oblast's publisher's program included a work on Fedorov with a print run of five thousand, equivalent to a book on Peter the Great's very faint yet celebrated links to Lviv (DALO P-3, 1, 170: 168–70). A year later, one of the accusations against Ivan Krypiakevych—in addition to the charge that he had sought to engender a perverse union of Marx and Hrushevskyi and had worked under the Germans—was his failure to popularize Fedorov (DALO P-3, 1, 414: 87). By the 1970s, Fedorov constituted one of postwar Lviv's major sites of memory, generating two monuments and three memorial plaques, almost all of which survived the end of Soviet rule (Shyshka, "Pamiatnyky i memorialni znaky, 18).

9. Sekretariuk, *Istoriia Lvova*, 154–63, 178–85.

10. DALO P-3, 4, 101: 23, 78.

11. Romm and Shklovsky anticipated an effect that Anne E. Gorsuch has identified for the postwar satellites of the Soviet Union: traveling there was perceived as a trip not only in space but time, to an as yet less developed form of Socialism (*All This Is Your World: Soviet Tourism at Home and Abroad after Stalin* [Oxford: Oxford University Press, 2011], 80). The conceptual and imaginary lines separating wartime and postwar Sovietization, the "inner empire" of the Soviet West and the "outer empire" of the satellites, were liminal.

12. For an example of the formal feudal-capitalist-Soviet schema applied to Lviv, see Sekretariuk, *Istoriia Lvova*. At the same time, the only extensive, if selective, Soviet volume of primary

Blurred at the edges, busy with interaction and conflict, and saturated with strategic meaning and risk, it was marked roughly by the years 1917 (representing the emergence of the Soviet order in the Great October Revolution), 1939 (standing for liberation and unification with Soviet Ukraine), and 1944/1945 (confirming the claims of 1917 as well as 1939 through the Great Fatherland War victory in general and the restoration of Lviv to Soviet power in particular).

Repeated claims for Lenin's prerevolutionary influence—and sometimes, incorrectly, even presence—in Lviv marked the earliest reaches of this Soviet history of the present.[13] More significant were the stories about the KPZU and the Narodna Hvardia. After the war, the Hvardia, a weak and isolated resistance organization, was glorified, its importance exaggerated, and its complex reality—marked by treason and defeat as much as by courage and self-sacrifice—was replaced by a simplifying myth. The Hvardia story became an indispensable local element of the Soviet myth of History's ordeal by battle, the Great Fatherland War, perhaps even more important for postwar Soviet legitimacy than the Great October Revolution. At the same time, the KPZU, which had been destroyed by Stalinist interwar repression, was—mostly, if never fully—rehabilitated, so as to integrate Western Ukraine into the Soviet myth of origins, the Great October Revolution.[14]

The Narodna Hvardia imeni Ivana Franka

As a story, the Great Fatherland War had two main parts, one about regular Soviet forces and one about resistance groups under German occupation. Both narratives included the axiom of ubiquitous party leadership. For Lviv, the army's

documents on Lviv's history was explicitly divided into "pre-Soviet" and "Soviet" periods (M. V. Bryk et al., eds., *Istoriia Lvova v dokumentakh i materialakh: Zbirnik dokumentiv i materialiv* [Kyiv: Naukova Dumka, 1986]).

13. In 1969/1970 the Kyiv Central Committee and the Lviv obkom formed two historians' commissions, both including Bohdan Dudykevych, to investigate repeated claims that Lenin had once set foot in Habsburg Lviv before the Russian Revolution, but they found no evidence. The local legend reached back at least to 1940 and was based, as it turned out, on a combination of unreliable hearsay evidence, part of it produced by people whom Dudykevych denounced as "interested" witnesses, "well-known Polish chauvinists" suspected of trying to ingratiate themselves with the Soviet conquerors. See DALO P-1, 2, 223: 9–10, 15–17; and, for a discussion of the same issue from 1951, DALO P-1, 2, 4: 10–12. Yet in 1947, it was the head curator of Lviv's History Museum, Kibalchich, who tried to prove that Lenin had been in Lviv, writing about his ideas to the Lviv obkom and directly to Moscow (DALO P-1, 2, 4: 20–23). In the end, the murky apocryphal stories were quietly dropped.

14. I am relying here especially on Amir Weiner's insights as presented in his *Making Sense of War*. Like Weiner, I use the term "myth" not to make a statement about the veracity or not of the Soviet narrative of the Second World War but to express that, like other modern myths, the Great Fatherland War was both fantasy, involving deception but also genuine belief, and a distorted reflection of reality.

story stressed the 1944 reconquest of the city, including variations on stock features, such as the raising of the Soviet flag on the Lviv town hall (*ratusha*) by a soldier who happened to be both Ukrainian and a Communist or the exploits of the traveling easterner agent Nikolai Kuznetsov.[15]

Stressing the multinational composition of the Soviet forces, these stories meshed well with the master narrative of multinational cadres liberating and modernizing Western Ukraine.[16] They were printed on paper and celluloid, carved in stone, and cast in bronze. The first monument to the 1944 "liberation" of Lviv was a Stalin tank on a pedestal overlooking a main road—renamed Lenin Street—pointing its gun toward the city center.[17] Close to the tank, a combination of a monumental war memorial and cemetery was finished in 1952. Adorned with marble from Vienna, the symbolism of the complex resonated beyond the Second World War. It was a place where the dead buried the dead, enclosing First World War Russian and later Soviet graves while obliterating Habsburg ones.[18] With the intensification of the Great Fatherland War myth in the 1960s, a major statue and a street were dedicated to Kuznetsov in 1962 and a second large monument to the army in 1970.[19]

The Narodna Hvardia also received its monument, two memorial plaques, and a street name.[20] While linked to the general war narrative, the Hvardia story

15. For late Soviet summaries of these themes, see O. E. Solomonchuk, ed., *Lvivshchyna turystska* (Lviv: Kameniar, 1986), 7–8; and, from a local poet, Lubkivskyi, *Lviv*, 84. For the last major Soviet publication of this narrative, see Mikhail Verbinskii, *V bitve za "rozu"* (Lviv: Kameniar, 1990). On the Kuznetsov cult and Lviv, see, e.g., I. N. Tiufiakov, *Doroga v bessmertie: fotoalbom o vydaiushchemsia sovetskom razvedchike Geroe Sovetskogo Soiuza Nikolae Ivanoviche Kuznetsove* (Moscow: Planeta, 1985), 126–29; and V. G. Loshak, *V pamiati narodnoi* (Sverdlovsk: Sredne-Uralskoe knizhnoe izdatelstvo, 1986), 111–37. A street was named in honor of Aleksandr Marchenko, the soldier who raised the flag; it was renamed after the Soviet collapse (Shyshka, "Pamiatnyky i memorialni znaky," 18).

16. For instance, Verbinskii, *V bitve za "rozu,"* 114, 118–19.

17. Shyshka, "Pamiatnyky i memorialni znaky," 14–15, 17. In his 1963 memoirs, Volodymyr Hurhal, Lviv's most prominent local labor hero, recalled that one of his workshop's first postwar jobs had been to make bronze details for the monumental tank (*Storinky robitnykoho zhyttia*, 71–72).

18. Isaievych et al., *Istoriia Lvova*, 3:292–93.

19. Shyshka, "Pamiatnyky i memorialni znaky," 17–18. Besides major monuments, there were various memorial plaques. After the collapse of Soviet rule, Kuznetsov's monument was moved to Russia. The street was renamed. The 1952 and 1970 war memorials have both survived. The latter now commemorates the "victors over fascism" (ibid., 15–17). During the Ukrainian-Russian crisis of 2014, the Ukrainian security services claimed to have uncovered a Russian-controlled group of infiltrators preparing attacks in Lviv and calling themselves the Kuznetsov Platoon, http://zaxid.net/news/showNews.do?sbu_zatrimala_u_lvovi_grupu_teroristiv_zagin_imeni_kuznyetsova&objectId=1328994.

20. See Shyshka, "Pamiatnyky i memorialni znaky," 17–18; and DALO P-183, 1, 125: 1–4 for a 1961 obkom-initiated meeting meeting of Hvardia veterans to discuss the location and nature of the monument.

was special. The aim of this narrative was to root the Great Fatherland War myth within Lviv by fitting it with its own Soviet underground myth. Although underground resistance was generally claimed as evidence of Soviet legitimacy, such claims were particularly important for Lviv.[21] Official rhetoric insisted that the city had become genuinely Soviet in less than two years of Soviet rule, but more than three subsequent years under the Nazis made it one of the Soviet cities longest under German occupation. To Soviet eyes, it also represented Ukrainian nationalism and collaboration; and Lviv stood for Polish nationalism, too, insofar as Poles were remembered. It was therefore indispensable to authenticate Lviv's Sovietness with a myth of a local Communist underground movement.

The Hvardia narrative also promoted Ukrainization: although it was depicted as "internationalist," uniting Ukrainians (local and eastern), Russians, Poles, Jews and others, in effect, the Hvardia story eclipsed Poles and Jews by constructing a mostly local and ethnically Ukrainian underground.[22] By the same token, the small Hvardia came to serve as a screen: in reality, a Polish and non-Communist Home Army underground had been much more important, yet Soviet narratives hardly acknowledged it or any other forms of resistance. The Hvardia overshadowed even other pro-Soviet underground organizations in Lviv oblast: they were officially acknowledged, but the Hvardia was far more prominent.

Finally, the Hvardia myth also displaced Hvardia reality. The real Hvardia emerged from small grassroots initiatives and exogenous organizing efforts by the Polish-Communist Gwardia Ludowa. For a long time, it was controlled, if at all, from Warsaw by the Polish Communist PPR party and came within Moscow's direct reach only in early 1944. Thus, in reality, when Germans ruled Lviv, Poles, rather than Moscow, could claim to have led even its Communist resisters. Unwilling to accommodate this strong Polish influence on Lviv's Communist resistance, the Soviet Hvardia story was a double twister, excising Polish presence *outside* the Communist underground and Polish influence *inside* it, too. Was there a clearer way to say—if silently—that the Polish past had left together with the Polish present?

The official codification of the postwar story of the Hvardia began in 1945, through party decrees and various publications. In April, the Kyiv Central Committee instructed the Lviv obkom to survey underground members, arrange for

21. On the memory of partisan activity and Soviet legitimacy, see Kenneth Slepyan, *Stalin's Guerrillas: Soviet Partisans in World War II* (Lawrence: University Press of Kansas, 2006), 186–87, 291.

22. For a typical example of the short summary of the mature Hvardia narrative, see M.K. Ivasiuta, ed. *Pravdu ne zdolaty: Trudiashchi zakhidnykh oblastei URSR v borotbi proty ukrainskykh burzhuaznykh natsionalistiv u roky sotsialistychnykh peretvoren* (Lviv: Kameniar, 1974), 71–72, 79–80.

rewards for survivors, and create monuments for the fallen.[23] The Lviv miskom and obkom soon passed fundamental decrees establishing that Lviv's underground was to be considered an oblast-wide organization. The obkom also decided that it should be called Narodna Hvardia imeni Ivana Franka, declaring that three smaller organizations in the city had originally used that name. Yet one Hvardia veteran would later tell a commission of inquiry that, during the war, nobody had known about it.[24] Behind closed doors, uncertainty and arguments about the Hvardia's true name continued for decades. However, for the Hvardia's public image, the obkom's decision, as well as its invocation of canonized western Ukrainian writer Ivan Franko, replaced ambiguity with certainty and, as with the renaming of Lviv's university during the first Soviet occupation, signaled not only a Ukrainian but a specifically western Ukrainian belonging.

In 1945, moreover, the expulsion of Lviv's Poles was at its height, and the obkom decree on the underground diminished their role in it, although the Soviet authorities knew better: initially, they had acknowledged a fundamental Polish contribution to Lviv's Communist underground.[25] Decrees from that year conceded that the Hvardia had been founded by Polish Communists from Warsaw, even as they denounced the Poles' nationalism.[26] In 1946, a special report for Khrushchev further simplified the Hvardia's founders into "Communists, Komsomol members, and progressive Soviet patriots." These activists had then foiled the Polish nationalist tendencies of the PPR's emissaries from Warsaw, so that the Hvardia fought Ukrainian and Polish nationalists as well as Germans.[27]

Postwar publications on the Hvardia expelled Poles even more vehemently from its memory by omitting or marginalizing the Polish Communist contribution to its creation. The Hvardia's leadership was praised for stopping a takeover by treacherous "local nationalists, Ukrainian as well as Polish."[28] A *Vilna*

23. DALO P-3, 1, 208: 56.

24. DALO P-183, 1, 174: 27.

25. DALO P-183, 1, 5: 1, 6. Soviet authorities knew that Lviv's Communist underground movement had been founded in the fall of 1942 "on the initiative of persons from the PPR party arriving from Warsaw." Individual resisters had been recognized as Polish or as fighting for Polish organizations: in 1944, the Komsomol had reinstated Stanislav Palubiak, who was Polish, and Norbert Shaleta, who was Jewish, after they had served, as officially noted, in the local branch of the "underground organization, the Polish Workers' Party" (DALO P-4, 1, 156: 88; P-66, 1, 5: 77, 81). For Vilnius, Theodore Weeks has found some evidence for a similar process of retrospective "localization" of an underground organization ("Multi-Ethnic City in Transition," 166).

26. TsDAHOU 1, 22, 417: 3–17; DALO P-183, 1, 5: 1.

27. TsDAHOU 1, 22, 414: 41–45, 83. The same report is also in DALO P-183, 1, 120, and P-183, 1, 123.

28. Mykhailo Marchenko and Vasyl Kolisnyk, "Narodna Hvardia im. Ivana Franka (Pidpilnyki Lvivshchyny)," in *Vyzvolena Lvivshchyna* (1945), as copied in DALO P-183, 1, 3: 75–84, esp. 80; *Borotba trudiashchykh Lvivshchyny proty nimetsko-fashystskykh zaharbnykiv, 1941–1944 rr.: Zbirnyk dokumentiv i materialiv* (Lviv, 1949), 153–78; Dudykevych et al., *Narysy istorii Lvova, 1256–1956*, 313–18.

Ukraina article stressed that the Hvardia's organizers and leaders had been "Lvivians—natives of Lviv and Lviv oblast." "Loyal sons" of Lviv, they shared in the "unforgettable" heroism of the *Ukrainian* people's struggle during the Great Fatherland War.[29]

While ties with Poland were cut, Soviet commemoration began to weave together narratives of eastern and western Ukraine as well as of the regular army and underground resisters: in 1945, Lviv's History Museum organized excursions to what it dubbed the birthplace of the Ukrainian partisan movement, defined as Chernihiv oblast in eastern Ukraine.[30] In 1946, the Hvardia was made an official topic for Lviv's artists, together with partisan raids of easterners striking west and the Red Army's retaking of Lviv.[31]

A Public Underground, Underground Conflict

Major publications dedicated exclusively to the Hvardia appeared from 1957 on. Their author, the local and Hvardia veteran Stepan Makivka, published three essentially identical versions of his account between 1957 and 1963, a period coinciding with high-level interest in resistance during the Second World War. In 1961, Ivan Nazarenko, director of the Kyiv Party History Institute, described it as an issue of "great political and scientific importance," arguing that the traditional estimate of 220,000 underground and partisan resisters in Ukraine was too low and should be replaced by a figure above one million.[32] In the same year, the Kyiv Central Committee passed a decree, "On Insufficiencies . . . in the Registration of Participants of the Anti-Fascist Underground and Partisan Movement," which started a republic-wide search for overlooked resisters.

The persistent, if inconsistent, Soviet tendency to associate western Ukraine with nationalism and collaboration with Germans made this operation even more urgent, since admitting the paucity of pro-Soviet resistance would undermine Soviet popular legitimacy. It was in 1962 that Yuryi Melnychuk, the editor of Lviv's intelligentsia journal *Zhovten*, demanded more emphasis on the wartime support for Soviet rule by the "main mass" of western Ukraine's population.[33]

In Lviv, the search for more resistance veterans was carried out by a commission under an obkom secretary which included, among others, ten Hvardia

29. "Borotba v Pidpili," *Vilna Ukraina*, 24 July 1945, as copied in DALO P-183, 1, 3: 85–86. (my emphasis).

30. DALO R-2591, 1, 13: 5.

31. Badiak, *U leshchatakh stalinshchyny*, 89.

32. TsDAHOU 1, 31, 1682: 87–88.

33. DALO P-3, 8, 421: 2.

veterans, the head of the oblast party archive Ignationok, and a KGB representative. Subsidiary town, village, and raion commissions worked throughout the oblast, backed up by itinerant teams from Lviv.[34] Within three years, these efforts produced 2,517 additional underground veterans, including 206 who had fought the Germans directly—"arms in hand"—and 2,311 who had resisted in other ways. This was a massive increase. By 1947, when postwar registrations had wound down, Lviv oblast had had, in the obkom's words, "only 385" pro-Soviet resisters. The search also increased the geographical reach of the Hvardia. Newly discovered branches were added in several towns of the oblast. The preponderant majority of resisters—2,246—were officially categorized as Ukrainian.[35]

This retrospective expansion of the memory and ranks of pro-Soviet resistance was accompanied by an extensive, if nonpublic, effort to reconstruct the Hvardia's history through a series of detailed interviews with underground veterans. Conducted under the direction of Ignationok, these interviews were especially important, since the Hvardia's own archive had been lost.[36] Not meant for publication, the interviews were open and direct, producing an extraordinarily intricate if often contradictory image of the Hvardia. Now they constitute a rich source on both the underground and the making of its Soviet memory.

Thus, Hvardia size, reach, and publicity increased simultaneously. Yet this growth came with escalating insider conflicts. In 1961 and 1962, an underground veteran, Vera Variagina, turned to the Lviv obkom to denounce several post-1957 accounts of the Hvardia, especially those by Stepan Makivka. Special obkom committees were set up, and an archival investigation by the Party History Institute in Kyiv was launched. Variagina aimed, she stressed, to protect the Hvardia story, not to debunk it. Glaring distortions and exaggeration, she argued, made the Hvardia look "ridiculous."[37] She attacked "falsification," "subjectivism," and "naïve" misrepresentations of German occupation.[38]

34. DALO P-183, 1, 166: 1, 14; P-183, 1, 168: 1.

35. DALO P-183, 1, 170: 1, 8–9. As pointed out by the obkom, a difference between immediate postwar registrations of pro-Soviet resisters and those of the early 1960s was that the later count included the territory of the neighboring, formerly separate oblast of Drohobych, joined to Lviv oblast only in 1959. This was especially important since the postwar registrations had failed to accredit a single pro-Soviet resister in Drohobych oblast, in effect leaving it an untouched resource of later resistance memory (DALO P-183, 1, 170: 8).

36. What exactly had happened to this archive—a sack of reports "about all the work" done by the underground, as one veteran described it—was a recurring issue at the interviews. It had clearly not fallen into German hands. Although other veterans had misgivings about how Kurylovych, a leading Hvardia member, had dealt with it, everyone—including Kurylovych—agreed that he had handed it over quickly to Soviet military intelligence after the Soviet return, after which it had disappeared (DALO P-183, 1, 174: 85, 161; P-183, 1, 175: 124; P-183, 1, 178: 208).

37. DALO P-3, 8, 464: 158–73.

38. DALO P-3, 8, 464: 132–47, 158–73.

Her credentials were impeccable. A Soviet officer's wife, originally from Tashkent, she arrived in Lviv in 1941 and joined the underground in April 1942.[39] By 1961, she and the historian Havrylo Vakulenko had done much research on the Hvardia.[40] In October 1962, Variagina coauthored a *Vilna Ukraina* article on the Hvardia which stressed individual conscience and self-sacrifice.[41] In a later article in Soviet Ukraine's flagship *Ukrainian Historical Journal*, she hinted that Makivka had sacrificed accuracy to thrill.[42] In his "harmful" book, Variagina charged, bumbling Germans and amateurish resisters made the Nazi occupation look farcical. Moreover, she added, he omitted key symbols of its brutality, such as the ghetto, camps, and public executions.[43] Yet, like Variagina, Makivka had been certified in the 1945 obkom decree as a Hvardia founding member.[44]

Remembering resistance also touched on the sensitive issue of how the occupied had lived through German occupation. Specific details, such as the German segregation of streetcars, were powerful symbols. Variagina attacked Makivka's claim of having accidentally entered a car section reserved for Germans only, which, she insisted, was impossible. Makivka, in effect, was diminishing not only German violence but also the distance between occupiers and occupied. Likewise, his depiction of how underground leaflets had been distributed in a packed cinema touched more than one sore spot. A Hvardia veteran who had done this was "offended" at Makivka's distortions.[45] But a crowded cinema under German occupation was also a disturbing image in and of itself. In Vladimir Beliaev's purifying fantasy, for instance, most inhabitants of occupied Lviv had "not seen a single movie" during the whole occupation.[46]

Yet Yevhen Nakonechnyi recalled a "cinema mania," with films, preceded by German newsreels and antisemitic propaganda, shown at venues which were overcrowded despite calls for boycotts.[47] According to a 1943 Soviet partisan report, several cinemas were open in Lviv: two for Germans only, three for

39. TsDAHOU 1, 22, 417: 3–17. Variagina was misnamed "Boriagyna" in this report. A comparison with the 1947 list of certified underground members, however, shows that Variagina and Boriagyna are the same person.

40. DALO P-3, 8, 464: 150–51. In Lviv's first Soviet history, Vakulenko had been responsible for the chapter on the German occupation (DALO P-4, 1, 697: 62).

41. *Vilna Ukraina*, 27 October 1962, 3.

42. H. S. Vakulenko and V. D. Variagina, "Bilshche vymohlyvosti i sumlivosti u vysvitlenni istorychnykh podii," *Ukrainskyi istorychnyi zhurnal*, no. 3 (1962): 121–22.

43. DALO P-3, 8, 464: 132–47.

44. In the decree his name was russified into Makovka (TsDAHOU 1, 22, 417: 3–17).

45. DALO P-3, 8, 120: 44–53.

46. Vladimir Beliaev, *Formula iada* (Moscow: Sovetskii pisatel, 1970), 24.

47. Nakonechnyi, *"Shoa" u Lvovi*, 256. Some of the same popular German movies continued to be screened in Lviv as Soviet "trophy" films.

Ukrainians, and an unclear number for Poles.[48] Variagina also insisted that the Germans had not closed all of them to all non-Germans but had "even exploited the crowds (comparatively speaking of course) . . . often making mass arrests."[49] The cognitive dissonance was clear enough: crowds had been merely "comparative," yet somehow also large enough for mass arrests.

While Variagina was defending Hvardia memory from Makivka, the obkom received a complaint from another key veteran, Ivan Vozniak. He was a prominent member of the combat group under Ivan Vovk, who, under his pseudonym "Iskra" had been one of the Hvardia's top leaders. His deeds, capture, and death were core elements of the Hvardia story. Vozniak was their witness, meeting, for instance, young Lviv workers at Vovk's grave.[50]

In February 1962, in his capacity as a "former participant of the revolutionary struggle in the western oblasts of Ukraine, prisoner of fascist camps, member of the [Communist] party, deputy of the Lviv oblast rada," Vozniak wrote to the obkom to denounce a recent *Lvovskaia pravda* article for slandering the Hvardia.[51] His complaint raised fundamental issues. *Lvovskaia pravda* had publicly attacked another key Hvardia veteran, Mykhailo Darmohai. Everybody agreed, in publications and internal interviews, that he had played an important role in establishing the first contact between Soviet forces and the Hvardia in 1944.[52] Now, *Lvovskaia pravda* claimed that he had inappropriately influenced the widow of a well-known Lviv artist, inducing her to refuse to exhibit her husband's paintings at the Museum of Ukrainian Art. Vozniak, in his letter to the obkom, countered that Darmohai was the victim of a smear campaign by "masked elements under the sign of the cross and the [nationalist] trident" as well as self-seeking associates of the

48. TsDAHOU 1, 22, 75: 19–36, as reproduced in Bilas, *Represivno-karalna systema*, 1:353.

49. DALO P-3, 8, 464: 168–73.

50. *Lvovskaia pravda*, 17 September 1957, 4. According to postwar reports, Vovk was a Ukrainian from a poor and semiliterate background in Lviv's countryside, who had acquired full literacy and an urban career when he joined the Soviet police of Lviv between 1939 and 1941, while also becoming a deputy in one of the city's raion soviets. During the German occupation, apart from his underground activity, he worked as an unskilled laborer. After his capture by the Germans in April 1944, Vovk had been deported to a concentration camp. He had barely survived it to return to Lviv, where he died of tuberculosis in 1945 (DALO P-183, 1, 6: 65; P-183, 1, 2: 30).

51. See DALO P-3, 8, 464: 58–63, for Ivan Vozniak's letter.

52. V. Variagina and H. Vakulenko, *Narodna Hvardia imeni Ivana Franka: Storinky heroichnoi borotby pidpilno-partyzanskoi orhanizatsii zakhidnykh oblastei Ukrainy, 1942–1944 roky*, rev. exp. ed. (Lviv: Kameniar, 1979), 113; DALO P-1, 183, 174: 23. For Darmohai's own detailed, internal 1964 account of this contact, see DALO P-1, 183, 1, 174: 59–62. In reality, according to this version, this operation involved a complicated and tense cooperation with groups outside Lviv, whom Mykhailo described as anti-Soviet Polish nationalists, while at least one pro-Soviet partisan commander trusted the emissaries from Lviv so little that he was getting ready to "liquidate" them. Naturally, none of this complexity ever made it into published accounts.

widow, led by a former nun. Arguments had arisen about food and money as well as a request for a priest.

Thus, both *Lvovskaia pravda* and Vozniak made this intimately sad story a Hvardia and thus also Great Fatherland War issue. The newspaper chose to focus on Darmohai's Hvardia past and lamented his putative "fall." Vozniak detected a general assault on Hvardia memory, in an environment where the past was "alive and of contemporary relevance." He viewed the former nun as a member of the same "black international" of "Nazi hordes," nationalists, and clerics against which the Hvardia had already fought, and he claimed she was slandering Darmohai because of his underground past. In sum, two decades after German occupation, between one of Lviv's principal postwar papers and one of its main embodiments of local antifascist resistance, a petty domestic argument had turned into the continuation of the Great Fatherland War.

Moreover, in Vozniak's recollections, the "black international," led by "Gestapo hangman Himmler," had consisted of Jewish nationalists, not only Ukrainian and Polish ones. In Vozniak's Lviv under Germans, the clerics of *all* faiths had made their flocks pray for the victory of Hitler in "churches, chapels," and synagogues.[53] In 1979, Vozniak was still among the ninety-two select veterans receiving a bibliographical entry in Variagina and Vakulenko's history of the Hvardia.[54]

The documents do not explain how a contemporary who said he had been there could claim that he had been fighting against a united front of Nazis and Polish, Ukrainian, and Jewish nationalists. But Vozniak's fantastic writing did cast a spotlight on the highly constructed nature of Lviv's Soviet underground. Variagina and Vakulenko decried Makivka's inaccuracies and exaggerations. But Vozniak's complaint showed that at the very core of the Hvardia myth, there was room for a key witness whose memory of the German occupation could turn delusional.

In 1979, Variagina and Vakulenko published what would be their last word on the Hvardia in the second edition of *Narodna Hvardia imeni Ivana Franka: Pages from the Heroic Struggle of the Underground-Partisan Organization of the Western Oblasts of Ukraine, 1942–1944*. Its introductory note described the Hvardia members as the "sons and daughters of the Ukrainian, Russian, Polish, and other peoples," while Variagina and Vakulenko also paid homage to the "Soviet people." The next two chapters, however, showed that national identity and nationally diverse experiences of the German occupation remained hard to accommodate.

53. Vozniak's statements were made in a well-prepared letter to the party, not in an anonymous denunciation or a summary of informers' talk.

54. Variagina and Vakulenko, *Narodna Hvardia imeni Ivana Franka*, 180.

Variagina and Vakulenko's work was unusual in that it included a small chapter on the genocide of Lviv's and Western Ukraine's Jews.[55] Although the Holocaust was not denied in the Soviet Union, on the whole, in Zvi Gitelman's summary, "the overall thrust of the Soviet literature was to assign" it "far less significance than it has been given in the West."[56] Generally, there was no contestation of the fact that Germans had murdered millions of Jews, but Soviet publications marginalized this crime. Attempts to commemorate it were resisted as privileging Jews.[57] In the 1946 report enshrining the first official Hvardia narrative, the ghetto had been described as a place set up by Germans specifically for Jews, but concentration camps were described as a place to kill "millions of Soviet and allied citizens." The report pointed out that mass graves in Lviv had contained the corpses of "Frenchmen, Czechs, Slovaks, Yugoslavs, Dutchmen, Britons, and Americans," but made no mention of Jews in this context. The victims of the Yanivska Camp and the Lysynychi Forest killing site were described as civilians and POWs.[58]

In Variagina's and Vakulenko's 1979 background chapter on the occupation regime, four out of seventeen pages described the Lviv ghetto and the mass murder of Jews.[59] The main labor and murder camp for Jews in Lviv, the Janowska or Yanivska camp, was not mentioned.[60] The German *Aktionen* of 1942 were, but only to show the collusion of the Ukrainian Police; readers did not learn that the roundup was the start of deportation to death camps. By comparison, the comprehensive history of Western Ukraine in the 1968 publication *The Triumph of Historic Justice* reported over a million victims killed by the Germans without once mentioning Jews.[61]

55. Pohl, *Nationalsozialistische Judenverfolgung*, 12. For a detailed analysis of Soviet discourse about the Holocaust in Lviv, see Amar, "A Disturbed Silence."

56. Zvi Gitelman, "Soviet Reactions to the Holocaust, 1945–1991," in *The Holocaust in the Soviet Union: Studies and Sources on the Destruction of the Jews in the Nazi-Occupied Territories of the USSR, 1941–1945*, ed. Lucjan Dobroszycki and Jeffrey S. Gurock (Armonk, NY: M. E. Sharpe, 1993), 6-7.

57. Gorovskii et al., *Evrei Ukrainy*, 196. As in Lviv, in Vilnius, too, the Jewish identity of Holocaust victims was eclipsed or deemphasized (Weeks, "Multi-Ethnic City in Transition," 166).

58. DALO P-183, 1, 123: 19–20, 24, 30.

59. Variagina and Vakulenko, *Narodna Hvardia imeni Ivana Franka*, 19.

60. The Yanivska camp did appear in the book at a later point. It was, however, mentioned in passing as a non-descript "concentration camp" from which guards opened fire on Hvardia members retreating after burning a factory, which had nothing to do with the Yanivska Camp (Variagina and Vakulenko, *Narodna Hvardia imeni Ivana Franka*, 74).

61. M. M. Oleksiuk, *Torzhestvo istorychnoi spravedlyvosti* (Lviv: Vydavnytstvo Lvivskoho universytetu, 1968), 616–17.

Yet Variagina and Vakulenko still deprived crimes against Jews of their specific context of antisemitism, subsuming them under a generalized "inhuman racial policy." Significantly, Jews had no voice in their own narrative. While non-Jewish victims of forced labor deportation featured in direct quotations, crimes against Jews were presented through the testimonies of German perpetrators or non-Jewish witnesses.

"Former member of the 'Narodna Hvardia' Moisei Naumovych Isaiev" functioned as an exception confirming the rule that being Jewish was special. With a name that readers would recognize as Jewish, Isaiev experienced German camps and narrowly escaped during a massacre of Soviet POWs. Yet, in Variagina and Vakulenko's account, his victimization was solely due to his identity as a Soviet soldier or underground member. In a biographical appendix, in most entries ethnicity was simply an adjective; Variagina was "Russian," Makivka was "Ukrainian." Isaiev, however, was not "Jewish" but had "been born into a Jewish family."[62] His national identity, unlike all others, was reduced to a childhood biographical accident, possibly overcome by the mature personality engaging in anti-German resistance.[63] Variagina and Vakulenko described some German crimes as specifically targeting Jews. While showing some, if not all, victimization of Jews as Jews, a *resister*, at any rate, was shown emphatically not as a Jew.[64]

In this last official version of the Hvardia myth, Poles were still almost as unwelcome as recognizable Jews. Yet they too were hard to suppress entirely since the original Hvardia had been so Polish. Variagina and Vakulenko conceded that it had been particularly difficult to organize an underground in Galicia, as they called it. Internal reports and the veteran interviews of the early 1960s had

62. Variagina and Vakulenko, *Narodna Hvardia imeni Ivana Franka*, 19, 97, 190.

63. The treatment of Isaiev's ethnicity was representative. As Zvi Gitelman has pointed out, in one of the main Soviet works on one of the key Great Fatherland War battle myths, the heroic and hopeless defense of the Brest Fortress, individual defenders represented a multinational combination of Soviet valor, including Russians, Ukrainians, Belorussians, Tatars, and even a German. A Jewish defender was also included but could be identified only through his name and an accumulation of stereotypically Jewish features (Gitelman, "Internationalism, Patriotism, and Disillusion,"105). In effect, his Jewish identity was made no less clear than the fact that, for some reason, it—unlike other identities—was unmentionable.

64. As Zvi Gitelman and Mordechai Altshuler have shown, the question of a particularly Jewish resistance to Nazism—in regular forces, partisan groups, or individually—remained virtually ignored to the end (Zvi Gitelman, "Soviet Reactions to the Holocaust, 1945–1991," in *The Holocaust in the Soviet Union*, ed. Dobroszycki and Gurock, 16; Mordechai Altshuler, "Jewish Warfare and the Participation of Jews in Combat in the Soviet Union as Reflected in Soviet and Western Historiography," in *Bitter Legacies*, ed. Gitelman, 160–63). An estimated 400,000–500,000 Jews fought in the Soviet forces. With high exposure to combat, they suffered about 180,000 casualties, while at least 147 Jews received the highest military decoration of the Soviet Union. Thus, as a nationality, Jews were clearly over-represented among the recipients as a whole (Gitelman, "Internationalism, Patriotism, and Disillusion," 101, 109–10; Gorovskii et al., *Evrei Ukrainy*, 144–79).

confirmed that attempts made in 1941 to send Soviet underground organizers to Lviv from the East had failed.[65] But in 1968, *The Triumph of Historic Justice* had still publicly maintained that most of these emissaries had reached western Ukraine.[66] Variagina and Vakulenko admitted that, for Lviv at least, these attempts had failed completely, as had all other efforts to link the Soviet leadership and the Lviv underground, until the spring of 1944.

The old question persisted: if Moscow had lost touch, who had been in charge? It was no challenge for Variagina and Vakulenko to dismiss "Polish nationalists" and their underground; to hardly mention the Polish majority population of wartime Lviv was also no new feat.[67] But *Communist* Polish influence on a pro-Soviet underground cut off from Moscow remained a challenge. Variagina and Vakulenko stressed the independent emergence of small underground groups in Lviv, who turned "to the PPR for help in organizational questions." They conceded that the Hvardia's name had been "adopted from the revolutionary underground of Poland," but they insisted that even "progressive" Poles, hobbled by nationalism, had not dominated the Hvardia.[68] Admitting that Ukrainians as well as Poles had been exposed to "reactionary" influences, they singled out Poles as particularly susceptible as well as hostile to the Soviet Union.[69]

Hvardia cadre Ivan "Rishard" Kurylovych represented Variagina and Vakulenko's assertion that the PPR, once put in its place, had continued to render useful "internationalist" assistance. In Polish historiography, Kurylovych was a PPR-appointed "commander" of Lwów's Gwardia Ludowa.[70] Variagina and Vakulenko identified him as a Belarusian and veteran of an International Brigades unit in Spain's Civil War, which was named after the Ukrainian national poet Taras Shevchenko; returning to Warsaw from internment in France, he had been sent to Lviv by the PPR leadership at the end of March 1943.

There, Variagina and Vakulenko's Kurylovych became an important but subordinate member of the Hvardia's leadership and then an "intelligence officer at

65. DALO P-1, 183, 170: 4.

66. Oleksiuk, *Torzhestvo istorychnoi spravedlyvosti*, 629.

67. In 1968 and 1969, the Lviv authorities planned to build a memorial for the mostly Polish academics massacred by the Germans in June 1941. Yet demands from the Polish Ministry of Culture to indicate the victims' national identity were rejected with several arguments: there had been Ukrainians and Jews among them, too; all of them were citizens of the Soviet Union when murdered; and the memorial should have an "international" character (DALO P-3, 13, 69: 13–14). In the end, the memorial was not built.

68. Variagina and Vakulenko, *Narodna Hvardia imeni Ivana Franka*, 29.

69. Ibid., 26.

70. Rishard Nazarevich [Ryszard Nazarewicz], "Soiuz polskykh ta ukrainskykh komunistiv u borotbi proty nimetsko-fashystskykh okupantiv," in M.I.Panchuk, Iu.Iu.Slyvka, *Aktualni problemy istorii KPZU* (Lviv: Svit, 1990), 37.

the disposal" of Soviet forces. After helping establish the first contact between the Soviet command and the Hvardia in 1944, he called himself a "patriot of the Soviet Union."[71] In this public narrative, an exemplary emissary from Warsaw was not ethnically Polish, had a proven "internationalist" record with a Ukrainian accent, came to Lviv late, participated in operational planning but not key decisions, established contact with Moscow, and moved on to fight in Prague.[72]

To what extent had the Hvardia itself been a Polish organization, in terms of its membership and the language of its publications or internal communication? Variagina and Vakulenko did not offer a survey of Hvardia membership. Instead they provided lists of individuals and ninety-two short biographical sketches and insisted that they characterized the Hvardia as a whole "by social status, nationality, party membership, [and] age." Out of this sample, fifty-six were Ukrainian, fifteen Polish, and nine Russian.[73] The obkom's 1947 list of Hvardia members, by contrast, listed two-thirds of the members as Poles and one-sixth as Ukrainians. The divergence between the versions of 1947 and 1979 was equally pronounced regarding party affiliation. Whereas the 1947 report had listed a large majority without any party or quasi-party affiliation, almost everybody listed in 1979 had some organizational tie. Variagina and Vakulenko also emphasized Hvardia propaganda but left its language fuzzy. Before the first underground publication in Ukrainian in the spring of 1943, at any rate, their Hvardia had relied on Polish publications, smuggled in from Warsaw.[74]

The Hvardia's official memory could never accommodate the national and political complexity or the comparative insignificance of Communist resistance in Lviv. In the same year in which Variagina and Vakulenko published their final word on the Hvardia, a more general publication on the Ukrainian Komsomol and its wartime underground organizations marginalized Lviv by hardly mentioning it.[75] Minimized in an all-Ukrainian context, in Lviv the Hvardia was exaggerated, de-Polonized, and Ukrainized.

71. Variagina and Vakulenko, *Narodna Hvardia imeni Ivana Franka*, 110–11, 195–96. Kurylovych was decorated in 1966 (DALO P-3, 9, 228: 18–20).

72. Kurylovych's party admission in Lviv made him summarize his war experiences. Identifying himself as "Belorussian by nationality," he had intended to go to Belorussia to engage in partisan warfare when redirected to Lviv. After his mission there, he was sent to Prague in April 1945. He joined the party in January 1952; by then he managed a Lviv dining hall. By 1966, he was running the prestigious Lvov restaurant (DALO P-3, 4, 128: 15; P-3, 4, 416: 1–2; P-3, 9, 228: 18).

73. Variagina and Vakulenko, *Narodna Hvardia imeni Ivana Franka*, 172–227.

74. Ibid., 40.

75. Yu. V. Babko, *Istoriia Leninskoi komunistychnoi spilky molodi Ukrainy* (Kyiv: Molod, 1979), 392–30, 396.

The KPZU Legacy: A Bundle of Problems

After 1956, the KPZU's de facto rehabilitation, in addition to reflecting "Thaw" policies, was part of a longer-term change, with the party-state coming to accept that Western Ukraine was something special—if in a Soviet way.[76] The growth of the Hvardia story and the restoration of the KPZU to official memory were connected in an immediate manner. As ten Hvardia veterans complained in a 1957 letter to the obkom, many of its members had belonged to the interwar KPZU, but immediately after the war, with the KPZU still officially denounced, they had been treated by Soviet authorities with the same distrust as Ukrainian nationalists.[77]

Yet there were important differences between these narratives. The Hvardia excised a Polish past. The KPZU constructed and integrated a Ukrainian past. The Hvardia allowed Lviv and Western Ukraine to share in a key aspect of the Great Fatherland War. The KPZU integrated them with the Great October Revolution, closely linking the Bolshevik Big Bang with local revolutionary traditions.

As Jochen Hellbeck has pointed out, one of the first Bolshevik initiatives was to connect history and memory by soliciting reminiscences from veterans of the revolution. Inscribing themselves into its narrative, they came to "own the revolution."[78] The revolution also made sure that it owned them. But how could this mutual if unequal ownership be extended to Western Ukraine, which had been outside the direct territorial reach of the Russian revolution? The KPZU needed first to be rehabilitated.

Moreover, in reality, the illegal interwar KPZU had never been a mass party, with membership between four thousand and five thousand at its peak and fluctuating strongly; a late Soviet publication estimated it at only slightly above six hundred in 1928. The number of survivors—especially inside Western Ukraine—was even smaller after Stalinist and German repression. Electorally, the interwar KPZU did have some temporary success. At its peak in 1928, its front parties got 250,000 votes. By 1936, however, pro-Communist parties received only a tenth of this result.[79] In Lwów, they never received more than 3.7 percent.[80] Northeast of Galicia, in Volhynia, the KPZU exerted influence

76. On the general context of Khrushchev's limited de-Stalinization, see Kathleen E. Smith, *Remembering Stalin's Victims: Popular Memory and the End of the USSR* (Ithaca, NY: Cornell University Press, 1996), 20–40; and Taubman, *Khrushchev*, 270–324, 513–28.

77. DALO P-183, 1, 184: 12.

78. Hellbeck, *Revolution on My Mind*, 27.

79. Lewytzkyj, *Die Sowjetukraine*, 27.

80. Mazur, *Życie polityczne polskiego Lwowa*, 420.

beyond its numbers, but in the area of the former Galicia it was weak.[81] By the late 1930s, Lwów KPZU representatives deplored their own marginalization and failure to understand the "national liberation" issues so effectively exploited by nationalists.[82] In 1938, after splits and purges, the Stalinist Comintern dissolved what was left of the KPZU, accusing it of nationalism and working for hostile intelligence services.[83]

Thus, before the party's 1956 rehabilitation Soviet public discourse could appeal only to a generic Western Ukrainian "revolutionary tradition" *without* a local leading party. The stakes were not merely local; they involved the relationship between an imperial order of revolutionary precedence and a local legitimization of Soviet rule, between a local pre-1939 revolutionary movement and the Great October Revolution as the basis of other proper revolutionary movements.

The Soviet repression of the KPZU also reawakened concerns left over from the 1930s Soviet purges and the first Soviet occupation of western Ukraine, when some KPZU veterans had been persecuted. Underlying these concerns was the broader question of the locals' status. The members of the KPZU were locals of proven, retrospectively denied, then reacknowledged Communist loyalty. If they had no place among the new elite of Soviet western Ukraine, who did? If other locals were, in fact, more welcome, their success cast a shadow over the loyalty that Soviet rule rewarded. Which was more important: opportunism or commitment? Moreover, to function without many of these potential local cadres meant a greater reliance on easterners.

The KPZU: Born to Split

Much of the KPZU's history involved its inner conflict and divisions. In the early 1920s, the Communist Party of Eastern Galicia (KPSH), the proto-KPZU, was integrated into the Polish Communist Party, dividing the KPSH/KPZU between those accepting this subordination, called KPR-ites, after the then acronym of the Polish party, and those who did not, called Vasylkivites, after their leader Osyp Krilyk's pseudonym, Vasylkiv. In the late 1920s, the KPZU split between those under Krilyk-Vasylkiv, who opposed the turn against Ukrainization in Soviet Ukraine, and those obeying it. The former were expelled from the Comintern in February 1928. Their leaders, including Krilyk-Vasylkiv, were [*sic*!] disappeared in

81. On the KPZU's influence in Volhynia, see Timothy Snyder, "The Life and Death of Western Volhynian Jewry, 1921–1945," in *Shoah in Ukraine*, ed. Brandon and Lower, 82.

82. AAN 165/VII-1, tom 8: 1–2.

83. For the shortest survey, see *Dovidnik z istorii Ukrainy* (Kyiv, 2001), 334.

Moscow.[84] In 1933, the two chief leaders of the remaining KPZU were also called to Moscow and killed. The dissolution of 1938 was only the peak of a long history of conflict and repression.

It was not the end, however. Now the memory of the party became the target. Official narratives of interwar "revolutionary struggles" omitted the region's own Communist party.[85] During the German occupation, KPZU veterans were important in the city's small Communist underground. But, at the same time, a Polish Communist in Lviv identified the main obstacle to Communist resistance as "ideological crisis" and claimed that "former KPZU members [were] disappointed in the Soviet Union."[86]

Until the Twentieth Congress in February 1956, the KPZU remained virtually unmentionable. Although there was a public debate on it in the late 1980s, it was only a late rehashing of its reemergence between 1956 and the early 1960s.[87] Inside party-controlled circles of select intellectuals and KPZU veterans the party's legacy was already discussed in the late 1940s. Stalin's death was the condition for any reassessment, which would have been impossible without Khrushchev's policies. Locally, some KPZU veterans appealed for admission to the Soviet Communist Party as early as 1945, stressing their prewar subversion of other parties.[88] According to a Soviet history, by 1947, thirty-four KPZU veterans had been admitted.[89] In these cases, what mattered most was not the applicants' KPZU past but their special service to post-1939 Soviet rule: Konstantin Staiko, also appointed to an important party position, was held up for emulation as a former "poor peasant" who had received decorations in the Great Fatherland War.[90] Stepan Lupyi had joined the Soviet police under the first Soviet occupation and Soviet internal security forces during the war against Germany; after victory, he

84. Janusz Radziejowski, *Komunistyczna Partia Zachodniej Ukrainy 1919–1929: Węzlowe problemy ideologiczne* (Cracow: Wydawnictwo literackie, 1976), 23; *Dovidnik z istorii Ukrainy*, 334.

85. I. M. Premysler, "Revoliutsiyna borotba proty polskoho panuvannia v Zakhidniy Ukraini," in *Zakhidna Ukraina*, ed. Ohloblin, 83–94.

86. Quoted in Mieczysław Juchniewicz, "Z działalności Organizacyjno-Bojowej Gwardii Ludowej w Obwodzie Lwowskim PPR-GL" *Wojskowy historyczny przegłąd*, no. 4 (1968): 130. In a more popular publication of 1972, co-authored by Juchniewicz, such traces of the real experience of the KPZU were gone and ex-KPZU members presented as happily joining the underground. See Władyslaw Góra and Mieczysław Juchniewicz, *Walczyli Razem: O wspóldziałaniu polskich i radzieckich oddziałów partyzanckich w latach drugiej wojny światowej* (Lublin: Wydawnictwo Lubelskie, 1972), 226.

87. For the 1980s, see David R. Marples, "The Ukrainians in Eastern Poland under Soviet Occupation, 1939–1941: A Study in Soviet Rural Policy," in *Deportation and Exile: Poles in the Soviet Union, 1939–1948*, ed. Keith Sword (London: Macmillan, 1994), 236–52, 236, and 250n.

88. DALO P-3, 1, 95: 8, 58–60.

89. *Narysy istorii Lvivskoi oblasnoi partinoi orhanizatsii* (1980), 235.

90. DALO P-3, 1, 361: 6–7.

quickly rose to become the deputy head of the criminal investigation department of Lviv's oblast police.[91]

The postwar party also held comparatively frank if exclusive discussions about how best to exploit local Communists. In August 1945, the Lviv miskom hosted a group of veterans of the pre-1939 anti-Polish and the post-1941 anti-German undergrounds to discuss the Soviet failure to make use of local underground members. Both Yaroslav Halan and Bohdan Dudykevych complained that this potential was neglected, but there was no explicit reference to the KPZU.[92] In effect, the meeting signaled the attempt to exploit some narrative of interwar local Communism without mentioning its party. In Olga Barkova's *Every Day*, a fictionalized Khrushchev calls a local veteran Communist "our gold reserve in the western oblasts." Yet the KPZU was not mentioned, while its front organization, Selrob, was.[93] If the KPZU was gold, conversion into the currency of politics and propaganda proved complicated.

When it was mentioned, the KPZU was excoriated. But this also caused tensions. In 1947, the obkom invited select Lviv intelligentsia representatives to discuss its legacy. The occasion was a conflict over newspaper articles by the Lviv University historian Volodymyr Horbatiuk, who described himself as "categorically opposed to giving the KPZU as a whole a good image."[94] Yet everybody agreed that something more important was at stake than one specific article.

One problem grew out of the intersection of personal and official memory. Yaroslav Halan—a local intellectual as well as a KPZU veteran—warned that many inhabitants of Western Ukraine still had personal memories of the interwar period, and making up things that directly contradicted them was inadvisable.[95] Fortunately, as Halan argued, there was no need to lie: the history of the local revolutionary tradition was "rich enough to write the truth and only the truth." But, in fact, it was too rich: a truer and more persuasive history would have to include the KPZU. Halan insisted that the history of a local revolutionary

91. DALO P-3, 5, 356: 9–10.

92. DALO P-4, 1, 58: 206–7. Like Halan, Dudykevych was a privileged KPZU veteran and an important local official (DALO P-3, 5, 356: 6–7).

93. Barkova, *Kazhdyi den*, 16, 329.

94. See DALO-P 3, 2, 104: 28–52, for all citations from this meeting. The meeting was also described very misleadingly in Vladimir Beliaev's 1974 ode to Halan, giving the impression that Halan's main point had been to attack Ukrainian nationalism (including inside the KPZU) once more. See Vladimir Beliaev and Anatoly Iolkin, *Yaroslav Halan* (Kyiv: Molod, 1974), 244. In a 1962 newspaper article, Bohdan Dudykevych wrote that Halan's complaint had inititated a meeting on local press attacks on the KPZU ("Communist, Fighter," *Vilna Ukraina*, 19 July 1962, 3).

95. See *Narysy istorii Lvivskoi oblasnoi partinoi orhanizatsii* (1980), 84, for Kozlaniuk's work for *Vilna Ukraina*.

movement was inconceivable without the KPZU in the lead: no KPZU, no revolutionary movement at all. Halan stressed the KPZU's self-sacrifice and "heroism," yet there was nothing to read about it. Personal memory, in the form of KPZU veterans' recollections, had been neglected but should be used.[96]

For Bohdan Dudykevych, then the director of Lviv's History Museum, the problem of the KPZU was part of a larger context. In 1946, he had already criticized propaganda statements claiming that, before Soviet rule, "the toilers did not vote but simply watched through the windows" as only the rich voted; such claims "ridicul[ed] the traditions of the Ukrainian working population." In 1955, Dudykevych deplored the way in which lecturers stressed the "backwardness" of pre-Soviet western Ukraine and presented "the masses not as creators of history but as an object."[97] Dudykevych wanted agency for pre-Soviet locals. He also warned that a denial of the KPZU permitted unreliable locals, such as Mykhailo Rudnytskyi, to downplay their own failure to support the interwar Soviet Union.[98] Local agency, in effect, came with local liability.[99]

The veteran local and promotee Kuzma Pelekhatyi, prosecuted as a KPZU activist by interwar Polish authorities, also insisted "that we be told the truth" about the KPZU. His personal biography was at stake: his interwar publication "What Is Collectivization?" denied and justified the mass famine of 1932/1933 in Soviet Ukraine, although every Ukrainian political party of interwar Poland—except the Communists—condemned it. Making his postwar way to the Soviet Union's Supreme Soviet, Pelekhatyi feared accusations of opportunism and wanted his interwar activism to be more publicly known, so that "nationalists" could no longer deride Communists as "old sell-outs."[100]

Suppressing the KPZU's memory while bestowing public honors on a select few of its veterans proved counterproductive; it could make them appear to be the opportunists their nationalist opponents loved to hate. At the same time, accusations of servility—under Habsburgs, Poles, Germans, the "western imperialists," and the Vatican—were an essential element of Soviet propaganda: the title of Petro Kozlaniuk's first postwar play, deploying crude satire against nationalism,

96. DALO P-3, 2, 104: 28–31.

97. DALO P-3, 1, 416: 57, 59; P-3, 5, 176: 44.

98. DALO P-3, 2, 104: 31–33.

99. DALO P-3, 2, 104: 31–33.

100. DALO-P 3, 2, 104: 38. On responses to the mass famine from Ukrainians in interwar Poland, see Kushnezh, "Uchast ukrainskoi hromadskosti Polshi," 132. On Sheptytskyi's public denunciation of the famine and Communism in general, see Budurowycz, "Sheptyts'kyi and the Ukrainian National Movement," 57. On Pelekhatyi's interwar prosecution, see Mazur, *Życie polityczne polskiego Lwowa*, 154, 392–96, 418; and *Narysy istorii Lvivskoi oblasnoi partinoi orhanizatsii* (1980), 36, 84.

was *The Sell-Outs*.[101] In a place rich in adaptations, everybody loudly agreed that adapting was wrong. And if local pre-1939 Communists were "sell-outs," then Soviet power was tarnished by the act of buying them.

Yet despite the arguments advanced by prominent locals, the dilemma persisted. Osechynskyi, then at the university's kafedra of Soviet history, warned of giving too much publicity to the KPZU, even though publicizing nobody would also be "water on the mills of our enemies." As before, only "individual leaders" should be presented, and even they should be praised only as individuals, not as KPZU veterans.

No significant changes in the treatment of the KPZU followed this meeting, but it demonstrated that, even when removed from public discourse, the issue lingered. Hrushetskyi, meanwhile, did his best to keep KPZU veterans out. In July 1947, he warned Kyiv Central Committee head Lazar Kaganovich that their applications needed special scrutiny.[102] According to a draft document, Kaganovich praised Hrushetskyi's initiative and ordered all western obkoms to remain wary of KPZU veterans.[103] Vladimir Beliaev later recalled a story of Hrushetskyi showing the irrelevance of a local revolutionary past: he described his visit to a village with an "exemplary" reputation for delivering produce, which was now slacking. Hrushetskyi told the local village soviet head, who used to be "a Communist," that if he did not take "decisive measures," then "he himself was striking out his own revolutionary past." The past of this local revolutionary veteran (which included surviving a German concentration camp) thus counted for nothing if he did not—literally—deliver: grain as well as fractious locals. The veteran then argued with his daughter and shot her dead. She had been the hidden enemy, a "fanatical nationalist." True or not, the tale's morale was obvious and pertinent, with references to ancient, biblical, and Pavlik-Morozov-type Soviet mythology as well as Gogol's hero *Taras Bulba*. Beliaev pointed out only the latter.[104]

Yet the local revolutionary tradition was celebrated even without the KPZU. In 1950 and 1951, the history department at Lviv's university made it a research

101. Yuryi Baida, *Petro Kozlaniuk: Zhyttia i tvorchist* (Kyiv: Radianskyi psymennyk, 1959), 137, 139.

102. This offer of Soviet party membership to select surviving members of the interwar Polish Communist Party, including its minority wings, was really made in the spring of 1941. It came late and was combined with a verification process that may have made potential candidates wary. According to Włodzimierz Bonusiak, in Western Ukraine, only thirty-four former KPP and KPZU members were admitted before the German invasion. See Andrzej Werblan, *Władysław Gomułka: Sekretarz Generalny PPR* (Warsaw: Książka i Wiedza, 1988), 92–94; and Bonusiak, *Polytika ludnościowa i ekonomiczna ZSRR*, 86. According to Amir Weiner, candidates also had to prove loyalty by informing on comrades (Weiner and Rahi-Tamm, "Getting to Know You," 15).

103. TsDAHOU 1, 23, 4080: 1–3.

104. Beliaev and Elkin, *Yaroslav Halan*, 255–56.

focus, and the city's Komsomol newspaper explained that there were three relevant topics in history: industrialization, collectivization, and the local interwar "Bolshevik struggle," while the obkom demanded more work on the latter from Lviv's Institute of Social Sciences of the Academy of Sciences.[105]

The KPZU, however, remained beyond bounds. Following a Moscow Central Committee decree, between 1951 and 1953, the Kyiv Central Committee screened all KPZU veterans who had already been admitted to the party. Acccording to correspondence between Melnikov and Khrushchev in April 1953, their total was around 600, but only 129 passed this fresh winnowing and were allowed to stay as party candidates, not full members.[106]

After Stalin's death that same year, however, small signs of relaxation appeared. In 1953, the obkom head Serdiuk attacked Lviv's university for excluding a student just because her father "used to be in the KPZU."[107] In late 1954 and 1955, the Lviv obkom and the Kyiv and Moscow Central Committees discussed how to address the party's memory after the director of Lviv's History Museum, Yuryi Hoshko, quarreled with the obkom over the party's legacy and called on the Moscow Central Committee. Hoshko, like Dudykevych, was a KPZU veteran. He joined the KPZU in 1936, then worked for the Soviet authorities during their first stint in Lviv, later serving in the Great Fatherland War. After joining the Soviet Communist Party in 1944, he became a propagandist. In 1951, he succeeded Dudykevych as the director of Lviv's History Museum.[108]

Hoshko complained that he had attempted to introduce some exhibits relating to the KPZU, but the obkom had had all of them removed. Like Halan before him, Hoshko questioned the plausibility of asserting a local pre-1939 revolutionary tradition without a local Communist party. In addition, Hoshko pointed out "the *essence of the issue*," by which he meant the KPZU's control of legal front organizations. If these organizations had not been controlled by Communists, they could not have been genuinely revolutionary—that is, Leninist. According to Hoshko, there was no ideologically convincing way to reconcile an affirmative memory of front organizations and selective oblivion for the KPZU: without the latter, the revolutionary tradition would have developed in a quite different direction under a hostile leadership. If the KPZU was unmentionable, then, Hoshko

105. "To Achieve the Preparation of Scientific Cadres," *Leninska molod*, 17 September 1950: 3; DALO R-119, 17, 158: 33–40; P-3, 4, 22: 28.

106. TsDAHOU 1, 24, 2749: 31, 41. The exact number of screened KPZU veterans is not clear, since those screened also included veterans of other non-Soviet Communist parties. Melnikov indicated a total of 683 screening cases without a separate figure for KPZU veterans. However, the latter clearly made up the vast majority, so that six hundred is a plausible estimate.

107. DALO-P 3, 3, 692, as reproduced in *Kulturne zhyttia*, 2:15.

108. DALO P-3, 5, 356: 8–9.

explained, "the revolutionary movement should not be shown at all"—a decision that would mean accepting Ukrainian nationalist denials of any local revolutionary movement in western Ukraine. Moreover, Hoshko implied, suppressing the KPZU's memory also invoked a countermemory portraying Soviet rule as conquest instead of liberation. Here was another loyal local speaking impeccable Bolshevik to Moscow, and his message was much worse than Halan's: Moscow's memory policies were not only ineffective but fundamentally self-defeating.

It is noteworthy that all post-1956 Soviet literature on the KPZU responded to Hoshko's complaint: a volume of KPZU veterans' memoirs, published in 1958 and coedited by Hoshko, claimed that the KPZU "worked *constantly* in *all* legal organizations" to pull the "masses away" from "bourgeois-nationalist and reformist" influence.[109] But in 1954 Hoshko's arguments had not yet prevailed, and he was not allowed to display the KPZU exhibits. The Party History Institute of the Kyiv Central Committee conceded that there had been many individual good Communists in the KPZU but insisted that, as a whole, it had been contaminated by hostile ideologies and intelligence services.[110]

Nobody addressed the fundamental contradiction that Hoshko had identified: how to construct a Western Ukrainian revolutionary tradition before 1939 without a leading Communist party and therefore inauthentic. Hoshko's failure showed that, although there was some room for local initiative in favor of KPZU commemoration, it was very restricted. It widened substantially only with Khrushchev's partial rehabilitation of the KPZU at the Twentieth Congress in 1956.

Resurrection from Afar, Partial Recall in Lviv

The city's first major Soviet-era history, *Outlines of the History of Lviv* (1956), praised the KPZU for organizing the working class and admitted that its 1938 dissolution had been a result of "provocation."[111] The KPZU reappeared as a proto-Soviet collective hero, but the hero was still a problem. One of the first official meetings to discuss the KPZU's newly resurrected past took place at the Lviv Institute of Social Sciences in December 1956. Chaired by the director, Ivan Krypiakevych, it brought together historians and KPZU veterans. Combining individual memory and archival research, the neglected history of the KPZU

109. Yu. H. Hoshko et al., eds., *KPZU—orhanizator revolutsinoi borotby: Spohady kolyshnikh chleniv Komunistychnoi partii Zakhidnoi Ukrainy* (Lviv: Knizhkovo-zhurnalne vydavnytstvo, 1958), 9 (my emphasis).

110. TsDAHOU 1, 30, 3655: 182–84. For Hoshko's complaint, DALO P-3, 5, 250: 135–36 (my emphasis).

111. B.K. Dudykevych et al., *Narysy Istorii Lvova*, 242, 274.

would finally be written, or such was the general idea. Two committees on KPZU history would be established in Lviv, one for archival and printed sources and the other to gather veterans' recollections.[112]

The meeting, however, demonstrated the potential for difficulties and conflicts inherent even in recovered memories of the KPZU. The ban on Krilyk-Vasylkiv and his alleged nationalism, for instance, was still in force. Nobody demanded his rehabilitation, but he emerged as more tragic than criminal, perhaps even ahead of his time. Clearly, once the revival started, it was hard to say where to stop or why. Reassessing a remote past, moreover, called into question a more recent one. If the KPZU was not as bad as formerly decreed, then what about those who had made it look so bad? Perhaps they were careerists, as Dudykevych suspected.[113] But what the meeting brought out most clearly was that harvesting KPZU veterans' recollections and authority for official Soviet discourse would be tricky, as was highlighted when the historian Oleksandr Karpenko read out his paper on the party's early history.[114]

The controversy over Karpenko's paper exposed another fundamental issue. For a local revolutionary tradition to develop deep roots, its origins should be early and local; to ensure that same tradition's Leninist purity required its subordination to the Great October Revolution. But a local revolutionary tradition could not be a mere copy of the demiurgic Bolshevik original. The whole identity of the remembered KPZU must have depended on Bolshevik example, which would, in Ukraine, also imply Russian superiority. Attendants at the meeting accused Karpenko of exaggerating local roots by backdating precursors of the KPZU's activity to Lviv students in 1916. Mykhailo Herasymenko, another historian, insisted that "the beginnings of real Communist organizations in Western Ukraine" should be sought in "organizations . . . set up by the Communist Party of Ukraine" or by Polish Communists, whereas the Communist Party of Ukraine should be seen as belonging to a "general-Russian-empire" (*zahalnorossiska*) organization. Karpenko rejected this "Kyiv variant."[115]

112. IUA 1, 181, 63 (minutes of institute meeting on KPZU history on 14 December 1956).

113. IUA 1, 181: 6. "Careerism" was a recurring trope of de-Stalinization, as Polly Jones has pointed out, resonating with pre-Soviet and Soviet ideas of opprobrium (*Myth, Memory, Trauma*, 36, 71, 178).

114. IUA 1, 181: 42, 73. Karpenko was a committed Communist and party member who had joined the party as a young man during the war. His biography featured combat service in multiple battles, including Stalingrad, and postwar graduation from the Higher Party School in Kyiv. In Lviv, he was a locally prominent scholar and activist. In 1950, nationalists tried but failed to assassinate him. See *Kulturne zhyttia*, 3:469 (doc. 126).

115. IUA 1, 181: 45–47. Herasymenko's term for "Russian" here implied imperial, not national, identity—comparable to some extent to "British" as against "English" and hard to translate.

The historian Mykola Kravets offered an important compromise. The KPZU's origins should not be framed as "a Ukrainian variant, or a Lviv variant, or a Kharkiv or Turkestani" one. Instead, convergence of outside and local initiatives should be stressed through the figure of Nestor Khomin, who had arrived "from Turkestan, where he gathered Galician Communists."[116] Later, Khomin would be popularized as a former Ukrainian soldier of the Habsburgs and POW in Russia, joining the revolution in a high-ranking Bolshevik office in Turkestan before being sent back to Galicia in 1919 to help Communism go west. Here was revolution from far abroad but embodied in a reimported and improved local, not unlike the fictitious heroine of Romm's film *The Dream*. Karpenko, however, still insisted, the "Communist movement was not imported into Western Ukraine."[117]

Among the KPZU veterans present, the issue of the local versus the imported resonated. The veteran Stakh Tsybrukh challenged Karpenko's thesis that early party members in western Ukraine had had no precise idea of, as he put it slightly anachronistically, the "Soviet Union."[118] Dudykevych also insisted that "beginning from 1918 our masses understood" the meaning of Soviet power.[119] Sydir Senyk and Yosyp Zavadka, also veterans, however, were skeptical. Senyk warned that it was hard to remember.[120] Zavadka felt that the meeting could "not produce . . . what the historians were looking for." These repositories of personal memory, when finally questioned, said they felt empty. Zavadka implied that Soviet repression had destroyed memory. It was a "pity" about the KPZU's leaders, but they were "not there" anymore: Vasylkiv would have had memories to share, but he and Senyk simply did not know enough.[121]

Senyk and Zavadka did address the important issue of what early local activists had known about revolutionary Russia. For Senyk, this invoked differences in nation building between Ukraine and Russia: he and his comrades had understood the end of the First World War and the Habsburgs as the doomsday of the

116. IUA 1, 181: 52.

117. IUA 1, 181: 69.

118. IUA 1, 181: 32. In a text Tsybrukh wrote in 1953, he had described himself after the First World War as a veteran of the Habsburg Italian front and an exploited worker growing into a strike organizer before, in 1920, for the first time being called a Bolshevik by "enemies." The Tsybrukh of 1953 remembered that the Tsybrukh of 1920 initially became "angry, although . . . not even really understand[ing] very well what bolshevism" was, then responded that he was neither a Communist nor a Bolshevik but would become one. In October 1920, he entered the proto-KPZU KPZH (DALO P-1, 2, 8: 2).

119. IUA 1, 181: 10.

120. IUA 1, 181: 13, 18. In fact, also in 1956, Senyk produced extensive and detailed written recollections, and with a purpose. In a letter he declared that "we cannot allow that our first steps of conscious history . . . will be blurred or dissolved in a 'common pot'" (DALO P-1, 2, 13: 1, 3–17). His memory clearly depended on context.

121. IUA 1, 181: 20–22.

bourgeois world but had lacked ideas about what would come next. Russians, meanwhile, had been ahead in finding the postbourgeois future, but the reason was circumstantial: Ukrainians had been delayed by also having to "solve the national question" and thus "two issues and not only one like the Russian people."

Publicly silencing KPZU veterans was no longer policy. Yet making them speak produced disturbing responses. The question at hand was when and how correctly Galician Ukrainians had understood Soviet and Russian Socialism. Senyk's answer was about who happened to be ahead in nation building. The answer to a question about Socialism was still—and again—national: like the party itself, memories of the KPZU could still destabilize the delicate balance between socialist content and national form on which the Soviet political order rested.

For Zavadka, the national effectively overrode the social. Galicia's Ukrainians, he explained, had been oppressed by Germans and Poles, which crippled Ukrainians' capacity for a social/ist revolution; instead they rose "to fight for independence" and "Polish land."[122] Publicly, in 1969, Zavadka would remember "the torch of October . . . always" shining "brilliantly for the Communist fighters" of pre-1939 western Ukraine.[123] In the small circle of 1956, he admitted to initially opposing the "Bolsheviks." Already a Communist by 1920, he was still antagonized by Polish Communists claiming eastern Galicia for Poland, which made him side with Krilyk-Vasylkiv to "fight for Ukraine." Moreover, the Comintern, he implied, let itself be used by Poles against Ukrainians.

Apparently, Zavadka's first personal contact with Communism was through an activist visiting his home village—"an easterner," as his manner of speech suggested. Later, when divisions between Poles and Ukrainians within the KPZU escalated, Zavadka remembered, another "comrade from the East, by nationality Jewish," arrived to intervene, without success.[124] In sum, according to Zavadka, if local Ukrainians rose, then they did so in pursuit of national liberation from Poles and of Polish land; Communism's first local representative spoke in an unlocal way; and the Comintern, *the* institution of internationalism, was manipulated by Poles against Ukrainians and, when trying to act as an intermediary, took the shape of an ineffective outsider from "the East." From a Soviet perspective, what else could have been wrong with this picture? Moscow had once shut down the KPZU. Now it wanted historians and veterans in Lviv to bring it back into public memory, but their meeting showed that they could not agree on how to comply. Rehabilitation, it turned out, was neither a simple release nor a reassuring closure but a way to both new and old problems.

122. IUA 1, 181: 24.
123. *Narysy istorii Lvivskoi oblasnoi partinoi orhanizatsii* (1969), 62.
124. IUA 1, 181: 23–25.

Spillover

Despite these difficulties, the party-state project of writing the KPZU back in continued. In 1957, the Kyiv Central Committee and the Lviv obkom ordered two major publications combining biographical sketches and recollections, as well as two marble memorial plaques in Lviv.[125] It quickly became clear, however, that restoring the memory of the KPZU had the potential for contagion. For example, Karpenko built on his controversial paper with a study, now better known than his work on the KPZU, of the Western Ukrainian National Republic (ZUNR) after the First World War. In this study, later dubbed "revisionist," he went beyond the orthodox Soviet interpretion of the ZUNR as reactionary deception and treason to argue that it was a real revolution, if only of the national-democratic and bourgeois type, with some genuine if misguided mass and worker support.

A posse of ideological vigilantes struck back. With Bohdan Dudykevych and Valentyn Malanchuk leading the chase in *Vilna Ukraina*, Karpenko was accused of isolating the revolutionary movement in Galicia from eastern Ukraine (then, in reality, in another state), exaggerating links between eastern Galicia and Austria-Hungary (the state where it was actually located at the time), confusing the aspirations of the masses with the interests of the local bourgeoisie, idealizing the latter, and even equating the formation of the ZUNR and the Great October Revolution.[126] Karpenko lost his institute job, receiving a new position with stricter supervision at Lviv's university history department, where, within a few years, he was demoted for "blacken[ing] everything done by the party."[127]

It bears emphasis that Karpenko's better-known reinterpretation of the "bourgeois" ZUNR was a direct outcome of his work on the Communist KPZU. As he explained in 1958, the influence of KPZU documents had caused his

125. DALO P-3, 6, 88: 56. Lviv historians, writers and party officials—including Petro Kozlaniuk and Valentyn Malanchuk—staffed the editorial committees; academic institutions were to assist (DALO P-3, 6, 28: 9–11; P-3, 6, 142: 104–9).

126. DALO P-3, 6, 360: 4; Volodymyr Badiak, "Nelehka borotba proty tendentsiinosti: Vystup I. Krypiakevycha v obhovorenni statti pro Lystopadovy zryv 1918 r.," in Isaievych, *Ivan Krypiakevych u rodynnii tradytsii*, 473–75, 805; William Jay Risch, "Historical Memory as Nonconformity: Institute of Social Sciences under Ivan Krypiakevych," in *Ivan Krypiakevych u rodynnii tradytsii* ed. Isaievych, 915–17; Marusyk, *Zakhidnoukrainska humanitarna intelihentsia*, 206; *Kulturne zhyttia*, 3:248 (doc. 65), 536 (doc. 142), 738–52 (doc. 212). On Karpenko, the KPZU, and the ZUNR, see also Risch, *The Ukrainian West: Culture and the Fate of Empire in Soviet Lviv* (Cambridge, MA: Harvard University Press, 2011), 150–55.

127. *Kulturne zhyttia*, 3:476 (doc. 127). Karpenko had also given the impression that "naked violence" was the basis of collectivization. A persecuting colleague complained that students could get the feeling that "only Karpenko tells them the truth and other lecturers don't." Karpenko knew about collectivization from personal experience: he had volunteered as a party organizer for a postwar collective farm in western Ukraine (*Kulturne zhyttia*, 3:469 [doc. 126]).

"confusion." Malanchuk countered that the KPZU's position on the ZUNR reflected the former's nationalist deviation.[128] By reading the unsealed traces of past deviation, Karpenko had become deviant himself.

More specifically, Karpenko's interpretations of both the KPZU and the ZUNR could affect the historical ties of the former eastern Galicia, here implicitly understood as proto-Western Ukraine. His KPZU theses reimagined teleologies construed as shared among the postwar Soviet periphery, the center, and its sacrosanct origins in Petrograd in 1917. But Karpenko's rethinking of the ZUNR, as inspired by KPZU documents, implied a deeper challenge: it was only in countries belonging to the postwar outer empire, such as Poland, that Soviet narratives accorded some legitimacy to "national-bourgeois revolutions" at the end of the First World War. Since eastern Galicia was part of Austria-Hungary at that time, it too should have undergone such a revolution. As Karpenko put it, the revolution that gave rise to the ZUNR "was bourgeois-democratic" as well as part of a larger whole other than the Russian Empire: its "tasks" were "facing *all* peoples *of Austro-Hungary*."[129] On heterodox but Marxist terms, Karpenko here was resurrecting not a suppressed interwar Communist party but the Habsburg Empire—not as a legitimate political order but as an authentically different space of revolution at a legitimately different historical stage.

What made this "confusion" intolerable was that it was plausible and traced a fault line in the Soviet understanding of time. Karpenko had hit on the precise spot where post-1939 Soviet space and post-1917 Soviet time failed to meet. The incorporation of western Ukraine into the Soviet Union came with a backward and westward projection of Leninist (emphatically not "national-democratic") revolution. The historic decision to include western Ukraine in the Soviet Union, unlike the image of the KPZU, was not amenable to revision from above. After 1956, the rehabilitation of the KPZU constituted an attempt to further integrate western Ukraine. Legitimizing the ZUNR on terms that were both Marxist and oddly Habsburg implied the opposite, even if Karpenko failed to notice. As Malanchuk told a 1958 meeting at the institute, there were things "discussable" and things "not discussable."[130]

128. *Kulturne zhyttia*, 3:748 (doc. 212).

129. Isaievych, *Ivan Krypiakevych u rodynnii tradytsii* 475 (my emphasis).

130. Volodymyr Badiak, "Nelehka borotba proty tendentsiinosti," in *Ivan Krypiakevych u rodynnii tradytsii*, ed. Ivan Krypiakevych, 805; *Kulturne zhyttia*, 3:742 (doc. 212). At the same time, it is worth noting that Karpenko's digression and punishment can also be seen in a wider context of post-1956 challenges to Soviet dogma that went beyond the narrow limits the leadership was ready to tolerate. Against this background, Karpenko paid a comparatively small price for his heterodoxy: compare with the fate of Lev Krasnopevtsev, a Moscow University history graduate student and Komsomol leader, and those charged with following him, who ended up in the camps (Jones, *Myth, Memory, Trauma*, 90).

Back in Town

While intellectuals struggled with the limits of the discussable, the newly available memory of the KPZU was projected into Lviv's public space.[131] On the 1957 anniversary of the Soviet invasion in 1939, *Lvovskaia pravda* published "In the Footsteps of Our Fathers," a long article on a guided tour through Lviv for young workers of the Lviv Electric Lamp Factory.[132] The excursion and article, later republished as a booklet, mobilized the recovered KPZU for recovering youth, neatly framing the party's memory between the universal Great October Revolution and the local 1939 "liberation."[133]

The Electric Lamp Factory was a beacon of Soviet modernization.[134] A new generation of its young workers, according to "In the Footsteps," now "expressed a burning desire to learn about the history of their home city," and Lviv's Lenin Museum had "long wanted to organize meetings between old KPZU activists and youth." The vehicle for the one-day excursion in search of their home's revolutionary past was a symbol, the newest 1957 model of Lviv's Bus Factory, named "Lviv." Its design and production marked a special milestone of Lviv's industrialization.[135] Touring Lviv's revolutionary past in the shiny, comfortable, and modern Lviv bus, the workers visited the Lviv Opera, the site of the 1939 Popular Assembly, the Lenin Museum, and sites of local revolutionary martyrology, such as a prison and heroes' graves. With each site featuring a meeting with a

131. International events and criticism from the center added urgency, especially regarding youth. In June 1957, the Moscow Central Committee castigated youth work in Ukraine's western oblasts for failing to counter the effects of the "Hungarian events," persistent religion, and general apathy. For some Lvivians, moreover, the wrong memories resurfaced. Shevchenko raion reported rumors about Lviv reverting to Poland (DALO P-3, 6, 82: 52–63; P-4, 1, 728: 173).

132. *Lvovskaia pravda*, 17 September 1957: 2–4.

133. A. Bulychova and P. Degtiarov, *Shlakhamy batkiv: Rozpovid pro odnu ekskursiiu* (Lviv: Knyzhkovo-zhurnalne vydavnytstvo, 1958).

134. Dudykevych et al., *Narysy istorii Lvova*, 320.

135. For the prototype, see *Istoriia gorodov i sel ukrainskoi SSR: Lvovskaia oblast* (Kyiv: Glavnaia redaktsiia Ukrainskoi sovetskoi entsiklopedii, 1978), 120; and a longer story in Dudykevych et al., *Narysy istorii Lvova*, 327–28, where it features as an exemplary tale of industrialization. Receiving orders from the Union Ministry of Automobile Industry to overhaul the dated ZIS-155, the whole staff of the Lviv Bus Factory agreed solemnly with the factory Communists' proposition to build the "more perfect" prototype LAZ-695. The new model, developed between August 1955 and November 1956, then passed muster with the ministry as well as the car factories of Moscow: Lviv had signally justified Moscow's trust. In Soviet guidebooks, Lviv buses retained a special aura of progress, symbolizing the Soviet modernization of the city as well as its catching-up to industrial equality with the rest of the Soviet Union (Solomonchuk, *Lvivshchyna turystska*, 11). In 1982, a Lviv miskom secretary gave a prominent place to the buses in a *Lvovskaia pravda* article. Once more affirming that "Contemporary Lvov is a major industrial and cultural center, which has grown and grown strong under the hot sun of the Soviet Fatherland" (Sovetskaia Otchizna), the article pointed out that Lviv buses were used in many Soviet cities and that the staff of the Lviv Bus Factory was

Figure 8.1 Lviv Bus Factory (built 1945–1950), 1964: Buses of the LAZ-695 "Lviv" Model. Collections: Mykhailo Tsimerman and Center for Urban History of East Central Europe, Lviv.

revolutionary veteran, the first meeting did *not* turn on local tradition but on faraway origins. At the Lenin Museum, a helpfully lucid veteran of the 1917 storming of the Winter Palace told tales of epic fights. A trip down hometown memory lane still began in fantasy Petrograd.

Subsequent encounters, however, were local. The young workers were reminded of class oppression, poverty, and heroism in pre-Soviet times. The leitmotif was youthful forgetfulness: finding their factory's daily output beating the annual output of a Polish predecessor plant, they did not know that after the war there had been only "a dirty wasteland" and a "dwarf factory" ruined by Germans.

Every Soviet achievement was compared to its absence before 1939. There had been no clubs, libraries, or cinemas for youth. Even young Kuzma Pelekhatyi and Yaroslav Halan had had to sneak into a Greek Catholic reading room. But now all

particularly proud that its hundred thousandth bus had been given as a present to "Ulianov oblast, the home region" (*rodina*) of Lenin. Moreover, all Lvivians should feel a "special pride" that "the cosmonauts at the cosmodrome get to the start ramp on Lviv buses" (*Lvovskaia pravda*, 25 August 1982, quoted in Bryk et al., *Istoriia Lvova v dokumentakh i materialakh*, 351). From the birth of the secular messiah to the leap into space, Lviv buses ran through it.

roads were "open to youth." In return, young people had to "appreciate everything which Soviet power has given us, the Great October, what your fathers have won." A graveside meeting with the Hvardia veteran Vozniak tied ancestral achievements to the Great Fatherland War. Reminded that thousands had died for "today's happiness," the young duly promised "to appreciate" and to "follow in the footsteps of our fathers." In this fantasy staging of an ideal Lviv, it all came together: the Great October Revolution, the "liberation" of 1939, the test and triumph of the war against Germany, the young and their ignorance, the old and their memory, the dead and the living, the universally Soviet and the revolutionarily local, deliverance and gratitude.

Closing Closure

Although Lviv was permitted to remember the KPZU, making it history remained a challenge. By September 1958, editors and contributors had compiled 222 KPZU documents, most to be published for the first time; most were in Polish, many in Ukrainian.[136] But the Ukrainian language of the KPZU documents was different, marked by Polish influences. Ivan Nazarenko called a meeting at the Kyiv Party History Institute to decide whether to edit it into "modern" Soviet Ukrainian.[137]

For Nazarenko, the KPZU's deviations from his idea of Ukrainian were the "result of oppression" and now incomprehensible, even in western Ukraine.[138] In effect and paradoxically, the KPZU needed Soviet Ukrainian translation and lexical purging to become locally understandable and lose the humiliating marks of its local adaptations. Bohdan Dudykevych, however, insisted on the original language; editing it would be "a crude infringement," which Ukrainian nationalists would exploit to deny the local revolutionary tradition. For him, different kinds of Ukrainian were evidence of local revolutionary authenticity.[139] Dudykevych prevailed and even Nazarenko's compromise proposal—"modern language with a preface"—was rejected.[140] The documents were to be published with only minor editing.[141] The KPZU would speak again and, mostly, in its own, unmistakably local, disturbingly hybrid voice.

136. TsDAHOU 39, 7, 6: 7, 11–12.

137. For the codification of Ukrainian, its politics, and persistent tensions over "what was to be regarded as true Ukrainian," see James Dingley, "Ukrainian and Belorussian—A Testing Ground," in *Language Planning in the Soviet Union*, ed. Michael Kirkwood (London: Macmillan, 1989), 185.

138. TsDAHOU 39, 7, 5: 1–2, 9.

139. TsDAHOU 39, 7, 5: 3.

140. TsDAHOU 39, 7, 5: 13.

141. TsDAHOU 39, 7, 5: 24.

Yet, symptomatically, the meeting was only about the selection of documents, not a new synthetic narrative. The Stalinist tale of treason and nationalism had not been replaced by an equally developed story. Thus, in 1960, when Herasymenko and Dudykevych published "The Struggle of the Toilers of Western Ukraine for Unification with Soviet Ukraine," they claimed that new research would "show more broadly the activity of the KPZU."[142] Yet, in reality, the book was merely an expanded edition of a work produced in 1955, hardly incorporating fresh research. At a Lviv University party meeting in 1971, a speaker complained that there was still no "academic work" on the history of the KPZU.[143] Indeed, a synthetic and academically certified new story was never produced. The new narrative also never addressed its own origins. Why was it new all of a sudden, and why had the KPZU been suppressed for nearly two decades? A story meant to recover a suppressed past never recovered the suppression itself.

Herasymenko and Dudykevych, for instance, showed the KPZU directing the struggle against the Polish "occupiers" and for "unification with Soviet Ukraine," organizing strikes, subverting legal organizations, and leading workers as well as the "progressive intelligentsia."[144] In short, their local interwar Leninists finally did what a Leninist had to do. Yet the text was almost silent about the party's 1938 dissolution: the strange death of the KPZU was still blamed on outside intrigue.[145] While the Stalinist story had blamed the KPZU to serve its own ends, the post-Stalin version flatly regretted the Comintern's "mistake."[146] A fuzzy blur with a warmer glow had replaced an icy blank spot. The new version also said nothing about the party's return to memory.[147] The life of the KPZU had some past again; its death, oblivion, and resurrection had none—and would never have.

Local Limits

In this period, when Lviv's newspapers were covering Cuba's "romance of the revolution," the local romance with the KPZU kept stalling.[148] Available Polish police documents on the KPZU remained off-limits; they were mixed up with

142. M. Herasymenko and Bohdan Dudykevych, *Borotba trudiashchykh zakhidnoi Ukrainy za vozzednannia z radianskoiu Ukrainoiu* (Kyiv: Derzhavnyi vydavnytstvo politychnoi literatury URSR, 1960), ii.

143. *Kulturne zhyttia*, 3:577 (doc. 158).

144. Herasymenko and Dudykevych, *Borotba trudiashchykh zakhidnoi Ukrainy*, 68, 73, 86–89, 132–35, 158, 161–67, 172–77.

145. Ibid., 191–92, 203–22.

146. Ibid., 186.

147. Ibid., 186.

148. On the general enthusiasm about Cuba in the Soviet Union, see Zubok, *Zhivago's Children*, 118–19.

information about "bourgeois nationalists." Once more, resurrecting the KPZU came with the risk of contagion.

In late 1958, the Party History Institute reported that the publication of biographical sketches of KPZU members had been stopped. The editors in Lviv, led by obkom secretary Valentyn Malanchuk, had exceeded their powers and eluded supervision: their manuscript needed special review.[149] A consensus emerged that the collection, at least in its current shape, could not be published. For example, a story about a KPZU activist showed his journey from ignorant peasant to conscious and revolutionary worker, reading aloud from newspapers during work breaks, in a traditional Soviet vein. Yet the topic of his reading was the Boer War, and he and his listeners "of course, sympathized with the Boers." One reviewer deplored the way in which he grew "into a 'conscious worker-revolutionary' . . . without any participation in the revolutionary movement." Locally, there had, it seemed, been different paths to Socialism, leading through eastern Galicia as well as the Boer Republic.[150]

In February, Nazarenko found that the collection was unpublishable. Five of the featured activists had been repressed in the 1930s and not rehabilitated by the party. There was too little on the fight against Ukrainian nationalism and for unification with Soviet Ukraine. Nazarenko warned that publication could lead to undesirable reactions in Poland, too. He suggested cannibalizing the manuscript. Parts of it should, after fresh editing, be released individually in newspapers or on the radio.[151]

In 1961, the Twenty-Second Party Congress added fresh momentum to the selective attack from above on Stalin's legacy. His corpse was removed from the Red Square mausoleum and *Pravda* and Khrushchev even called for a monument to his victims.[152] Locally, in Lviv, Bohdan Dudykevych called for the "renewal of revolutionary traditions" to provide "legends" for "a new generation."[153] In 1962, the obkom noted that, with 140 applications from KPZU veterans to join the Communist party resulting in 134 admissions, everybody eligible had now joined; eighty-six veterans had received new apartments and at least fifty additional pensions; historical research and commemoration were underway.[154]

149. See TsDAHOU 39, 7, 8: 27–30; and 39, 7, 13: 1–36, for the review process. According to a Lviv obkom note of September 1959, Malanchuk was in fact one of the three editors, who were really working on the collection, together with the historians Hoshko and Kravets (DALO P-3, 6, 371: 53).

150. TsDAHOU 39, 7, 13: 28, 32.

151. TsDAHOU 39, 7, 14: 1–6. When the early 1960s brought increasing coverage in Lviv newspapers of the KPZU and the Western Ukrainian revolutionary tradition, some of it may have been the by-product of Kyiv's restricting more substantial publications.

152. Taubman, *Khrushchev*, 514–15.

153. DALO P-3, 8, 424: 66.

154. DALO P-3, 8, 299: 49. 102–5.

Yet the surge in publicity for the KPZU was about to peak. On 23 July 1963, *Lvovskaia pravda* sealed the new interpretation of the KPZU in a long article, "For a Correct Exposition of the History of the Communist Party of Western Ukraine," a reprint from *Kommunist*.[155] The KPZU's interwar importance was reconfirmed, and its 1938 dissolution blamed on provocation, the cult of personality, and Lazar Kaganovich's "intrigue." The fuzzy blur at the heart of the unacknowledged dissolution now acquired a human and, perhaps not accidentally, Jewish face. The article also stressed the need for more historical study of the KPZU and deplored lost opportunities when the local revolutionary movement had been reduced to "a spontaneous process, without the leading role of the Communist party," which, "to a certain extent, disarmed Soviet historians and propagandists."[156] Halan and Hoshko, it was officially if implicitly stated, had been right.

The article not only secured but also restricted the results of the KPZU's rehabilitation. It codified a new relationship between local revolutionary tradition and Communist leadership, not a simple increase in local agency. For the more the KPZU's memory grew, the *less* room there was for "spontaneous" traditions. Now the KPZU, and only the KPZU, provided the missing link for those trying to assert the indispensable leading role of Bolsheviks or their followers over a territory not part of the interwar Soviet Union. Rehabilitating the KPZU meant both highlighting and subordinating the local.

Before the Fall

In October 1987, Soviet General Secretary Mikhail Gorbachev and Ukrainian First Secretary Vladimir Shcherbitskii received a letter signed by a group of twenty-one Hvardia and KPZU veterans. Demanding more Ukrainian in public life and education, they argued that neglecting Ukrainian fed into the propaganda of foreign "anti-Communists" and "Ukrainian nationalists."[157] Clearly, by this time, the authority of the KPZU and the Hvardia could be employed to cautiously criticize Soviet policies. Yet, even with Soviet legitimacy weakening, the fundamental taboos on the Hvardia and KPZU remained in force. In July 1989, a *Vilna Ukraina* article celebrated a Hvardia that still eclipsed the Polish past by

155. *Kommunist* was the "theoretical and political newspaper of the Central Committee" in Moscow. In the 1969 second edition of *Outlines of History of the Lviv Oblast Party Organization*, the article was the principal, and only, reference to the rendition of the 1927/1928 crisis (*Narysy istorii Lvivskoi oblasnoi partinoi orhanizatsii* [1969], 37).

156. *Lvovska pravda* [sic], 23 July 1963, 2–3. The article's message was repeated in a similar piece, also citing *Kommunist*, in *Radianska Ukraina* (i.e., on the Ukrainian-republic level) on 21 August 1963.

157. DALO P-1, 2, 339: 26–32.

omitting both the Home Army and the Gwardia Ludowa. The PPR's role in the Hvardia was distorted as before and Polish input omitted.[158] As to the KPZU, by the beginning of 1990, with Lviv's central Lenin statue under threat and living KPZU veterans reduced to several dozen, there were obkom plans to enhance the city's Lenin Museum across the street from the teetering sculpture with a permanent exhibition on the KPZU.[159] In the end, this last bid for a fusion of the universal and the local failed: Lenin's statue disappeared, while his museum was rededicated not to the KPZU but to art, including religious icons.

It marked the irony of western Ukraine's Soviet history of the present as well as its persistence that what survived the end of Soviet rule was what could be assimilated into a post-Soviet, nationally centered reading of local history, with Soviet tales of the local reduced to their omissions. While the Hvardia and the KPZU have now been consigned to oblivion, Poles and Jews have only slowly been retrieved from that same oblivion.

158. M. Belinsky, M. Teslenko, and L. Shlemkevych, "Zvytiaha muzhnikh: Borotba trudiashchykh Lvivshchyny proty nimetsko-fashystskykh zaharbnykiv," *Vilna Ukraina*, 16 July 1989, 2.

159. DALO P-3, 62, 757: 1–4.

Conclusion

A *Sonderweg* through Soviet Modernity

One of the first major Soviet publications to address the meaning of the "liberation" of Western Ukraine, published in Moscow on the occasion of its first anniversary in 1940, explained that the army of the country of Socialism had "liberated the toilers of the *former* Western Ukraine."[1] In the same year, the obkom head of one of the new western oblasts told the Fifteenth Congress of the Communist Party of Ukraine that "there is no Western Ukraine any more": all that remained was one united Soviet and Socialist Ukraine.[2]

Almost half a century later, in 1989, for the fiftieth and last major anniversary of the "liberation," Iakiv Pohrebniak (Iakov Pogrebniak), the head of the Lviv obkom and a candidate of the Ukrainian Politburo, spoke on the "unification of Western Ukraine with Soviet Ukraine."[3] In the same year, before a plenum of the Kyiv Central Committee on the "National Politics of the Party in Contemporary Conditions," he reiterated the multiple "historical, political, and economic particularities" of "our western region and the city of Lviv": problems had accumulated there for decades, and perestroika had only made them worse.[4]

In fact, soon after Stalin's death the party-state had adapted to the real outcome of western Ukraine's and Lviv's catching-up with Soviet Socialism. After 1956, its ideologists and historians began to write and speak in ways combining two goals—to praise the unification of Ukraine into one Soviet Socialist state in beneficial subordination to a Soviet Union dominated by a senior Russia and to construct elements of a distinct Western Ukrainian past to fit this larger scheme. In this case, these ideological shifts in the superstructure of official discourse did

1. M. Bril, *Osvobozhdennaia zapadnaia Ukraina* (Moscow: Politizdat, 1940), 3 (my emphasis).

2. TsDAHOU 1, 1, 601: 64.

3. "Naviky razom: Urochisty sbory u Lvovi, prysviacheni 50-richchiu vozziednannia Zakhidnoi Ukrainy z Radianskoiu Ukrainoiu u skladi Soiuzu RSR," *Vilna Ukraina*, 24 October 1989, 2.

4. *Vilna Ukraina*, 21 October 1989, 2.

reflect developments at the base: if initially some Soviet invaders had thought that western Ukraine had been "liberated" so that it would disappear, it persisted with the willing and unwilling, intentional and unintentional support of decades of Soviet postwar policy.

But if the Soviet period did have an influence so much deeper than a reductionist focus on repression and resistance alone would suggest, what were its effects? One year after Pohrebniak's speech, in the fall of 1990, with the Soviet empire in crisis and its myths up for—partial—revision, the Lviv obkom called a major conference, this time on the fifty-first anniversary of the unification of 1939. It would turn out to be the last such anniversary, celebrated in a Soviet Union whose own unity was terminally fragile. In his speech, obkom secretary Honcharuk acknowledged that the crimes of the Stalin period, including the Hitler-Stalin Pact and Soviet deportations, had marred the unification, but it remained an act of "humanism" and "justice."[5] The challenge now, following Honcharuk's logic, was merely to separate the criminal and contingent from the historically necessary and the nationally and socially just.

But for contemporary Lviv, fully shedding the legacy of Sovietization means questioning more than Stalinism or the conformism and mythomania on which the Soviet order had no monopoly but which it spread with great energy and bumbling mastery. Clearly, the Communist party's last instructions on what to think about the past it had made, voiced by a humbled yet still presumptuous obkom secretary, were insufficient. Rethinking the Soviet past also requires rethinking the present. Lviv's post-Soviet rise of both civil society and radical-right politics and nationalist revisionism has shown this to be harder than tackling Stalin's shadow. If Lviv and what it stands for in Ukraine is special, as often claimed, it is rash to assume that it is especially liberal. If it is a window on the West, that West cannot be reduced to civil society, democracy, pluralism, and individualism. In fact, historically, its darker side, from fascism and ethnic nationalism to the perversions of Enlightenment rationality that fed into Stalinism, has been at least as important.

Persistent differences between western Ukraine and central/eastern Ukraine—that is here, Ukraine Sovietized from 1939 versus Ukraine before 1939—have long been noted. Post-Soviet electoral patterns are one indicator.[6] The relative strength of protest movements, especially during the Orange Revolution of 2004

5. DALO P-3, 62, 727: 2, 5.

6. For post-Soviet election and referendum patterns as evidence of Lviv's peculiarity in Ukraine, see Roman Szporluk, "The Strange Politics of Lviv: An Essay in Search of an Explanation," in his *Russia, Ukraine, and the Breakup*, 312.

and the Second Maidan of 2013/2014, are another. A disproportionate share of Soviet-era Ukrainian dissidents coming from western Ukraine was a third.[7] Recent research confirms that, among Ukraine's regions, western Ukraine is the one most clearly distinguishable in terms of demography, political orientation, language, and economy.[8] It is also especially influential: political scientists have identified a spreading of western Ukrainian political views to central Ukraine as a key dynamic of Ukraine's post-Soviet history.[9]

Traditionally, these peculiarities of Lviv and western Ukraine have been attributed to three main causes. First, what was made into Soviet western Ukraine only after 1939 had a history of Habsburg constitutionalism and relative nationality-policy liberalism as opposed to eastern Ukraine's historic path through Russian imperial and Soviet authoritarianism. This explanation citing long-term differences in political culture has meshed reassuringly with more general narratives about the Soviet period in central and eastern Europe and with current assertions of local pride.[10] Since the last years of the Cold War, for activists, intellectuals, and politicians, claiming a Central European legacy, superior to the "supposedly Asiatic nature of Tsarist Russia and the USSR," has been important.[11] The past, however, is again more complicated than we tend to remember: ironically, the Habsburg stereotype of Galicia's politics was one of corruption, with "Galician elections" used as a pejorative term suggesting backwardness and fraud.[12]

Second, Ukrainian nationalism, traditionally traced to eastern Ukraine in its initial nineteenth-century stages, subsequently grew stronger in eastern Galicia, the core of the later Soviet western Ukraine. According to this argument, eastern Galicia, with its key city of Lviv, then went through a critical amount of Ukrainian national identity building before the Soviet annexation and transformation. This legacy, the argument continues, warped and foiled

7. Volodymyr Potulnyckyi, "Das ukrainische historische Denken im 19. und 20. Jahrhundert: Konzeptionen und Periodisierung," *Jahrbücher für Geschichte Osteuropas* 45 (1997): 27. See also the statistics assembled earlier by Kenneth C. Farmer in his *Ukrainian Nationalism in the Post-Stalin Area: Myth, Symbols and Ideology in Soviet Nationalities Policy* (The Hague: Nijhoff, 1980), 177–79.

8. Sebastian Klüsener, "Die Regionen der Ukraine: Abgrenzung und Charakterisierung," *Ukraineanalysen*, no. 23 (8 May 2007), 3–4. These differences need be antagonistic or persist further, can change, and may not be monolithic; the statement entails no value judgement whatsoever.

9. Yitzhak M. Brudny and Evgeny Finkel, "Why Ukraine Is Not Russia: Hegemonic National Identity and Democracy in Russia and Ukraine," *East European Politics and Societies* 25 (2011): 827.

10. For a comparison with Polish former Galicia, see Luiza Bialasiewicz, "Another Europe: Remembering Habsburg Galicia," *Cultural Geographies* (2003): 10, 36.

11. Brudny and Finkel, "Why Ukraine Is Not Russia," 822; Padraic Kenney, "Lviv's Central European Renaissance, 1987–1990," *Harvard Ukrainian Studies* 24 (2000): 303–12; Wolff, *Idea of Galicia*, 411.

12. Binder, *Galizien in Wien*, 295–308.

Soviet modernization, effectively hijacking it as a vehicle of even more Ukrainian nation building.[13]

Third, as another explanation points out, prewar western Ukraine, then still part of eastern Poland, missed out on the first, interwar wave of "building Socialism" and therefore did not undergo the same amount of transformatory Soviet violence and, especially, the turn away from Ukrainization and the artificial famine created in Soviet Ukraine during the early 1930s.

Of these three traditional explanations of western Ukraine's persistent peculiarity, the third can be discarded. It is true that western Ukraine did not experience interwar Soviet party-state violence, but it did receive an extra jolt of violence during the Soviet war against local resistance in the late 1940s. No scale is fine enough to tell us exactly how much violent disruption proper Sovietization takes. But there was much of it in both the East and the West; that much is certain.

But as deep research into the historical record shows, even taken together, the first two traditional explanations also remain incomplete and thus flawed. Roman Szporluk's dichotomy summarizes their essence: Was western Ukraine "starting to look like the rest of Ukraine or . . . *preserving* [its] *pre*-Soviet identity?"[14] Yet, as this book has shown, in postwar reality, the persistence of western Ukraine's peculiarity was not simply the result of somehow withstanding the Soviet onslaught. It was at least as much shaped by Soviet policies.[15]

Martin Åberg has advanced an argument that integrates the pre-Soviet and the Soviet that is similar to but also different from my interpretation. He has identified as an "unintended consequence of Soviet modernization" the "laying of the socio-cultural and demographic basis for Lviv to become the 'secret capital' of Ukraine and a major center of ethno-nationalist politics during the first years after independence."[16] Thus, Åberg's argument is an extension of George Liber's modernization-centered interpretation of the Ukrainization of Soviet Ukrainian cities before the war: modernization in and of itself appears as essentially sufficient to explain a de facto continuity of Ukrainian national emergence through

13. For a concise recent restatement of this traditional hypothesis, see Brudny and Finkel, "Why Ukraine Is Not Russia," 817; and Taras Kuzio, "The National Factor in Ukraine's Quadruple Transition," *Contemporary Politics* 6 (2000): 151–52.

14. Szporluk, *Russia, Ukraine, and the Breakup*, xxix (my emphasis). Szporluk found the answer to this question where its formulation would lead one to expect it, in the pre-Soviet past: "By 1939 the West Ukrainians had established a presence in the urban sector and their language served as a modern medium of communication for them before the Soviets arrived" (ibid., xxx).

15. For a similar argument about Central Asia, see Olivier Roy, *The New Central Asia: The Creation of Nations* (New York: New York University Press, 2000), 106.

16. Martin Åberg, "Paradox of Change: Soviet Modernization and Ethno-Linguistic Differentiation in Lviv, 1945–1989," *Harvard Ukrainian Studies* 24 (2000): 296.

urbanization. My interpretation of what happened in Lviv after 1944 attaches significantly more weight to the party-state's role in shaping identities. Soviet influence cannot be reduced to the negative of *not* attempting to Russify or the *non*intention, the "oversight," of creating the new urban working class of Lviv from already nationalized western Ukrainian peasants.

In the end, Lviv and Soviet western Ukraine did turn out to be special. Although Soviet authorities initially announced their intention to make it just like the rest of Ukraine, within about a decade after the second conquest of the area in 1944 the Soviet regime implicitly but clearly conceded and even, in effect, promoted a Soviet western Ukrainian identity—Sovietized and Ukrainian, but also somehow apart and different. This was neither a coincidence nor due merely to the persistence of pre-Soviet difference but was the result of Soviet policies after 1939.

Bibliography

Published Sources

Allerhand, Mauricy, and Leszek Allerhand. *Zapiski z tamtego świata*. Cracow: Wydawnictwo Edukacyjne, 2003.

Armia krajowa w dokumentach 1939–1945. Vol. 6, *Uzupełnienia*. Wrocław: Ossolineum, 1991.

Bazhan, Mykola, et al., eds. *Ukrainska radianska entsyklopediia*. Kyiv: URE, 1977–1985.

Bizuń, Stanisław. *Historia krzyżem znaczona: Wspomnienia z życia Kościoła katolickiego na Ziemi Lwowskiej 1939–1945*. Edited by Ks. Józef Wołczański. Lublin: Wspólnota Polska, 1993.

Bereza, Tomasz, ed. *Lwowskie pod okupacją sowiecką 1939–1941*. Rzeszów: Instytut Pamięci Narodowej, 2006.

Bilas, Ivan. *Represivno-karalna systema v Ukraini 1917–1953: Suspilno-politychnyi ta istoryko-pravovyi analiz*. 2 vols. Kyiv: Libid, 1994.

Bohunov, Serhyi, et al., eds. *Likvidatsiia UHKTs (1939–1946): Dokumenty radianskykh orhaniv derzhavnoi bezpeky*. 2 vols. Kyiv: PP Serhiychuk, 2006.

Borotba trudiashchykh Lvivshchyny proty nimetsko-fashystskykh zaharbnykiv, 1941–1944 rr. Zbirnyk dokumentiv i materialiv. Lviv: s.n., 1949.

Bryk, M. V., et al., eds. *Istoriia Lvova v dokumentakh i materialakh: Zbirnik dokumentiv i materialiv*. Kyiv: Naukova dumka, 1986.

Chuwis Thau, Lili. *Hidden: Only the Leaves Bore Witness to Her Secret*. Austin, TX: Groundbreaking Press, 2012.

Czekanowska, Anna. *Świat rzeczywisty—świat zapamiętany: Losy Polaków we Lwowie, 1939–1941*. Lublin: Norbertinum, 2010.

Danylenko, Vasyl, et al., eds. *Radianski orhany derzhavnoi bezpeky u 1939—chervni 1941 roku: Dokumenty HDA SB Ukrainy*. Kyiv: Kyevo-Mohylanska akademiia, 2009.

Diadiuk, Myroslava, ed. *Milena Rudnytska: Statti, listy, dokumenty*. Lviv: Misioner, 1998.

Döblin, Alfred. *Reise in Polen*. Munich: DTV, 2000.

Dovzhenko, Oleksandr. *Ukrainy v ohni: Kinopovist, shchodennyk*. Kyiv: Radianskyi pysmennyk, 1990.

Drix, Samuel. *Witness to Annihilation: Surviving the Holocaust. A Memoir*. Washington, DC: Brassey's, 1994.

Dzięgiel, Leszek. *Lwów nie każdemu zdrów*. Wrocław: PTL, 1991.

Gansiniec, Ryszard. *Notatki Lwowskie, 1944–1946*. Wrocław: Sudety, 1995.

Gerstenfeld-Maltiel, Jacob. *My Private War: One Man's Struggle to Survive the Soviets and the Nazis*. London: Valentine Mitchell, 1993.
Grossman, Iurii. *Perezhitoe i peredumannoe*. New York: Slovo World, 1994.
Heczko, Alma. "Pożegnanie Lwówa." *Karta* 13 (1994): 3–6.
Hesheles, Ianina [Janina Hescheles]. *Ochyma dvanadtsiatyrichnoi divchynky*. Kyiv: Dukh i litera, 2011.
Hurhal, Volodymyr. *Druzia moi stanochnyky!* Moscow: Izdatelstvo VTsPS Profizdat, 1963.
——. *Dvadtsiat dniv za okeanom*. Lviv: Knyzhkovo-zhurnalne vydavnytstvo, 1962.
——. *Na velykykh shvydkostiakh* Lviv: Knyzhkovo-zhurnalne vydavnytstvo, 1953.
——. *Storinky robitnykoho zhyttia*. Kyiv: Derzhavne vydavnytstvo politychnoi literatury URSR, 1963.
——. *Ya robitnyk*. Lviv: Knyzhkovo-zhurnalne vydavnytstvo, 1964.
Instytut Pamięci Narodowej, ed. *Deportacje obywateli polskich z Zachodniej Ukrainy i Zachodniej Białorusi w 1940 roku*. Warsaw: Instytut Pamięci Narodowej, 2003.
Kalinovskii, Eduard. *Vremia, kotoroe on obgoniaet: Geroi sovetskoi rodiny. Dokumentalnyi povest*. Moscow: Izdatelstvo politicheskoi literatury, 1973.
Kaplan, Helen C. *I Never Left Janowska*. New York: Holocaust Library, 1989.
Khlevniuk, Oleg V., et al. *Politburo TsK VKP(b) i Sovet ministrov SSSR 1945–1953*. Moscow: Rosspen, 2002.
Klotz, Aleksander. *Zapiski konspiratora 1939–1945*. Edited by Grzegorz Mazur. Cracow: Księgarnia Akademicka, 2001.
Kokin, Serhiy, et al., eds. *Mytropolyt Andrei Sheptytskyi u dokumentakh radianskykh orhaniv derzhavnoi bezpeky, 1934–1944 rr*. Kyiv: Ukrainska vydavnycha spilka, 2005.
Kott, Jan. *Still Alive*. New Haven: Yale University Press, 1994.
Kubiiovych, Volodymyr. *Meni 70*. Paris: NTSh, 1970.
——. *Ukraintsi v Heneralnii Hubernii, 1939–1941: Istoriia Ukrainskoho Tsentralnoho komitetu*. Chicago: Vydavnytstvo Mykoly Denysiuka, 1975.
Lanckorońska, Karolina. *Wspomnienia wojenne*. Cracow: Znak, 2003.
Leixner, Leo. *Von Lemberg bis Bordeaux: Fronterlebnisse eines Kriegsberichterstatters*. 4th ed. Munich: Zentralverlag der NSDAP, 1942.
Lem, Stanisław. *Świat na krawędzi: Ze Stanisławem Lemem rozmawia Tomasz Fiałkowski*. Cracow: Wydawnictwo Literackie, 2000.
Leonhard, Wolfgang. *Die Revolution entläßt ihre Kinder*. Cologne: Kiepenheuer & Witsch, 1955.
Lewin, Kurt I. *Przeżyłem: Saga Świętego Jura spisana w roku 1946 przez syna rabina Lwowa*. Edited by Barbara Toruńczyk. Annotated by Andrzej Żbikowski. Warsaw: Fundacja Zeszytów Literackich, 2006.
Lück, Kurt, and Alfred Lattermann, eds. *Die Heimkehr der Galiziendeutschen*. Posen: Historische Gesellschaft Posen; Leipzig: Hirzel, Gaugrenzlandamt der NSDAP im Reichsgau Wartheland, 1940.
Lutskyi, Iuriy, ed. *Shchodennyk Arkadiia Liubchenka: 2/XI-41–21/II-45 p*. Lviv: M. P. Kots, 1999.
Makivka, Stepan. *Narodna Hvardia imeni Ivana Franka: Iz spohadiv pidpilnyka*. Lviv: Knyzhkovo-zhurnalne vydavnytstvo, 1959.
Márai, Sándor. *Memoir of Hungary, 1944–1948*. Budapest: Central European University Press, 1996.

Mężyński, Andrzej. *Biblioteki naukowe w Generalnym Gubernatorstwie w latach 1939–1945: Wybór dokumentów źródłowych.* Warsaw: LTW, 2003.

Mochulsky, Fyodor Vasilevych. *Gulag Boss: A Soviet Memoir.* Translated and edited by Deborah Kaple. Oxford: Oxford University Press, 2011.

Nakonechnyi, Yevhen. *"Shoa" u Lvovi: Spohady.* Lviv: Naukova biblioteka im. V. Stefanyka, 2004.

Nimchuk, Ivan. *595 dniv sovetskym viaznem.* Toronto: Vydavnytstvo Vasilian, 1950.

Operacja "Sejm," 1944–1946: Polska i Ukraina w latach trzydziestych–czterdziestych XX wieku. Vol. 6. Warsaw: Archiwum Ministerstwa Spraw Wewnȩtrznych i Administracji Rzeczypospolitej Polskiej, 2007.

Ossowska, Wanda. *Przeżyłam: Lwów-Warszawa 1939–1946.* Warsaw: Oficyna Przeglądu Powszechnego, 1990.

Präg, Werner, and Wolfgang Jacobmeyer, eds. *Das Diensttagebuch des deutschen Generalgouverneurs in Polen 1939–1945.* Stuttgart: DVA, 1975.

Pretzel, Marian. *Portrait of a Young Forger: A Memoir of Wartime Adventures.* St. Lucia: University of Queensland Press, 1993.

——. *There Was No Farewell: Fifty Years on Marian Pretzel Revisits Lvov.* Sydney: Sydney Jewish Museum, 1995.

Romanowiczówna, Zofia. *Dziennik lwowski 1842–1930.* Vol. 2, *1888–1930.* Edited by Zbigniew Sudolski. Warsaw: Ancher, 2005.

Rosenfeld, Klara. *From Lwów to Parma: A Young Woman's Escape from Nazi-Occupied Poland.* London: Vallentine Mitchell, 2005.

Ruda, Nava. *Zum ewigen Angedenken: Erinnerungen eines Mädchens aus dem Ghetto Lwow. Jüdische Familiengeschichte 1899–1999.* Edited by Erhard Roy Wiehn. Konstanz: Hartung-Gorre, 2000.

Rudnytska, Milena. *Zakhidna Ukraina pid bolshevykamy, IX 1939–VI 1941.* New York: Naukove tovarystvo im. Shevchenka v Amerytsi, 1958.

Serhiychuk, Volodymyr. *Deportatsiia poliakiv z Ukrainy: Nevidomi dokumenty pro nasylnytske pereselennia bilshovytskoiu vladoiu polskoho naselennia z URSR v Polshu v 1944–1946 rokakh.* Kyiv: Ukrainska vydavnycha spilka, 1999.

——. *Desiat buremnykh lit: Zachidnoukrainski zemli v 1944–1953 rokakh.* Kyiv: Dnipro, 1998.

——. *Poliaky na Volyni u roky druhoi svitovoi viiny: Dokumenty z ukrainskykh arkhiviv i polski publikatsii.* Kyiv: Ukrainska vydavnycha spilka, 2003.

Serhiychuk, Volodymyr, ed. *Ukrainskyi zdvyh.* 5 vols. Kyiv: Ukrainska vydavnycha apilka, 2004–5.

Solomonchuk, O. E., ed. *Lvivshchyna turystska.* Lviv: Kameniar, 1986.

Schoenfeld, Joachim. *Holocaust Memoirs: Jews in the Lwow Ghetto, the Janowski Concentration Camp, and as Deportees in Siberia.* Hoboken, NJ: Ktav, 1985.

Simonov, Konstantin. *Glazami cheloveka moego pokoleniia: Razmyshleniia o I. V. Staline.* Moscow: Kniga, 1990.

Slyvka, Iuriy, et al., eds. *Kulturne zhyttia v Ukraini: Zakhidni zemli. Dokumenty i materialy.* 3 vols. Introduction by Oleksandr Lutskyi. Kyiv: Instytut ukrainoznavstva im. I. I. Krypiakevycha—Natsionalna akademia nauk Ukrainy, 1995, 1996, 2006.

Sokhan, P. S., et al., eds. *Litopys Ukrainskoi Povstanskoi Armii,* n.s., 7. Toronto: Litopys UPA, 2003.

Steinhaus, Hugo. *Wspomnienia i zapiski.* Edited by Aleksandra Zgorzelska. Londyn: Aneks, 1992.

Tarnawski, Ostap. *Literacki Lwów 1939–1944: Wspomnienia ukrainskiego pisarza.* Poznań: Bonami, 2004.

Tsehelskyi, Lonhyn [Longin]. *Vid legendy do pravdy: Spomyny pro podii v Ukraini zviazani z Pershym Lystopadom 1918 r.* New York: Bulava, 1960. Reprint, Lviv: Svichado, 2003.

Tomaszewski, Tadeusz. *Lwów: Pejzaż psychologiczny.* Warsaw: WIP, 1996.

Volchuk, Roman. *Spomyny: Z peredvoennoho Lvova ta voiennoho Vidnia.* Kyiv: Krytyka, 2002.

Wat, Aleksander. *Mój wiek.* Warsaw: Czytelnik, 1990.

Węgierski, Jerzy. *Bardzo różne życie: We Lwowie, w sowieckich łagrach, na Śląsku.* Katowice: J. Węgierski, 2003.

Wells, Leon W. *Ein Sohn Hiobs.* Munich: Heyne, 1963.

——. "Interview." Visual History Archive Online: USC Shoah Foundation Institute, Wells Leon, 23410. http://vhaonline.usc.edu/viewingPage.aspx?testimonyID=25727&returnIndex=0.

Żbikowski, Andrzej, ed. *Archiwum Ringelbluma: Konspiracyjne Archiwum Getta Warszawy.* Vol. 3, *Relacje z Kresów.* Warsaw: PWN, 2000.

Złotorzycka, Jadwiga. *Dwugłos pokoleń.* Wrocław: Wydawnictwo Uniwersytetu Wrocławskiego, 1996.

Secondary Literature

Åberg, Martin. "Paradox of Change: Soviet Modernization and Ethno-Linguistic Differentiation in Lviv, 1945–1989." *Harvard Ukrainian Studies* 24 (2000): 285–301.

Abramson, Henry. "Nachrichten aus Lemberg: Lokale Elemente in der antisemitischen Ikonographie der NS-Propaganda in ukrainischer Sprache." *Jahrbuch des Fritz Bauer Instituts* 6 (2002): 249–68.

Ackermann, Felix. *Palimpsest Grodno: Nationalisierung, Nivellierung und Sowjetisierung einer mitteleuropäischen Stadt, 1919–1991.* Munich: Harrassowitz, 2010.

Albert, Zygmunt. *Lwowski wydział lekarski w czasie okupacij Hitlerowskiej, 1941–1944.* Wrocław: Zakład Narodowy im. Ossolińskich, 1975.

Albert, Zygmunt, ed. *Kaźń profesorów lwowskich, lipiec 1941: Studia oraz relacje i dokumenty.* Wrocław: Wydawnictwo Uniwersytetu Wrocławskiego, 1989.

Allen, Arthur. *The Fantastic Laboratory of Dr. Weigl: How Two Brave Scientists Battled Typhus and Sabotaged the Nazis.* New York: W. W. Norton, 2014.

Altshuler, Mordechai. "Jewish Holocaust Commemoration Activity in the USSR under Stalin." *Yad Vashem Studies* 30 (2002): 271–95.

Amar, Tarik Cyril. "Different but the Same or the Same but Different? Public Memory of the Second World War in Post-Soviet Lviv." *Journal of Modern European History* 9 (2011): 373–96.

An-ski, Szymon. *Tragedia Żydów galicyjskich w czasie I wojny światowej: Wrażenia i refleksje z podróży po kraju.* Przemyśl: Południowo-Wschodni Instytut Naukowy w Przemyślu, 2010.

Antoniuk, N. V. *Ukrainske kulturne zhyttia v "Heneralnyi hubernii," 1939–1944 rr.: Za materialamy periodychnoi presy.* Lviv: Stefanyka, 1997.

Apor, Balázs, Péter Apor, and E. A. Rees, eds. *The Sovietization of Eastern Europe: New Perspectives on the Postwar Period.* Washington, DC: New Academia Publishing, 2008.

Applebaum, Anne. *Gułag.* Warsaw: Świat Książki, 2005.

Arad, Yitzhak. *The Holocaust in the Soviet Union*. Lincoln: University of Nebraska Press, 2009.

Armstrong, John A. *Ukrainian Nationalism*. 3rd ed. New York: Columbia University Press, 1990.

Aster, Howard, and Peter J. Potichnyj, eds. *Ukrainian-Jewish Relations in Historical Perspective*. 2nd ed. Edmonton: Canadian Institute of Ukrainian Studies, University of Alberta, 1990.

Baberowski, Jörg. *Der Feind ist überall: Stalinismus im Kaukasus*. Munich: Deutsche Verlags-Anstalt, 2003.

Babko, Yu. V. *Istoriia Leninskoi komunistychnoi spilky molodi Ukrainy*. Kyiv: Molod, 1979.

Badiak, Volodymyr. *U leshchatakh stalinshchyny: Narys istorii Lvivskoi orhanizatsii Spilky khudozhnykiv Ukrainy, 1939–1953 rr*. Lviv: SKIM, 2003.

Baida, Iuriy. *Petro Kozlaniuk: Zhyttia i tvorchist*. Kyiv: Radianskyi pysmennyk, 1959.

Bajohr, Frank. "Die wirtschaftliche Existenzvernichtung und Enteignung der Juden: Forschungsbilanz und offene Fragen." *Terezin Studies and Documents (Theresienstädter Studien und Dokumente)* 13 (2006): 348–63.

Bakhturina, Aleksandra Iu. *Okrainy rossiiskoi imperii: Gosudarstvennoe upravlenie i natsionalnaia politika v gody pervoi mirovoi voiny, 1914–1917 gg*. Moscow: Rosspen, 2004.

Balbus, Tomasz. "Sowieci i żymierski a Lwowska AK 1944." *Biuletyn Instytutu Pamięci Narodowej*, no. 12 (2004): 67–79.

Bantyshev, Aleksandr, and Arzen Ukhal. *Ubiistvo na zakaz: Kto zhe organizoval ubiistvo Iaroslava Halana?* Uzhhorod: Gorodskaia tipografiia, 2002.

Baran, Volodymyr. *Istoriia Ukrainy, 1945–1953*. Lviv: Instytut ukrainoznavstva im. I. Krypiakevycha, 2005.

——. *Ukraina: Novitnia istoriia, 1945–1991 rr*. Lviv: Instytut ukrainoznavstva im. I. Krypiakevycha, 2003.

Barkova, O. *Kazhdyi den: Povest*. Moscow: Sovetskii pisatel, 1950.

Barnes, Steven A. *Death and Redemption: The Gulag and the Shaping of Soviet Society*. Princeton, NJ: Princeton University Press, 2011.

Bartal, Israel, and Antony Polonsky. "The Jews of Galicia under the Habsburgs." *Polin* 12 (1999): 3–24.

Bartov, Omer. "Eastern Europe as the Site of Genocide." *Journal of Modern History* 80 (2008): 557–93.

——. *Erased: Vanishing Traces of Jewish Galicia in Present-Day Ukraine*. Princeton, NJ: Princeton University Press, 2007.

Bartov, Omer, and Eric D. Weitz, eds. *Shatterzone of Empires: Coexistence and Violence in the German, Habsburg, Russian, and Ottoman Borderlands*. Bloomington: Indiana University Press, 2013.

Bauer, Yehuda. *The Death of the Shtetl*. New Haven: Yale University Press, 2009.

Beer, Daniel. "Origins, Modernity, and Resistance in the Historiography of Stalinism." *Journal of Contemporary History* 40 (2005): 363–79.

Beliaev, Vladimir. *Do poslednei minuty: Povest dlia kino*. Moscow: Iskusstvo, 1974.

——. *Formula iada*. Moscow: Sovetskii pisatel, 1970.

Beliaev, Vladimir, and A. S. Elkin. *Yaroslav Halan*. Moscow: Molodaia gvardiia, 1971.

Beliaev, Volodymyr [Vladimir]. *Lvivski zustrichi*. Lviv: Vilna Ukraina, 1949.

Beliaev, Volodymyr, and Anatoly Iolkin. *Iaroslav Halan*. Kyiv: Molod, 1974.

Bemporad, Elissa. *Becoming Soviet Jews: The Bolshevik Experiment in Minsk*. Bloomington: Indiana University Press, 2013.

Benecke, Werner. *Die Ostgebiete der Zweiten Polnischen Republik: Staatsmacht und öffentliche Ordnung in einer Minderheitenregion 1918–1939*. Cologne: Böhlau, 1999.

Benz, Wolfgang, ed. *Die Dimension des Völkermords: Die Zahl der jüdischen Opfer des Nationalsozialismus*. Munich: Oldenbourg, 1991.

Bergen, Doris L. "The Nazi Concept of 'Volksdeutsche' and the Exacerbation of Anti-Semitism in Eastern Europe, 1939–45." *Journal of Contemporary History* 29 (1994): 569–82.

Berkhoff, Karel C. *Harvest of Despair: Life and Death in Ukraine under Nazi Rule*. Cambridge, MA: Harvard University Press, 2004.

——. *Motherland in Danger: Soviet Propaganda during World War II*. Cambridge, MA: Harvard University Press, 2012.

Bezsonov, S. V. *Arkhitektura zapadnoi Ukrainy*. Moscow: Izdatelstvo Akademii arkhitektury SSSR, 1946.

Bialasiewicz, Luiza. "Another Europe: Remembering Habsburg Galicia." *Cultural Geographies* 10 (2003): 21–44.

Binder, Harald. *Galizien in Wien: Parteien, Wahlen, Fraktionen und Abgeordnete im Übergang zur Massenpolitik*. Vienna: Verlag der österreichischen Akademie der Wissenschaften, 2005.

Biskupski, M. B. B. *Independence Day: Myth, Symbol, and the Creation of Modern Poland*. Oxford: Oxford University Press, 2012.

Blobaum, Robert, ed. *Antisemitism and Its Opponents in Modern Poland*. Ithaca, NY: Cornell University Press, 2005.

Bociurkiw, Bohdan R. *The Ukrainian Greek Catholic Church and the Soviet State, 1939–1950*. Edmonton: Canadian Institute of Ukrainian Studies Press, 1996.

Bodnar, Halyna. *Lviv: Shchodenne zhyttia mista ochyma pereselentsiv iz sil, 50–80-ti roky XX st*. Lviv: Vydavnychyi tsentr LNU im. Ivana Franka, 2010.

——. "Mihratsiia silskoho naselennia do Lvova v 50–80-kh rokakh XX stolittia." Candidate of Sciences (History) dissertation. Lviv: Ivan Franko University, 2007.

Boeckh, Katrin. "Jüdisches Leben in der Ukraine nach dem Zweiten Weltkrieg: Zur Verfolgung einer Religionsgemeinschaft im Spätstalinismus, 1945–1953." *Vierteljahrhefte für Zeitgeschichte*, no. 3 (2005): 421–48.

Bogner, Nahum. "The Convent Children: The Rescue of Jewish Children in Polish Convents during the Holocaust." *Yad Vashem Studies* 27 (1999): 235–85. http://www1.yadvashem.org/yv/en/righteous/pdf/resources/nachum_bogner.pdf.

Bohn, Thomas M. *Minsk—Musterstadt des Sozialismus: Stadtplanung und Urbanisierung in der Sowjetunion nach 1945*. Cologne: Böhlau, 2008.

Bonnell, Victoria E., and Lynn Hunt, eds. *Beyond the Cultural Turn: New Directions in the Study of Society and Culture*. Berkeley: University of California Press, 1999.

Bonusiak, Andrzej. *Lwów w latach 1918–1939: Ludność-Przestrzeń-Samorząd*. Rzeszów: Wydawnictwo Wyższej Szkoły Pedagogicznej, 2000.

——. "Sowietyzacja kultury Lwowa w latach 1939–1941." *Lviv: Misto, suspilstvo, kultura* 3 (1999): 599–606.

Bonusiak, Włodzimierz. *Polytika ludnościowa i ekonomiczna ZSRR na okupowanych ziemiach polskich w latach 1939–1941: "Zachodnia Ukraina" i "Zachodnia Białoruś."* Rzeszów: Wydawnictwo Universytetu Rzeszowskiego, 2006.

———. "Powstanie i działalność władz okupacyjnych we Lwowie w okresie IX 1939–VI 1941." *Lwów: Miasto, społeczenstwo, kultura* 2 (1998): 307–18.

Borodziej, Włodzimierz. *Der Warschauer Aufstand 1944*. Frankfurt am Main: Fischer, 2001.

Borschtschagowski, Alexander. *Orden für einen Mord: Die Judenverfolgung unter Stalin*. Aus dem Russischen von Alfred Frank. Berlin: Propyläen, 1997.

Borys, Jurij. *The Sovietization of Ukraine, 1917–1923: The Communist Doctrine and Practice of National Self-Determination*. Edmonton: University of Ontario Press, 1980.

Brandenberger, David. *National Bolshevism: Stalinist Mass Culture and the Formation of Modern Russian National Identity, 1931–1956*. Cambridge, MA: Harvard University Press, 2002.

Brandon, Ray, and Wendy Lower, eds. *The Shoah in Ukraine: History, Testimony, Memorialization*. Bloomington: Indiana University Press, in association with the United States Holocaust Memorial Museum, 2008.

Bril, M. *Osvobozhdennaia zapadnaia Ukraina*. Moscow: Politizdat, 1940.

Brown, Kate. *A Biography of No Place: From Ethnic Borderland to Soviet Heartland*. Cambridge, MA: Harvard University Press, 2004.

Browning, Christopher R.. *Remembering Survival: Inside a Nazi Slave-Labor Camp*. New York: W. W. Norton, 2010.

Browning, Christopher R., and Jürgen Matthäus. *The Origins of the Final Solution: The Evolution of Nazi Jewish Policy, September 1939–March 1942*. Lincoln: University of Nebraska Press, 2004.

Bruder, Franziska. *"Den ukrainischen Staat erkämpfen oder sterben!" Die Organisation Ukrainischer Nationalisten (OUN) 1929–1948*. Berlin: Metropol, 2007.

Brudny, Yitzhak M., and Evgeny Finkel. "Why Ukraine Is Not Russia: Hegemonic National Identity and Democracy in Russia and Ukraine." *East European Politics and Societies* 25 (2011): 813–33.

Brzezinski, Zbigniew. *The Soviet Bloc: Unity and Conflict. Ideology and Power in the Relations among the USSR, Poland, Yugoslavia, China, and Other Communist States*. Cambridge, MA: Harvard University Press, 1960.

Burds, Jeffrey. "AGENTURA: Soviet Informants' Networks and the Ukrainian Underground in Galicia, 1944–48." *East European Politics and Society* 11 (1997): 89–130.

Carynnyk, Marco. "Foes of Our Rebirth: Ukrainian Nationalist Discussions about Jews, 1929–1947." *Nationalities Papers* 39 (2011): 315–52.

Center for Advanced Holocaust Studies. *The Holocaust in the Soviet Union: Symposium Presentations*. Washington, DC: Center for Advanced Holocaust Studies, United States Holocaust Memorial Museum, 2005. http://www.ushmm.org/m/pdfs/20050908-holocaust-soviet-union-symposium.pdf.

Chernysh, M. "Borotba lvivskoi miskoi partorhanizatsii za provedennia v zhyttia rishen partii i uriadu pro industrializatsiiu mista Lvova." In *Trista rokiv vozzedanniia Ukrainy z Rosiiu*. Lviv: Vydavnytstvo Lvivskoho universytetu, 1954.

Chiari, Bernhard. *Alltag hinter der Front: Besatzung, Kollaboration und Widerstand in Weißrußland, 1941–1944*. Düsseldorf: Droste, 1998.

Chiari, Bernhard, and Jerzy Kochanowski, eds. *Die Polnische Heimatarmee: Geschichte und Mythos der Armija Krajowa seit dem Zweiten Weltkrieg*. Munich: Oldenbourg, 2003.

Chrobaczyński, Jacek. "Kraków i Lwów 1939–1945: Funkcje miast w systemie okupacyjnym i w konspiracji." *Lviv: Misto, suspilstvo, kultura* 3 (1999): 607–23.

Clark, Katerina. *Moscow, the Fourth Rome: Stalinism, Cosmopolitanism, and the Evolution of Soviet Culture, 1931–1941*. Cambridge, MA: Harvard University Press, 2011.

Connelly, John. *Captive University: The Sovietization of East German, Czech, and Polish Higher Education, 1945–1956*. Berkeley: University of California Press, 2000.

Czaplicka, John, ed. *Lviv: A City in the Crosscurrents of Culture*. Cambridge, MA: Harvard University Press, 2005.

Czerniakiewicz, Jan. *Przemieszczenia ludności polskiej z ZSRR 1944–1959*. Warsaw: Wydawnystwo Wyzszej Szkoły Pedagogicznej TWP, 2004.

Czop, Edyta. *Obwód lwowski pod okupacją ZSRR w latach 1939–1941*. Rzeszów: Wydawnictwo Universytetu Rzeszowskiego, 2004.

David-Fox, Michael. "Multiple Modernities vs. Neo-Traditionalism: On Recent Debates in Russian and Soviet History." *Jahrbücher für Geschichte Osteuropas* 54 (2006): 535–55.

——. *Showcasing the Great Experiment: Cultural Diplomacy and Western Visitors to the Soviet Union, 1921–1941*. Oxford: Oxford University Press, 2012.

David-Fox, Michael, Peter Holquist, and Alexander M. Martin, eds. *The Holocaust in the East: Local Perpetrators and Soviet Responses*. Pittsburgh: University of Pittsburgh Press, 2014.

Davies, Norman. *God's Playground: A History of Poland*. Oxford: Oxford University Press, 2005.

Davies, Norman, and Antony Polonsky, eds. *Jews in Eastern Poland and the USSR, 1939–46*. London: St. Martin's Press, 1991.

Davymuka, Stepan. *Lvivshchyna na porozi XXI stolittia: Sotsialnyi portret*. Lviv: Natsionalna akademiia nauk Ukrainy, Instytut rehionalnykh doslidzhen, 2001.

Deák, István, Jan T. Gross, and Tony Judt, eds. *The Politics of Retribution in Europe: World War II and Its Aftermath*. Princeton, NJ: Princeton University Press, 2000.

Dean, Martin. *Robbing the Jews: The Confiscation of Jewish Property in the Holocaust, 1933–1945*. Cambridge: Cambridge University Press, 2008.

Dean, Martin, Constantin Goschler, and Philipp Ther. *Robbery and Restitution: The Conflict over Jewish Property in Europe*. New York: Berghahn Books, 2007.

Dekel-Chen, Jonathan. "'New' Jews of the Agricultural Kind: A Case of Soviet Interwar Propaganda." *Russian Review* 66 (2007): 424–50.

Dobroszycki, Lucjan. *Die legale polnische Presse im Generalgouvernement, 1939–1945*. Munich: Institut für Zeitgeschichte, 1977.

Dobroszycki, Lucjan, and Jeffrey S. Gurock, eds. *The Holocaust in the Soviet Union: Studies and Sources on the Destruction of the Jews in the Nazi-Occupied Territories of the USSR, 1941–1945*. Armonk, NY: M. E. Sharpe, 1993.

Dontsov, Dmytro. *Dukh nashoi davnyny*. Prague: Vydavnytstvo Yuriia Tyshchenka, 1944.

——. *Groß-Polen und die Zentralmächte*. Berlin: Carl Kroll, 1915.

Dovidnik z istorii Ukrainy. Kyiv: s.n., 2001.

Drobaschenko, Sergej, and Manfred Hagen. *Sowjetische Filmpropaganda zur Westexpansion der UdSSR, 1939–1940: Ausgewählte Berichte der Staatswochenschau "Sojuskinoschurnal."* Göttingen: Institut für den Wissenschaftlichen Film, 1999.

Dudykevych, B. K., et al., eds. *Narysy istorii Lvova, 1256–1956*. Lviv: Knyzhkovo-zhurnalne vydavnytstvo, 1956.

Dullin, Sabine. *La frontière épaisse: Aux origins des politiques soviétiques, 1920–1940*. Paris: Éditions de l'École des hautes études en sciences sociales, 2014.

Du Prel, Max, ed. *Das Generalgouvernement: Im Auftrage und mit einem Vorwort des Generalgouverneurs Reichsminister Dr. Frank*. Würzburg: Konrad Triltsch Verlag, 1942.

Duzhii, Petro. *Roman Shukhevych—polityk, voin, hromadianyn*. Lviv: Halytska vydavnycha spilka, 1998.

Dyak, Sofia. "Tvorennja obrasu Lwowa jak rehionalnoho zentru Sachidnoi Ukrainy: Radjanskji projekt ta joho urbanistytschne wtilennja." *Schid-Sachid*, nos. 9–10 (2008): 75–86.

Ekbladh, David. *The Great American Mission: Modernization and the Construction of an American World Order*. Princeton, NJ: Princeton University Press, 2010.

Engerman, David C., et al., eds. *Staging Growth: Modernization, Development, and the Global Cold War*. Amherst: University of Massachusetts Press, 2003.

Etkind, Alexander. *Warped Mourning: Stories of the Undead in the Land of the Unburied*. Stanford, CA: Stanford University Press, 2013.

Evtuhov, Catherine, and Stephen Kotkin, eds. *The Cultural Gradient: The Transmission of Ideas in Europe, 1789–1991*. Lanham, MD: Rowman and Littlefield, 2003.

Farmer, Kenneth C. *Ukrainian Nationalism in the Post-Stalin Area: Myth, Symbols, and Ideology in Soviet Nationalities Policy*. The Hague: Nijhoff, 1980.

Fastnacht-Stupnicka, Anna. *Zostali we Lwowie*. Wrocław: Sator Media, 2010.

Fäßler, Peter, Thomas Held, and Dirk Sawitzki, eds. *Lemberg, Lwów, Lviv: Eine Stadt im Schnittpunkt europäischer Kulturen*. Cologne: Böhlau, 1993.

Feest, David. *Zwangskollektivierung im Baltikum: Die Sowjetisierung des estnischen Dorfes 1944–1953*. Cologne: Böhlau, 2007.

Fejtö, François. *A History of the People's Democracies: Eastern Europe since Stalin*. London: Pall Mall Press, 1969.

Figura, Marek. *Konflikt polsko-ukraiński w prasie Polski Zachodniej w latach 1918–1923*. Poznań: Wydawnictwo Poznańskie, 2001.

Filtzer, Donald. *Soviet Workers and Late Stalinism: Labour and the Restoration of the Stalinist System after World War II*. Cambridge: Cambridge University Press, 2002.

Finder, Gabriel N., and Alexander V. Prusin. "Collaboration in Eastern Galicia: The Ukrainian Police and the Holocaust." *East European Jewish Affairs* 34 (2004): 95–118.

Finkel, Stuart. *On the Ideological Front: The Russian Intelligentsia and the Making of the Soviet Public Sphere*. New Haven: Yale University Press, 2007.

Fish, M. Steven. *Democracy Derailed in Russia: The Failure of Open Politics*. Cambridge: Cambridge University Press, 2005.

Fitzpatrick, Sheila. *Everyday Stalinism: Ordinary Life in Extraordinary Times. Soviet Russia in the 1930s*. New York: Oxford University Press, 1999.

——. *Stalin's Peasants: Resistance and Survival in the Russian Village after Collectivization*. Oxford: Oxford University Press, 1994.

——. *Tear off the Masks! Identity and Imposture in Twentieth-Century Russia*. Princeton, NJ: Princeton University Press, 2005.

Frank, Alison Fleig. *Oil Empire: Visions of Prosperity in Austrian Galicia*. Cambridge, MA: Harvard University Press, 2005.

Friedman, Philip. *Zagłada Żydów lwowskich*. Łódź: Centralna Żyd. Komisja Historyczna w Polsce, 1945.

Fürst, Juliane, ed. *Late Stalinist Russia: Society between Reconstruction and Reinvention*. New York: Routledge, 2006.

Gati, Charles. *The Bloc That Failed: Soviet-East European Relations in Transition*. Bloomington: Indiana University Press, 1990.

Gatrell, Peter. *A Whole Empire Walking: Refugees in Russia during World War I*. Bloomington: Indiana University Press, 1999.

Gerlach, Christian. *Kalkulierte Morde: Die deutsche Wirtschafts- und Vernichtungspolitik in Weißrußland 1941 bis 1944*. Hamburg: Hamburger Edition, 1999.

Getty, J. Arch. *Practicing Stalinism: Bolsheviks, Boyars, and the Persistence of Tradition*. New Haven: Yale University Press, 2013.

Gibianskii, Leonid Ia., ed. *U istokov "Sotsialisticheskogo sodruzhestva": SSSR i vostochnoevropeiskie strany v 1944–1949 gg*. Moscow: Nauka, 1995.

Gierszewska, Barbara. *Kino i film we Lwowie do 1939 roku*. Kielce: Wydawnictwo Akademii Świętokrzyskiej, 2006.

Gieryński, Jan. *Lwów nie znany*. Lwów: Nakładem Księgarni A. Krawczyńskiego, 1938.

Gitelman, Zvi, ed. *Bitter Legacy: Confronting the Holocaust in the USSR*. Bloomington: Indiana University Press, 1997.

Goehrke, Carsten, and Bianka Pietrow-Ennker, eds. *Städte im östlichen Europa: Zur Problematik von Modernisierung und Raum vom Spätmittelalter bis zum 20. Jahrhundert*. Zürich: Chronos, 2006.

Goldman, Wendy Z. *Women at the Gates: Gender and Industry in Stalin's Russia*. Cambridge: Cambridge University Press: 2002.

Góra, Władysław, and Mieczysław Juchniewicz. *Walczyli razem: O wspóldziałaniu polskich i radzieckich oddziałów partyzanckich w latach drugiej wojny światowej*. Lublin: Wydawnictwo Lubelskie, 1972.

Gorodetsky, Gabriel. "The Impact of the Molotov-Ribbentrop Pact on the Course of Soviet Foreign Policy." *Cahiers du monde russe et soviétique* 31 (1990): 27–41.

Gorovskii, F. Ia., et al. *Evrei Ukrainy: Kratkii ocherk istorii*. Part 2. Kyiv: Ukrainsko-finskii instytut menedzhmenta i biznesa, 1995.

Gorsuch, Anne E. *All This Is Your World: Soviet Tourism at Home and Abroad after Stalin*. Oxford: Oxford University Press, 2011.

Goussef, Catherine. "'Kto naš, kto ne naš': Théorie et pratiques de la citoyenneté à l'égard des populations conquises. Le cas polonais en URSS, 1939–1946." *Cahiers du monde russe* 44 (2003): 519–58.

Grabski, August. *Działalność komunistów wśród Żydów w Polsce, 1944–1949*. Warsaw: Trio, 2004.

Grimsted, Patricia. *Trophies of War and Empire: The Archival Heritage of Ukraine, World War II, and the International Politics of Restitution*. Cambridge, MA: Harvard Ukrainian Research Institute, 2001.

Gross, Jan T. "A Colonial History of the Bloodlands." *Kritika: Explorations in Russian and Eurasian History* 15 (2014): 591–96.

——. *Fear: Anti-Semitism in Poland and after Auschwitz. An Essay in Historical Interpretation*. New York: Random House, 2007.

——. *Polish Society under German Occupation: The Generalgouvernement, 1939–1944*. Princeton, NJ: Princeton University Press, 1979.

———. *Revolution from Abroad: The Soviet Conquest of Poland's Western Ukraine and Western Belorussia*. Expanded ed. Princeton, NJ: Princeton University Press, 2002.

Groys, Boris. "Russia and the West: The Quest for Russian National Identity." *Studies in Soviet Thought* 43 (1992): 185–98.

———. *The Total Art of Stalinism: Avant-Garde, Aesthetic Dictatorship, and Beyond*. London: Verso, 2011.

Grudzińska-Gross, Irena, and Jan T. Gross, eds. *"W czterdziestym nas matko na Sibir zesłali..." Polska a Rosja 1939–1942*. Cracow: Znak, 2008.

Grünberg, Karol, and Bolesław Sprengel. *Trudne sąsiedztwo: Stosunki polsko-ukraińskie w X–XX wieku*. Warsaw: Książka i Wiedza, 2005.

Grüner, Frank. "Jüdischer Glaube und religiöse Praxis unter dem Stalinistischen Regime in der Sowjetunion während der Kriegs- und Nachkriegsjahre." *Jahrbücher für Geschichte Osteuropas* 54 (2004): 534–56.

Grynberg, Michal, and Maria Kotowska, eds. *Życie i zagłada Żydów polskich 1939–1945: Relacje Świadków*. Warsaw: Oficyna Naukowa, 2003.

Gutman, Israel. *Resistance: The Warsaw Ghetto Uprising*. New York: Houghton Mifflin, 1994.

Gutman, Israel, Ezra Mendelsohn, and Jehuda Reinharz, eds. *The Jews of Poland between Two World Wars*. Hanover, NH: University Press of New England, 1989.

Gutman, Israel, and Efraim Zuroff, eds. *Rescue Attempts during the Holocaust: Proceedings of the Second Yad Vashem International Historical Conference*. Jerusalem: Yad Vashem, 1974. http://www1.yadvashem.org/yv/en/righteous/pdf/resources/activites_zegota.pdf.

Hagenloh, Paul. *Stalin's Police: Public Order and Mass Repression in the USSR, 1926–1941*. Baltimore: Johns Hopkins University Press, 2009.

Halan, Yaroslav. *Z neopublikovanoho: Feiletony. Statti. Vystupy. Lystuvannia. Shchodennyk*. Lviv: Kameniar, 1990.

Hann, Christopher, and Paul Robert Magocsi, eds. *Galicia: A Multicultured Land*. Toronto: University of Toronto Press, 2005.

Hartmann, Christian, et al. *Der deutsche Krieg im Osten 1941–1944: Facetten einer Grenzüberschreitung*. Munich: Oldenbourg, 2009.

Hausmann, Guido, and Andreas Kappeler, eds. *Ukraine: Gegenwart und Geschichte eines neuen Staates*. Baden-Baden: Nomos, 1993.

Havryliv, Oksana, and Timofy Havryliv, eds. *Podorozh do Evropy: Halychyna, Bukovyna i Viden na tsentralnoevropeiskii kulturnii shakhivnytsi*. Lviv: VNTL, 2005.

Hellbeck, Jochen. *Revolution on My Mind: Writing a Diary under Stalin*. Cambridge, MA: Harvard University Press, 2006.

Herasymenko, M., and Bohdan Dudykevych. *Borotba trudiashchykh zakhidnoi Ukrainy za vozziednannia z radianskoiu Ukrainoiu*. Kyiv: Derzhavnyi vydavnytstvo politychnoi literatury URSR, 1960.

Hillis, Faith. *Children of Rus': Right-Bank Ukraine and the Invention of a Russian Nation*. Ithaca, NY: Cornell University, 2013.

Himka, Ivan [John-Paul Himka]. "Dostovirnist svidchennia: Relatsiia Ruzi Vagner pro Lvivskii pohrom vlitku 1941 r." *Holokost i Suchanist*, no. 2 (2008): 43–65.

Himka, John-Paul. "Debates in Ukraine over Nationalist Involvement in the Holocaust, 2004–2008." *Nationalities Papers* 39 (2011): 353–70.

——. "Encumbered Memory: The Ukrainian Famine of 1932–33." *Kritika: Explorations in Russian and Eurasian History* 14 (2013): 411–36.

——. "The Lviv Pogrom of 1941: The Germans, Ukrainian Nationalists, and the Carnival Crowd." *Canadian Slavonic Papers/Revue canadienne des slavistes* 53 (2011): 209–43.

——. "Metropolitan Andrey Sheptytsky and the Holocaust." *Polin Studies in Polish Jewry* 26 (2014): 337–59.

Himka, John-Paul, and Joanna Michlic, eds. *Bringing the Dark Past to Light: The Reception of the Holocaust in Postcommunist Europe*. Lincoln: University of Nebraska Press, 2013.

Hirsch, Francine. *Empire of Nations: Ethnographic Knowledge and the Making of the Soviet Union*. Ithaca, NY: Cornell University Press, 2005.

Hobsbawn, Eric. *The Age of Empire, 1875–1914*. London: Abacus, 1994.

Hoffmann, David L. *Cultivating the Masses: Modern State Practices and Soviet Socialism, 1914–1939*. Ithaca, NY: Cornell University Press, 2011.

——. *Peasant Metropolis: Social Identities in Moscow, 1929–1941*. Ithaca, NY: Cornell University Press, 1994.

——. *Stalinist Values: The Cultural Norms of Soviet Modernity, 1917–1941*. Ithaca, NY: Cornell University Press, 2003.

Hoffmann, David L., and Yanni Kotsonis. *Russian Modernity: Politics, Knowledge, Practices*. New York: Macmillan, 2000.

Holovko, Mykola. *Suspilno-politychni orhanizatsii ta rukhy Ukrainy v period druhoi svitovoi viiny, 1939–1945 rr*. Kyiv: Olan, 2004.

Holquist, Peter. *Making War, Forging Revolution: Russia's Continuum of Crisis, 1914–1921*. Cambridge, MA: Harvard University Press, 2002.

Horozhankina, L. I., ed. *Lvivshchyna industrialna: Dokumenty i materialy*. Lviv: Kameniar, 1979.

Hoshko, Yu. H., et al., eds. *KPZU—orhanizator revolutsinoi borotby: Spohady kolyshnikh chleniv Komunistychnoi partii Zakhidnoi Ukrainy*. Lviv: Knyzhkovo-zhurnalne vydavnytstvo, 1958.

Hryciuk, Grzegorz. "Die 'Evakuierung' der polnischen und jüdischen Bevölkerung aus den Ostgebieten der Zweiten Polnischen Republik in den Jahren 1944–1947." *Zeitschrift für Geschichtswissenschaft* 55 (2007): 722–42.

——. *"Kumityt" Polski Komitet Opiekuńczy Lwów Miasto w latach 1941–1944*. Toruń: Marszałek, 2000.

——. *Polacy we Lwowie 1939–1944: Życie codzienne*. Warsaw: Książka i Wiedza, 2000.

——. *Przemiany narodowościowe i ludnościowe w Galicji Wschodniej i na Wołyniu w latach 1931–1948*. Toruń: Wydawnictwo Adam Marszałek, 2005.

Hrytsak, Yaroslav. *Prorok u svoi vitchyzni: Franko ta ioho spilnota*. Kyiv: Krytyka, 2006.

Hrytsak, Yaroslav, and Yaroslav Dashkevych, eds. *Mykhailo Hrushevsky i ukrainska istorychna nauka*. Lviv: Instytut istorychnykh doslidzhen Lvivskoho derzhavnoho universytetu im. Ivana Franka, Instytut ukrainskoi arkheohrafii ta dzhereloznavstva im. Mykhaila Hrushevskoho NAN Ukrainy, Lvivske viddilennia, 1999.

Ilnytskyi, Mykola. *Drama bez katarsysu: Storinky literaturnoho zhyttia Lvova pershoi polovyny XX stolittia*. Lviv: Misioner, 1999.

Isaievych, Iaroslav. *Instytut ukrainoznavstva imeni Ivana Krypiakevycha natsionalnoi akademi nauk Ukrainy: Naukova diialnist, struktura, pratsivnyky*. Lviv: Instytut ukrainoznavstva im. I. Krypiakevycha, 2001.

———. *Ivan Krypiakevych u rodynnii tradytsii, nautsi, suspilstvi*. Lviv: Instytut ukrainoznavstva im. I. Krypiakevycha, 2001.

Isaievych, Iaroslav, et al., eds. *Istoriia Lvova*. Lviv: Tsentr Evropy, 2006–7.

———. *Lviv: Istorychni narysy*. Lviv: Instytut ukrainoznavstva im. I. Krypiakevycha, 1996.

Ishchuk, Oleksandr. *Molodizhni orhanizatsii OUN, 1939–1955 rr*. Toronto: Litopys UPA, 2011.

Istoriia gorodov i sel ukrainskoi SSR: Lvovskaia oblast. Kyiv: Glavnaia redaktsiia Ukrainskoi sovetskoi entsiklopedii, 1978.

Ivasiuta, M. K., ed. *Pravdu ne zdolaty: Trudiashchi zakhidnykh oblastei URSR v borotbi proty ukrainskykh burzhuaznykh natsionalistiv u roky sotsialistychnykh peretvoren*. Lviv: Kameniar, 1974.

Jasiewicz, Krzysztof. *Świat niepożegnany: Żydzi na dawnych ziemiach wschodnich Rzeczypospolitej w XVIII–XX wieku*. Warsaw: RYTM, 2004.

Jolluck, Katherine R. *Exile and Identity: Polish Women in the Soviet Union during World War II*. Pittsburgh: University of Pittsburgh Press, 2002.

Jones [Yones], Eliyahu. *Żydzi Lwowa w okresie okupacji 1939–1945*. Łodź: Oficyna Bibliofilów, 1999.

Jones, Polly. *Myth, Memory, Trauma: Rethinking the Stalinist Past in the Soviet Union, 1953–70*. New Haven: Yale University Press, 2013.

Joravsky, David. "The Stalinist Mentality and Higher Learning." *Slavic Review* 42 (1983): 575–600.

Josephson, Paul R. *Resources under Regimes: Technology, Environment, and the State*. Cambridge, MA: Harvard University Press, 2005.

Juchniewicz, Mieczysław. *Polacy w Radzieckim Ruchu Partyzanckim, 1941–1945*. Warsaw: Wydawnictwo Ministerstwa Obrony Narodowej, 1975.

———. "Z działalności Organizacyjno-Bojowej Gwardii Ludowej w Obwodzie Lwowskim PPR-GL." *Wojskowy historyczny przegłąd*, no. 4 (1968): 112–61.

Judson, Pieter M., and Marsha L. Rozenblit, eds. *Constructing Nationalities in East Central Europe*. New York: Berghahn, 2005.

Kaganovsky, Lilya. *How the Soviet Man Was Unmade: Cultural Fantasy and Male Subjectivity under Stalin*. Pittsburgh: University of Pittsburgh Press, 2008.

Kahane, David. *Shchodennyk Lvivskoho hetto*. Kyiv: Dukh i litera, 2003.

Kalbarczyk, Sławomir. *Polscy pracownicy nauki: Ofiary zbrodni sowieckich w latach II wojny światowej*. Warsaw: Neriton, 2001.

Kalinovskii, Eduard. *Vremia, kotoroe on obgoniaet: Geroi sovetskoi rodiny. Dokumentalnyi povest*. Moscow: Izdatelstvo politicheskoi literatury, 1973.

Kamiński, Łukasz, Andrzej Małkiewicz, and Krzysztof Ruchniewicz. *Opór społeczny w Europie Środkowie w latach 1948–1953 na przykładzie Polski, NRD i Czechosłowacji*. Wrocław: ATUT, 2004.

Kaple, Deborah A. *Dream of a Red Factory: The Legacy of High Stalinism in China*. Oxford: Oxford University Press, 1994.

Kappeler, Andreas. "'Great Russians' and 'Little Russians': Russian-Ukrainian Relations and Perceptions in Historical Perspective." *Donald W. Treadgold Papers in Russian, East European, and Central Asian Studies*, no. 39 (October 2003).

Kasianov, Georgii [Heorhiy Kasianov]. "The Holodomor and the Building of a Nation." *Russian Social Science Review* 52 (2011): 71–93.

Kasianov, Georgiy, and Philipp Ther, eds. *A Laboratory of Transnational History: Ukraine and Recent Ukrainian Historiography*. Budapest: Central European University Press, 2009.

Kenez, Peter. *Hungary from the Nazis to the Soviets: The Establishment of the Communist Regime in Hungary, 1944–1948*. Cambridge: Cambridge University Press, 2006.

Kenney, Padraic. "Lviv's Central European Renaissance, 1987–1990." *Harvard Ukrainian Studies* 24 (2000): 303–12.

Kentii, Anatolii. *Zbroinyi chyn ukrainskykh natsionalistiv 1920–1956: Istoryko-arkhivni narysy*. Vol. 1. Kyiv: TsDAHOU, 2005.

Kershaw, Ian. *Hitler, 1936–1945: Nemesis*. London: Penguin, 2000.

Kersten, Krystyna. *The Establishment of Communist Rule in Poland, 1943–1948*. Berkeley: University of California Press, 1991.

Khalid, Adeeb. *The Politics of Muslim Cultural Reform: Jadidism in Central Asia*. Berkeley: University of California Press, 1998.

Khlevniuk, Oleg V. *The History of the Gulag: From Collectivization to the Great Terror*. New Haven: Yale University Press, 2004.

Khonigsman, Iakub. *Katastrofa evreistva zapadnoi Ukrainy: Evrei vostochnoi Galitsii, zapadnoi Volyni, Bukoviny i Zakarpatiia v 1933–1945 godakh*. Lvov: s.n., 1998.

——. *Liudi, gody, sobytiia: stati iz nashei davnei i nedavnei istorii*. Lvov: Lvovskoe obshchestvo evreiskoi kultury im. Sholom Aleikhema, 1998.

Khromeychuk, Olesya. *"Undetermined" Ukrainians: Post-War Narratives of the Waffen SS "Galicia" Division*. Bern: Peter Lang, 2013.

Kirkwood, Michael, ed. *Language Planning in the Soviet Union*. London: Macmillan, 1989.

Kirsanova, O. A. *Rozvitok suspilno-politychnoi aktyvnosti trudiashchykh zakhidnykh oblastei URSR u protsesi budivnytstva osnov sotsializmu*. Kyiv: Naukova dumka, 1981.

Kleßmann, Christoph. *Die Selbstbehauptung einer Nation: NS-Kulturpolitik und polnische Widerstandsbewegung im Generalgouvernement 1939–1945*. Düsseldorf: Bertelsmann, 1971.

Kleßmann, Christoph, and Wacław Długoborski. "Nationalsozialistische Bildungspolitik und polnische Hochschulen." *Geschichte und Gesellschaft* 23 (1997): 535–59.

Klimecki, Michał. *Polski-ukraińska wojna o Lwów i Galicję Wschodnią 1918–1919*. Warsaw: Bellona, 2000.

Klüsener, Sebastian. "Die Regionen der Ukraine: Abgrenzung und Charakterisierung." *Ukraineanalysen*, no. 23 (8 May 2007): 2–11.

Kohlbauer-Fritz, Gabriele. "Judaicasammlungen zwischen Galizien und Wien: Das Jüdische Museum in Lemberg und die Sammlung Maximilian Goldsteins." *Wiener Jahrbuch für Jüdische Geschichte, Kultur und Museumswesen* 1 (1994–95): 133–45.

Komar, Liuba. *Protses 59-ty*. Lviv: Naukove tovarystvo im. Shevchenka, 1997.

Kondratiuk, Kostiantyn, and Ivana Luchakivska. "Zakhidnoukrainska intelihentsiia u pershi roky radianskoi vlady (veresen 1939—cherven 1941)." *Visnyk Lvivskoho universytetu*, no. 33 (1998): 178–85.

Kosyk, Volodymyr. *Ukraina i Nimechchyna u Druhiy svitoviy viini*. Paris: Naukove tovarystvo im. T. Shevchenka u Lvovi, 1993.

Kosytskyi, Andriy. *Entsyklopediia Lvova*. Lviv: Litopys, 2007–8.

Kotkin, Stephen. *Magnetic Mountain: Stalinism as a Civilization*. Berkeley: University of California Press, 1995.

Koval, M. V. "Polityka proty istorii: Ukrainska istorychna nauka v druhii svitovii viini i pershi povoyenni roky." *Ukrainsky istorychny zhurnal*, no. 1 (2002): 3–26.

Kovalchak, H. I. *Rozvytok promyslovosti v zakhidnykh oblastiakh Ukrainy za 20 rokiv radianskoi vlady, 1939–1958 rr.* Kyiv: Naukova dumka, 1965.

Kovba, Zhanna. *Liudianist u bezodni pekla: Povedinka mistsevoho naselennia skhidnoi Halychyny v roky "ostatochnoho rozviazannia ievreiskoho pytannia."* 3rd rev., exp. ed. Kyiv: Dukh i litera, 2009.

Kravtsov, Sergey R. *Di Gildene Royze: The Turei Zahav Synagogue in L'viv*. Petersberg, Ger.: Michael Imhof, 2011.

Krzoska, Markus, and Isabel Röskau-Rydel, eds. *Stadtleben und Nationalität: Ausgewählte Beiträge zur Stadtgeschichtsforschung in Ostmitteleuropa im 19. und 20. Jahrhundert*. Munich: Meidenbauer, 2006.

Kryshtanovskaya, Olga. "Sovietization of Russia, 2000–2008." *Eurasian Review* 2 (2009): 95–133.

Kucherenko, Olga. *Little Soldiers: How Soviet Children Went to War, 1941–1945*. Oxford: Oxford University Press, 2011.

Kudelia, Serhiy. "Choosing Violence in Irregular Wars: The Case of Anti-Soviet Insurgency in Western Ukraine." *East European Politics and Societies* 27 (2013): 149–81.

Kurylo, Taras, and Ivan Khymka [John-Paul Himka]. "Iak OUN stavylasia do evreiv? Rozdumy nad knyzhkoiu Volodymyra Viatrovycha." *Ukraina moderna*, no. 13 (2008): 252–65.

Kurylyshyn, Kostiantyn. *Ukrainska lehalna presa periodu nimetskoi okupatsii (1939–1944 rr.)*. Vol. 1. Lviv: Stefanyka, 2007.

Kushnezh, R. "Uchast ukrainskoi hromadskosti Polshi v dopomohovykh ta protestatsiinykh aktsiiakh proty holodomoru v Ukraine." *Ukrainsky istorichny zhurnal*, no. 2 (2005): 131–41.

Kuzio, Taras. "The National Factor in Ukraine's Quadruple Transition." *Contemporary Politics* 6 (2000): 143–64.

Lafleur, Brenda et al., *Lviv City Profile: Demographic, Economic, Fiscal* (The Conference Board of Canada, Canadian International Development Agency, 2012). http://www.ebed.org.ua/sites/expertise.one2action.com/files/repo/ebed_lviv_city_profile_eng.pdf.

Lemberg, Hans, ed. *Sowjetisches Modell und Nationale Prägung: Kontinuität und Wandel in Ostmitteleuropa nach dem Zweiten Weltkrieg*. Marburg: Herder-Institut, 1991.

Levin, Dov. *The Lesser of Two Evils: Eastern European Jewry under Soviet Rule, 1939–1941*. Philadelphia: The Jewish Publication Society, 1995.

Levin, Nora. *The Jews in the Soviet Union since 1917: Paradox of Survival*. New York: New York University Press, 1988.

Lewytzkyj, Borys. *Die Sowjetukraine 1944–1963*. Cologne: Kiepenheuer & Witsch, 1964.

———. *Politics and Society in Soviet Ukraine, 1953–1980*. Edmonton: Canadian Institute of Ukrainian Studies Press, 1984.

Leyda, Jay. *Kino: A History of Russian and Soviet Film: A Study of the Development of Russian Cinema from 1896 to the Present*. 3rd ed. Princeton, NJ: Princeton University Press, 1983.

Lieberman, Sanford R., et al., eds. *The Soviet Empire Reconsidered: Essays in Honor of Adam B. Ulam*. Boulder, CO: Westview, 1994.

Linne, Karsten. "Arbeiterrekrutierungen in Ostgalizien 1941 bis 1944: Zwischen Freiwilligkeit und Menschenjagden." *Jahrbücher für Geschichte Osteuropas* 62 (2014): 61–88.

Loew, Peter Oliver. *Danzig und seine Vergangenheit, 1793–1997: Die Geschichtskultur einer Stadt zwischen Deutschland und Polen*. Osnabrück: fibre, 2003.

Logusz, Michael O. *Galicia Division: The Waffen-SS 14th Grenadier Division, 1943–1945*. Atglen: Schiffer, 1997.

Loshak, V. G. *V pamiati narodnoi*. Sverdlovsk: Sredne-Uralskoe knizhnoe izdatelstvo, 1986.

Lower, Wendy. "Pogroms, Mob Violence, and Genocide in Western Ukraine, Summer 1941: Varied Histories, Explanations and Comparisons." *Journal of Genocide Research* 13 (2011): 217–46.

——. *Hitler's Furies: German Women in the Nazi Killing Fields*. New York: Mariner Books, 2014.

Lozynskyi, Roman. *Etnichnyi sklad naselennia Lvova*. Lviv: Vydavnychnyi tsentr LNU im. Ivana Franka, 2005.

Lubkivskyi, Roman. *Lviv: Misto ochyma pysmennyka*. Lviv: Kameniar, 1985.

Lysiak, Olesa, ed. *Brody: Zbirnyk statei i narysiv*. Drohobych-Lviv: Vidrodzhennia, 2003.

Madajczyk, Czesław. *Die Okkupationspolitik Nazideutschlands in Polen 1939–1945*. Berlin: Akademieverlag, 1987.

Madajczyk, Czesław, ed. *Vom Generalplan Ost zum Generalsiedlungsplan*. Munich: Saur, 1994.

Magocsi, Paul Robert. *Galicia: A Historical Survey and Bibliographic Guide*. Toronto: University of Toronto Press, 1983.

——. *The Roots of Ukrainian Nationalism: Galicia as Ukraine's Piedmont*. Toronto: University of Toronto Press, 2002.

Magocsi, Paul Robert, ed. *Morality and Reality: The Life and Times of Andrei Sheptyts'kyi*. Edmonton: Canadian Institute for Ukrainian Studies Press, 1989.

Makarchuk, S. A. "Pereselennia poliakiv iz zakhidnikh oblastei Ukrainy v Polshchu, 1944–1946 rr." *Ukrainskyi istorychnyi zhurnal*, no. 3 (2003): 103–15.

Manuilskyi, Dmytro. *Ukrainsko-nimetski natsionalisty na sluzhbi u fashistskoi Nimechchyny*. Kyiv: Ukrainske derzhavne vydavnytstvo, 1946.

Marples, David R. *Stalinism in Ukraine in the 1940s*. New York: St. Martin's Press, 1992.

Martin, Sean. *Jewish Life in Cracow, 1918–1939*. London: Vallentine Mitchell, 2004.

Martin, Terry. *The Affirmative Action Empire: Nations and Nationalism in the Soviet Union, 1923–1939*. Ithaca, NY: Cornell University Press, 2001.

Marusyk, Tamara. *Zakhidnoukrainska humanitarna intelihentsia: Realii zhyttia ta diialnosti*. Chernivtsi: Ruta, 2002.

Mastny, Vojtech. *The Cold War and Soviet Insecurity: The Stalin Years*. Oxford: Oxford University Press, 1996.

Materialy konferentsii (Kiev, 8–9 dekabria 1994 g.): Evreiska istoriia i kultura v Ukraine. Assotsiatsiia iudaiki Ukrainy. http://www.jewish-heritage.org/eu94a26r.htm.

Matiukhina, Aleksandra. *W Sowieckim Lwowie: Życie codzienne miasta w latach 1944–1990*. Cracow: Wydawnictwo Uniwersytetu Jagiellońskiego, 2000.

Matwijów, Maciej. *Walka o lwowskie dobra kultury w latach 1945–1948*. Wrocław: Towarzystwo Przyjaciól Ossolineum, 1996.

——. *Zaklad Narodowy imienia Ossolinskich w latach 1939–1946*. Wrocław: Towarzystwo Przyjaciól Ossolineum, 2003.

Mazower, Mark. *Dark Continent: Europe's Twentieth Century*. New York: Vintage, 1998.

——. *Governing the World: The History of an Idea, 1815 to the Present*. New York: Penguin, 2012.

——. *Hitler's Empire: Nazi Rule in Occupied Europe*. London: Allen Lane, 2008.

——. "Minorities and the League of Nations in Interwar Europe." *Daedalus* 126 (1997): 47–63.

——. *Salonica, City of Ghosts: Christians, Muslims, and Jews, 1430–1950*. New York: Vintage, 2006.

Mazur, Grzegorz. *Życie polityczne polskiego Lwowa, 1918–1939*. Cracow: Księgarnia Akademicka, 2007.

Mękarski, Stefan. *Sowietyzacja kulturalna Polski*. London: Reduta, 1949.

Mendelsohn, Ezra. "From Assimilation to Zionism in Lvov: The Case of Alfred Nossig." *Slavonic and East European Review* 49 (1971): 521–34.

——. *The Jews of East Central Europe between the World Wars*. Bloomington: Indiana University Press, 1983.

Mendelsohn, Ezra, ed. *People of the City: Jews and the Urban Challenge*. Oxford: Oxford University Press, 1999.

Merl, Stephan. "Review of David Feest, *Zwangskollektivierung im Baltikum: Die Sowjetisierung des estnischen Dorfes 1944–1953* (Cologne: Böhlau, 2007)." *Kritika: Explorations in Russian and Eurasian History* 10 (2009): 376–86.

Merridale, Catherine. *Ivan's War: Life and Death in the Red Army, 1939–1945*. New York: Picador, 2006.

Mertelsmann, Olaf. *The Sovietization of the Baltic States, 1940–1956*. Tartu: Kleio, 2003.

Mevius, Martin. *Agents of Moscow: The Hungarian Communist Party and the Origins of Socialist Patriotism, 1941–1953*. Oxford: Oxford University Press, 2005.

Michlic, Joanna Beata. *Poland's Threatening Other: The Image of the Jew from 1880 to the Present*. Lincoln: University of Nebraska Press, 2006.

——. "The Soviet Occupation of Poland, 1939–1941, and the Stereotype of the Anti-Polish and Pro-Soviet Jew." *Jewish Social Studies* 13 (2007): 135–76.

Micińska, Magdalena. *Inteligencja na rozdrożach, 1864–1918*. Warsaw: Neriton, 2008.

Mick, Christoph. "Incompatible Experiences: Poles, Ukrainians, and Jews in Lviv under Soviet and German Occupation, 1939–1944." *Journal of Contemporary History* 46 (2011): 336–63.

——. *Kriegserfahrungen in einer multiethnischen Stadt: Lemberg 1914–1947*. Wiesbaden: Harrassowitz, 2010.

Miller, Alexei. *The Ukrainian Question: The Russian Empire and Nationalism in the Nineteenth Century*. Budapest: Central European University Press, 2003.

Milosz, Czesław. *The Captive Mind*. New York: Knopf, 1953.

Misiunas, Romuald J., and Rein Taagepera. *The Baltic States: Years of Dependence, 1940–1980*. Berkeley: University of California Press, 1983.

Mitsel, Mikhail. *Obshchiny iudeiskogo veroispovedaniia v Ukraine: Kiev, Lvov, 1945–1981 gg*. Kyiv: Sfera, 1998.

——. *Evrei Ukrainy v 1943–1953 gg.: Ocherki dokumentirovannoi istorii*. Kyiv: Dukh i litera, 2004.

Mitsuyoshi, Yoshie. "Gender, Nationality, and Socialism: Women in Soviet Western Ukraine, 1939–1950." PhD diss., University of Alberta, 2004.

——. "Public Representations of Women in Western Ukraine under Late Stalinism: Magazines, Literature, and Memoirs." *Jahrbücher für Geschichte Osteuropas* 54 (2006): 20–36.

Motyka, Grzegorz. *Tak było w bieszczadach: Walki polsko-ukraińskie 1943–1948*. Warsaw: Oficyna Wydawnicza Volumen, 1999.

——. *Ukraińska partyzantka, 1942–1960*. Warsaw: RYTM, 2006.

Motyl, Alexander J. *The Turn to the Right: The Ideological Origins and Development of Ukrainian Nationalism, 1919–1929*. New York: Columbia University Press, 1980.

Müller, Sepp. *Von der Ansiedlung bis zur Umsiedlung: Das Deutschtum Galiziens, insbesondere Lembergs 1772–1940*. Marburg: Johann Gottfried Herder-Institut, 1961.

Müller, Sepp, with Erich Müller. *Galizien und sein Deutschtum: Eine Dokumentation aus Sepp Müller's Nachlaß ergänzt durch Unterlagen des Hilfskomitees der Galiziendeutschen 1948–1951*. Vol. 1, *Heimatbuch der Galiziendeutschen Teil V*. Stuttgart: Hilfskomitee der Galiziendeutschen, 1999.

Naimark, Norman. *The Russians in Germany: A History of the Soviet Zone of Occupation, 1945–1949*. Cambridge, MA: Harvard University Press, 1995.

Naimark, Norman, and Leonid Gibianskii, eds. *The Establishment of Communist Regimes in Eastern Europe, 1944–1949*. Boulder, CO: Westview, 1997.

Nam partiia sylu dala: Z istorii komsomolskoi orhanizatsii Lvivskoho derzhavnoho universytetu im. Ivana Franka. Lviv: Vydavnytstvo Lvivskoho universytetu, 1960.

Narvselius, Eleonora. "The 'Bandera Debate': The Contentious Legacy of World War II and Liberalization of Collective Memory in Western Ukraine." *Canadian Slavonic Papers/ Revue canadienne des slavistes* 54 (2012): 469–90.

Narysy istorii Lvivskoi oblasnoi partinoi orhanizatsii. 2nd. rev. exp. ed. Lviv: Kameniar, 1969.

Narysy istorii Lvivskoi oblasnoi partinoi orhanizatsii. 3rd rev. exp. ed. Lviv: Kameniar, 1980.

Nazarenko, I., et al., eds. *Ukrainskaia SSR v Velikoi Otechestvennoi Voine Sovetskogo Soiuza*. 3 vols. Kyiv: Izdatelstvo politicheskoi literatury Ukrainy, 1975.

Nazaruk, Osyp. *Halychyna i Velyka Ukraina*. Lviv: Nova zoria, 1936.

——. *Rik na velykii Ukraini: Konspekt spomyniv z ukrainskoi revolutsii*. New York: Hoverlia, 1978. Originally printed Vienna: Ukrainskyi prapor, 1920.

——. *Zi Lvova do Varshavy: 2–13 zhovtnia 1939 roku*. Lviv: NTSh, 1995.

Nechytaliuk, Mykhailo. *"Chest pratsi!" Akademik Mykhailo Vozniak u spohadakh ta publikatsiiakh*. Lviv: Lviv University, 2000.

Nimchuk, Ivan. *595 dniv sovetskym viaznem*. Toronto: Vydavnytstvo Vasilian, 1950.

Northrop, Douglas. *Veiled Empire: Gender and Power in Stalinist Central Asia*. Ithaca, NY: Cornell University Press, 2003.

Noskova, A. F. *Iz Varshavy: Moskva, tovaryshchu Beriia. Dokumenty NKVD SSSR o polskom podpole, 1944–1945 gg*. Moscow: Rossiiskaia akademiia nauk, 2001.

Obertreis, Julia. *Tränen des Sozialismus: Wohnen in Leningrad zwischen Alltag und Utopie 1917–1937*. Cologne: Böhlau, 2004.

Ohloblin, Oleksandr, ed. *Zakhidna Ukraina: Zbirnyk*. Kyiv: Vidavnytstvo Akademii nauk URSR, 1940.

Oleksiuk, M. M. *Torzhestvo istorychnoi spravedlyvosti*. Lviv: Vydavnytstvo Lvivskoho universytetu, 1968.

Panchuk, M. I., and Iu. Iu. Slyvka. *Aktualni problemy istorii KPZU*. Lviv: Svit, 1990.

Pankivskyi, Kost. *Roky nimetskoi okupatsii*. New York: Kliuchi, 1965.

——. *Vid derzhavy do komitetu*. New York: Kliuchi, 1957.

Patryliak, Ivan. "Dialnist Romana Shukhevycha v Ukrainskomu lehioni." *Ukrainskyi vyzvolnyi rukh*, no. 10 (2007): 186–201.

Paxton, Robert O. *Vichy France: Old Guard and New Order, 1940–1944*. New York: Columbia University Press, 1972.

Petrov, Nikita. *Pervyi predsedatel KGB Ivan Serov*. Moscow: Materik, 2005.

Petrovsky-Shtern, Yohanan, and Antony Polonsky. "Introduction." In "Jews and Ukrainians." Special issue, *Polin: Studies in Polish Jewry* 26 (2013): 3–64.

Pinkus, Benjamin. *The Soviet Government and the Jews, 1948–1967: A Documented Study*. Cambridge: Cambridge University Press, 1984.

Pipes, Richard, ed. *The Unknown Lenin: From the Secret Archive*. New Haven: Yale University Press, 1998.

Plaggenborg, Stefan. *Experiment Moderne: Der sowjetische Weg*. Frankfurt am Main: Campus, 2006.

Plaggenborg, Stefan, ed. *Stalinismus: Neue Forschungen und Konzepte*. Berlin: Berlin-Verlag, 1998.

Plokhy, Serhii. *Unmaking Imperial Russia: Mykhailo Hrushevsky and the Writing of Ukrainian History*. Toronto: University of Toronto Press, 2005.

Podoliak, H., and L. Shlemkevych. *Robitnyk—tse zvuchyt hordo*. Lviv: Kameniar, 1965.

Pohl, Dieter. *Nationalsozialistische Judenverfolgung in Ostgalizien 1941–1944: Organisation und Durchführung eines staatlichen Massenverbrechens*. Munich: Oldenbourg, 1996.

——. "Schlachtfeld zweier totalitärer Diktaturen—die Ukraine im Zweiten Weltkrieg." *Österreichische Osthefte* 42 (2000): 339–62.

Pohl, Dieter, and Tanja Sebta, eds. *Zwangsarbeit in Hitler's Europa: Besatzung, Arbeit, Folgen*. Berlin: Metropol, 2013.

Polian, Pavel. *Against Their Will: The History and Geography of Forced Migrations in the USSR*. Budapest: Central European University Press, 2004.

——. *Zhertvy dvukh diktatur: Zhizn, trud, unizhenie i smert sovetskikh voennoplennykh i ostarbaiterov na chuzhbine i na rodine*. Moscow: Rosspen, 2002.

Polonsky, Antony. *The Jews in Poland and Russia*. Vol. 3. Oxford: The Littman Library of Jewish Civilization, 2012.

Portnov, Andriy. "Post-Soviet Ukraine Dealing with Its Controversial Past." *Journal of Modern European History* 8 (2010): 152–55.

Potocki, Robert. *Polityka państwa polskiego wobec zagadnienia ukraińskiego w latach 1930–1939*. Lublin: Instytut Europy Środkowo-Wschodniej, 2003.

Potulnyckyi, Volodymyr. "Das ukrainische historische Denken im 19. und 20. Jahrhundert: Konzeptionen und Periodisierung." *Jahrbücher für Geschichte Osteuropas* 45 (1997): 2–30.

Prokopovych, Markian. *Habsburg Lemberg: Architecture, Public Space, and Politics in the Galician Capital, 1772–1914*. West Lafayette, IN: Purdue University Press, 2009.

Prusin, Alexander V. *The Lands Between: Conflict in the East European Borderlands, 1870–1992*. Oxford: Oxford University Press, 2010.

——. *Nationalizing a Borderland: War, Ethnicity, and Anti-Jewish Violence in East Galicia, 1914–1920*. Tuscaloosa: University of Alabama Press, 2005.

Quinkert, Babette. *Propaganda und Terror in Weißrussland, 1941–1944: Die deutsche "geistige" Kriegführung gegen Zivilbevölkerung und Partisanen*. Paderborn: Schöningh, 2009.

Radziejowski, Janusz. *Kommunistyczna Partia Zachodniej Ukrainy 1919–1929: Węzlowe problemy ideologiczne*. Cracow: Wydawnictwo Literackie, 1976.

Redlich, Shimon. *Together and Apart in Brzezany: Poles, Jews, and Ukrainians, 1919–1945*. Bloomington: Indiana University Press, 2002.

Redzik, Adam. *Wydział Prawa Uniwersytetu Lwowskiego w latach 1939–1946*. Lublin: TN KUL, 2006.

Reinkowski, Maurus, and Gregor Thum, eds. *Helpless Imperialists: Imperial Failure, Fear, and Radicalization*. Göttingen: Vandenhoeck & Ruprecht, 2013.

Reynolds, David. *The Long Shadow: The Legacies of the Great War in the Twentieth Century*. New York: W. W. Norton, 2014.

Risch, William Jay. *The Ukrainian West: Culture and the Fate of Empire in Soviet Lviv*. Cambridge, MA: Harvard University Press, 2011.

Ro'i, Yaacov. *Islam in the Soviet Union: From the Second World War to Gorbachev*. New York: Columbia University Press, 2000.

——. *The Struggle for Soviet Jewish Emigration 1948–1967*. Cambridge: Cambridge University Press, 1991.

Ro'i, Yaacov, and Avi Beker, eds. *Jewish Culture and Identity in the Soviet Union*. New York: New York University Press, 1991.

Röskau-Rydel, Isabel, ed. *Galizien, Bukowina, Moldau: Deutsche Geschichte im Osten Europas*. Berlin: Siedler, 1999.

Rossino, Alexander B. *Hitler Strikes Poland*. Lawrence: University Press of Kansas, 2003.

Rossoliński-Liebe, Grzegorz, *Stepan Bandera. The Life and Afterlife of a Ukrainian Nationalist. Fascism, Genocide, and Cult*. Stuttgart: ibidem, 2014.

——. "The Ukrainian National Revolution of 1941: Discourse and Practice of a Fascist Movement." *Kritika: Explorations in Russian and Eurasian History* 12 (2011): 83–114.

Roth, Joseph. *Orte: Ausgewählte Texte*. Berlin: Reclam, 1990.

Roy, Olivier. *The New Central Asia: The Creation of Nations*. New York: New York University Press, 2000.

Rubl'ov, O. S., and Iu. A. Cherchenko. *Stalinshchyna i dolia zakhidnoukrainskoi intelihentsii*. Kyiv: Naukova dumka, 1994.

Rubl'ov, Oleksandr. *Zakhidnoukrainska intelihentsiia u zahalnonatsionalnykh politychnykh ta kulturnykh protsesakh, 1914–1939*. Kyiv: Instytut istorii Ukrainy, NAN Ukrainy, 2004.

Rudling, Per A. "The OUN, the UPA, and the Holocaust: A Study in the Manufacturing of Historical Myths." *Carl Beck Papers in Russian and East European Studies*, no. 2107. Pittsburgh: University of Pittsburgh, 2011.

Said, Edward W. *Orientalism*. New York: Vintage Books: 1979.

Sandkühler, Thomas. *"Endlösung" in Galizien: Der Judenmord in Ostpolen und die Rettungsinitiativen von Berthold Beitz 1941–1944*. Bonn: Dietz, 1996.

Schenk, Dieter. *Der Lemberger Professorenmord und der Holocaust in Ostgalizien*. Bonn: Dietz, 2007.

Schenke, Cornelia. *Nationalstaat und nationale Frage: Polen und die Ukrainer 1921–1939*. Hamburg: Dölling & Glitz, 2004.

Schoenfeld, Joachim. *Holocaust Memoirs: Jews in the Lwow Ghetto, the Janowski Concentration Camp, and as Deportees in Siberia*. Hoboken, NJ: Ktav, 1985.

Schreiber, Gerhard. *Die italienischen Militärinternierten im deutschen Machtbereich, 1943 bis 1945: Verraten, verachtet, vergessen*. Munich: Oldenbourg, 1990.

Sekretariuk, V. V., et al., eds. *Istoriia Lvova*. Kyiv: Naukova dumka, 1984.

Senkiv, Mykhailo. *Zakhidnoukrainske selo: Nasylnytska kolektyvisatsia—40-poch. 50-kh rr. XX st*. Lviv: Instytut ukrainoznavstva im. I. Krypiakevycha, 2002.

Serhiychuk, Volodymyr. *Stepan Bandera: U dokumentakh radianskykh orhaniv derzhavnoi bezpeky (1939–1959)*. Vol. 1. Kyiv: PP Serhiychuk, 2009.

Shaw, Tony. *Hollywood's Cold War*. Amherst: University of Massachusetts Press, 2007.

Shkandrij, Myroslav. *Jews in Ukrainian Literature: Representation and Identity*. New Haven: Yale University Press, 2009.

Shklovsky, Viktor. "Rasskazy o Zapadnoi Ukraine." *Znamia*, no. 2 (1940): 8–35.

Shneer, David. *Through Soviet Jewish Eyes: Photography, War, and the Holocaust*. New Brunswick, NJ: Rutgers University Press, 2011.

——. *Yiddish and the Creation of Soviet Jewish Culture, 1918–1930*. Cambridge: Cambridge University Press, 2004.

Shore, Marci. *Caviar and Ashes: A Warsaw Generation's Life and Death in Marxism, 1918–1968*. New Haven: Yale University Press, 2006.

Shyshka, Oleksandr. "Pamiatnyky i memorialni znaky Lvova (do 1991 roku)." *Halytska brama*, nos. 6–7 (2010): 4–18.

Sienkiewicz, Witold, and Gregorz Hryciuk. *Wysiedlenia wypędzenia i ucieczki 1939–1959: Atlas ziem Polski*. Warsaw: Demart, 2008.

Skaba, A. D., ed. *Radianska entsyklopediia istorii Ukrainy*. Kyiv: Hol. red. Ukr. rad. entsyklopedii, 1969.

Slepyan, Kenneth. *Stalin's Guerrillas: Soviet Partisans in World War II*. Lawrence: University Press of Kansas, 2006.

Slezkine, Yuri. "Imperialism as the Highest Stage of Socialism." *Russian Review* 59 (2000): 227–34.

Slotkin, Richard. *Gunfighter Nation: The Myth of the Frontier in Twentieth-Century America*. Norman: University of Oklahoma Press, 1998.

Slyvka, Iuriy, et al. *Stanovlennia i rozvytok masovoho ateizmu v zakhidnykh oblastiakh Ukrainskoi RSR*. Kyiv: Naukova dumka, 1981.

Smith, Kathleen E. *Remembering Stalin's Victims: Popular Memory and the End of the USSR*. Ithaca, NY: Cornell University Press, 1996.

Snyder, Timothy. *Bloodlands: Europe between Hitler and Stalin*. New York: Basic Books, 2010.

——. *The Reconstruction of Nations: Poland, Ukraine, Lithuania, Belarus, 1569–1999*. New Haven: Yale University Press, 2003.

——. *The Red Prince: The Secret Lives of a Habsburg Archduke*. New York: Basic Books, 2008.

Sroczynski, Ryszard, et al., eds. *Politechnika Lwowska: Macierz Polskich Politechnik*. Wrocław: Wrocławskie Towarzystwo Naukowe, 1995.

Staar, Richard F. *Poland, 1944–1962: The Sovietization of a Captive People*. Baton Rouge: Louisiana State University Press, 1962.

Statiev, Alexander. *The Soviet Counterinsurgency in the Western Borderlands*. Cambridge: Cambridge University Press, 2010.

Stefanyk, S. *Dva svity—dvi demokratii*. Lviv: Knyzhkovo-zhurnalne vydavnytstvo, 1962.

Steinlauf, Michael C. *Bondage to the Dead: Poland and the Memory of the Holocaust*. Syracuse: Syracuse University Press, 1997.

Steinweis, Alan E., and Daniel E. Rogers, eds. *The Impact of Nazism: New Perspectives on the Third Reich and Its Legacy*. Lincoln: University of Nebraska Press, 2003.

Stepaniv, Olena. *Suchasnyi Lviv*. Cracow: Ukrainske vydavnytstvo, 1943.

Stites, Richard, ed. *Culture and Entertainment in Wartime Russia*. Bloomington: Indiana University Press, 1995.

Stoler, Ann Laura. *Carnal Knowledge and Imperial Power: Race and the Intimate in Colonial Rule*. Berkeley: University of California Press, 2010.

Strong, John W., ed. *Essays on Revolutionary Culture and Stalinism*. Columbus, OH: Slavica Publishers, 1990.

Subtelny, Orest. *Ukraina: Istoriia*. 3rd rev. ed. Kyiv: Lybid, 1993.

Suchmiel, Jadwiga. *Działalność naukowa kobiet w Uniwersytecie we Lwowie do roku 1939*. Częstochowa: WSP, 2000.
Suny, Ronald Grigor. "On Ideology, Subjectivity, and Modernity: Disparate Thoughts about Doing Soviet History." *Russian History/Histoire russe* 35 (2008): 251–58.
Suny, Ronald Grigor, and Terry Martin, eds. *A State of Nations: Empire and Nation-Making in the Age of Lenin and Stalin*. Oxford: Oxford University Press, 2001.
Sword, Keith. *Deportation and Exile: Poles in the Soviet Union, 1939–1948*. London: Macmillan, 1994.
Sword, Keith, ed. *The Soviet Takeover of the Soviet Eastern Provinces, 1939–1941*. London: Macmillan, 1991.
Szporluk, Roman. "The Making of Modern Ukraine: The Western Dimension." *Harvard Ukrainian Studies* 25 (2001): 73.
——. *Russia, Ukraine, and the Breakup of the Soviet Union*. Stanford, CA: Hoover Institution Press, 2000.
Szporluk, Roman, ed. *The Influence of East Europe and the Soviet West on the USSR*. New York: Praeger, 1975.
Taki, Victor. "The Horrors of War: Representations of Violence in European, Oriental, and 'Patriotic' Wars." *Kritika: Explorations in Russian and Eurasian History* 15 (2014): 263–92.
Taubman, William. *Khrushchev: The Man and His Era*. New York: W. W. Norton, 2003.
Taubman, William, Sergei Khrushchev, and Abbott Gleason, eds. *Nikita Khrushchev*. New Haven: Yale University Press, 2000.
Taylor, Charles. *Modern Social Imaginaries*. Durham, NC: Duke University Press, 2004.
Ther, Philipp, and Ana Siljak, eds. *Redrawing Nations: Ethnic Cleansing in East-Central Europe, 1944–1948*. Lanham, MD: Rowman and Littlefield, 2001.
Ther, Philipp, and Holm Sundhausen, eds. *Nationalitätenkonflikte im 20. Jahrhundert: Ursachen von inter-ethnischer Gewalt im Vergleich*. Wiesbaden: Harrasowitz, 2001.
Thum, Gregor. *Uprooted: How Breslau Became Wrocław during the Century of Expulsions*. Princeton, NJ: Princeton University Press, 2011.
Tismaneanu, Vladimir. *Stalinism for All Seasons: A Political History of Romanian Communism*. Berkeley: University of California Press, 2003.
Tiufiakov, I. N. *Doroga v bessmertie: Fotoalbom o vydaiushchemsia sovetskom razvedchike Geroe Sovetskogo Soiuza Nikolae Ivanoviche Kuznetsove*. Moscow: Planeta, 1985.
Torzecki, Ryszard. *Polacy i Ukraińcy: Sprawa ukraińska w czasie II wojny światowej na terenie II Rzeczpospolitej*. Warsaw: Wydawnyctwo Naukowe PWN, 1993.
Torzhestvo istorychnoi spravedlyvosti. Lviv: Vydavnytstvo Lvivskoho universytetu, 1968.
Trainin, Ilia. *Natsionalnoe i sotsialnoe osvobozhdenie Zapadnoi Ukrainy i Zapadnoi Belorussii*. Moscow: Gosudarstvennoe sotsialno-ekonomicheskoe izdatelstvo, 1939.
Trista rokiv vozziednannia Ukrainy z Rosiiu. Lviv: Vydavnytstvo Lvivskoho universytetu, 1954.
Trznadel, Jacek. *Kolaboranci: Tadeusz Boy-Żeleński i grupa komunistycznych pisarzy we Lwowie 1939–1941*. Komorów: Wydawnictwo Antyk Marcin Dybowski, 1998.
Tscherkes, Bohdan. "Stalinist Visions for the Urban Transformation of Lviv, 1939–1955." *Harvard Ukrainian Studies* 24 (2000): 205–22.
Urbansky, Sören, ed. *"Unsere Insel": Sowjetische Identitätspolitik auf Sachalin nach 1945*. Berlin: be.bra, 2013.

Vakulenko, H. S., and V. D. Variagina. "Bilshche vymohlyvosti i sumlivosti u vysvitlenni istorychnykh podii." *Ukrainskyi istorychnyi zhurnal*, no. 3 (1962): 121–22.

Variagina, V., and H. Vakulenko. *Narodna Hvardia imeni Ivana Franka: Storinky heroichnoi borotby pidpilno-partyzanskoi orhanizatsii zakhidnykh oblastei Ukrainy, 1942–1944 roky*. 1967. 2nd rev. exp. ed. Lviv: Kameniar, 1979.

Venclova, Tomas. *Alexander Wat: Life and Art of an Iconoclast*. New Haven: Yale University Press, 1996.

Verbinskii, Mikhail. *V bitve za "rozu."* Lviv: Kameniar, 1990.

Veryha, Wasyl, ed. *The Correspondence of the Ukrainian Central Committee in Cracow and Lviv with the German Authorities, 1939–1944*. 2 parts. Research Report no. 61. Edmonton: Canadian Institute of Ukrainian Studies, University of Alberta, 2000.

Viatrovych, Volodymyr, ed. *Polsko-ukrainski stosunky v 1942–1947 rokakh u dokumentakh OUN ta UPA*. 2 vols. Lviv: Tsentr doslidzhen vyzvolnoho rukhu, 2011.

Vid maisternia do veletnia. Lviv: Kameniar, 1975.

Viedienieiev, Dmytro, and Hennadiy Bystrukhin. *Dvobii bez kompromisiv: Protyborstvo spetspidrozdiliv OUN ta radianskykh syl spetsoperatsii, 1945–1980-ti roky*. Kyiv: KIS, 2007.

Voinalovych, Viktor. *Partiino-derzhavna polityka shchodo relihii ta relihiinykh instytutsii v Ukraini 1940–1960-kh rokiv: Politolohichnyi dyskurs*. Kyiv: NAN Ukrainy, 2005.

Volin, B. M., and D. N. Ushakov, eds. *Tolkovyi slovar russkogo iazyka*. 4 vols. Moscow: Sovetskaia entsiklopediia, 1935–1940. Reprint, Moscow, 1948.

Wachs, Philipp-Christian. *Der Fall Theodor Oberländer (1905–1998): Ein Lehrstück deutscher Geschichte*. Frankfurt am Main: Campus, 2000.

Wandruska, Adam, and Peter Urbanitsch, eds. *Die Habsburgermonarchie 1848–1918*. Vol. 3, part 1, *Die Völker des Reiches*. Vienna: Verlag der Österreichischen Akademie der Wissenschaften, 1980.

Wanner, Catherine. *Burden of Dreams: History and Identity in Post-Soviet Ukraine*. University Park: Pennsylvania State University Press, 1998.

Wanner, Catherine, ed. *State Secularism and Lived Religion in Soviet Russia and Ukraine*. Washington, DC: Woodrow Wilson Center Press; New York: Oxford University Press, 2012.

Wardzyńska, Maria, ed. *Deportacje na roboty przymusowe z Generalnego Gubernatorstwa 1939–1945*. Warsaw: Instytut Pamięci Narodowej, 1991.

Weeks, Theodore R. "The Best of Both Worlds: Creating the *Żyd-Polak*." *East European Jewish Affairs* 34 (2004): 1–20.

——. *From Assimilation to Antisemitism: The Jewish Question in Poland, 1850–1914*. DeKalb: Northern Illinois University Press, 2006.

——. "A Multi-Ethnic City in Transition: Vilnius's Stormy Decade, 1939–1949." *Eurasian Geography and Economics* 47 (2006): 153–75.

——. "Population Politics in Vilnius, 1944–1947: A Case Study of Socialist-Sponsored Ethnic Cleansing." *Post-Soviet Affairs* 32 (2007): 76–95.

Węgierski, Jerzy. *W lwowskiej Armii Krajowej*. Warsaw: PAX, 1989.

Weiner, Amir. "The Making of a Dominant Myth: The Second World War and the Construction of Political Identities within the Soviet Polity." *Russian Review* 55 (1996): 638–60.

——. *Making Sense of War: The Second World War and the Fate of the Bolshevik Revolution*. Princeton, NJ: Princeton University Press, 2001.

——. "Nothing but Certainty." *Slavic Review* 61 (2002): 44–53.

Weiner, Amir, ed. *Landscaping the Human Garden: Twentieth-Century Population Management in a Comparative Framework*. Stanford, CA: Stanford University Press, 2003.

Weiner, Amir, and Aigi Rahi-Tamm. "Getting to Know You: The Soviet Surveillance System, 1939–57." *Kritika: Explorations in Russian and Eurasian History* 13 (2012): 5–45.

Weiss, Yfaat. *Deutsche und polnische Juden vor dem Holocaust: Jüdische Identität zwischen Staatsbürgerschaft und Ethnizität 1933–1940*. Munich: Oldenbourg, 2000.

Wendland, Anna Veronika. *Die Russophilen in Galizien: Ukrainische Konservative zwischen Österrreich und Rußland 1848–1915*. Vienna: Verlag der Österreichischen Akademie der Wissenschaften, 2001.

Werblan, Andrzej. *Władysław Gomułka: Sekretarz Generalny PPR*. Warsaw: Książka i Wiedza, 1988.

Werth, Nicolas. *Cannibal Island: Death in a Siberian Gulag*. Princeton, NJ: Princeton University Press, 2007.

Widdis, Emma. *Visions of a New Land: Soviet Film from the Revolution to the Second World War*. New Haven: Yale University Press, 2003.

Winklowa, Barbara. *Nad Wisłą i nad Sekwaną: Biografia Tadeusza Boya-Żeleńskiego*. Warsaw: Iskry, 1998.

Winklowa, Barbara, ed. *Boy we Lwowie: Antologia tekstów Tadeusza Żeleńskiego (Boya) we Lwowie*. Warsaw: RYTM, 1992.

Witwicki, Michal, ed. *Plastychna Panorama davnoho Lvova: Janusz Witwicki/Panorama plastyczna dawnego Lwowa: Janusz Witwicki 1903–1946*. Lviv: s.n., 2004.

Włodarkiewicz, Wojciech. *Lwów 1939*. Warsaw: Bellona, 2003.

Wnuk, Rafał. *"Za pierwszego Sowieta": Polska konspiracja na Kresach Wschodnich II Rzeczypospolitej, wrzesień 1939–czerwiec 1941*. Warsaw: PAN ISP, 2007.

Wojak, Irmtrud, and Susanne Meinl, eds. *Im Labyrinth der Shuld: Täter—Opfer—Ankläger*. Frankfurt am Main: Campus, 2003.

Wolff, Larry. *The Idea of Galicia: History and Fantasy in Habsburg Political Culture*. Stanford, CA: Stanford University Press, 2010.

——. *Inventing Eastern Europe: The Map of Civilization on the Mind of the Enlightenment*. Stanford, CA: Stanford University Press, 1994.

Wood, Elizabeth. *The Baba and the Comrade: Gender and Politics in Revolutionary Russia*. Bloomington: Indiana University Press, 1997.

Wrzesiński, Wojciech, ed. *Studia z historii najnowszej*. Wrocław: Gajt, 1999.

Yakowenko, Natalya. *Narys istorii serednovichnoi ta rannomodernoi Ukrainy*. 2nd ed. Kyiv: Krytyka, 2005.

Yekelchyk, Serhy. *Stalin's Empire of Memory: Russian-Ukrainian Relations in the Soviet Historical Imagination*. Toronto: University of Toronto Press, 2004.

Yones [Jones], Eliyahu. *Die Straße nach Lemberg: Zwangsarbeit und Widerstand in Ostgalizien 1941–1944*. Frankfurt am Main: Fischer, 1999.

Zabłotniak, Ryszard, and Kubiatowski, Jerzy. "Polacy na studiach we Lwowie w latach okupacji hitlerowskiej." *Przegląd historyczno-oświatowy*, no. 4 (1979): 526–36.

Zabolotna, Inna. "Roky nimetskoi okupatsii na zakhidnii Ukraini za spohadamy I. P. Krypiakevycha." *Ukrainskii arkheohrafichnyi shchorichnyk*, n.s., no. 7. Kyiv: M. P. Kots, 2002.

Zaitsev, Oleksandr. *Ukrainskyi intehralnyi natsionalism, 1920–1930-ti roky*. Kyiv: Krytyka, 2013.

Ziętek, Dorota. *Tożsamość i religia: Ormianie w krakowskiej i lwowskiej diasporze*. Cracow: Nomos, 2008.

Zimmerman, Joshua D., ed. *Contested Memories: Poles and Jews during the Holocaust and Its Aftermath*. New Brunswick, NJ: Rutgers University Press, 2003.

Zolotyi veresen. Kyiv: Dnipro, 1979.

Zubok, Vladislav. *Zhivago's Children: The Last Russian Intelligentsia*. Cambridge, MA: Harvard University Press, 2009.

Index